BY DUE PROCESS OF LAW?

By Due Process of Law?

Racial Discrimination and the Right to Vote in South Africa 1855–1960

by

IAN LOVELAND

Professor of Law, Brunel University

• HART •
PUBLISHING

OXFORD AND PORTLAND, OREGON

1999

Hart Publishing
Oxford and Portland, Oregon

Published in North America (US and Canada) by
Hart Publishing c/o
International Specialized Book Services
5804 N.E. Hassalo Street
Portland, Oregon
97213-3644
USA

Distributed in the Netherlands, Belgium and Luxembourg by
Intersentia, Churchillaan 108
B2900 Schoten
Antwerpen
Belgium

Distributed in Australia and New Zealand by
Federation Press
John St
Leichhardt
NSW 2000

Hart Publishing is a specialist legal publisher based in Oxford, England.
To order further copies of this book or to request a list of other
publications please write to:

Hart Publishing, 19 Whitehouse Road, Oxford, OX1 4PA
Telephone: +44 (0)1865 434459 or Fax: +44 (0)1865 794882
e-mail: hartpub@janep.demon.co.uk

British Library Cataloguing in Publication Data
Data Available
ISBN 1 84113–049–4 (cloth)

Typeset by Hope Services (Abingdon) Ltd.
Printed in Great Britain on acid-free paper
by Biddles Ltd, Guildford and King's Lynn

To
the memories of

GANIEF HARRIS
EDGAR FRANKLIN
WILLIAM COLLINS
and
EDGAR DEANE

For having the courage to try
and the faith to believe

Contents

Preface

The South African case of *Harris* v *(Donges) Minister of the Interior* is one familiar—if only fleetingly—to most students of British constitutional law. The case was triggered by the South African government's attempt in the early 1950s to disenfranchise non-white voters in the Cape province. In British legal education, it is passed briefly by as an illustration of the point that—irrespective of the constitutional limitations which may restrain the legal authority of legislatures in countries which were formerly British colonies—it is not legally possible for the United Kingdom Parliament to produce a statute which limits the powers of successive Parliaments. The correctness of that dominant view as a matter of constitutional law, and its desirability as a matter of constitutional morality, continue to provoke disagreement among constitutional theorists in Britain, and in its final chapter this book adds further strands to that already tightly woven tapestry of political and legal analysis.

However, the book's primary objective is to offer a rather fuller picture of the story underlying the *Harris* litigation. In part, the book has been written to satisfy my own historical curiosity about the process of British acquisition of and disengagement from the government of its 'white' colonies in southern Africa and then—in the new (post-1909) country of South Africa—the consequential emergence and consolidation of *apartheid* as a system of socio-political organisation. Perhaps equally importantly, the book tries to use the South African experience to speak to broader, contemporary and British concerns about the nature of our Constitution, and the role of our legislature and our courts in determining just how that Constitution is to work. In the main, this purpose is pursued implicitly rather than explicitly, and may therefore be most evident to readers who already have at least a passing familiarity with the main elements of British constitutional law. The issue has of course gained an added urgency and topicality at the present time, given the victory in the 1997 general election of a Labour party which professes itself committed to promoting fundamental reform to the British constitutional system.

Harris v *Donges* was only the first and—from both a legal and political viewpoint—the least interesting and significant of three closely interlinked pieces of litigation. The second and third cases, *Harris (No. 2)* and *Collins*, raise far more legally complex and politically contentious questions, and they are each afforded as extensive an analysis as *Harris (No. 1)* in this book. But since the book is largely concerned with telling a political and moral story, law reports, statutes, legal textbooks and articles in legal periodicals are not the main sources of data on which I have relied. Neither is the text dominated by the abstract thoughts of constitutional and jurisprudential theorists. Both types of data feature prominently in the analysis offered, but they share equal billing with studies of economic, social and political history, with the biographies and autobiographies of politicians, judges and political activists, and with contemporaneous reportage from more exoteric sources such as political weeklies and newspapers.

The text becomes rather more 'legal' in its later chapters, as litigation increasingly assumes centre stage within the constitutional drama. However, I have assumed that virtually all of the political and historical context surrounding *Harris* will be at best vaguely familiar to a British audience. The book's early chapters are therefore largely devoted to offering a brief history of British colonial policy in southern Africa and the subsequent emergence of South Africa as an autonomous (1910) and then independent (1931) country. This general historical task has recently been admirably performed by several academic historians. Leonard Thompson's *A History of South Africa* (1995) is perhaps the leader in the field; William Beinart's *Twentieth Century South Africa* a worthy challenger. The curious reader will also find a substantial range of 'liberal' histories of South Africa written in the 1960s and 1970s. This book is not intended to replicate those texts, but to offer a distinctively more 'legally aware' interpretation of southern African political history.

General histories of South Africa treat the country's legal system, and especially the role of its courts, as at best an incidental contributor to constitutional development; at worst, they ignore it altogether. This text places judicial decisions in a distinctly more prominent position. The reasoning adopted by the various courts hearing the *Harris* litigation was firmly rooted in a series of ostensibly contradictory precedents reaching all the way back to the years before the second boer war. Many of the most significant legislative initiatives taken by successive South African parliaments were enacted as direct responses to judicial decisions which frustrated achievement of discriminatory objectives. In contrast, a substantial number of political protests launched by white liberals and black pressure groups were expressly prompted by case law which seemed unnecessarily accommodating to discriminatory sentiments. The South African courts, and the laws they made, perhaps deserve a higher profile in their country's political history than they have hitherto been granted. This book takes a modest step in that direction.

There are obvious shortcomings to the approach I have taken. It is written at a considerable distance—chronologically, geographically, and racially—from the story it tells. The last caveat is the most important, and operates at two levels. The first is that much of the documentation surrounding this controversy is the product of white elites, whether British or South African. History, we are often told, is simply the story told by the winners. We need equally to bear in mind that the raw materials from which future histories are constructed may also be tainted and are undoubtedly incomplete. Some non-white stories simply cannot be told. The second level is simply a result of my being a white middle-class liberal in a relatively mature democracy—I can only guess at the motivations and beliefs of many of the key players in this episode. I began the book holding the view that many of the substantive policies that successive South African governments pursued between 1910 and 1960 were irredeemably evil, and the legal arguments they deployed to support those policies were feeble and mendacious. Nothing I have encountered since then has led me to modify those views, beyond the emergence of a feeling that some of the politicians who governed South Africa in the 1950s were insane rather than evil. But that initial conclusion was apparently by no means self-evident even in the 1950s to observers who would presumably have regarded themselves as 'liberals': from the 'liberal' vantage point of 1910, 1920 or 1930 (be it British, American or southern African) it would have been hotly disputed. I have tried as best I can to acknowledge the sincerity with which those beliefs were held by at least some of their proponents.

Notwithstanding these unavoidable weaknesses, I hope that the book will serve some useful political and jurisprudential purposes. The first is to act as a counterweight to the traditional esotericisation of constitutional law and constitutional theory within British political culture. That citizens of the United Kingdom have in the main enjoyed the good fortune of not having suffered under an overtly tyrannical government in the modern era has perhaps led us to take the constituent principles which mould our society rather for granted. We therefore need to travel beyond international boundaries to become sensitised to our own internal political realities. The *Harris* saga conveys perhaps better than any episode of British political history the enormous significance of the choices a country makes (or fails to make) concerning its constitutional arrangements. If this book has one overriding objective, it is to stress that constitution-building is a task far too important to be left to politicians, and *much* too important to be left to the vagaries of party politics.

A note on terminology

Readers will notice as the text progresses that it contains two spellings of Afrika(a)ner. This is not a typographical error, but is rather an attempt to identify two distinct political ideologies which existed at varying times within the white South African population. 'Afrikaner' denotes an ideology which sought to foster a sense of equality within the white community across linguistic and cultural divides. 'Afrikaaner' is intended to convey in contrast an ideology which sought to establish the dominance of one faction of the white community over another. Readers familiar with South African history will no doubt appreciate the point I am trying to make; I would hope that those who lack such familiarity will appreciate its significance as the narrative in the book unfolds.

IAN LOVELAND
London, Autumn 1998

Acknowledgments

I owe thanks to several people and organisations for assisting me to finish this book. Richard Hart stands at the head of that list. His enthusiasm for the project in its early stages was extremely heartening. The British Academy offered very generous financial support for my research, enabling me both to visit South Africa to conduct some archival and interview-based research and to employ a long-range research assistant to dig into data sources that I would not have had the time to explore myself. David Borgstrom performed that task for me with great enthusiasm, diligence, and initiative. I owe him a great debt, as I do to Hugh Corder of the University of Cape Town who had the very good sense to recommend David to me as my assistant. Dean Danie Visser was kind enough to extend the hospitality of UCT's Law Faculty to me during (our) summer of 1998.

As might be expected in relation to events which occurred some fifty years ago, few of the principal actors in this episode of constitutional history remain alive. I was however fortunate enough to be able to meet and speak with several political activists and lawyers inolved in the events of the time. Brian Bunting and Reggie September—both now MPs in South Africa—were kind enough to find the time to speak to me about the political context in which the cases occurred. Harry Snitcher, who acted on behalf of the plaintiffs in the litigation, also provided me with invaluable insight into the formulation and presentation of their arguments. My greatest debt however is owed to Denis Cowen, formerly Professor of Comparative Law at the University of Cape Town. His role in the *Harris* litigation is examined at length in Chapter 8. At this point, I simply take the opportunity to thank him for giving so generously of his time, his memories and his own archival material in assisting me to complete this project.

Table of Cases

Table of Statutes

TREATIES AND CONVENTIONS

LEGISLATION (by country)

Australia

Canada

Ireland

South Africa ("Independent" Republics)

Orange Free State

Natal

The Cape

Transvaal/South African Republic

Republic of South Africa

United Kingdom

United States of America

1

The European Colonisation of Southern Africa: A Brief History[1]

I. THE INITIAL INVASIONS 1650–1806

The Portugese were the first Europeans to reach the Cape, arriving in the late sixteenth century. However the Dutch East India Company began the era of European imperialism by establishing a base at the Cape to serve as a supply post and victualling station for its ships as they sailed to and from the Indies. The Company formalised its presence on the Cape in 1652, when it established a small settlement and authorised a handful of its employees to manage agricultural smallholdings in the immediately adjoining areas. The settlers encountered three distinct groups of native Africans in the Cape, whom they referred to as Bantu, Hottentots and Bushmen.[2]

The weight of modern day archaeological and anthropological evidence suggests that native Africans had been present in southern Africa in appreciable numbers for several thousand years.[3] While the bulk of the population initially supported itself through a nomadic hunter-gatherer lifestyle, there are clear indications that many groups had developed a pastoral form of agricultural economy, based primarily on cattle ownership, by the seventeenth century. Within the next hundred years, tribes in the eastern half of southern Africa had also taken advantage of that region's more favourable climate to develop a farming system that mixed both pastoral and arable agricultural techniques. The Dutch East India company entered a land that was sparsely populated by European standards, but it was by no means empty.

[1] I am much indebted in this chapter to the following works: F. Troup, *South Africa: an Historical Introduction* (London: Metheun, 1972); L. Marquard, *The Story of South Africa* (London: Faber and Faber, 1955); W. Beinart, *Twentieth Century South Africa* (Oxford: OUP, 1994); L. Thompson, *A History of South Africa* (New Haven: Yale University Press, 1995); T. Pakenham, *The Scramble for Africa* (London: Abacus, 1992); T. Lloyd *The British Empire 1558–1995*, 2nd edn. (Oxford: OUP, 1996); T. Davenport, *South Africa: a Modern History*, 2nd edn. (Cambridge: CUP, 1978).

[2] Marquard, n. 1 above, pp. 17–25. The 'Bushmen' identified themselves as the San, while the 'Hottentots' referred to themselves as the Khoikoi; see L. Thompson, *The Political Mythology of Apartheid* (New Haven: Yale University Press, 1985), ch. 1. This book follows the indigenous people's self-endowed names except when it is referring explicitly to the descriptions applied to them by white colonists. For an assessment of the significance of the 'names' attached to non-whites by whites in southern Africa see A. Ashforth, *The Politics of Official Discourse in Twentieth Century South Africa* (Oxford: Clarendon Press, 1990).

[3] The literature is compellingly surveyed in Thompson (1995), n. 1 above, ch. 1. See also Thompson (1985), n. 2 above, pp. 78–80.

The Company formally required its employees to respect the autonomy and traditions of the indigenous population, although the colonists themselves seemed to honour this rule more in the breach than the observance. By 1658, the settlers had begun to use military force to seize land and water supplies from the Khoikoi population. From the outset, the Company allowed its formal rules to be compromised when faced with an expansionist *fait accompli* by the settlers.

Barely 150 colonists had arrived in the Cape by 1670. Somewhat ironically, given later developments, the Company urged its employees to boost their population by inter-breeding with the indigenous black tribes, thus sowing the seeds (literally as well as metaphorically) of what later generations were to describe as the Cape Coloured population of South Africa.[4] Much of this sexual contact took place outside the marriage relationship, but marriages according to christian rites between whites (men) and natives (women) were by no means uncommon.[5] The racial heterogeneity of the Cape population was increased from 1657 onwards by the institution of slavery, the initial slaves being peoples of Malay extraction from Madagascar. In subsequent years, the Company also imported slaves from Asia and Mozambique. The Dutch laws of slavery which were adopted in the Cape afforded owners virtually absolute property rights over the life and body of their slaves. The Company itself seems (by contemporary standards) to have been an 'enlightened' slave master. Slave children were offered rudimentary schooling, and a small number of slaves who embraced Christianity were baptised and manumitted, subsequently living as free men and women in the Cape Town area. The treatment meted out to slaves owned by white settlers was markedly less benign.[6]

In 1680, the Company formalised the settlers' *de facto* policy of internal expansion and established a second settlement at Stellenbosch, a little to the north and east of Cape Town. In the same year, the Company permitted some 200 French Huguenot exiles to immigrate. The Huguenots were in the main extreme Calvinists, fleeing persecution by France's Catholic regimes. The Company's motives in permitting such immigration appeared to owe more to commercial than humanitarian or religious concerns: an increased white farming population was seen as a necessity if the Cape was to become sufficiently productive to service the increasing tonnage of the Company's trade to and from India. The French aspect of these *immigrés*' identity was rapidly submerged (other than in the retention of obviously Gallic surnames)[7] beneath the continuing stream of Dutch immigration, but their religious faith served if anything to

[4] On the racial heterogeneity of the 'Coloured' population of Southern Africa see G. Lewis, *Between the Wire and the Wall* (Cape Town: David Phillip, 1987), pp. 2–4.

[5] Thompson (1995), n. 1 above, pp. 44–45: A. Sachs, *Justice in South Africa* (London: University of Sussex Press, 1973), pp. 20–27.

[6] Thompson (1995), n. 1 above, pp. 42–46.

[7] As we shall see in later chapters, the descendants of the de Villiers family were to occupy many positions in the elite ranks of the South African legal profession.

reinforce the doctrinal fundamentalism of many of the Dutch settlers.[8] Despite the introduction of slave labour into the Colony, the settlers found the Cape's land insufficiently fertile to permit the intensive cultivation of vegetable and cereal crops. Sheep and cattle farming seemed the obvious alternative, but agriculture of that sort required substantial amounts of grazing land. From 1680 onwards, the Company had leased farms in the outlying areas of Cape Town and Stellenbosch to the Hugenots and existing Dutch settlers. By the turn of the century, this policy had expanded into a more systematic encouragement of so-called 'Trekboers'. The Trekboers headed north, west and east to lay claim to 600-acre 'loan farms', nominally leased to them by the Company at extremely low rents.[9] The Company maintained its formal policy of land acquisition by purchase and negotiation, although the practical history of European imperialism in South Africa in the eighteenth century seemed to owe more to violence and betrayal than to consensual techniques.[10]

Violence was also an endemic feature of the boer communities' criminal justice 'system'—the word is used guardedly. Floggings, torture, mutilation and execution were commonplace punishments. The system was imported from Holland, rather than being the novel creation of the boers' slave-owning society. Whites as well as blacks were subject to this brutal regime, although it seems likely that such discretion as the system permitted was exercised to the benefit of white rather than native black 'criminals'.[11]

The Company had neither the inclination nor the resources to staff a standing army in the Cape. Nor were the settlers sufficiently populous to maintain such a force themselves. Their military power derived instead from what was termed the 'commando' system. All adult males were required to serve in a decentralised militia, which could be summoned into action at any time, ordered into units which served under elected commanders. Commando training placed great emphasis on developing each individual's equestrian and marksmanship skills. The settlers' horses and firearms—buttressed by shiftingly opportunistic alliances with the indigenous peoples—enabled the Trekboers to fight effectively against the much larger native tribes, who in the main fought on foot and were armed only with spears.

The commando was not a purely defensive force. It served also as the vehicle for episodic raids against the native black population. From 1770 onwards, the Trekboers waged what was in effect a genocidal war (on occasion with Khoikoi assistance) against the San tribe which occupied lands north of Cape Town itself. By 1800, few San were left alive; most of those were enslaved either *de jure*, or *de facto* through an oppressive 'apprenticeship' system which fastened

[8] The linkages between the settlers' religious convictions and developments in Dutch theology are concisely explored in I. Hexham, 'Afrikaner Nationalism 1902–1914' in P. Warwick (ed.), *The South African War* (London: Longman, 1980), pp. 386–390.

[9] Thompson (1995), n. 1 above, pp. 46–50.

[10] T. Bennet, 'African Land—a History of Dispossession', in R. Zimmerman and D. Visser (eds.), *Southern Cross: Civil Law and Common Law in South Africa* (Oxford: Clarendon Press, 1996).

[11] Sachs (1973), n. 5 above, pp. 23–27.

on the San's colour as a justification for not permitting them to make freely negotiated employment contracts with their employers in the way that white workers were permitted to do. The Khoikoi's sporadic complicity in this campaign afforded them little long term benefit. By the late eighteenth century they too had been virtually eradicated as a distinct tribal group, their surviving members (many of whom found themselves in the same unfavourable employment situation as the remnants of the San) had been absorbed into the evermore variegated genetic heritage of the Cape coloured population.

Nor were episodes of ostensibly peaceful co-existence necessarily a boon to the native inhabitiants of southern Africa. In addition to guns and Calvinism, the boer settlers brought European diseases into the colonies. Smallpox wrought particularly severe consequences on the Khoikoi, and was to prove a constant ally to the boers as they moved northwards from the Cape in future years.[12]

The settlers nevertheless met stiff resistance when they tried to expand eastwards. Their treks into the eastern Cape coincided with the consolidation of the Xhosa tribe's southward drift into the same area. By this time, the Xhosa had become adept practictioners of a stable form of mixed pastoral and arable agricultural subsistence. The Xhosa were also both more numerous than the San and Khokoi, and more succesful in repelling the trekboers' military adventurism. The East India Company attempted (somewhat half-heartedly and largely ineffectually) to maintain agreed borders with the Xhosa and other native tribes in the Eastern Cape, but had no way of forcing the trekboers to respect them. White eastern expansion consequently continued episodically—and violently—throughout the final decades of the century.[13]

By 1800, the white Cape had become an expansive society in terms of the land its members occupied. Yet its population was, by European standards, negligibly small, comprising some 16,000 white and Coloured inhabitants, living alongside some 17,000 slaves and (a very rough estimate) 20,000 native blacks.[14] The trekboers' preferences for large farms necessarily condemned them to forego the close physical proximity of other whites in any significant numbers. Yet paradoxically, this seemed to strengthen rather than attenuate the ties which bound the whites into a coherent boer 'community'.[15] In the absence either of any formal education system or the progressive dynamic of urbanisation and industrialisation—factors increasingly prevalent in societies on the European continent—the trekboers sought an identity in the simple certainties of Calvinist fundamentalism. The dogmatic tenets of Calvinist faith were well-suited to a people whose waking hours were spent wholly in subsistence farming in largely uncharted lands, especially since Calvinism's perception of its

[12] Beinart (1994), n. 1 above, pp. 3–6.

[13] For a polemical perspective see H. Simons and R. Simons, *Class and colour in South Africa 1850–1950* (Harmonsdworth: Penguin, 1969), ch. 1.

[14] Marquard, n. 1 above, p. 56.

[15] For a discussion of the contending views of southern African historians on this point see Beinart (1994), n. 1 above, pp. 44–46.

adherents as an elite, chosen few (fortuitously?) offered a 'divine' justification for the settler's dominant economic and political ambitions:[16] these being first to appropriate, by violence if necessary, the lands and cattle tended by native tribes; and secondly to consign the natives themselves to a markedly inferior, indeed in its most extreme form, essentially non-human status.[17]

Yet by 1800, the cultural and geographical isolationism of the trekboers began to contrast with an increasingly cosmopolitan core community in Cape Town itself. From 1780 onwards, the French had shown an increasing interest in the Cape. Their presence as traders stimulated a period of economic boom, which was accompanied (especially in the years immediately following the French Revolution) by an influx of political and cultural ideas which sat most uncomfortably with the inward-looking Calvinist fundamentalism to which so many of the Cape's early settlers had pledged their ideological allegiance. The growth of French influence was facilitated by the evermore dire financial straits into which the Dutch East India Company was sinking. The Company finally collapsed in 1794, leaving the government of the Cape as something of a colonial vacuum, a vacuum which the already established French promptly filled.

The French dominance was, however, to prove short-lived. France and Britain were again at war, and the British navy seized control of the Cape in 1795, recognising it as having vital strategic importance as a base from which to control European access to India and the East. The 1803 Treaty of Amiens restored the Cape to France, which entrusted its government to a French client state, the Dutch Batavian Republic. But some three years later, the British invaded once again. In the aftermath of Waterloo, the British occupation was legitimised (at least in the eyes of the European powers) by the Congress of Vienna. By 1815, the Cape had become a colony of the British crown.

The 'legal' basis of European colonisation

The European colonial powers had by this time begun to develop an elaborate jurisprudence to 'justify' their colonisation of foreign lands, whether in Africa, the Indies, or Australasia. The audiences for such justification were primarily the colonising governments themselves: the emergence of a mutually acceptable set of international law principles to regulate colonial land acquisition served as a useful (and much cheaper) addition to war as a tool for the conduct of foreign

[16] For a detailed examination of the Dutch roots of this particular brand of Calvinism see Moodie, *The Rise of Afrikanerdom* (London: University of California Press, 1975), pp. 22–27, 51–53.

[17] Cf. the comments of J.F. Van Oordt, a prominent boer historian in the late nineteenth century; "According to the Boer idea, the kaffer, the Hottentot, the Bushman belong to a lower race than the whites. They carry, as people rightly called it, the mark of Cain; God, the Lord, destined them to be 'drawers of water and hewers of wood', as presses subject to the white race . . . I do not believe that I go too far when I express my feeling that the Boers as a whole doubt the existence of a Kaffer- or a Hottentot-soul"; quoted in Thompson (1985), n. 2 above, p. 85.

policy. The model of international law created by the European colonial powers recognised several techniques through which a country could acquire sovereignty over lands beyond its original borders. The most significant were conquest, cession and occupation of *terra nullius*. The principle that a conquering people acquired sovereignty over the lands which they subugated was, in legal terms, unproblematic. Acquisition of territory through cession—that is to say through treaties negotiated with the present government of the land concerned—raised slightly more legal difficulty. The colonising power had to be sure, for example, that its co-signatory was indeed possessed of the sovereignty it purported to be relinquishing. Questions might also arise as to the extent to which the former governments of acquired territories had exercised informed consent in treaty negotiations,[18] or had acted under duress; if not the threat of conquest by the negotiating European power, then the offer of 'protection' against other European powers who might offer even less advantageous terms in future.

The legal uncertainties attaching to territorial acquisition through conquest and cession were a matter of significance more for the regulation of the European colonial powers' claims against each other than against the colonised lands. The third mode of aquisition, occupation, raised similar difficulties. The substance of the technique of 'occupation' underwent a significant change during the nineteenth century.[19] Occupation could only be effected on land which was *terra nullius*. As originally conceived by the Spanish jurist Vittoria, *terra nullius* was narrowly construed to denote only land that was utterly devoid of human population.[20] The colonising power which discovered such lands was able to acquire sovereignty by establishing effective occupation of the territory, in the sense of creating an organised form of colonial government. Attempted colonisation of unpopulated land could provoke disputes among European powers over such matters as which of them had initially discovered the territory, and whether or not a country's presence there did indeed amount to 'occupation'. But such land did not, of course, present the additional complication of how to address the presumably competing claims to sovereignty of indigenous peoples.[21] The presence of such peoples would mean that the land was not *terra nullius*, and that colonising powers could gain sovereignty over it only by either cession or conquest.

[18] See generally Pakenham's riveting analysis (n. 1 above) of the European colonisation of Africa, and especially his account of the 'negotiations' between the French and a Sudanese chief at p. 536.

[19] I am much indebted in the following passages to J. Crawford, *The Creation of States in International Law* (Oxford: Carendon Press, 1979); R. Jennings, *The Aquisition of Territory in International Law* (Manchester: Manchester University Press, 1963); M. Akehurst, *A Modern Introduction to International Law*, 4th edn. (London: George Allen and Unwin, 1982); B. O'Kere, 'The Western Sahara Case' (1979) 28 *ICLQ* 296: R. Lumb, 'Native Title to Land in Australia: Recent High Court Decisions' (1993) 42 *ICLQ* 84.

[20] See O'Kere, n. 19 above: P. Fitzpatrick, 'The Constitution of the Excluded: Indians and Others', in I. Loveland (ed.), *A Special Relationship* (Oxford: Clarendon Press, 1995).

[21] Akehurst, n. 19 above, pp. 142–145.

The perception of *terra nullius* as wholly unpopulated land was also accepted in English law in the mid-eighteenth century. Sir William Blackstone's authoritative *Commentaries on the Laws of England* suggested that English law recognised occupation as a route to sovereignty only in respect of land that was 'desart and uncultivated' or 'uninhabited'.[22] The *Commentaries* also suggested that there was no moral justification for colonial 'occupation' of lands which demanded the displacement or enslavement of an existing native population:

> "how far the seising on countries already peopled, and driving out or massacring the innocent and defenceless natives, merely because they differed from their invaders in language, in religion, in customs, in government, or in colour . . . was consonant to nature, to reason or to christianity, deserved well to be considered by those who have rendered their names immortal by thus civilising mankind".[23]

Blackstone's moral scruples worked but little influence on the political leaders of nineteenth century European colonial powers. Even by 1800, there were few parts of the world that were entirely unoccupied by human beings. This proved an inconvenient demographic truth for European governments, since it seemed to remove the possibility of using occupation as a means to gain sovereignty of colonised lands. The solution adopted was not to abandon occupation, but to bolster its utility by redefining the concept of *terra nullius* to include lands whose indigenous peoples were not 'civilised' in the European sense.

The 'civilisation' test was expressed with varying degrees of sophistication. The English courts offered a relatively crude label in the 1863 case of *Advocate-General of Bengal v Ranee Surnomoye Dossee*:[24]

> "Where Englishmen establish themselves in an uninhabited or *barbourous* country, they carry with them not only the laws but the sovereignty of their own state; and those who live amongst them and become members of their community become also partakers of, and subject to the same laws" (emphasis added).[25]

A 'barbarous' people was necessarily not a 'civilised' one, and its lands were thus ripe for occupation as *terra nullius*. But the label conveys little precise meaning. Later writers added a somewhat more elaborate gloss to this 'enlarged' notion of *terra nullius*, drawing on such considerations as whether the inhabitants were Christian or whether they organised their collective relations into a stable, permanent form of political government that could maintain internal order, make effective provision for the internal transfer of political power, and represent the people as a whole in dealing with other sovereign states.

The test had some meaning as a mechanism to regulate disputes between the European powers, but it was manifestly a Euro-centric concept which

[22] Cited in Crawford, n. 19 above, p. 179.

[23] 17th edn., 1830, Bk II, ch. 1, p. 7; quoted by Brennan J. of the Australian High Court in *Mabo v State of Queensland* (1991–1992) 175 CLR 1 at 33.

[24] (1863) 19 ER 786.

[25] Per Lord Kingsdown *ibid.* at 800.

constructed 'civilisation' largely in accordance with European historical and political traditions. That the Dutch East India Company claimed (on the Dutch government's behalf) to have *occupied* the Cape rather than gained it through cession or conquest indicates that the Dutch did not see the the Khoikoi and San as 'civilised' peoples. Neither, presumably, did either the French or the British who successively acquired through treaties the sovereignty of the Cape which the Dutch occupation had evidently established.

The enlarged notion of *terra nullius* was also manifestly a concept whose boundaries might expand or contract according to changing perceptions among European colonial governments as to the desirability of further colonial expansion. Throughout much of the nineteenth century, the European powers regarded a great deal of southern and south central Africa as *terra nullius* (in the enlarged sense).[26] This may have been a happy conclusion from a jurisprudential perspective, since it removed the legal impediment to colonisation that might be offered by a people already in occupation of the territory concerned. The conclusion seemed however to lack any defensible factual basis in respect of much (if not all) of the land in question, which had long accommodated indigenous African peoples with viable agricultural economies and stable political societies.[27] That inconvenience was not seen as an insuperable barrier to occupation of new lands, still less to expansion through conquest and cession, either by European governments themselves or by the colonists with whom they were increasingly populating their newly claimed lands.

II. THE CONSOLIDATION AND FRAGMENTATION OF BRITISH RULE 1806–1880

The red ink with which British cartographers identified the physical limits of the British Empire pockmarked much of the map of the globe by the time Britain assumed control of the Cape colony. That mapmakers should colour the southern tip of Africa in the same hue was in itself an unremarkable consequence of Britain's restlessly, if episodically, expansionist imperial policy; the addition was a modest one to an Empire that already embraced Australia, New Zealand, India, the islands of the West Indies and what is now Canada. Nor was there anything unusual in the fact that British rule in the new colony was being imposed by a white governing class on a land where the great majority of the population was not white. Such would always be the case in India, Egypt and the West Indies; and in Canada and Australasia many years were still to pass before white settlers outnumbered the native peoples. The atypical feature of the Cape—shared only and to a much lesser extent by the Canadian colonies—was that British rule was being imposed on a society in which the great majority of the colony's *white* population were not of British descent, and had no

[26] Pakenham, n. 1 above, p. xxiii.
[27] Thompson (1985), n. 2 above, pp. 204–205; Sachs, n. 5 above, pp. 28–29.

obvious reason for looking fondly on British interference with their traditional culture and mode of government. This brute political fact posed especial difficulties to peaceful and successful imperial government from the outset. And as the nineteenth century progressed, Britain's failure to produce a unified white 'race' was to have increasingly draconian consequences.

The formative years

The guiding principle underlying British policy towards the government of its imperial possessions during the eighteenth century has been described by one commentator as 'salutory neglect'.[28] The North American colonies in particular had been largely left to govern their internal affairs acording to their own devices. Colonists were encouraged to create their own elected assemblies responsible for enacting laws for local application. The British government maintained a formal presence in each colony in the shape of a Governor, who as well as being the *de jure* head of the executive branch of the colony's government, functioned as the British government's mouthpiece. In theory, the British Parliament had the power to override any colonial legislation of which it disapproved. But the power was rarely exercised so long as colonial assemblies confined their attention to domestic issues.[29]

The loss of the American colonies in the 1770–1780s suggested a need for a slightly less cavalier British approach to the administration of the country's growing empire. In the Cape, Britain attempted to impress itself on the existing population in both a physical and cultural sense. In the first two decades of the colony's existence, it was ruled as virtually a personal fiefdom by a Governor, appointed by and directly responsible to the Secretary of State for the Colonies. The first appointees to the Governor's office took modest steps to heighten the influence of British culture on the colony's predominantly Dutch white population, particularly by establishing a small school system whose pupils were imbibed with the evident benefit of an anglo-centric curriculum. Given the virtual absence of schools of any sort among the boer community outside Cape Town, this initiative was not overtly threatening to the maintenance of the boer population's cultural identity.

Furthermore, those settlers who feared that British rule heralded the end of *all* the values they held dear were promptly offered some reassurance in the matter of relations with the native tribes: one of Britain's first legal initiatives was to introduce a law requiring native blacks to carry passes if they wished to enter 'white' areas of the colony.[30] This was rapidly followed by a law imposing compulsory ten year apprenticeships to white masters on native children, which

[28] T. Lloyd (1996), n. 1 above, p. 1.

[29] *Ibid.* pp. 67–68, 96. See also B. Bailyn *The Ideological Origins of the American Revolution* (Cambridge, Mass: Harvard UP, 1969), pp. 198–229.

[30] Marquard, n. 1 above, pp. 99–100; Troup, n. 1 above, pp. 83–84.

was redolent of the system used by the Dutch East India company in respect of the San at the turn of the century.[31]

The apprenticeship laws also imposed certain obligations on employers concerning the physical treatment of native workers, and recognising their right to receive the stipulated payment for services performed. This represented something of a departure from orthodox boer principle, in which the habit of not paying black workers for the services they performed enjoyed an elevated status. This departure was heightened when it transpired that the Cape government was prepared to ensure that such provisions were enforced. Nonetheless, many boer settlers, even in the outlying areas, seemed to see some virtues in British rule.

This was evidenced most clearly in 1815, when the majority of boers in the Slagtersnek region of the Cape took up arms in alliance with British forces to suppress a rebellion initiated by a small group of boer farmers unwilling to recognise that 'Kaffers' had any legal rights at all. The ringleaders of the rebellion were subsequently convicted of treason and hanged.[32]

In 1820, some 5,000 British settlers were brought to the Cape to settle on farms around the Fish river. The rationale behind the immigration was both economic—to boost the productivity of the Cape's still sparsely populated and poorly farmed agricultural land—and political—to counterbalance the boer dominance of the colony's outlying agricultural population. Parliament voted funds of £50,000 to launch the scheme, which allocated settlers plots of around 100 acres.[33] The policy soon proved a failure on both counts. Many British settlers were unwilling to endure the initial hardships, borne so readily by their boer predecessors, involved in establishing productive farms in the Cape hinterlands. This reluctance stemmed in part from the relatively poor quality of the land concerned, but more from the unfortunate fact that most of the immigrants had been town dwellers rather than farmers in England. Unsurprisingly, many settlers left the colony's rural hinterlands, preferring instead to earn a living in the Cape's emergent urban areas, especially around Cape Town itself, and engaged in a reverse 'trek' of very modest proportions which threatened to create a cleavage in Cape white society that was not simply one of *boer versus Briton*, but also simultaneously of *urban versus rural*.[34]

The fragmentation of the white community was reinforced by a series of initiatives taken by the British government in the 1820s. From 1820 onwards, Britain permitted the creation of several so-called 'Griqualand republics' on the northern banks of the Orange river. The republics were comprised predominantly of Cape coloureds who had been brought up as Christians in mixed race families, and of native tribes whose chiefs had fallen under the influence of

[31] Thompson (1995), n. 1 above, pp. 58–60.
[32] See Thompson (1985), n. 2 above, ch. 5; Moodie, n. 16 above, pp. 3–4.
[33] Thompson (1995), n. 1 above, pp. 53–55.
[34] Lloyd, n. 1 above, pp. 140–143.

British missionaries and consequently embraced both Christianity and British rule.[35]

The full importance of this policy was not to become evident until almost half a century later, when South Africa's vast diamond reserves were first discovered. The immediate impact was nevertheless siginficant. The creation of the republics placed a formidable legal and practical obstacle in the path of trekboers who wished to continue their by now long established lifestyle of seizing native lands and displacing the former inhabitants. Within the republics, the resistance to Boer expansion now rested on guarantees underwritten by the British government, rather than, as had been the case in respect of those lands just south of the Orange river prior to British rule, by the spears of native tribes and the ineffectual promises of the Dutch East India Company.

These physical restraints on boers' capacity to express their traditional identity—an identity premised at least in part on relentless territorial expansionism—were accompanied by equally restrictive cultural limitations. In the late 1820s, the British government promoted several reforms to the Cape's government structures and legal system which markedly 'anglicised' the colony's political character.[36] Insofar as the white settlers had a functioning legal system prior to 1800 (and in the remote areas of the Cape there was no meaningful system of any sort), its officers were in the main overtly political appointees who administered a bastardised system of Roman-Dutch law. The 'Charter of Justice' introduced into the Cape modified both the substance and the administration of the colony's legal system. Roman-Dutch criminal law and criminal procedure was largly replaced by English common law;[37] a new Supreme Court, staffed only by qualified lawyers, was created to hear appeals from all inferior courts; and the decisions of the Supreme Court were themselves to be subject to appeal to the Privy Council.[38] The colony's executive and 'legislative' organs were also modified. In 1825, the British government established a body called the 'Council of Advice', consisting of the Governor and four officials, appointed by the Governor himself. The Council was given the power to make 'ordinances', a power which superseded the Governor's own authority to pass laws by proclamation. The Council of Advice was in turn replaced by a twelve member 'Legislative Council' in 1834, and a new 'Executive Council' was created in the same year. Both of these bodies broadened the basis of governmental power in the Cape, but the Governor still retained *de jure* and *de facto* responsibility for

[35] The initial leaders of the Griqualand Republics were the distinctly boer-sounding Andries Waterboer and Adam Kok: see Troup, n. 1 above, pp. 93–95: Simon and Simon, n. 13 above, p. 28: Thompson (1995), n. 1 above, pp. 50, 94. For a more expansive account of the emergence of the republics see R. Ross, *Adam Kok's Griquas* (Cambridge: CUP, 1976), esp. chs. 1–4.

[36] Thompson (1985), n. 2 above, pp. 146–147; Sachs, n. 5 above, pp. 38–39: J. Dugard, *Human Rights and the South African Legal Order* (Princeton: Princeton University Press, 1978), pp. 8–9.

[37] Dugard (1978), n. 36 above, pp. 8–9, 268–269. See also H. Corder, 'The Judicial Branch of Government: an Historical Overview', in D. Visser (ed.), *Essays on the History of Law* (Cape Town: Juta & Co., 1989).

[38] The Privy Council was in effect the judges who were members of the House of Lords.

both legislation and administration, and was himself directly subordinate to the Secretary of State for the Colonies.

The Cape colony's governmental structure thus possessed a recognisably 'British' form, in that it was clearly separated into legislative, executive and judicial branches. What it manifestly lacked, even to the limited degree then accepted in Britain itself, was a 'representative' character in the sense of having some of its members chosen by popular election. Successive British governments were evidently unwilling to sanction this reform for fear in part that the Dutch and French settlers, who outnumbered the British, would use a representative assembly to foster anti-British sentiment. The alternative fear was that white settlers would manage to suppress their own disagreements in order to impose oppressive laws on the non-white population.[39] The first, cautious steps towards a representative system were subsequently taken in 1836, when a number of elected municipal councils were established.

The 1836 reforms followed measures to liberalise the laws governing the press introduced in 1828. The colony's first commercial newspaper, the *South African Commercial Advertiser*, was founded by two recent English *emigrés*, one a poet and the other a clergyman.[40] The *Advertiser* professed a commitment to support the liberty of the press and harmonious race relations; and rapidly incurred the displeasure of the colony's then Governor, Lord Charles Somerset for publishing material critical of his administration. Somerset twice attempted to ban the paper, and also tried to exercise pre-publication powers of censorship over its contents. Somerset's authoritarian tendencies were overridden by the British government, which instructed the Council of Advice to issue a Press Ordinance in 1828. The ordinance required publishers to lodge a sum of £300 as a surety against future libel liabilities. Having done so, their legal position was analogous to that enjoyed by their English counterparts; no prior restraints would be exercised on the contents of their newspapers, but they ran the risk of suffering post-publication liability for any defamatory, blasphemous or criminal material that they might publish. The Press Ordinance encouraged further growth in the Cape's newspaper industry. A Dutch language paper—*De Zud Afrikaan*—was established in 1830.

Of more pervasive significance to the Cape's social and political mores was the 50th Ordinance, introduced in 1828, following sustained pressure in Britain from the Anti-Slavery Society, with the active support of liberally inclined members of the boer population.[41] The ordinance, colloquially referred to as the 'Hottentot Charter',[42] repealed the pass laws introduced in 1809, and established as a general principle that laws in the Cape colony were to be 'colourblind' in their form and application.

[39] See S. Trapido, 'The Origins of the Cape Franchise Qualifications of 1853' (1964) 5 *Journal of African History* 37.

[40] Information in this paragraph is drawn from E. Potter, *The Press as Opposition* (London: Chatto and Windus, 1975), pp. 31–33.

[41] Thompson (1995), n. 1 above, pp. 60–62.

[42] Marquard, n. 1 above, p. 101.

That all residents were now permitted to own land in the Cape was not of much immediate benefit to any non-whites, given that so few of them had the resources with which to purchase it. Nonetheless a substantial portion of the Cape Coloured community was soon to be sufficiently affluent to be able to exercise its rights in this respect. Nor did the measure obviously assist the black population, since traditional tribal patterns of land ownership were cast predominantly in communal rather than individuated form, insofar as tribals chiefs were recognised as having the authority to allocate given parcels of land to particular individuals and families, and to revoke such allocations. In terms of 'occupancy' as opposed to 'ownership', land tenure systems were markedly more individual/family-oriented: many parcels might be farmed and occupied by the same family group for a period spanning several generations.[43]

The more immediately significant impact of the Ordinance was felt in the labour market. The new law placed all races on a footing of formal equality in the negotiation of employment contracts. In consequence, the identifiable vestiges of the Khoikoi and the many Cape Coloureds who had been trapped in grossly exploitative employment relationships with white settlers became free to seek employment wherever they wished within the Cape, and thereby gained the means to become landowners in the longer term.

It would be misleadingly romantic to characterise the 50th Ordinance as a purely 'liberal measure'—as the triumph of humane and enlightened British values over the reactionary bigotry of the majority of the boer community. There is no doubt that such sentiments played some role in the formation of British policy. By 1830 the British Parliament was beginning to enact measures which lent British society a tentatively 'democratic' character. The lines of Tory/Whig division in the struggle over the Great Reform Act were by then clearly drawn, Peel had risked the unity of the Tory party over the issue of Catholic emancipation, and was shortly to promulgate a progressive social policy agenda in his famous 'Tamworth Manifesto'. But it is equally the case that the removal of caste-based restraints on labour mobility and property ownership are a regularly occurring phenomenon in industrialising societies. The dynamics of capitalist (and increasingly urbanised) economic development require both workers and consumers in large numbers.

It also seems clear that the racial 'equality' produced by the Ordinance was to a large degree rhetorical and symbolic rather than practical in its effect. The

[43] See Thompson (1995), n. 1 above, pp. 23, 71; Troup, n. 1 above, pp. 19–21. Bennet, n. 10 above, has suggested that the notion of 'communal' land tenure was a European fiction, intended to enable Europeans to justify their presence in southern Africa by offering some native blacks the chance to 'progress' towards a more 'civilised' form of individuated ownership of land. The question is perhaps one more of anthropology than law. Bennet suggests evidence from the former discipline supports his view, while evidence from the latter tends to refute it. This is hardly surprising, given that the 'law' was written by Europeans whose interest in 'civilising the native' co-existed with a wish to legitimise white usurpation of native lands. The law was in effect a micro-level manifestation of the enlarged concept of *terra nullius*. See however Mandela: "[In early African societies] the land, the main means of production, belonged to the whole tribe and there was no individual ownership whatsoever"; N. Mandela, *Long Road to Freedom* (London: Abacus, 1995), p. 391.

difficulties that non-whites faced in becoming landowners have already been alluded to, and it seemed evident that the nominally race-neutral labour relations laws were consistently applied in a manner that disadvantaged non-white workers.[44]

To an appreciable extent therefore, whether driven by liberal idealism or economic necessity, the 50th Ordinance represented the triumph of increasingly pervasive imperial values rather than a carefully targeted attack on boer society or a spirited defence of liberal idealism. But while this may have seemed a familiar, even natural process to British officials in the Cape, and to those members of Cape society who maintained close links with developments in Europe, it was perceived as invasive and alien by the more culturally and geographically isolated members of the colony's boer community.

In the early 1830s, that community suffered two further intrusions into its traditional way of life. The first involved the abolition of the 'loan farm' system, a mechanism which had permitted impecunious settlers to lay an effective legal claim to vast tracts of undeveloped land. The British government would in future require trekking settlers to *buy* the land they wished to farm in as yet unoccupied (by whites) areas of the Cape. For the children of many boer families, such a purchase was a financial improbabilty, becoming the more so because the 50th Ordinance appreciably increased the cost of hiring non-white labourers.

In 1834, that improbability became an impossibility when the British Parliament offered further evidence of its embrace of formally democratic and liberal values by abolishing the institution of slavery in the British Empire. The gap in the cheap labour force created by the 'Hottentot Charter' could no longer be filled by the even less expensive expedient of buying or breeding slaves. Such compensation as the emancipation legislation offered to slave-owners was regarded as entirely inadequate by many boers, a large number of whom were effectively denied any recompense by technicalities in the Act's rules.[45]

That the ownership of one human being by another was *per se* unacceptably immoral was not an argument with which many boers could empathise, especially when the 'property' in issue was a non-white. That slavery continued to be an accepted practice in the USA, a country which might lay some claim to being the most constitutionally advanced of the western democracies, lent further weight to the boers' sense of grievance.[46] For some members of the boer community, the interactive effect of these measures was sufficient to push them

[44] Simons and Simons, n. 13 above, ch. 1.

[45] Thompson (1995), n. 1 above, pp. 57 65; Lloyd (1996), n. 1 above, pp. 153–156; Pakenham, n. 1 above, pp. 45–46.

[46] Bailyn, n. 29 above, pp. 232–245: E. Malz, 'Slavery, Federalism and the Structure of the Constitution' (1992) *American Journal of Legal History* 466; W. Frehling, 'The Founding Fathers and Slavery' (1972) *American Historical Review* 81; *Dred Scott* v *Sandford* (1857) 19 Howard 393; E. Corwin 'The *Dred Scott* decision in the light of contemporary doctrines' (1911) *American Historical Review* 52. A further thirty years were to pass, culminating in a bloody civil war, before the legal status of slavery was formally abolished in the USA.

out of the Cape and strike out northwards, passing through and by the Griqualand republics into the largely uncharted (by Europeans) terrain north of the Orange river.

The Great Trek and the creation of the Boer Republics

The 'Great Trek' began in the mid–1830s. The 'Great' soubriquet owes rather more to the ambitions of the project, than to its size. Those ambitions were threefold. The first was to escape what was perceived as an increasingly oppressive 'British' regime in the Cape. One of the trekboers' leaders, Piet Retief, borrowed heavily from Thomas Jefferson's *Declaration of Independence*, drafted in 1776 to justify the American colonists' revolution against British rule, in writing a manifesto explaining the reasons for the trek. The second and third ambitions were less lofty, amounting to little more than the trekboers' desires to find new supplies of cheap land[47] and to impose their own preferred form of oppression on the territory and the native Africans who dwelt there to the north of the original colony.

The trekkers numbered initially in the hundreds rather than the thousands, although many other discontented whites were soon to follow them out of the Cape. They travelled in carts drawn by oxen, making extraordinarily slow progress to the north and the north east. One group, led by Andre Pretorious, ventured into what would subsequently become Natal province, a land then occupied almost exclusively by the Zulu tribe. The venture was, inevitably, a bloody affair. The Zulus' initial resistance to the invasion merely reinforced the trekboers' taste for genocide: Pretorious himself led a commando in December 1838 which slaughtered some 3,000 Zulus, an event subsequently to be embellished and then honoured in boer history as 'The Day of the Covenant'.[48] Some three years later, Pretorious announced the formation of the Republic of Natalia, with its capital in Pietermarizburg. The Republic had a population of barely 25,000, of whom just 6,000 were white: all the others were native Africans.[49]

A second group of trekkers had settled somewhat earlier in the lands between the Orange and Vaal rivers. At that time, this area appeared to have virtually no indigenous native population, a fact which lent some credence to trekkers' claims that they were legitimately colonising *terra nullis* (in the narrow, original sense of the term). The trekkers rapidly established a 'Volksraad', a representative body with fused legislative and executive power, formed small towns at Blomfontein and Winburg, and set up large farms in the sparsely populated

[47] Thompson (1995), n. 1 above, pp. 68–69. On the 'theological' rationale underpinning the boers' genocidal tendencies see Moodie, n. 16 above, ch. 1, esp pp. 1–6.

[48] See Thompson (1985), n. 2 above, ch. 5. On the later significance of the date see pp. 210–211. below.

[49] Troup, n. 1 above, pp. 108–120.

veld. By the mid–1840s they claimed to have created a new 'white' country in the central-northern lands of southern Africa—the Orange Free State.

A third wave of settlers struck out northwards across the Vaal river, trekking north and northwest as far as the Limpopo river, and northeast as far as the Lebombo mountains, which marked the western limits of the coastal colony of Portugese East Africa (now Mozambique). This territory was not as 'empty' as the land which was claimed as the Orange Free State; boer control was established by a mixture of conquest and cession. For these '*trans-Vaalers*', the obvious name for their newly conquered 'country' would be the Transvaal. It too would be governed by a Volksraad; and as in the Free State, all white male boers would be entitled to participate in the election of the Volksraad's members. In terms of its acreage, the Transvaal was larger than than the Free State and Natal combined. However its white population was tiny in comparison to the numbers of native Africans who occupied the land concerned. The initial centres of the white population were concentrated in Potchefstroom—on the south-western border with the Free State, in Pretoria in the centre of the country, and in Lydenburg in the north-east. But as in the Free State, the majority of the Transvaal's white population was widely scattered: it adhered to a rural culture sustained by an agricultural economy.

The relative speed with which the boer trekkers colonised large swathes of the northern regions of southern Africa owed much to their technologically advanced weaponry. Boer leaders also proved adept at exploiting existing divisions (and creating new ones) between different groups of the native people. Their forays northwards from the Cape coincided with a period of aggressive expansionism by Zulu tribes into areas previously inhabited by other native peoples. This *Mfecane* ('time of troubles') ensued that the boers were never faced with the prospect of overcoming a united indigenous population.[50] Nor, in the main, did the boers entertain any moral qualms about the techniques of warfare which they employed. Many trekker commandoes implemented a 'scorched earth' strategy, destroying native people's means of subsistence and thereby subjecting woman and children to a slow and lingering version of the death which their menfolk met in a more abrupt and bloody fashion on the field of battle.[51] International law recognised the legitimacy of claims to sovereignty by a conquering people. It offered no strictures concerning the way in which that conquest was carried out.

While the trekboers sought to escape British rule in practice, their activities nominally remained subject to British control. Britain had formally annexed Natal in 1843, and administered it as a sub-division of the Cape. In the 1850s, the British government encouraged substantial white immigration into Natal,

[50] Thompson (1995), n. 1 above, pp. 81–83; Davenport (1978), n. 1 above, pp. 43–56. The extent and duration of the *Mfecane* are subjects of sharp dispute among South African historians. For a survey see J. Omer-Cooper, 'The Mfecane Survives Its Critics' in C. Hamilton (ed.), *The Mfecane Aftermath* (Johannesburg: University of Witwatersrand Press, 1995).

[51] Thompson (1995), n. 1 above, pp. 70–72.

with the result that the region's boer population became quantitatively insignificant. Natal's extensive coastline lent it appreciable strategic importance,[52] and also, prior to the construction of a railway system in southern Africa, made communications between Cape Town and Durban (Natal's main port) relatively straightforward.

Neither factor applied to the landlocked Free State and Transvaal. By 1850, successive British governments had grown sufficiently weary of attempting to police the behaviour of the trekboers that they were willing to grant both societies a substantial degree of formal legal autonomy: the principle of 'salutory neglect' still had a role to play in calming the political waters of potentially turbulent (and strategically insignificant) colonial possessions. The 1852 Sand River Convention granted the Transvaal effective control over all of its internal affairs.

One of the Transvaal government's first steps was to change the colony's name; henceforth it would be known as the South African Republic. The Volksraad subsequently drew up a constitution (*Grondwet*) which confirmed that; "there should be no equality between black and white with regard to matters of church and state". Britain's solicitousness for the legal status of blacks in the Republic had not stretched so far as ensuring that the Sand River Convention forbade such provision within the Republic's laws.

The Free State was granted a similar degree of 'independence' by the Bloemfontein Convention of 1854.[53] Its leaders fashioned a governmental structure to regulate its internal affairs which drew heavily on principles embodied in the American constitution. In ensuing years, a substantial number of Anglophile Cape whites moved northwards into the Free State, lured by the prospect of cheap farmland and cheap black labour, and reassured by a constitutional structure that did not obviously expose 'British' whites to substantial legal disabilities.

Boer ideology was markedly more fragmented in the Republic than in the Free State. This fragmentation was rooted largely in religious differences. A particularly extremist sub-sect of the Calvinist faith had been formed in the Transvaal in 1859.[54] The *Gerformeerde Kerk von Suid Afrika* (the 'Dopper Kerk') established effective control over the Transvaal's theological college (and subsequently university) at Potchefstrom, so gaining an institutional base which would enable it to exercise political influence out of all proportion to its numbers in the coming years.[55]

Britain made no attempt through the terms of either the Sand River or Blomfontein Conventions to interfere with the boers' religious autonomy.

[52] Lloyd (1996), n. 1 above, pp. 155–159.

[53] Thompson (1995), n. 1 above, pp. 95–96.

[54] Troup, n. 1 above, pp. 125–127.

[55] Hexham, n. 8 above; Moodie, n. 16 above, pp. 61–62 offers a useful summary of the Dopper Kerk's theological rationale and its subsequent influence on late nineteenth century boer political ideology.

However, the British government retained control over native affairs in both 'countries'. It also forbade the boer governments to conduct their own 'foreign policies', a concept which included their relationships with each other and with native Africans living outside their boundaries, as well as with other European states and their respective colonies.

This proscription took various forms. The most blunt example followed a series of military skirmishes between the Free State and a segment of the Sotho tribe living in an area bordering the south-west corner of Natal, the south east of the Free State and the north east of the Cape. At the 'invitation' of the Sotho chief, Britain formally annexed the region, which it styled Basutoland (now Lesotho) in 1868, thereby preventing any further boer territorial expansion.[56]

The drift towards colonial self-government for the whites of southern Africa, at least in respect of internal affairs, was also evident, albeit conducted through a more consensual process, in the Cape. In 1853, the colony was given a new constitution which granted it 'representative government'. This system permitted the colony's electorate to choose members of both a House of Assembly (loosely comparable to the British House of Commons) and a Legislative Council. However the Governor retained the power to block the wishes of either body; they were in constitutional terms no more than advisory fora.

'Representative government' may be contrasted with 'responsible government', a status to which at that point the Cape could merely aspire. Under the latter system, the colony's governmental structure would mirror that used in Britain. The party leader who could command majority support in the House of Assembly would be invited by the Governor to form a Cabinet of his own choosing and assume *de facto* control of the colony's internal affairs. The system provided (*de facto* if not *de jure*) freedom for colonial governments to pursue policies of which the British government might disapprove. The Governor's role in respect of internal matters would be become analogous to that of the Queen *vis-à-vis* the British Cabinet—namely to act on her Ministers' advice. The colonial government's foreign policy, however, would continue to be controlled by the British government via the Governor-General.

As in Britain, the system of responsible government in the colonies rested largely on conventional or political understandings rather than on an explicit legal base.[57] Canada had been the first colony to be granted responsible government, in 1847:[58] in the mid–1850s the system was extended to New South Wales, Tasmania and New Zealand.

In its early years, the relationship between the newly 'responsible' colonial governments and the British government also rested on conventional rather than legal foundations. The British Parliament attempted to impose a legal structure upon the new system by enacting the Colonial Laws Validity Act in

[56] Thompson (1995), n. 1 above, pp. 105–106.

[57] A. Keith, *The Constitutional Law of the British Dominions* (London: Macmillan, 1933), pp. 99–104.

[58] Lloyd (1996), n. 1 above, pp. 162–167.

1865.[59] The Act is a remarkably short and opaque document. The legislation defined the powers of colonial legislatures primarily in negative terms. Section 2 provided that any colonial law which conflicted with English primary or secondary legislation which Parliament intended to have effect in the colony concerned would be void to the extent of the inconsistency.[60] This suggested, by omission, that colonial legislatures were competent to override rules of common law[61] and to depart from more amorphous understandings of the moral or political principles inherent in 'English law'. The latter point had previously been the source of some confusion in respect of colonial constitutions which provided that colonial legislatures could not pass law 'repugnant to the laws of England', a phrase which had on occasion been taken to include common law and abstract notions of the rule of law and separation of powers as well as Acts of Parliament.[62]

Somewhat bizarrely, given its political objectives, the Act made no reference at all to 'responsible government'. Section 5 instead drew a legal distinction between 'colonial legislatures' and 'representative legislatures'. The legal distinction bore little obvious relationship to political practice. 'Representative legislatures', defined as those in which at least half of the members were elected by the colony's residents, enjoyed greater powers than colonial legislatures. They were empowered to alter their own powers and composition in whatever way they thought fit, subject only to the proviso that the procedures through which such alterations were made complied with the 'manner and form' specified by any British or colonial law in force in the colony at the time the alteration was made. 'Colonial legislatures' were not given such powers. They were however granted full authority to alter their respective court systems to suit their own preferences.

In the early 1850s, the political maturity of Cape society remained some distance short of meriting the grant of responsible government. Yet in some respects, the Cape's system of representative government did appear to be in advance of its time. The right to vote for members of the representative assembly established under the Cape's 1853 constitutional arrangements was restricted, but on a 'colour blind' basis. The franchise was granted to all adult male British subjects who either earned an income of at least £50 per year or who occupied (whether as owner or tenant) property with an annual rental value of £25 or more.[63] This was broadly in line with the franchise in Britain, where the right to vote was contingent upon being a male adult who owned appreciable amounts of property: the notion of a universal franchise based

[59] A. Keith, *Responsible Government in the Dominions* (Oxford: Clarendon Press, 1912).

[60] Section 1 provided that a British Act or statutory instrument would be presumed to be effective in the colony only if its text (either expressly or by necessary implication) unambiguously conveyed that intention.

[61] The term is used here in the loose sense, to embrace all forms of judicial law-making.

[62] *R* v *Marais, ex parte Marais* [1902] AC 51.

[63] S. Trapido, 'The Origins of the Cape Franchise Qualifications of 1853' (1964) *Journal of African History* 37.

solely on adulthood was considered an eccentric, even dangerous notion at that time, and would remain so for over sixty years.[64]

The level of the Cape franchise qualification, and its embrace of all racial groups, had been the subject of fierce controversy in the Cape and Britain in the 1840s and early 1850s.[65] Despite vigorous requests from Cape whites for a representative system, the British government doubted that Cape society could produce a legislature that would not be riven by bitter Anglo-Dutch and/or white versus non-white factionalism. That the concession to local sentiment was eventually made in 1853 owed much to the Liberal government's decision in the 1840s to settle convicts in the Cape against the wishes of the colony's white inhabitants. The policy offered the Dutch and the more liberal members of the British community a cause in which to unite against continued British government control of all their affairs.

William Porter, then the Cape Attorney-General, drafted much of the 1853 constitution. He was an ideological liberal, who took the view that all men possessing at least a rudimentary education and modest financial means should be entitled to participate in the election of their law-makers. His advocacy of a colour-blind franchise also had a pragmatic basis:

> "I would rather meet the Hottentot at the hustings voting for his representative, than meet the Hottentot in the wilds with his gun over over his shoulder".[66]

Dutch settlers had no intrinsic enthusiasm for this principle, but were driven to accept it by the fact that they could thereby muster overwhelming support within the white community overall for a franchise level that was sufficiently low to ensure that most Dutch men were granted the right to vote. This support, coupled with the approval of leaders of the Coloured community, was sufficient to garner the British government's approval for Porter's proposed constitution.

The significance of the franchise law should perhaps not be overstated. Although *de jure* colour blind, the Cape's monetary qualification was *de facto* disproportionately beneficial to whites, whose superior economic status translated directly into superior political power.[67] It was nonetheless the case that Cape political society contained a strong vein of what would then have been regarded as 'liberal' ideology. This was reinforced in 1857 when Saul Solomon, a Cape MP, established the *Cape Argus* newspaper. Solomon was known in Cape circles as a 'negrophilisit', and his newspaper—in addition to campaigning vigorously for responsible government in the Cape—pursued a markedly liberal policy on race relations.[68]

[64] See I. Loveland, *Constitutional Law* (London: Butterworths, 1996), ch. 7. Indeed, in the 1830s, advocates of the principle had been convicted of sedition; see Z. Chafee, 'Freedom of Speech in Time of War' (1919) *Harvard LR* 932 at 950–951.

[65] Information in the following paragraphs is drawn from Trapido (1964), n. 63 above.

[66] *Ibid*. at 53.

[67] Thompson (1995), n. 1 above, pp. 64–65: G. Lewis, n. 4 above, pp. 8–9.

[68] Potter, n. 40 above, pp. 37–38.

The British government took few steps to establish a colour blind political culture in Natal. Indeed, the early stages of Natal's colonial development were marked by the introduction of an extremely rigid system of racial discrimination fashioned by Theophilious Shepstone. Shepstone appeared to conceive his system as one of benevolent paternalism rather than oppression. Native blacks should be territorially separated—and thus segregated politically, economically and socially—from whites in order that they be protected from white corruption and exploitation.[69] Shepstone's paternalism was not widely shared by Natal's white inhabitants. As noted above, white immigrants into Natal since 1840 had been predominantly British, and, in terms of the fierceness of its attachment to Imperial values, Natal was the most anglophile of the southern African colonies. Yet its white citizens were intensely racist in their attitude to non-whites. Few had any empathy with the Cape's (relatively) liberal race laws. They shared with the burghers of the Free State and the Republic the belief that while the white 'races' of South Africa might be divided on many political issues, they were united in their abhorrence for and resistance to any suggestion that non-whites should enjoy equal political rights with whites.

British suspicions that neither the Natal nor Cape governments could be fully trusted to maintain peaceful relationships with African tribes in neighbouring, non-British territories were in large part reponsible for the delay in granting either colony reponsible government.[70] The Cape eventually achieved this status in 1872, its first Prime Minister being Sir John Molteno.[71] By that time however, the economic and hence political significance of southern Africa was beginning to undergo a marked change.

Diamonds

The precision with which boundaries had been drawn by the colonial powers in southern Africa assumed vast importance in 1867, when diamonds were discovered near Kimberly. It seemed likely that the diamond fields would straddle lands held by the Cape colony, by the Griqualand republics, and by the Orange Free State. Britain resolved the dispute by giving control of much of the diamond resources to Griqualand.[72] Free State suspicions that this was simply a device to deprive the boer community of the wealth the diamonds would bring were soon borne out. By 1880, Britain had annexed Griqualand and subsequently turned it into an administrative district of the Cape.

[69] Davenport (1978), n. 1 above, pp. 331–333; Bennet, n. 10 above, pp. 75–77; J. Cell, *The Highest Stage of White Supremacy* (Cambridge: CUP, 1982), pp. 52–55.

[70] Lloyd (1996), n. 1 above, pp. 168–169; Pakenham, n. 1 above, pp. 47–48.

[71] *Ibid.* pp. 1–2.

[72] Pakenham, n. 1 above, pp. 46–47; D. Kruger, 'The British Imperial Factor in South Africa from 1870–1910', in L. Gann and P. Dignan (eds.), *Colonialism in Africa 1870–1960* (Cambridge: CUP, 1969), pp. 326–327.

The ensuing diamond rush was to have profound consequences, in both the short and long term, for the political future of southern Africa. Its immediate impact was to expose a hitherto entirely agricultural economy to the pressures of intense industrialisation, and to expose the hitherto predominantly boer white population of the area to a rapid influx of mostly British white immigrants, known as '*uitlanders*' to the boers. Both factors offered the prospect of Britain gaining effective control of the region through the vehicle of economic and demographic rather than military imperialism.

Kimberley, now sited just on the Cape side of the Cape's border with the Orange Free State, became the central urban focus of the mining industry. The industry itself was a sprawling rather than tightly contained phenomenon. Kimberley's rapid growth was led almost entirely by *uitlanders* and native black Africans, many of whom (despite Britain's penchant for redrawing colonial borders) lived and worked within the Free State. The Free Staters, both the boer and the former Cape Anglophiles who had settled in the Free State in the 1850s, subjected the latter group to its traditional inferior status. The *uitlanders'* inferiority was somewhat more subtly constructed, primarily by restricting their right to participate in elections for the *Volksraad*.[73] The most sustained attempt to turn the prospect of *de facto* British control of the Free State into a reality was launched by Cecil Rhodes. Barely twenty years old when the diamond fields were discovered, Rhodes combined degree studies at Oxford with ruthless entrepeneurism in the diamond industry and increasingly successful forays into the Cape's political life. Rhodes believed not simply that British values were best, but that he had a personal duty to see such values dominant in all of southern African culture; "We are the first race in the world, and the more of the world we inhabit, the better for the human race".[74] He possessed a similarly inflexible determination to use political, economic or if need be military means to bring those ends about. Rhodes was never to be an advocate of direct British rule of the southern African colonies: his ambition was rather to ensure that the indigenous governments of the colonies managed their own affairs according to a system of values which of themselves furthered Britain's imperial interests.[75] Rhodes found the press a particularly potent vehicle in this respect. By 1870, the *Cape Argus* had become part of a burgeoning press empire—the Argus group—which had swallowed up several smaller, independent newspapers. Rhodes, in association with other major players in the diamond industry was a major shareholder in the Argus group, and promptly succeeded in moving its editorial line in a rather less liberal direction.[76] The *Argus* remained the dominant newspaper in the colony until the mid–1870s, when the *Cape Times*—an independent journal which initially adopted the *Argus'* formerly liberal political views—was established.

[73] Marquard, n. 1 above, pp. 172–180.

[74] K. Roskam, *Apartheid and Discrimination* (Leyden: AW Sythoff, 1960), p. 84), cited in Troup, n. 1 above, at p. 161.

[75] M. Belof, *Britain's Liberal Empire 1897–1921* (London: Metheun and Co., 1969), pp. 39–46.

[76] Potter, n. 68 above, pp. 37–38.

While Rhodes was single-minded in his ambitions for southern Africa, British government policy was both inconsistent and unstable. In the mid–1870s, Lord Carnarvon, the Secretary of State for the Colonies in Disraeli's Conservative administration, had urged that the four colonies be united into a single federation, along the lines of the model successfully used in Canada. Carnarvon's involvement in the federation of Canada had been the high point of his political career. To engineer agreement for a similar policy in the ostensibly more fragmented and troublesome colonies of southern Africa would be an immense political and diplomatic triumph, and one Carnarvon longed to achieve. Parliament laid the ground work for such an initiative in the South Africa Act 1877. But Carnarvon's plans enjoyed virtually no support at all in any of the four white colonies.[77] This did not deter him altogether. The abortive attempt at consensual integration was promptly followed by more aggressive measures.

The rabidly pro-British colonists in Natal had taken pains to ferment political instability in the Republic. This was done primarily by 'inviting' anglophile settlers in the Republic to send pleas to the British government to save them from the allegedly repressive political conditions imposed on them by the Republic's government. In 1877, ostensibly in response to such pleas, Theophilous Shepstone led a small force across the border from Natal to annex the Republic for Britain and thereby repudiate the agreements reached in the Sand River Convention.[78] The invitation was largely a sham. Shepstone had intervened at Carnarvon's request, a request which had apparently not been approved by the Cabinet and of which Disraeli was at most vaguely aware.[79]

Carnarvon's capacity to embroil the Disraeli government in military activities in the north-eastern reaches of southern Africa were not exhausted by the annexation of the Republic. Nor, indeed, were that government's subsequent actions entirely the result of unilateral initiatives undertaken by the Colonial Secretary. Over the next few years, a bitter war was fought against the Zulu and Sotho tribes in Natal and the eastern Cape. Britain's taste for military conquest seemed no less developed than that of the trekboers. The Zulus inflicted a calamitous defeat on the British forces at Isandlhwana in January 1879. However their numbers and their weaponry were no match in the longer term for the British forces, which finally crushed the Zulus' efforts to preserve their independence at the battle of Ulundi.[80] The Zulu wars had provoked fierce party political controversy in Britain. Gladstone had condemned the Disraeli government's policy, arguing that the natives' only 'crime' was; "to defend against your

[77] On Carnarvon's scheme see L. Thompson, 'Great Britian and the Afrikaner Republics 1870–1899', in L. Thompson and W. Wilson (eds.), *The Oxford History of South Africa Vol II: South Africa 1870–1966* (Oxford: Clarendon Press, 1971): Marquard, n. 1 above, pp. 144–146: D. Kruger, 'The British Imperial Factor in South Africa from 1870–1910', in L. Gann and P. Dignan (eds.) *Colonialism in Africa 1870–1960* (Cambridge: CUP, 1969), pp. 328–330.

[78] Kruger, n. 77 above, pp. 329–331; Thompson (1995), n. 1 above, pp. 134–135.

[79] Pakenham, n. 1 above, pp. 41–43.

[80] Thompson (1995), n. 1 above, pp. 124–125; Lloyd (1996), n. 1 above, pp. 201–203. A gripping account of the campaign is offered in Pakenham, n. 1 above, ch. 14.

artillery with their naked bodies, their hearths and home, their wives and families".[81] Among the lower ranks of the Liberal party, two of the party's most radical young members, Sir Charles Dilke and Joseph Chamberlain, co-ordinated a fierce and extensive campaign on behalf of the autonomy of the Zulu people.[82]

Given its army's technological superiority, the wholesale slaughter and subjugation of native tribes and the annexation of Zululand was a relatively simple affair for the British government. Britain also took steps to minimise the possibility of a recurrent Zulu military threat by creating a fragmented government structure in the annexed territory. Rather than rule the area directly, Britain carved it up into a dozen separate units, each nominally presided over by a Zulu chief.[83] The fostering and preservation of political disunity within the sub-divided Zulu people (echoing the opportunistic divide and rule tactics of the boer trekkers) thus became a staple ingredient of British policy. Basutoland was dealt with in a more orthodox fashion. It was granted the status of a 'Crown Colony'[84] in its own right in 1884.

Britain's military adventurism in the north-eastern region of southern Africa substantially compromised native blacks' readiness and capacity to accept employment in Natal's overwhelmingly agricultural economy. White Natalians consequently chose to 'import' indentured labourers from the Indian sub-continent to work in the colonies' thriving sugar industry.[85] Some 150,000 plantation workers had come to Natal by 1900. Many remained in the colony after serving their term of labour, and they were joined by an Indian merchant class which emigrated to Natal to service their commercial needs. At the turn of the century, Natal's Indian population outnumbered the colony's whites.[86]

But by the mid–1880s, the imperial picture in southern Africa was becoming increasingly complicated. Belgium, Germany and France began to establish a substantial presence in central and southern Africa.[87] Under the terms of the Berlin Convention of 1885, the European powers 'gave' control of the Congo to Belgium, handed South West Africa to Germany, and set in train a frantic race among the European states to maximise the political and economic benefits they might derive from the continued colonisation of the African continent.[88] The

[81] The extract is from an election address made during the 1880 general election campaign; quoted in R. Jenkins, *Gladstone* (London: Macmillan, 1995), p. 425.

[82] R. Jenkins, *Sir Charles Dilke* (London: Collins, 1958), pp. 117–119.

[83] Pakenham, n. 1 above, p. 88.

[84] The 'Crown Colony' form of imperial control emerged in Jamaica in the mid–1860s. Although such colonies retained the trappings of an internally representative system of government, their elected assemblies exercised minimal influence over the British-appointed Governor who was in effect both legislature and executive within the colony's borders: Lloyd (1996), n. 1 above, pp. 180–181.

[85] Thompson (1995), n. 1 above, pp. 99–100, 113.

[86] Beinart W. (1994), n. 1 above, pp. 43–5. Both were greatly outnumbered by native blacks. The figures for 1904 were: whites—97,109; blacks—904,041; Indians—100,918; Coloureds—6,686: L. Thompson, *The Unification of South Africa* (Oxford: Clarendon Press, 1960), p. 486.

[87] Lloyd (1996), n. 1 above, pp. 207–208; Pakenham, n. 1 above, esp. chs. 1, 10–11, 14.

[88] Pakenham, n. 1 above, ch. 14.

European powers had little difficulty in agreeing with each other that international law should recognise all areas of sub-Saharan Africa (including the northern reaches of southern Africa) which were not yet colonised by Europeans as *terra nulliius*; even if they were not empty of people, these lands were empty of 'civilised' people. They could thus be claimed as colonies by the technique of 'occupation'; neither conquest nor cession would be necessary for the European powers to gain legal control of such territory.[89] The political and legal scene was thus set for the manic 'Scramble for Africa' between the Germans, French, Belgians, British and Italians which began in the mid–1880s.[90]

In addition to the German and Belgium presence in southern Africa, Portugal was already an established power in the region. Discontent with Britain in either the Republic or the Orange Free State now possessed an added danger from the British perspective, for it might lead the boer governments to seek political or even military assistance from the other European imperialist states. While the boer states *per se* posed no appreciable threat to Britain's imperial interests, the prospect of either the Free State or the Transvaal turning into a client state of the rapidly expanding German Empire was an altogether more alarming proposition. In the event, the boers' first attempt at armed rebellion against British rule was to be a largely 'independent' venture.

[89] J. Crawford, *The Creation of States in International Law* (Oxford: Clarendon Press, 1979), pp. 177–181; Bennet, n. 10 above, pp. 79–80.

[90] And which is compellingly charted in Pakenham, n. 1 above.

2

The Boer Wars

Shepstone's annexation of the Republic is difficult to defend in legal terms. The Sand River Convention had seemed to grant the Republic *de jure* control over its internal affairs and recognised that it was in most respects an 'independent' country. That the Republic's Volksraad chose to manage those internal affairs in ways which treated Anglophile whites less favourably than boers could hardly been a cause for surprise, either to the British government which signed the Convention or those that succeeded it. For the boer politicians and the boer people of the Republic, regaining and maintaining their government's autonomy was a just as well as a pressing cause.

I. THE FIRST BOER WAR

By 1880, Paul Kruger had become the leading political figure in the Republic's boer population. His ancestors had arrived in the Cape in 1713, and later generations had been among the first of the *voortrekkers*. As a boy, Kruger himself had taken part in the Great Trek in the 1830s. His formative years were spent in a tiny white community infused with the belief that British rule was an evil that the boers had either to flee or to fight, and faced by the practical reality of sustaining an expansionist agricultural existence against the constant hostility of a more numerous native black population.[1]

Kruger had never had any formal education: indeed, it has been claimed that he had never read any book other than the bible.[2] Kruger was a member of the *Dopper Kerk*,[3] and adhered to a Calvinist fundamentalism so extreme that he reputedly went to his deathbed still believing that the earth was flat.[4] Yet in the political context of the time, such attributes were not necessarily a shortcoming. Kruger held an unshakeable belief in the divine rectitude of the boers' ambitions to escape from British influence, to dominate the native tribes, and to preserve their essentially rural culture and fundamentalist religious beliefs. Shepstone's

[1] J. Meintjes, *President Paul Kruger* (London: Cassell, 1974), pp. 10–28; L. Thompson, *The Political Mythology of Apartheid* (New Haven: Yale University Press, 1985), pp. 81–85.

[2] T. Pakenham, *The Scramble for Africa* (London: Abacus, 1992), pp. 91–92.

[3] See p. 17 above. On Kruger's religious motivations see I. Hexham, "Afrikaner Nationalism 1902–1914" in P. Warwick (ed.), *The South African War* (London: Longman, 1980).

[4] F. Troup, *South Africa: an Historical Introduction* (London: Methuen, 1972), p. 162; L. Thompson, *A History of South Africa* (New Haven: Yale University Press, 1995), p. 137. For a more sophisticated account of Kruger's theological beliefs see T. Moodie, *The Rise of Afrikanerdom* (London: University of California Press, 1975), pp. 25–27.

annexation of the Republic threatened the religious, economic, cultural and racial foundations of Kruger's boer ideology. It could not be long before such threats became intolerable. Kruger was prepared, if need be, to go to war with Britain in defence of his ideals.

Between 1877 and 1880, the Republic's boers had adopted peaceful methods in an attempt to regain self-government. Kruger had travelled to London on two occasions to plead their case. Both missions ended in failure.[5] Their future hopes rested in large part on Gladstone's Liberals winning power in Britain's 1880 general election.[6] However the Liberal victory did not bring the expected change in policy. In December 1880, 5,000 boers met—in defiance of British rule—to elect a new Volksraad. Its first action was to declare war.[7]

In the initial skirmishes, the boers killed and captured several scores of British soldiers and relieved them of their rifles, ammunition and cannon. The boer commandoes then won a stunning military success at Majuba in February 1881,[8] succeeding both in embarassing the Gladstone government and confirming that restoring peace through solely military means might prove an immensely costly adventure, in terms both of money and soldiers' lives. Gladstone saw little purpose in pursuing such a policy.[9] A negotiated peace, the Pretoria Convention, was signed in August 1881. Its terms in effect restored to the Republic the degree of self-government it had enjoyed under the Sand River Convention.[10]

The picture was complicated by Germany's increasingly forceful presence in south west Africa. The Gladstone government had prevaricated in the early 1880s over a Cape government plan to annex much of the south western coastal strip of southern Africa.[11] Bismarck seized the opportunity offered by Britain's indecision to claim the territory for Germany. Gladstone's government, embarassed by the defeat at Majuba, and facing growing (and expensive) unrest in Ireland, Egypt and Afghanistan, had neither the desire nor the capacity to stand in Bismarck's way over this matter.[12]

Gladstone was nevertheless careful to ensure that boer autonomy remained within existing borders. In the aftermath of the Pretoria Convention, many of the Republic's white inhabitants had begun yet another trek, this time to the

[5] Meintjes, n. 1 above, ch. 8.

[6] D. Kruger, "The British Imperial Factor in South Africa from 1870–1910" in L. Gann and P. Dignan (eds.), *Colonialism in Africa 1870–1960* (Cambridge: UP, 1969), pp. 330, 331.

[7] L. Thompson, 'Great Britain and the Afrikaner Republics 1870–1899', in M. Wilson and L. Thompson, *The Oxford History of South Africa: Volume II 1870–1966* (Oxford: Clarendon Press, 1971); Pakenham, n. 2 above, p. 93.

[8] Pakenham, n. 2 above, pp. 95–96, 100–105.

[9] Pakenham, n. 2 above, pp. 106–107. Gladstone evidently attached little significance to southern Africa. Roy Jenkins' epic biography *Gladstone* (London: Macmillan, 1995) makes no reference at all to the first Boer war. Gladstone's colonial concerns were at that time focused on Ireland and Egypt.

[10] Meintjes, n. 1 above, ch. 10; D. Schreuder, *Gladstone and Kruger* (London: RKP, 1969), ch. 4.

[11] Land that is now part of Namibia.

[12] Pakenham, n. 2 above, pp. 206–207, 213.

west towards the Kalahari desert. Two new 'republics', styled Goshen and Stellaland, were proclaimed on territory already occupied by native tribes.[13] Any further westward expansion threatened to create a boer corridor between German South West Africa and the Transvaal. Gladstone found this prospect so alarming that he responded readily to Rhodes' suggestion that the British government should annex the land concerned in 1884, renaming it Bechuanaland, to provide a buffer territory between German South West Africa and the Republic.[14]

The war proved a considerable catalyst to Kruger's political career. In 1882, he was elected President of the newly re-named (by the British government) Transvaal, rooting his political base in the Calvinist fundamentalism of the Dopper Kerk and drawing his intellectual credibility from the philosophers and theologians at Potchestfrom.[15] His first success in office was to travel to London to renegotiate the Pretoria Convention. He returned having won approval for once again renaming the Transvaal the South African Republic. More significantly, he had persuaded the British to relinquish control over native affairs within the Republic, and to permit the Republic to negotiate treaties with the Orange Free State. The London Convention of 1884 offered an early indication that Liberal as well as Tory governments in Britain would be prepared to abandon the fate of non-whites in southern Africa to the tender mercies of boer fundamentalists if that was to be the price of securing peaceful co-existence among the white 'races'.[16]

II. THE 'INDEPENDENT' BOER REPUBLICS

If blessed with the benefit of just a few years hindsight, the British may have been far less accommodating to Kruger's ambitions.[17] In the mid-1880s, substantial gold reserves were discovered in the Witwatersrand, on a scale which promised to bestow economic benefits which would dwarf those provided by the diamond fields at Kimberly. By this time, Britain's pre-eminent position within the world's money markets was coming under increasing threat from the emergent industrial super-powers of the USA and Germany.[18] Given that international confidence in a country's financial power was substantially determined by its government's capacity to defend its currency with gold, the evident 'loss' of the Republic's gold reserves was an unfortunate blow to British commercial and

[13] The boers claimed the indigenous occupants were not 'civilised', so the land was *terra nullius*.

[14] T. Lloyd, *The British Empire 1558–1995*, 2nd edn. (Oxford: OUP, 1996) pp. 211–212; Pakenham, n. 2 above, pp. 216–217. The territory is better known to modern observers as the independent country of Botswana.

[15] The size of the Republic, and hence of Kruger's achievement in becoming its President, is nicely illustrated by the elections returns: Kruger won 3,471 votes; his opponent 1,171.

[16] Schreuder, n. 10 above, ch. 7.

[17] D. Judd, *Balfour and the British Empire* (London: Macmillan, 1968), ch. 10.

[18] E. Hobsbawm, *Industry and Empire* (Harmondworth: Penguin, 1972), pp. 191–193.

imperial ambitions and an obvious spur to future British interference in the Republic's internal affairs.[19] But it was by no means obvious that the loss could be easily repaired. Unlike the Kimberley diamond fields, the gold of the Rand was located squarely in the centre of boer territory: there was no scope for Britain to gain control of it through the type of diplomatic manoeuvrings it had used to deprive the Free State of control of the diamond reserves.

Gold

The potential wealth of the Rand's gold reserves presented Kruger's government with the possibility of fashioning a boer state with sufficient economic power to become *de facto* as well as *de jure* an independent force—perhaps even the dominant force—in southern Africa's political development. The challenge the government faced was to regulate the growth of the industry in a way that struck an acceptable balance between maximising revenue to the Republic's treasury and minimising the 'anglicising' and 'nativising' effect that rapid industrialisation of the Rand would have on boer culture and political structures.[20]

These tensions were simultaneously both chronic and acute. The Rand gold rush bore little similarity to the romanticised notion of gold prospecting in the American west. Individual entrepeneurs did not scoop shining nuggets from glittering streams. While the Rand's gold reserves appeared to be vast, the great majority of the ore was both low grade and deeply cast. It could be profitably extracted only by techniques requiring massive industrialisation and investment.[21] Kruger's government, whose members and ideology were still rooted in a predominantly agrarian political and economic base, was thus faced with the prospect of an instantaneous industrial revolution:[22] and a revolution whose leaders came not from within, but beyond the Republic's borders.

Rhodes, in his guise as economic entrepeneur, immediately became a major factor in the Rand's gold industry. He had by this time gained a virtual monopoly, through his control of the De Beers corporation, of southern Africa's diamond industry. The economic leverage this provided enabled him to make substantial progress towards gaining *de facto* control of the gold mining industry, fashioning what was in effect a cartel—the 'Randlords'—between a small oligopoly of British-owned companies.[23] Rhodes' cartel gained a visible form in 1889, when the various companies formed 'The Chamber of Mines' to act as a

[19] S. Marks and S. Trapido, 'Lord Milner and the South African State', (1979) 8 *History Workshop* 50; Robinson and Van-Helten, n. 21 below.

[20] On Kruger's personal difficulties in coming to terms with the transition see Meintjes, n. 1 above, ch. 13.

[21] P. Richardson and J. Van-Helten, 'The Gold Mining Industry in the Transvaal 1886–99', in P. Warwick (ed.), *The South African War* (London: Longman, 1980).

[22] Marks and Trapido, n. 19 above, pp. 59–61: Cell, *The Highest Stage of White Supremacy* (Cambridge: CUP, 1982), pp. 65–70.

[23] Richardson and Van-Helten, n. 21 above.

political mouthpiece for conveying the views of the industry to Britain and as a political pressure group within the Republic.[24] For Kruger's government, the Chamber was in some senses 'an enemy within'.

The government's perception that boer culture was under siege was heightened by a massive expansion in the Rand's newspaper industry.[25] The *Diggers' News* led the way in 1886; five others had followed it into circulation by the end of the next year. Unsurprisingly, Rhodes and the other Randlords sought to enhance their political leverage in the Republic by expanding the Argus group of newsapers. In 1889 the group launched *The Star* newspaper in Johannesburg. *The Star's* initial editorial policy was clearly pro-mining, but it expressed its views in way which were calculated not to antagonise Kruger and his government.[26] Kruger was not without his supporters in the press; by the mid-1890s the *Diggers' News* had merged with a rival paper, *The Standard*, and followed a consistently pro-governmental editorial line.[27]

The Republic's administration took steps to minimise the risk of internal subversion by resolutely refusing to employ either British immigrants or Cape anglophiles in the many new government posts that sprang up to regulate the mining industry and to police the rapid population growth and urban expansion that accompanied it. The Republic's own boer population had not yet been sufficiently educated in large enough numbers to fill these positions, so Kruger imported large numbers of Dutch and German administrators to staff government offices. There could have been few clearer indications that the Republic saw the boer political identity as both separate from and (politically) superior to the anglophile white community.

The growth of the gold mining industry also subjected the Republic to two further 'invasions' in addition to that of the British-leaning mining magnates. The first took the form of a flood of European immigrants, known dismissively (like their counterparts in the Kimberley diamond fields) as '*uitlanders*' by the boers. The *uitlanders* were predominantly although not exclusively British in origin, many drawn from the Cornish tin mines and other coal mining areas. Because of the geological nature of the Republic's gold fields, few immigrants had realistic prospects of making a fortune through independent prospecting. They nevertheless saw that working for the large mining companies offered them the opportunity of earning substantially higher wages than they could at home. Many came simply for the short or medium term, leaving their families behind them: the Rand's *uitlander* population was almost entirely composed of adult males. Most lived in Johannesburg, a town which grew at a phenomenal pace in the last decades of the nineteenth century.

[24] H. Simons and R. Simons, *Class and Colour in South Africa 1850–1950* (Harmondsworth: Penguin, 1969), pp. 57–59.

[25] See J. Mervis, *Fourth Estate* (Johannesburg: Jonathan Ball, 1989), ch. 1 for a lively account of the early years of press activity in the Republic.

[26] E. Potter, *The Press as Opposition* (London: Chatto and Windus, 1975), pp. 39–40.

[27] Mervis, n. 25 above, pp. 9–10.

Uitlanders comprised however only a small part (barely ten per cent) of the mines' labour force. The industry's vast profits (and thus indirectly the Republic's hugely increasing tax revenues) were dependent largely on the employment of native African workers at bare subsistence wages. The Republic itself could not satisfy this demand, with the result that large numbers of native workers were drawn to the Rand not simply from the other British colonies in southern Africa, but also from Portugese East Africa (Mozambique).[28] Their presence on the Rand formed a further link in an intricate chain of class, race and cultural divisions which lent considerable complexity to the balance of political forces in the Republic, and cast a large shadow over any efforts to predict how those forces would shape the development of its political and economic history.

Crudely stated, Kruger's government and the bulk of the boer population detested Rhodes and his fellow Anglo-Imperialists in the Chamber of Mines. The boers nevertheless reluctantly accepted that the Republic's long-term economic security depended upon the Chamber's efficient exploitation of the Rand's gold reserves. Kruger's government regarded the *uitlanders* with equally pronounced distaste. They were seen as the harbingers of an alien, urban culture, concerned only with the short-term issue of maximising their wages and indifferent to the long-term welfare and stability of the Republic. Yet it also saw them as potential bulwarks against the commercial power of the Anglophile Chamber of Mines and as potential allies in the continuing economic and political subordination of non-white workers. For the boers detested above all the prospect that native blacks might at some future date achieve through their employment in the gold mining industry a level of economic security and educational experience which would lead them to demand, with prospects of success, that they be afforded an equal political status to the boers.

But Kruger's government was not the only player on the Rand stage which held dissonant views about the other actors involved in this particular political drama. The British *uitlanders* brought with them a strong tradition of industrial trade unionism. The Witwatersrand Mine Employees and Mechanics Union (WMEMU) was founded in 1892[29] to represent their interests. Quite where those interests lay was however a potentially perplexing question. Solidarity amongst workers against employers—the dominant paradigm in British trade union history—seemed to have only limited applicability on the Rand. For while the Rand's British trade unionists were to regard their employers as one target for their solidarity, the Republic's government (because it subjected them to the present reality of political subordination) and the mines' black labour force (because black workers offered the future prospect of supplanting white workers or, at the least, of depressing whites' wages) were also perceived as a threat.[30]

[28] W. Beinart, Twentieth Century South Africa (Oxford: OUP, 1994), pp. 31–32; Richardson and Van-Helten, n. 21 above.

[29] Simons and Simons, n. 24 above, pp. 52–56.

[30] Simons and Simons, n. 24 above, pp. 56–58; Marks and Trapido, n. 19 above.

The Kruger government, fearing that the 'indigenous' boer population would be swamped by white immigrants, subjected the *uitlander* population to a series of political disabilities. The most graphic of these was a law passed in 1890 which required *uitlanders* to have been resident in the Republic for fourteen years before they were permitted to vote in Volksraad elections. The impact of this law was staggering. In 1899, the 76,000 (overwhelmingly *uitlander*) whites living in Johannesburg elected just one member to the Volksraad, yet the 3,500 boers living in the remote district of Lydenburg returned two.[31]

One might have expected that such discrimination would preclude any co-operation between the mining union and the government. Yet such was not the case. In 1893, the Vollksraad enacted the Republic's first substantial law regulating the mines. The measure was in large part drafted by the WMEMU. It contained extensive health and safety provisions, and also imposed a rigid colour bar on certain forms of employment; only whites (whether boer or *uitlander*) would in future be permitted to work with explosives in the mines. The colour bar was nominally also a safety measure. The majority in the Volksraad maintained that 'Kaffirs' were not capable of performing such tasks competently.

Its true purposes reveal a degree of political sophistication on Kruger's part. The law managed to emphasise and extend the economic and political subordinancy of blacks, while simultaneously both buying off (at black workers' expense) some *uitlander* discontent with the pro-boer discrimination inherent in the Republic's electoral laws, and also (by denying the Chamber of Mines access to cheaper, black workers) driving a further wedge between the potential anti-boer unity of the Cape-dominated Chamber and their *uitlander* workforce. From the mine-owners' perspective, the colour bar simply raised the cost of labour, and thence threatened profits. The notion that black Africans were in some objective way 'incapable' of doing 'skilled' jobs in the mines was in principle absurd and in practice belied by years of experience. The Chamber of Mines thus opposed the law: not, it should be stressed, because of any abstract empathy with the notion that the bar subjected blacks to intolerable discrimination, but because it deprived employers of the cheapest possible labour.[32]

Kruger's administration also antagonised the Chamber of Mines by granting monopolies to boer companies to supply certain 'essential' products to the mines. Dynamite and access to the railways were the most obvious of these. Liquor was a less obvious but, if only from the workers' viewpoint, no less essential commodity.[33] From the Kruger government's perspective, the monopolies were a crude attempt to ensure that a substantial portion of the mining industry's profits remained in boer rather than anglo- hands. To the Chamber of Mines, to liberal opinion in the Cape, and to successive British governments, they smacked at best of feudalism and at worst simply of corruption.

[31] L. Thompson, *The Unification of South Africa* (Oxford: Clarendon Press, 1960), p. 128.

[32] Richardson and Van-Helten, n. 21 above.

[33] Richardson and Van-Helten, n. 21 above, pp. 32–34; Simons and Simons, n. 24 above, pp. 61–64.

By the mid-1890s, the Republic's political, economic and cultural demography was bitterly and deeply fragmented. Even without the added complication of British imperial involvement, the Republic was an inherently unstable society. When its internal divisions were placed within the broader context of Britain's foreign policy ambitions, that instability assumed an increasingly volatile hue. In the Cape colony, in contrast, both internal and external factors pointed towards the consolidation of a markedly more consensual form of realpolitick.

Political developments in the Cape and the construction of a 'liberal' Afrikaner identity

Political sentiment within the Cape's white community had nominally become considerably more fragmented by the time that gold was discovered on the Rand. John X. Merriman was by then the figurehead of a faction of the British community that increasingly saw its 'national identity' as Cape or 'South African' rather than British.[34] The grouping had no desire to detach the Cape from the British Empire, but regarded overt imperial interference in southern African affairs as a hindrance rather than a help to the development of political stability. Merriman had been Prime Minister of the Cape in the early 1880s, and was the architect of the proposal that the Cape annex the south west African coastal strip. The British government's failure to act decisively on the issue had convinced Merriman that British involvement in southern African issues was best avoided.

Merriman had been born and educated in England. A superfical view of his politics might suggest he was a 'liberal'. On closer examination, his beliefs appeared to be a curious mix of the progressive and reactionary, driven more by the recognition of having to accommodate necessary evils than by an evangelistic pursuit of ideals. He was a trenchant supporter of the Cape's colour-blind political and legal culture. This was not because he felt any particular personal affinity or comradeship with non-whites—he had on occasion expressed the wish that there were no blacks in South Africa.[35] Rather he was motivated in part by the belief that denial of political equality to non-whites would eventually provoke them into armed rebellion—a rebellion which, ultimately, would be successful.

Merriman was also driven by a desire to deny political equality to southern Africa's emergent white proletariat. His concept of 'whiteness' had a cultural tinge: Cape Coloureds, Asians and native blacks who were educated, prosperous and conservative in outlook were much preferable as citizens (as long as there were not too many of them) to impecunious, ill-educated whites, whose

[34] See Beinart (1994), n. 28 above, ch. 3.
[35] Hancock (1962), n. 44 below, pp. 218–214.

short-term economic interest and debased personal morality rendered them prey to demagogic political ideologies. Merriman thus had a distinct preference for loading voting power in favour of settled, rural communities, whose members' status as farmers and landowners implied that they would have the long-term stability and prosperity of the province at heart. Recent immigrants to urban areas, whether in the Cape or on the Rand, offered no such guarantees, and should therefore be afforded at most a diluted form of political citizenship. Merriman had continued to serve in various Cape governments after having been Prime Minister. He had been Rhodes' Treasurer-General[36] and then Secretary of Agriculture between 1890 and 1892, before leaving the government in a row concerning corruption in the administration of the Cape's railway system.

The emergence of the "Afrikaner Bond" as a distinct political force within the Cape was an event of greater significance than Merriman's ascendancy within the anglo-community. The roots of the Bond can be traced back to the early 1870s, when S.J. du Toit, a Calvinist clergyman in the Dopper Kerk, founded a journal called *Die Afrikaansie Patriot*.[37] Du Toit's initial concern was to foster a national Afrikaner identity by creating a written Afrikans culture. The literary tradition he envisaged would be recognisably Dutch in form but reflecting the realities of boer life in the Cape and gradually developing its own vocabulary and grammatical rules, which could serve as a unifying force within the boer community. The Afrikaner Bond was initially established by du Toit as a separatist boer political party in 1879, and flourished as such in the immediate aftermath of the first Boer War. Du Toit rapidly proved adept at manufacturing mythical symbols to serve as rallying points for boer culture. The squalid rebellion at Slagtersnek in 1815,[38] which many boers had assisted the British to repress, was transformed by his pen into a brave and noble fight by hardy boer pioneers against the gratuitous tyranny of the British government.

Such divisive rhetoric had little appeal to other prominent Cape Afrikaners. By the mid-1880s, a wealthy Cape farmer, J.H. Hofmeyr had become the most influential voice within the party.[39] Hofmeyr had no desire to be a political leader in the *de jure* sense of becoming Cape Prime Minister, a prize which would seem to have been easily within his grasp. But he exercised such leadership *de facto*—in part through his newspaper *Volksriend*, which merged with *De Zuid Afrikaan* in the mid-1870s[40]—by ensuring that Cape governments were led, if not by Bond members, then by politicians with whose policies the Bond was in broad agreement.

Much like Merriman, but in contrast to Du Toit and especially to Kruger in the Transvaal, Hofmeyr's objective was to safeguard white rather than just boer

[36] The Cape equivalent of the British office of Chancellor of the Exchequer.
[37] Troup, n. 4 above, pp. 163–165; Hexham, n. 3 above; Potter, n. 26 above, p. 34.
[38] See p. 10 above.
[39] Beinart, n. 28 above, p. 38.
[40] Potter, n. 26 above, pp. 33–34.

dominance within southern Africa. For Hofmeyr, the status of 'Afrikaner' was as open to whites of British as of boer descent and leaning. He saw no merit in the separatist route to boer dominance favoured so uncompromisingly by Kruger's government in the Transvaal, and, albeit to a lesser extent, by the government of the Orange Free State. Hofmeyr's concern was to achieve the 'reconciliation' of the Anglo and boer communities. The key to the long-term success of the project of creating a distinct Afrikaner identity demanded that boer and Briton submerge their current differences into a fused identity, neither wholly British nor wholly Dutch, but combining and/or accommodating the best features of both and directed above all to securing the political dominance of the white race. Hofmeyr, like Merriman, was also prepared to extend his notion of 'inclusiveness' to embrace non-whites who could meet relatively high standards of education and affluence, and to restrict it to exclude the venal lower strata of the white working class. Like Merriman, he supported retention of the Cape's formally colour-blind, property-based electoral system.[41]

Du Toit, who was committed to an exclusionist vision of Afrikaaner development, could find no common ground with Hofmeyr and Merriman. He subsequently left the Cape for the Republic, where he became Kruger's Minister of Education,[42] having already earned the President's gratitude for creating in his mythical rendition of the Slagtersnek rebellion a potent rallying cry for the Republic's war against the British.[43]

Notwithstanding Du Toit's departure, the Bond's membership remained largely boer rather than British in origin. Merriman, for example, while instinctively empathetic to the Bond's vision for southern Africa's political development and in his own view a 'South African' rather than a Briton, was too anglophile in background and cultural sympathies to build a significant power base within the Bond. He—and those like him—might be the Bond's allies; they could never be its leaders. The Bond was thus willing to lend support to Cecil Rhodes' efforts to become Prime Minister of the Cape—an objective which Rhodes achieved in 1890. But such support was by no means wholehearted, and was most certainly not unconditional.[44]

The territorial expansion of the British Empire in Africa lay at the heart of Rhodes' political ambitions. His economic adventurism and electoral successes were merely tools with which to achieve that end. The Free State and the Republic were obstacles, both geographically and politically to such expansion. Thus, just as the boers of the Great Trek had to pass through the unreceptive territory of the Griqualand Republics to strike north into the Free State and the Transvaal, so Rhodes was compelled to continue the task of British expansion by leapfrogging over the Transvaal and pushing into the area that was

[41] Hancock (1962), n. 44 below, pp. 23–27.

[42] Thompson, n. 7 above, pp. 302–304.

[43] Thompson (1985), n. 1 above, ch. 5.

[44] K. Hancock, *Smuts. Volume 1: The Sanguine Years 1870–1919* (Cambridge: Cambridge University Press, 1962), pp. 52–57.

subsequently to become Rhodesia. His motives were also economic. Rhodes believed, erroneously, that the land would prove as rich in gold as the Rand.[45]

Rhodes began the process in the early 1890s.[46] His methods were as much military as diplomatic or commercial. Wars were fought with the Shona and Matebele tribes, who like the San, the Khoikoi and the Zulus before them, were unable to resist the Europeans' greater force of arms.[47] The British government maintained no more than arm's length control of the Rhodesian territories. In a manner reminiscent of the first Dutch settlement in the Cape, they were formally administered by a Company operating under a Charter granted by the British Crown.[48] As well as attracting the approval of the British government,[49] the policy initially enjoyed broad support from the Bond and from the Merriman-led faction of the Anglo white population, in part because of the promise of economic growth it offered, and in part because it extended the political reach of Afrikanerdom.

The 'reconciliation' project was made manifest in concrete legal initiatives, as well as in the more amorphous sense of cultural coalescence. In 1882, the Cape legislature had provided that Dutch be recognised as an official language in Cape, and there was a broad acceptance that Afrikaans would at some future date have developed into a sufficiently mature and elaborate written language to enjoy similar status.

The Rhodes' Cape government lent further impetus to the trend by promoting legislation in 1887 which reformed the Cape's franchise laws in a manner perfectly consistent with Merriman and Hofmeyr's views. The formally colour-blind basis of the laws was retained. However the property occupancy qualification was increased to £75 per year and a literacy test was added.[50] These reforms undoubtedly removed the right to vote from some poor whites and Coloureds. But in practical terms they had a disproportionate impact on native blacks, whose access to education and land-ownership was restricted by their generally less affluent economic status.

The 1887 Act also made a rather more direct assault on the voting rights of native blacks. As noted in Chapter 1, the African tribes native to the Cape had traditionally held their land on a communal rather than individual basis. The Cape's original electoral laws had treated all the male adult occupants of such property as landowners and/or tenants for franchise purposes. The new legislation reversed that presumption: land occupied communally could no longer be

[45] Pakenham, n. 2 above, p. 375.

[46] Kruger, n. 6 above, pp. 336–338.

[47] Thompson, n. 4 above, pp. 137–138; L. Marquard, *The Story of South Africa* (London: Faber and Faber, 1955), pp. 200–202.

[48] Thompson (1960), n. 31 above, pp. 49–51; Pakenham, n. 2 above, pp. 341–342, 354–355.

[49] Arthur Balfour, a leading figure in the British Cabinet and soon to become a Conservative Prime Minister spoke warmly of Rhodes' initiative in 1893. Not only did the Company secure expansion of British influence at no cost to the taxpayer, but Britain was 'exceptionally fortunate' to have a man such as Rhodes steering events: Judd, n. 17 above, p. 159.

[50] Simons and Simons, n. 24 above, pp. 30–31; Troup, n. 4 above, pp. 30–31; Pakenham, n. 2 above, p. 381.

invoked by any of its inhabitants as a means to satisfy the colony's voting requirements. The innovation had no impact on whites, Coloured or Indians, but obviously had the effect of disenfranchising substantial numbers of black Africans.[51] Native blacks nevertheless retained some appreciable electoral influence: they comprised over forty-five per cent of the electorate in five constituencies in the early 1890s.[52]

The increasing 'gap' between the formally colour-blind nature of Cape electoral law and its discriminatory practical impact seemed likely to be exacerbated by the provisions of the 1894 'Glen Grey' Act.[53] The Act introduced a new type of individual land tenure, the quitrent system, in specified areas of the colony. Native blacks wishing to occupy land in these areas could do so only under this form of tenure. In many respects, quitrent was analogous to long leasehold. But occupants of such land were specifically denied the right to vote. By way of compensation for this disenfranchisement, the Act also established an 'autonomous' system of native local government in these areas.

Such measures seemed calculated to strengthen the ties between the Anglophile and Afrikaans whites in the Cape. They promised to create a broad front of moderate white opinion (incorporating a small minority of Coloureds and 'civilised' blacks) which could stand united against overt British interference, against boer separatism, and against the native tribes.

Yet from Kruger's vantage point, Rhodes was a quintessential example not just of British cultural imperialism, but also of rampant urban capitalism. Insofar as the Bond offered Rhodes support for such policies, its members were guilty of a betrayal of their boer compatriots in the northern republics. Kruger's government resolutely set its face against Rhodes' efforts to tempt it into a more interdependent commercial relationship with the Cape. Railways were an essential ingredient of this complex political recipe.[54] The Rand's gold obviously needed to be exported, just as the mines required large amounts of machinery and labour to be brought into the Rand. Access to the coast was a vital precondition of the gold mines' economic success. Control of the railways thus offered the company or government which owned them the prospect of reaping lucrative profits—and thus gaining political influence—by serving the transport needs of the gold industry.

Rhodes' concern was to ensure that the bulk of this traffic would run on a rail-line from Johannesburg to Cape Town, to be built and run by the Cape government. Politicians in Natal hoped that the bulk of the Rand traffic would run east-west rather than north-south, on a line running between Johannesburg and

[51] T. Davenport, 'Civil Rights in South Africa 1910–1960' (1960) *Acta Juridica* 11.

[52] P. Rich, *State Power and Black Politics in South Africa 1921–1951* (London: Macmillan, 1996), p. 196.

[53] Simons and Simons, n. 24 above, p. 43; L. Thompson, 'The Compromise of Union', in L. Thompson and M. Wilson (eds.), *The Oxford History of South Africa: Volume II 1870–1966* (Oxford: Clarendon Press, 1971), pp. 337–339.

[54] Beinart, n. 28 above, pp. 48–49; A. Porter, 'British Imperial Policy and South Africa 1895–1899', in Warwick, n. 21 above.

Durban. Kruger wished to have an option that operated independently of Anglophile control. His preferred route ran east from Johanesburg to the port of Delagoa Bay in Portugese East Africa. Constructing the line remained for many years at the forefront of Kruger's ambitions. It was eventually opened in 1895.

The Republic's unwillingness to rely predominantly on the Cape as its import/export route also obstructed Rhodes' ambitions in Rhodesia. A direct Cape to Rhodesia railway line could skirt the Republic by running along the eastern edge of Bechuanaland, but a route travelling through the Republic would offer the obvious benefit of linking up with other routes in Johannesburg. This simple geographical fact afforded Kruger valuable political leverage.[55] Kruger was similarly unreceptive to Rhodes' advocacy of a customs union between the Republic, the Cape, the Free State and Natal.

Rhodes was a sufficiently skilled politician to present the Republic's position as one of intransigent antideluvianism, both to the British government and to his anglophile supporters in the Cape, and also, crucially, to the Afrikaner Bond. Rhodes' ambitions were particularly fondly regarded by Joseph Chamberlain, who took office as Secretary of State for the Colonies in Salisbury's Tory administration in July 1895.

Chamberlain remains one of the most quixotic political figures of the Edwardian era. The son of a wealthy Midlands industrialist, Chamberlain did not formally enter party politics until his early thirties, by which time he had greatly increased his family's fortune. His party politics were initially those of a radical—and provincial—Liberal. As Mayor of Birmingham between 1873 and 1875 he became the foremost proponent of 'gas and water municipal socialism', and associated himself firmly with the most progressive faction of the Liberal party. Chamberlain was elected to the Commons in 1876, where he achieved considerable prominence along with his close friend and colleague Sir Charles Dilke by opposing the Disraeli government's Zulu wars.[56] Chamberlain entered Gladstone's Cabinet in 1880. His radical views on domestic politics were however allied with a consistently aggressive imperialism on matters of foreign policy, a sentiment that led him to oppose Gladstone's advocacy of home rule for Ireland, firstly from within the Liberal party, but ultimately by crossing the floor with other so-called Liberal Unionists and agreeing to serve in a Tory coalition administration.[57]

As Colonial Secretary, Chamberlain embarked immediately on policies designed to foster economic development within the colonies. 'Salutory neglect' had not even a vestigial role in his understanding of Britain's imperial future.[58]

[55] The British government approved a route through Bechuanaland in 1890; Lloyd (1996), n. 14 above, pp. 241–243.

[56] See p. 24 above.

[57] Pakenham, n. 2 above, pp. 487–488.

[58] Porter, n. 54 above, pp. 39–42; Lloyd, n. 14 above, pp. 240–241; Pakenham, n. 2 above, pp. 488–490; A. Parker, *The Origins of the South African War* (Manchester: Manchester University Press, 1980), pp. 49–51.

His vision of the Empire is well captured in a speech he made in January 1896:

> "Let us do all in our power by improving our communications, by developing our commercial relations, by co-operating in mutual defence; and none of us will ever feel isolated . . . and in the time to come, the time that must come, when these colonies of ours have grown in stature, in population and in strength, this league of kindred nations, this federation of Great Britain, will not only provide for its own security, but will be a potent factor in maintaining the peace of the world".[59]

Chamberlain was not on close personal terms with Rhodes,[60] but the two men shared a considerable ruthlessness in their political dealings. Yet in 1895, by promoting a project of the most spectacular conceptual and practical ineptitude, Rhodes succeeded not just in losing the support of the Bond but in attracting its ardent opposition, in turning J.H. Hofmeyr from being his friend and colleague into his implacable political opponent, and in pushing the Anglo-Afrikaners led by Merriman into firm alliance with the Bond on a distinctly anti-imperialist political platform.[61] Chamberlain, who was able to conceal his complicity in the project, suffered no obvious political disadvantge from the episode. But his involvement, and by implication the approval of the British government, provided the boer governments of the Republic and the Free State with good reasons for assuming that their 'autonomy' from British rule was at best a very fragile political phenomenon.

The Jameson Raid

The plotting which led to the 'Jameson raid' of late December 1895 had echoes of Shepstone's contrived 'rescue' of oppressed Britons in the Republic in 1877. Rhodes and Jameson—seemingly with at least the tacit approval of Chamberlain—[62] prompted a substantial number of the Rand's *uitlanders* to send pleas to the British government requesting protection from the discriminatory laws enacted by the Republic's Volksraad. *The Star* had by this time forsworn its diplomatic approach to relations with Kruger, and had been active in fermenting and publicising the *uitlanders'* grievances. The Rhodes/Chamberlain plan was for a substantial number of *uitlanders* to go so far as to launch an armed rebellion against the government and request help from the Cape, whereupon Jameson would lead a heavily armed cavalry force to their assistance. His attack would be presented as an initiative to safeguard the rights of the mostly British *uitlanders*.[63]

59 Quoted in the *Dictionary of National Biography*, p. 111.

60 Porter, n. 54 above.

61 Hancock (1962), n. 44 above, pp. 72–74.

62 Porter, n. 54 above, pp. 41–45; Thompson (1995), n. 4 above, pp. 136–140; Hancock (1962) n. 44 above, pp. 58–60.

63 Pakenham, n. 2 above, ch. 27.

The *uitlander* rebels proved as few in number and as faint-hearted in resolve as Jameson was impetuous in spirit and ill-prepared in practice. The 'rebellion' was a comically inept affair, which placed so little strain on the Republic's police and commandoes that Jameson's raiders were rapidly disarmed and imprisoned. In a move designed (successfully) both to increase the British government's embarassment and enhance international sympathy for the boer cause, Kruger handed the invaders—who included the then editor of *The Star*—over to Britain for trial and punishment.[64]

The raid attracted great criticism both in Britain and in the other self-governing colonies.[65] The British government and the House of Commons consequently took great pains to cover up Chamberlain's involvement in the plot.[66] Rhodes' role could not however be concealed, and the political fall-out from the episode was to bring his political career to a premature end and trigger a fundamental political realignment both within the Cape and within southern Africa more generally.

The tacit support Rhodes had received from the Bond was withdrawn. From Hofmeyr's perspective, Rhodes stood exposed not as an Afrikaner seeking to secure the ascendancy of 'civilised' white values, but as a conduit for an aggressive and intrusive form of British imperialism, in pursuit of which the British Tory government was ready to suppress the boer identity and disregard Afrikaner sentiment. The separatism favoured by the Republic and the Free State now struck the *Bond* as a far more defensible political strategy. In part, this expressed itself simply in a diffuse shift in political sympathies. But it also took a corporeal form. Many young Afrikaners subsequently left the Cape to live and work in the Republic.[67] They took with them an intense dislike of British imperialism, and thus offered Kruger the chance of ending his government's reliance on Dutch and German administrators.

The raid also prompted a clear fragmentation within the Cape's Anglophile community.[68] One faction, focused around the Progressive party, remained loyal to Rhodes, to Jameson (whose British administered 'punishment' was hardly severe) and to the ideal of a 'British' southern Africa. In contrast, Merriman and his supporters considered the raid an outrage, and irrespective of

[64] Thompson (1995), n. 4 above, pp. 138–140; A. Porter 'British Imperial Policy in South Africa 1895–9', in Warwick (1980), pp. 37–49; K. Hancock, *Smuts Volume 1: the Sanguine Years* pp. 56–65 (Cambridge: CUP, 1962); Lloyd (1996), n. 14 above, pp. 241–245. Kruger resisted pressure from other boer politicians to execute the invaders, in part it seems because he feared they might then become martyrs to the anglo cause by providing British propogandists with the opportunity to create their own Slagtersnek myth; Meintjes, n. 1 above, pp. 195–197. On the role of *The Star* see Potter, n. 26 above, pp. 39–40.

[65] The criticism in Britain was not just from radical Liberals. Chamberlain's own Cabinet colleagues were (quietly) dismayed by his activities. Arthur Balfour, Salisbury's nephew and then Leader of the House, observed caustically that Chamberlain's "favourite method of dealing with the South African sore is by the free appplication of irritants"; Judd, n. 17 above, p. 162.

[66] Pakenham, n. 2 above, pp. 502–503.

[67] Hancock (1962), n. 44 above, pp. 60–70.

[68] Porter, n. 54 above.

their distaste for Kruger and his ideology of boer supremacism, saw no merit in continued British intervention in internal southern African affairs.

The Free State responded to the raid by forming a military alliance with the Republic. Their combined forces would presumably have been no match for a determined British invasion, but the raid enabled both governments to play successfully to a range of external audiences. Rhodes' alienation of the Bond and the Merriman strand of the Anglo-community offered Kruger a climate of supportive opinion within the Cape which needed little cultivation; and while it remained Britain could expect at best minimal Cape support for any further military adventures in the north; at worst, the British government might expect parts of the Cape Afrikaner population to take up arms on the boers' behalf.

Kruger's government emphasised the distance between the Republic's political ideology and the anglo mores of the Cape by promoting a change to the *grondwet*. The original *grondwet* had forbidden equality between blacks and whites in matters of state and church. The 1896 amendment removed the church and state clause—henceforth it seemed the Republic's law would require discrimination on all matters.

The Republic also took pains to secure German support for its autonomy. The Kaiser had sent Kruger a congratulatory telegram in the wake of the Raid.[69] The German government also enabled Kruger to purchase large numbers of German rifles, thereby enhancing the effectiveness of the boer commandoes. The prospect of the Republic serving as a vehicle for German interests in central and eastern southern Africa was a disquieting one for Britain.[70] But dealing with Germany was also a dangerous game for Kruger to play. German support for the Republic could either lead Britain to foreswear military interference in the Republic's affairs for fear of having to fight Germany as well, or prompt it to act quickly to neutralise the German threat.[71]

Nor was the British audience ignored. Liberal and radical opinion in Britain perceived the Republic's citizens as an 'oppressed' people, with Britain's Tory government and the rampant capitalism of the Chamber of Mines as the oppressors.[72] (Liberal opinion seemed temporarily blinded to or unconcerned by Kruger's attitudes towards native blacks and other non-whites). Further British aggression would also therefore be hampered by internal political dissension.

The Jameson Raid confirmed, not just to the resolutely anti-British boers of the Free State and the Republic, but also to hitherto Anglo-tolerant Afrikaners in the Cape, that the British could not be relied upon to respect the constitutional arrangements they had made for the southern African colonies. Imperial professions of respect for the rule of law had now to be regarded with disbelief. In this regard, as we shall see below, the Free State could plausibly have claimed

[69] A move which had led to a sharp rebuke from his grnadmother, Queen Victoria; Pakenham, n. 2 above, p. 504.

[70] Thompson (1995), n. 4 above, pp. 139–140; Porter, n. 54 above.

[71] Kruger, n. 6 above, pp. 343–344.

[72] B. Porter, 'The Pro-Boers in Britain', in Warwick (1980), n. 21 above.

to be occupying the constitutional moral high ground. The Republic, in contrast, seemed as little concerned as Rhodes and Dr Jameson to observe formal constitutional proprieties.

Constitutionalism and the rule of law in the Republic: The *Brown v Leyds* controversy

In addition to endorsing the principle that; "there should be no equality betwen black and white with regard to matters of church and state",[73] the Republic's *Grondwet* seemed to place certain procedural constraints on the power of the Volksraad. The text of the *Grondwet* differentiated between two types of legislation—*wetten* and *besluiten*. *Wetten* could be passed only by a two-thirds majority in the Volksraad, and had no legal effect until three months after the vote was taken.[74] This form of law seemed to be required in respect of a range of major political and economic issues. *Besluiten*, in contrast appeared to require only a simple majority in the Volksraad, and could be used to change laws regulating all other matters. The rationale underlying the *wetten/besluiten* distinction would seem readily understandable—'fundamental' or 'constituent' legal principles should be more difficult to alter than minor laws.

The *Grondwet* also indicated that all proposed *wetten* and *besluiten* had to be promulgated in the Republic's official government *Gazette* three months prior to their being discussed in the Volksraad. This requirement was evidently intended to afford voters the opportunity to communicate their views on the projected laws to the legislature before they were enacted. The *Grondwet* also provided that *besluiten* could have immediate effect in 'urgent' situations. The *Grondwet* did not have an explicit amendment mechanism. This might logically suggest that the constitution was utterly rigid, and could not be changed through any process. However most boer politicians (including Kruger) construed the absence of an amendment mechanism to indicate that the *Grondwet* was entirely flexible, and a majority of members in the Volksraad could do with it whatever they wished. This view had some 'historical' support: since the Republic's inception, the Volksraad had in fact passed virtually all laws as *besluiten*, including those amending the *Grondwet* itself.

This process had not been subject to judicial challenge, since the Republic had not initially had a judiciary in the orthodox Anglo-American sense. The judicial element of government was entrusted to a 'High Court' comprised of three *landrost*, political appointees who need not be legally qualified (or even, in some cases, literate) and a twelve person jury. In 1877, the constitution was purportedly 'amended' via a *besluit* which created a new High Court, staffed by three

[73] See p. 17 above.

[74] For a detailed account of the provisions see J. Bryce, *Studies in History and Jurisprudence Vol. 1* (Oxford: Clarendon Press, 1901), ch. 7.

legally qualified judges.[75] The Chief Justice was J.G. Kotze, a twenty-eight-year-old British educated lawyer.

Executors of McCorkindale v Bok, NO

The High Court was afforded the opportunity to offer its view on the status of the *Grondwet* in an 1884 decision, *Executors of McCorkindale v Bok, NO.*[76] The case centred on the constitutionality of a *besluit* through which the Volksraad purported to appropriate some farms owned by the McCorkindale Estate. McCorkindale argued that since the *besluit* had not been publicised in the *Gazette* three months before being enacted, it contravened the *Grondwet*—and as such had no legal status—since there was no scope for regarding it as dealing with an 'urgent' matter.

Kotze C.J., for a unanimous court, considered the argument that the *Grondwet* placed limits on the powers of a bare majority in the Volksraad to be misconceived. Kotze accepted that the *Grondwet* expressed the will of the Republic's 'people', and as such should be regarded as a statement of fundamental *moral* principles. However this did not mean the *Grondwet* had fundamental legal status. The relationship between the *Grondwet* and the Volksraad was not analogous to that between the Constitution of the USA and the American Congress. Rather, Kotze suggested, the Volksraad enjoyed the same legal powers as the British Parliament—namely that its members could by a bare majority of votes, through any procedure that they thought appropriate, enact laws on any subject matter whatsoever.

Kotze was driven to this conclusion largely by the weight of historical practice since the Republic's foundation; *besluiten* having immediate effect had always been accepted as enjoying full legal force. He suggested the American analogy was inappropriate because the USA's consitution was built on a federal basis, while the Republic was a unitary state. He was also unpersuaded by the thesis of an eminent Dutch jurist, a Professor Opzoomer.[77] Opzoomer suggested simply that the *Grondwet* was the expression not just of fundamental moral principles, but also fundamental legal rules. Those rules defined the powers of the Volksraad, and specified the procedures through which such powers should be exercised. If the Volksraad failed to follow those rules, it acted beyond the limits of its competence, and it was the responsibility of the courts to recognise such acts as having no legal effect.

Kotze suggested it was 'unfortunate' that Opzoomer's thesis had not been clearly embraced by the founders of the Republic,[78] but he saw no scope for the

[75] See H. Corder, 'The Judicial Branch of Government: an Historical Overview", in D. Visser (ed.), *Essays on the History of Law* (Cape Town: Juta & Co., 1989).

[76] [1884] Official Reports of the High Court of the South African Repblic 202.

[77] *Aanteekening op de Wet Houdende Algemeene Bepalingen*—discussed in *McCorkindale* at 212–213.

[78] *Ibid.* at 210.

Republic's courts to claim a power to review the constitutionality of *wetten* or *besluiten*: "If the Court were to assume such an authority, it would raise itself above the Volksraad, which would be illegal and contrary to the *Grondwet*".[79] Kotze was also no doubt mindful of the (im)practical legal consequences which would flow from the court's embrace of Opzoomer's thesis—namely that the court might be obliged to invalidate a great many of the Republic's laws, including—and here the situation assumed a surreal hue -the law creating the High Court itself!

Hess v The State

The matter seemed therefore to be closed. However eleven years later, in 1895, Kotze C.J. announced that he had changed his mind regarding the legal status of the *Grondwet*. The issue before the court in *Hess v The State*[80] was a criminal libel law, enacted by the Volksraad in 1893. Hess had been convicted under the statute for publishing an article in an English language newspaper, *The Critic*, casting doubts on the integrity of a High Court Judge. Kotze C.J. and his two fellow judges quashed the conviction on a point of statutory interpretation. However the bulk of the Chief Justice's opinion was taken up with a discussion of principles of constitutional law.

Kotze indicated that "further consideration and study"[81] had led him to believe that Professor Opzoomer's analysis of the *Grondwet* was indeed correct, and that his own views in *McCorkindale* were poorly conceived. He now believed that the *Grondwet*—as the expression of the founding principles of government articulated by the Republic's 'people'—had to be viewed as the creator of all the ordinary institutions of government, be they the Volksraad, the Presidency or the courts. It fell to the courts to ensure that neither the Volksraad nor the President exceeded their lawful authority by 'testing' such purported laws against the requirements of the *Grondwet*. The absence of any express 'testing power' in the text of the *Grondwet* was no barrier to the court's exercise of this jurisdiction; as in the USA "this testing right is a tacit and necessary outcome of a popular government under a constitution".[82] Thus if the Volksraad attempted to achieve through a *besluit* an end that the *Grondwet* required to be enacted through a *wet*, the court would be obliged to declare the purported law invalid. Similarly, unless a situation of urgency prevailed, the court would be required to strike down any *wet* or *besluit* which had not been publicised in the *Gazette* three months prior to its enactment.

[79] *Aanteekening op de Wet Houdende Algemeene Bepalingen*—discussed in *McCorkindale* at 211.

[80] [1895] Official reports of the High Court of the South African Republic 112.

[81] *Ibid.* at 116.

[82] *Ibid.*

Brown v Leyds

Kotze's fellow judges in *Hess* made no comment on his constitutional analysis, so it was not clear to what extent his change of heart was shared within the court. Nor was it clear how Kruger and the Volksraad might respond to any attempt by the court to quash a *wet* or *besluit*. Both questions were answered shortly afterwards, by *Brown v Leyds*[83] a case triggered by a governmental attempt to revoke gold prospecting licences.

Kotze C.J.'s leading judgment began by echoing his comments in *Hess* that the High Court's previous decisions (including his own) on the status of the *Grondwet* had been erroneous. That mistake could however be remedied. The Court was not bound by an inviolable rule of *stare decisis*. It could depart from its previous holdings; "for very cogent reasons and upon a clear manifestation of error".[84] That error was now clearly revealed to the Chief Justice. The solution to the error required recognition of two principles: first that the powers of the Volksraad were limited by the *Grondwet*; and secondly, that the High Court possessed the constitutional authority to determine if those limits had been exceeded.

Kotze C.J. thought the first proposition easy to establish. The *Grondwet* was the creation of the Republic's people, not of its Volksraad. The Volksraad itself was in turn a creation of the *Grondwet*. This logically demanded that:

> "[the power] entrusted to the Volksraad by the people shall be exercised under and in accordance with the terms of the authority or mandate as expressed in the constitution [*Grondwet*]. Were this not so, the agent or mandatory would have greater power than the principle, a position which cannot for a moment be maintained . . . What would otherwise be the use of a *Grondwet*, if it is not to be observed by the various departments of State, to which it has been appointed as a guide?".[85]

The second proposition was, in Kotze C.J.'s view, similarly self-evident:

> "It is, moreover, within the province of the Court to consider or *test*[86] a particular law by reference to the Constitution. In exercising this function the Court does not by any means raise itself above the legislature, but remains within its province, by inquiring whether what has been submitted to it is in reality a law".[87]

From a legal perspective, the judgment in *Brown* seems eminently defensible. Kotze C.J. took care to root his analysis in a wide field of comparative legal principle. His reasoning drew heavily on American case law and theorisation,

[83] The authoritative English language report of *Brown* appears in The Official Reports of the High Court of the South African Republic Vol IV 17 (translated by J. Kotze). On the background to the case see L. Thompson 'Constitutionalism in the Boer Republics' (1954) *Butterworths South African LR* 49; Hancock (1962), n. 44 above, pp. 69–72; J. Dugard, *Human Rights and the South African Legal Order* (Princeton: Princeton University Press, 1978), pp. 20–23.

[84] Official Reports of the High Court of the South African Republic, Vol IV, 17 at 24.

[85] *Ibid*. at 26–27.

[86] Emphasis added.

[87] *Ibid*. at 27.

but also made copious references to the constitutional law of continental European countries, especially Germany, Holland and Belgium. If the case revealed malpractice in the constitutional sense, fault would seem to lie with the Volksraad for ignoring the *besluiten/wetten* distinction and with the High Court for not enforcing the provision from the outset. On this view, *Brown* was simply remedying past wrongs.

Yet the whole *Brown v Leyds* episode has a rather deeper—and overtly political—history. Kotze was a judge who seemed to take a relaxed view of judicial 'independence'.[88] He had been one of Kruger's rivals in the Republic's 1892 Presidential election, and was a prominent member of the Republic's anglophile community. In the eyes of Kruger and his supporters, Kotze's judgment in *Brown* owed little to constitutional principle and much to party political expediency: Kotze was perceived as abusing his judicial power in order to curry favour both with the Republic's anglophile community, with its mining companies (for whom the Volksraad's habit of altering laws arbitrarily was a major hindrance to sound economic planning), and, more importantly, with the British government.

Kruger was ready to accept that no legislative attempt should be made to reverse the specific outcome of the *Brown* litigation. But he had little empathy with the case's broader holding that the wishes of a majority in the Volksraad should and could be subject to the constraints of a higher body of constitutional law, especially if the power to interpret that law rested with a court.[89] In 1899, he was to describe such a principle as 'the devil itself'.[90] He had no empathy at all with its promulgation by the High Court in these circumstances. At his instigation, the Volksraad immediately passed a *besluit* affirming its unhindered right to legislate via *besluiten*, denying that the High Court had any power to question the constitutionality of such laws, and imposing penalties (including dismissal) on any judge who had the temerity to do so. The expected response of the Court was that the new *besluit* was itself unconstitutional.

The then Chief Justice of the Cape, Sir Johan Hendrik (Henry) De Villiers,[91] tried to broker a compromise between the Court and the President, but was unsuccessful. Kotze then began an essentially political campaign castigating Kruger and the Volksraad for (as he saw it) contravening the *Grondwet*. Kruger's response was to dismiss him from office, claiming the power to do so under the terms of the 1897 *besluiten*. Kotze found few of his fellow judges—and evidently an even smaller percentage of his fellow citizens—willing to support his views at this juncture. As a matter of politics, Kruger's views had won

[88] A. Sachs, *Justice in South Africa* (London: University of Sussex Press, 1973), p. 76.

[89] Meintjes, n. 1 above, pp. 208–209.

[90] Kruger's views were firmly rooted in his fundamentalist Calvinism rather than resting simply on a point of political expediency; see Moodie, n. 4 above, pp. 30–31.

[91] See further n. 14 at p. 103 below. De Villiers considered that *Brown* was wrongly decided, but was unable to persuade Kotze to this view. De Villiers' brother, Melius who was at the time Chief Justice of the Free State, believed that Kotze was correct—for reasons that will shortly become apparent; see A. Walker *Lord De Villiers and His Times* (London: Constable & Co., 1925), ch. 17.

the day. Kotze himself was promptly dismissed from office. The evidently (for Kruger) awkward provision in Article 57 of the *Grondwet* that judges be 'left altogether free and independent in the exercise of their judicial power' was pointedly ignored.

The court's decision was subject to a scathing criticism in a leading British academic journal.[92] J.K. Gordon accused Kotze C.J. of poor legal reasoning—for overturning his own previous decisions—and of political myopia—for failing to see that Kruger would have both the power and the will to ensure that the issue was eventually resolved in accordance with his own wishes. Gordon voiced no objection to the principle of supra-legislative constitutions *per se*,[93] but doubted that the Republic's *Grondwet* really merited such a classification, and was quite sure that Kotze had committed a severe jurisprudential error in choosing so weak a legal base as the foundation for overturning not just his own opinion but also the weight of settled practice ever since the Republic was founded. Kruger fared little better in Gordon's estimation. The *besluit* dismissing the judges was characterised as a coup d'etat, the President as an autocrat and the Republic itself as a country subsisting in a state of "scarcely veiled anarchy".[94]

The Argus Printing and Publishing Co. Ltd v The State

Kruger's discontent with the High Court was not limited to the issue of the testing right, nor solely to Kotze C.J.'s innovative jurisprudence. Given *The Star's* complicity in the Jameson Raid, Kruger's government was increasingly unwilling to tolerate the paper's continued championing of *uitlander* interests. The Volksraad had enacted a press law in 1896 which, in addition to imposing severe fines and gaol terms of up to a year on the publishers of defamatory or indecent material, appeared in section 5 to empower Kruger to prevent some newspapers from being published at all:

> "The State President shall at all times have the right with the advice and consent of the Executive Council, to either wholly or in part prohibit the circulation of printed or published matter, the contents whereof, in his opinion, conflict with good morals, or are dangerous to the order and peace of the Republic".

In March 1897, Kruger invoked the section 5 power against *The Star* and order that it cease publication for three months. The Argus group's response was to challenge the ban in the Republic's courts.[95] *The Argus Printing and*

[92] J. Gordon 'The Judicial Crisis in the Transvaal' (1898) 14 *Law Quarterly Review* 343.

[93] And especially, it seemed, for the Republic; "The English reader . . . will easily believe that when legislative functions are entrusted to a peasant parliament of four and twenty elders from among the people, it is at least eminently desirable that some deliberative body should possess a 'testing right' "; *ibid.* at 353.

[94] *Ibid.* at 365. Bryce offered rather more muted criticism of the decision, n. 74 above, pp. 453–457.

[95] Potter, n. 26 above, pp. 39–40.

Publishing Co. Ltd v The State was heard by the two judges who had sat with Kotze in *Brown*—Ames-Hoff and Morice JJ. Ames-Hoff had approved Kotze's reasoning in *Brown*, but Morice had declined to address the issue. In *Argus Printing*, they were faced with the argument—manifestly rooted in the rationale Kotze C.J. deployed in *Brown*—to the effect that the Volksraad's power to regulate the press was controlled by Article 19 of the *Grondwet*, which provided that:

> "The liberty of the press is recognised, provided that the printer and publisher remain responsible for all articles containing anything defamatory or insulting, or attacking anyone's character".

The Argus Group maintained that the *Grondwet* permitted the Volksraad or the President to regulate the press only through the mechanism of imposing punishments in respect of already published material; such powers did not extend to prohibiting the publication itself. The court was in effect being invited to declare section 5 of the 1896 law unconstitutional. As one might have expected, given the nature of the relationship between the Court and the Volksraad after *Brown*, Morice and Ames-Hoff JJ. declined this invitation. They nonetheless concluded that the meaning of section 5 was conditioned by the terms of Article 19, on the ostensibly plausible ground that the Volksraad would not have intended to enact a law which contravened the *Grondwet*. The Court also accepted that the Argus Group's interpretation of Article 19 was correct. It therefore concluded that section 5 had to be construed as a measure which did not give the President a power to prevent publication, but only to restrain the circulation of particular editions of a newspaper which he had determined to be 'in conflict with good morals or dangerous to the peace and order of the Republic'.

Conclusion

Notwithstanding the Court's ingenious use of the *Grondwet* in *Argus Printing* to produce a judgment which would no doubt have antagonised the government but which did not expressly approve the 'testing power', the outcome of the *Brown v Leyds* controversy indicated that—in the Republic at least—formal constitutional structures which purported to prevent narrow legislative majorities from doing whatever they willed to whoever they wished whenever and however they wanted would have little practical legal effect. In the Orange Free State, in contrast, a much more recognisably American constitutional system seemed to have been established as a matter both of law and of politics by 1897.

Constitutionalism and the rule of law in the Orange Free State

As noted above, the founders of the Free State had made express reference to American ideas when framing the country's constitution after the Bloemfontein

Convention.[96] They had in some instances gone so far in imitation of the American system as to incorporate sections of the American constitution verbatim into the Free State's own constitutional arrangements. Such references could no doubt be seen as an attempt to legitimise the boer settlers' preferences for slavery and oppressive race discrimination laws. The Great Trek had been prompted in large part by Britain's abolition of slavery in the Empire and by the Cape's colour blind legislation. In the USA of the 1850s, the institution of slavery still enjoyed constitutional protection, and even those northern states which opposed slavery *per se* had enacted extensive discriminatory race laws.[97] Yet it seems tolerably clear that the framers of the Free State constitution genuinely sought to entrench the fundamental values initially recognised by its 'people' (in the limited sense of white adult males) against the wishes of small and possibly transient legislative majorities within the white male population.[98]

The constitution was drafted in 1854 by a specially convened Volksraad. The constitution placed all legislative power in a new Volksraad, but it drew a distinction between fundamental laws articulated in the constitution itself (*grondwetten*) and ordinary legislation (*wetten*). Ordinary laws could be amended by simple majority. However, amendments to the *Grondwet* required a three-quarters majority in three successive years—a particularly high level of procedural entrenchment.

Until 1874, the Free State had no High Court in the orthodox sense. As in the Republic, judicial powers were vested in a *landrost* which had not been granted, nor ever claimed, the power to determine the constitutionality of ordinary legislation. In practice, the legislature respected the letter of the constitution. The *Grondwet's* terms were amended several times prior to 1874; on each occasion the three-quarters majority in three successive sessions formula was scrupulously followed.

In 1874, the Volksraad created a Court of Appeal, staffed by qualified lawyers. The Court was created by ordinary legislation rather than constitutional amendment. It was not expressly empowered to adjudge the constitutionality of ordinary legislation, and since its status was simply *wetten* rather than *grondwetten* one might doubt that it could lay a defensible claim to have been impliedly given such authority. The US Supreme Court, in contrast, enjoys constitutional rather than simply statutory status, a political fact which underpins its claim to be impliedly empowered to gauge the constitutionality of Congressional, Presidential and State action.[99]

[96] See p. 17 above; Dugard (1978), n. 83 above, pp. 18–19.

[97] E. Corwin, 'The Dred Scott decision in the light of contemporary doctrines' (1911) *American Historical Review* 52; E. Maltz, 'Slavery, Federalism and the Structure of the Constitution' (1992) *American Journal of Legal History* 466.

[98] James Bryce, the former Professor of Civil Law at Oxford, a former cabinet Minister and a noted commentator on comparative constitutional law, spoke in admiring terms of the Free State's constitution; (albeit tempered by condemnation of its overt racism): n. 74 above, ch. 7.

[99] This point is returned to in some detail in Chapter 4.

The Free State's Court of Appeal nevertheless seemed to assume that it did enjoy powers analagous to those of the US Supreme Court. Its most eminent members, among them Melius De Villiers,[100] the first Chief Justice, and M.T. Steyn and J.M. Hertzog, seemed to regard the question as beyond argument. At the same time as the *Brown v Leyds* controversy was raging in the Republic, De Villiers published a lengthy essay in The *Cape Law Journal* on the subject of 'The Relationship of the Judicial to the Legislative Authority'.[101] De Villiers devoted the first half of his article to theoretical issues. He began with a summary of what seemed to be the Krugerite position in the Republic; namely a belief that only the legislature could decide what the law is, and that for a court to possess such a power would place the judges above the law. De Villiers saw no merit in this argument in the context of the Orange Free State's constitutional arrangements; "All these propositions seem to me wholly unacceptable".[102] While the *Grondwet* acknowledged the Volksraad as the state's supreme legislative power, it also bestowed the state's judicial functions on the courts. That judicial function was to interpret law, a function which applied as readily to matters of constitutional law as to ordinary legislation. If this were not the case, there would be no need for the special constitutional amendment mechanism identified in the *Grondwet* itself, for if the Volksraad had the sole power to determine the constitutionality of ordinary legislation it could enact any measures whatsoever through the ordinary legislative procedure by the simple expedient of announcing that the *Grondwet* had not been breached. Nor, De Viliers stressed, was this point one involving simply the relationship between the legislature and the courts:

> "Unfortunately however, the question as to the existence or otherwise of the judge's competency is treated too much as a purely academic question between [legislator] and judge. That the burgher can have any practical interest, and that his rights may be involved, are matters too often overlooked or forgotten. By the Constitutions of most civilised countries, the personal liberty of the citizen is guaranteed. Wherein does this guarantee against violent and despotic actions on the part of any power in the State consist. Clearly in the privilege of being able to appeal to the judicial power. Otherwise the 'guarantee' is useless, nay nonsense".[103]

At root, the issue was whether citizens lived under a system of government secured by law or under a simple despotism.

That the Free State had adopted the former course was, De Villiers suggested, clear from the text of the *Grondwet*. But that presumption was reinforced by practical experience. In the second part of his article, De Villiers recounted an episode of recent political history in the Free State. In the early 1890s, the majority in the Volksraad had proposed to pass by *besluit* a 'law' that would make

[100] As noted earlier, the De Villiers family had colonised large swathes of the southern African legal profession. Melius was the brother of Sir J.H. De Villiers, the Cape's Chief Justice.
[101] (1897) *Cape Law Journal* 38.
[102] *Ibid*. at 38.
[103] *Ibid*. at 42.

breach of the Volksraad's privileges a criminal offence, punishable by up to six months imprisonment. The Volksraad itself was to determine both what its privileges were, and whether a given action or comment had breached them. The 'law' could also be applied with retrospective effect.

The proposed *besluit* provoked considerable public controversy. It also prompted a public statement by the Chief Justice to the effect that it breached several provisions of the *Grondwet:* namely that the judicial power be vested in the courts; that citizens accused of criminal offences be guaranteed a trial by jury; and that no retrospective criminal laws were permissible.[104] In response to the criticism, the Volksraad majority proposed a less draconian measure. This was again attacked by the Chief Justice, with the result that the proposal was withdrawn on the basis that the *Grondwet* did not permit such a *besluit* to be passed.

The Free State courts' resolute commitment to these principles is forcefully illustrated by the contemporaneous judgment of Hertzog J. in *The State v Gibson.*[105] Gibson had published a newspaper article accusing the majority in the Volksraad of partiality and bias in passing a *besluit* annulling the result of an election to one of its seats. The Volksraad's decision was described as "not in strict accordance with justice and civilised laws and a disgrace to the country".[106] Gibson was prosecuted on two counts, both of which were claimed by the State to be crimes under the Free States's Roman Dutch system of common law. The first was that of '*lese majeste*'; the second that of inflicting 'verbal injury' on the Volksraad.

Hertzog J. concluded that the first charge could not be put to the jury at all, as it was constitutionally misconceived. The concept of *lese majeste*, as recognised by Dutch and German authorities, required an attack on the *sovereign* power within the state. Under the terms of the *Grondwet*, the Volksraad did not possess this status:

> "The Volksraad is beyond doubt the highest legislative authority, but still not unqualifiedly the highest authority. Above the legislative authority stands the constitution-giving authority—that is the sovereign people, to whom the majesty belongs".[107]

The second offence—that of verbal injury to the Volksraad—was, in principle, reconcilable with the *Grondwet*. However, Hertzog's instructions to the jury on the way the offence had to be interpreted in effect made conviction impossible. Most significantly, Hertzog instructed the jury that the offence was

[104] All those provisions of the *Grondwet* were lifted from the American Constitution.

[105] Reported in (1898) *Cape LJ* 1. Hertzog also expressed support for Kotze's position in his struggle with Kruger in his extra-judicial statements. Hertzog reputedly regarded Kruger's disrespect for the rule of law a good enough reason to decline Kruger's offer to appoint him Chief Justice of the Transvaal in Kotze's stead; Pirow (ed.), *James Barry Munik Herzog* (Cape Town: Howard Timmins), pp. 23–24.For reasons that will become clear at a later stage, references to Pirow's work are made with some scepticism.

[106] *Ibid.* at 7.

[107] (1898) 15 *Cape LJ* 1 at 4.

not committed if the injury was targeted at a faction or majority of the Volksraad in criticism of a policy decision that the majority had made. Rather it required an attack on the dignity of the Volksraad qua institution in the abstract. Since Gibson's critique had been addressed just to a policy and the majority which supported it, he could not have been guilty of the crime. Hertzog also precluded any prosecution for seditious libel or a civil suit for defamation on the part of an individual member of the Volksraad in response to Gibson's article. He held that legislators in an elected assembly were necessarily and unavoidably motivated by 'partial' considerations; to accuse them of acting on such motives was no more than " a lawful critique. . .with regard to the tendency and propriety of the [*besluit*] passed".[108]

Hertzog's opinion was not subject to political challenge. The weight of opinion both in the Volksraad and among the white population appeared to have no difficulty in accepting what Kruger had so scathingly referred to as the judiciary's 'testing' power. The 'people' of the Free State may have comprised only a small portion of its population, but there seemed no scope to doubt that they, rather than their legislature, were the source of constitutional authority in their fledgling country.[109]

III. THE SECOND BOER WAR

By 1896, M.T. Steyn had moved from the bench of the Free State Court of Appeal to become the country's President. Steyn, a distant relation of Kruger, was an advocate who had trained at the English bar but who, like Kruger, retained throughout his life a rigid belief in safeguarding boer independence against both the British and the native southern African population. After a brief and successful career as an advocate in the Orange Free State, Steyn became a judge in 1889 and was appointed Chief Justice in 1892. He then declared himself a candidate for the Presidency of the Free State in the 1896 election. Steyn ran on a platform which called for closer relations with the Republic. The Jameson Raid occurred at a fortuitous time for Steyn's political ambitions, given that his opponent in the Presidential race was closely identified with the Cape's anglo-community. Steyn won the election with a substantial majority.

The 'English' population of the Free State was smaller than that of the Republic, and many of them had by now become long-term residents rather than *uitlanders*. They posed no realistic threat to boer political dominance. Nevertheless, Steyn was prepared if need be to stand shoulder to shoulder with Kruger in defiance of British imperialism. The aforementioned mutual defence pact signed by the Free State and the Republic in 1897 was the most obvious example of this. In the following two years, the British gave the two boer gov-

[108] 1898) 15 *Cape LJ* 1 at 4.
[109] Cf. Corder (1989), n. 75 above.

ernments further justification for uniting both politically and militarily against imperial aggression.

Milnerism

While Chamberlain, as Secretary of State for the Colonies, bore primary responsibility within the British Cabinet for policy in southern Africa, the figurehead of the British presence in southern Africa was Alfred Milner, who Chamberlain appointed as High Commissioner in April 1897. Milner was only forty-three at this time. As a child and young man, Milner had been an outstanding scholar, first at Kings College, London and subsequently at Balliol. In terms of his political outlook, Milner had much in common with Chamberlain. His party politics in his early years were Liberal, and he had unsuccessfully stood as a Liberal candidate in 1885, following brief periods as a fellow of New College, Oxford, as a barrister and as a journalist. Milner subsequently split with the Gladstonian wing of the Liberal party over the issue of home rule for Ireland, and became a leading figure in the Liberal Unionist Association.[110] Under the patronage of Lord Goschen, a former Liberal who accepted office as Chancellor of the Exchequer in Lord Salibury's Tory government in 1886, Milner embarked upon a meteoric career as a civil servant, serving in Egypt until 1892 and then returning to England to head the Inland Revenue.

Milner's broader domestic political sentiments remained broadly progressive. He shared however with Rhodes—(and indeed with leading British political figures of almost all parties)[111] a dogmatic attachment to 'British race patriotism', whose adherents regarded British culture as a value system to which all other ethnic groups, be they boer or black, should either aspire or be subjected.[112]

The 'Milnerisation' of southern Africa was to proceed on several fronts. Milner expressed some dissatisfaction with the Republic's treatment of its non-white residents. Neither Milner nor Chamberlain could plausibly be seen as champions of racial equality as we now understand the term, and there must be some basis for assuming that Milner's criticism of the Republic in this regard owed as much to a desire to cultivate British liberal hostility to Kruger than to an intrinsic concern with the welfare of blacks.

On the question of the treatment of non-whites, Milner shared some common ground with Merriman and Hofmeyr. Yet he showed no inclination to try to reach an accommodation with either man, both of whom had found their loyalty to Britain much strained by the Jameson Raid. His demands were that

[110] On the nature and immediate causes of the fragmentation of the Liberal party see R. Jenkins *Gladstone* (London: Macmillan, 1995), ch. 32.

[111] Marks and Trapido, n. 19 above, observe that Fabianism and 'racism' in this sense were perfectly compatible bedfellows.

[112] J. Wilson, *A Life of Sir Henry Campbell-Bannerman* (London: Constable, 1973), pp. 299–301; Judd, n. 17 above, pp. 162–163.

Kruger should enfranchise *uitlanders* on the same basis as boers, and that English should be accorded equal status with Dutch/Afrikaans in the Republic's schools.

In combination, these innovations would have swept away the boers' political and cultural dominance within the Republic's white population. In March 1898, Milner made a notorious and manifestly inflammatory speech in which he expressed an ambition to 'separate the sheep from the goats'. The only way in which the Bond and Merriman's supporters could come into the fold with the English sheep was evidently to join in wholehearted condemnation of Kruger's goats.[113]

Milner also meddled overtly in the Republic's internal constitutional affairs, seeking (unsuccessfully) to raise suppport within the Republic for Chief Justice Kotze against Kruger in the aftermath of *Brown v Leyds*.[114] Milner was equally concerned to ensure that the 'right' messages about affairs in the Republic were placed before the British public: he took pains to ensure that *The Times* appointed as its Johannesburg correspondent a journalist in complete sympathy with the 'race patriotism' ideology.[115]

Milner's ostensibly 'political' concerns were firmly intertwined with economic matters. It would be unduly simplistic to equate 'Milnerism' solely with the long-term commercial ambitions of the Chamber of Mines, but there was undoubtedly a symbiotic relationship between the two phenomena.[116] Kruger's government had taken few positive steps to facilitate the mining companies' exploitation of the gold fields: a more Anglo-friendly administration would undoubtedly do so. And, perhaps more beguilingly, a Republic that was *de jure* as well as *de facto* a British colony would offer the British Treasury the means to underwrite London's pre-eminence in the international money markets by giving it access to the world's foremost source of gold:[117] by 1898, the Republic was producing nearly thirty per cent of the world's gold output.[118]

Chastened by the manifest illegality (and no doubt by the spectacular failure) of the Jameson Raid, Chamberlain initially hoped to anglicise Kruger's republics through diplomatic and economic pressure rather than military adventurism. At the very least, Chamberlain wished to ensure that any military action that Britain might undertake against the Republic was rooted in a just response to flagrant boer provocation. Any such initiative would demand the tacit support of the Liberal opposition at home and the neutrality of the Afrikaner population in the Cape.

Milner was considerably more impatient than his Secretary of State. From the outset, he began to weave together the political web which would enable Britain

[113] Hancock (1962), n. 44 above, pp. 73–75.

[114] Porter, n. 54 above, pp. 49–50.

[115] *Ibid.*

[116] For a more unflinching example of analysis of 'Milnerism' as driven almost entirely by narrow economic imperatives see S. Marks and S. Trapido (1979) 8 *History Workshop* 50.

[117] Marks and Trapido, n. 116 above.

[118] Richardson and Van-Helten, n. 21 above.

to wage a 'just' war against what he described as Kruger's 'unprogressive' regime. The *uitlanders*' unabated protests against their exclusion from the franchise formed one strand of the web, as did the far more pervasive political and economic discrimination practised against blacks. Kruger's dismissal of Chief Justice Kotze in the aftermath of *Brown v Leyds*[119] offered two more, insofar as it represented both an attack on Anglo-American notions of an independent judiciary and threatened British mining interests by undermining what little stability the Republic's laws then possessed.

Nor was it difficult for Milner to point to clear breaches by the Republic of the constitutional understandings endorsed by the Pretoria and London Conventions of 1881 and 1884 respectively. Immediately upon Milner's arrival, the Volksraad had passed a *besluit* restricting the rights of residents of other colonies from entering the Republic to seek work on the Rand. This was a blatant breach of the London Convention, to which Lord Salisbury's government responded with a barely veiled threat of military invasion.[120]

Any hope Chamberlain and Milner might have had that the Republic would become more accommodating to *uitlander* interests were dashed by the Volksraad election of 1898. Kruger was again returned as President, having achieved a large majority after a campaign stressing the need to secure the autonomy of the Republic. One of Kruger's most trusted advisers, W.J. Leyds was appointed as State Secretary and promptly dispatched to Europe, (where he recklessly spoke of the Republic as an independent and sovereign state) to try to cultivate anti-British sentiment among the continental powers.[121]

On this latter issue at least, Kruger was outmanouevred by the British. Britain's capacity to undertake military action in southern Africa, if such action was thought desirable, was much enhanced in 1898 by an accord reached with Germany over the disposition of the Portugese colonies in the area. Portugal had offered Britain the colonies as security for a large loan. Rather than respond to this request unilaterally, the then Foreign Secretary, Arthur Balfour, brokered an agreement which confirmed Britain's interest in Portugese East Africa while recognising Germany's claim to the western territory of what is now Angola. Germany's renunciation of any ambition to assist Kruger's resistance to Britain was an essential part of the agreement.[122] Neither Balfour nor Chamberlain believed that the arrangement would satisfy German imperial ambitions in the longer term, but it certainly served a useful, short-term purpose.

By early 1899, Milner had convinced Chamberlain of the need for military intervention. There was no obvious Cabinet consensus on the issue however. Salisbury (the Prime Minister) and Hicks Beach (the Chancellor) harboured

[119] Thompson, n. 7 above, pp. 321–323.

[120] Hancock (1962), n. 44 above, pp. 73–75; Porter (1980), n. 54 above.

[121] Leyds was the State Attorney (the British equivalent of this position would combine the roles of Lord Chancellor and the Attorney General) and nominal defendant in *Brown*. 'State Secretary' was the equivalent of the British Foreign Secretary, although technically the Republic was not permitted to have a 'foreign policy' in the orthodox sense; see p. 28 above.

[122] Judd, n. 17 above, pp. 163–164; Kruger, n. 6 above.

grave reservations as to the practicality of the policy, and Arthur Balfour in particular doubted the legitimacy of Milner's objectives:

> "were I a boer . . . nothing but necessity would induce me to adopt a constitution which would turn my country into an English republic, or a system of education which would reduce my language to the 'patois' of a small and helpless minority".[123]

Chamberlain's room for manoeuvre was however much enhanced by a rapid decline in Salisbury's health. In the final stages of the crisis, the Prime Minister's physical competence was giving his colleagues serious cause for concern, and doubt also existed about the sharpness of his mental abilities.[124] Chamberlain's position within Cabinet on the issue was tantamount to that of first among equals. Nevertheless, the Cabinet en bloc would not jump into war. Rather its members would need to be pushed by Kruger. What was less obvious was the extent to which Salisbury's government[125] would allow Milner to provoke Kruger into taking such precipitate action.

It soon became evident that the Cabinet saw no need to keep Milner on a short rein. W.P. Schreiner, a prominent member of the Bond who had been elected as Prime Minister of the Cape in 1898 (and who remained loyal to Hofmeyr's now tainted ambitions for 'reconciliation'),[126] attempted to mediate between Milner and the leaders of the Republic. His efforts were rebuffed by the High Commissioner.[127] Milner and Kruger met at the Blomfontein Conference in early June 1899[128] in what was presented for British public consumption as a *bona fide* effort to reach a compromise. Yet it seems that Milner had no sincere wish to engineer a peaceful solution to the tension. Kruger responded to Milner's demand that *uitlanders* be granted the franchise after only five years' residence by offering to reduce the then fourteen year limit to seven years. A *besluit* to that effect was indeed enacted in July. Milner may well have doubted Kruger's integrity on this point; as *Brown v Leyds* made clear, 'law' would have a very contingent constitutional status in the Republic. But from Milner's perspective, the 'failure' of the Conference was a success—for it hardened the sentiments of the British Cabinet and the British public in favour of armed intervention. Salisbury signalled his government's intention by moving substantial numbers of troops onto the Natal/Transvaal border. The Republic and the Free State regarded this a prelude to war, and demanded the troops be withdrawn. There is little likelihood that Britain would have done so. In the event, Kruger and Steyn did not wait. In October 1899, the boers and the British were again at war.

[123] Quoted in Judd, n. 17 above, 165.

[124] A. Kennedy, *Salisbury 1830–1903* (New York: Kraus Reprint Co., 1973), pp. 307–310.

[125] The label is used guardedly given the state of Salisbury's health.

[126] Schreiner had appointed Merriman as his Treasurer-General, the post Merriman had held under Rhodes eight years earlier.

[127] Thompson (1971), n. 7 above, p. 323.

[128] Kruger, n. 6 above, pp. 344–345; Wilson, n. 112 above, pp. 306–307.

War

As in the first war nearly twenty years earlier, the early stages of hostilities in the second conflict were marked by a series of spectacular boer victories. Chamberlain and Milner were both guilty of having vastly underestimated both the boers' willingness to fight for their political autonomy and their level of military competence. The British forces in the Cape were too small and too poorly prepared to bring the war to a prompt and successful conclusion.[129]

Yet the boers' long-term prospects of victory hinged on political rather than military tactics. There was no doubt that the British could eventually mobilise sufficient troops to overwhelm the boer commandoes. For Kruger and Steyn, *allies* were the crucial strategic resource. Balfour's agreement with Germany over the Portugese colonies had deprived the boers of any assistance (either military or diplomatic) from the Germans. Their hopes were thus pinned on a general uprising against the British among the Afrikaner population of the Cape. Those hopes were to be disappointed. Although several thousand Cape Afrikaners joined the boer forces, and many others offered covert assistance to the roving boer commandoes, the majority sought to distance themselves from the conflict.

The Schreiner government was subsequently to fall following internal divisions over the response that should be made to Cape residents who had joined the boers. Merriman had urged a wide-ranging amnesty. Schreiner, bowing to Chamberlain's pressure, had argued for more repressive measures. The split in the Bond in the event favoured the British cause, as the Schreiner ministry was replaced in June 1900 by a government more willing to follow Milner's lead.

By this time, British forces had occupied most of the major population centres in both the Republic and the Free State. In May, Kruger and several of his senior colleagues fled to Europe, where Kruger himself was shortly to die.[130] *De facto* control of the Republic's military and political strategies then rested with the various 'generals' who led the bands of boer commandoes scattered throughout the veld. The Republic's forces were on the verge of surrender at this point, before being rallied by Steyn's call for resistance to the bitter end through a campaign of guerilla warfare.

J.C. Smuts was to prove the foremost of the Republic's military leaders.[131] Barely thirty years old, Smuts was one of the Cape Afrikaners who had emigrated to the Republic after the Jameson raid. Smuts had enjoyed a meteoric rise in the Republic's government: at the outbreak of war he was the State

[129] H. Bailes, 'Military Aspects of the War', in Warwick, n. 21 above.

[130] Balfour's rapprochment with Germany was sufficiently effective to lead the Kaiser to refuse to meet Kruger when he came to Cologne.

[131] Information in the rest of this paragraph is drawn from W.K. Hancock's marvellously informative, if rather adulatory, biography: *Smuts: the Sanguine Years 1870–1919* (Cambridge: Cambridge University Press, 1962), chs. 4–5.

Attorney[132] and in effect Kruger's closest counsellor. Smuts had been an outstanding scholar in his youth. His academic career had culminated in a double first in law at Cambridge, and he was deeply immersed in theories of philosophy and metaphysics. On his return to South Africa, he had become intimately involved in the Bond's reconciliation project, and was vocal in his support of Rhodes' vision of a greater (white controlled) South Africa.[133] The Raid precipitated a fundamental change in Smuts' views of Britain, which swung to the other extreme of seeing the British embrace of reconciliation as a mere facade concealing a desire for the cultural extermination of the boer identity.

In Britain, the Tory government was able to exploit the military successes which followed the initial embarassments at boer hands to ride back into power on a wave of jingoistic imperialism in the 1900 general election. The campaign has since come to be known as the 'Khaki election'. It offers one of the earliest examples of a party employing systematically negative advertising to discredit its opponents. The government in effect portrayed the Liberal party's ambivalence about the merits of the war as tantamount to treason; "Every seat won by a Liberal"—Chamberlain is reputed to have argued—"is a seat sold to the Boers".[134]

The government's campaign (amplified in most of the popular press) at best oversimplified and at worst grossly distorted the Liberals' position.[135] A radical left faction, then best represented by the young Lloyd George, opposed the war root and branch, regarding it as an unwarranted imperial intrusion into the autonomy of a small and proud minority community. (Like Gladstone before him, Lloyd George seemed to have overlooked the blacks living in the Republic who were in turn oppressed—and far more severely—by the boers). On the right of the party, a grouping of so-called 'Liberal Imperialists' led by Herbert Asquith and Sir Edward Grey, offered their broad support for Chamberlain's militarism. In the centre, stood the party's leader, Henry Campbell-Bannerman.

Campbell-Bannerman was a Scot, born in Glasgow in 1836. His father was a wealthy retailer, who had stood unsuccessfully as a Conservative parliamentary candidate in the 1830s. His elder brother sat as a Conservative MP from 1880–1906. Despite this family background, Campbell-Bannerman's own political sympathies lay with the radical wing of the Liberal party. After attending Glasgow and Cambridge universities and a brief spell working in his father's business, he was elected as Liberal member for the Scots seat of Stirling Burghs in 1868. He entered the Cabinet as Secretary of State for War in Gladstone's

[132] Smuts' appointment to this post again illustrates Kruger's (and presumably Smuts') cavalier attachment to notions of constitutionalism and the rule of law. The Republic's constitution required that all government ministers be at least thirty years old. Smuts was twenty-eight when appointed State Attorney; Hancock, n. 44 above, p. 67. Nor, it seems, was Smuts sufficient of a lawyer (unlike Hertzog) to consider Kruger's behaviour in *Brown v Leyds* a good reason for not accepting office in his government.

[133] Hancock (1962), n. 44 above, pp. 57–60.

[134] M. Blanch, 'British Society and the War', in Warwick, n. 21 above; S. Koss (ed.), (1973) *The Pro-Boers* (Chicago: University of Chicago Press), ch. 7.

[135] See Blanch, n. 134 above; B. Porter (1980), n. 72 above.

1886 administration, associating himself firmly with the movement for home rule in Ireland and for progressive social reform in Britain. Campbell-Bannerman had been a member of the Commons committee investigating the Jameson Raid, and had been a party (whether as innocent dupe or willing conspirator is unclear) to absolving Chamberlain from any blame for Rhodes' military adventurism. He became leader of the Liberals in 1899.

Campbell-Bannerman had spoken out against military action during the final stages of Milner's confrontations with Kruger. But once war had been declared, he took the position that it was the duty of a loyal opposition to ensure that the campaign was concluded as expeditiously and with as little loss of life as possible. Thereafter, energy should be devoted to securing a just and lasting peace.

The emerging Labour party also consistently opposed British military involvement in southern Africa. This had little to do however with sympathy for the boers as an 'oppressed people'. Rather the party saw the war as a crude vehicle for enhancing the interests of the Chamber of Mines against both the black and white populations of the Republic.[136]

The Conservative victory in the 1900 general election did not quell domestic opposition to the war. Indeed, that opposition became more intense as it became clear that the campaign could not be brought to a swift and conclusive end. Rather than seek a negotiated truce, the British insisted on receiving the boers' unconditional surrender. Merriman had led a deputation to England in 1901 in an attempt to broker a negotiated settlement. Chamberlain proved entirely unresponsive. Indeed, on his return to the Cape, Merriman was placed under house arrest.

The boer commandoes were equally obdurate. Inspired by M.T. Steyn's unflinching defence of boer independence, the commandoes determined to resist for as long as it was possible to do so. Smuts, along with his Republic colleague Louis Botha, was to prove a constant thorn in Kitchener's side. J.B. Hertzog, whose career as a jurist in the Orange Free State had been rudely interrupted by the war, was a less skilled but equally obdurate enemy.[137]

General Kitchener, the commander of the British forces, attempted to hasten the end of the war by adopting a scorched earth policy. In so doing, he followed the example set by previous generations of boer commandoes in the years following the Great Trek to crush the resistance of native blacks to the boer invasion.[138] Homes, crops and livestock were systematically destroyed in order to deprive the boer commandoes of any form of shelter or means of subsistence. The women and children thereby displaced were detained in hastily erected compounds, which were rapidly relabelled 'concentration camps' by hostile British opinion and by the Afrikaner faction in the Cape. The camps were manifestly ill-equipped to meet even the basic needs of the detainees. The precise numbers of woman and children who died in the camps from malnutrition, exposure, or easily preventable disease was then, and remains, a source of

136 B. Porter (1980), n. 72 above.
137 Bailes, n. 129 above; F. Pretorious, 'Life on Commando', in Warwick, n. 21 above.
138 See p. 16 above. Thompson (1995), n. 4 above, pp. 71–72.

contention; but even conservative estimates suggest many more boers died in the camps than were killed in battle.[139] The weight of opinion now suggests that the deaths were the result of incompetence and indifference rather than malice on the British army's part. The camps were eventually managed in a fashion that guaranteed tolerable levels of santitation and nutrition. But the cause of the victims' death was a far lesser issue than the deaths themselves to the boer population, and the camps were eventually to prove to have a symbolic significance in southern Africa that long outlived their physicial existence.

The use of the camps also facilitated the reconsolidation of Liberal opinion in Britain in opposition to the war. Campbell-Bannerman condemned the strategy as tantamount to 'methods of barbarism'.[140] Lloyd George echoed his leader's sentiments in more emotive language. In a speech he gave in October 1901, Lloyd George characterised the concentration camp policy as:

> "a maddening horror, and it will haunt the Empire to its dying hour . . . Let any honest Britisher fearlessly search his heart and answer this question: Is there any ground for the reproach flung at us by the civilised world that, having failed to crush the men, we have now taken to killing babes?".[141]

Public disquiet in Britain about the camps was sufficient to prompt the government to relieve Kitchener of responsibility for their management, and transfer it instead to Milner.[142] The recognition of the inadequacies of the camps did not however wholly legitimise more pervasive opposition to the war. In December 1901, Lloyd George almost paid a high price for his outspoken views. He travelled to Birmingham, Chamberlain's home city, to make an anti-war speech in the Town Hall. The speech was violently disrupted by a pro-Chamberlain mob, and the meeting degenerated into a riot during which one man was killed and several dozen people seriously injured. Lloyd George himself fled from the meeting disguised as a policeman.[143]

Far less attention was paid by opponents of British government policy, either in southern Africa or Britain, to the concentration camps which Kitchener established to 'accommodate' native black southern Africans whose means of subsistence had also been destroyed by the scorched earth policy. Almost 120,000 blacks were interned in these camps. Over 14,000 died from dysentry, malnutrition and infectious diseases.[144]

[139] Gilbert, n. 141 below, p. 21 offers a figure of 9,000. Kruger, n. 6 above, p. 349 plumps for 26,000; Thompson (1971), n. 7 above, p. 328 settles on 25,000.

[140] Koss, n. 134 above, ch. 10.

[141] Quoted in M. Gilbert (ed.), *Lloyd George* (New Jersey: Prentice Hall, 1969), p. 21.

[142] Hancock (1962), n. 44 above, p. 177.

[143] Blanch, n. 134 above, pp. 219–220. There is no evidence that Chamberlain was complicit in encouraging this violence. Such charges would seem consistent with his track record, however. His involvement in the Raid has already been noted. He had also in 1883, when a (radical) member of Gladstone's Cabinet, urged his supporters among Birmingham radicals 'to inject a little more devil' into campaigns against the House of Lords' threatened veto of a bill extending the parliamentary franchise. The exhortation was widely seen as an incitement to violent disorder; I. Loveland, *Constitutional Law* (London: Butterworths, 1996), pp. 254–255.

[144] P. Warwick, 'Black People and the War', in Warwick (1980), n. 21 above, pp. 204–206.

Yet in the limited, military sense, Kitchener's methods were to prove (albeit very slowly) a success in their own terms. By the spring of 1902, the boer commandoes had exhausted their physical capacity to fight any further. The leaders of the Free State and the Republic met at Klerksdorp on 9 April to try to arrive at a common position on which to seek a negotiated settlement. Smuts played little part in this process; the key figures were Steyn and Hertzog for the Free State and Burger, Reitz (the acting President and State Secretary respectively) and Botha for the Republic. The peace agreement subsequently reached between Britain and the boers could not formally have been a Treaty, since neither boer government represented a sovereign state. It nevertheless soon came to be known by all sides as the Treaty of Vereeniging, a symbolic label which gave some hint of the agreement's substantive principles.

The contents of the agreement are outlined at the beginning of Chapter 3. At this juncture, one final point concerning the conduct of the war might be made. Neither side had at any time sought to involve non-whites in the conflict on any significant scale. The 'responsible governments' in Canada, New Zealand and the various colonies of Australia all contributed contingents of combatant troops to assist the British war effort.[145] No such assistance was sought from non-white colonies. British forces had occasionally struck opportunistic military alliances with native chiefs as did (to a much lesser extent) some boer generals.[146] The British also permitted armed native blacks to act as scouts and intelligence gatherers attached to contingents of British troops. But non-whites did not serve in any substantial numbers as combat troops within the British forces.[147] A young Indian lawyer then living in Natal, Mohinas Gandhi, had organised an Asian ambulance brigade in support of British forces, which made extensive use of native blacks as ancillary workers.[148] But the conflict had in formal terms been 'a white man's war'. Smuts had felt sufficiently confident of this point to write, in the midst of the guerilla campaign, of the 'tacit understanding' that existed between boer and Briton:

> "which forbids the white races to to appeal for assistance to the coloured races in their mutual disputes . . . otherwise the coloured races must become the arbiters in disputes between the whites and in the long run the predominating political factor in South Africa. That this would soon cause South Africa to lapse into barbarism must be evident to everybody".[149]

One therefore would presumably not have been greatly surprised if the next phase in southern African history turned out to be the construction of a white man's peace.

145 Lloyd (1996), n. 14 above, pp. 253–254.

146 Bailes, n. 129 above, pp. 112–114.

147 P. Warwick, 'Introduction' and 'Black People and the War', both in Warwick (1980), n. 21 above.

148 Warwick, n. 144 above; Simons and Simons, n. 24 above, p. 70.

149 Quoted in Warwick 'Introduction' in Warwick (1980), n. 21 above, p. 194.

3

Securing a White Peace

The peace terms were laid out in the 1902 'Treaty' of Vereeninging. Milner was Britain's chief negotiator. He favoured, with Chamberlain's support, an aggressive policy of 'anglicisation' of the Republic and Orange River Colony, to lay the ground for an eventual unification of the four colonies into a single nation that was 'British' not simply in its formal imperial status, but also in its dominant political and social culture:

> "The ultimate end is a self-governing white community, supported by *well treated* and *justly governed* black labour from Cape Town to Zambesi. There must be one flag, the Union Jack . . . I think though all South Africa should be one dominion . . . a considerable amount of freedom should be left to the several states . . . As for the Boer himself . . . first beaten and then fairly treated . . . I think he will be peaceful enough" (original emphasis).[1]

Milner pinned much of his hope for the future of southern Africa on the planned immigration of substantial numbers of British settlers:

> "If, ten years hence, there are three men of British race to two of Dutch, the country will be safe and prosperous. If there are three of Dutch to two of British we shall have perpetual difficulty".[2]

But his concerns were also evident in the terms of the Treaty. Milner thus resisted pressure, especially from Free State politicians, to accord substantively equal status to the Dutch and English languages. While Dutch might be used in courts, the general medium of instruction in schools would be English, with Dutch being available only as a discrete subject for those children whose parents wished them to learn it. Teachers and administrators would be imported from England rather than drawn from the local population.[3] Milner's expectation was that Dutch and Afrikaans would gradually decline to the status of residual languages, a process which would in itself contribute greatly to the neutralisation of boer nationalism.

[1] Quoted in L. Thompson, *The Unification of South Africa* (Oxford: Clarendon Press, 1960), p. 6.

[2] The comment is oft-quoted see W. Hancock, *Smuts. Volume 1: The Sanguine Years 1870–1919* (Cambridge: CUP, 1962), p. 174; Thompson (1960), n. 1 above, p. 7.

[3] That particular policy has of course strong echoes of Kruger's decision in the 1890s to staff government offices in the Republic with administrators from Holland and Germany rather than allow non-boer whites to gain any position of influence within the state bureaucracy; see p. 30 above.

Milner had begun this process prior to the peace. After ensuring that the camps in which boer women and children had been detained were sufficiently well-managed to safeguard the physical well-being of their inmates, Milner introduced complusory schooling (in English) for the children. For many boer children, this was the first formal education they had received, and many left the camps and subsequently entered school perceiving English rather than Dutch or Afrikaans to be the 'natural' language of instruction.[4]

The press afforded Milner another means with which to pursue the anglicisation process. Argus group newspapers had unsurprisingly been banned in the Republic during the war, but on the cessation of hostilities *The Star* rapidly resumed a prominent role in Johannesburg's political life. Milner gave the group a more than generous helping hand in its efforts to relaunch *The Star* by awarding it a substantial role in printing the colony's government documents.[5] *The Star's* main 'competitor' in the immediate post-war era, was the *Rand Daily Mail*, which was founded in 1902. The *Mail*—along with its (*de facto* if not *de jure*) sister paper The *Sunday Times*—was however also owned by a mining magnate, and was in no sense an 'opposition' paper.[6]

Milner refused to countenance the production of a definite date at which the colonies would be granted self-government over their internal affairs. The Treaty provided that the Free State (which was to be renamed the Orange River Colony) and the Republic (renamed—once more and this time finally—the Transvaal) would initially be subjected to military government. This would in turn be replaced by Crown Colony status, under which all governmental power would rest with a British-appointed Governor. Representative and thereafter responsible government were envisaged as distant ambitions for the conquered boer peoples.

The Treaty did however make one significant concession to boer sentiment. In approving its final text, the British government did not insist that the grant of responsible government be tied to any liberalisation of the two colonies' rigid franchise colour bar. Rather Article 8 provided that: "The question of granting the franchise to natives will not be decided until after the introduction of self-government". It is difficult to believe that either Milner or Chamberlain sincerely expected that any such government, whose members and electors would in the main be profoundly racist whites, would voluntarily enfranchise any of its country's non-white inhabitants. It is equally difficult to believe that Milner thought it intrinsically right that any government should do so.[7]

[4] I. Hexham "Afrikaner Nationalism 1902–1914" in P. Warwick (ed.), *The South African War* (London, 1980); Hancock (1962) *op. cit.* pp. 176–178.

[5] E. Potter, *The Press as Opposition* (London: Chatto and Windruss, 1975), p. 40.

[6] Potter, n. 5 above, pp. 41–42; J. Mervis, *Fourth Estate* (Johannesburg: Jonathan Ball, 1989), ch. 2 offers a more colourful account of the founding of the two papers.

[7] "A political equality of white and black is impossible. The white man must rule, because he is elevated by many, many steps above the black man; steps which it will take the latter centuries to climb, and which it is quite possible that the vast bulk of the black population may never be able to climb at all": Lord Milner, Speech to the Johannesburg Municipal Congress, May 1903, quoted in L. Thompson *The Unification of South Africa 1902–1910* (Oxford: Clarendon Press, 1960), p. 6. See also G. Lewis, *Between the Wire and the Wall* (Cape Town: David Phillip, 1987), pp. 158–160.

The initial suggested text of Article 8 had read rather differently: "The franchise will not be given to natives until after the introduction of self-government"—a form of words which could be seen as implying a colour-blind franchise was a necessary concomitant of the restoration of the Transvaal and the Free State's autonomy. The final version of Article 8 was drafted by J.C. Smuts.[8] The significance of the changed wording can hardly have escaped Chamberlain and Milner's notice. Their acquiescence suggests that the British government considered that perpetuating such discrimination was a price worth paying for achieving an anglo-leaning peace.

I. BRITISH POLICY TOWARDS THE NON-WHITE RACES

There was little support in any quarter of British political opinion for the proposition that the internal governance of the southern African colonies should be guided by the preferences of an electorate comprising all adult males. Even Britain had not yet quite reached that level of democratic sophistication in respect of its own (virtually entirely white) population. Eugenic theories concerning the innate inferiority of the non-white races also enjoyed a substantial hold on the ideological beliefs of most of the era's leading politicians, not simply in Britain and her white colonies, but also throughout Europe and in the USA, in whose southern States such beliefs were clearly expressed in a vast array of laws segregating the white and black races.[9] The native blacks and coloured peoples of southern Africa en masse were not regarded by any leading British politicians as capable of self-government. This belief was it seems sincerely held by many of it advocates, rather than being an expedient and mendacious justification for the tyrannisation of Africa's indigenous black populations.[10]

Both viewpoints were pervasively and acutely 'racist' in the sense in which we now understand that term. The central division in British political culture on racial issues at the turn of the twentieth century was nevertheless a stark one. One viewpoint accepted that increasing numbers of non-white Africans might gradually 'earn' through their cultural and educational 'progress' the right to be accorded formally equal political status with whites; in the meantime, in addition to being encouraged to move towards that goal, they should be safeguarded from more egregious forms of political repression and economic exploitation by benevolent white rule. The second perspective doubted that significant numbers

[8] Hancock (1962), n. 2 above, pp. 158–160.

[9] See especially N. Lofgren, *The Plessey Case* (New York: OUP, 1993), ch. 1; C. Woodward, *The Strange Career of Jim Crow* ch. 3 (New York: OUP, 1966), ch. 3). In the South African context see L. Thompson, *The Political Mythology of Apartheid* (New Haven: Yale University Press, 185), pp. 101–103.

[10] The point is forcefully conveyed in Pakenham's account of Livingstone's grip upon the imaginations and aspirations of liberal British public opinion in the 1870s and 1880s, a grip through which the explorer had urged upon his countrymen their duty to take Christianity and commerce to the African peoples: *The Scramble for Africa* (London: Abacus, 1992), pp. 1–5, 25–26.

of native blacks could ever take such steps, and thus saw little need for benevolence and none at all for the encouragement of self-'improvement' in the systems of government imposed by white colonial powers.

These views, which in themselves contained many gradations and nuances, were complicated by a second factor; namely the firmly established constitutional convention that the internal affairs (including race relations) of the Empire's white-dominated colonies were a matter solely for the respective colonial governments to determine. The various policies adopted to 'the native question' by successive British governments in the immediate post-war period give a clear indication of the complex and fragmented ways in which imperial 'racism' was given legal and political expression.

The native protectorates

The most obvious way for the British government to 'protect' native blacks from potentially tyrannical exploitation of white colonists was to ensure that the territory they peopled was kept legally distinct from the white-governed colonies. At the end of the war, Britain retained a system of direct rule through appointed officials in several substantial areas of southern Africa. The Bechuanaland protectorate, an area almost twice the size of Britain, was home to only 120,000 people, ninety-nine per cent of whom were native blacks. Basutoland occupied rather less territory, but had a larger population of some 350,000. Fewer than 1,000 of these people were whites; the rest were native blacks. Swaziland, a still smaller area, contained around 1,000 whites in an overall population of 90,000.[11]

The detailed mechanics of government in the protectorates were administered through local chiefs. There was no discernible pressure from the native populations for their territories to be merged with any of the white colonies. Direct rule from Britain was regarded as greatly preferable to any form of government that southern African whites might offer. In economic terms, the three protectorates were virtually prostrate. None had any industry to speak of. Much of their territory, especially in Bechuanaland, was desert. The protectorates were barely able to cultivate sufficient crops and livestock to feed their populations, and substantial numbers of male inhabitants continued to work in the mines on the Rand.

There was little prospect of Britain devolving administrative responsibilty for the protectorates to the other white colonies. Questions nevertheless remained over how best to ensure the economic development of the territories, and over their relationship with the evermore rapidly industrialising Transvaal. Both the Chamber of Mines and Kruger's pre-war governments had seen attractions in the protectorate form of government: the territories offered a substantial labour

[11] Thompson (1960), n. 1 above, pp. 49–51.

force which was economically dependent upon the Rand's mines, but which existed quite apart from the Transvaal in a political, legal and cultural sense. In the aftermath of the war, Milner also seemed to be attracted to the idea that a similar system of subordinated segregation might have merits *within* the boundaries of the existing colonies.

The South African Native Affairs Commission

Milner's search for a native policy which would ensure that black southern Africans were 'well treated' and 'justly governed' led him to establish a South African Native Affairs Commission (SANAC) in 1903. The Commission, chaired by Sir Godfrey Langden, was given a wide-ranging brief. Its report, published in 1905, seemed to owe more to the overtly and pervasively discriminatory traditions of the Transvaal and Natal than to the partially colour-blind policies adopted in the Cape.[12]

The Commission explicitly approved the principle of territorial segregation along racial lines. Specific areas of the country should be set aside for the exclusive occupation of the native black population. Blacks would not however be able to 'own' this land in the traditional European sense. Rather it would be held in a form of 'trust' on their behalf by the colonial governments. Blacks would be assisted in developing their own forms of government to manage internal affairs within their specified territories. SANAC ultimately envisaged a situation of 'differential sovereignty' between the native black and white peoples of southern Africa,[13] in which, with the benefit of benevolent white trusteeship, blacks would gradually approach if not necessarily reach 'European' standards of civilisation.

Quite how long this process would take was unclear. Nor was it obvious that native black areas would be economically self-sufficient. Native blacks comprised over seventy per cent of the southern African population at the turn of the century. It would seem most unlikely that any whites, even among the Cape's liberal intelligentsia, envisaged that blacks would be allocated a commensurate proportion of the colonies' lands, or that they would be encouraged to develop an industrialised economy. What seemed rather more probable was that such black areas would 'develop' as bare subsistence agricultural economies, many of

[12] S. Dubow, *Racial Segregation and the Origins of Apartheid in South Africa 1919–1936* (London: Macmillan, 1989), ch. 1; T. Davenport *South Africa: A Modern History*, 2nd edn. (Cambridge: CUP, 1978), pp. 152–153; Cell *The Highest Stage of White Supremacy* (Cambridge: CUP, 1982), pp. 196–210. For a detailed critique of SANAC's report, and a careful assessment of the language in which it expressed itself, see Ashforth *The Politics of Official Discourse in Twentieth Century South Africa* (Oxford: Clarendon Press, 1990), ch. 2.

[13] The term is Dubow's, n. 12 above, p. 6. For a careful analysis of the 'British' roots of segregation in South Africa see M. Legassick, 'British Hegemony and the Origins of Apartheid in South Africa', in W. Beinart and S. Dubow (eds.), *Segregation and Apartheid in South Africa* (London: Routledge, 1995).

whose residents would ultimately be compelled to earn a living by working (for low wages) in the increasingly industrialised 'white' areas.[14]

SANAC's proposals were however for the longer term, and were rather more political than economic in objective. The separation thesis had already begun to appeal to Cape whites by this time following an outbreak of bubonic plague in the Cape Town area during the boer war.[15] Native black areas of the city were widely regarded as breeding grounds of disease and squalour which posed a physiological threat to the white community. That contemporary medical records suggested that native blacks were proportionately less susceptible to the plague than whites evidently did not impress itself upon white opinion. Whether this was because many whites fell victim to mass hysteria, or rather saw the plague as an 'objective' justification for racial segregation, is unclear. The outcome of the concern was more tangible however. In 1901 some 7,000 native blacks were uprooted from their Cape Town homes and forcibly relocated in a camp built on the site of an old sewerage works at Uitvlugt.[16]

The suggestion that the acceleration of segregation strategies in the Cape was predominantly a legislative response to demands from both white farmers and industrialists for a cheap and dependent black labour force enjoys considerable currency within Southern African historiography.[17] If that was Milner's overriding purpose however, it was one which could not rapidly be achieved. In the shorter term, Milner faced an acute economic problem to which native blacks did not not seem to offer an immediate solution.

Chinese labour and racial discrimination in the Witwatersrand mines

Restoring the economic power of the Rand gold mines was an essential ingredient of Milner's reconstruction agenda in the Transvaal. Output in 1903 was only half that produced in 1898. The economic regeneration not just of the Transvaal, but also of the Cape and Natal, hinged on the rapid restoration of pre-war levels of gold production on the Rand. The industry was however beset by labour problems. The outcome of the war had in itself solved one of the more acute difficulties—namely the obviously 'second class' status of the white

[14] Cf. Legassick, n. 13 above, at pp. 47–48: "SANAC . . . advocated racially exclusive occupation of separate land areas, and political representation of blacks and whites by separate means. Yet it was no protagonist of *total* separation. If there was emphasis on the preservation and development of an agriculturally based African society, SANAC was equally clear that black labour was needed by the South African urban and mining economy". See also Ashforth, n. 12 above, at p. 25: "a proletariat for South African industry [could] not simply be found but had to be made".

[15] See M. Swanson, 'The Sanitation Syndrome: Bubonic Plague and Urban Native Policy in the Cape Colony 1900–1909', in Beinart and Dubow, n. 13 above.

[16] The programme was enthusiastically endorsed even by supposedly liberal members of the white community, two of whom, W.P. Schreiner and Sir James Rose Innes, we will encounter on a number of occasions later in this book. Merriman was vigorously opposed to the policy: *ibid*. at pp. 37–38.

[17] See especially H. Wolpe 'Capitalism and Cheap Labour Power in South Africa: From Segregation to Apartheid', in Beinart and Dubow, n. 13 above.

uitlanders. There was no scope for doubting that the boer and non-boer factions of the white population would henceforth be treated on a footing of political equality by the Transvaal's legal system.

But, as noted in Chapter 2, whites formed only a small percentage of the mines' labour force. The overwhelming majority of the Transvaal's miners were black, and many of these were migrant workers who retained family homes in Bechuanaland, Basutoland, Swaziland or Portugese East Africa (Mozambique). They had returned to their homes during the war, and in the early stages of the peace displayed a marked reluctance to journey back to the Rand to undertake the dangerous work and live in the poor conditions that employment in the mines provided. The number of native blacks working in the mines had fallen from 108,000 in 1899 to barely 64,000 in 1903.[18] There would seem to have been a ready explanation for this decline. Potential miners who were able to make a subsistence living in their home areas would have little incentive to leave their homes and families to work for prolonged periods on the Rand for low wages. The Chamber of Mines had indeed sought to preserve the mines' profitability by depressing black wage levels; average wages paid to blacks had fallen from £2 7s in 1898 to £1 7s in 1903.[19]

Employers were however unwilling to take the seemingly obvious step of attracting more black labour by raising wage levels, a policy which they feared would adversely affect the mines' profitability. Nor were they willing to deal with the issue by promoting enhanced white immigration. Doing this on a large scale raised the prospect of the labour force becoming increasingly dominated by militant trade unionists, who would not only form a substantial economic power bloc, but might also be able to win control of the Transvaal legislature when representative or responsible government was granted to the colony. From the Chamber's perspective, Krugerism was less uncongenial than socialism (albeit a distinctly racist brand of socialism) as a government ideology. Frederick Cresswell, a mine manager who pioneered a new system of working practices in which white workers gradually replaced blacks, was sacked for his pains in 1902.[20]

Milner was also unwilling to countenance the use of white labour to perform unskilled, low paid work in the mines. His concern to raise the size of the 'English' population in southern Africa did not extend to wanting to create a white proletariat. His vision of a 'white man's South Africa' was:

> "not a country full of poor whites, but one in which a largely increased white population can live in decency and comfort. That development requires capital, but it also requires a large amount of rough labour. And that labour cannot to any extent be white, if only because. . .white labour is much too dear".[21]

[18] H. Simons and R. Simons, *Class and Colour in South Africa 1850–1950* (Harmondsworth: Penguin, 1969), p. 81.

[19] Simons and Simons, n. 18 above, p. 81; Katzellenbogen, n. 64 below, pp. 354–356.

[20] Simons and Simons, n. 18 above, p. 78.

[21] Quoted in S. Trapido and S. Marks, 'Lord Milner and the South African State' (1979) 8 *History Workshops* 50 at 66. See also Davenport (1978), n. 12 above, pp. 150–151.

The Chamber's preferred solution to the labour shortage was to import substantial numbers of non-white workers from abroad for a fixed period, pay them little more than subsistence wages, deny them any political rights during their residency, and re-export them to their countries of origin at the expiry of their contracts. The Chamber of Mines had initially looked to India for its workers, but looked elsewhere when the Indian government indicated it would only approve such a scheme on terms far more generous to the labourers than the Chamber had proposed. Its gaze subsequently alighted on China, which offered the prospect of an unlimited supply of cheap labour. The plan unsurprisingly received enthusiastic endorsement in what were by then the Transvaal's two leading newspapers, *The Star* and the *Rand Daily Mail*.[22] Milner also supported the initiative, and persuaded the British government to approve the importation of Chinese labourers.[23] Over 60,000 eventually made the journey to the Transvaal.[24]

The proposal attracted substantial opposition both in the Transvaal and in Britain.[25] In the Transvaal, Botha and Smuts campaigned vigorously against the policy. Smuts considered the labour shortage was a temporary problem, which could adequately be met by black workers in the longer term. He feared also that many of the Chinese would, notwithstanding the terms of their contracts, eventually settle in the Transvaal (as had the Indian immigrants in Natal thirty years earlier),[26] thereby adding a further complication to the colony's already volatile race relations.[27] He objected most strongly however (in a letter published in *The Times*) to the autocratic way in which Milner and Chamberlain had simply ignored boer sentiments in doing the bidding of the Chamber of Mines.

To the British Liberal party, the importation of indentured labourers smacked of a barely sanitised form of slavery. Lloyd-George was as forthright in his denunciation of the scheme as he had been of the war.[28] Campbell-Bannerman laid down a motion of censure in the Commons on the government's approval of the policy.[29] His criticism centred in part on Milner's failure to consult local opinion, but his main concern was couched in more straightforwardly humantarian terms: "These are, at all events, uncommonly like slave

[22] Mervis, n. 6 above, pp. 23–25.

[23] Thompson (1960), n. 1 above, pp. 21–22; Trapido and Marks, n. 21 above, pp. 65–67. Milner had also taken the trouble to secure the approval of the leading members of the Imperialist wing of the Liberal party: J. Wilson, *A Life of Sir Henry Campbell-Bannerman* (London: Constable, 1973), p. 398.

[24] Cell, n. 12 above, pp. 46–48: P. Richardson, 'The Recruiting of Chinese Indentured Labour for the Transvaal Gold Mines 1903–1908' (1977) 18 *Journal of African History* 87; Katzenellenbogen, n. 64 below, p. 358.

[25] Katzenellenbogen, n. 64 below, p. 358; D. Judd, *Balfour and the British Empire* (London: Macmillan, 1968), pp. 200–202.

[26] See p. 24 above.

[27] Hancock, n. 2 above, pp. 182–183, 195–196.

[28] Grigg J. (1978) *Lloyd George: the People's Champion* pp. 70–71 (London: Eyre Methuen).

[29] Wilson, n. 23 above, pp. 398–400.

laws. 'Indentured labour' no doubt sounds better, but do not let us haggle over words: let us see what the thing itself is".[30] Leading figures in the Cape Coloured community also opposed the scheme, albeit for less altruistic reasons. From this perspective, the Chinese were viewed as a device to enable Rand mineowners to undercut wages paid to Coloured workers, thereby subjecting them to either impoverishment or unemployment.[31]

The policy also lent added impetus to the formation of a Labour party in southern Africa. The origins of the party lay in the creation in 1903 of the Witwatersrand Trades and Labour Council, an umbrella organisation drawing together the guild organisations of such skilled (white) workers as boilermakers, carpenters and stonemasons.[32] Five candidates were fielded in the Johannesburg municipal elections in 1903, two of whom were returned to office. The WTLC was potentially a vehicle for promoting 'reconciliation' among the anglo and boer segments of the emerging white urban proletariat, insofar as it enabled them to subsume their own cultural and political differences within a much more pronounced and shared antipathy towards the prospect of non-white workers, be they black or Chinese, undercutting the whites' dominant status within the mines' labour force.

That status had been further enhanced by the Mines, Works and Machinery Ordinance of 1903. The Transvaal's status as a Crown Colony afforded Milner and his officials more or less arbitrary law-making power within the colony's borders.[33] The 1903 Ordinance was promulgated without any consultation with affected parties. On its face, the Ordinance appeared to reject the notion of a colour bar within the mining industry, insofar as it repealed various discriminatory laws passed by Kruger's Volksraad. However the Ordinance also empowered Milner's administration to issue regulations to control employment conditions in the mining industry. This device was used on several occasions in the next few years to ensure that only whites were eligible to fill the most skilled and well-paid jobs in the mines.[34] Similarly restrictive limits were placed on the tasks that could be performed by the Chinese labourers. The Chinese presence might thus place a downward pressure on *black* wages, but it would have little direct effect on the wages earned by *whites*.

The meaning of black and white

The Milner administration's condonation of a colour bar in the Rand's gold mines had a parallel in the Municipalities Election Ordinance 1903 which established the post-war local government electoral system in the

[30] Wilson, n. 23 above, at p. 399.
[31] Lewis, n. 7 above, pp. 18–19.
[32] Simons and Simons, n. 18 above, pp. 98–99.
[33] See pp. 62–4 above.
[34] Simons and Simons, n. 18 above, pp. 77–78.

Transvaal.[35] Section 11 clearly cured one of the political ills of which the *uitlanders* had complained in the late 1890s: it extended the right to vote to all *white* adult British subjects resident in the local authority area concerned. All non-whites were excluded. Since the war had been justified by the British government at least in part as a crusade to save non-whites in the Republic from the extremism of Kruger's government, Chamberlain's approval of Milner's whites-only franchise (which made no concessions to 'civilised' non-whites and included even the most 'uncivilised' of boers) might seem unexpected. It could be defended, on technical 'legal' grounds, by referring back to Article 8 of the Treaty of Vereeniging, which might be taken to encompass the local franchise as well as the Volksraad franchise. The more compelling explanation is purely political. Neither Chamberlain nor Milner saw any particular intrinsic merit in exporting the Cape's colour blind electoral laws to the Transvaal; and both appreciated that the instrumental shortcomings of such a policy would be immense, given that both the boers and most *uitlanders* shared a deeply held belief in the need to keep the Transvaal's non-white inhabitants in a state of economic and political subordination.

The ordinance did not however define what was meant by 'white'. Nor did it specify whether the burden lay on an aspiring voter to prove his 'whitenesss', or on the local electoral registration officer to establish that the person concerned was not 'white'. The literal terms of the ordinance afforded the Transvaal courts considerable room for manouevre in determining the precise extent of the colour bar in the Transvaal's electoral law. It could plausibly be argued, for example, that any resident whose ancestry included one or more British or Dutch settlers was 'white', simply because his ancestors were not exclusively native blacks. Nor did the text of the ordinance obviously restrict the test of whiteness to matters of genealogy. Residents whose ancestors were exclusively black, but whose 'customs and manners' were European in nature could conceivably be thought of as white if one construed that term as a shorthand for the Cape's long-standing notion of the 'civilised native'. Similarly, it might be assumed that a potential voter should be assumed to be 'white' until such time as local election officials proved beyond any doubt that he was not.

Such interpretation of section 11 would no doubt have appalled both boer and *uitlander* in the Transvaal, since it would *de facto* have pushed the colony's electoral laws some substantial way towards those of the Cape. Election officials in Pretoria initially took a very different view of the concept. They required potential voters to demonstrate that their ancestral lines did not contain *any* forbears who were not the progeny solely of white European settlers, and were prepared to exclude an applicant who ostensibly met this test if they thought he 'looked' as though he had some non-white ancestry. The practical impact of the policy was to restrict the franchise to boers and *utilanders*.

[35] *Ibid*. p. 78.

The legality of this practice came before the Transvaal Supreme Court in *Swarts v Pretoria Town Council*[36] in 1905. Swarts had been denied registration, despite having produced evidence that all his grandparents were of white European ethnicity; the council's registration officer had thought that Swarts did not 'look' white. The Transvaal Supreme Court upheld the decision. Innes C.J. delivered the leading judgment.

Sir James Rose Innes, born in 1855, was the son of a junior minister in several Cape governments. Innes had completed both his undergraduate and legal education in the Cape. He had been a prominent liberal political activist in the Cape in the 1880s, working closely with native black politicians and activists[37] and eventually being elected to the Cape legislature with the enthusiatic support of non-white voters.[38] In 1990 he became a Q.C. and Attorney-General in Rhodes' ministry. He aligned himself firmly with Merriman, with whom he resigned from the cabinet in 1892.[39] He again became Cape Attorney-General in 1900, was knighted in 1901 and was then appointed by Milner as Judge-President of the Transvaal in 1902.[40]

Given his reputation as both an anglophile and and a liberal,[41] it is perhaps unsurprising that Innes C.J. began his judgment in *Swarts* by observing that the court took no view on the merits of the policy that the ordinance enacted and was concerned merely to give effect to its terms. He then expressed the hope that; "nothing will fall from me which may hurt the feelings of people who must feel very keenly the disabilities under which they are placed".[42] Since section 11 failed to define either the substance of 'whiteness', or the location of the burden of proving it, such protestations of judicial impartiality and impotence ring very hollow. The court's effective discretion on the point was extremely widely cast.

Innes C.J. gave no reason at all for the court's conclusion that it fell to the applicant to prove his whiteness, rather than to the town council to disprove it. He then offered the unhelpful observation that section 11's use of 'white' was coterminous with the concept of 'European descent'. This comparator was derived not from the text of the ordinance but from Innes C.J.'s perception of the 'circumstances of the country' when the ordinance was passed. These circumstances evidently required that 'white' be construed to minimise rather than maximise the size of the electorate:

> "The personal appearance of the applicant in each case must be a very important element. We all know in this country what an admixture of coloured blood means, and

36 (1905) SC (Transvaal) 621.

37 See pp. 97–98 below.

38 Innes J. Rose, *Autobiography* (Cape Town: OUP, 1949), ch. 5.

39 See p. 35 above.

40 He was subsequently appointed to the Appellate Division of the South African Supreme Court (see p. 4 below) and to the Privy Council in 1910. He became Chief Justice of South Africa in 1914, in which post he served until his retirement in 1927. He thereafter resumed his career as a liberal political activist (see p. 199 below).

41 A. Sachs, *Justice in South Africa* (London: University of Sussex Press, 1973), pp. 136–137.

42 (1905) SC (Transvaal) 621 at 622.

the appearance which proves the presence of such blood: and when we find one in whom these appearances are present, then unless it is clearly proved that his ancestors were of European descent we would usually be guided by his appearance".[43]

Since the court's understanding of 'ancestors' seemed to go beyond grandparents, the practical effect of the decision was to give local electoral officials virtually untrammelled discretion to decide who was 'white'. It needed no great political insight to conclude that such discretion would be exercised in a most restrictive fashion.

Innes C.J. had been rather coy in *Swarts* about revealing what it was about a person's appearance that indicated he was not 'white'. A more candid explanation had been offered by Sir J.H. De Villiers, Chief Justice of the Cape Provincial division, in two cases decided respectively at the beginning and end of the war.

While the Cape's *franchise* laws were colour blind,[44] the colony's legal system (as had already been noted)[45] had long harboured racially-based classifications on other issues. The sale of alcohol was among the most prominent of these racially discriminatory laws. Legislation passed in 1888 made it a crime for holders of liquor licences to sell alcohol to 'natives', unless the native was a domestic servant or had been certified as competent to buy liquor by a Justice of the Peace. The legislation had ostensibly been enacted as paternalistic measure to protect native blacks from their own irresponsibility; the exceptions spared white employers the inconvenience of having to buy their own alcohol and acknowledged that some blacks were sufficiently 'civilised' to be trusted to drink liquor in moderation.

It would obviously be a defence to any charge brought under this legislation for the seller to claim that the purchaser was not a 'native'. Yet the Act left this concept undefined. The defendant in *R v Parrott*[46] had sold alcohol to two brothers, David and Damion van Rooy. The van Rooys had subsequently become heavily intoxicated, and collapsed insensate in the veld, where they died of exposure during the night. Parrot's primary defence was to argue that both men had some white ancestry: they could not therefore be 'natives'.

At trial, the Magistrate had rejected this contention. He held that the brothers; "had the appearance and usual characteristics of Hottentots, in the flat nose, woolly hair and shape of the head".[47] De Villiers C.J. approved the Magistrates' approach, observing that: "In the absence of other evidence, the appearance of

[43] *Ibid.*

[44] The Cape's electoral arrangements also proved extremely accommodating to boers from the Republic and Free State who had moved to the Cape but not made any attempt to become British subjects. Since Cape franchise legislation applied only to British subjects, such residents would not appear to be qualified to vote. However many Cape officials took the view that such men had *impliedly* become British subjects, and were thus entitled to vote. The Cape Supreme Court upheld this view in a series of decisions in 1905; see especially *In Re Radloff* (1905) 22 SCR (Cape of Good Hope) 299.

[45] See pp. 9–10 above.

[46] (1899) 16 SCR (Cape of Good Hope) 452.

[47] *Ibid.* at 453.

the persons furnishes the best criterion of descent".[48] The Chief Justice then suggested that such legislative terminology presented the courts with a substantial and growing problem. Trans-racial marriage and sexual liaisons were producing a population of increasingly complex racial structure, whose position *vis-à-vis* such statutory dividing lines as 'native' was evermore difficult to discern. Mere skin colour was not an exhaustive test—one could apparently be 'dark but white' or 'light but black'.[49]

De Villiers C.J. was also prepared to attach a 'legal' rather than physiological dimension to the term; the offspring of a white man and black woman who were married to each other would not be natives, while the illegitimate children of a black and a white parent would be. Nor could the court accept the uncorroborated evidence of an unmarried mother as to the ancestry of her child's father. In much the same way as Innes C.J. was later to do in *Swarts*, the Cape Supreme Court appeared to want to disengage itself from the awkward business of drawing racial lines by leaving government officials a very loosely defined subjective discretion.

De Villiers C.J. reiterated this position in *R v Willets*.[50] The case again concerned the sale of alcohol to natives. The purchaser in this case was one Rose Coetzee, who described her mother as a Hottentot and her father as a boer. The court held that it was for the defendant to prove the ancestry of the purchaser; her own statements were of no evidential weight. The 'best test' in such circumstance would be the person's appearance. Magistrates were quite entitled to premise their conclusions as to a person's race on that characteristic alone.

On sex and marriage across the racial divide[51]

The definitional difficulties to which De Villiers C.J. alluded in *Parrott* were caused at least in part by the Cape's colour blind approach to the questions of sex and marriage. As noted in Chapter 1, the Dutch East India Company had actively encouraged its employees to procreate with the Cape's non-white inhibitants, and the predisposition of white male slave-owners to rape their female slaves (and of a smaller number to marry them) lent a further degree of 'normalcy' to trans-racial sexual activities within Cape culture.[52]

[48] (1899) 16 SCR (Cape of Good Hope) 452 at 455.

[49] See also Innes C.J. in *Swarts* at 622: "You may have a person of European descent who is not very white: or you may have a native who is quite white in colour". Sachs conveys the potentially bewildering nature of racial classification in the southern African colonies at this time by noting that the definition of 'European' in Natal's prison regulations explicitly included' "Eurasians, American negroes, French creoles and West Indians", n. 41 above, pp. 89–90.

[50] (1902) 19 SCR (Cape of Good Hope) 168.

[51] Information in this section is drawn primarily from E. Matthews, 'Legislation Relating to Marriage or Sexual Intercourse between Europeans and Natives or Coloured Persons' (1921) *South African Law Journal* 313.

[52] Sachs, n. 41 above, p. 30.

This cultural tradition was given legal force in an ordinance promulgated in the Cape in 1838, which reformed the colony's marriage laws without making any reference to the racial identity of the spouses. The ordinance continued to provide the basis of the Cape's matrimonial laws in the early twentieth century. Nor had Cape law drawn any distinction on racial grounds in areas peripheral to marriage itself, such as rights of property between living spouses and the inheritance of property consequent upon a spouse's death.

It was by no means unusual for mixed race marriages to be made in the Cape. And as time wore on, and children of mixed marriages made marriages themselves, so the racial identity of many of the Cape's inhabitants became increasing complicated. Nevertheless, as the cases discussed in the previous section suggest, the white parent of a mixed race child ran the risk that his/her offspring, even if born in wedlock, would not be regarded as 'white' for all purposes by Cape law. Nor did the Cape prohibit sex outside marriage between adult men and women of different races. It did however attach greater penalties to pimping and prostitution across the racial divide than to such activities within a single racial group.

Natal's marriage laws before the war had also been race neutral in form. Such marriages were however a far rarer ocurrence in Natal than in the Cape, a social phenomenon which is hardly surprising given white Natalian's violently racist political culture. Trans-racial sex outside marriage had also been left unregulated prior to the war. However in 1903 the Natal legislature criminalised both parties (with a sanction of up to two years' imprisonment and twenty-five lashes) in sexual activities between a white woman and a 'coloured person'. The man was 'coloured' if he was a "Hottnetot, Bushman, coolie, or lascar, or any of the people commonly called Kaffirs". White men, in contrast, were free to have sex consensually with women from any racial category.

The laws of Kruger's Republic had of course erected rigid barriers to inter-racial marriage. Only whites were permitted to marry. Not only were non-whites forbidden from marrying whites, they were forbidden even from marrying each other until 1897. In that year, Kruger's Volksraad approved a *besluit* permitting marriage between non-whites "who by education and civilisation have become distinguished from barbarians"

Unlike Milner's later election ordinance for the Transvaal, the Republic's marriage legislation had attempted to define 'white'. It did so in a negative fashion. One was not white if one was a person "belonging to or being a desecendant of any native race in South Africa", or any race emanating from the Indian sub-continent. The test was clearly a broad one; any non-white ancestry would be sufficient. The law was not altered immediately after the war.

Perhaps surprisingly, the Republic had not criminalised participants in inter-racial sex outside marriage. Milner's Crown Colony Transvaal administration did however take that step in 1903. A white woman who had sex with a non-white man faced up to five years' imprisonment. The man concerned could be sentenced to six years in goal and be whipped. The formal test of non-whiteness in this law was perhaps less severe than in the Transvaal's marriage legislation. One was non-white if "*manifestly* belonging to any of the coloured or native races of Africa, Asia, America or St Helena" (emphasis added). This perhaps meant that a man who looked only 'slightly' black could sleep with a white woman: but given the pre-disposition of both boer and *uitlander* law enforcement officals in the Transvaal, and the evident unwillingness (displayed in *Swarts*) of Transvaal courts to review administrative decisions on questions of racial identity, a man whose ancestral heritage had any discernable non-white components would have been ill-advised to do so.

At the outbreak of the second boer war, the laws of the Free State did not prohibit trans-racial marriage; although few such marriages appeared to have been made. Moreover, the children of such marriages were expressly identified as 'white' by Free State legislation. Christian marriages between non-whites were also permitted. Prior to the war, inter-racial sex between men and women of different races was not a criminal offence. Nor did the Crown Colony government introduce such measures.

Land ownership and development in the Transvaal

The habitual disinclination of the Republic's legislators and government officials to respect basic legal principles and the brutality of their discrimination against non-whites were both forcefully illustrated by the case of *Tsewu v Registrar of Deeds*[53] in 1905. Mr Tsewu was—as the court put it—an 'aboriginal native of Africa'. He had bought a plot of land in Klipriversoog in the Transvaal. His application to the local Deeds Office to have the land registered in his name was refused. The Registrar maintained simply that native blacks were not permitted to own land in the Transvaal.

Before the Transvaal Supreme Court, counsel for the Registrar suggested that there were several legal sources for this principle. The first was a *besluit* passed in 1884, in which the Volksraad had referred approvingly to a letter from a boer farmer arguing that blacks could not own land in the Republic. The second was the 1896 amendment to the *grondwet* which asserted that 'there shall be no equality between black and white'.[54] The third was a provision (Article 13) of the Pretoria and London Conventions, which read: "Leave shall be given to natives to obtain ground, but the passing or transfer of such ground shall in every case be made to and registered in the name of the Commission for Kafir Locations hereinafter provided for the benefit of such natives".

Innes C.J., for a unanimous court, took as his starting point the presumption that all adult men in the Transvaal had an equal right to own land in any area unless and until such rights had been abridged by legislation. He then proceeded

[53] (1905) TLR 130.
[54] See p. 41 above.

to hold that none of the sources identified by the Registrar could be regarded as 'legislation' for these purposes. The purported *besluit* was not a *besluit* at all, (and here Innes adopted Kotze C.J.'s reasoning in *Brown v Leyds*) since it had not been promulgated in accordance with the then extant provisions of the *grondwet*. It thus amounted to no more than an expression of the Volksraad's opinion. Innes C.J. also doubted that Article 13 of the Pretoria Convention could have the meaning for which the Registrar contended. But that question was in any event irrelevant, since the Convention was merely a treaty between different states and could have no effect in the Republic's domestic law.[55] Innes C.J. acknowledged that the 'no equality' clause of the amended *grondwet* could conceivably have stretched to cover ownership of land. However this too was an irrelevant argument, since Milner's Crown Colony government had repealed the 1896 *grondwet*. Mr Tsewu—and indeed any other adult male—was thus entitled to buy land in the Transvaal and have his ownership recorded in the local Register of Deeds. Any alteration of that common law principle would have to await action by the legislature.

Innes C.J.'s presumption of race equality as the starting point for legal analysis in *Tsewu* might at first glance be thought difficult to reconcile with his approach in *Swarts*. One can however readily square this apparent circle by presuming that while Innes C.J. appeared to regard the *common law* as a substantively liberal in respect of race discrimination, the common law could not be invoked to counter *explicit* statutory commands. The general accuracy of this suggestion is reinforced by a judgment Innes C.J. had delivered one month prior to *Tsewu*, in which he concluded that the courts should generally assume that legislation was intended by its framers to be implemented in a colour-blind fashion.

The plaintiff in *Hajee Habib v Pietersberg Municipality*[56] was an Asiatic who wished to construct a building for commercial and residential use in an area of Pietersberg inhabited primarily by whites. Construction would require the approval of the local authority. The council refused to grant the permission for the building, on the candid grounds that it did not wish Asians to live and trade in white areas because their sanitary habits were so primitive that they posed a threat to public health.[57]

[55] This is a perfectly orthodox statement of English legal principle which maintains a dualist approach to international law; i.e. that a Treaty is not 'part of' English law until incorporated by Parliament. The principle has less force in the context of legal systems rooted in Roman Dutch law, some of which have adopted a monist approach to international law: i.e. that a Treaty automatically becomes 'part of' the signatory state's domestic law.

[56] (1905) TLR 63.

[57] This was, curiously, a matter to which Gandhi's opposition was muted. Hancock records that Gandhi expressed some sympathy with such views: "Our [i.e. Indians'] different ways of living, our simplicity, our indifference to the laws of hygiene and sanitation, our slowness in keeping our surroundings clean and tidy, and our stinginess in keeping our houses in good repair—all these, combined with the difference in religion, contributed to fan the flame of antagonism": (1962), n. 2 above, p. 326.

Innes C.J., again giving judgment for a unanimous court, held that governmental bodies exercising statutory powers had no implied authority to structure their decisions in accordance with racist ideology. The court was to assume that the legislature intended governmental powers to be exercised in a non-discriminatory way unless the statute concerned clearly approved such discrimination. In other words, legislators were presumptively colour blind in their intentions.

This distinction between purely common law rules and the common law rules courts invoked to stucture their interpretation of statutes does not however fully answer the question of why Innes C.J. felt bound in *Swarts* to interpret 'white' in such a restrictive fashion. The same point might be made in respect of the Transvaal Supreme Court judgment in *Salujee v Rex*.[58] Salujee had been convicted for breaching a bye-law passed in the Transvaal town of Middleburg which prohibited 'coloured persons' from walking on pavements.[59] Salujee contested his conviction on the grounds that he was not 'Coloured' but 'Asiatic'. His argument that the bye-law should be strictly construed to minimise the extent of its interference with individual liberty found little favour with the Transvaal Supreme Court. Wessells and Mason JJ. were both of the opinion that 'Asiatic' and 'Coloured' were interchangeable terms for these purposes. Mr Salujee would therefore have to keep off the pavements. It would have been quite defensible for the court to have reached the conclusion urged by Salujee's counsel. That it chose not to do so is indicative of a judicial presumption of deference to the policy preferences of elected governmental bodies, a deference which manifestly was not conditioned by the markedly selective racial composition of the Middleburg electorate.

Conclusion

It is evident even from this brief and selective survey that there was appreciable divergence both in law and in practice among and within the four white colonies on race relations issues. The Cape's supposedly 'liberal' principles were much compromised in matters of detail, while Natal seemingly accorded no respect at all to even the few aspects of its political culture which in legal terms enjoyed colour-blind status. It is similarly clear that no perfect congruence existed between the Transvaal and the Free State on these matters. But the differences between the colonies were perhaps of degree rather than quality, insufficient to preclude the emergence (at least in the three southern colonies) of a more cohesive and pervasive 'Afrikaner' identity. Paradoxically, it was Milner who more

[58] (1903) TS 13.

[59] 'Coloured persons' were to keep to the streets. Quite how they were to enter shops would be something of a mystery, although one might also assume they were banned from most retail outlets as well.

than anyone else was responsible for breathing life into this process and providing its initial sustenance.[60]

II. FROM MILITARY DEFEAT TO POLITICAL VICTORY: THE REASSERTION OF THE AFRIKA(A)NER IDENTITY

In the first years of the peace, the anglicisation policy was to prove a failure. The expected British immigration did not materialise on any significant scale, with the result that Afrika(a)ners continued to form a clear majority of the white population in the Transvaal and the Free State.[61] A substantial portion of that majority was also antagonised rather than seduced by the internal elements of Milner's policy, especially by the importation of Chinese labour and the relegation of Dutch to so manifestly subsidiary a status within the schools.

This latter issue had prompted the first significant post-war attempt by boers in both the Free State and the Transvaal to create institutional protection for their political and cultural preferences. A Commission for National Christian Education was created in 1902.[62] Its objective was to establish a primary and secondary schools system for boer children in which they would not be exposed to anglicising influences. The Commission, most of whose leading members were Dopper Kerk clergymen, received no government funding. It drew most of its financial support and virtually all its ideology from Calvinist educationists in the Netherlands. The National Christian Education movement in the Netherlands promoted a rigid brand of Calvinism, whose adherents regarded themselves as a 'chosen people', superior to and isolated from any religious or ethnic groups in their society.[63] The Commission's influence among the rural boer population and an increasingly numerous population of 'poor whites' in urban areas[64] was further enhanced by the Dopper Kerk's role in dispensing charitable relief.[65] Kitchener's scorched earth policy prevented many previously self-sufficient boer families from feeding themselves in the immediate aftermath of the war. Britain had accepted responsibility for rebuilding and reinvigorating the agricultural economy in both the Free State and the Transvaal, but this was a medium and long-term ambition.[66] In the short term, the Dopper Kerk stepped into the breach, administering funds provided by Dutch churches.

[60] See especially Thompson (1985), n. 9 above, p. 33.

[61] R. Hyam 'British Imperial Policy and South Africa 1906–1910', in Warwick, n. 4 above; Marks and Trapido, n. 21 above. Davenport estimates that barely 1300 British families settled in southern Africa as a result of Milner's policy: (1978), n. 12 above, p. 151.

[62] Thompson (1960), n. 1 above, pp. 18–21; T. Moodie *The Rise of Afrikanerdom* (London: University of California Press, 1975), pp. 46–47, 70–73.

[63] Hexham, n. 4 above.

[64] S. Katzenellenbogen, 'Reconstruction in the Transvaal' in Warwick (1980), n. 4 above, pp. 349–351; L. Thompson *A History of South Africa* (New Haven: Yale University Press, 1995), pp. 111–114; Marks and Trapido, n. 21 above.

[65] Moodie, n. 62 above, pp. 69–71.

[66] The financial and technological impetus which Milnerism lent to southern African agriculture is cogently examined and explained in Katzellenbogen, n. 64 above.

The reassertion of the boer identity also had a more amorphous dimension. J.D. du Toit, a minister of the Dutch Reform Church and the son of S.J. du Toit,[67] was active both as a promoter and author of Afrikaans literature. His own poems presented an uncritical portrait of boers as a devout christian people assailed on all sides either by the imperialist British or the barbarous native tribes. Like his father before him, J.D. du Toit proved a skilled propagandist as manufacturer of uplifting myths from events in the boers' past.[68] The Great Trek was soon to be given that status, as was the Day of the Covenant.[69] Du Toit was joined by other 'historians' and biographers in an endeavour to create an instant, glorified written culture around which boer political sentiment could in the long term coalesce.[70]

Despite the antagonism which Milner's anglicisation provoked among many boers, and notwithstanding the evangelical extremism of the Christian Education movement, there seemed to be little immediate prospect of a wholly unified Afrika(a)ner political opposition emerging in any of the southern African colonies. During the war, the Afrikaner community in the Republic and the Free State was bitterly divided between the so-called *bittereinders* (those who had wished to fight the British to the death), the *hensoppers* (who had acquiesced in British military dominance) and the National Scouts (who had assisted the British war effort).[71]

In the early years of the peace, a distinct cleavage emerged amongst the former boer generals and their followers. The division was between those who, echoing the policies of Hofmeyr in the Cape, sought to advance the cause of Afrikaner self-government by moderating their politics sufficiently to find common ground with any anglophile whites, and those whose vision of Afrikaanerdom was of a narrow, doctrinaire faction, separate from and superior to other whites and non-whites.

Smuts and Botha were the standard bearers of the first grouping. They took a substantial step towards their goal in 1905, by founding a new political party to contest the next elections in the colony. The party was given the nominally inclusive title of Het Volk (The People), and rapidly attracted the support of the majority of the Transvaal's boer population.[72] Het Volk faced several obstacles on its path to power. The longer term challenge confronting Botha and Smuts was to ensure that Het Volk managed to win the support of at least a substantial minority of the Rand's *uitlander* population. The possibilities of this being achieved were enhanced by a clear split among the anglo-population after the war. The Chamber of Mines channelled its support to a party calling itself the

[67] See pp. 34–35 above.

[68] Thompson (1985) n. 9 above, pp. 35–36, 168–180.

[69] See p. 34 above.

[70] Thompson (1985), n. 9 above, pp. 181–182.

[71] A. Grundlingh 'Collaborators in Boer Society', in Warwick, n. 4 above; Thompson (1960), n. 1 above, pp. 17–18. It takes no great linguistic ability to recognise that the Afrikaans terms translate as 'bitterenders' and 'hands-uppers' in English.

[72] Hexham, n. 4 above; Hancock (1962), n. 2 above, pp. 195–196.

Transvaal Progressive Association, which naturally recieved the fulsome support of the Johannesburg *Star*.[73] Botha and Smuts saw little scope for Het Volk to cooperate with the 'Progressives'. The second anglo-faction, the Transvaal Responsible Government Association, representing the colony's professional middle classes, offered more favourable prospects.[74] The embryonic Labour Party, notwithstanding its modest success in the 1903 Johnanesburg elections, remained something of an unknown quantity.

The more pressing concern which Botha and Smuts faced, however, was to ensure that the colony's new electoral system was structured in a way that maximised rather than minimised the influence of Het Volk's boer supporters; and which had just precisely the opposite effect on the influence of the Progressives.

The rise and fall of the Lyttleton constitution

Balfour's Conservative government had envisaged that the Transvaal would take its first steps towards autonomous government under the so-called 'Lyttleton' constitution.[75] This would offer a representative rather than responsible form of government. This was in itself unacceptable to Het Volk. In this they were supported (as one might gather from its name) by the Responsible Government Association. But Smuts and Botha's concern was exacerbated by the proposals for the system under which members of the representative legislature would be elected.

The Lyttleton system proposed all white male residents of the Transvaal would be granted the right to vote for members of a new Legislative Assembly. This was manifestly a non-negotiable condition. But the Lyttleton constitution also provided that the Assembly would have single member constituencies. These would be apportioned on the basis of strict numerical equality of the number of white *men* (i.e. potential voters) in each area. Het Volk wished the notion of equal constituency size to be based on the total white *population*, which would include women and children as well as men. Thus while women and children would not be voters *per se*, their very existence would enhance the voting power of their husbands and fathers since *uitlanders* were much less likely to be married and have children than their boer fellow residents. The system chosen would clearly have a significant influence on the allocation of political power. Since *uitlanders* were mainly single men,[76] their collective voting power would be much enhanced relative to boer men under the Lyttleton arrangements. Similarly, the Lyttleton proposals would increase the influence of

[73] On the *Star*'s role see Potter, n. 5 above, pp. 40–41.

[74] Hancock (1962), n. 2 above, pp. 194–196; Davenport (1978), n. 12 above, pp. 156–158.

[75] Thompson (1960), n. 1 above, pp. 22–26; Davenport (1978), n. 12 above, pp. 159–161.

[76] Milner had backed a spectacularly unsuccessful scheme to import substantial numbers of British women to the Rand: Trapido and Marks, n. 21 above, pp. 68–69.

urban areas relative to the Transvaal's rural regions. Both implications were wholly unpalatable to boer interests.

It would seem unlikely that Smuts and Botha would have been able to convince the Conservative government (now headed by Balfour following Salisbury's death in 1903) to amend these proposals, which clearly met Milner's concerns to 'anglicise' the colony before it was granted responsible government. Milner himself resigned as High Commissioner just as the constitution was due to come into force,[77] but his replacement, Lord Selborne, seemed equally wedded to the Lyttleton proposals. However the Conservative government fell in December 1905. It was replaced by a Liberal administration, led by Henry Campbell-Bannerman. Virtually the first decision taken by the new government was to suspend the continued importation of Chinese labourers into the Transvaal.[78]

The Liberal party, in informal alliance with the Labour and Irish Nationalist parties, subsequently won a resounding victory at the ensuing January 1906 general election. Campbell-Bannerman had committed himself while in opposition to restoring representative government to the Transvaal and the Orange River Colony as quickly as possible. Lord Elgin, who replaced Lyttleton (Chamberlain's short-lived successor) as Colonial Secretary was of like mind, as was Selborne, who Campbell-Bannerman somewhat reluctantly and distrustfully retained as High Commissioner.

Smuts went to England immediately after the election to press the new government on the terms of the Transvaal's new constitution. He succeeded to an extent that he could not have expected. Campbell-Bannerman rapidly committed his administration to grant responsible rather than just representative government to the Transvaal and the Orange River Colony. Moreover, the Liberal government was prepared to amend the principles underpinning the Lyttleton constitution's electoral system and the structure of the Transvaal's legislature. Campbell-Bannerman dispatched a committee headed by Sir J. West Ridgeway to the Transvaal to reconsider the form that its new government should take.[79] Smuts exercised great influence on the committee's deliberations. Its recommendations were accepted without amendment by the British government. Winston Churchill, then Under-Secretary of State for the Colonies, steered the requisite bill through the Commons.[80]

The Transvaal's legislature would be bi-cameral. Its upper house (the Legislative Council) would contain fifteen appointed members, chosen initially by the Governor-General but eventually by the Transvaal's government itself. The lower house (the Legislative Assembly) would contain sixty-nine elected members, drawn from sixty-nine single member constituencies. Constituency

[77] As part of his legacy to the colony, Milner had taken pains to ensure that one of his proteges was installed as editor of *The Star*: Potter, n. 5 above, p. 41.

[78] Wilson, n. 23 above, pp. 471–472.

[79] Wilson, n. 23 above, pp. 485–487; Davenport (1978), n. 12 above, pp. 160–162.

[80] Wilson, n. 23 above, pp. 486–488.

sizes would be based on the number of voters, rather than as Smuts had wished, on the total white population. However, the constitution would not require strict numerical equality—a leeway of fifteen per cent above or below the precise equality figure would be permitted.[81] Geographical size and topography were accepted as legitimate considerations in shaping constitutency boundaries, which were to be redrawn every four years. In effect, the scheme was an open invitation for a boer government to weight the colony's voting power in favour of rural electors, or for an anglophile government to weight it in favour of urban, *uitlander* interests. Winning power at the first election would thus be of crucial significance to a party's long-term electoral prospects, for such power carried with it the authority for the governing party to redraw electoral boundaries in a fashion that significantly increased its supporters' effective voting strength.

The initial scheme allocated thirty-four seats to the Rand, six to Pretoria, and twenty-nine to the rural areas. The West Ridgeway committee had assumed that this allocation would guarentee an anglophile majority in the Assembly in the Republic's first election: Het Volk would sweep the countryside but gain no seats in urban areas. Indeed, in an unusual display of candour which much discomfited some members of the British Cabinet, its final report repeatedly stressed that its proposals were drafted with this result in mind.[82] These calculations assumed however that no *uitlanders* would support Het Volk, and that the anti-Het Volk vote would not be split in such a way as to permit Het Volk candidates to win constituencies with only a minority of the popular vote. Botha and Smuts considered both assumptions to be poorly based, and saw real prospects of Het Volk actually gaining a majority of Assembly seats at its first attempt.

It certainly appears several senior members of the Liberal Cabinet were alert to this possibility, and that they doubted the wisdom of Campbell-Bannerman's strategy. Historians of the era are divided on whether Campbell-Bannerman steamrollered his preferences over the opposition of Lord Elgin, the Colonial Secretary and several other of his Cabinet colleagues, or merely persuaded a largely indifferent Cabinet audience to back his initiative.[83] There is rather less doubt that Campbell-Bannerman regarded the Transvaal in particular and southern Africa in general as a small but nonetheless vital corner of a larger foreign policy field. The Prime Minister was already much concerned by the threat of German military expansion and imperial ambition, and was alert to the possibility that a Transvaal hostile to Britain would offer Germany a valuable conduit for further intervention in southern Africa.

Perhaps fortuitously for Campbell-Bannerman's desire to frustrate German imperial expansion, his wish to enhance boer autonomy meshed perfectly with

[81] i.e. there could be a 30% discrepancy between the number of voters in the largest and smallest constituencies.

[82] Hyam, n. 61 above, pp. 368–369.

[83] Wilson, n. 23 above, pp. 481–484.

the already well established British constitutional principle that the white populations of 'white' colonial societies—Australia, Canada, New Zealand and the four South African colonies—should be left to fashion their own preferred solutions to their internal political problems.[84] For Campbell-Bannerman, applying this principle to the Transvaal also offered the further benefit of relieving the British government of responsibility for solving the Chinese labour force problem, a stick with which the Cabinet was being beaten with increasing severity by the more radical wing of the Liberal party.[85]

The Liberal government's apparent inclination to leave the fate of non-whites in the Transvaal in the hands of the colony's white inhabitants is also evident in the West Ridgeway committee's approval of the Lyttleton constitution's provision that only whites be granted the franchise. In this respect, the Transvaal's constitution followed the racially exclusive example which Milner had introduced for local elections in the Municipalities Election Ordinance 1903. The Cape tradition was evidently no more persuasive a political principle to the 1906 Liberal government than it had been to its immediate Conservative predecessor.

It could have come as little surprise to any informed observer when Het Volk won a majority (albeit a narrow one) in the Transvaal's first post-war election in February 1907,[86] and subsequently formed a government headed by Botha as Prime Minister and Smuts as Colonial Secretary. Botha was nevertheless keen to respond to what he and Smuts perceived as Campbell-Bannerman's magnanimity with a similarly generous, reconciliatory gesture of his own.[87] Rather than fashion a purely Het Volk administration, he gave two of his six 'cabinet' posts to members of the Responsible party.[88]

Smuts' role in the reconciliation project extended beyond the Transvaal's borders. His advocacy in London in 1906 had also been directed towards securing self-government for the Orange River Colony. This followed—under constitutional arrangements virtually identical to those in the Transvaal (and which included the re-naming of the colony as the Orange Free State)—in 1907. The Orange River boers had created a new political party, Orangia Unie, in 1906, led by Hertzog and Fischer. The party won a huge majority in the Free State's first election in 1908. Fischer became Prime Minister and Hertzog, the former judge-turned-general-turned-politician, occupied the offices both of Attorney-General and Minister of Education.

[84] Thompson (1960), n. 1 above, pp. 23–24.

[85] Hyam, n. 61 above; Davenport (1978), n. 12 above, pp. 159–160: Pakenham, n. 10 above, pp. 646–647.

[86] Het Volk's victory was won without the support of any of the three major English language newspapers. *The Star* campaigned feverishly for the Progressives, the *Sunday Times* chose to castigate all parties as hot-beds of corruption, while the *Mail* followed a more cautiously pro-mining policy: Potter, n. 5 above, pp. 39–41; Mervis, n. 6 above, pp. 46–47.

[87] Smuts was euphoric in his praise of Campbell-Bannerman's policy: "They gave us our country back in everything but name. Has such a miracle of trust and magnanimity ever happened before? Only people like the English could do it. They may make mistakes, but they are a big people": quoted in Wilson, n. 23 above, p. 492.

[88] Hancock (1962), n. 2 above, p. 230.

Thus, less than six years after the end of the war, Britain had installed the generals who had commanded the boer forces as leaders of internally autonomous colonial governments, and had granted them constitutions which seemed to concede many of the political arguments which had triggered the war. For Smuts and Botha, the Liberal government's actions were an act of extraordinary generosity to a defeated enemy. Their feelings in this regard were further strengthened in 1907, when Botha was made a member of the Privy Council and granted the freedom of the City of London.[89] Both men subsequently embraced the ideal of a unified white South African race (albeit strongly tinged in Afrikaner hues) functioning as a loyal member of the British Empire. To this end, the continued conciliation of the anglophile and Afrikaans communities became a key element of their political ideas and practice.[90]

Afrikaaner leaders in the Orange River Colony took a less statesmanlike view. Hertzog in particular saw the grant of self-government as a spur not to Anglo-Afrikaaner reconciliation, but to boer hegemony, if only—initially—within his colony's borders. Orangia Unie had been able to indulge this instinct in the 1907 election campaign; given that a substantial majority of the Free State's white population were boers, there was little electoral need to 'reconcile' anglophile voters.

Nor did Botha and Smuts extend the notion of conciliation beyond the white race. Indeed, discrimination against non-whites was a useful tool to foster unity within the white community. There was no significant constituency within the Transvaal's white electorate—even in the increasingly urbanised and *uitlander* dominated environs of Johannesburg—favouring adoption of even the limited range of formally colour-blind laws used in the Cape. Neither did the Transvaal government feel constrained on this issue by the views of the British government. While a small number of Liberal and Labour MPs might consistently attack racist colonial legislation, Campell-Bannerman and Elgin's support for a manifestly racist Transvaal constitution had convinced Botha and Smuts that they enjoyed a free hand in erecting a similarly discriminatory superstructure on that foundation. In pursuing that ambition, they shared common ground with their counterparts in both Natal and the Orange Free State, and albeit to a lesser extent, in the Cape.

II. FROM 'RECONSTRUCTION' TO 'REDEMPTION'

As responsible governments, the Botha and Fischer administrations in the Transvaal and the Free State could both confidently assume that they would

[89] Thompson (1960), n. 1 above, pp. 30–32.

[90] One of Smuts' many biographers offers an early example of Smuts' potentially anglophile leanings, recalling that the teenage Smuts had fantasised about being knighted by Queen Victoria: Hancock, n. 2 above, p. 12.

enjoy virtually unfettered control over their respective colony's internal affairs. Smuts wasted little time in putting this expectation to the test.

The Transvaal

Botha and Smuts' commitment to fostering reconciliation between the Transvaal's whites made it unlikely that they would promote legislation that would seriously antagonise opposition parties. Botha's decision to construct a coalition rather than purely Het Volk administration also ensured that his government would be able to command an appreciable and reliable Assembly majority for its proposed legislative programme. Three elements of that programme merit detailed examination.

The Asiatic Law Amendment Act 1907

One of the new legislature's first products was the Asiatic Law Amendment Act 1907. The Act required all Indians in the Transvaal to carry identity cards, containing their names, addresses, occupations and fingerprints. No such documentation had to be carried by whites. By registering the Asian population in this way, Botha's government hoped to equip itself with the information necessary to prevent any further Asian immigration into the Transvaal, either from Natal, the Cape or from India itself. The Act was not Smuts' creation. Rather it was an identical copy of an ordinance which Lord Selborne's Crown Colony government had sought to introduce shortly before the Transvaal was granted responsible government. Elgin had vetoed the proposed ordinance because of its discriminatory contents. He considered himself bound however to acquiesce in such a measure promoted by a legislature in a colony enjoying responsible government.[91]

The Act provided the stimulus for Gandhi's first widely celebrated forays into civil disobedience.[92] After an unsuccessful trip to London to persuade the Liberal government to intervene, Gandhi orchestrated a widespread campaign of resistance amongst the Transvaal's Asian community against the Act.[93] Some 9,000 refused to register. Smuts and Botha determined to enforce compliance by prosecuting the leaders of the campaign, scores of whom, including Gandhi, were gaoled.[94]

[91] Hancock (1992), n. 2 above, pp. 329–330.

[92] F. Troup, *South Africa: an Historical Introduction* (London: Methuen, 1972), pp. 205–207; Sachs, n. 41 above, pp. 205–208. On the philosophy underpinning Gandhi's methods in South Africa see L. Kuper, *Passive Resistance* (London: Jonathan Cape, 1956), chs. 1–3.

[93] Gandhi's civil disobedience activities in southern Africa were characterised by an exclusive concern with the Asian community. He made few efforts to find common cause with Coloureds, and none at all to act in concert with native blacks.

[94] P. Joshi, *The Tyranny of Colour* (London: Kennikat Press, 1942), pp. 63–66.

Although eschewing official interference, Churchill let it be known to Smuts that the Liberal government was dismayed by the Act. The Indian government suffered no such inhibitions. Nor did large sections of the British press. Merriman also suggested to Smuts that a diplomatic retreat would be advisable. Smuts subsequently began negotiations with Gandhi, leaving the latter with the impression that if Indians agreed to register voluntarily the Act would be repealed. Gandhi and his colleagues upheld their end of this arrangement. Smuts made no attempt to honour his half of the bargain.[95]

The Act remained in force. On his release from goal Gandhi and 2,000 other Indians staged a celebrated mass burning of registration cards. Gandhi was promptly re-arrested, re-convicted and re-imprisoned. Smuts again exhibited the cavalier attachment to legal propriety he had displayed on assuming cabinet office under Kruger[96] by approving the manifestly illegal deportation of many Asiatic residents back to India.[97]

Smuts seemed increasingly to be assuming a dual identity as politician. In his dealings with the British government, he was the exemplar of honest and conciliatory political behaviour. In dealing with non-whites, his taste for discriminatory ends and for mendacious means to achieve them made him virtually indistinguishable from his former patron Kruger and his former comrade-in-arms Hertzog. To anglophile whites in the Transvaal, he exhibited the first of his two faces.

Education and the civil service

The questions of who should staff government agencies and the nature of the Transvaal's education system offered Het Volk the opportunity to demonstrate the *bona fides* of their professed intention to promote reconciliation rather than division within the white community. Botha and Smuts were in the main willing to accept the bureaucratic ideology bequeathed by Milnerism during the Transvaal's brief period as a Crown Colony. Neither man saw any merit in suggestions that Milner's manifestly English appointees should be replaced wholesale by boers. Even if the boer population could furnish such skilled men in sufficient numbers (which Smuts doubted), their appointment would send clear signals to the anglo-community that Het Volk remained in effect a Krugerite party so far as non-boer whites were concerned . A 'non-political' civil service appointed on the British model was regarded as the only defensible model for the Transvaal to adopt.[98]

95 Hancock labels Smuts' action as a 'misunderstanding' rather than a betrayal, but offers no convincing evidence to support such a benevolent interpretation: (1962), n. 2 above, p. 336. Joshi, n. 94 above, pp. 66–67, offers a less flattering analysis of Smuts' behaviour and motives.

96 See p. 58 above.

97 Simons and Simons, n. 18 above, pp. 71–72.

98 Hancock (1962), n. 2 above, pp. 238–239.

Smuts pursued a similar course in the Education bill he promoted in 1907. The bill, enacted virtually without amendment, appeared to promote a principle of equality between the Dutch and English languages within the Transvaal's schools. But a detailed reading of the Act made it clear that English would be the dominant medium of education in the Transvaal's new state-administered system of primary education. Attendance would be compulsory for all white children, and no fees would be charged. The Act was as welcome to the Transvaal's anglo-commuity as it was anathema to the Commission on Christian National Education. Smuts saw no need for Commission schools to exist alongside the state system, and no provision was made for public funding of such enterprises. Nor would local communities enjoy sufficient autonomy to pursue effectively independent education policies. The Act granted extensive powers to a centrally appointed Director of Education, an office in which Smuts decided to retain the Englishman appointed to run the school system established by Milner.[99]

The provisions of the Education Act appeared to vindicate the judgment the Campbell-Bannerman government had made in granting responsible government to the Transvaal. Balfour, as Leader of the opposition in 1906, had denounced the policy in apocalyptic terms;

> "No human being ever thought of such an experiment before—that of giving to a population equal to, and far more homogenous than our own, absolute control of everything, civil and military . . . [It is] the most reckless experiment ever tried in the development of a great colonial policy".[100]

His fears for the Transvaal seemed, initially at least, to have been unfounded. In respect of the Orange Free State, as we shall see below, the picture would prove rather less clear cut. But in the first years of its administration, the Campbell-Bannerman government was to find that it was the supposedly ultra-loyalist whites of Natal who presented the most serious cause for concern.

Natal

The whites of Natal, as already mentioned, combined arch-Britishness with intense antipathy towards non-whites. The colony had been granted responsible government in 1893, but prior to the war, Natal's political parties were poorly developed. There was no obvious ideological or economic cause for cleavage within the white community of what was still in the main an agricultural economy. Such divisions as did exist seemed to centre on the personalities rather the policies of leading politicians. On the main issues of the day, foremost among which was policy towards the native tribes, the discerning voter would have been hard pressed to identify any appreciable difference in the policy of the government and that of the opposition. Successive administrations had continued

[99] Hancock (1962), n. 2 above, pp. 238–240.
[100] Quoted in Wilson, n. 23 above, p. 488.

to develop Shepstone's notion of fashioning separate political and legal communities for native blacks. This had been particularly clearly evidenced in 1898 by legislation which established a distinct legal system for native blacks, topped by a 'Native High Court'. The native courts' jurisdiction was to extend only to civil cases in which *all* litigants were natives, and to criminal cases in which *all* defendants were natives.

The Zulu wars

At the conclusion of the war, the Natal administration was headed by C.J. Smythe. Smythe's government rapidly found itself facing severe economic problems. As one means to lessen its budget defecit, Smythe's administration successfully promoted a bill which would levy a £1 per annum poll tax on all single native men. The British government regared the measure as 'medieval', but had no wish to interfere with what it regarded as purely 'internal' political matter.[101] A number of native blacks refused to pay the tax. A police contingent sent to enforce the law was subsequently attacked and two of its members killed.[102] A minor chief, Bambata, emerged as the leader of a small armed rebellion against the government. Smythe responded by declaring martial law, and launched a military campaign during which several thousand blacks were slaughtered.[103]

Britain's Liberal government regarded these events with acute dismay, considering Natal's political class at best incompetent and at worst barbaric and corrupt. Winston Churchill referred to Natal as "This wretched colony—the hooligan of the British Empire".[104] But since Natal had a responsible government, and since its actions against its black residents were seemingly a purely 'internal' affair, Campbell-Bannerman felt himself bound by conventional understandings of British-colonial relations not to intervene.

Natal's political leaders evidently saw little reason to be deflected from their course. Their military adventurism was subsequently followed by a series of show trials, in which native blacks were tried for a range of offences. Twenty-six blacks were tried by court martial and sentenced to death. At this point, Campbell-Bannerman decided the convention of non-interference could no longer be respected. Churchill instructed the Governor-General to suspend the sentences, pending an inquiry.[105] Natal's government thereupon resigned, and Elgin found himself showered with protest from the governments of Canada and Australia, which feared the episode could be used as a precedent for British intrusion into their internal affairs. The British government consequently

101 W. Beinart *Twentieth Century South Africa* (Oxford: OUP, 1994), p. 94.

102 Simons and Simons, n. 18 above, pp. 70–71; Thompson (1960), n. 1 above, pp. 42–43.

103 L. Thompson and W. Wilson (eds.), *The Oxford History of South Africa Vol II: South Africa 1870–1966* (Oxford: Clarendon Press, 1971), pp. 344–346; Davenport, n. 12 above, pp. 152–154; Pakenham, n. 10 above, pp. 648–650.

104 Wilson, n. 23 above, p. 490.

105 Pakenham, n. 10 above, p. 648.

revoked the suspension, Smythe resumed office, and the twenty-six natives were shot.[106]

In the election of 1906, the Labour party injected an element of class division into the Natal legislature by winning four of its seats. The party did not however exercise any influence on government policy. The government formed after the election was led by F.R. Moor, a landowner and Minister in former Natal administrations, previously the leader of the opposition. This ostensible transfer of power had no impact however on the colony's race relations policies. Several of Smythe's cabinet agreed to serve under Moor, and his administration continued with its predecessor's policies.

The new government decided that the Zulu chief Dinizulu had been co-ordinating the rebellion. He was arrested and arrangements were made to try him for treason. Elgin considered the charges outrageous, referring to Dinuzulu as an 'estimable' man, "who seems to have taken it all with quiet dignity".[107] The Liberal government still declined however, despite Churchill's urging, to intervene. Dinuzulu engaged W.P. Schreiner, the former Cape Prime Minister as his counsel. The government's case was sufficiently weak, and Schreiner's defence sufficiently adept, to secure Dinuzulu's acquittal on most of the charges.[108]

Smuts, Merriman and Steyn viewed affairs in Natal with alarm. In part this was because they thought the Natal government was pursuing intrinsically absurd policies. But their main concern, misplaced as it turned out, was that the Moor administration's increasingly brutal and incompetent behaviour would eventually provide justification for overt British interference in southern African affairs, thereby undoing much of the work that they had already done to restore the colonies' internal political autonomy.[109]

The extremist policies pursued by the Natal government appeared to derive from the colony's pervasive (white) political culture. As in the Cape and the pre-war republic, Natal's electoral system was blatantly gerrymandered in favour of rural residents. Its legislature's single member constituencies varied in size from as little as 200 voters in some country seats, to over 1,500 in some cities. Durban and Pietermarizburg contained almost forty per cent of the electorate, but returned less than twenty per cent of the legislature's members.[110] Initially, under the terms of its 1856 constitution, Natal had granted the right to vote on a colour-blind basis. However that principle had been substantially eroded, both in law and practice, over the intervening fifty years.[111] By 1906, whites in

[106] Thompson (1960), n. 1 above, pp. 44–45.

[107] Wilson, n. 23 above, p. 490.

[108] *In re Dinizulu* (1908) 29 NLR 271. See Sachs, n. 41 above, pp. 93–94; Dugard *Human rights and the South African Legal Order* (Princeton: Princeton University Press, 1978), pp. 251–252.

[109] Hancock (1962), n. 2 above, pp. 223–224.

[110] Thompson (1960), n. 1 above, p. 127.

[111] Non-whites had been removed from the electoral roll by a series of ostensibly colour-blind measures. Indians, for example, were denied the vote by an 1896 Act which disenfranchised immigrants (and their descendants) from countries which did not themselves have a parliamentary system of government: Davenport (1960), n. 12 above.

Natal formed barely ten per cent of the colony's population, but accounted for ninety-nine pr cent of its electorate.[112] Neither Natal's blacks, nor its by now substantial Indian population, wielded any electoral influence.[113]

The Orange Free State

While Botha and Smuts pursued a policy of reconciliation and inclusion between the white communities of the Transvaal, their former comrades in arms who had formed Orangia Unie decided to adopt a quite different strategy when the Free State was granted responsible government.

J.B. Hertzog was barely forty years old in 1907. His parents were originally farmers in the Cape, but had lost their land during an economic slump in the 1870s, and eventually became small shopkeepers in the Free State. Hertzog had attended college at Stellenbosch, and then gone to Holland rather than England to take a law degree. He was subsequently appointed to the Free State High Court when only twenty-nine years old.[114]

Hertzog's time in Holland, his experiences in the war, and his personal devotion to M.T. Steyn, had led him to conclude that the future prosperity of white races in southern Africa lay in the rigid separation rather than reconciliation of the anglo and boer elements of the white populations. Their common interests extended only to ensuring the continued political and economic subordination of non-whites. As Minister of Education[115] in the 1908 Orangie Unie government in the Free State, Hertzog had the opportunity to give his views concrete legal effect.

The Education Act which Hertzog promoted in the Free State took a rather more trenchant view of the concept of language equality than Smuts' Act in the Transvaal. The Free State legislation essentially made English/Dutch bilingualism compulsory in the latter stages of elementary education and throughout secondary schooling.[116] Such a policy would of course require that teachers be bi-lingual, or become so rapidly. Since many of the teachers Free State's anglo teachers were not bi-lingual, the Act would have the indirect effect, at least in the short term, of rendering them ineligible for employment in state schools.

Enforced language equality was not a principle that held much attraction to English-speaking whites in the Free State. The Act was also afforded a frosty reception in the British press, in Natal, and among the anglo-communities of the

[112] Wilson and Thompson, n. 103 above, p. 338.

[113] One might wonder if a substantial bloc of Indian votes would have made any difference to government policy. Gandhi, by now an eminent member of southern Africa's Indian community, had followed his non-combatant participation in the second boer war by serving in the Natal forces as an ambulance driver during the Zulu war.

[114] Hancock, n. 2 above, pp. 241–242; O. Pirow (nd.), *James Barry Munik Herzog* (Cape Town: Howard Timmins), ch. 1.

[115] Hertzog also held the post of Attorney-General.

[116] Hancock (1962), n. 2 above, pp. 242–244; Pirow, n. 114 above, pp. 47–50.

Cape and the Transvaal. It was portrayed as an early indication of what was expected to be a more pervasive phenomenon, labelled 'Hertzogism', if boer politicians were ever to gain power in the other white colonies; namely an attempt by the most intransigent of the boers to achieve through the political process the ends they had failed to gain in the war.

Hertzog himself did not seem to consider such criticism a cause for concern. Rather he construed it as evidence of the anglo-population's lukewarm support for reconciliation, and thence of the misguided nature of Botha and Smuts' endorsement of that policy. Separation rather than assimilation between the white 'races' appeared at this time to be the dominant factor in his political beliefs.

The Cape

Milner's success in making enemies among southern Africa's white population was not limited to boers in the Transvaal and the Free State. He also managed to antagonise most shades of white political opinion in the Cape by trying to persuade Chamberlain to suspend the colony's constitution in 1902 and grant him the power to govern the Cape as though it was a Crown colony. The initiative seemed unduly alarmist, for he soon found himself working hand-in-hand with a congenial Cape government. Jameson—evidently purged of whatever opprobrium had attached to him as a result of his illegal and botched adventurism in the Raid—had led his Progressive Party[117] to power in the Cape elections in 1904. This was an achievement of some note on Jameson's part, given the electoral handicap under which his party had laboured.

Merriman's preference for loading the electoral system in favour of rural areas had by 1904 been taken to lengths almost as extreme as those in force in Natal. The Cape's House of Assembly had 107 members, representing some 150,000 voters. The size of constituencies varied dramatically however, from barely 400 in some rural areas to over 2,500 in some urban seats. The forty plus per cent of voters living in urban areas (where Jameson's support was disproportionately located) returned only twenty-five per cent of the House's members.[118]

Jameson professed himself at this time to be a firm supporter of the Cape's colour-blind electoral laws. His government was not wedded to that principle of non-discrimination in other areas however. In this, he was following rather than initiating a trend. The Cape's discriminatory alcohol laws have already been discussed, as have the obviously segregationist policies outlined in the report of Milner's Native Affairs Commission. Several other significant measures involving a system of race-based classifications were introduced in the Cape in the aftermath of the war.

[117] The party shared the name and outlook of the Chamber of Mines' vehicle in the Transvaal.
[118] Thompson (1960), n. 1 above, p. 127.

The Governor-General's opening address to the 1902 session of the Cape Parliament recognised that it was "necessary for the Government to be endowed with larger powers than they [sic] now possess to effectually carry out the policy of segregation".[119] Legislation had been passed in 1904 permitting the physical segregation of native blacks within specific residential areas in towns and cities.[120] Jameson's government, elected later that year, was evidently content to continue with the segregation policies.

One of its first measures, prefiguring the steps that Botha's government would shortly take in the Transvaal, was to promote an immigration bill (enacted in 1906) which prevented any further adult male immigration from India.[121] In the previous year, Jameson's government had endorsed segregation in the most explicit of terms, and did so moreover in a way that was concerned not simply to emphasise that whites and non-whites enjoyed separate but equal status, but to stress that non-whites occupied a distinctly inferior status in Cape society.

Schooling in the Cape

The Cape School Board Act 1905 required individual school districts within the Cape to establish undenominational schools for children in their area. Prior to 1905, the bulk of elementary and secondary education in the Cape had been provided by so-called 'mission' schools, financed and run by religious organisations. Provision was patchy, teaching and resources varied markedly between schools, and many schools accommodated only children from particular racial groups.

The 1905 Act was one of the final ingredients of Milner's recipe to anglicise the Cape's Afrikaaner population. The new state schools would not be free; fees could be charged for attendance if the district so wished. The Act did not explicitly require that separate state schools be established for pupils of different races. On its face, the Act seemingly permitted school districts to admit children of all races to any particular school, although it certainly did not explicitly require them to do so. A careful reading of the statute indicated however that Milner's policy might enable school districts to impose a quite stark form of racial discrimination. While the Act imposed uniformity within the Cape's white population, it could be construed in a way that drew a clear distinction between whites and non-whites.

School districts could, for example, make attendance at a state school compulsory for children of European extraction.[122] Attendance at a mission school would be an acceptable alternative only if the mission school concerned admitted solely children of European extraction. Attendance at a state school

[119] S. Dubow, *Racial Segregation and the Origins of Apartheid in SA 1919–1936* (London: Macmillan, 1989), p. 23.

[120] The Native Locations Act 1904; see Simons and Simons, n. 18 above, p. 70.

[121] Simons and Simons, n. 18 above, p. 70.

[122] An exception was made for children living more than three miles from a state school.

for children of non-European extraction could be made compulsory only if the relevant district had provided a school exclusively for non-white children. However districts were not under any obligation to make such provision unless requested to do so by at least fifty parents of non-white children.

The text of the Act thus left three potentially important questions unanswered. First, was a school district empowered to establish schools solely for the use of white children? Secondly, if a school district could create whites-only schools, was it also obliged if it did so to establish schools exclusively for non-white children? And thirdly, just what was meant by 'white' or 'European descent' in this context ?

A definitive answer to those questions would presumably have to come (eventually) from the courts. As a matter of practice, however, many school districts chose to segregate their schools. And in areas with only small non-white populations, no provision at all was made for children whom local school boards considered to be non-white. In this further respect, therefore, the Cape's colour-blind tradition was subjected to an additional, substantial dilution.

The schools legislation was indicative of what several commentators have identified as a distinct shift of position within the ranks of Cape liberals (and British governments) in the late nineteenth and early twentieth centuries. The mid-nineteenth century has been characterised as an era in which white liberals viewed non-whites as 'Europeans-in-waiting', some, perhaps many of whom would gradually 'advance' sufficiently in terms of education and culture to be assimilated into 'white' colonial society. By 1900, in contrast, the increasing grip of eugenic theories and social Darwinism on the minds of white politicians had led many liberals to assume that a benevolent form of segregation of the races was the most appropriate way to govern ethnically diverse societies.[123]

IV. THE EMERGENCE OF NON-WHITE POLITICAL MOVEMENTS

The Cape's inconstancy towards the political and legal status of its non-white inhabitants provided an obvious spur for the development of political movements composed exclusively of non-white members, and concerned exclusively with promoting the interests of the Cape's non-white citizens. The Cape's colour-blind franchise also facilitated the emergence of such groups, since their members could expect to exercise some direct (albeit limited) electoral influence on Cape legislators[124] in addition to simply acting as a pressure group outside the parliamentary process.

[123] Dubow, n. 12 above, pp. 30–33; R. Hyam, *Elgin and Churchill at the Colonial Office* (London: Macmillan, 1968), pp. 537–542.

[124] Dubow, n. 12 above, pp. 131–132.

The African Political Organisation

The peace negotitiations leading to the Treaty of Vereeniging had also provided a trigger for the formation of the African Political Organisation (APO) in 1902. The APO's founders were drawn from the elite strata of Cape Coloured society. 'Elite' was very much a relative term: the original members were "small shop-keepers, fruit vendors, tradesmen, coachmen, a fireman, a carpenter and a property speculator". Few coloureds had then entered the professions which comprised the upper echelons of white Cape society.[125] A notable exception was offered by Abdullah Abuhrahman, who rapidly became the dominant figure within the APO, and served as its President from 1905–1940. Abdurahman was the grandson of slaves who, after buying their freedom, made a substantial fortune as fruit merchants. Abdurahman himself had been educated at one of the Cape's most exclusive private schools, and qualified as a medical doctor after attending Glasgow University.[126]

The founders of the APO were motivated in part by the well-founded fear that Milner wanted to revive Lord Carnarvon's plans for creating a unified South African state from the four colonies. Abdurahman doubted that the white majority in such a state would favour the Cape's (relatively) liberal race relations policies, and saw a need for the non-white community to maximise its influence both on the Cape's electoral stage and on any future British government that might be attracted to the idea of creating a unified South African colony.

APO membership was formally open to people of any racial identity, although in its early years only coloureds tended to join, and its activities were limited geographically to the western Cape. The APO anounced its aims as 'promoting unity among the coloured races; obtaining higher and better education for Coloured children; and defending Coloured people's social and political rights'.[127] These ends would be pursued through avowedly 'constitutional' means. The APO's tactics brought it some early successes. The non-white vote was of sufficient size to have a significant bearing on the result in several of the Cape's parliamentary and municipal constituencies, a political fact which sensitised some white politicians to the aspirations of non-white voters. Abduhrahman himself was elected to the Cape municipal council in 1904—the first non-white to achieve this feat. His victory required him to have won at least a substantial minority of white votes in his constituency, a fact which he regarded as a hopeful indicator that the Cape's colour-blind political culture was increasing rather than declining in strength.[128]

[125] Lewis, n. 7 above, p. 23; S. Trapido, 'The Origins and Development of the African Political Organisation' (1969) *Institute of Commonwealth Studies* 1.

[126] Simons and Simons, n. 18 above, pp. 117–118.

[127] Lewis, n. 7 above, p. 21.

[128] Simon and Simon, n. 18 above, pp. 117–118.

The APO's policy gained some credibility in 1902 and 1903, when its lobbying of the Cape government led to the exemption of Coloured residents from the location policy applied to native blacks following the panic engendered by the plague.[129] This victory was not however a precursor to continued success. The APO campaigned vigorously against the Jameson government's School Board Bill of 1905, but with little effect.[130]

Abdurahman's view of race relations in the other colonies was similarly ambiguous. The APO had vigorously and vociferously opposed the importation of Chinese indentured labourers into the Transvaal. Chamberlain was accused of shaping policy simply to service the interests of Rand mineowners, and of turning the Transvaal into little more than an "Imperial prison for coloured people".[131] Abdurahman found common ground with Campbell-Bannerman on this issue. On others, however, they were far apart. Abduhraman had led a delegation of non-white southern Africans to London in 1906 to protest against the West Ridgeway committee's approval of an electoral colour bar in the Transvaal's electoral system.[132] Campbell-Bannerman remained unmoved by his argument that a colour-blind franchise was both intrinsically just and a necessary implication from Article 8 of the Treaty of Vereeniging, a point upon which Churchill relied heavily in the Commons.[133] The Transvaal was to be if not a 'prison', then certainly not a 'home' either for the non-white southern Africans who lived there.

The APO was nevertheless a radical rather than militant organisation. Its methods of opposing racial discrimination were to be parliamentary rather than revolutionary.[134] Abdurahman himself seemed even at this early stage to be a politician capable of holding apparently irreconcilable views. Despite his professed antagonism to the Transvaal's electoral colour bar,[135] Abdurahman had begun to form 'a friendly relationship' with Smuts by the time the colony was granted responsible government.[136] Abdurahman perhaps sincerely believed that Smuts could be persuaded to steer the Transvaal's political culture in a more liberal direction. Whether one should attribute such views to optimism or naivety is difficult to gauge. What is however clear is that the APO's stance in this regard was not unique among southern Africa's various non-white communities.

[129] See p. 67 above; Lewis, n. 7 above, pp. 16–20, 26.

[130] Davenport (1978), n. 12 above, p. 155; Lewis, n. 7 above, pp. 30–34.

[131] Simons and Simons, n. 18 above, p. 119.

[132] *Ibid*. pp. 111–112.

[133] Wilson, n. 23 above, p. 487.

[134] Dubow observes that the 'liberal' whites who professed sympathy for the objectives of non-white groups invariably urged them to eschew extra-parliamentary methods: n. 12 above, pp. 16–17. See also Hancock (1962), n. 2 above, pp. 221–223.

[135] Lewis, n. 7 above, pp. 34–39.

[136] Hancock (1962), n. 2 above, p. 224.

Native black politicians and political organisations

'Political' activity in the form followed by Abdurahman was simply not an option for the great majority of native blacks living in the southern African colonies, since they had no 'constitutional' means at all of participating in the political systems of Natal, the Free State and the Transvaal. Bambatha's 'rebellion' in Natal was perhaps the most graphic example of black political action in this period, but historians have recorded many other less seismic episodes of black resistance to white rule at this time, especially in rural areas.[137]

Native black assertions of autonomy were frequently channelled into explicitly religious movements. The African Methodist Episcopal Church, underwritten by American funding, was particularly influential at the turn of the century, especially in the Cape and Transvaal. Yet its leaders were reluctant to couch their ambitions in explicitly political terms. [138]

The urbanised[139] black workforce on the Rand had taken some tentative steps towards effective unionisation by 1908, although these activities (like those of their white union counterparts) tended to draw a distinction (albeit an unconvincing one) between pursuit of (legitimate) economic ends and (illegitimate) political objectives. Within the urbanised black population, J.T. Jabavu had been perhaps the foremost 'political' figure. Jabavu, initially a teacher and lay preacher, had come to prominence in the Cape in the 1890s as the publisher of *Imvo*, the biggest selling black newspaper.[140] Jabavu had aligned his paper with Merriman and Hofmeyr in the 1890s, had worked closely with James Rose-Innes to secure Rose-Innes' election to the colonial legislature,[141] and was forthright in condemning the Jameson Raid.[142]

Jabavu's main rival for preeminence within the native African community in the Cape was Solomon Plaatje. Plaatje was a descendant of settlers in the Griqualand republic, had begun a career in the Cape civil service and served (as a non-combatant) in the boer war. Plaatje had been greatly disillusioned by the evident post-war rapprochement between the boers and Britain, and was a key figure in the formation of the South African Native Congress (SANC) in the Cape in 1902.[143]

The SANC and the APO shared a commitment to parliamentary forms of protest. Yet they seemed unable to see any substantial scope for joint action between their respective movements. In 1910 Abdurahman had urged all

[137] Beinart (1994), n. 101 above, pp. 94–97.

[138] Davenport, n. 12 above, pp. 154–155.

[139] The term is used guardedly, given that many black workers in the mining industry retained 'homes' in rural areas outside the Transvaal; see pp. 00 above.

[140] Simons and Simons, n. 18 above, pp. 49–50; P. Rich, *State Power and Black Politics in South Africa 1921–1951* (London: Macmillan, 1996), pp. 64–65.

[141] See p. 72 above.

[142] Beinart (1994), n. 101 above, pp. 84–86.

[143] Beinart (1994), n. 101 above, pp. 84–85.

non-whites to adopt a united front to resist segregationist and discriminatory legislation, but his call attacted little positive response from native black leaders.[144] Gandhi's activities in Natal and the Transvaal were similarly exclusive. His concern was with the status of Indians in southern Africa. His methods were developed to suit the specific class and race positions held by Indians. His objectives extended no further than countering or diluting white assaults on Indians' legal, political and economic identities.

To speak of a non-white 'community' in any of the southern African colonies would be a gross inaccuracy, whether one uses the term in a cultural or political sense. The divison between boer and anglo within the white population may have been pronounced at this time, but it was more than matched by the political fragmentation of southern Africa's non-white racial groups.

V. CONCLUSION

By 1907, both Milner and Chamberlain had departed the southern African stage. In many matters of detail, their respective ambitions for the future political and cultural development of the four white colonies had been frustrated. In matters of principle, the extent of their failure was less clear cut. The Transvaal, the Free State and the Cape were manifestly not going to become anglicised by dint of British immigration. Nor did it seem realistic to assume that they would become so through the increasing dominance of British cultural traditions. But Milner and Chamberlain had also harboured the hope that the four colonies could in some fashion be united into a single state.

On this question of principle, they shared common ground (as to ends if not to means) both with Campbell-Bannerman and many influential politicians within southern Africa itself. The prize of a unified South Africa, loyal to the British Empire, was one coveted—albeit for rather different reasons—by many of the leading players on the contemporary political stage. Milner had undertaken some modest institutional initiatives to kickstart a unification process. He had introduced a customs union between the four colonies in 1903, abolishing internal duties and imposing a common tarrif against imported goods. Steps were also taken to amalgamate the colonies' railways, thereby removing one of the most uncomfortable irritants affecting pre-war inter-colonial relations.[145] Milner saw these economic measures as a necessary first step towards political integration. Whether he realised that he was pushing, as far as Smuts, Botha, Merriman and Steyn were concerned, at an open door is unclear. Had he foreseen the landscape that would shortly emerge on the other side, one might doubt that he would have begun pushing at all.

[144] Hancock (1962), n. 2 above, pp. 348–349.
[145] Davenport (1978), n. 12 above, pp. 164–166.

4

The Act of Union 1909

The creation of a South African constitution which accommodated the divergent desires of the colonies' white factions was a matter of some importance to the Liberal government elected in Britain in 1906. It was however far from being the *most* pressing of issues facing the Campbell-Bannerman and Asquith administrations. Students of British political history would most readily identify that era with Lloyd George's 'People's Budget' in 1909, and the related Liberal efforts to lay the foundations of the welfare state.[1] For constitutional lawyers, the era is most significant for the passage of the Parliament Act 1911. The 1911 statute removed the House of Lords' legal status as an equal partner with the Commons in the legislative process, and granted it instead merely a delaying power in respect of most legislation.[2] Such domestic crises, co-existing with an increasing perception of the growing German military threat, pushed questions concerning the *intrinsic* merits of promoting constitutional reform in South Africa some way down the British political agenda. Its instrumental significance was more pronounced, primarily because of Britain's concern about German military ambitions. The German presence in South West Africa, while rendered temporarily benign by Balfour's diplomacy, continued to cast a shadow not just over British dominance in southern Africa itself, but also British control of the sea passage around the Cape to India. A bellicose and potentially rebellious boer population in southern Africa—which might welcome and assist German action against Britain—would have presented a serious danger to British imperial interests. A boer population acquiescent in its colonial status would have been a far lesser evil from the British perspective, but would have done nothing to counter potential German expansion. The summit of British foreign policy ambitions in southern Africa was to fashion a settlement which would lead the majority of southern Africa's white population to take up arms on the British side against Germany should the need ever arise.[3] Campbell-Bannerman's decision to entrust the fate of non-whites in the Transvaal and the Free State to the far from tender mercies of Smuts and Hertzog in 1906 and 1907 may be seen as an example of his far-sighted understanding of Anglo-German tensions.[4] His

[1] R. Jenkins, *Mr Balfour's Poodle* (London: Heineman, 1968).

[2] See I. Loveland, *Constitutional Law* (London: Butterworths, 1996), pp. 200–205.

[3] See M. Beloff, *Britain's Liberal Empire 1897–1921* (London: Metheun and Co, 1969), pp. 75–80, 122–126.

[4] J. Wilson, *A Life of Sir Henry Campbell-Bannerman* (London: Constable, 1973), pp. 476–484; R. Hyam 'British Imperial Policy and South Africa 1906–1910' in P. Warwick (ed.), *The South African War* (London: Longman, 1980).

successors had, by 1909, rather less far to see. But their gaze, like Campbell-Bannerman's, seemed also to fasten on a horizon in which the hazy glow of a desire to foster the re-integration of an Akrikaner/boer-dominated southern Africa into the British Empire hid the territory's non-white population from the Liberal government's view. As Max Beloff was subsequently to put it

> "To have been right about the Boer war was essential to the credentials of a true radical. In all this, there was of course a great measure of self-deception. In their sense of outrage at what seemed a wanton assault on the liberties of a free people British radicals did not look too closely at the nature of Boer society".[5]

Milner himself later took the view that the boers could simply not be trusted to govern southern Africa's non-white population in an acceptable, 'civilised' fashion. Given that Milner had been the motive force behind the 1905 Native Affairs Commission, it is obviously a nonsense to suggest that he championed anything other than a social structure which (in the collective sense) subordinated non-whites to whites legally, politically and economically. Milner shared with Steyn and Hertzog, Botha and Smuts, and Merriman and Hofmeyr the belief that southern Africa was to be white man's territory. He shared only with the latter pair the assumption that such supremacy should be constrained within a moral and legal framework which accepted first that many—perhaps most—non-whites might in the very[6] long term 'develop' sufficently to merit equal political status, and secondly that in the meantime white superiority should be expressed through benevolent if stern paternalism rather than arbitrary oppression.

The influence of Milnerism was by 1909 insignificant. But Beloff's suggestion that it was only the radical opponents rather than the more moderate proponents of Liberal government policy who refused to take 'a close look' at boer policy and practice rather understates the case. By 1909, the Liberal government was taking a similarly Nelsonian approach. It is unsurprising that Lloyd George, by now Chancellor of the Exchequer, should have done so. He had maintained a similarly romanticised view of the boer cause during the war. That Herbert Asquith, who became Prime Minister following Campbell-Bannerman's death in 1908, should do so was more unexpected. Asquith had been among the most vigorous of the 'Liberal Imperialist' supporters of the war against the boers.[7] Now he seemed more than willing to assume Campbell-Bannerman's mantle as a facilitator of boer nationhood within the confines of the Empire. By 1909, both Ministers were as one in leading the Cabinet and Parliament to give their blessing to a South African settlement which even on its face seemed both to condone and facilitate the growth of an egregiously racist political culture.

[5] (1969), n. 3 above, p. 79.

[6] See his comment at n. 7 in Chapter 3.

[7] See Wilson, n. 4 above, ch. 21; M. Blanch, 'British Society and the War', in Warwick (1980), n. 4 above; B. Porter, 'The Pro-Boers in Britain', in Warwick (1980), n. 4 above.

I. THE CONSTITUTIONAL STRUCTURE OF SOUTH AFRICA

The construction of the South African constitution was a process formally undertaken in three distinct phases, the first two in southern Africa itself, the third before the Imperial Parliament.[8] The first phase entailed the creation of a national Convention, sitting first in Durban and then in Cape Town, at which delegates from all four colonies met to fashion the framework of a national constitutional settlement. In the second phase, the conclusions reached at the Convention were placed before the legislatures of the four colonies for approval and or amendment, whereupon the National Convention met once again, this time at Blomfontein, to consider any such amendments. The third and final phase required the colonies to send delegates to London, charged with the task of convincing the Imperial Parliament to enact the proposed constitution without amendment.

The formal stages of the process occupied barely nine months: the National Convention began its proceedings in October 1908, and the South Africa Act received the Royal Assent in the summer of 1909. But the task of creating the conditions needed to bring such an enterprise to a successful conclusion had begun much more informally—indeed covertly—several years earlier. Its chief protagonists were Smuts and Botha in the Transvaal, Steyn in the Orange River Colony, and Merriman in the Cape. All four politicians had seemingly concluded as early as 1904 that the colonies should combine to create a single South African nation. At that time however, the domestic political circumstances in all three of the colonies hardly favoured the airing, still less the promotion, of such views. Merriman in particular urged the necessity of patience, if only in the relatively short term, before such ambitions were made clear.[9]

Merriman and Smuts realised that the creation of a South African nation state would require both the approval of the British Parliament and substantial, enthusiastic support from the white populations of the Cape, the Transvaal and the Free State, and at least the grudging acceptance of whites in Natal. The initiative would have to have 'South African' rather than British or 'boer' origins. Merriman and Smuts pinned their hopes for British approval on the election of a Liberal government. Those hopes proved, as we have seen, to have been well-founded. Lord Selborne, Milner's successor as High Commissioner, lent momentum to the process by issuing a memorandum in 1907 which invited the colonial governments to explore the prospect of unification.[10] Campbell-Bannerman's initial policies towards the Transvaal and the Free State and his

[8] I have drawn heavily in the following section on Professor L.M. Thompson's book, *The Unification of South Africa 1902–1910* (Oxford: Clarendon Press, 1960). I am much indebted to this splendid work.

[9] K. Hancock, *Smuts. Volume 1: The Sanguine Years 1870–1919* (Cambridge: CUP, 1962), pp. 246–249.

[10] Hyam (1980), n. 4 above; G. Dold and C. Joubert, *The Union of South Africa* (London: Stevens and Sons, 1955), pp. 27–30.

subsequent enthusiasm for Selborne's proposal also facilitated the construction of a pro-'South Africa' white culture within the colonies. The victories of Het Volk and Orangie Unie respectively in the Transvaal and Free State elections of 1906 and 1907 ensured that two Afrika(a)ner-controlled colonial governments were in principle supportive of unification. The timetable in the Cape was a little more leisurely. Jameson's Progressive/Unionist party clung to power until February 1908, when it was defeated in the general election by Merriman's South African Party. With Merriman installed as Prime Minister in the Cape, the internal elements needed to promote the unification cause were securely in place. In a superficial sense, Natal remained a staunchly 'British' society. But this strain of Britishness bore little resemblance to the emergant social democratic ethos of early twentieth century Liberal governments. The inveterate racism of Natal's white inhabitants meant they had much in common with the more extreme elements of boer nationalism; for both factions the subordination, indeed the suppression, of all non-white groups, was an unshakeable article of faith. It was by no means absurd for Smuts and Merriman to calculate that the white Natalians' attachment to unfettered racism might outweigh their wish to retain *de jure* their 'British heritage'.

Their ambition was greatly assisted by the manifest difficulties caused by the four colony structure of southern Africa. The planned expiry of the existing customs union between the colonies offered the prospect of renewed and bitter wrangling between the colonial governments, while the question of railway regulation remained a running sore on the colonies' body politic.[11] The balance of economic power within southern Africa had also by then swung markedly in favour of the Free State and (especially) the Transvaal in the years since the end of the war. The Rand's gold mines enabled the Transvaal government to accumulate substantial surpluses in its treasury, while the Delago Bay rail route denied both the Cape and Natal the substantial income they had previously extracted for transporting goods to and from the Transvaal. Natal's public finances were in a state of pronounced and continuing defecit, and the Cape's budgetary circumstances were almost equally straitened.[12] For the coastal colonies, therefore, economics provided a strong incentive for the creation of a single country.

An inter-colonial Conference scheduled in May 1908 to discuss the customs union and rail issues rapidly found its terms of inquiry broadened to considering the question of unification. There was no significant opposition to Smuts and Merriman's suggestion that the Conference's main objective should be to establish a Convention at which a scheme for unification could be hammered out.[13] The Conference agreed that the Convention would be chaired by Sir

[11] Dold and Joubert, n. 10 above, pp. 30–32.

[12] Thompson (1960), n. 8 above, pp. 52–60.

[13] The process has uncanny parallels with that followed by proponents of the present American Constitution at the Philadelphia Convention in 1787. That Convention was ostensibly called to discuss ways to remedy defects in the USA's first constitution, the Articles of Confederation. In the

Johan Hendrick De Villiers, then Chief Justice of the Cape.[14] M.T. Steyn would serve as his deputy. The Convention would be attended by thirty delegates; twelve from the Cape, eight from the Transvaal, and five each from both Natal and the Orange Free State.[15] Each colony was left to devise its own method of selecting its delegates. All chose a process which ensured that their delegations broadly represented the spread of political opinion in their respective legislatures. All thirty delegates were white. The Conference did not see any active role for non-white citizens in the Convention's deliberations.

Merriman led the Cape delegation. Hofmeyr, as he had always done, chose not to participate in the Convention in person, but to wield influence behind the scenes. Schreiner had absented himself from the Convention in order to defend Dinizulu against the treason charges brought by the Natal government.[16] Merriman was accompanied by several of his Cabinet colleagues, notably F.S. Malan and Jacobus Sauer. Jameson led a group of three Unionists. The six Natal delegates, headed by then Prime Minister Frederick Moor, were a more politically homogenous grouping. So were the five from the Free State, four of whom (Christiann de Wet, Abraham Fischer, Hertzog and Steyn) were prominent members of the Orangia Unie Cabinet. The Transvaal delegates were a more mixed bunch. Smuts and Botha led a group of four Het Volk nominees; they were joined by three members of the Progressive Party (who *de facto* represented the Chamber of Mines) and one Nationalist.

The agenda which the Convention would address was framed only in the most general of terms. In respect of many matters of principle as well as detail, the delegates would be writing on a blank constitutional page. But on perhaps the most important question of all, the conclusion they would reach seemed to have been settled before they even met.

A unitary or federal state?

A country which amalgamated four previously discrete colonies might be thought likely to adopt a federal rather than unitary state structure. The obvious model for South Africa to have followed would appear to have been that adopted in the USA. The American Constitution divides law-making powers

event, supporters of the Articles found themselves railroaded into accepting an agenda which called for the overturning rather than amendment of the *status quo*; see L. Levy, 'Introduction' in L. Levy (ed.), *Essays on the Making of the Constitution* (Harvard UP: Cambridge, Mass, 1987).

[14] Johan Hendrick (Henry) De Villiers (1842–1914). Educated at the South African College. He studied law at Berlin and in London. He was the Attorney-General in Molteno's 1872 Cape administration, the colony's first 'responsible' government (see p. 21 above). Molteno appointed him Chief Justice of the Cape in 1873. De Villiers remained intimately involved in party politics in the Cape, the Transvaal and the Free State, and had ambitions (never realised) to become President of one of the boer republics or Prime Minister of the Cape.

[15] The Rhodesian colonies sent observer delegates to the Convention. Smuts in particular had hopes that the Rhodesians would wish to become part of South Africa in the near future.

[16] See pp. 90–91 above.

between the various organs of the national government and the country's (now) fifty states. The USA's constitutional settlement was designed to ensure that its governmental structure enabled Americans to disagree about some important political questions—and to enable that disagreement to be given simultaneous effect in different parts of the country—while placing other important powers in the hands of a national government which could impose its will, but only in respect of a limited range of issues, on the entire country. The separation of powers was to have a geographical as well as an institutional dimension.

Canada and Australia also offered 'federal' models which the southern Africans might have followed. Canada had been functioning as a federal polity since the 1860s, and had done so with sufficient success to persuade the then 'independent' British North American colony of Prince Edward Island to seek admission to Canada in the next decade.[17] The various British colonies in Australia had formed a federal state in 1901. The Canadian and Australian constitutions differed in the degree of 'federalism' which they adopted. The powers given to the organs of the respective central and provincial/state governments (and those given to neither) varied appreciably, as did the mechanisms through which the terms of their constitutions could be altered. Both were however variations on a theme—the theme offered by the constitution of the USA.

Entrenching political pluralism

It is sometimes forgotten that the USA's federal constitution demands that legal authority be divided not into two but into *three* spheres. Some matters are beyond the reach of either the national or state governments. Both the national and state governments in the USA were the creations of—and hence inferior to—a higher form of law-making body. This body—'the people' of the USA—is defined by Article V of the Constitution as comprising at least two-thirds of the members of Congress (the national legislature) and at least three-quarters of the states themselves. It is quite possible as a matter of constitutional law for 'the people' of the USA to refashion their country as a unitary state and/or to grant their national legislature the same legal powers as the United Kingdom Parliament should they wish to do so. Indeed, the American 'people' possess just the same sovereign legal authority as is wielded by Parliament in the United Kingdom.

The difference between the two 'sovereigns' is that while the USA's Article V law-making process is hardly ever activated—it has been used barely thirty times in over 200 years—Parliament has been in permanent session since 1688: Britain's 'constitution' is constantly being amended. Britain is necessarily therefore a unitary rather than federal state. While it may have an elaborate system of local government, whose members are elected and who may exerise significant powers, Parliament can at any time alter the boundaries and powers of

[17] T. Lloyd, *The British Empire 1558–1995*, 2nd edn. (Oxford: OUP, 1996), pp. 187–191.

local authorities and may even abolish them altogether. The British constitution provides no legal protection for geographically concentrated minority groups—be they defined in terms of race and/or political sentiment—against the political preferences of narrow majorities (or even large minorities) within the population whose representatives form a majority in the Commons and Lords.

The Article V process in the USA ensures that certain fundamental moral and political principles are *entrenched* within the American constitution. They are protected against the wishes of small and transient majorities which might temporarily control either the national or state governments.[18] The entrenchment is 'procedural' rather than 'substantive'. The values are not fixed forever. Rather they are guaranteed a *relative degree of permanence* compared to non-fundamental laws because they can be repealed or amended only by Article V's 'super-majoritarian' law-making process.

It is not only the issue of federalism that is protected in this way in the USA. All the provisions of the American constitution are 'fundamental law' in this sense. These include certain individual civil liberties with which neither the national or state governments can interfere, such as freedom of speech, protection from unreasonable searches, and a prohibition on 'cruel and unusual punishments', as well as such matters as the structure of Congress and the procedures it must follow to enact legislation, and the allocation of powers between Congress and the President. In Britain in contrast, the scope of civil liberties, the structure of Parliament and the law-making processes it employs were—like every moral and political value—susceptible to legal alteration by the simple majority plus royal assent formula.

The notion of 'entrenched' political rights, secured against repeal by a narrow legislative majority, is not (and was not in 1900) a constitutional characteristic unique to countries organised along federal lines. Southern Africa itself offered two illustrations of this point. The constitution of the Orange Free State clearly drew a distinction between entrenched and ordinary political values, while the Republic's *Grondwet* had apparently recognised that distinction in theory if not in practice.[19] Neither country was a federal state.

In the early 1900s, a small bloc of white southern African political opinion favoured a federal model for the South African constitution.[20] That bloc was however composed predominantly of Natalians. Natal's polity possessed the twin characteristics of being both resolutely 'British' and resolutely racist. Its white citizens feared that a unitary South African state would threaten them from two directions, either by exposing their 'Britishness' to the dominance of a Hertzogian Afrikaaner nationalism, or by forcing them to adopt the Cape's more liberal race policies. The Natal viewpoint commanded no sympathy in Britain. The Liberal government had been no less appalled than Merriman and

[18] The seminal analysis is offered by James Madison in *The Federalist Papers No. 10*.

[19] See pp. 42–52 above.

[20] Dold and Joubert, n. 10 above, pp. 41–42; T. Davenport, *South Africa: a Modern History*, 2nd edn. (Cambridge: CUP, 1978), pp. 163–165.

Smuts by the Natal government's Zulu wars in 1906–1908. Campbell-Bannerman had observed that: "These Natal people are tiresome to the last degree. I hope federation[21] will soon squelch them".[22]

A federal solution was also favoured by a few Cape liberals, W.P. Schreiner, J.H. Hofmeyr and F.S. Malan being the foremost among them, who feared that a unitary state might grant too much legislative power to the more resolutely racist whites in the northern provinces.[23] Abdurahman and the APO campaigned for a federal solution for precisely the same reason.[24]

Jameson was initially a further (perhaps unexpected) adherent to the federal cause. A federal system reserving substantial powers to each colony was essential so that the Cape could "hold to our native policy until the neighbouring colonies are sufficiently educated to agree to allow equal facilities for blacks and whites to rise in the scale of humanity".[25] Such an assertion might appear as an example of breathtaking hypocrisy given that Jameson was the Cape Prime Minister who had promoted the Cape School Board Act 1905.[26] That Act seemed to deny schooling to many non-whites, thereby depriving them of a 'facility' which was surely of crucial significance to their ability to 'rise in the scale of humanity'.

Merriman, however, favoured a unitary model.[27] Smuts, who had initially flirted with the idea of creating a federal nation, had come to share this view by 1907. Merriman's motives were a mix of the pragmatic and the ideological. True to his (L)liberal beliefs, Merriman harboured a Gladstonian fondness for curbing public expenditure by minimising the size of public bureaucracies. A federal system would require South Africa to have five fully fledged governmental structures, with fiscal consequences that Merriman regarded as wantonly excessive. Merriman also appreciated that creating a federal system would necessitate granting the courts the power to review the constitutionality of national legislation. This was a step he was loathe to take. Smuts was equally adamant in his opposition to federalism. He believed that a federal constitution would perpetuate the Anglo/Afrikaner/boer divisions between white South Africans, thereby storing up (as it had in the USA) tensions which might one day lead to civil war. A supreme national government—rather than a supreme 'people'—was the only way to avoid this potential calamity.[28]

By the time the Convention met, this argument had to all intents and purposes been won. So dominant were Smuts and Merriman on the southern African

[21] Federation into a unitary, not federal, state.

[22] Quoted in Hyam (1980), n. 4 above, p. 374.

[23] Hancock (1962), n. 9 above, pp. 252–255; Davenport (1978), n. 20 above, p. 164.

[24] G. Lewis, *Between the Wire and the Wall* (Cape Town: David Phillip, 1987), pp. 41–42.

[25] Quoted in H. Simons and R. Simons, *Class and Colour in South Africa 1850–1950* (Harmondsworth: Penguin, 1969), pp. 119–120.

[26] See pp. 93–94 above.

[27] Dugard, *Human Rights and the South African Legal Order* (Princeton: Princeton University Press, 1978), pp. 25–26.

[28] Thompson (1960), n. 8 above, pp. 102–107; Hancock (1962), n. 9 above, pp. 253–254.

political stage, that it was virtually unthinkable that any proposal enjoying their joint support would not be approved by the Convention. Jameson, potentially the most powerful of the federalists, was quickly won over to this point of view. If South Africa was to come into being, it would do so as a unitary state. The task before the Convention was thus to fashion a constitutional settlement which would attract the approval not just of electors in the four colonies, but also of Asquith's government and the British Parliament.

The delegates met and conducted their negotiations in what was (both to them and outside observers) a remarkably open-minded and co-operative spirit. Even Jameson and Steyn, who ostensibly stood on the twin extremes of the whites' political spectrum, found each other to be congenial company, a circumstance greatly aided by their shared love of bridge. But if the Convention was to function as an orchestra which ultimately played in harmony, it was Merriman and Smuts who proved to be its conductors.

The preamble to the legislation eventually enacted by the British Parliament as the South Africa Act 1909 described the measure as "An Act to constitute the Union of South Africa". The preamble continued by noting that unification of the four colonies under the Crown was necessary to further the welfare and progress of South Africa. It then made explicit reference to the fact that the Act was intended to give legal effect to the political "terms and conditions which [the four colonies] have agreed by resolution of their respective Parliaments and to define the executive, legislative and and judicial powers to be exercised in the government of the Union". The remainder of the Act was a curious melange of matters both of broad principle and minute detail.

The legislature and executive

Section 19 of the South Africa Act created a tri-cameral parliament for the new country, comprising a house of assembly, a senate and the King. The South African parliament was clearly to be—like all colonial law-making assemblies—a legislature possessing only limited legal competence. The most obvious restriction on its power was that it could not pass laws 'repugnant' to any British statutory provisions which had effect within South Africa's borders. This limitation was not contained in the South Africa Act itself, but appeared in the Colonial Laws Validity Act 1865, and applied with equal force to all British colonies.[29]

The 1909 Act also gave the King the power—presumably acting on the advice of the British government—to repeal within one year any statute enacted by the South African parliament.[30] In general however, the South African parliament

[29] See pp. 18–19 above.

[30] For constitutional lawyers, the provision has echoes of the notorious English case of *Godden v Hales* (1686) 11 ST. Tr. 1165. In *Godden*, the courts upheld James II's claim that he had a divine right to disallow or disregard legislation whenever he thought it necessary. The judgment was a precipitate cause of the English revolution in 1688; see Loveland, n. 2 above, pp. 103–108.

was empowered to enact laws in the same way as its British master. Section 59 of the Act provided that "Parliament shall have full power to make laws for the peace, order and good government of the Union". It had by then been established that the 'peace, order and good government' formula did not place *substantive* limits on a colonial legislature's power which a court (be it British or colonial) could enforce. The term was accepted as indicating that it was a matter solely for the colonial legislators themselves to decide what policies best served their countries' interests.[31]

In most respects, the South African parliament's law-making *process* would mirror that of the United Kingdom legislature. So sections 50 and 31 respectively provided that a majority of one vote in favour of a Bill in the house and the senate would be sufficient to make it eligible to receive the Royal Assent, which would in most circumstances be given by an official called the Governor-General (appointed by the British government) qua representative of the King. Legislation on a small number of matters had however to be 'reserved' for the assent of the King in person, a provision which nominally at least afforded the British Cabinet the power to veto South African bills of which it disapproved.

The structure of the South African Parliament

The original structure of the South African legislature presented a curious picture. On the surface, it seemed to make several concessions to the federalist ethos which had been rejected by the Convention.[32] Yet on closer examination, the design of the South African parliament seemingly offered substantial opportunities for a narrow majority of the white population to ensure that, in the longer term, their political preferences gained the force of law throughout the country.

The house of assembly was to contain 121 members. The Act rigidly divided this total among the four provinces; fifty-one were to come from the Cape, thirty-six from the Transvaal, and seventeen from both the Orange Free State and Natal. The provinces were sub-divided into individual constituencies, each returning one representative to the house. The boundaries of each constituency were to be drawn up by a commission headed by a Supreme Court judge.[33] The Act required only an approximate equality of voters between constituencies. A national 'quota' would be fixed by dividing the electorate by the number of constituencies. But the quota would be only a starting point in defining the population size of each constituency. Variations of fifteen per cent above or below the quota would be permissible: constituencies could thus vary in size by as much as

[31] *Hodge v The Queen* (1883) LR 9 AC 117; *Riel v R* (1885) LR 10 AC 695.

[32] One such concession concerned the location of the various branches of the national government. The legislature would be in Cape Town, the seat of the executive in Pretoria, and the Appellate Division of the Supreme Court in Bloemfontein. Natal was given financial compensation in exchange for not having any of the branches based within its borders: Hancock (1962), n. 9 above, p. 269.

[33] The structure of the court system is outlined below.

thirty per cent. In effect, South Africa's constituency apportionment arrangements would mirror those then in place in the Transvaal. In comparison with the numerical discrepancies that then existed in the Cape and Natal electoral systems, this solution represented a shift towards the principle of equally weighted votes. There was nevertheless little doubt that the imbalances which the Act retained would be used to ensure that rural constituencies would be substantially smaller than urban ones.[34]

South Africa's constitution also rejected strict numerical equality when apportioning shares of house seats *between the provinces*. That division bore little relationship to the respective adult populations of each province. The formula that the constitution adopted was premised only on a province's white male population: all women and all non-white adult males were excluded from the calculations. But even on this basis, the Cape would be grossly under-represented in the House. As Table 2.1 indicates, in the predominantly anglophile Cape the 'electoral quota' was almost 3,300 voters. But the quota was some ten per cent lower in the Transvaal; twenty-five per cent lower in the Orange Free State; and almost forty per cent lower in Natal.

Table 2.1 Representation in the House of Assembly*

Province	*Seats*	*Voters*	*Voters per seat*
Cape	51	167,546	3,285
Natal	17	34,784	2,046
Orange Free State	17	41,104	2,417
Transvaal	36	106,493	2,958

*Source: South Africa Act 1909.

It would be oversimplistic to assume that the white population of each province would vote as homogenous blocs divided along ethnic lines in elections. The 1907 elections in the Transvaal had readily demonstrated the falsity of such suggestions. Political beliefs were not rigidly determined by ethno-cultural origins. It is also evident that psephologists could readily have identified many distinct sub-groups within the white populations: in matters of detail one would not expect to find perfect congruence between the political programmes of Jameson's Cape Progressives and Merriman's and Schreiner's respective limbs of Cape Afrikanerdom; nor between the more overtly boer-led Afrikanerdom of Smuts and Steyn; nor between the various brands of racist

[34] There had been little pressure within the Convention for the country to adopt perfectly equal-sized constituencies. The strongest advocate of the idea was Sir Percy Fitzpatrick, the leader of the Chamber of Mines faction of the Transvaal delegates. His motivation had perhaps more to do with his party's prospects of winning power in the Transvaal than with an abstract empathy with a more recognisably 'modern' version of democracy.

extremism favoured by white Natalians and Hertzog's supporters in the Free State. One would also expect the two partners within each of those three pairings to disagree with each other on some matters of principle. When one adds the additional variables of economic class and labour market position to those political divisions it is evident that predicting white voting behaviour could not be an exact science.

In 1909, there were marked discrepancies in the populations of constituencies for the British House of Commons. It is perhaps therefore unsurprising that the ostensibly modest numerical inequality envisaged in South African constituencies by the 1909 Act prompted little comment in the British Parliament. Nevertheless, South Africa's constituency structure did appear to be skewed in favour of the more reactionary strands of boer and Afrikaner opinion and the extreme racism of the whites of Natal. In 1906, Smuts had succeeded in persuading the Liberal government to abandon the Lyttleton criteria for electoral apportionment in the Transvaal of requiring strict numerical equality between constituencies. In 1909, Smuts and his colleagues succeeded in persuading the Liberal government to endorse electoral gerrymandering within South Africa as a whole. Whether that favouritism would translate into effective dominance of the house of assembly by one faction of the white population remained to be seen.

The second chamber of South Africa's parliament was even more clearly structured to favour reactionary rather than liberal political sentiments. The senate was to contain forty members. Each province would return eight representatives, elected by members of the four 'provincial councils' (see further below) using the the single transferable vote system. An additional eight members were to be appointed by the 'Governor-General in Council'—a body described below.[35] Four of these senators were to be appointed "on the ground mainly of their thorough acquaintance, by reason of their official experience or otherwise, with the reasonable wants and wishes of the coloured races in South Africa". Section 24 provided that this selection system could not be altered for ten years. Thereafter parliament could evidently alter the powers or composition of the senate in any way it thought appropriate. Any such legislation could be passed either with the support of the senate itself or, in the event of senate opposition, through the joint sitting mechanism specified in section 63.

Section 63 potentially tilted the balance of political power within South Africa away from the smaller provinces. Unlike its counterpart within the US Congress (and at that time the House of Lords within the United Kingdom's Parliament), the South African senate could not permanently veto the passage of bills passed by the house. Section 63 provided that in the event of a stalemate between the two houses, the Governor-General could summon a joint sitting of the house and senate, at which the obstructed bill could be passed by a simple majority of the members present. The greater numbers of members in the house (121 com-

[35] See s. 24 and s. 134.

pared to forty in the senate) made it likely that a majority party there could also muster a majority in a joint sitting. Should it not be able to do so, the Constitution made no direct provision for resolving the ensuing deadlock. As will be suggested below, however, there were indirect means through which, in the longer term, the legislature might bypass or remove impediments imposed by the senate.

A fused legislature and executive

Delegates to the Convention unanimously supported the principle that South Africa should follow the British system of placing *de jure* control of the executive government in the hands of the King, while *de facto* requiring the King to exercise that control on the advice of Ministers drawn from the ranks of the legislature.[36] This convention of the British constitution was firmly, if not quite unshakeably established by 1909: both Edward VII and George V were (at least initially) unwilling to act on Asquith's advice during the Liberal government's disputes with the House of Lords over the People's Budget and the Parliament Bill 1910.[37] The principle seemed to have equal (if not legal force) in respect of the relationships between the colonial legislatures and the Governors-General in Canada, Australia and New Zealand.

The Convention did not propose that either the office of Prime Minister or the notion of a 'Cabinet' be given formal recognition in the constitution. As a matter of strict legality, the Governor-General acting as the King's representative in South Africa enjoyed an unfettered discretion (per section 12) to appoint whomsoever he wished to serve on a body called the 'Executive Council'. The Act also created a legal entity styled 'the Governor-General in Council', which referred to the Governor-General acting on the advice of the Executive Council. There was no requirement that members of the Executive Council be government Ministers. The Governor-General was empowered to create up to ten government ministries, and might appoint whichever members of parliament he wished to head them. Such Ministers would automatically become members of the Executive Council.

The provisions of the Act painted a rather misleading picture of the political reality envisaged by the Convention and approved by the British Parliament. It was anticipated that, in the normal run of events, the executive government would in effect be headed by a Prime Minister, who would be the leader of whichever political party could command majority support in the house of assembly. The presumption was that the Governor-General would endorse whichever choices the Prime Minister would make concerning the occupants of

[36] Thompson (1960), n. 8 above, pp. 199–201. Indeed, the Convention wished to make this 'fusion' rather than 'separation' of the legislative and executive branches even more explicit in South Africa than in Britain: unlike members of the British government, South African Ministers would have to be members of the legislature.

[37] See Loveland (1996), n. 2 above, ch. 6.

Ministerial office, and that the Executive Council would operate as the South African equivalent of the British Cabinet.

It would be only on matters with foreign policy implications that the Governor-General would operate as an 'independent' political actor, taking his instructions from the British rather than South African cabinet. It would thus also be fair to assume that in most instances where the Act *de jure* allocated authority to the Governor-General in person, power was effectively being granted to the Cabinet.[38] The distinction was nevertheless not without legal significance, if only because one would expect the Cabinet to have to comply with the *form* of decision the constitution required. An action taken by the Prime Minister alone or by the Cabinet without reference to the Governor-General would not be an action of the Governor-General-in-Council, and would thus presumably be *ultra vires* if the constitution specified it had to be taken by the latter procedure. Some potentially significant issues were reserved for decisions taken in this way. The most important was perhaps laid out in section 147 of the South Africa Act, and encompassed "the control and administration of native affairs and of matters specially or differentially affecting Asiatics throughout the Union".

Notwithstanding these considerations of legal form, the Convention proposed, and the British Parliament approved, a constitutional structure for South Africa in which as a matter of political substance most governmental powers would be wielded by whichever political party could command a bare majority of seats in the house. The method by which the house's members were to be selected was thus of paramount importance.

The electoral system

It was suggested above that the apportionment of constituencies skewed the balance of power in the house in favour both of the three smaller colonies and, within all four colonies, in favour of rural rather than urban voters. The balance of power in the senate was even more favourable to the northern colonies. But these matters formed only part—and perhaps the least contentious part—of South Africa's proposed electoral system. The 1909 Act also addressed two further electoral questions: who would be permitted to vote in parliamentary elections; and who would be permitted to take up a parliamentary seat.

[38] This mismatch between appearance and reality was heightened by the Act's provisions concerning salaries. The Governor-General received the then phenomenal sum of £10,000 per year (s. 10). Members of the House and Senate received £400 per year (s. 56). In real terms, the Governor-General's salary had declined enormously. The same sum was paid to the Governor of the Cape Colony in 1814; L. Thompson, *A History of South Africa* (New Haven: Yale University Press, 1995), p. 54.

The representatives

Perhaps the clearest textual indications in the Act that South Africa had adopted an expressly racist constitution were offered by section 26(d) and section 44(c). These provided that members of the Senate or the House of Assembly respectively were to be British subjects of 'European descent'. This conformed with the legal position with respect to legislative membership in the Orange Free State and the Transvaal prior to the Union. The Cape, as with its approach to the franchise, did not invoke racial identity as a qualifying characteristic of legislative membership. The Cape's stance on this question was more of symbolic than practical significance. Although some Cape Coloured citizens had come to occupy prominent positions in the Cape's social and politicial life,[39] no non-white had ever been elected to serve in the Cape parliament.[40] Neither, of course, had the nominally colour-blind Natal legislature ever contained a non-white member.

The *Cape Times* had condemned the white-only rule as an unjustifiable error.[41] In Britian, the proviso was widely regarded as an error, but not an error without justification. In the Commons second reading debate on the South Africa bill, Colonel Seely, Asquith's Under-Secretary for the Colonies, had exhibited some distaste for this provision: "I may say at once, speaking for the Government that we regret that these words are in the Bill, but we know that they form part of an essential compromise".[42] The Liberal government's position was simply stated. Its view was that if the house rejected this clause, the two boer-dominated provinces and Natal would withdraw their consent to the Union. At the least, such a withdrawal would embroil the British government in the unwelcome and expensive task of policing a geographically remote and politically fractious set of colonies. At the worst, it could trigger a further boer war. Seely also suggested that the Commons had a responsibility to the colonies' non-white inhabitants to approve the provision: "I can only assure the House, speaking with all seriousness, that we know that if these words were struck out, the Union would be smashed, with results most evil for the native whom we wish to protect".[43]

This rationale echoed the argument made by Lord Crewe, Asquith's Secretary of State for the Colonies, in the House of Lords:

[39] As noted in Chapter 3, Abdurahman had been elected to the Cape Municipal Council in 1904; see p. 95 above.

[40] Davenport, n. 20 above, notes that there had been only one occasion on which a non-white had even seemed likely to be elected. There had by this time been two Asiatic members of the British House of Commons. Dhadabai Naoriji was Liberal member for Finsbury Central between 1892 and 1895. Sir Mancherjee Bhownaggree was the Conservative member for Bethnal Green North East between 1895 and 1906.

[41] 12 February 1909; cited in G. Shaw, *Some Beginnings* (London: OUP, 1975), p. 150.

[42] House of Commons Debates, 16 August 1909, c.938.

[43] *Ibid.* 16 August 1909, c.959.

> "I say frankly that there does seem to me to be a strong case against the insertion of this provision in this Act, or in any Act . . . There are men not of European descent of high standing, high character and high ability. They regard this provision as a slight, and we regret that any loyal subjects of the King should consider themselves slighted".[44]

Crewe explained however that the government's 'regrets' could not be translated into action:

> "As a government we cannot take . . . the responsibility for the possible wrecking of this Union measure altogether by a provision of this kind; and I am assured that such would be the result of any attempt to insert such a provision".[45]

Whether the Liberal government's view on this point was well-founded can be at best a matter of conjecture. We will return to this point below. At this juncture, one might simply note that the thesis offered Asquith's Cabinet an extremely convenient justification for acceding to the Convention's more illiberal wishes. Such wishes might not be 'good' in any absolute sense, but they were the least bad of the various evils on offer. As such, the British Parliament ought to grant them.

A handful of Liberal and Labour MPs challenged both the accuracy and *bona fides* of the Cabinet's appeasement of white South African racism. The government's assent to the clause excluding non-whites from the legislature attracted particularly bitter opposition during the second reading debate. Within Liberal ranks, the most forceful criticism came from Sir Charles Dilke.[46] Dilke described the provision as "a slap in the face for men who are well educated and quite as competent to be members of Parliament as we are ourselves".[47]

As well as opposing the substantive (im)morality of sections 26(d) and 44(c), Dilke expressed doubts about their technical adequacy. The Act itself did not define 'European descent'. Was this to be a matter of culture, of ability, of genetics, of simple appearance, or a mix of any or all of these factors? Dilke presumed, referring to the *Willets* and *Swarts* cases,[48] that sections 26(d) and 44(c) would be construed by the South African courts in the most restrictive and arbitrary fashion.[49]

[44] House of Lords Debates, 27 July 1909, c.857.

[45] *Ibid.*

[46] Dilke, along with Chamberlain, had been the two radical *enfants terribles* of Gladstone's governments in the 1880s and the most inveterate critics of Disraelis's Zulu wars; see p. 24 above. Dilke's Ministerial career was ended by a sex scandal in the mid–1880s. Thereafter he remained in the Commons as a resolutely radical member of the Liberal party who took a particular interest in exposing the more egregiously racist activities of Britain's colonial governments. The most helpful insight into his character and career is offered in R. Jenkins, *Sir Charles Dilke* (London: Collins, 1958).

[47] House of Commons Debates, 16 August 1909, c.979.

[48] See pp. 72–73 above.

[49] The provision was not however without support in the Commons. While Seely expressed reluctant acquiescence, Lyttelton was one of its more enthusiastic advocates. He regretted that an exception had not been made for the 'highly educated' minorities within the non-white population. He was however willing to stifle his regret, taking refuge in the general proposition that native

The Convention's advocacy of a colour bar within Parliament had emerged during protracted negotiations concerning the qualifications needed for *voters* in House elections. The two questions were intimately linked. In combination they formed the most contentious element of the Convention's work.

The franchise

Modern political opinion seemingly considers a near universal adult franchise as an axiomatic component of any democratic system of representative government. But this is a political presumption of relatively recent vintage. At the time the South Africa Act was passed, substantially fewer than half of Britain's adult citizens were entitled to vote in elections for members of the Commons. The main exclusory factor in Britain was gender—women were not presumed to be competent citizens for the purposes of choosing the country's law-makers. British electoral law also retained a complex system of property qualifications which excluded the lower strata of the male working class from the electoral register, and granted additional votes to owners of commercial property and graduates of certain universities.[50]

The four southern African colonies had also excluded women from the electoral process through which they chose members of their legislatures. The Orange Free State and the Transvaal applied a further restriction—voters had to be white. No further qualification was necessary. As we have seen, the Cape had in contrast operated a nominally 'colour blind' franchise immediately prior to union. Cape legislation of 1887, 1892 and 1899 granted the right to any adult British male who was first able to write his name and occupation, and secondly was either employed in a job paying more than £50 per year or occupied (as owner or tenant) land or buildings (whether residential or commercial) valued at more than £75.[51]

This formal equality clearly permitted some indirect racial discrimination.[52] Patterns of land ownership and the structure of the labour market in the Cape meant in practice that whites, Indians, Coloureds and natives enjoyed differential access to the franchise. Crudely stated, whites occupied a disproportionately large percentage of the Cape's land, and filled a disproportionately large percentage of the Cape economy's better paid jobs in comparison with other racial groups. The native population fared poorly on both comparators, in relation not just to whites but also the Coloureds and Indians. Countering such indirect

blacks had too childlike a mentality to merit equal access with whites to political institutions; House of Commons Debates, 16 August 1909, c.969–970.

[50] Women did not gain equality with men until the late 1920s, and it was not until 1948 that British electoral law accpted that the franchise should be granted on the principle of 'one adult one vote'.

[51] Other than land occupied under the terms of the Glen Grey Act 1894; see pp. 36–37 above.

[52] Simons and Simons, n. 25 above, pp. 49–50.

discrimination has become a central concern of modern anti-racism laws in many democratic countries, but it was an issue of little significance in the Cape in the early 1900s.

Formal equality was not worthless however. In the early 1900s, some 14,388 Coloured citizens were registered to vote, as were 6,633 native blacks. The non-white vote was a crucial factor in a number of Cape constituencies, with the result that candidates for election and members of the Cape House were constrained to court rather than ignore non-white political opinion.

Natal also retained in theory a franchise that was open to adult males of any race. In effect, its electoral system was on a par with those in the boer colonies. By 1909, Natal had some 20,000 registered voters. Of these, 150 were Asian, fifty coloured, and just six native blacks. The other 19,800 were white.[53]

Merriman and Smuts had engaged in a protracted correspondence in the aftermath of the war debating the merits of the Cape system.[54] Smuts' vision of a united South Africa saw no place for a non-white franchise. The extent to which Smuts perceived this position to be intrinsically correct, as opposed to being merely a concession he thought it essential to make if the Free State, Natal and many members of Het Volk were to support unification is unclear. One could at best suggest that Smuts was in the abstract indifferent to the idea of eventually creating a colour-blind polity. At worst, one might assume he saw non-whites simply as a useful tool with which to manipulate the various factions within the white population.[55]

The Asquith government had made it plain to Sir J.H. De Villiers shortly before the Convention began that its approval of the Convention's proposals was dependent upon adequate protection being given to the voting rights of non-whites who were already enfranchised in the Cape. As long as that proviso was respected, the Convention could be sure that its solution to the problem would enjoy the British government's support.

At the outset of the Convention debate, F.S. Malan, Sauer and Stanford (who had replaced Schreiner as a delegate) urged the adoption of a colour-blind franchise throughout South Africa. They were immediately followed by delegates from Natal and the Free State who spoke equally forcefully in favour of a

[53] Dugard (1978), n. 27 above, p. 18. Hancock aptly characterises the Natal system as offering non-whites "the pretence, but not the practice, of a colour-blind franchise law": (1962), n. 9 above, 219.

[54] Hancock, n. 9 above, pp. 214–225.

[55] Hancock captures this ambivalence in tracing Smuts' correspondence at this time with friends of differing political persuasions. An oft-quoted comment comes from a letter to J.A. Hobson, a British liberal who favoured extension of the Cape principle to the whole of South Africa: "My impression is that the only sound policy at this stage is to avoid any attempt at a comprehensive solution of the various questions surrounding the political status and rights of the native . . . The political status of the natives is no doubt a very important matter, but vastly more important to me is the Union of South Africa": (1962), n. 9 above, pp. 255–256. The duplicity which Smuts had shown as a politician in the Transvaal (see pp. 87–89 above) would presumably travel with him into the politics of the unified South Africa.

whites-only electoral system.[56] The key to the compromise which Smuts eventually succeeded in brokering was that advocates of these varying extreme positions should not find their own preferences at the mercy of other factions. Section 37 of the constitution specified that the franchise in South Africa would initially be allocated in each province according to the laws that had existed in each colony prior to the union. The Act made no attempt to force the Cape to adopt the colour bar applied in the Free State and the Transvaal, nor conversely to compel the boer colonies to adopt the Cape's colour-blind approach. Natal's *de jure* colour blind but *de facto* discriminatory franchise was also left in place. Neither was any serious effort made to extend the right to vote to women, nor to abolish the property qualifications used in the Cape.

In the Commons, opinion on the franchise question mirrored the debate on the European descent clauses in sections 26 and 44. Lyttelton again offered enthusiastic approval for the compromise the Convention had reached:

> "it is better to face the real facts and to acknowledge that the black races are not the equals of the white than to give them a franchise which probably . . . would lead to little if any good to them and would, I am certain, lead to some demoralisation among the whites".[57]

Dilke, along with a handful of his radical Liberal colleagues and the then quantatively insignificant Labour party members, were isolated voices within the Commons in their opposition to this provision.

The judiciary

The structure of South Africa's 'Supreme Court' proposed by the Convention was straightforward. The term 'Supreme Court' is somewhat misleading: it referred not to a single court sitting at the top of the legal hierarchy as in the USA, but rather to the higher echelons of the national court system as a whole. Each province was to have its own division of the Supreme Court, as were the localities of the Eastern Cape, Griqualand and Witwatersrand. Each division was to have a Chief Justice (a title subsequently altered to Judge President) and an unspecified number of ordinary judges.

The summit of the domestic legal system was to be the Appellate Division of the Supreme Court. The Appellate division would consist of five members: a Chief Justice, two 'ordinary' judges of appeal who were permanently attached to the Appellate Division, and two 'additional judges' of appeal—drawn from

[56] They were enthusiastically supported in this view by the *Rand Daily Mail*. The *Mail* invoked two arguments for its position. The first was that acceptance of the Cape's admittedly limited non-white elctorate would serve as the thin end of a wedge which would soon lead to much wider non-white enfranchisement. The second, flowing from the first, was that non-white voters would not support a labour policy which gave non-meritocratic privileges to whites: J. Mervis, *Fourth Estate* (Johannesburg: Jonathan Ball, 1989), pp. 58–60.

[57] House of Commons Debates, 16 August 1909, c.967.

the provincial or local divisions—who sat in the Appellate Division in a part-time capacity.

Under the terms of section 99, all the existing judges of the colonial High Courts were to become members of the Supreme Court of South Africa in their respective provincial divisions. Section 100 granted the power to appoint new judges to the Governor-General in Council. The Act did not place any limit on the number of judges who could be appointed to the Supreme Court. The obvious implication of this omission was that the government could make as few or as many judicial appointments as it wished.[58] The position of Chief Justice was also to be in the gift of the government. The constitution did not impose any qualification criteria on the people appointed to judicial office. It did however provide that once judges had been appointed they could be removed from office only by the Governor-General in Council on the recommendation of the house and senate, such recommendation being permissible only in respect of a judge's 'incapacity' or 'misbehaviour'.[59]

Like Canada, Australia and New Zealand, South Africa would retain the House of Lords (acting under the soubriquet of the Privy Council) as its final court of appeal.[60] The South African constitution did not make any automatic provision for an appeal from the Appellate Division to the Privy Council, but permitted the Privy Council to hear any such appeal if it so wished. Section 106 also permitted parliament to abolish the Privy Council's power to hear such appeals, although any such legislation would have to be assented to by the King in person rather than by the Governor-General.

Section 98 of the constitution explicitly granted the provincial and local divisions jurisdiction to hear as a first instance court any cases in which the 'Government of the Union' was a party, or in which the validity of a provincial ordinance was in issue. It also expressly authorised an appeal to the Appellate Division in such litigation.[61] Section 110 required that a quorum of at least three Appellate judges sit in appeals from cases heard at first instance by one judge. A quorum of five (the full court) was required to hear appeals from judgments issued by a lower court containing two or more judges. Section 111 also provided that the judgment of the Appellate Division would have 'full force and effect' throughout the country.

Sections 107 and 108 gave the Chief Justice and other judges of the Supreme Court the power, subject to the approval of the Governor-General, to determine the courts' respective rules of procedure. The presumption seemed to be that the

[58] Although the combined effect of s. 96 and s. 102 of the Act seemed to require the government to maintain the strength of the Appellate Division at five members.

[59] See s. 101. The constitution did not define either 'misbehaviour' or 'incapacity'. Neither does the British statute on which the 1909 Act was based—the Act of Settlement 1701; see Loveland (1996), n. 2 above, ch. 3.

[60] A. Keith, n. 2 above, *The Constitutional Law of the British Dominions* (London: Macmillan & Co., 1933), pp. 265–276; D. Swinfen, *Imperial Appeal* (Manchester: Manchester University Press, 1987), pp. 101–102.

[61] See s. 103.

choice of which judge(s) would hear particular cases would be for the Chief Justice in the Appellate Division and for the various Judge Presidents in the provincial and local divisions.

There was no provision in the constitution which suggested that parliament was unable to alter any of the rules relating to the structure, composition, jurisdiction or indeed the very existence of the Supreme Court at any time, acting either through the simple majority plus Governor-General's assent, or via the section 63 joint sitting procedure.[62] As in the United Kingdom, the 'independence of the judiciary' did not seem to be a constitutional value which was safeguarded against the wishes of a narrow legislative majority. The principle's effective continued existence would be dependent upon the self-restraint of the government and parliament. One further question as to the courts' role, of potentially great importance but left unanswered by the text of the constitution, will be returned to below.

Provincial government

The Convention's decision to seek a unitary rather than federal state had significant implications for the geographical separation of powers within the new country. The Act redefined the four former colonies as 'provinces' of South Africa. Most provisions in respect of provincial government were contained in Part V of the Act (sections 68–94).

Sections 68–84 established a form of quasi-parliamentary government within the provinces. Each would have an elected council, which would in turn elect an 'Executive Committee' headed by a Chief Executive Officer ('Administrator') appointed by the Governor-General in Council. Section 85 then granted each council the power to enact 'ordinances' within its territory in respect of a short list of issues. These comprised the powers to levy taxes; to borrow money; to control primary and secondary education; to regulate agriculture; to establish hospitals; to undertake minor road and harbour works; to licence markets; and to make bye-laws to enforce measures taken in respect of these powers.

At first glance, section 85 seemed to grant the provinces a substantial degree of political power. However their capacity to use that power as they thought fit, irrespective of the wishes of the national government, was not underwritten by any legal guarantees. Section 86 provided that: "Any ordinance made by a provincial council shall have effect in and for the province as long and as far only as it is not repugnant to any Act of Parliament". The autonomy of the provinces, much like the independence of the judiciary, would be dependent upon the grace and favour of the South African parliament. A government

[62] Certain matters of detail were settled in legislation passed in 1912. The Act fixed the retirement age at seventy and also made generous provisions for judicial pensions. Judges who had sat for over ten years were to receive a pension of £1,100–1,300 per year. Those who had sat for a lesser period received £110–130 per year of service, with a £700 minimum being imposed.

commanding a simple majority in the house and senate could at any time reduce, amend or increase the powers of any or all of the provinces, alter the boundaries of any province, create new provinces, or indeed abolish all or any of the original four.[63]

The Natal delegates had come to the Convention hoping to ensure both that provincial governments were afforded substantial powers, and that those powers were effectively protected against central government intrusion. Merriman and Smuts had already decided that their opposition to a federal constitution for South Africa also embraced an unwillingness to grant provincial governments a significant degree of political independence. They carried the Free State delegates with them on this issue, leaving the Natalians an isolated rump. Smuts made various placatory noises about the provinces occupying a unique constitutional status, midway between that of local councils in Britain and states in the USA.[64] But even if one accepts that Smuts was sincere in that belief, the proposal that he and Merriman presented to the Convention placed the four provinces in just the same position *vis-à-vis* the South African legislature as was occupied by British local government *vis-à-vis* the British Parliament.[65]

It is therefore unsurprising that no objections were raised by the British government in respect of this aspect of the Convention's proposals. On one related question however, Asquith's Cabinet refused to accommodate white southern African sentiments.

The protectorates

The distinction between 'South Africa' as a legal phenomenon and South Africa as a distinct geographic region was forcefully illustrated by the United Kingdom Parliament's refusal to grant the new colonial parliament jurisdiction to enact laws affecting large tracts of the southern African land mass. Lord Crewe was determined to ensure that the 'High Commission territories' of Basutoland, Bechuanaland and Swaziland[66] should not be ceded to South Africa until such time as it was clear that South African whites could be trusted to govern them in a spirit of benevolent paternalism. Crewe's concern for the native blacks of the protectorates stands of course in marked contrast to the Liberal government's evident abandonment of blacks in the three northern South African provinces to the mercies of the South African parliament and the new provincial governments.

[63] Section 149 provided that parliament could only change provincial boundaries at the request of the provincial councils whose territory was affected. But since this provision could be repealed by the simple majority formula, it did not afford the provinces' geographical boundaries any meaningful protection against legislative alteration.

[64] Thompson (1960), n. 8 above, pp. 187–188, 248–260.

[65] Keith (1933), n. 60 above, pp. 360–370.

[66] See pp. 65–66 above.

Delegates at the Convention, especially the Natal representatives, had initially bridled at the symbolic insult which seemed to be implied by the British government's refusal to hand the protectorates over to South Africa directly. Their indignation was stifled by Crewe's evident intransigence: this was it seems an issue on which he might have been prepared to let the union project founder. Whether Asquith would have supported him on this question is a matter for speculation. The retention of the protectorates nevertheless provides some support for the argument that the Liberal government's concern for safeguarding native black southern Africans from white exploitation and oppression was genuine. That concern was however trumped in the four white colonies by the long established constitutional principle that the the British government should not interfere with domestic affairs in colonies enjoying responsible government. Since the protectorates had never had responsible government, that argument did not apply to them.[67]

Crewe seemed to doubt that South African whites could ever be trusted to govern the territories in an acceptable fashion. The 1909 Act made no provision for the transfer of *sovereignty* over the protectorates to South Africa. Rather it contained a power in section 151 under which the British government might (at some unspecified date) if it so wished transfer the power of *administering* the protectorates to an indigenous South African body. The details of the administrative arrangements were outlined in a lengthy appendix to the Act. In formal terms, the administering body would exist at one step removed from the South African government itself. After transfer, the territories would be administered by the Prime Minister acting on the advice of a small group of Commissioners, appointed by the Governor-General in Council. Legislation would be in the form of proclamations, issued by the Governor-General in Council on the Commissioners' advice. This legal form was something of a political fiction. As noted above, the Governor-General in Council was *de facto* the cabinet of the day; thus, in effect, the South African government would exercise substantial control over the administration of the territories. The Act also made it clear that the Prime Minister was not bound to follow the advice of the Commissioners if he did not wish to do so.

It was thus evident that the transfer of the territories would effectively bring their land and their peoples under South African control. What was equally evident however, to the chagrin of many leading southern African politicians, was that the British government was in no hurry to allow any transfer to occur.

The entrenched clauses

As noted above, the South African parliament was granted the power to pass legislation on most issues within its competence by the mechanism of a simple

[67] R. Hyam, 'British Imperial Policy and South Africa 1906–1910', in Warwick (ed.), n. 4 above; Davenport (1978), n. 20 above, pp. 168–169.

majority in the house and the senate plus the royal assent. There were however several issues in respect of which its powers were more tightly constrained. The Act safeguarded some aspects of the Constitution against the whims of a bare legislative majority through a form of *procedural entrenchment*, and others seemed to be afforded protection through forms of temporary and permanent *substantive entrenchment*.

Temporary substantive entrenchment: the composition of the senate and the house

As noted above, the selection method used to choose members of the senate was fixed for a ten-year period. Section 152 confirmed explicitly that the legislature could not alter this provision, irrespective of how many of its members wished to do so within that ten-year period. Thereafter, the South African parliament could alter the senate's composition in whatever way it thought appropriate. In theory, parliament would after that date be able to abolish the senate entirely if it wished to do so.

Section 152 also forbade the legislature from altering the terms of section 33 (which specified the allocation of house seats between the provinces) [68] or section 34 (which specified the electoral quota and the method to be used to increase the number of representatives in the House)[69] for at least ten years after the Act came into force. Once again, upon the expiry of that term, parliament could alter any of those provisions in any way it wished.

Procedural entrenchment: potential non-white voters in the Cape

Section 35(1) began by confirming that parliament could amend the country's franchise laws through the simple majority plus royal assent formula. That principle was subject to two qualifications. The first qualification involved a form of procedural rather than substantive entrenchment. Parliament could not disenfranchise:

> "any person in the province of the Cape of Good Hope who, under the laws existing in the colony of the Cape of Good Hope at the establishment of the Union, is or may become capable of being registered as a voter from being so registered in the province of the Cape of Good Hope by reason of his race or colour only, unless the Bill be passed by both Houses of Parliament sitting together, and at the third reading be agreed to by not less than two thirds of the total number of members of both Houses".[70]

Section 152 of the Act further provided that section 35(1) itself could not be amended unless the amending provision was passed by the 'two thirds majority

[68] See pp. 108–9 above.
[69] See pp. 108–10 above.
[70] i.e. two-thirds of all those members eligible to vote, not just two-thirds of those who participated in the division in question.

in joint session formula'. A 'super-majority' within the legislature would thus be required in order for parliament to alter the colour-blind basis of the Cape franchise, thereby protecting non-white cape residents against a parliament dominated by a narrow majority of members favouring a whites-only electoral system.

The entrenchment proposal had been subject to a vitriolic attack by the *Sunday Times*, the *Rand Daily Mail's* sister paper. The *Sunday Times* was by then selling some 35,000 copies per week, which made it a major force in Transvaal politics. An editorial on 14 March 1909 deplored what it regarded as the positive discrimination being made in favour of non-whites:

> "The Union Parliament may by a majority of one juggle with the white franchise as it pleases; to the extent even of restoring an unadulterated Krugerism; but the 'sacred rights' of the nigger are above the control of democracy".[71]

The Cape delegates, it suggested, were riven with "a grovelling and ignoble fear of the inferior races"; the grant of the vote to native blacks in particular was "subversive of all political morality".[72]

The *Cape Times*, in contrast, had considered it unfortunate that the Cape's own franchise had not been extended throughout the Union, but suggested that the Union would not have come into being if the Cape delegates had insisted on this point. It welcomed section 35 as "a pretty strong barricade to our way of thinking", and expressed the hope that its preferred 'liberal policy' on the franchise would in the fullness of time be embraced by MPs from the northern provinces.[73]

The political underpinnings and implications of section 35(1) are open to two interpretations. The first is that the Cape delegates at the Convention had struck a hard bargain in the face of the other provinces' vehement opposition to any deviation from the principle that only whites should be able to participate in the electoral process. By forcing the Convention to set such a high parliamentary threshhold for the dilution of the Cape's colour-blind franchise, the Cape

[71] Quoted in Mervis, n. 56 above, p. 63.

[72] *Ibid*. The *Rand Daily Mail* signalled its disapproval in less forthright terms. The author of *The Sunday Times* leader evidently did not regard himself as a 'racist'. Many whites in the Transvaal seemingly regarded 'racism' as a purely intra-white phenomenon; a boer was racist if he wished to deny equal rights to anglos; and *vice versa*. Both groups were united in their belief that non-whites were simply inferior to whites; to discriminate against them could thus not be racism. See the discussion of this point in Mervis, n. 56 above, ch. 4. Mervis notes that the *Sunday Times* was markedly non-discriminatory in being crudely offensive to all non-white groups, nothwithstanding its recognition of their vital role as low wage labour in the white economy. The first page of its first edition had included a twenty line poem which began:

> **"Ten Little Chinamen**
> Ten little Chinamen, working in a mine,
> One tasted dynamite, and then there were nine,
> Nine little Chinamen sat up rather late,
> One swallowed opium and then there were eight. . .".

The poem continued in similar vein until all ten Chinamen had been eliminated: *ibid*. pp. 43–44.

[73] Cited in Shaw, n. 41 above, pp. 150–151.

delegates might be seen as having successfully ensured that its long-term survival was guaranteed.

Merriman and the Cape delegates had entered the Convention with a rigid commitment to safeguarding the Cape's electoral laws.[74] Merriman initially proposed that those laws should be repealable only be a 'three-quarters majority of both houses in joint session formula'. He was vigorously opposed by Moor, leader of the Natal delegation, who wished the constitution specifically to exclude any non-whites from the franchise. Hertzog and Botha appeared willing to preserve the Cape's arrangements, as long as no question arose of requiring either the Transvaal or the Free State to accept similar laws. Lord Selborne made it known to the Convention that a compromise based on Merriman's original proposal would be acceptable to the British government. The two-thirds majority protection might thus be seen as an effective defence of the Cape's laws, and moreover as the best deal the Cape delegates could strike, given the positions adopted by the other delegates and the British government.

The second interpretation is that the protection offered by section 35(1) was illusory, and that the Cape delegates had been duped by Smuts and Botha into salving their consciences by accepting a worthless compromise. This analysis operated on two levels. The first critique suggested that, even if the composition of the two houses of parliament remained unchanged, the balance of political forces created by South Africa's initial electoral arrangements made it quite likely that the white faction which abhorred the Cape's multi-racial fanchise could gain a two-thirds majority in parliament. Since the house and senate combined had 161 members, 108 votes would be sufficient to overturn section 35(1). Since seventy house members and twenty-four senators came from the three northern provinces, and since the government nominated a further eight Senators, it would in principle require only eight or ten of the Cape's house representatives to support a whites-only franchise for a two-thirds majority to arise.[75] Such bald figures would of course tell only an incomplete story of the political dynamics which would jeopardise section 35(1). It was perhaps unlikely that political divisions within the house and senate would ever coalesce around this issue. It was also conceivable that some legislators from the northern provinces might not favour any alteration to the Cape's non-racial franchise, either because they considered it intrinsically meritorious or because they wished to respect the substance of the compromise that the Convention had reached. Merriman shared with the *Cape Times* the sanguine opinion that the passage of time would inexorably lead more and more white

[74] Information in this paragraph is drawn primarily from Thompson (1960), n. 8 above, pp. 21–223.

[75] This argument is perhaps reinforced by the fact that the Cape delegates eventually accepted a two-thirds rather than three-quarters majority, which suggests they were concerned more with matters of symbolic principle than of practical politics. In a legislature of 161 members, the first formula required 108 votes, the second 121. This would seem a rather significant concession to have made.

South Africans to acknowledge the basic political rectitude of the Cape's franchise laws, with a consequent extension of that principle to the nation as a whole. Britain's Liberal government eagerly adopted a similar view. Smuts was, it seems, happy to indulge Merriman's rose-tinted view of the Afrikaner psyche, and was more than willing to extend that indulgence to members of the British legislature. Dilke was to prove a somewhat isolated voice in the Commons in arguing that the Cape's non-white electoral laws would be unlikely to survive for many years within the constitutional settlement that the 1909 Act laid down.

The second critique, which seemed not to have been appreciated (but certainly was not acknowledged) either in South Africa or Britain when the Act was passed, rests on the fact that a bare parliamentary majority would have had the power to change the composition of the house and the senate after ten years. A governing party could thereby create its own parliamentary super-majority and so satisfy the constitutional requirements. For section 35(1) to have offered more effective, long-term procedural entrenchment of the Cape's colour-blind franchise, the Act would also have had to apply the 'two thirds majority in joint session' proviso to any legislation altering the composition of the house and/or the senate. However, in respect of non-whites who were already on the Cape electoral register when the South Africa Act came into force, the constitution did seem to offer irremoveable protection.

Permanent substantive entrenchment: existing non-white voters in the Cape

The South Africa Act identified only one political principle that was to be substantively entrenched 'permanently'. Section 35(2) of the constitution provided that: "No person who *at the time of passing of any such law* [i.e. a two-thirds majority law per section 35(1)] *is registered as a voter* in any province shall be removed from the [electoral] register by reason only of any disqualification based on race or colour" (emphasis added). This section appeared to prevent a racistly motivated parliament from disenfranchising any *existing* non-white Cape voters. That entitlement would be something they could take with them to their graves, since the South Africa Act did not contain any mechanism permitting repeal or amendment of section 35(2). The section was necessary to satisfy Selborne's aforementioned warning to Sir J.H. De Villiers that the Liberal government could not support an Act disenfranchising any existing voters. The guarantee appeared to be watertight, even if its breadth was initially very limited. Some 21,000 non-white adult men were registered on the Cape's electoral rolls in 1909. Whether that number would rise or fall in future years remained to be seen, depending in part on whether the Cape's income and property qualifications were reduced, and whether demographic and economic trends brought a growing number of sufficiently affluent native blacks into Cape society.

Procedural entrenchment: language equality

The second of the Act's procedurally entrenched values (by the same 'two-thirds majority in joint session formula' as section 35(1)) appeared in section 137:

> "Both the English and Dutch languages shall be official languages of the Union, and shall be treated on a footing of equality, and possess and enjoy equal freedom, rights and privileges; all records, journals, and proceedings of Parliament shall be kept in both languages, and all Bills, Acts, and notices of general public importance or interest issued by the Government of the Union shall be in both languages".

Section 137 was nominally no more permanent a legal fixture of the South African constitutional landscape than section 35(1). However, its political status seemed markedly more secure. The substance of section 137 comes much closer to the language policy that Hertzog had promoted in the Orange Free State than to Smuts' far more anglophile policy. Hertzog and Steyn had come to the Convention ready to scupper the plans for Union if they did not win the argument on the language question.[76] To their great surprise, they found the Cape delegates ready to accede to most of their concerns. The provision that became section 137 was adopted with little formal disagreement in the Convention,[77] and none at all in the British Parliament. Nor did there appear to be any realistic prospect that the South African legislature would at any point in the forseeable future muster a two-thirds majority for amending section 137. The division of political forces on the language question was far more evenly split than on the issue of the Cape franchise.

The role of the courts?

The Act itself was silent about how the entrenchment provisions were to be enforced. The provisions establishing the Supreme Court did not explicitly empower either the Provincial or Appellate Divisions to strike down an Act passed by the simple majority formula which infringed any of the entrenched provisions. Section 111 confirmed that Appellate Division judgments would have 'full force and effect' throughout South Africa. But no answer was offered to the logically anterior questions of whether the Supreme Court could issue judgments which invalidated legislation or whether, like the English House of Lords, its judgments could reach only to the interpretation of statutes and the development of the common law. That section 98 granted the Supreme Court jurisdiction over cases in which the 'Government of the Union' was a party

[76] Pirow, *James Barry Munik Herzog* (Cape Town: Howard Timmins, nd), pp. 51–52. Steyn had initially wanted the constitution to guarantee bi-lingualism in schools and in the government service at national and provincial level. His acceptance of s. 137 thus represented some compromise on his part; Hancock (1962), n. 9 above, pp. 260–261. The reservation of control of education to the provinces presumably also offered him some justification for assuming that the Free State could enforce bi-lingualism in its own schools.

[77] Thompson (1960), n. 8 above, pp. 192–198.

intensified rather than resolved this ambiguity. The notion of the 'government' could be construed narowly, encompassing only the executive branch. But it could plausibly also bear a wider meaning, embracing the country's entire government structure—a concept which would presumably include parliament and its component parts.

As noted in Chapter 2, politicians in the Transvaal during the *Brown v Leyds* controversy were fiercely opposed to the courts having a so-called 'testing power'. In contrast, Hertzog, then a judge on the Orange River Colony's Supreme Court and now a key player at the Convention, worked within a jurisprudential tradition which upheld the judiciary's power to invalidate unconstitutional legislation, and had sided with Kotze in his dispute with Kruger. Kotze himself had been active in 1908 in promoting the idea of a constitution placing strict, judicially enforceable limits on the country's legislature.[78] The delegates at the Convention had adopted differing views on the powers the Supreme Court would possess.[79] Merriman's antipathy to granting the courts the power to review legislation has already been noted.[80] Smuts, Sir J.H. De Villiers (surprisingly perhaps given his status as the Cape's Chief Justice), and the Transvaal delegates also assumed the 'testing power' was not being granted. This then begged the question of how the entrenched provisions were to be enforced. Smuts' view seemed to be that they were barely worth the paper they were written on. He observed in February 1909 that section 35(1) 'was not a powerful check, perhaps it was not a check at all'.[81] F.S. Malan took quite the opposite view: "If we have a Constitution which can only be altered in a special way, the 'testing right' of the Supreme Court is essential".[82]

The question did not appear greatly to exercise the minds of legislators in the British Parliament. In his speech in the second reading debate, Colonel Seely had observed that the creation of an Appellate Division with jurisdiction over the entire country would be a 'great advantage',[83] but his comments appeared to be directed to the desire to promote uniformity in the common law rather than to any presumed judicial power to quash legislation.[84]

The uncertainty thus created had obvious echoes of the situation existing in the USA in 1800. The Framers of the American Constitution were also divided

[78] Thopmson (1960), n. 8 above, pp. 100–101.

[79] Thompson (1960), n. 8 above, pp. 283–284.

[80] See p. 106 above.

[81] *Ibid.*, p. 283. It was comments such as these which led Dilke to doubt the *bona fides* of most Afrikaners; see p. 114 above. Smuts had of course already shown himself to be no respecter of constitutional norms which stood in the way of political expediency: first by taking office in the Transvaal when too young to do so; and secondly by accepting that office when Kruger had shown his own contempt for the rule of law by dismissing Kotze C.J. from the Transvaal bench in the aftermath of *Brown v Leyds*; see pp. 50–51 above.

[82] *Ibid.*

[83] House of Commons Debates, 16 August 1909, c.955.

[84] Sir J.H. De Villiers evidently felt that this was all that was intended; Dold and Joubert, n. 10 above, p. 32.

as to the desirability of empowering the US Supreme Court to invalidate federal and state legislation. The text of the Constitution arguably grants such a power implicitly, but it was the Supreme Court which initially answered the question in the affirmative in the 1803 case of *Marbury v Madison*.[85] The Court's judgment was controversial at the time,[86] but its legitimacy was never seriously challenged. The logic of the *Marbury* decision, delivered by Chief Justice John Marshall (and expressly adopted by Kotze C.J. in *Brown v Leyds*),[87] would seem as applicable to the newly created South African constitution as it was to that of the USA:

> "Certainly, all those who have framed written constitutions contemplate them as forming the fundamental and paramount law of the nation, and consequently the theory of every such government must be, that an act of the legislature, repugnant to the constitution is void . . . It is emphatically the province of the judicial department to say what the law is . . . If, then, the courts are to regard the constitution [as] superior to any ordinary act of the legislature, the constitution and not such ordinary act must govern the case to which they both apply".[88]

The 1909 Act placed *few* limits on the South African legislature's power to make laws in just the same way as the British Parliament, but it undoubtedly placed *some* limits on that capacity, be they substantive (per section 35(2)) or—by the device of requiring 'parliament' to operate in a distinct form to achieve particular objectives—procedural (sections 35(1), 137 and 152). The power of the South African parliament(s) would thus seem subject to the higher form of law articulated in the constitution by which the legislature itself was created. But a definitive answer to the question of whether the South African Supreme Court had the constitutional authority to enforce those provisions would however have to await one of two developments: either a clear acknowledgment by the legislature that it could not alter ostensibly entrenched values through the simple majority process; or a judgment of the court invalidating legislation which was introduced in such a fashion.

II. CONCLUSION

For the white representatives of the four colonial governments who came to London in 1909 to observe the Convention's proposals being enacted into law, the British government, press and public proved welcoming and enthusiastic

[85] (1803) 2 L Ed 60.

[86] See W. Van Alstyne 'A Critical Guide to *Marbury v Madison*' (1969) *Duke Law Journal* 1; B. Schwarz, *A History of the United States Supreme Court* (Oxford: OUP, 1995), ch. 1; R. McCloskey, *The American Supreme Court*, 2nd edn. (Chicago: University of Chicago Press, 1994), ch. 2.

[87] See pp. 45–47 above. Hertzog, it may be recalled, had approved of Kotze's reasoning in *Brown*.

[88] (1803) 2 L Ed 60 at 73. See also the argument made by Alexander Hamilton in the period immediately preceding the ratification of the Constitution in *The Federalist Papers No. 78*.

hosts. They were feted in most newspapers, warmly received by the government and the Conservative opposition, and entertained to dinner at Buckingham Palace. The Act with which they returned to South Africa was in virtually all respects identical to the proposals with which they had arrived.[89] They were not however the only emissaries sent to Britain by the southern African people. They were shadowed by a handful of the colonies' citizens who had a very different agenda.

W.P. Schreiner had sailed to England in the company of leading native black and Coloured politicians after the Convention hoping to persuade the Liberal government to amend the South Africa bill to remove its racially discriminatory provisions.[90] The substance of his argument seemed perfectly consistent with the ideology Merriman had long propounded and so recently abandoned. If the British Parliament enacted the Convention's proposals, it would have passed not an Act of Union "but rather an Act of separation between the minority and the majority of the people of South Africa": non-whites would be "barred from the opportunity to rise and evolve naturally, which is the right of every free man in a free country": what he sought was not a socialistic notion of equality of outcomes, but simply "equality of opportunity".[91] If a man could 'rise and evolve' to a 'civilised' level, no political or economic liberty should be denied him simply because of his race.

In Schreiner's view, the claim by the Convention delegates from the northern colonies that they would rather wreck the union than reconise even a limited degree of inter-racial political equality was simply a bluff—and one which the Liberal government might call at no risk to the Union project. His arguments, while courteously received by Lord Crewe, fell on deaf ears.[92] Smuts, Botha and Merriman did their utmost to discredit him in the eyes of the British government and the British press.[93] Within the House of Commons, Dilke was the only figure of substance willing to champion his cause. Among the press, only the *Manchester Guardian* accepted the justice of his claims.

Representatives of coloured and black southern Africans also journeyed to Britain in an attempt to exert pressure on Asquith's government. Abdurahman's efforts were to prove no more successful than those he made in 1906 when protesting against the proposed whites-only franchise which Smuts persuaded Campbell-Bannerman's government to insert in the Transvaal's new constitution.[94] The native black delegation was led by J.T. Jabavu.[95] During the course of the Convention, he had urged that blacks should not seek to involve themselves in its proceedings, but to trust instead in the innate justice of the 'liberal'

[89] Dold and Joubert, n. 10 above, p. 47.

[90] Simons and Simons, n. 25 above, pp. 113–115; G. Lewis, n. 24 above, pp. 52–54.

[91] Thompson (1960), n. 8 above, pp. 402–407. Quotations are drawn from a statement made by Schreiner in *The Times*, reproduced in Thompson (1960) at p. 402.

[92] Hyam (1980), n. 4 above, pp. 379–381.

[93] Simons and Simons, n. 25 above, pp. 114–115.

[94] Simons and Simons, n. 25 above, pp. 110–112; see also p. 84 above.

[95] See pp. 97–98 above.

Cape delegates to defend their interests. When Merriman and his colleagues betrayed that trust, Jabavu sought assistance in Britain. The Asquith government found him no more compelling an advocate than Schreiner or Abdurahman.

Keir Hardie, then leader of the British Labour Party, had vigorously opposed the Act during its parliamentary passage. The entire parliamentary Labour Party had voted in support of an amendment moved at second reading to strike out the electoral colour bar from the bill.[96] Hardie's own position on southern African issues had moved markedly in the previous ten years. During the war, he had adopted the apparently dissonant standpoint of being a champion both of the oppressed boers and the oppressed natives. Like the radical Liberals, he saw no contradiction in this stance. After having visited South Africa in 1908 however, Hardie found himself opposing the restoration of autonomy to the Transvaal and the Free State if it led (as it surely did) to boer oppression of the colonies' non-white peoples.[97] During the passage of the 1909 bill, Hardie consistently maintained that Smuts, Botha and Hertzog and their supporters could not be trusted to treat South Africa's non-white population in a humane fashion. His parting comment on the Act was cast in apocalyptic terms: "For the first time we are asked to write above the portals of the British Empire: 'Abandon hope all ye who enter here' ".[98]

Sir Charles Dilke, with whom Hardie had collaborated in opposing the colour bar,[99] had expressed similar sentiments in rather more prosaic language:

> "This is a Bill which ignores entirely, or puts to one side, or trusts to luck . . . the ultimate fate of 6¼ million people, who are to be governed by an absolute and permanent oligarchy of a million people such as has never been established by us before".[100]

The most piquant characterisation of the political settlement which created the new nation of South Africa came from a member of the Natal legislature, T. Kirkman. Kirkman had favoured a federal constitution, in which provincial autonomy was (as in the USA) a deeply entrenched fundamental value. He described the proposed Act as "An elastic constitution that is simply a farce . . . a constitution of easy virtue".[101] His concerns were directed at the constitution's geographical separation of powers. But the larger question that he raised was whether any component of the South Africa Act 1909 could sensibly be regarded as a fundamental principle of the new nation's constitutional morality. Asquith's government had perhaps succeeded in creating a white nation that would align itself firmly with British interests in any future war with Germany.

[96] Simons and Simons, n. 25 above, p. 115.

[97] W. Stewart *J. Keir Hardie* (London: ILP, 1921) pp. 257–258; K. Morgan, *Keir Hardie* (London: Macmillan, 1975), pp. 104–107.

[98] House of Commons Debates, 2R, c.994

[99] Hyam, n. 4 above, pp. 380–381.

[100] House of Commons Debates, 16 August 1909, c.974. Hyam characterises the Asquith Cabinet members as indulging themselves in "well-meaning self-delusion": (1980), n. 4 above, p. 378.

[101] Quoted in Thompson (1960), n. 8 above, p. 361.

The price of doing so was running the risk that it had placed control of that nation's internal affairs in the hands of a white faction that saw little need to govern the majority non-white population in accordance with even the most rudimentary standards of substantive justice.

5

From Autonomy to Independence

As suggested in Chapter 3, the foundations of a political and legal system resting on extensive racial segregation and discrimination were firmly laid even before South Africa became a unified country. It is similarly clear that the constitution which the new country adopted took no positive steps to redress that pre-existing situation. This chapter considers the ways in which those foundations were both strengthened and built upon in the next twenty years—by the national parliament and the provincial legislatures, by national and municipal government, and (less consistently) by the provincial and appellate divisions of the Supreme Court.

I. STATE-SPONSORED RACIAL DISCRIMINATION 1909–1918

South Africa's first Governor-General was Herbert Gladstone, son of the former Prime Minister, and previously British Home Secretary.[1] His first task was to appoint an interim government pending elections to be held in September 1910. Botha was invited to form the country's first administration. Het Volk, Orangia Unie and the Bond had fused into the South African Party (SAP) to fight the election: the SAP's very name conveyed the impression that the Botha/Smuts ethos of anglo-boer conciliation had overcome the Hertzog ethos of anglo-boer separation. The SAP won sixty-eight of the House of Assembly's 121 seats; Jamesons' Progressives secured thirty-seven;[2] the Labour Party three; and thirteen were won by various other parties, predominantly based in Natal. Botha himself suffered the inconvenience of failing to win his seat in Pretoria, and a by-election was engineered to return him to parliament.[3]

Botha formed an exclusively SAP Cabinet. This created a somewhat bizarre political situation, for it seemed that Botha and Smuts shared substantially more common ground with the Progressives than with some of their Cabinet colleagues. Hertzog was the main source of intra-Cabinet dissent. As suggested below, his support for reconciliation proved both shallow and short-lived. On matters relating to race relations however, the Botha government acted swiftly and decisively in the finest discriminatory traditions of the Transvaal and Free

[1] C. Mallet, *Herbert Gladstone* (London: Hutchinson & Co, 1932), ch. 8.

[2] Jameson retired from South African politics shortly afterwards. His party chose Sir Thomas Smartt, a member of the Bond, to replace him.

[3] T. Davenport, *South Africa: a Modern History*, 2nd edn. (Cambridge: CUP, 1978), pp. 173–174; W. Hancock, *Smuts. Volume 1: The Sanguine Years 1870–1919* (Cambridge: CUP, 1962).

State. This had an immediate, symbolic dimension. One of the first bills the new parliament enacted was the Dutch Reformed Church Act 1911, which restricted membership of the Reformed Church in the three northern provinces solely to whites. A separation of Church and State was clearly not to be a feature of South African society. But the government rapidly turned to more practical matters.

Land

The Native Land Act 1913 introduced the concept of 'scheduled native areas'.[4] A 'native' could not buy land in a non-scheduled area, and, conversely, a non-native (which evidently included coloureds and Asians) could not own or lease land in a scheduled area, unless the transaction was approved by the Governor-General. The government's presumption was that the Governor-General's approval for inter-racial land transactions would rarely be forthcoming.

The measure was prompted in part by the segregationist ideology propounded by Milner's South African Native Affairs Commission.[5] However, the Botha administration adopted a wholly perverse notion of equitable distribution. At that time, native blacks accounted for some sixty-seven per cent of South Africa's population. The original allocation of scheduled land for their occupation comprised some seven per cent of the country's territory.[6] This indicates that Botha's government was using the SANAC report's notion of 'trusteeship' as a legitimising fig-leaf to cover rather less lofty motives.

Two such motives are readily discernible. After the *Tsewu* judgment,[7] many native blacks had pooled their resources to buy formerly white-owned farms in the Transvaal. This was an activity which many whites in all three northern provinces regarded as politically and economically unacceptable. The 1913 Act prevented the spread of such activities, and also permitted the eventual compulsory purchase of black-owned farms and the forcible eviction of blacks who had leased land in non-scheduled areas.[8]

The manifestly inadequate allocation of land to native blacks, and the poor quality of much that was granted, also ensured that its occupants could not sustain a viable subsistence level agricultural economy in their home regions. The scheduled lands thus served as pools of cheap unskilled labour for the mines and

[4] A. Walshe and A. Roberts, 'Southern Africa' in A. Roberts (ed.), *The Cambridge History of Africa Vol. 7 1905–1940* (Cambridge: Cambridge University Press, 1986); Cell, *The Highest Stage of White Supremacy* (Cambridge: CUP, 1982), pp. 79–81; H. Fenberg, 'The 1913 Native Land Act in South Africa: Politics, Race and Segregation in the Early Twentieth Century' (1993) *International Journal of African Historical Studies* 65; Dugard, *Human Rights and the South African Legal Order* (Princeton: Princeton University Press, 1978), pp. 78–79.

[5] See pp. 66–67 above.

[6] T. Bennet, 'African Land—a History of Dispossession' in R. Zimmerman and D. Visser (eds.), *South Cross: Civil Law and Common Law in South Africa* (Oxford: Clarendon Press, 1996), pp. 81–82.

[7] See pp. 76–77 above.

[8] Davenport (1978), n. 3 above, pp. 334–336.

similarly cheap domestic servants for urban white populations. South Africa had no need of indentured Chinese labourers[9] when its parliament could fashion a land policy that so effectively proletarianised its indigenous black population. The Act contained a rather ambiguous exclusion clause. Its provisions would not apply in the Cape insofar as they would remove a native's right to vote, or prevent him acquiring such a right. The clause did not obviously exclude the Cape from the Act altogether, but suggested that individual land transactions in that province could be exempted on a case by case basis. The South African parliament seemed to have inherited the predilection of its Cape predecessor to express at least some aspects of its racially motivated legislative provisions in obscure language: the precise scope of the Land Act 1913 would fall to be determined by the courts. In the meantime, the Appellate Division had begun to fill in some of the gaps in the discriminatory legislation which the Cape's colonial legislature had bequeathed to its provincial successor.

Separate and unequal? Schooling in the Cape

The Appellate Division addressed the questions left unanswered by the text of the Cape School Board Act 1905[10] in the 1911 case of *Moller v Keimoes School Committee*.[11] The Gordonia School District admitted only whites to its state schools. It did not establish a state school for non-whites. Two mission schools for non-whites operated within the district's boundaries.

Mr Moller was a white man whose wife was the daughter of a white father and a Coloured woman. These facts as to Mr and Mrs Moller's respective racial identities were not disputed. The couple had two school age children. Mr Moller was a resident of Keimoes, and paid local taxes to the Gordonia school district. Moller enrolled his children at Keimoes state school. The headmaster had admitted the children, evidently believing they were of European extraction, and accepted the appropriate fees from Mr Moller. Within a few days however, almost fifty per cent of the white parents at the school withdrew their children in protest at the presence of 'coloured' pupils. The school thereupon expelled the Moller children and returned the fees Mr Moller had paid. Mr Moller engaged W.P. Schreiner as his counsel. His application to the Cape provincial division for an order requiring the school to admit his children was refused,[12] whereupon he applied to the Appellate Division.

In addition to becoming the first Chief Justice of South Africa, Sir J.H. De Villiers had by now also been elevated to the House of Lords by the Asquith

[9] See pp. 68–70 above.

[10] See pp. 93–94 above.

[11] (1911) AD 635. See also A. Sachs, *Justice in South Africa* (London: University of Sussex Press, 1973), pp. 132–134: H. Corder, *Judges at Work* (Cape Town: Juta & Co, 1984), pp. 156–158. On the background to the case see G. Lewis, *Between the Wire and the Wall* (Cape Town: David Phillip, 1987), pp. 67–68.

[12] (1911) CPD 673.

government.[13] It was thus as Lord De Villiers C.J. that he delivered the leading judgment for a unanimous five judge court in *Moller*.

W.P. Schreiner advanced two arguments on Mr Moller's behalf. The first was simply that in the absence of any explicit provision in the 1905 Act authorising districts to discriminate on grounds of *skin colour*, all state schools should be open to the children of all ratepayers in the district concerned. 'European' should thus be construed, in accordance with the political philosophy that Merriman (and Schreiner himself qua politician) had advocated,[14] as an indicator of intellectual and cultural capacity rather than physiological ethnicity.

Schreiner suggested that discrimination premised on the latter ground was rendered unlawful by a recent English decision, *Kruse v Johnson*.[15] *Kruse*—a case concerning a local authority's power to make bye-laws—had held that executive action would be unlawful if, *inter alia*, its effects were "partial and unequal in their operation as between different classes",[16] unless such inequality and partiality was expressly authorised by the statute granting the power concerned. Racial identity, Schreiner argued, was a 'class' for these purposes. In the alternative, if 'European extraction' was taken to mean one's racial identity, Schreiner contended that Mr Moller's children met the test because three of their four grandparents were whites.

Lord De Villiers C.J. rejected both contentions. His methodology closely resembled that employed by Innes C.J. in *Swarts*.[17] While the Act did not explicitly authorise segregation on racial lines, it did so by necessary implication. That implication evidently arose from matters of undisputed historical fact:

> "We know that the first civilized legislators in South Africa [sic] came from Holland and regarded the aboriginal natives of the country as belonging to an inferior race . . . whom they refused to admit to social or political equality . . . These prepossessions, or as many might term them, these prejudices, have never died out and are not less deeply rooted at the present day among the Europeans in South Africa, whether of Dutch or English or French descent".[18]

Given the depth and prevalence of such prejudice, Lord De Villiers C.J. considered it inconceivable that the wholly white[19] Cape Parliament would have passed legislation which did not establish separate schools for white children. The child's intellectual abilities, her home environment, and her culture were irrelevant to the notion of 'European'. The gist of the Chief Justice's opinion seemed to be that the South African common law's rules of statutory interpretation *required* the courts to assume that explicitly colour-conscious

[13] Botha requested Asquith not to ennoble any further South Africans. His embrace of things British evidently did not extend to wishing to found an indigenous aristocracy in South Africa.

[14] See pp. 33–34 above.

[15] [1898] 2 QB 91.

[16] *Ibid*. at 95.

[17] See pp. 72–73 above.

[18] (1911) AD 635 at 643.

[19] See p. 113 above.

national and provincial legislation was intended by its framers to be implemented in a spirit which maximised rather than minimised racial intolerance.

The Chief Justice was similarly unreceptive to Schreiner's second point. The Act did not define how much 'white blood' a child needed to be classified as 'European'. Schreiner argued that, in the absence of a clear statutory definition, the term should include any child with a discernible portion of white ancestry, a classification that would encompass virtually all of the Coloured population. The school board contended, in contrast, that 'European' embraced only children of 'pure' white descent.

Lord De Villiers C.J. again resolved this uncertainty by resorting to the presumed 'prejudices' of the Cape legislators:

> "The court is unable to ignore the universal meaning attached to the term 'European' . . . A white citizen of the United States, who has never been in Europe, would be regarded as a European, while a black man born or bred in Europe would be regarded as other than European . . . [O]nce it is established that one of a man's nearer ancestors was black, like a Negro or Kaffir, or yellow like a Bushman or Hottentot or Chinaman, he is regarded as being of other than European descent".[20]

The Chief Justice saw no need to concern himself with defining precisely who would be a 'near ancestor', for the facts in this case were clear. Since one of Mrs Moller's parents was not white, her children could not be of European descent.

De Villiers seemed quite to have forgotten his own judgment in *R v Parrott*.[21] In *Parrot*, he had formed the apparently unambiguous conclusion that the children of a white man and non-white woman who were married to each other would be regarded as 'white', while the offspring of an unmarried white/non-white couple would be non-white. The point did not appear to be raised by counsel on either side. De Villiers C.J. also effectively placed the burden of proving purity in the parent, rather than requiring the school to disprove it, a conclusion which significantly facilitated exclusion.

De Villiers C.J.'s reasoning was elaborated upon by Innes J.'s concurring judgment.[22] Innes J. explicitly adopted the so-called 'mischief rule' of statutory interpretation to defeat Schreiner's arguments.[23] The technique has a long pedigree in English law. It provides that when a statute's text is ambiguous, the court may seek its meaning by looking at the problem or 'mischief' the Act was intended to remedy. Innes J. considered that the 'mischief' perceived by the Cape legislature in 1905 was racial integration:

> "There seems little doubt that what the Act was intended to remedy was the possibility of white and coloured children associating in the schools; a possibility against

20 (1911) AD 635 at 643.

21 See pp. 73–74 above.

22 This being Sir James Rose Innes, the former Chief Justice of the Transvaal.

23 See M. Zander, 4th edn., *The Lawmaking Process* (London: Butterworths, 2996), pp. 108–110. Lord de Villiers C.J. also adopted this approach, but did not expressly acknowledge that he was doing so.

which the law at that time had not provided. And the remedy was to be the provision of separate institutions for the white children".[24]

Innes J.'s reasoning in reaching this conclusion became clearer when he rejected the second of Schreiner's arguments—namely that the Moller children were of European extraction. After referring approvingly to his own judgment in *Swarts*,[25] Innes J. accepted the school board's argument. He then concluded his concurring opinion with a pious note of regret, (reminiscent of his judgment in *Swarts*), noting that the school district's policy:

> "may inflict great hardship on deserving members of the community. I should like to express my individual view that the machinery of the Act for the education of children of other than European extraction seems inadequate . . . This is a matter which one may hope that the Legislature will duly take into consideration".[26]

The Moller children were thus not simply excluded from the 'European' state school. Since no state school for non-whites existed in their area, they could not extract any benefit from the 1905 Act. As construed by the Appellate Divison, the Act did not require integrated schools; it did not require the provision of separate schools of equal quality to non-whites; it did not even require school districts to open inferior schools for non-white children. Rather it permitted school districts to run schools solely for whites. And, to add injury to insult, a school district could finance such schools with the local taxes levied on the parents of non-white children living in its area.

The judgment is defensible from a narrowly legalistic perspective. But it is equally the case that the court could have accepted Schreiner's arguments without departing from orthodox legal principles. De Villiers C.J. had coloured his invocation of the mischief rule with a suggestion that, regrettably, his judicial hands were tied. In referring to the presumed racial animosity informing the 1905 Cape parliament's deliberations on the Act, he had observed:

> "We may not from a philosophical or humanitarian point of view be able to approve this prevalent sentiment, but we cannot as judges, who are called upon to construe an Act of Parliament, ignore the reasons which must have induced the legislature to adopt the policy of separate education for European and non-European children".[27]

That protestation is entirely inaccurate. The Appellate Division was under no obligation to adopt the mischief rule. It could if it had so wished have employed the dominant principle of statutory interpretation in English law—the literal rule—which simply requires that a court is to give the orthodox, grammatical meaning to a statute's words. Application of the literal rule would have led to some ambiguity being found in the statute's meaning, an ambiguity which could have been resolved in the Moller children's favour by applying the rule in *Kruse*

24 (1911) AD 634 at 648.
25 (1905) TS 621.
26 (1911) AD 634 at 649.
27 (1911) AD 635 at 643–644.

v Johnson in the manner that Schreiner had advocated. The Appellate Division had a choice in *Moller*. De Villiers C.J. and Innes J. could have coupled their professions of distaste for racial prejudice with judgments precluding school districts from giving such sentiments substantial practical effect against Cape coloured children. The onus would then have fallen on the Cape provincial council or parliament[28] to pass an ordinance or statute respectively which expressly empowered school districts to discriminate in so egregious a manner against non-white children. That De Villiers, Innes and their three other colleagues chose not to do so indicated that a substantial number of South Africa's senior judges were prepared to facilitate the development of an evermore segregated state.[29]

It is pefectly plausible to assume that Cape legislators in 1905 wished to introduce an education system segregated so rigidly according to skin colour that it embraced only the 'purest' of white children, but did not want to do so explicitly for fear that such a measure would antagonise public and political opinion in Britain. As noted in Chapter 3, Jameson's government had been unperturbed by Coloured opposition in the Cape.[30] The use of the label 'European' was sufficiently ambiguous to defuse such criticism, since it could be construed as denoting a person's cultural rather than physiological characteristics and so encompass many children within the Cape Coloured population. Given the evident indifference of both of the Campbell-Bannerman and Asquith governments to the welfare of non-white South Africans, such fears were probably misplaced. Nevertheless, the political rationale underpinning the legal arguments that W.P. Schreiner advanced are clear; if a legislature wishes to authorise an executive body to discriminate against certain citizens solely because of their racial characteristics, it must draft the legislation concerned in the most clear and unambiguous fashion. Only by insisting on such transparency in the law-making process can one be sure that legislators are rendering themselves accountable to the voters who returned them to power and (in the case of a colony) to the Imperial legislature which exercises legal sovereignty over their behaviour. *Moller* undermined this principle in permitting discriminatory ends to be achieved through rather more opaque means.

The judgment was nonetheless supportively reviewed in the *Cape Times*, which reproduced all the opinions verbatim and ran a lengthy leader commenting on the case. The editorial offered equivocal approval for the principle of segregation, but equally firmly disapproved of the current inadequacy of provision for non-white children:

> "The State has imposed a very serious disability on non-European children, for reasons which may or may not be sound, but which are undoubtedly in accordance

[28] Under the terms of s. 85 of the South Africa Act, provincial councils were to retain control over education matters for at least five years after the Act's coming into force, as long as the contents of any ordinances were not (per s. 86) incompatible with the provisions of any legislation.

[29] See Dugard (1978), n. 4 above, pp. 305–307.

[30] See pp. 93–94 above.

> with the views of the vast majority of white people in South Africa. Having imposed that disability, the obligation to balance it, as far as possible, by special provisions is all the stronger. We trust that the remarks of the judges on these important points will result in [provincial] legislation which will go far to remove the present defects in the machinery of the law, and will assure to the Coloured people such educational opportunities as they may be able to afford".[31]

'Mohammedan marriages'

As noted in Chapter 3, the Cape had not drawn any colour-based distinctions in relation to inter-racial marriage and sexual liaisons. The colony's courts had however always maintained a euro-centric understanding of just what constituted a 'marriage'; they had in particular insisted that only monogamous marriage relationships would be recognised at common law. This created obvious difficulties for Cape residents whose immediate or ancestral origins were Indian or Malay and who had entered into potentially or actually polygamous marriages. The Cape legislature had softened this common law rule in 1860, by passing an Act which permitted the 'solemnisation' of so-called Mohammaden marriages before a government official, whereupon the marriage would be regarded as equivalent to a European marriage for legal purposes. The recognition or otherwise of 'Mohammedan marriages' had some appreciable significance to purely internal southern African concerns, in relation for example to the conveyance of property and the law of succession.[32] However, the issue raised in *Esop v Union Government (Minister of the Interior)*[33] had a rather more extra-territorial dimension.

Botha's government had retained the 1906 Cape legislation promoted by Jameson's administration to regulate Asiatic immigration into the Cape. Under section 4 of the Act, an Indian man already resident in the Cape was permitted to bring his 'wife' into the country. Mr Esop was an Indian who had entered a marriage with an Indian woman in India. The marriage was an Islamic rather than Christian ceremony. This was Mr Esop's first marriage, but Indian law did not preclude him marrying other wives if he so wished. His attempt to bring his wife into South Africa was resisted by the Botha government, The government maintained she was not his 'wife' within the meaning of section 4: only a monogamous marriage could bestow that status on a woman.

Searle J. upheld the government's argument. He suggested that recognising such marriages would offer Indians a means to evade the restrictions imposed on their immigration. The conclusion might cause hardship, but that was a matter for the legislature, rather than the courts, to consider. In Searle J.'s view,

31 14 December 1911.

32 See for example *Seedat's Executor v The Master (Natal)* [1917] AD 302; discussed in Corder (1984), n. 11 above, pp. 132–133.

33 (1913) CPD 133.

a polygamous marriage was a state of affairs "where the very elements and essentials of a legal union of marriage are, by admission wanting".[34] In circumstances where the precise nature of the marriage was unclear, the burden of proof fell on the applicant to demonstrate that the relationship was sealed according to European rather than 'Mohammedan' principles.[35]

The judgment afforded Gandhi a further reason for maintaining his ongoing campaign of passive resistance to Botha and Smuts' policies towards South Africa's Indian population. *Esop* undoubtedly caused acute hardship to many Indian families. But in quantitative terms this judicially created discrimination paled into virtual insignificance when placed alongside one of the Botha administration's first forays into the realm of race relations in the labour market.

Labour relations

The Mines and Works Act 1911 seemingly gave a legislative seal of approval to a policy position that had been formulated by Botha's Transvaal government between 1907 and 1909. Smuts had established a Mining Regulations Commission in 1907 to investigate the regulation of labour relations in the industry. The Commission's deliberations and conclusions were dominated by the concerns of white trade unions, whose primary objective was to ensure that black workers were permitted to work only in unskilled occupations. This would create an artificial scarcity in white labour, thereby both raising white workers' wages and enhancing their job security.[36]

The Transvaal Commission and the Union Parliament which enacted its recommendations were both rather coy about their motives. The Act did not expressly authorise race discrimination, but did empower the government to issue regulations controlling health and safety matters in the mines. Smuts then promptly used this power to issue regulations preventing blacks from working in thirty-two 'skilled' occupations.[37] The regulations were presented as a safety measure, the government's argument being—on the basis of no obvious evidence—that blacks were intrinsically incapable of performing such tasks with a due standard of expertise and diligence.[38]

[34] (1913) CPD 133 at 137.

[35] See also *Soetje Magmoet v Registrar of Deeds* 5 SC 1798; *Mahomed v Union Government* [1911] CPD 841. In contrast, the Transvaal Supreme Court had previously concluded that the burden of proof in such cases should lie on the party disputing the 'European' validity of a marriage; see *Mashia Ebrahim v Mahomed Esop* (1905) TLR 59 per Innes C.J.

[36] H. Simons and R. Simons *Class and Colour in South Africa 1850–1950* (Harmondsworth: Penguin, 1969), pp. 89–92.

[37] Simons and Simons, n. 36 above, p. 174. Smuts held an expansive view of 'skilled'. The regulations not only included such jobs as train driver, boilermaker, and blaster, but also extended to supervision of toilet cleaning.

[38] Davenport (1978), n. 3 above, pp. 175–176; Walshe and Roberts, n. 4 above, pp. 549–551; Simons and Simons, n. 36 above, pp. 90–92.

The Native Labour Regulation Act 1911 had a rather broader sweep.[39] In some respects, it enhanced the status of black employees. The legislation imposed more stringent health and safety requirements, and also made employers liable to pay compensation (albeit in small amounts) to workers seriously injured at work. On the other hand, the Act prohibited strikes by native black workers, and also confirmed that an individual breach of contract by a black worker would be treated as a criminal offence.

The Acts' combined effect was to reinforce the subordinate position of native black workers relative to whites. The point is forcefully made simply by comparing wage levels in the mining industry. White workers earned on average nine times as much as blacks. The Chamber of Mines thus had an obvious economic interest in relaxing the colour bar and recruiting more black labourers. The 1911 and 1913 Acts suggested that the Botha government was initially rather more concerned to cultivate the loyalty of the white working class than indulge the wishes of the mineowners or protect the interests of black workers.

That initial image of Botha and Smuts as the champions of the white worker against the Chamber of Mines was soon to be dispelled. The most serious challenge to the labour relations policies pursued by the Botha government was sparked by white rather than black opposition, and by the workers rather than the Chamber of Mines.

The Labour party had been campaigning for the introduction of a maximum forty-eight-hour working week for white miners. The Chamber opposed the initiative, and a strike was triggered in May 1913 when several mining companies attempted to increase working hours. The action was co-ordinated by British trade unionists, whose success was such that by late June, almost 20,000 white miners were on strike. Botha and Smuts responded by declaring martial law and using troops to restore order. The ensuing riots suggested that Smuts' action had exacerbated rather than calmed the situation, and the government found itself in the unwelcome position of having to broker a settlement between the unions and the mineowners which conceded the legitimacy of many of the worker's grievances.[40]

The Rand unrest was followed by a trade union efforts to co-ordinate a nationwide general strike early the next year.[41] Frederick Cresswell, the pioneer of a white labour policy in the mines, and by now a Labour MP, was active in co-ordinating the strike and was imprisoned for his pains.[42] Smuts again mobilised troops to quell the unrest, this time in greater numbers and with greater success. Smuts then indulged in another of his episodic forays into blatant illegality. The leaders of the general strike were unceremoniously and

[39] Walshe and Roberts, n. 4 above, pp. 550–551; Simons and Simons, n. 36 above.

[40] See Simons and Simons, n. 36 above, pp. 156–160.

[41] Hancock (1962), n. 3 above, pp. 366–367.

[42] Davenport (1978), n. 3 above, p. 199; Pirow (ed.), *James Barry Munik Hertzog* (Cape Town, Howard Timmins, 1946), pp. 85–86.

unlawfully deported to Britain.[43] The government was then obliged to promote a bill which retrospectively indemnified any government officials against liability for any crimes or torts they might have committed during the strike and its aftermath.[44]

Sir James Rose Innes, then sitting on the Appellate Division bench and shortly to become Chief Justice, subsequently denounced the government's behaviour. The deportations were a "high-handed and lawless enterprise"; the indemnity legislation was "a fascist exploit" and a "blot upon the pages of South African history".[45] The voters of the Transvaal registered their opinion by returning the Labour party to power in the 1914 provincial elections.[46]

Parliament was clearly less critical of the Botha government's behaviour. In addition to passing the indemnity legislation, the house and the senate also passed Smuts' Riotous Assemblies bill. Once enacted, the measure placed limits on trade union recruitment activities, banned strikes in public services, and granted sweeping powers to local police and magistrates to prohibit and disperse public parades and meetings which might engender a breach of the peace.[47] The Act also addressed what the government regarded as efforts by white political activists to forge a common front with non-white workers. Section 1 of the Act empowered the Minister of Justice both to ban political meetings in paticular areas and to exclude named individuals from particular parts of the country for as long as the Minister thought appropriate if "the Minister is satisfied that [the person] is promoting feelings of hostility between the European inhabitants of the Union and any other section of the inhabitants of the Union". The Act did not require the Minister to hold a hearing prior to making the exclusion order, although it did require him to offer the individual concerned reasons for the decision after the order had been issued and granted the individual the right to make representations to the Minister with a view to having the order lifted.

The wide powers which the Act conferred upon the government indicated that a major realignment had occurred in white South Africa's domestic political orthodoxies. Smuts and Botha, who barely ten years previously had fought a war against Britain to safeguard boer culture from the economic imperialism of the Chamber of Mines, now seemed to stand shoulder to shoulder with the mineowners in opposition to both the boer and anglo working class. A clear

[43] On press coverage of the episode, which the *Rand Daily Mail* scooped through a fortuitous combination of circumstances, see J. Mervis, *Fourth Estate* (Johannesburg: Jonathan Ball, 1989), pp. 102–106.

[44] Hancock (1962), n. 3 above, pp. 368–371.

[45] J. Rose Innes, *Autobiography* (Cape Town: OUP, 1949), pp. 253–255. Merriman's position on the issue was one of unembarrassed hypocrisy. After urging Smuts to take forceful action (Hancock (1962), n. 3 above, pp. 367–368), he then referred to Smuts as a 'dictator' after the Indemnity Act was passed; (Innes *op. cit.* p. 254). He abstained in the votes on the indemnity bill.

[46] See Mervis, n. 43 above, pp. 105–106 for an account of the campaign and the Rand press' subsequent attempts to persuade the new administration to follow 'responsible' policies.

[47] See Davenport (1978), n. 3 above, pp. 183–184.

political faultline—based on economic class—had emerged within the boer and anglo communities. Hertzog wasted little time in exploiting it.

Fragmentation within the Afrika(a)ner community

Hertzog increasingly took the view that Botha and Smuts had been seduced by the British to pursue a policy that would ultimately lead to the disappearance of boer culture. Botha's presence at the coronation of George V in 1911, and his subsequent participation in the Imperial Conference on equal terms with the Prime Ministers of the other white colonies, intensified Hertzog's suspicions.[48] By 1912, he had begun to make speeches calling for South African secession from the Empire, a position quite incompatible with Botha and Smuts' intentions. When Hertzog refused to resign from the Cabinet, Botha adopted the expedient course of removing him from office by tendering the resignation of the entire government. On being invited to form a new adminstration by the Governor-General, Botha did so without including Hertzog.[49]

Hertzog's dismissal initially seemed of little consequence. After much agonising, the former Free State Prime Minister, Abraham Fischer, remained in the Cabinet, and only five of the SAP's MPs crossed the floor with Hertzog into opposition.[50] His support among the party outside parliament was however substantially stronger, and proved sufficient to enable him to lauch a new party, the National Party, in 1914. The National Party's vision of Afrikaanerdom mirrored the programme advanced by Orangia Unie during its brief period of government in the Free State. South Africa was to be a white man's country, but a country whose white culture would not be dominated by 'British' values, and which—sooner rather than later—should become a republic independent not only of the British monarchy but also of the British Empire.

The National Party was formed in the Free State, but spread rapidly into the Cape and the Transvaal. The party gained substantial support in the Cape under the leadership of D.F. Malan, a journalist and a predikant of the Dutch Reform Church. D.F. Malan combined his two professions with his political vocation by founding an extremist boer newspaper, *Die Burger*, in 1915.[51] In the Transvaal, Hertzog's caused was championed by Tielman Roos, a Cape-educated barrister who had built a formidable reputation as a trial lawyer at the Transvaal bar.[52]

[48] Hancock (1962), n. 3 above, pp. 351–353; L. Thompson, *A History of South Africa* (New Haven: Yale University Press, 1995), pp. 157–159; Pirow, n. 42 above, pp. 55–56.

[49] T. Moodie, *The Rise of Afrikanerdom* (London: University of California Press, 1975), pp. 76–79.

[50] Pirow, n. 42 above, pp. 58–67.

[51] E. Potter, *The Press as Opposition* (London: Chatto and Windruss, 1975), p. 45. On the paper's editorial policy and circulation see Moodie, n. 49 above, pp. 84–85.

[52] Roos had acted as counsel for Pietersburg in the *Hajee Habib* case; see pp. 77–78 above.

The industrial unrest of 1913 and 1914 offered the National Party a ready-made tool with which to undermine boer working class support for the SAP. The outbreak of the First World War drove a second, more damaging stake into the heart of Smuts and Botha's ambition to achieve an anglo-boer reconciliation.

Botha and Smuts considered that South Africa's status as a colony necessarily meant it was automatically at war with Germany once Britain had opened hostilities. They also considered that South Africa's involvement in the conflict had to be as an active supporter of the British military campaign. Botha and Smuts personally led an invasion and conquest of German South West Africa. The campaign prompted several senior members of the South African army to defect to the German side. Hertzog did not go so far, but rather advocated a policy of South African neutrality. For Smuts, neutrality was never an option. Indeed his commitment to the Imperial cause was such that he spent much of the war in London, as a key member of Lloyd George's War Cabinet, and seriously contemplated standing for election to the House of Commons.

Such activities and ambitions reinforced the National Party's view that the SAP was becoming a vehicle for British rather than Afrikaaner interests. Hertzog's party won twenty-seven house seats in the 1915 elections. The SAP won fifty-four, and governed in effective coalition with thirty-nine Unionist MPs. Hertzog seemed a long way away from achieving power, but he had already established his party as the main opposition. That opposition was founded primarily on two issues: the imperial connection and the treatment of the non-white races. On the first issue, South Africa was pursuing policies of which Hertzog manifestly disapproved. On the second question, as already noted, parliament was erecting a discriminatory legal structure which was moving (albeit too slowly and too timidly) in a direction with which the National Party could broadly agree. The role played by the courts on racial issues was rather more ambiguous.

Separate but equal? Trams in the Transvaal

There are few decisions of the US Supreme Court that history has treated less kindly than the 1896 judgment in *Plessey v Ferguson*.[53] *Plessey* upheld a Louisiana statute which required whites and non-whites to travel in separate compartments on internal Louisiana railway journeys. The majority held that the Act did not contravene the Fourteenth Amedment to the American Constitution, which required states to afford all citizens 'the equal protection of the laws'. Separation was consistent with this requirement as long as the segregated facilities were of equal standard; it could not *per se* be construed as 'discrimination' or as denoting the inferiority of one race to another. The judgment

[53] 163 US 537 (1896).

drew a stinging dissent from Harlan J., who maintained that the Fourteenth Amendment required all state legislation to be 'colour blind'. He considered that the constitution prohibited any classification of any sort premised on grounds of race. In Harlan J.'s view it was a nonsense to suggest such separation did not denote inferiority. The law had no other purpose than to confirm the dominance of whites in southern society.[54]

Sixty years passed before a majority of the US Supreme Court accepted Harlan's analysis.[55] In the interim, *Plessey* provided a legal green light for all state legislatures which wished to spare their white citizens the evident indignity of having to share buses, trains, movie theatres, swimming pools, bars and all manner of other public facilities with non-white citizens.[56] What is more surprising perhaps is that the spirit of Harlan's dissent was embraced, if only fleetingly and tentatively, by some members of the Transvaal judiciary as early as 1915.

As noted in Chapter 3, James Rose Innes C.J. in *Hajee Habib* and *Tsewu* had produced judgments which suggested that the common law was colour blind and that courts should assume that legislation was intended by its framers to be racially non-discriminatory in its effect unless its text indicated explicitly to the contrary. Ten years later, several of his successors on the Transvaal bench seemed willing both to approve and elaborate those principles.

The plaintiffs in *Williams & Adendorff v Johannesburg Municipality*[57] challenged the legality of a 1906 Johnannesburg bye-law passed under the terms of a 1906 Transvaal ordinance which granted the council a monopoly 'to establish, maintain and work . . . tramways for the public use within the municipality'. The ordinance did not explicitly permit any racial discrimination in the service provided. However, the bye-law required that some passenger cars be reserved solely for passengers 'of the European race'; the rest would be reserved exclusively for non-European passengers. Williams and Adendorff were Coloureds who were forcibly ejected from a 'European car'. They claimed the bye-law was *ultra vires* the ordinance because, per *Kruse v Johnson*, it introduced an arbitrary distinction between different classes of the public.

The Transvaal provincial division unanimously upheld the plainitffs' claim, deploying reasoning that was wholly consistent with Innes C.J.'s conclusion in *Hajee Habib*.[58] De Villiers J.P.[59] thought the question a simple one: "whether a well behaved decently dressed coloured person, by tendering the legal fare, is

[54] See N. Lofgren, *The Plessey Case* (New York: OUP, 1993); P. Oberst, 'The Strange Career of *Plessey v Ferguson*' (1973) *Arizona LR* 389.

[55] In *Brown v Board of Education* 347 US 483 (1954).

[56] C. Woodward, *The Strange Career of Jim Crow* (New York: OUP, 1966), chs. 1–3.

[57] (1915) TPD 106.

[58] See pp. 77–78 above.

[59] Jacob De Villiers (1868–1932). De Villiers was educated at Stellenbosch, then read law at both Amsterdam (where he became a close friend of Hertzog) and London universities. He became Attorney-General of the Free State in 1897. After the war, Botha appointed him as Attorney-General of the Transvaal in 1907, and then as Judge President of the Transvaal in 1910. Smuts appointed him to the Appellate Division in 1920, and he became Chief Justice under Hertzog's government in 1929.

entitled to board an ordinary service tramcar".[60] The answer was clearly 'Yes'. The ordinance required the trams to be run for the public benefit. This meant the whole public, not simply certain racial groups. Any bye-law which even "distinguished" between Europeans and non-Europeans would be unlawful if such powers were not specifically granted by the ordinance.[61]

Bristow and Curlewis JJ. delivered separate concurring judgments. Neither offered a wholehearted endorsement of the common law as a colour-blind phenomenon. Bristow J. accepted that it was permissible for the common law to acknowledge that municipal councils were impliedly empowered to have regard to "the feelings and sensitiveness, even to the prejudices and foibles" of their citizens.[62] In the prevailing state of race relations in Johannesburg, segregating native blacks from 'Europeans' might be permissible even without express authorisation in the relevant ordinance.

To segregate all non-Europeans was however a wholly different matter. In part, this was a matter of practicalities. Echoing De Villiers C.J.'s concerns in *Parrott*, Bristow J. asked how 'European' was to be defined:

> "Many persons who pass as of European race are darker than many Asians or Cape coloured persons; and many of the latter are lighter in colour than some so-called Europeans . . . [W]hat amount of alloy constitutes a departure from pure European blood? As matters stand, the decision rests with the tramway conductor and can only be based on a rough and ready comparison of shades of facial colouration".[63]

Bristow J. saw no reason why the operation of trams required such segregation. The bye-law thus failed the *Kruse v Johnson* test.

The court's fortitude in resisting segregation on the trams proved somewhat ephemeral however. Pretoria town council introduced its own tram segregation bye-law in 1912. Whites who travelled in non-white cars, and non-whites who travelled in white cars, committed a criminal offence. This bye-law was issued under the auspices of a 1912 Transvaal ordinance which explicitly permitted the provisions of separate cars for whites and non-whites.

The plaintiff in *George v Pretoria Municipality*[64] had refused to leave a whites-only car and was convicted of breaching the bye-law. Mr George accepted that the provincial legislature was competent to authorise councils to separate racial groups on trams if it so desired. However, he argued that the bye-law was nevertheless *ultra vires* the ordinance because Pretoria had never made *any* trams available to non-whites. All were allocated to white citizens. In other words, while the ordinance permitted separation, it did not permit total exclusion.

[60] (1915) TPD 106 at 115.

[61] *Ibid.* at 117. De Villiers J.P. seemingly did not require that the races be accorded different levels of service. Mere separation was sufficient to render the bye-law invalid.

[62] *Ibid.* at 122.

[63] *Ibid.* at 123. Like De Villiers J.P., Bristow J. saw the *separation* of the races as the problem. He did not limit his reasoning to situations where the separation was coupled with inferior provision.

[64] (1916) TPD 501.

By a two to one majority, the Transvaal provincial division rejected George's argument. In Wessells J.'s view, the ordinance was entirely permissive. The council could if it wished discriminate in this fashion against non-whites without exceeding the powers it had been granted. De Villiers J.P. was slightly more cautious. The council was not under an automatic duty to provide trams for non-whites. It would however have to do so if there was 'reasonable demand' for such services. Until that level of demand was made manifest, Pretoria could run a whites-only service.

Bristow J. dissented. He shared De Villiers J.P.'s view that the council was not obliged to run a service for non-whites if there was no demand for one. But in contrast to De Villiers J.P., he considered that the ordinance required a council to assume that there was a demand for non-white trams. Only if the council established that no such demand existed would it be lawful to run a whites-only service.

All the judgments in these two cases accepted that the common law could recognise the legitimacy of the racial intolerance of the white citizens who elected the Transvaal's municipal councils.[65] The judges nevertheless differed markedly in their views of the extent to which the courts' indulgence of that intolerance should stretch. Wessels J. in *George* essentially required the common law to pander to racist motivation; De Villiers J.P. seemed prepared to accommodate it; Bristow J. placed several awkward obstacles in its path. No one of these positions is obviously 'right' as a matter of law. Rather the judges' disagreements accurately convey the contingent, unstable nature of South African (and indeed English) administrative law. A later section of this chapter revisits the courts in the Transvaal to pursue this argument further. For the moment however, attention returns to the Cape.

Of race and reputation

The overlap between the social and legal facets of racial discrimination in the first years of South Africa's history is neatly illustrated by the Cape Provincial Division's judgment in *Louw v Kielblock* in 1911.[66] Louw had commenced slander proceedings against Kielblock for circulating comments which maintained that Louw was the child of a white father and native black woman. Louw maintained that he was the child of two white parents, and contended that it was *per se* defamatory for a 'white' to be described as of mixed race or black.

[65] Even modest efforts on the part of private groups to foster integration in the Transvaal met with stern press disapproval. Mervis recounts the campaign waged by The *Sunday Times* against the Johannesburg Turf Club, which had allowed a native black to run one of his horses in Johannesburg: "We strongly resent this new plan for mixing up black and white. Natal and the Cape may not mind, but on the High Veld the public are not accustomed to this sort of thing. It is the thin end of the wedge. The precedent will be used by the negrophilists as an argument in favour of all manner of concessions objectionable to the white population": n. 43 above, pp. 112–114.

[66] (1911) CPD 209.

Searle J. accepted that "to say of a white man, commonly regarded as such, that he is not fit to associate with white people on the ground of his being coloured is defamatory".[67] The judge evidently thought the point so obvious that he did not need to explain why or how a white's reputation was damaged by such an assertion. Nor did he feel any need to explain just what was meant by 'white' for these purposes.

The rationale would presumably be that to be non-white was to occupy a markedly inferior social position in Cape society, notwithstanding the fact that a Cape resident's racial identity was supposedly an irrelevance in respect of South Africa's electoral laws. As suggested by the decision in *Moller* and the alcohol sale cases discussed in Chapter 3, this inferiority was not just a matter of social opprobrium—it brought with it potentially significant legal disabilities. In at least one respect, however, the Appellate Division was prepared to assert that the constitution, if not the common law, rendered such disabilities impermissible.

The constitutionality of the Land Act 1913: *Thomson v Kama*

The defendant in *Thomson v Kama*[68] was a native black who was trying to withdraw from a contract for the purchase of a plot of land in Kingwilliamstown in the Cape. The litigation was triggered by a dispute over the validity of a trans-racial sale of land in a scheduled area. The outcome seemed to turn on the precise meaning of the exclusion clause contained in section 8(8) of the 1913 Act. In the Cape provincial division, the court had held that section 8(8) was to be applied only on a case by case basis, and had no relevance to transactions in which a sale had no obvious implications for either party's franchise rights.

The Appellate Division's judgment concluded that intricate analysis of section 8(8) was not needed. Sir James Rose Innes, by now Chief Justice of South Africa, described the terms of section 8(8) as "lamentably obscure".[69] However, he considered that doubts as to the meaning of the text were resolved by the manifest purpose which must have lain behind the provision:

> "The Cape alone among the provinces of the Union recognised no colour bar to the parliamentary franchise. That was a right which for constitutional and other reasons the legislature would naturally be slow to disturb. And it was entrenched by sec.35 of the South Africa Act".[70]

[67] (1911) CPD 209 at 210.

[68] (1917) AD 209.

[69] *Ibid.* at 212.

[70] *Ibid.* at 216. Rose Innes, perhaps more than any other member of white Cape society, would have recognised the legitimacy of this concern. He had, it may be recalled, owed his own election to the Cape legislature prior to Union largely to the support of native voters; see p. 72 above.

Since the Act "would seriously curtail the existing facilities for the acquisition of an electoral qualification by [natives]",[71] and since it had not been passed through the entrenchment procedures specified in section 35, it had no application at all in the Cape: "It was the exemption of the Province that was aimed at, not the relief of particular individuals".[72] It is implicit in Rose-Innes' judgment, although he does not make the point expressly, that the exclusion clause in section 8(8) was not simply insufficiently wide, it was also unnecessary. Such an Act passed in this way could have no effect in the Cape.

Juta A.J.A. concurred in this reasoning. Solomon J. agreed with the result, but offered a rather different rationale for his conclusion. He suggested that an Act which obstructed or removed a non-white ability to qualify for the franchise by the indirect route of restricting his right to own land "would be contrary to the spirit, though not the letter of s.35 of the South Africa Act".[73]

One might reasonably assume that section 8(8) indicated legislative acknowledgment of this constitutional restraint. Innes C.J.'s judgment need not therefore be seen as an accusation that the government, in inviting parliament to enact the bill through the simple majority bicameral procedure, had tried to evade the section 35 entrenchment provisions. But his opinion was potentially of much broader significance. Unlike Solomon J., Innes C.J. had not drawn any distinction between matters of 'letter' and of 'spirit'. Unconstitutional ends could not be achieved through constitutional means. A bare house and senate majority could not manipulate its way around the restriction imposed by section 35.

Yet, despite the force of his conclusion, the Cape's electoral laws were increasingly beginning to appear as a race-neutral British oasis surrounded by an ever-expanding desert of boer race discrimination—not just in the northern provinces, but also in the Cape—discrimination which parliament and provincial legislatures could apparently enact free from any constitutional constraint. For many of South Africa's non-white residents, the time had come for their political identity to be asserted more forcefully than had hitherto been the case.

Non-white opposition movements

The South African Native National Congress (SANNC, which became the African National Congress in 1923) was formed at Blomfontein in 1912. It represented the upper echelons of South Africa's native black population, just as the APO represented the elite strata of the Coloured people. Its members were lawyers, clergymen, teachers and other white collar professionals.[74] The movement was not however solely one of a new black bourgeoisie; determined efforts

[71] *Ibid.* at 216–27.
[72] *Ibid.* at 217.
[73] *Ibid.* at 226.
[74] T. Lodge, *Black Politics in South Africa* (London: Longman, 1983), pp. 1–4.

were made to incorporate traditional tribal chiefs into the organisation.[75] The SANNC's first President was John Dube, an American-educated clergyman who had been much influenced by Booker T. Washington's activities in the USA.[76] Abdurahman and the APO had welcomed the formation of the SANNC. Abdurahman had also made some tentative efforts to co-ordinate Coloured and native black activities, but no formal relationship was established.[77]

The SANNC had initially offered cautious support for the Land Act 1913, as indeed had J.T. Jabavu.[78] Many SANNC members felt that the economic self-sufficiency offered by land was more valuable to native blacks than any extension of the franchise. The inadequacy of the land eventally allocated for 'scheduled' areas rapidly disabused the SANNC of this belief, whereupon it settled into a campaign of clear but distinctly 'constitutional' opposition to SAP race relations policy.[79]

Rather more vigorous opposition developed spontaneously in the Orange Free State late in 1913, when many native black women followed the example set by Gandhi's supporters in the Transvaal and refused to carry passes establishing their entitlement to be in Blomfontein. The protest produced a rare victory for the activists; in practice, if not as a matter of law, their subjection to the pass laws was lifted.[80]

Native black women in the Transvaal achieved a more legally secure victory to the same effect. In *R v Detody*,[81] the majority of the Appellate Division—with Rose Innes giving the leading judgment—held that Transvaal's pass laws[82] should be construed as applying only to men. The majority reached this conclusion notwithstanding the general principle that references to 'men' in legislation should be taken to include women unless the contrary intention was clearly expressed. Rose Innes exlained that he could not discern any good reason why women should be subject to pass laws and so assumed that the legislature had not intended them to be affected.

A man named Clements Kadalie, who had come to South Africa as a migrant worker from Nyasaland (now Malawi), channelled black protest down a rather broader stream. In 1919, Kadalie led a successful strike by the Cape's native black dockworkers. The dockers belonged to a small union, the Industrial and Commercial Union (ICU). The success of the strike prompted rapid growth in the ICU, and it briefly appeared that Kadalie could be laying the foundations of

[75] Simons and Simons, n. 36 above, pp. 134–135; Rich, n. 84 below, pp. 16–21; Hancock (1968), n. 89 below, pp. 117–118.

[76] Beinart, *Twentieth Century South Africa* (Oxford: OUP, 1994), pp. 86–87; Walshe and Roberts, n. 4 above, pp. 552–553.

[77] Lewis, n. 11 above, pp. 78–79.

[78] Jabavu refused to join the SANNC, and perpetuated divisions within the black political community by actively competing with the SANNC for political influence: Davenport (1978), n. 3 above, pp. 176–178.

[79] Simons and Simons, n. 36 above, pp. 130–133.

[80] Walshe and Roberts, n. 4 above, p. 553; Beinart (1994), n. 76 above, pp. 88–89.

[81] [1926] AD 198. See the discussion in Corder (1984), n. 11 above, pp. 141–143.

[82] Which had been enacted prior to Union and retained in unchanged form thereafter.

a black movement which could pursue an integrated, nationwide campaign of political and economic action.[83]

The ICU's momemtum was halted in 1920 however. Kadalie had been involved in organising action by strikers (significantly both black and coloured) in Port Elizabeth. Smuts' response to the strike was more prompt and more brutal than his reaction to the white strikers in 1913 and 1914. Troops were deployed and ordered to disperse the strikers—by force if necessary. Some twenty strikers were killed in the ensuing disturbances. Kadalie himself was convicted of offences under the Riotous Assemblies Act and scheduled for deportation.[84]

Abdurahman's APO remained the primary voice of South Africa's coloured community. He had never seen any merit in the Native Land Act, which the APO had described as an 'audacious act of piracy'.[85] The Act did not however impinge immediately on coloured interests, and while Abdurahman himself made tentative efforts to build a cross-racial non-white alliance, he found few supporters for such an initiative.

Gandhi, in particular, remained exclusively concerned with Indian interests.[86] His activities were focused on two questions: first seeking a legislative reversal of the Cape Supreme Court's decision in *Esop*; and secondly ensuring that Indian labourers in Natal could remain in the province after their period of indentured labour had expired. His campaigns on these issues again caused Smuts acute international embarassment. Both the British government (covertly) and the Indian Viceroy (overtly) pressured Smuts to meet these demands. The Indian Relief Act 1914 appeared to satisfy Gandhi's concerns on both counts.[87]

The First World War had made little impact on white South African's views on racial matters. Echoing his stance in the second boer war, Smuts had generally maintained that South Africa's opposition to Germany would be primarily a white man's conflict. Many native black Africans served in auxiliary roles, and a Cape coloured regiment (under white officers) fought alongside white troops in East Africa and Palestine. There was no question however, in the minds either of Smuts or Hertzog, that the exigencies of war had any bearing on issues of South African race relations in time of peace. For Smuts, the task facing the Botha government in respect of 'the native question' was clear. Its goal should be as far as possible to segregate South Africa's racial groups.[88]

[83] Davenport (1978), n. 3 above, pp. 179–180; Cell, n. 4 above, pp. 268–270; Lodge, n. 74 above, pp. 5–9.

[84] Beinart (1994), n. 76 above, pp. 100–101: Simons and Simons, n. 36 above, pp. 241–243; P. Rich, *State Power and Black Politics in South Africa 1921–1951* (London: Macmillan, 1996), pp. 43–50.

[85] Lewis, n. 11 above, p. 79.

[86] Beinart (1994), n. 76 above, pp. 90–91; Cell, n. 4 above, pp. 253–256.

[87] Hancock (1962), n. 3 above, pp. 340–345; P. Joshi, *The Tyranny of Colour* (London: Kennikat Press, 1942), pp. 78–82. Gandhi left South Africa shortly thereafter to return to India.

[88] Cell, n. 4 above, pp. 224–225.

II. THE CONSOLIDATION AND REINFORCEMENT OF STATE-SPONSORED RACIAL DISCRIMINATION 1919–1930

After the First World War, Smuts assumed a prominent role within the League of Nations. He was intimately involved with formulating the League's 'Mandate' policy for the governance of former German colonies, under which the colonies would be administered by one of the victorious powers until they were capable of independent government. Smuts and Botha had hoped that the League would permit South Africa simply to absorb South West Africa as a fifth province. They acceded reluctantly to the League's designation of South West Africa as a mandate territory, administered by South Africa as if it were a province.

Smuts was also disappointed by the severe reparations which the victorious allies imposed on Germany, even though he himself had greatly influenced their contents. With the benefit of even limited hindsight, he regarded them as a recipe for political instability in Germany, which in turn would lead to political instability in Europe. But Smuts was not the only South African disgruntled by the outcome of the Versailles negotiations.

Hertzog had also been in attendance, leading a Nationalist party delegation which included among its members Dr D.F. Malan, by now a National Party MP, and one F.W. Beyers, a Cape advocate. Hertzog, Malan and Beyers sought to persuade the Allies that the Transvaal and the Orange Free State should be recognised as independent nations, free of both British and Union control. Their second line of argument was that South Africa should at the least be granted complete independence from Britain. Neither contention attracted much support.

The formation of the Afrikaner Broederbond in 1918 was an event of rather broader significance for Hertzog's ambitions. Unlike Hofmeyr's Afrikaner Bond, the Broederbond was designed to foster an exclusively boer vision of Afrikaanerdom. It was never intended to be a mass movement, but rather a small, elitist organisation, whose members would use such political and economic power as they possessed to secure the advancement of like-minded individuals.[89] As O'Meara has suggested, the Broederbond's agenda was directed as much towards 'culture' as economics:

> "In addition to a concern to stimulate Afrikaaner economic activity in the private sector, the Broederbond was much concerned to place its sympathisers in positions of influence within state schools, teacher training institutes and universities, in the police forces and local and provincial government, and in the legal profession".[90]

[89] Walshe and Roberts, n. 4 above, pp. 563–565; L. Thompson, *The Political Mythology of Apartheid* (New Haven: Yale University Press, 1985), pp. 46–50; (1995), n. 48 above, pp. 162–163; K. Hancock, *Smuts Vol 2: Fields of Force 1919–1950* (Cambridge: CUP, 1968), pp. 25–26.

[90] D. O'Meara, *Forty Lost Years* (Athens, Ohio: Ohio University Press, 1996), pp. 43–48; Moodie, n. 49 above, pp. 50, 96–102.

Versailles also offered the SANNC the opportunity to launch one of its first appeals to foreign public opinion. It too sent a delegation, not just to Versailles, but also to Britain to lobby Lloyd George. The SANNC argued for action to curb the already elaborate system of discriminatory race laws enacted in South Africa since 1909. At Versailles, the SANNC was not even granted a hearing. In London, Lloyd George refuse to interfere with what he termed the colony's 'internal affairs', and offered the delegates the less than helpful advice that they should address their grievances to the Union government.[91]

Botha's death in 1919 forced Smuts return to South Africa to become Prime Minister. His government immediately faced a general election, in which the central issue was whether South Africa could and should (as Hertzog and Malan claimed) unilaterally secede from the British Empire. In the 1920 election, the SAP won only a minority of house seats, and clung to power by making an agreement with the Unionist party, which merged into the SAP shortly afterwards. The National Party won forty-four seats, and was making increasingly co-operative overtures to the twenty-one MPs representing the Labour party. Hertzog now appeared as a Prime Minister-in-waiting—the champion of the 'Afrikaner' rather than just of the 'boer'—in opposition to the evermore anglicised Smuts and leading somewhat uneasily a party in which the right wing gathered around Malan was seemingly committed to a far more exclusive vision of what it meant to be an Afrikaaner.

Smuts did not wait for Hertzog's support to grow still further. Buoyed by a favourable economic tide, he called another election less than a year later. His now enlarged party managed to win seventy-nine house seats, in an election which saw the National Party advance to forty-five seats and Labour's representation collapse to only nine. Smuts hoped to consolidate the SAP's hold on power by persuading the wholly 'British' whites of Southern Rhodesia to enter the Union as a fifth province, and was severely disappointed when they chose instead to become a self-governing colony.

The new government's race policies built upon those introduced during the Botha administration, and took several steps in the direction the National Party had marked out in its election campaigns. The Land Act 1913 had indeed had the effect of turning scheduled native areas into labour pools for the white urban areas. The Natives (Urban Areas) Act 1923 ensured that those migrant workers could not integrate themselves into white society. The Act, similar in scope to the measures adopted in the Cape during the bubonic plague scare, empowered local authorities to designate specified 'locations' within their boundaries within which all native blacks (other than those employed by whites as domestic servants) would be required to live. Blacks were required to carry permits proving their entitlement to reside in particular locations. Permits were granted only if a native black was employed by an employer who provided housing for him/her

[91] F. Troup, *South Africa: an Historical Introduction* (London: Metheun, 1972), pp. 228–229.

in the location.[92] The Act was designed to ensure that blacks' presence in urban areas was solely for the purposes of employment; they would not be permitted to have a home or family in the European sense within 'white' towns and cities.

Smuts' government coupled this residential segregation with a more formalised system of political segregation. The Native Affairs Act 1920 established a hierarchy of African representative institutions, based on existing tribal structures, which would supposedly be granted a consultative role in respect of the government's native policies. The ANC initially decided to co-operate with the structures established by the Act.[93] The British government was evidently less impressed. Smuts proposed that Swaziland be transferred to the Union under the arrangements envisaged by section 151 of the constitution,[94] claiming that the type of representative institutions envisaged by the 1920 Act would adequately ensure the protection of Swaziland's black population. The British rejected the proposal.[95]

Both the Smuts government and the National party opposition were committed to a programme of stark race discrimination. Nonetheless, the consolidation of party politics within white South Africa into two large blocs, of which Smuts' party formed the 'liberal' alternative to Hertzog's more trenchant Nationalists, continued. From 1922, the South African economy plunged into recession. This prompted the Chamber of Mines to try to replace white workers with cheaper black labour, which in turn prompted the mining unions to engage in increasingly militant industrial action. Frederick Cresswell, by now an MP and leader of the Labour party, was discreetly involved in fermenting the unrest which manifested itself in an episode subsequently to be known as 'the Rand Rebellion'. Miners took up arms to enforce the strike, rallying under the slogan 'Workers of the World Unite and Fight for a White South Africa'. The notion that black and white workers might share a common cause against the mineowners found no favour with white miners. Smuts' views and actions echoed those he displayed in 1913 and 1914. Martial law was declared; troops were deployed to maintain order; Cresswell was arrested; and 150 strikers were killed during the riots that ensued before peace was restored.[96] Once again, Smuts was compelled to ask parliament to pass an indemnity Act to excuse the over-enthusiasm displayed by his troops. Five strikers, in contrast, were tried for treason, convicted, and hung, notwithstanding the efforts of their leading counsel, Tielman Roos.[97]

[92] Thompson (1995), n. 48 above, pp. 169–170; Rich (1996), n. 84 above, pp. 30–31; 'Ministering to the White Man's Needs: the Development of Urban Segregation in South Africa 1913–1923' (1978) *African Studies* 177.

[93] Walshe and Roberts, n. 4 above, pp. 569–570.

[94] See pp. 120–121 above.

[95] Davenport (1978), n. 3 above, pp. 189–190.

[96] Thompson (1995), n. 48 above, pp. 159–160; Simons and Simons, n. 36 above, pp. 271–299; Mervis, n. 43 above, pp. 147–149. Hancock (1968), n. 89 above, ch. 4 suggests that the preponderance of evidence indicates that Smuts made prolonged and repeated attempts to broker a settlement in the dispute, and resorted to force only in response to a threat of widespread and serious violence by the strikers.

[97] Pirow, n. 42 above, pp. 90–95.

That the leaders of the unrest had little faith in the courts was unsurprising given the outcome of the trials. But the worker's reasoning on this point had a further dimension. In a fascinating mix of race and class bigotry, the Transvaal Legal Defence Committee condemned the South African judiciary as "a bogus aristocracy partly of coloured blood . . . who have in most cases both a political bias and a social prejudice against the white worker".[98]

Smuts' evident defence of the mineowners' interest was mirrored in the English language press. By the 1920s, the Argus and *Rand Daily Mail* groups had embarked upon a persistent campaign of acquisition of and merger with smaller independent newspapers. The two groups had also agreed not to compete with each other in their respective provincial markets. Insofar as the Smuts government faced an opposition press, its critics comprised a small number of Afrikaans language journals, all of which teetered on the edge of commercial viability.[99]

That the Smuts' government should resort to force to crush both black and white opposition to its labour relations policies could hardly be a surprise. More unexpected perhaps, was the check that was imposed on government policy in 1923: a check that came not from militant black trade unionism, but from the ostensibly unlikely source of the Transvaal Supreme Court.

R v Hildick-Smith and *Dadoo Ltd v Krugersdorp Municipal Council*

Hildick-Smith was a white manager who had employed a native black African as an engine driver in a Transvaal mine. The regulations Smuts had issued under the Mines and Works Act had identified the job of engine driver as one of thirty-five which could only be performed by whites.[100] The justification offered for the colour bar at the time, and reiterated in court in *Hildick-Smith*,[101] was that it was a safety measure: native blacks were presumed to be inadequately intelligent and responsible to be employed in tasks which had implications for the safety of other workers.

Hildick-Smith's appeal contended that he had not committed any crime because the regulations were *ultra vires* the 1911 Act. His argument was a familiar one, deriving from the *Kruse v Johnson* principle. The regulations were partial and unequal, and thus could be a valid exercise of governmental power only if their parent Act explicitly authorised such discrimination.

The three-man court unanimously accepted Hildick-Smith's argument. Tindall J.[102] followed De Villiers J.P.'s reasoning in *Williams & Adendorff*. The

[98] Cited in Dugard (1978), n. 4 above, p. 230. The 'coloured blood' jibe was probably directed against the various De Villiers who sat on the bench, whose ancestors were widely assumed to have procreated across the colour lines.

[99] Potter, n. 51 above, p. 43–44.

[100] See pp. 140–141 above.

[101] [1924] TPD 69.

[102] Ben Tindall, born in the Cape in 1879, was the son of a clergyman. He took a BA at Victoria College (later Stellenbosch University) and entered the civil service. He subsequently took an LLB at

government had no inherent power to discriminate among classes of citizens, and no such power had been granted by the 1911 Act. Morice J. concurred with this reasoning.

Krause J.'s opinion is perhaps the most interesting, if only because he was uniquely placed to know just what had been intended by the 1911 regulations. He had then been the Chairman of the Mining Regulations Commission, and had produced the first draft of the regulations which Smuts subsequently adopted.[103]

Krause J. followed Tindall J. in concluding that the Act did not expressly authorise racial discrimination. He then went on to consider if the regulations could plausibly be construed as a measure intended to uphold health and safety in the mines. If so, they would be within the power conferred by the statute. There could be no doubt for example that the regulations could prohibit 'unskilful, ignorant or drunken' people from performing jobs which if poorly performed could jeopardise their own safety and that of other workers.

Racial classifications were however more problematic. Krause J. acknowledged his acceptance of the belief that "Generally speaking it can be admitted that coloured persons especially natives have not yet reached the same stage of civilisation as white or European persons".[104] However, he could see no rational basis for assuming that *all* non-white workers were necessarily so backward in their education and industrial aptitude that they could not be trusted to perform skilled jobs in the mines with perfect safety. The regulations imposed a general prohibition premised solely on colour. As such, they were "capricious and arbitrary"; their use for such purposes "could never have been contemplated by the Legislature".[105]

It seems quite reasonable to assume that the first Union parliament did indeed contemplate such results. The court was *de facto* obstructing the legislature's wishes. The decision was nevertheless readily defensible *de jure*. Legislation did not emerge from parliament into a legal vacuum. Rather it emerged into a complex and elaborate legal environment in which its meaning fell to be determined by existing common law rules unless the Act itself disapplied such rules to its interpretation. The *Kruse* principle was firmly established as a matter of English and South African common law. The legislature could thus validly be assumed to have been aware of its effect.

The *Hildick* judgment nevertheless reinforces the confusion that pervaded the approach taken by South African common law towards government-sponsored race segregation. The confusion was compounded by the Appellate Division's judgment in *Dadoo Ltd v Krugersdorp Municipal Council*.[106] Mr Tsewu's right

Stellenbosch, and took up a position as Rose-Innes' private secretary. He began a practice at the Pretoria bar in 1903, taking silk in 1919 and being appointed to the Transvaal bench by the Smuts government in 1923.

103 Simons and Simons, n. 36 above, pp. 330–302.

104 [1924] TPD 69 at 83.

105 *Ibid.* at 90.

106 [1920] AD 530. On the background to the case see Joshi, n. 87 above, pp. 96–100.

at common law to own land in the Transvaal could have been extinguished at any time by legislation. The Transvaal Volksraad had 'passed'[107] a *wet* in 1885 which forbade 'Asiatics' from owning land in designated areas.[108] Some Asians had tried to circumvent the ban by forming companies which then purchased land in the areas concerned. The local land registry refused to register the purchase. Its decision was approved by the trial court. The Appellate Division upheld Dadoo's appeal. Invoking a strictly literal rule of construction, Innes C.J. concluded that the legislation reached only to people and not to companies, even if companies possesed a legal personality for most purposes. More broadly, he noted that any legislation which interfered with 'elementary rights' (which included the purchase, occupancy and sale of land) should be construed as narrowly as possible.[109] Both *Hildick Smith* and *Dadoo* would seem readily reconcilable with *Williams*, but quite inconsistent with the ethos promulgated in cases such as *Swarts, Parrot* and *Moller*. The cases were an embarassment to the Smuts government, but one which could simply be remedied by persuading parliament to enact new statutes explicitly confirming the legality of the industrial colour bar and prohibiting Asian-owned companies purchasing land in the Transvaal. But these were steps that the SAP government did not have the time to take.

The 1924 general election

The 'Rand rebellion' was cynically and successfully exploited by Hertzog's Nationalists. They were able to present Smuts as the enemy of the white working class, be it anglo or boer, and the friend both of the Chamber of Mines and the growing black urban proletariat. Hertzog then arranged an electoral pact with the Labour Party to ensure the anti-Smuts vote was not split.

The Nationalists also intimated that they were prepared to treat Coloured South Africans as the equals of whites in terms of their political and economic rights: the industrial colour bar would be lifted and the Cape franchise extended throughout the country.[110] Abdurahman and the APO leadership were not convinced of Hertzog's sincerity. Abdurahman himself had previously described Hertzog as "the narrowest, most virulent and most offensive of all the enemies of the Black races".[111] He did not regard Hertzog's overtures in 1924 as a reason

[107] The word is used guardedly in the light of the cavalier approach to law-making adopted by the Volksraad at this time. See the discussion of *Brown v Leyds* at pp. 45–47 above.

[108] Mr Tsewu was of course a native black, and so not caught by this ordinance.

[109] For further discussion see Dugard (1978), n. 4 above, pp. 308–310.

[110] The episode is treated in some depth in Lewis, n. 11 above, pp. 122–131. Davenport (1978), n. 3 above, pp. 196–197: Hertzog seemed (initially) sincere in this policy. In a speech in his constituency he argued that the coloured South African "has his origin and existence in our midst. He knows no other civilisation than that of the white man. However often he may fall short of it, his outlook is essentially that of the whites and not that of the natives, and his mother tongue is that of the white man": quoted in Pirow, n. 42 above, p. 128.

[111] Quoted in Lewis, n. 11 above, p. 125.

to change this view. The Nationalists were nevertheless able to exploit divisions in the Coloured community, and the promises were sufficient to win Hertzog the electoral support of a significant number of Coloured voters. Hertzog had also aired suggestions that his government would relax the industrial colour bar for blacks. Both the ANC and the ICU were sufficiently credulous about his *bona fides* to urge black Cape voters to support National Party candidates.

Nowithstanding the trenchant opposition of virtually every English language newspaper to the Nationalist/Labour pact,[112] Hertzog's tactics proved a success. The Nationalists won sixty-three seats in the house, the Labour Party eighteen. In coalition, they had a workable majority over the fifty-two MPs representing the SAP. In part, the Nationalists' success was a result of Smuts' electoral system manoeuvrings in 1907 and 1909.[113] The fifteen per cent plus or minus loading of the franchise permitted by the South African constitution had been exercised in favour of rural constituencies. This was manifestly to the benefit of the SAP when its main opposition was the anglo-leaning and urban-centred Progressive or Unionist parties. But it worked markedly to the SAP's disadvantage once it had absorbed the Progressives and found its dominance threatened primarily by an extremist Afrikaaner opposition. In the 1924 election, the SAP won substantially more votes than the Nationalists. But its seats were won by huge majorities in urban seats, while the Nationalists were successful by far smaller majorities in rural areas. Hertzog became Prime Minister and he appointed D.F. Malan, then the most extreme champion of a boer-dominated vision of Afrikaanerdom, to be Minister for Internal Affairs, for Education, and for Public Health. Tielman Roos became Minister of Justice. N.C. Havenga served as Minister of Finance.[114] Creswell, only two years after being arrested during the Rand Revolt, was appointed Minister of Defence. F.W. Beyers, Hertzog and Malan's companion at Versailles, became Minister of Mines.[115]

The new government wasted no time in inviting parliament to enact legislation giving both practical and symbolic effect to this shift in the balance of power both within the white population of South Africa, and between the white and non-white peoples.

[112] Mervis, n. 43 above, pp. 150–151.

[113] See pp. 81–83 and 108–110 above.

[114] Havenga was born in 1882 in the Orange Free State. His parents suffered straitened economic circumstances, and although Havenga had been an able student at school he could not afford to continue his education at university. Havenga had been Hertzog's private secretary during the boer war, and was wounded in action on several occasions. After the war he had qualified as a lawyer, and ran a successful legal practice in the Free State. He retained his close association with Hertzog, and initially won political office for the SAP as a member of the Free State provincial council in 1910. He followed Hertzog out of the SAP in 1912, and won the house seat of Fauriesmith in the Free State at the 1915 election. In his early parliamentary career, Havenga focused primarily on defence issues, but then became the party's chief spokesman on financial and budgetary matters.

[115] The full cabinet is listed in Pirow, n. 42 above, pp. 98–99.

Political 'independence'

Much of D.F. Malan's energy in the first two years of the government was spent on designing a new South African flag. The episode prompted furious controversy between the boer and anglo-white communities, both within and outside parliament.[116] The National Party saw a new flag as a symbolic affirmation of South Africa's *de facto* independence from Britain. For the SAP, and the English language press, it was an assault both on the unity of the Empire and the political status of anglo whites. Passions eventually cooled sufficiently for a design acceptable to both factions to be adopted.[117]

Hertzog's efforts to win both British and international recognition for the 'independence' betokened by the new flag also proved successful. At the Imperial Conference in London in 1926, the Prime Ministers of Britain, Australia, New Zealand, Canada, Newfoundland and South Africa publicly announced their support for a formal clarification of the political relationship between their countries. The 'Balfour Declaration' provided that:

> "Great Britain and the self-governing dominions are autonomous communities of equal status, united by the common bond of the Crown. They stand no subordination to one another in a national or international affairs, but are freely associated as members of the British Commonwealth of nations".

Smuts had been developing the notion of an Imperial 'Commonwealth' for some years, and his ambitions were greatly assisted by the crucial role played by the 'white' colonies in the First World War.[118] Hertzog had however insisted on a rather more stringent notion of autonomy than Smuts envisaged. The final text of the Declaration was closely modelled on his own original proposal. The principle of imperial non-intervention in South Africa's internal affairs was already firmly established. What most concerned Hertzog in 1926 was the issue of autonomy in foreign policy. In particular he sought confirmation of the principle that British involvement in another European war would not automatically commit South Africa to enter the hostilities on the British side. It could, if it wished, remain neutral. Hertzog saw no reason for South Africa to declare war simply because Britain had done so. It would take that step only if South Africa's interests demanded it. And South Africa's interests were not necessarily coterminous with those of Britain.

Internal affairs

Hertzog's government also recognised the significance of symbolic reform on purely domestic questions. One of the new government's first objectives was to

[116] Mervis offers a detailed account of the government's public and behind the scenes manoeuvrings over the issue; n. 43 above, pp. 155–168.
[117] Davenport (1978), n. 3 above, pp. 201–202.
[118] See Hancock (1968), n. 89 above, pp. 42–46.

promote legislation amending the constitution to extend the definition of Dutch as South Africa's second official language to include Afrikaans.[119] The legislation, which per section 152 of the constitution required a two-thirds majority in joint session, was enacted unanimously. The cultural struggle launched almost fifty years earlier by S.J. du Toit, and subsequently continued by his son, had at last borne constitutional fruit.[120]

Hertzog was not however a boer supremacist in any crude sense. His concern was to secure equal political status, but separate social and political norms, for the anglo and boer communities. Hertzog saw himself as an 'Afrikaner' rather than a boer or 'Afrikaaner'. He assumed boers instinctively shared that characteristic, but was ready to embrace English speakers as South Africans as long as they accepted both that South African and British interests did not invariably coincide and that South African interests should predominate whenever the two were incompatible. D.F. Malan represented a more extreme ideology,[121] favouring a South African polity in which Afrikaanerdom was accessible only to boers and in which anglo-whites would occupy a distinctly secondary status. In the mid–1920s, however, Malan represented only a minority view within the cabinet.

The new government was, of course, not concerned solely with symbols: nor simply with relations within the white population. The extension of Botha and Smuts' discriminatory policy against blacks had both practical and symbolic effects. It enhanced the economic status of both boer and anglo-whites, and did so in a way which stressed to both white communities that they had a common interest in the continued subordination of the native black population.

Hertzog's administration moved promptly to reverse *Hildick-Smith*. The Mines and Works Act 1926 explicitly authorised an industrial colour bar, a policy which the ANC and ICU might justly have felt was inconsistent with the position Hertzog had adopted prior to the election when he was seeking native black votes in the Cape. The bill was forcefully opposed by the SAP—somewhat ironically (perhaps hypocritically) given that it was seeking to enact a policy that Smuts himself had designed. More significantly, it was rejected by the senate, and was ultimately passed through the joint sitting procedure specifed in section 63 of the constitution.[122] In contrast to its treatment of blacks, the Act met some of the promises made to the APO: coloured workers were bracketed with whites as far as this sector of the economy was concerned.[123] Hertzog confirmed his hostility to black workers by sacking his Minister of Labour, the Labour MP

[119] Pirow, n. 42 above, p. 126.

[120] See p. 34 above.

[121] That one can find oneself (by implication) regarding Hertzog as a 'moderate' (in comparison with D.F. Malan) is testimony perhaps to the truth that, in politics at least, one is faced only with relative rather than absolute values.

[122] See p. 110 above.

[123] L. Marquand, *The Story of South Africa* (London: Faber and Faber, 1955), pp. 224–226; Simons and Simons, n. 36 above, pp. 339–342.

Walter Madeley, simply for receiving an ICU delegation which wished to protest about the 1926 Act.[124]

The government also took prompt steps to reduce the chances of his government's policies again being obstructed in the senate. Sections 24 and 25 of the South Africa Act had substantively entrenched the composition of the senate for ten years after 1909.[125] Thereafter its size, and the way in which its members were chosen, was open to amendment by bicameral, simple majority legislation. Smuts had convened a Speaker's Conference in 1920 to discuss potential changes to the senate, but no bipartisan agreement had been reached. At the very end of the 1926 parliamentary session, Hertzog's government introduced a bill intended to increase the likelihood that a party with a house majority could also command a majority in the senate. The South Africa Act had initially provided that the eight senators appointed by the Governor-General would hold office for ten years. Elected senators, in contrast, lost their seats whenever parliament was dissolved. The new bill proposed that appointed senators would now vacate their seats whenever parliament was dissolved or whenever a new government took office. A new Prime Minister could thus be sure that no opposition senators occupied appointed senate seats.

The change was relatively modest, and in principle was as beneficial (in the long run) to the SAP as to the Nationalists. Smuts nonetheless opposed the measure. He was fiercely critical of the government's decision to timetable the bill for the last few days of the session, and equally dismayed that so significant a constitutional matter should be pursued on the basis of anything other than cross-party agreement.[126] If any Nationalist MPs shared these sentiments, they did not reveal them in their votes. The bill was carried by fifty-nine votes to thirty-six at second reading, and became law by the end of the year.

The Immorality Act 1927 imposed a colour bar of a rather more intimate sort than the one introduced under the Mines and Works Act. Pre- and extra-marital sexual relations between 'Europeans' and native blacks were to be a criminal offence throughout the Union. Men who contravened the Act could be gaoled for up to five years. For women, the maximum sentence was four years. The Act also imposed similar penalties on an owner or occupier of premises who knowingly allowed such sexual activities to take place on his/her property.

The Native Administration Act 1927 was a measure of extraordinary scope. In effect, it granted the Governor-General (in practice Hertzog, who appointed himself Minister of Native Affairs) full legislative powers over all scheduled

[124] Pirow, n. 42 above, p. 129. Madeley was later to engineer a split in the Labour party, taking several of its MPs into a new party which aligned itself with the SAP. In a nicely ironic course of action, Hertzog dismissed Madeley—who initially refused to leave office—by offering the Governor-General the resignation of the government as a whole and then re-forming his cabinet without Madeley in it; H. Hahlo and E. Kahn (1960) *South Africa: the Development of Its Laws and Constitution* p. 131 (Cape Town: Juta & Co.). This was of course the device Botha had used to sack Hertzog in 1912; see p. 143 above.

[125] See p. 122 above.

[126] See his speech in HAD, 24 May 1926, c.3933 *et seq.*

areas.[127] It also designated him the 'Paramount Chief' of all black Africans, and empowered him to appoint and dismiss chiefs and to order tribes and individual blacks to relocate from one area to another. Section 29(1) of the Act also created a broad criminal offence:

> "Any person who utters any words or does any other act or thing whatever with intent to promote any feeling of hostility between Natives and Europeans . . . shall be liable on conviction to imprisonment for a period not exceeding a year or to a fine of one hundred pounds".

The legislation also empowered the Governor-General to appoint a Commissioner to investigate the legal status of land held by native South Africans. Occupants who refused to furnish the Commissioner with documents pertaining to their land's legal status committed a criminal offence under section 8(4). The Governor-General was authorised by section 7 to issue proclamations transforming the legal status of any land leased by blacks, replacing the original tenure with a grant 'in such form and subject to such conditions as the Governor-General may . . . prescribe'. The power was sufficiently widely cast to enable the Governor-General to attach occupancy and succession provisions to the grant which would control the racial identity of the occupiers of a given piece of land—in effect the power enabled the government to engage in a protracted process of individuated, piecemeal residential segregation. This part of the Act clearly signalled that the Hertzog government would not allow non-white citizens' long-standing expectations as to their land rights to obstruct a segregationist land use policy.

The 1927 Act was enacted by a bare parliamentary majority with the house and senate sitting separately. The measure was not seen as implicating the voting rights safeguarded by section 35 of the constitution. The broader sweep of Hertzog's race policies had implications for the Cape franchise, which Hertzog accepted would require unicameral two-thirds majority approval per section 35(1). Hertzog did not appear to accept however that the South Africa Act did not permit parliament under any circumstances to disenfranchise *existing* black voters on racial grounds. The text of section 35(2) seemed to state with perfect clarity that their rights were substantively and permanently entrenched. But the government evidently assumed notwithstanding the text of the constitution, that a two-thirds majority would serve as well for these purposes as it would for disenfrancising *prospective* black voters.[128]

The government introduced a package of four bills in 1926. The Representation of Natives bill was intended to remove native blacks in the Cape from the common electoral roll and introduce instead seven additional house members

[127] Cf. A. Milner, 'Apartheid and the South African Courts' (1961) *Current Legal Problems* 280: "[The Act] conferred upon the Governor-General powers of legislation so wide as to verge on the total surrender by Parliament of its normal legislative functions".

[128] Smuts, notwithstanding his ambiguous attitude towards entrenched voting rights in 1909 (see p. 127 above) did recognise this point in 1926: Hancock (1968), n. 89 above, pp. 212–214.

who would be elected by blacks in all four provinces. This discrimination was to be 'balanced' by the Native Lands bill, which would increase the amount of land allocated to scheduled areas under the Land Act 1913, and by the Union Native Council Bill, which would strengthen the Native Conference set up under Smuts' Native Affairs Act 1920.[129] The fourth bill proposed that Coloured voters in the three northern provinces should initially be placed on a separate electoral roll and be entitled to return one MP to the house. In the longer term, the bill envisaged the extension of the Cape coloured franchise throughout the Union.

The SAP opposed the package, on the ostensibly perverse grounds that it would grant blacks too much political influence and too little land. Hertzog's own back-benchers, encouraged by Tielman Roos, were less than enthused by the proposals, especially the extension of coloured voting rights. Abdurahman and the APO were trenchant in their opposition, describing the bills as "one of the biggest frauds which any party had tried to palm off on the Coloured people".[130]

Such political pressure as native blacks might have deployed was much weakened by factionalism and conservatism among their leading figures.[131] The ANC campaigned against the planned policies, regarding them as an irreversible confirmation of blacks' political inferiority. Its tactics remained wholly 'constitutional' in style, being limited to sending deputations to the government and petitioning MPs. Even such passive resistance measures as had been used by Gandhi were regarded as inappropriate by the ANC leadership. Kadalie's ICU, riven by corruption allegations, split into several parts in the mid-late 1920s, none of which could command sufficient numbers of workers to act as a powerful influence. The South African communist party had by this time begun to accept Lenin's thesis that the overthrow of capitalism in Africa would first demand the creation of majority black rule, but as yet the party's influence among black workers remained limited.

The Native Representation bill was the only measure requiring a two-thirds majority in parliament, and thus the only one dependent on SAP support. However, having failed to win that support, Hertzog declined to proceed with the other three measures, regarding their desirability as contingent on black disenfranchisement in the Cape. They were thus withdrawn, and the government turned its attention to less complicated matters.[132]

The 1929 general election

The 1929 election was fought on essentially racial grounds. Tielman Roos had set the stage with several vehement speeches outlining a draconian extension of

[129] *Ibid.*
[130] Quoted in Lewis, n. 11 above, p. 140.
[131] Davenport, n. 3 above, pp. 208–212; Rich (1996), n. 84 above, pp. 41–51.
[132] Davenport (1978), n. 3 above, pp. 205–208.

the segregation policy. The National party also made considerable capital out of a speech made by Smuts at the same time. Smuts had spoken of his vision of a greater South African federation, stretching as far north as Uganda and Kenya. Smuts' vision was no doubt of a federation under effective white control, but his ideas were successfully presented by the Nationalists as a plan to ensure white subordination to a black majority.[133]

The campaign continued in a similar vein. Hertzog's 'black terror' strategy paid handsome dividends. While the SAP increased its representation from fifty-two to sixty-one seats, the Nationalists moved from having sixty-three to seventy-eight members in the house. With the support of several Labour members, Hertzog had retained a more than adequate majority. His grand plans for re-orienting South Africa's racial policies appeared temporarily stalled by the need to attain a two-thirds majority for the black disenfranchisement legislation. He thus turned his attention to other matters.

The government's Riotous Assemblies bill was enacted in 1930. The Act was essentially a race relations measure. It empowered the Minister of Justice to prevent any person entering any area if the Minister thought the person's presence there could provoke hostility between white and non-whites. The Act precluded any appeal to the courts against the Minister's decision, a provision which indicated that the judiciary was proving rather too 'independent' for the government's liking.[134]

The franchise question was not however forgotten. The second Hertzog government managed to reduce appreciably the voting power of the Cape's non-whites by two indirect means. Its first measure was a bill which would extend the right to vote to all white women, enacted in 1930. This Act doubled the size of the white electorate, while leaving the size of the non-white voting population unchanged. The Franchise Laws Amendment Act 1931 then removed all property and educational franchise qualifications for white males, but retained them for the Cape's non-whites.

The combined effect of these innovations was to reduce the 'value' of the Cape's colour-blind franchise by more than half. Barely five per cent of the Cape electorate was Coloured in 1932, compared to twelve per cent in 1930. The fall was exacerbated by the Electoral Laws Amendment Act 1931, which permitted anyone to challenge a registered voter's entitlement to vote. The Act placed the burden of proof to prove entitlement on the voter concerned, and prompted strenuous efforts by some National Party activists to have Coloured voters de-registered.[135]

By 1932, it was thus much less likely that non-white voters would swing marginal constituencies in the Cape from the Nationalists to the SAP or vice versa. There was no serious suggestion that this dilution of the Cape's non-white vote amounted to a 'disqualification' within the meaning of section 35 of

[133] Hancock (1968), n. 89 above, pp. 216–219.
[134] See Dugard (1978), n. 4 above, pp. 137–138.
[135] Lewis, n. 11 above, pp. 144–145.

the constitution,[136] a consequence which would have required the 1930 and 1931 Acts to be passed by the 'two thirds majority in joint sitting' procedure. The letter, if not the spirit of the original constitutional settlement appeared to have been observed.

The Act could nevertheless be seen as a governmental attempt to stack the electoral odds in its favour. There was also some indication that the National party was as concerned to minimise the possibility of inconvenient judicial decisions as of inexpedient electoral outcomes. The second Hertzog government attracted criticism from the South African bar for its apparent readiness to pack the Appellate Division with its own ministers. Both Tielman Roos and F.W. Beyers were appointed to the court in 1929. Neither had any judicial experience.[137] In addition, Hertzog's boyhood friend, Jacob De Villiers,[138] was promoted to Chief Justice in the same year. Tielman-Roos' elevation to the bench was due at least in part to Hertzog's wish to appoint one of his proteges, a young barrister named Oswald Pirow, to the Cabinet as Minister of Justice. Pirow was an ardent white supremacist, who had unsuccessfully fought Smuts' seat at the general election. Hertzog circumvented this inconvenience[139] by appointing Pirow to one of the senate seats reserved for whites who were 'thoroughly acquainted with the reasonable wants and wishes' of the non-white races. Pirow may have been acquainted with those wants, but undoubtedly had no intention of acting as their champion.[140]

The independence (or otherwise) of the Appellate Division from the government and parliament was an issue of obvious theoretical concern to the bar and legal academics in South Africa. But it was soon to become evident that the issue was also of great practical significance to the allocation of constitutional authority. Within a year of the 1929 election, the Appellate Division decided *R v Ndobe*,[141] the first of the five great cases which would settle the legal status of section 35 of the constitution.

R v Ndobe (1930)

Mr Ndobe was a black Cape resident who leased several plots of land in Kingwilliamstown. The value of the land was sufficient to qualify him to exercise the Cape's parliamentary franchise. Mr Ndobe was concerned that the Governor-General would use section 7 of the Native Administration Act 1927 to issue proclamations altering the status of his land in a way that deprived him of his franchise qualification, and/or which might prevent him passing the land

[136] See pp. 122–123 above.

[137] Pirow, n. 42 above, pp. 139–140.

[138] See p. 145 n. 59 above.

[139] As noted in Chapter 4, the South Africa Act required cabinet members to have a seat in one of the houses of parliament; see p. 111 n. 36 above.

[140] A. Paton *Hofmeyr* (Cape Town: OUP, 1965), pp. 119–121.

[141] (1930) AD 484. For further discussion see Corder (1984), n. 11 above, pp. 152–154.

to his sons, with the result that they too would be disenfranchised. Mr Ndobe refused to co-operate with the Commissioner's investigation into his land, and was subsequently prosecuted and convicted under section 8.

Ndobe had been working closely with D.T. Jabavu, the son of J.T. Jabavu and by then one of the leading figures in native black politics. His refusal was a part of a deliberate test case strategy, which Jabavu hoped would eventually culminate in a Privy Council judgment against the government.[142] Mr Ndobe's defence was that the 1927 Act was wholly unconstitutional and thus of no legal effect. His argument essentially reiterated the Appellate Division's holding in *Thompson v Kama*.[143] The Act appeared to give the Governor-General a direct power to alter the legal status of land in the Cape owned or occupied by non-whites. As such it gave him the indirect power to remove the right to vote from certain non-white tenants and landowners. Consequently the Act should be construed as a racially discriminatory franchise reform measure, which could be enacted only through the section 35 'two thirds majority in joint sitting' formula.

Mr Ndobe's conviction had been upheld in the Eastern Districts Local Division. His appeal was heard by a four-man Appellate Division, comprising De Villiers C.J.,[144] Wessells J.A., Curlewis J.A., and Roos J.A.[145] The Court delivered a unanimous opinion, authored by the Chief Justice, dismissing Mr Ndobe's appeal.

Mr Ndobe persuaded the Court to reiterate the *Thomson v Kama* principle. Legislation which affected the Cape franchise as a result of a racial classification had to be passed via section 35 even if its impact on the franchise was merely an incidental side effect of its dominant purpose. However he failed to convince the Court that the 1927 Act had any effect on the Cape franchise. De Villiers C.J. could not discern any provision in the Act that had such consequences. He accepted that the Governor-General's power under section 7 might be thought sufficiently widely drafted to have such an effect, but such reasoning was flawed. The Governor-General could not be granted by ordinary legislation powers which parliament itself did not possess. If the Governor-General issued a proclamation which altered the legal status of landholdings in a way that hindered or reduced non-white citizens' right to vote, the proclamation would be *ultra vires* the constitution: parliament could only bestow such powers through the section 35 procedure. No such proclamation had yet been issued however, and the

[142] Rich (1996), n. 84 above, pp. 68–69.

[143] (1917) AD 209. See pp. 148–149 above.

[144] This being Jacob De Villiers, not Lord De Villiers. See p. 145 and n. 59 above.

[145] Wessells J.A. had sat in *George*, and Curlewis in *Williams*; see pp. 145–147 above. Roos had been the driving force behind the National Party in the Transvaal in 1912; see p. 143 above. His relations with Hertzog had subsequently soured. Hertzog had appointed him as Minister of Justice in his 1924 Cabinet, but he resigned on the somewhat suspect of grounds of ill-health. He was succeeded by one of his proteges, Oswald Pirow, who repaid the debt by appointing Roos to the Appellate Division in 1929; see O. Pirow, *James Barry Munick Hertzog* (Cape Town: Howard Timmins, 1946), ch. 12.

Court was not prepared to invalidate the entire Act on the basis that such a measure might at some unspecified future time be introduced. The criminal sanctions imposed on Mr Ndobe under section 8 were thus perfectly valid.

In the final paragraphs of the judgment, De Villiers C.J. made a point of potentially wider significance. Counsel for the government had argued that even if section 35 did apply to this issue, the satisfaction of the 'two thirds majority in joint session' formula was a matter solely for the houses of parliament themselves. He maintained that the Supreme Court had no jurisdiction to determine if the entrenching requirements had been followed, but must instead assume that any Act had been passed in accordance with the requisite procedures.

The argument would have been a familiar one to British constitutional lawyers if applied to the two Houses of the British Parliament. British courts have consistently accepted that they have no authority to examine the internal proceedings of each House to assure themselves that an Act was indeed passed by a majority of votes.[146] Control over their internal proceedings has been accepted to be part of the Commons' and Lords' respective 'privileges' ever since the 1688 revolution, and the principle is given statutory endorsement in Article 9 of the Bill of Rights.

In *Ndobe*, the Appellate Division suggested that the British analogy had limited applicability to South Africa. De Villiers C.J. accepted that the two houses of parliament were empowered by section 58 of the constitution to devise their own rules to regulate their internal procedures. These were not rules with which the court was competent to interfere. To that extent, the relationship between the houses of South Africa's parliament and the South African courts mirrored that between the House of Commons and House of Lords and the judiciary in Britain. However, he firmly rejected the contention that the 'two thirds majority in joint session' procedure had a similarly non-justiciable status. This was not a matter relating to the houses' internal arrangements, but rather a *constraint* on parliament's law-making capacity.[147] As such, the constitution demanded that the courts ensure that its requirements had been met. If a piece of legislation touched upon one of the subjects safeguarded by the entrenched provisions of the constitution, "the Court would have to assume that the clause was ultra vires in the absence of some indication in the Act or proof *aliunde* that such clause was passed as contemplated in the [entrenching] section".[148]

De Villiers C.J. also stressed—in a clear refutation of the position the government had adopted over its 1926 franchise reform bill—that the Court would act in defence both of the substantively and procedurally entrenched aspects of

[146] See for example *Wauchope v Edinburgh and Dalkeith Railways* (1842) 8 Cl & F 710; *Pickin v British Rail Engineering* [1974] AC 65. I have discussed the issue at some length in I. Loveland, *Constitutional Law* (London: Butterworths, 1996), ch. 8.

[147] De Villiers' reasoning assumed that s. 35 represented an exception to parliament's normal law-making identity, rather than indicating that the South Africa Act had created two parliaments; see pp. 492–493 of the judgment. Curiously, the headnote to the case adopted the latter analysis. As will become evident at a later stage, the distinction is not simply a matter of semantics.

[148] (1930) AD 484 at 497.

section 35. While, per section 35(1) of the South Africa Act, a two-thirds majority of parliament sitting in joint session would suffice to remove future voters from the Cape's electoral role because of their race, section 35(2):

> "goes even further, and safeguards the rights of persons who at the passing of the new law are registered as voters in any province. The names of such persons cannot be removed from the register at all, on the ground of race or colour, neither by parliament as usually constituted nor as constituted under s.35(1)".

The court's opinion seems readily defensible on several counts. As suggested in Chapter 4, the text of the South Africa Act on these points is quite unambiguous. The judgment also strongly echoes the reasoning offered by Kotze J. in *Brown v Leyds*:[149] the constitution was a superior source of legal authority to the legislature; the legislature's powers were therefore constrained by limits articulated in the constitution; and it fell to the courts to determine if those limits had been breached. Jacob De Villiers C.J. may have been Hertzog's lifelong friend, but this manifestly did not mean that he allowed his own view of the constitution to be tempered by opinions which the cabinet might find politically expedient.

Reinforcing the entrenchment thesis: *Trethowan v Attorney-General for New South Wales*

The Appellate Division's reasoning in *Ndobe* was given substantial support by closely contemporaneous decisions of the Australian High Court and the Privy Council on a matter of Australian constitutional law in the case of *Trethowan v Attorney General for New South Wales*.[150] Like the South African parliament, the New South Wales legislature was created by a British statute; in this case 'The Constitution Statute 1855'. The Constitution Statute provided that the New South Wales legislature was in many respects a carbon copy of the Westminster parliament. Legislation required the support of a simple majority in an upper house (the Legislative Council) and lower house (the Legislative Assembly), and the royal assent provided by the Governor-General qua the monarch's representative. The Act was modified by section 5 of the Colonial Laws Validity Act 1865,[151] which provided that statutes enacted by all colonial legislatures (including the New South Wales Parliament) which sought to alter their own "constitution, powers or procedures" would have legal effect only if passed "in such manner or form" as the law then in force in the colony demanded. The terms of section 5 were left unchanged when a new Constitution Act was passed by the New South Wales Legislature in 1902. The 1902 Act, *inter alia*, made provisions concerning the composition and respective powers of the two houses.

149 See pp. 44–47 above.
150 [1932] AC 526.
151 See pp. 18–19 above.

In 1929, New South Wales' Liberal Party government promoted the Constitution (Legislative Council Amendment) Bill 1929. The Bill was passed by both houses, received the royal assent, and thus became an Act. The Act introduced a new section 7(A) into the Constitution Act 1902. This provided that a bill seeking to abolish the Legislative Council could not be sent for the royal assent unless it had been approved by a majority of both houses *and* by a majority of the electorate in a referendum. Section 7(A) therefore seemed to change the 'manner and form' of the legislation needed to abolish the Upper Chamber, by adding an additional step to the usual legislative process. Furthermore, section 7A(6) provided that section 7A itself could not be repealed unless the repealing legislation had also been approved by a majority of electors in a special referendum. The Act was intended to entrench the existence of the Legislative Council by protecting it against abolition by narrow legislative majorities.

After the New South Wales elections of 1930, the previous opposition party secured a majority in both houses. Both houses then approved bills respectively repealing section 7A and abolishing the Legislative Council. No referendum was held. Several members of the Legislative Council immediately began an action before the New South Wales courts requesting an injunction to prevent the bills being sent to the Governor-General and so stop the bills becoming legislation. Their argument, quite simply, was that section 7A could be repealed only in the 'manner and form' which it had itself specified.

The new government argued that successive New South Wales Parliaments, just like the British Parliament, could not be bound by any legislation passed by their predecessors. A Parliament might pass any 'manner and form' provisions it thought fit, but they would cease to have effect when a future Parliament, acting by the 'simple majority in both houses plus royal assent formula', passed legislation to repeal them, whether the repeal was explicit or merely implied. This was precisely what had happened in this case.

In the High Court of Australia,[152] two of the five judges accepted that argument. However the majority considered that the court was bound to prevent any bill dealing with the subject matter of section 7A being sent for the royal assent unless it had been approved in a referendum. The special 'manner and form' of section 7A did provide an effective form of procedural entrenchment. The majority reasoned that, unlike the British Parliament, the New South Wales legislature owed its existence to a clearly visible British statute, the Colonial Laws Validity Act 1865. New South Wales had adopted that Act as the basis of its constitution, and until section 5 of the 1865 Act was itself repealed, the New South Wales legislature was subject to its terms. The majority saw this as a straightforward *legal* rule, which, Rich J. explained, served an obvious political purpose:

[152] [1931] 44 CLR 394.

> "There is no reason why a Parliament representing the people should be powerless to determine whether the constitutional salvation of the State is to be reached by cautious and well considered steps rather than by rash and ill considered measures".[153]

On a further appeal to the Privy Council,[154] the majority opinion, and the reasoning underlying it, was upheld unanimously.

It seems unlikely that Hertzog would have required such extra-territorial judicial support for the proposition that the entrenched clauses of the South African constitution remained an effective constraint on parliament's power to pass Acts by the bicameral simple majority procedure. Hertzog's own record as a judge, his opinion about *Brown v Leyds*, his views at the Convention on the judiciary's 'testing' power, and his readiness to seek two-thirds majorities for the Afrikaans language legislation and the Cape African franchise amendment bills in 1926 all suggest that he was not initially prepared to dispute the legitimacy of the entrenchment provisions. In contrast, the argument advanced by the government in *Ndobe* to the effect that the provisions were simply a matter of the two houses' privileges, rather than a mechanism defining the identity of parliament itself, indicate that he was at least prepared to explore ways to evade the spirit of section 35 by 1930. While the government had won *Ndobe* on the facts, the Court's judgment made it quite clear that the Cape's colour-blind franchise continued to enjoy significant protection as a matter of South African *constitutional* law. The judgment merely underlined the point that Innes C.J. had made in *Thompson v Kama*. Hertzog would presumbly not have been surprised by this. Rather more unexpected perhaps, would have been a series of judicial decisions which advanced propositions of South African *common* law to obstruct racially discriminatory government activities in the Transvaal.

Asiatic traders in the Transvaal[155]

The change of political direction signified by Hertzog's victory in the 1924 election was enthusiastically embraced at a provincial as well as parliamentary level. The Transvaal government's hostility towards its Indian residents—a hostility which had brought Gandhi into direct conflict with Smuts prior to Union—had intensifed rather than diminished by this time. In 1926, the Transvaal provincial council introduced the General Dealers (Control) Ordinance. The ordinance required all traders to be licensed by their local

[153] [1931] 44 CLR 394 at 420.

[154] Which then served as the ultimate court of appeal for most colonial courts.

[155] I am much indebted to two articles by W.H.B. Dean, formerly Professor of Public Law at the University of Cape Town, which alerted me to the existence of these cases: 'Reason and Prejudice: the Courts and Licencing Bodies in the Transvaal', in E. Kahn (ed.), *Fiat Iustititia: Essays in Memory of Oliver Denys Schreiner* (Cape Town: Juba & Co, 1983); 'Our Administrative Law: a Dismal Science' (1986) 2 *South African Journal of Human Rights* 164.

municipal council. The ordinance was intended to enable councils to refuse to grant licences to Indians, whereupon—it was assumed—the Indians would leave the province.[156] However, this motive was not made explicit in the text of the ordinance. Rather the provincial council specified various criteria which local authorities had to apply when exercising their discretion. These included such amorphous concepts as the 'character of the business' and 'the manner in which the surrounding area was occupied', tests which seemingly lent themselves to racially motivated refusals. The ordinance would thus seem to have been designed to remove the principle upheld by Innes C.J. in *Hajee Habib*. The ordinance also provided (in section 10) that a refusal of a new application was not to be subject to scrutiny by any court. Limited rights of appeal were given in respect of refusals to renew existing licences, and the local authority had to offer reasons for its refusal.

The town of Potchefstroom, whose university and theological college had long been the intellectual heart of the most rigidly segregationist boer ideology,[157] was one of the first councils to try to take advantage of the new ordinance. Its political leaders were to be somewhat taken aback when a Mr Bignaar, an Indian trader whose licence renewal application was refused, challenged the council's decision before the Transvaal division of the Supreme Court. Mr Bignaar had not been permitted to argue his case for renewal before the council, nor been furnished with any reasons for the refusal. In *Bignaar v Municipal Council of Rustenberg*[158] he sought an order quashing the refusal on the ground of 'gross [procedural] irregularity'.[159]

Greenberg J. had little difficulty in concluding that the council's procedures were unlawful. Orthodox English administrative law principles, which were accepted to be part of South African common law, demanded that citizens in Mr Bignaar's position be granted a meaningful hearing before a public body could lawfully revoke such a licence or permission. The more pressing question was whether section 10 of the ordinance, which purported to exclude the court's inherent power of review over council decisions, was effective. If so, Mr Bignaar's 'success' on the procedural irregularity point would be illusory, as the court would have no power to quash the refusal.

Greenberg J. saw no room for argument that a provincial council had any competence to alter the jurisdiction of a provincial division of the Supreme Court. That jurisdiction was defined by sections 95–98 of the constitution. Parliament could alter the Supreme Court's jurisdiction through its general amending powers under section 152;[160] this was a necessary consequence of its unlimited substantive sovereignty over internal South African affairs. Provincial governments were however bodies enjoying only those few, specific powers that

156 See Joshi, n. 106 above, esp. pp. 113, 119, and 138.

157 See A. Norval *Deconstructing Apartheid Discourse* (London: Verso, 1996), pp. 67–68.

158 [1927] TPD 615.

159 Per Greenberg J., *ibid.* at 617.

160 See pp. 107–108 above.

the constitution had granted them. They could have no implied authority to regulate the jurisdiction of even a provincial division of the Supreme Court.[161]

The *Bignaar* judgment was not cast in terms of judicial defiance or disapproval of racial discrimination *per se*. Rather it appealed to the notionally more 'objective' concepts of the rule of law and (precisely echoing Innes C.J.'s reasoning in *Hajee Habib*), the need to ensure that provincial councils and local authorities did not exceed the limits of the powers that parliament had granted them. There is an obvious irony here, in that it is certain that Hertzog's majority in the national legislature would have warmly approved of the Transvaal provincial council's initiative. But the courts could quite legitimately maintain that such approval had no legal significance until it had been expressed in appropriate legislation.

Some judges also took the view that the ordinance as drafted did not enable local authorities to invoke an applicant's racial identity as a substantive reason for refusing a licence. This point was succinctly put by (again by Greenberg J.) in *Nanabhay v Municipal Council of Johannesburg*: "the mere fact that the applicant is an Asiatic cannot affect the question".[162] More significantly, and perhaps more surprisingly, Greenberg J. then continued by holding that in the absence of persuasive and relevant evidence to justify the refusal, the court would assume that the council was motivated by racial bias. The fact that this bias might reflect the wishes of local electors could not render the council's decision lawful:

> "No doubt the Committee was acting in what it considered to be the best interests of the locality in an endeavour to prevent commercial penetration by Asiatics as a class but this object cannot be attained under the provisions of the ordinance".[163]

Greenberg's judgment seemed to be tacitly endorsing the argument based on *Kruse v Johnson* made unsuccessfully by W.P. Schreiner in *Moller*.[164] Racial identity was to be construed as a 'class' for administrative law purposes. It was a factor which a government body could take into account only if explicitly authorised to do so by the legislation in question.

The subsequent judgment of Tindall J. in *Patel v Witbank Town Council*[165] also suggested that the Transvaal Supreme Court would not permit local authorities to conceal racially motivated decisions behind reasons which were ostensibly linked to the refusal critieria specified in the ordinance. Mr Patel's licence had been refused on the grounds that his shop, which had operated for many years, caused a traffic hazard because of its location. Tindall J. quashed

[161] See also *Moola v Potchefstroom Municpality* (1927) TPD 615.

[162] (1928) WLD 153 at 158.

[163] *Ibid.* at 158.

[164] See pp. 134–139 above.

[165] (1931) TPD 477. Tindall had acted as counsel for the local authority in *George v Pretoria*; see p. 146 above. One might wonder if that experience had offered him an insider perspective into Witbank's intention in this case.

the refusal on the grounds that it was 'unreasonable' or 'irrational', insofar as there was no plausible evidence to support the council's decision:

> "The road is nearly 36 feet wide . . . There are no buildings opposite. It is not in a thickly populated or busy area . . . The building had been standing there for five years [and] . . . there is no suggestion that any accident occurred . . . The ground of refusal seems to me so fantastic that it suggests that the committee was searching for every plausible reason to fortify its refusal of the certificate".[166]

Greenberg J.'s judgment in *Nanabhay* and Tindall J.'s decision in *Patel* are significant in as much as they indicate that some judges accepted that South African *common law* contained an inherent intolerance of some types of racially discriminatory behaviour.[167] As such, they reinforce the point made earlier in respect of the Transvaal tram cases as to the South African courts' consistent inconsistency when faced with such questions. But their force as principles of *constitutional law* should not be exaggerated. Neither case suggested that the Transvaal provincial council was in some sense constitutionally incapable of discriminating against Indian traders. Both cases seemed to present the council with a navigable rather than insuperable obstacle. The 'solution' adopted precisely echoed the outcome of the trams litigation.

The judicial obstruction was apparently successfully overcome by an amended ordinance, passed in 1932. The new ordinance removed all the criteria which local authorities had previously been instructed to consider in deciding whether to refuse a licence. It also removed the authorities' duty to offer any reasons for the decisions they reached.

The plaintiff in *Jooma v Lydenburg Rural Licensing Board*[168] was an Asiatic trader whose application for a renewal of his licence was refused. He was not given any reasons for the refusal. His challenge to the decision rested on two grounds: first that the lack of reasons created an inference that the refusal was motivated by racial bias, a consideration not explicity referred to in the ordinance; secondly, that the provincial council had no power to grant municipal councils so broadly cast a discretion.

Tindall J. was again the presiding judge. On this occasion, however, his judgment favoured the council rather than the applicant. The Provincial Council's decision to remove the requirement that reasons be given for a licence refusal significantly curbed the court's capacity to question a council's behaviour. The initial ordinance required that some reasons be given for refusal. Because the reasons given in *Patel* were 'fantastic', they created the inference that the council's refusal had really been controlled by illegitimate, racially motivated considerations. Since the revised ordinance removed the duty to give any reasons at all for refusal, there was nothing (fantastic or otherwise) to trigger judicial suspicion about the council's *bona fides*. Nor would the court accept that either the

166 *Ibid*. at 290.

167 See Dean (1983) and (1986), n. 155 above.

168 (1933) TPD 477.

constitution or South African common law placed an *implied* duty to give reasons on government bodies making such decisions.

Nor could Tindall J. see any legal force in Mr Jooma's second contention. There was no constitutional impediment to a provincial council granting a municipality such loosely regulated discretionary powers. In reaching this conclusion, Tindall J. restated (much like Innes C.J. in *Swarts* and *Moller*) the classic Anglo-American tradition concerning the distinction between the legality of government action, which the courts would control, and its desirability, with which courts could not interfere:

> "The wisdom of giving an unlimited power of refusal to officials or a body of persons is . . . a question of policy with which the court is not concerned. Parliament placed the control of the granting of the authority for the issue of such licences completely in the hands of the Provincial Council".[169]

This short line of cases offers useful insight into both the potential and the limitations of administrative law as an autonomous 'colour blind' force within the South African legal and political system. Before drawing any conclusions on that point however, some attention should be paid to the decision of the Appellate Division in the 1933 case of *Minister of Posts and Telegraphs v Rasool*.[170]

Minister of Posts and Telegraphs v Rasool

As noted in earlier sections of this chapter, while there was some judicial authority for the proposition that racial classifications were unacceptable as a matter of common law, that common law presumption could be overridden by express legislative authorisation of the segregation concerned. There was also some authority supporting the argument that separation of the races, even on grounds of substantive 'equality' in respect of the segregated service, amounted to unlawful discrimination in the *Kruse v Johnson* sense. Both principles frustrated governmental attempts to extend the reach of discriminatory practice, if only because they demanded that either the national parliament or provincial legislature engage in the potentially time-consuming and transparent process of giving such practices explicit approval. The decision of the Appellate Division in *Rasool* suggested that those judicially created obstacles would in future prove rather less difficult to surmount.[171]

The background to the case

The legal structure of the South African Post Office had been established in one of the first Acts passed by the Union Parliament in 1911. The Act empowered the Postmaster-General, a government Minister, to 'establish, maintain and abolish

[169] (1933) TPD 477 at 483.
[170] (1933) AD 167.
[171] Dugard (1978), n. 4 above, pp. 313–316.

post offices and to supervise and control their services'. Under section 3(2), the Postmaster-General could 'issue such instructions as he may deem necessary for the conduct and guidance of officers in carrying out the provisons of the Act'. The Hertzog government took the view that this power was sufficiently broad to enable it to impose a system of segregation on the country's post offices without the need to introduce new legislation. Post offices in the Transvaal already divided native blacks from all other races; blacks had to seek service in a separate area labelled 'Native Post Office'. In December 1931, Hertzog's Postmaster-General issued an instruction under section 3(2) ordering all post offices throughout the country to divide their service facilities into 'Europeans only' and 'Non-Europeans'. Rasool was an ethnic Indian living in Pietersburg who took offence at the prospect of having to share facilities with blacks rather than whites and coloureds.[172] He argued that the instruction was *ultra vires* the Act, because it discriminated against a class of citizens in a sense forbidden by the rule in *Kruse v Johnson*.

At first instance in the Transvaal provincial division, Tindall J. delivered an opinion for a unanimous court in Rasool's favour. Tindall followed *Williams* in concluding that mere separation of the races was *per se* unreasonable in the *Kruse* sense, even if the service offered was 'equal'.[173] As in *Patel*, Tindall J. held that such discrimination had to be explicitly authorised by the relevant legislation. No such authorisation was contained in the 1911 Act. His opinion was forcefully disapproved in the Appellate Division.

The majority opinion

Acting Chief Justice Stratford[174] accepted that the *Kruse* principle controlled the case before the court. However he rejected Tindall J.'s conclusion that 'separate but equal' facilities were unreasonable per *Kruse*. He doubted that *Williams* really supported that proposition. But if it did so, it was wrongly decided and should be overruled. *Kruse* would prohibit only distinctions between citizens which were "absurd or designed to serve no useful purpose, as for example a classification depending on the colour of one's hair".[175] A racial classification, in contrast:

> "seems prima facie to be sensible and make for the convenience and comfort of the public as a whole, since appropriate officials conversant with the customs, requirements and languages of each section will conceivably serve the respective sections".[176]

[172] The action is perhaps another illustration of the lack of concerted action by non-white citizens against discriminatory government behaviour.

[173] Rasool had conceded that the facilities were indeed equal for the purposes of this action.

[174] Stratford was born in 1869. He read law at Oxford, and returned to practice in South Africa, becoming a Q.C. in 1912. The Smuts government appointed him to the Transvaal Supreme Court in 1921. He was evidently not seen as a 'Smuts man', since Tielman Roos (Minister of Justice in the first Hertzog cabinet) appointed him to the Appellate Division in 1927. He was evidently an undistinguished jurist, but nonetheless became Chief Justice in 1938. He died in 1952.

[175] (1933) AD 167 at 175.

[176] *Ibid.*

De Villiers J.A.[177] echoed the acting Chief Justice's sentiments. Discrimination coupled with equality of service was not unreasonable *per se*. The classification was apparently no different from one which would require people whose surname began with the letters A–M to be served at a different counter from those whose names began with N–Z.[178]

Gardiner J.'s dissent

Such reasoning did not commend itself to Gardiner A.J.A.[179] In a forceful dissent, he argued that the instruction was unlawful not simply because it was unreasonable at common law, but also because it amounted to a ministerial usurpation of a power which the constitution reserved either to the Governor-General in Council or to Parliament itself.

Gardiner A.J.A. began with the strident assertion that it was a fundamental principle of South African common law that "in the eyes of the law all men are equal".[180] That principle was violated by governmental action which adopted racial classifications, irrespective of whether the separated services were of equal standard. In an ingenious argument, Gardiner A.J.A. reasoned that the raft of national and provincial legislation (much of it promoted by the Hertzog government) which did indeed authorise such discrimination supported rather than undermined his conclusion: the Acts indicated that equality was a common law presumption that had to be displaced by explicit legislative approval of unequal treatment.[181] The principle applied as readily to blacks and to coloureds as to Asiatics.

Gardiner A.J.A. argued that separation was unlawful because it was 'humiliating', insofar as it gave a governmental seal of approval to the social fact that many 'Europeans' regarded non-whites as 'being of a lower order of civilisation' than themselves.[182] The common law could not accommodate such

[177] Jean Etienne De Villiers (1875–1947). He studied law at Cambridge and became a fellow of St Johns College. The Smuts government appointed him Judge-President of the Free State in 1920. He was elevated to the Appellate Division in 1933, an appointment which no doubt defused criticism that the Nationalists were attempting to pack the court with their own ministers; see p. 165 above.

[178] With admirable understatement, Dugard describes this analogy as "particularly inappropriate. . . . for all distinctions of this kind are arbitrary, and it is just as 'logical' to distinguish between people by the colour of their eyes as it is by the colour of their skins or by the initial letter of their names"; (1978), n. 4 above, p. 315.

[179] Frederick Gardiner was born in London in 1874, the son of an Irish father and Austrian mother. The family emigrated to South Africa in 1878. Gardiner took a BA at the University of the Cape of Good Hope, and then studied law at Keble College, Oxford. He was admitted to the bar in London and the Cape, where he joined the SAP and practiced until 1910, when he was appointed Attorney-General of the Cape Province. In 1914, Smuts appointed him to the Cape bench, where he served as Judge-President from 1926. He served as an acting judge in the Appellate Division, but never became a full member. Gardiner also developed a substantial academic reputation as the author of a leading text on criminal law and procedure.

[180] (1933) AD 167 at 185.

[181] Krause J. had offered a similar line of argument in *Hildick-Smith*.

[182] (1933) AD 167 at 190. This is precisely the reasoning adopted by Harlan J. in *Plessey*, although Gardiner A.J.A. did not refer to the case.

prejudice. This was the conclusion reached in *Williams*, and that case was correctly decided.

Having disagreed with the majority on the broad requirements of the common law and the narrow ratio of *Williams*, Gardiner A.J.A. then took issue with his colleagues' interpretation of the facts. He was especially unimpressed by Stratford A.C.J.'s suggestion that the instruction would 'make for the convenience and comfort of the public as a whole':

> "There is only one attendant at the non-European counter at Pietersburg. It is most unlikely that he would know both a Bantu dialect and also some language of India. But if such a linguist is in attendance at Pietersburg, it is impossible to believe that a person equally gifted will be found at each of the hundreds of other post offices throughout the Union".[183]

Gardiner A.J.A. then moved his argument to an issue of constitutional rather than common law. He observed that section 147 of the constitution provided that: "The control and administration of . . . matters specially or differentially affecting Asiatics throughout the Union shall vest in the Governor-General in Council".[184] Since the Postmaster-General's instruction was such a measure, he did not have the authority to issue it.[185]

III. CONCLUSION

Notwithstanding suggestions that the Hertzog government had tried to pack the Appellate Division bench, the inconstancy and inconsistency of the South African courts when faced with questions concerning racial equality indicated that the South African judiciary and South African common law had retained an independence of sorts—not just from the government but also from parliament. But by the time *Rasool* was decided, the issue of 'independence' had become associated rather more with the nature of the relationship between South Africa and Britain than with the relationship between the various branches of the South African government.

By enacting the Statute of Westminster 1931, the British Parliament had given formal legal effect to the Balfour Declaration. Australia, Canada, New Zealand and South Africa were explicitly recognised as independent nations. While George V was still to be their king, their constitutional arrangements would no longer be subject to *external* oversight—even as a matter of legal theory—by the Westminster Parliament. That point was, it seemed, quite beyond dispute.

[183] *Ibid.* at 190.

[184] See p. 112 above.

[185] For further discussion see Corder (1984), n. 11 above, pp. 144–147. Corder characterises the majority opinion as "a classic example of the Appellate Division giving judicial sanction to the race prejudices of the whites . . . a retreat from the principle of the equality of all citizens before the [common] law": *ibid.* at 147.

Quite what effect this grant of freedom from external British control would have on South Africa's *internal* constitutional arrangements was, in contrast, a matter on which political, academic and judicial opinion appeared to be divided.

6

Disenfranchising the African

It had been evident to all the participants at the 1926 Imperial Conference that the legal theory and political reality of Commonwealth relations bore little resemblance to each other. As a matter of legal theory, the constitutions of all the Dominions were the creation of the United Kingdom Parliament. As such, they could at any time be amended or even abolished by United Kingdom legislation. As a matter of practical politics, the Dominions were independent nations. As such, any attempt by the United Kingdom Parliament unilaterally to interfere with a Dominion's internal constitutional arrangements would have been ignored by the Dominion concerned and in all probability triggered a secession from the Commonwealth and a *de jure* declaration of independence.[1]

Steps were thus taken at the 1926 Imperial Conference to commission an inquiry into how best to reform the legal relationship between the United Kingdom and the Dominions in order accurately to reflect their *de facto* equal political status. A report was brought forward for consideration by the Imperial Conference of 1930.[2] Its recommendations were subsequently accepted in broad terms by the legislatures of the Dominions,[3] and were then enacted by the United Kingdom Parliament in the Statute of Westminster 1931.

I. THE TERMS OF INDEPENDENCE: THE STATUTE OF WESTMINSTER 1931

The preamble to the Act announced that it was passed "for the ratifying, confirming and establishing of certain of the declarations and resolutions" made at the 1926 and 1930 Imperial Conferences. The statute is very short, comprising only twelve sections and filling barely three pages of text.

[1] See Godfrey Phillips, 'The Dominions and the United Kingdom' (1929) 3 *Cambridge LJ* 164; C. Jenks, 'The Imperial Conference and the Constitution' (1929) 3 *Cambridge LJ* 13; W. Kennedy, 'The Imperial Conferences, 1926–1930. The Statute of Westminster'(1938) 48 *LQR* 191. Kennedy was particularly scathing of analysts who propounded the view that legal theory retained any significance in this field: "There is something childish in pronouncements which are known to every beginner in constitutional law—and the knowledge is barren apart from the social forces which condition the worth and value of the law. If our history has any lessons, it proves that law is a dangerous master, and that legal obscurantists, when let loose on the delicate world of imperial experience, can do more harm than many bulls in many china shops": *ibid.* at 194. Kennedy was then a professor at the University of Toronto law school, and a leading authority on Canadian constitutional law.

[2] See D. Judd and P. Slinn, *The Evolution of the Modern Commonwealth 1902–1980* (London: Macmillan, 1982), J. Marriot, *The Evolution of the British Empire and Commonwealth* (London: Nicholson and Watson, 1939), pp. 300–305.

[3] These being Canada, Newfoundland, Australia, New Zealand, South Africa and the Irish Free State.

Section 2 of the Act declared that British and Dominion courts were no longer required to refuse to apply Dominion law (be it common law, legislation or a constitutional provision) simply because its terms were inconsistent with British legislation. This end was to be achieved through the ostensibly simple device of repealing the Colonial Laws Validity Act 1865:

> "2(1) The Colonial Laws Validity Act 1865 shall not apply to any law made after the commencement of this Act by the Parliament of a Dominion.
>
> (2) No law . . . made after the commencement of this Act by the Parliament of a Dominion shall be void or inoperative on the ground that it is repugnant to . . . the provisions of any existing or future Act of Parliament of the United Kingdom . . . and the powers of a Dominion Parliament shall include the power to repeal or amend any such Act, order, rule or regulation in so far as the same is part of the law of the Dominion".

Section 3 of the Act then confirmed that the Dominions would in future have the power to make laws which had extra-territorial effect, while section 4 provided that:

> "No Act of Parliament of the United Kingdom passed after the commencement of this Act shall extend, or be deemed to extend, to a Dominion as part of the law of that Dominion unless it is expressly declared in that Act that that Dominion has requested and consented to the enactment thereof".

As a matter of British constitutional *law*, section 4 had little significance. Its purported effect was to bind Parliament in future to use a specific form of words if it wished to enact particular types of legislation. Orthodox legal opinion at that time held that Parliament had no power to restrain its future exercise of legislative power in this way. If it wished to pass legislation in contravention of section 4 it would undoubtedly have the power to do so. Such a statute would have legal force within the United Kingdom, insofar as domestic courts would be bound to apply it. Its force within the Dominion concerned, however, would be a rather different matter.

Section 4—and indeed the Statute of Westminster in its entirety—is more appropriately seen as an exercise in constitutional politics or practice, as a symbolic affirmation of an existing practical reality, namely that the Dominions were now capable of acting as independent states in respect both of their internal affairs and their international relations. The courts and legislatures of the Dominions would certainly have disregarded British legislation purportedly applicable to Dominion territory which had not been requested and consented to by the Dominion itself, even in the unlikely event that the United Kingdom Parliament should ever pass such an Act.[4] They would presumably have

[4] See for example the judgment of Lord Sankey in *British Coal Corporation v The King* [1935] AC 500 at 520: "It is doubtless true that the power of the Imperial Parliament to pass on its own initiative any legislation that it thought fit extending to [a Dominion] remains in theory unimpaired: indeed, the Imperial Parliament could as a matter of abstract law, repeal or disregard s.4 of the Statute. But that is [legal] theory and has no relation to [political] realities".

regarded statutes enacted in accordance with section 4 as domestic rather than United Kingdom law. In effect, the United Kingdom would function in these circumstances as an additional part of the Dominion's own legislature.[5]

This role for the United Kingdom Parliament was of particular significance in respect of Canada and Australia—whose constitutions had initially been organised on a federal basis—and New Zealand. Section 7 of the Act explicitly preserved the provisions of the British North America Acts which required the Westminster Parliament to assent to any legislation passed by Canada's national legislature which re-allocated powers between the federal and provincial levels of government. This provision essentially confirmed that the United Kingdom Parliament would serve as an entrenching device on such matters for the Canadian people.

Sections 8–9 of the Act also made an explicit reference to the continued vitality of the various entrenching provisions in the Australian and New Zealand constitutions prior to the statute's enactment. It could not therefore be assumed that the national legislatures of either country had in some way been imbued with legislative powers analogous to those of the United Kingdom Parliament, namely to amend or repeal any law by the simple majority process.

In contrast, the Act did not expressly preserve the entrenched provisions of the South Africa Act. Equally, however, it did not expressly repeal them. Moreover, the Imperial Conference of 1930 had accepted that there was no need for such provisions to be made in respect of South Africa, since that country's national legislature already enjoyed (unlike its counterparts in Australia, Canada and New Zealand) complete control over its internal constitutional arrangements. That the Union parliament was in a small number of cases required to act by a two-thirds unicameral rather than simple bicameral majority did not detract from the fact that it possessed sovereign legal authority within South Africa's borders.[6] This was a curious—indeed quite erroneous—conclusion for the Conference to have reached. While the Conference recognised the binding nature of the procedurally entrenched provisions, it ignored the permanent, substantive entrenchment in respect of existing voting rights in section 35(2) of the South Africa Act.[7] South Africa's parliament was not competent—irrespective of the form in which it acted—to amend or repeal that particular political value. The Conference's opinion was apparently irreconcilable with the Appellate Division's contemporaneous conclusion on this point in

[5] Godfrey Phillips offered traditionalists a comforting form of words with which to reconcile the divergent demands of legal theory and political practice: "The Imperial Conference of 1930 did not propose to abolish the legal supremacy of the Imperial Parliament, but it did propose changes in the law which. . .will render it inoperative. In law the Imperial Parliament cannot abolish its own supremacy, but by convention it can restrict the power to exercise it to a vanishing point": 'The Dominions and the United Kingdom' (1929) 3 *Cambridge LJ* 164 at 166.

[6] *Report of the Conference on Dominion Legislation and Merchant Shipping Legislation 1929* (Cmnd. 3479) para. 67; subject, of course, at that time, to the provisions of the Colonial Laws Validity Act 1865. The inference would be that after the passage of the 1931 Act South African 'sovereignty' would lie in its parliament as that body had been defined by the South Africa Act 1909.

[7] See p. 125 above.

Ndobe, and offered a potentially useful tool for politicians who might subsequently wish to contend that *Ndobe* was wrongly decided.

The impact of independence on the entrenched clauses

It nonetheless seemed likely that that the legal effect which British and South African courts would subsequently attach to the Act might depend more on its text than on the legislative history and professions of political intent surrounding it. Within the British constitutional tradition, rules of statutory interpretation had been a matter for the courts to determine. Three interpretive techniques, respectively referred to as the 'literal rule', the 'golden rule', and the 'mischief rule' had been recognised as legitimate.

The literal rule was the most widely used of these. The technique suggests that the court's duty is simply to attach the orthodox, grammatical meaning to the text of an Act. It should do this even if it is thereby led to produce an unjust or absurd result.[8] The potential harshness of the literal rule was on occasion avoided by use of the so-called 'golden rule'. This rule suggests that when a literal reading of a section of an Act would produce a bizarre result, the court should consider the Act as a whole to see if another, more sensible meaning might be attached to the section in the light of the legislative context in which it appears. The third technique, the 'mischief rule', permits a court to cast its interpretive net beyond the mere text of a statute. The rule's nature and purpose is perhaps best expressed in a quotation from the 1584 judgment in *Heydon's Case*:

> "(1)What was the law before the Act? (2) What was the mischief and effect for which the law did not provide? (3) What remedy the Parliament hath resolved and appointed to cure the disease of the commonwealth, and (4) The true reason of the remedy".[9]

Several commentators had suggested in the early 1930s that the Statute of Westminster was a distinctly atypical piece of legislation, which would in itself justify judicial resort to the proceedings of the Imperial Conferences in order to ascertain its meaning. It should, in other words, be interpreted according to the precepts of the mischief rule rather than the literal or golden rules.[10] Whether a court would accept that invitation remained to be seen; as did the nature of the 'mischief' that a court might assume the Act was intended to remedy.

A more radical contention would have been that the Act should not really be seen as an 'Act' at all. It should be seen rather as a source of 'fundamental' law or constituent legal principle for the newly independent former Dominions. As

[8] Cf. Lord Esher in *R v Judge of the City of London Court*;

"If the words of the Act are clear, you must follow them, even though they lead to a manifest absurdity. The court has nothing to do with the question of whether the legislature has committed an absurdity": [1892] 1 QB 273 at 290.

[9] (1584) 3 Co. Rep. 7a at 7b.

[10] See Kennedy, n. 1 above; Jennings (1936), n. 54 below.

such, its interpretation should be as much an exercise in defining political morality as searching for legal meaning. This essentially 'revolutionary' approach to the Act did not seem to find any favour with contemporary commentators. The text appeared to be the primary concern.

Much of that concern centred on the absence in the Act of any explicit textual reference to the entrenched provisions of the South Africa Act. This omission prompted some speculation in both political and academic circles as to their continued efficacy.[11] The so-called 'saving clauses' preserving the entrenched provisions of the Canadian, Australian and New Zealand constitutions had been inserted into the Act at the request of the governments of those Dominions. Hertzog had made no such request in respect of the the entrenched sections of the South Africa Act. He had indeed expressed opposition to any such formula appearing in the legislation. Yet this did not ostensibly appear to be because he anticipated that these provisions would be repealed.

As noted in Chapter 5, Hertzog had proceeded with his native franchise reforms on the assumption that their enactment demanded a two-thirds legislative majority. In 1931, Hertzog played a major part in prompting a joint resolution by the house and the senate cast in the following terms:

> "That on the understanding that the proposed legislation will in no way derogate from the entrenched provisions of the South Africa Act Parliament, having taken cognizance of the draft clauses and recitals which it was proposed by the Imperial Conference of 1930 should be embodied in legislation to be introduced in the Parliament at Westminster approves thereof and authorises the Government to take such steps as may be necessary with a view to the enactment by the Parliament of the United Kingdom of legislation on the lines set out in [clause 2 of the Statute of Westminster bill]".[12]

Smuts, who had initially regarded the entrenchment clauses as possessing only moral rather than legal force, now professed himself to be concerned that the effect of independence would be to remove the courts' power to enforce them.[13]

One Malanite backbencher, C.R. Swart, expressed an apparently widely-held view amongst his colleagues to the effect that even if Smuts' views were correct in the legal sense, there was no political likelihood of non-Europeans' voting rights being altered other than in accordance with the section 35 procedure:

> "We must watch that no rights be given up which we have today. Every portion of the population has clauses in the constitution to which it is attached . . . We feel that the entrenched clauses are a matter of good faith, and I cannot imagine that any Government would alter them by a bare majority".[14]

[11] See G. Marshall, *Parliamentary Sovereignty and the Commonwealth* (Oxford: Clarendon Press, 1957), ch. 6.

[12] Clause 2 of the bill was identical in form to s.2 of the Act.

[13] H. May, 3rd edn., *The South African Constitution* (Cape Town:Juta & Co, 1955), pp. 43–45.

[14] HAD, 22 April 1931, c.2757.

The British government maintained that the resolution was sufficient to confirm the continuing vitality of the entrenched clauses, and rejected suggestions that an explicit statutory confirmation of that point could be placed in the Act with the South African legislature's approval. A number of backbench MPs in the United Kingdom Parliament doubted the accuracy of that conclusion.[15] In their view, the absence of a 'saving clause' in respect of South Africa necessarily implied that the Union legislature would be able to repeal or amend sections 35, 137 and 152 of the South Africa Act by the simple majority, bicameral process.

Their *political* reason for fearing this consequence was obvious: namely that a Union parliament in which an extremist Afrikaaner party had gained a narrow majority would override the franchise rights of non-whites in the Cape and/or establish Afrikaans as the country's sole official language. But the *legal* reason for assuming the Act would have this effect is far more elusive.

There was no obvious basis for assuming that retention of the entrenched sections of the South African constitution would in any sense subordinate South Africa *as a country* to the Westminster parliament. South Africa would unquestionably be a sovereign state. Moreover, it would be—like the United Kingdom—a sovereign state with a sovereign parliament. Unlike the sovereign Parliament of the United Kingdom however, the sovereign parliament of South Africa would exist in *three different forms*.

The *first* parliament, which was competent to act on almost all issues, was indeed a replica of the British Parliament, and could legislate (according to sections 30 and 51)[16] through the 'simple majority plus royal assent' formula. The *second* parliament, for which there was no British analogy, was the unicameral legislature envisaged by section 63 of the consitution in the event of an irreconcilable conflict between the house and the senate. The *third* parliament, which was the only body capable of passing laws dealing with matters entrenched by the constitution, could act only by meeting in joint session and approving bills by a two-thirds majority. That the personnel of all three parliaments was the same was of no significance. Their constitutional identities derived from their respective *functions* rather than their *membership*.

Such an analysis would certainly have ploughed familiar constitutional ground to scholars of the American constitution. But the idea that 'parliament' in an independent state—whether it be South Africa or the United Kingdom—could mean anything other than the power to legislate on all subjects by simple bicameral majority was evidently an alien concept to several leading authorities on British and Commonwealth constitutional law. Sir Kenneth Wheare, Professor of Government and Public Administration at Oxford University, suggested that the repeal of the Colonial Laws Validity Act had indeed turned the South African legislature into a copy of the British parliament; it could now enact, amend or repeal any provision of South African law by the simple major-

[15] See especially the speeches of Marjoribanks and Hopkin-Morris on 20 November 1931.

[16] See pp. 107–108 above.

ity bicameral process.[17] One would have expected that such a viewpoint would have seemed quite ill-founded to South African observers acquainted with the constitutional traditions of the Orange Free State and the South African Republic. Yet this was apparently not the case.

The Pollak thesis

The fears voiced by some backbench MPs at Westminster over the absence of saving 'clauses' for sections 35, 137, and 152 were given a respectable academic gloss by Walter Pollak, a prominent young practicioner at the South African bar, in an article published in the 1931 *South African Law Journal*[18] shortly before enactment of the Statute of Westminster. Pollak argued that the legislation would indeed free the South African parliament from the constraints imposed by the enhanced majority procedures. His analysis would no doubt have been welcomed by Nationalist politicians for whom the assembling of a narrow legislative majority in favour of amending the Cape franchise was a more readily achievable prospect than gaining two-thirds support. Moreover, given the *South African Law Journal's* distinguished status in South African legal circles, Pollak's article was likely to be accorded appreciable weight both by politicians and the judiciary. It is therefore rather unfortunate that his critique made very little constitutional sense.

Pollak began with the ostensibly uncontroversial proposition that the South African parliament's legislative competence was defined by section 59 of the South Africa Act 1909: this power being "to make laws for the peace, order and good government of the Union". So much is uncontentious. But while Pollak identified the definition of parliament's 'power', he omitted to look for the definition of parliament itself. The obvious point that the South Africa Act created a parliament that existed in three forms evidently did not occur to him: the section 63 process 'parliament' was ignored entirely; while the entrenched provisions were portrayed as an aberrant departure from the simple majority bicameral norm rather than as an integral element of the South African constitutional settlement.[19]

Pollak then made the bizarre assertion that the currently binding status (per *Ndobe*) of the entrenched provisions was not imposed by the South Africa Act itself, but by the Colonial Laws Validity Act 1865. He then concluded:

> "Once repeal the Colonial Laws Validity Act and the Union Parliament can, it is submitted, validly repeal or alter any of the entrenched clauses of the South Africa Act without observing the requirements of section 152".[20]

[17] K. Wheare, *The Statute of Westminster* (Oxford: Clarendon Press, 1931), pp. 107–109.

[18] W. Pollak, 'The Legislative Competence of the Union Parliament' (1931) *South African Law Journal* 269.

[19] *Ibid.* His article made no reference to the constitutional traditions of the Free State or the Republic.

[20] *Ibid.* at 282. The argument is similar to that propounded by Wheare. As the following pages suggest, Wheare's argument was similarly ill-founded.

If his assertion was correct, then his conclusion would also have been irrefutable. But the assertion was quite inaccurate. Extraordinarily, Pollak did not explain *why* the 1865 Act was the source of the binding effect of the entrenched provisions: he simply made his 'submission' and decided it was irrebuttable. This was presumably because no plausible explanation could be found. This in turn seems to result from Pollak's misinterpretation of the relationship between the Colonial Laws Validity Act, colonial constitutions, and colonial legislation.

The Colonial Laws Validity Act had only one purpose. That purpose was to confirm to British and colonial courts that in the event of a conflict between colonial legislation and British legislation having effect in the colony concerned, they were to apply the British rather than the colonial statute. The Act had no immediate bearing on the constitutionality of a colony's internal law-making procedures, which would be determined by the relevant constituent Act of the British parliament. It is, admittedly, correct to assert that a colonial statute which breached the relevant constituent Act of the British Parliament would also breach the Colonial Laws Validity Act. However, the breach of the Colonial Laws Validity Act could not be established until the breach of the constituent Act had been proven. But as soon as the breach of the constituent Act had been proven, the *ultra vires* nature of the colonial Act would have been confirmed and no reference to the repugnancy provisions of the Colonial Laws Validity Act need arise.

Pollak evidently failed to appreciate the quite different constitutional functions served by the two Acts. The Colonial Laws Validity Act imposed a *variable, substantive* constraint on the competence of the Union parliament: it confirmed the subordinacy of South Africa *qua country* to the Westminster Parliament. The South Africa Act imposed a *rigid*, (and with the exception of section 35(2)) *procedural* constraint on its law-making capacity: it confirmed the subordinacy of the South African legislature qua simple bicameral majority to the South African constitution.

Nor did Pollak follow through the logic of his own argument. If sections 35, 137 and 152 were effective only because of the Colonial Laws Validity Act, then so too presumably was section 19, which defined 'parliament' as consisting of the house, the senate and the King. Why should not the 'parliament' of an independent South Africa consist solely of the house and the king, or the house and the senate? Section 63 would also presumably be in jeopardy. Why should a South African court respect an 'Act' passed by the joint procedure, especially since no such process was known to the British Parliament? And why indeed, should the requirements in sections 31 and 50 that the senate and house must each secure a majority of one to pass a bill have continued effect? Why could bills not be passed by minority votes in either or both chambers?[21]

[21] It is no answer to these questions to say that the scenarios could not arise because they would require a redefinition of 'parliament'. Pollak's thesis is in itself premised on a redefinition of 'parliament'. The point raised here is why the definition of 'parliament' relevant to the entrenched

The only magic political glue which could conceivably hold together the disparate fragments of Pollak's jurisprudentially shambolic argument was the assumption that the legislature of a former British colony simply *had* to be a carbon copy of the Westminster parliament unless the contrary was indicated in the British statute granting independence. But that was not an assumption which had any grounding in the text of the 1931 Act, in the deliberations of the Imperial Conferences, or in the constitutional history of the Cape, the Transvaal, the Free State or Natal.

Pollak had expressed regret at his conclusion, and urged Hertzog to ask the Westminster Parliament to enact the house and senate joint resolution in the proposed legislation. There is no reason to doubt Pollak's sincerity on this point. It nevertheless seems appropriate to assume that his analysis—riddled though it was with error and speculation—would offer a useful source of legitimation for South African politicians or judges who might wish in future to conclude that the entrenched provisions were no longer effective.

II. A WHITE CONSENSUS ON NATIVE POLICY? THE HERTZOG–SMUTS COALITION GOVERNMENT

Hertzog's triumph in securing South Africa's *de jure* and *de facto* independence from Britain was rapidly overshadowed, as were evidently esoteric debates as to the status of the entrenched clauses, by the onset of global economic depression. South Africa's economy was particularly badly hit, and the consequences of the depression were exacerbated by Hertzog and Havenga's determination to keep South Africa on the gold standard and by two years of drought.[22] Smuts expeditiously embraced rejection of the gold standard as a new political principle, seeing it as a powerful tool with which to dig away at the National Party's support in rural areas.[23] The party political picture was further complicated by Tielman Roos' decision to leave the Appellate Division and found a new party, which he proposed would form a coalition government with the SAP. Roos, rather than Smuts, would be Prime Minister.[24]

Roos' threat was sufficiently potent for Havenga to remove the country from the gold standard. But Roos' grander ambitions were thwarted by Smuts' decision to seek coalition terms with Hertzog to found a national unity government.[25] This reconciliation (*hereniging* as it was termed in Afrikaans) bore an

provisions should disappear consequent upon the passage of the Statute of Westminster while all the others would remain intact.

[22] T. Davenport, *South Africa: a Modern History*, 2nd edn. (Cambridge: CUP, 1978), pp. 212–213; L. Thompson, *A History of South Africa* (New Haven: Yale University Press, 1995), pp. 160–161.

[23] Hancock, *Smuts. Volume 2: Fields of Force 1919–1950* (Cambridge: CUP, 1968), pp. 242–246.

[24] *Ibid*. See also A. Paton, *Hofmeyr* (Cape Town: OUP, 1965), pp. 138–145.

[25] Roos subsequently tried to shore up his political popularity by founding a newspaper, the *Sunday Express*, in Johannesburg in 1934. Much like its owner, the paper flourished briefly before

obvious resemblance to the policy Botha and Smuts had pursued in 1910. It might have seemed unlikely that Hertzog, who had latterly spent much time both in public and in parliament attacking Smuts in vituperative terms, would embrace such a proposition. He seemed however to have accepted that the Nationalists would lose the next general election. A coalition government, within which he would remain Prime Minister, would both assign Smuts to a secondary role and safeguard the legislative programme the Nationalists had pursued since 1926. Agreement was reached for Hertzog to form a twelve-man cabinet, six from the Nationalists and six from the SAP.[26]

The echoes of events in the first years of Union grew stronger when Malan—now playing Hertzog's former role—expressed unease at the coalition arrangements and declined to serve in the cabinet. The electorate, in contrast, gave the initiative its overwhelming approval. The two parties agreed not to oppose each others' incumbent members in the 1933 general election. As a result, the coalition commanded 144 of the house of assembly's 150 seats.[27]

Smuts and Hertzog's minds thereafter turned from coalition government to a 'fusion' of their two parties. The greatest obstacle to combining the parties appeared not to be the race question—on which it seemed Smuts and Hertzog were finding more and more common ground—but on the issue of South Africa's relationship with the Commonwealth. The differences between the two men on this issue were—in theory at least—reconcilable. The Balfour Declaration, which Hertzog had claimed largely as his own handiwork, was in no substantial sense distinguishable from the principles Smuts had been advocating at the end of the First World War. The long term problem that they faced was what South Africa would do in the event of Britain becoming involved in another World War. In the early 1930s this seemed to be a sufficiently distant prospect for them to agree to differ on the correct answer to the question. The short term difficulties they faced were more a matter of practical politics.

A substantial faction within the SAP regarded Hertzog as a putative republican and secessionist, whose primary objective was to sever all of South Africa's ties with Britian and the Commonwealth. For Smuts to compromise with Hertzog on this matter would expose him to the risk of many SAP MPs refusing to join a merged party. On the other hand, a substantial faction within the Nationalists regarded Smuts as a stooge for British interests, whose primary objective was to embroil South Africa in a form of Imperial super-state. For Hertzog to compromise with Smuts on this matter would expose him to the risk of many Nationalist MPs refusing to join a merged party.

its threat to the existing market leaders was nullified; in 1939 the *Sunday Express* was taken over by the *Rand Daily Mail* group; J. Mervis, *The Fourth Estate* (Johannesburg: Jonathan Ball, 1989), pp. 199–204, 223.

[26] T. Moodie, *The Rise of Afrikanerdom* (London: University of California Press, pp. 121–130 details the ideological manuoevrings needed to permit the Nationalists and the SAP to present a united front.

[27] Malan and his followers, while not approving of the coalition, lacked the integrity to oppose it in the election. All existing Malanite MPs stood (unopposed) under the coalition banner.

In an effort to engineer a successful fusion of their parties, Smuts and Hertzog eventually decided to gloss over their intuitive disagreements over South Africa's role in a future world war. They also managed to agree on the broad objectives of 'native policy'. This policy would "without depriving the Native of his right of development . . . recognise as paramount the essentials of European civilization".[28]

The fusion proposals also accepted that the merged party would allow its members to follow their consciences in respect both of the native franchise, a Hertzog concession vital to secure the assent of the liberal wing of the SAP; and of South Africa's continued membership of the Commonwealth, a Smuts concession vital to secure the assent of the Malanite wing of the Nationalists.

A deferential judiciary?

The judgment in *Rasool* (notwithstanding Gardiner's dissent)[29] had indicated that the government need not anticipate much obstruction from the Appellate Division in its efforts to impose greater levels of racial segregation on South African society. This impression was reinforced by the Court's conclusion in *Sachs v Minister of Justice*,[30] a case decided late in 1933 when Stratford was again serving as Acting Chief Justice.

Solly Sachs was a radical white political activist and trade unionist, who had been issued by Pirow (the Minister of Justice) with an exclusion order under section 1 of the Riotous Assemblies Act 1914 banning him from entering several areas in the Transvaal, including Johannesburg and its environs.[31] In accordance with the scheme of the Act, Pirow did not grant Sachs any type of hearing before issuing the order. Sachs thereupon requested that the Minister give reasons for the decision, as was required by section 1(13). Pirow's reasons intimated that the government regarded Sachs as a communist agitator who was making strenuous efforts to ferment political unrest among the black population. Sachs denied ever having engaged in such activities, and insisted that section 1(13) required the Minister to furnish him with the evidence on which such reasons were based. Pirow refused to provide this information, on the grounds that to do so would be 'prejudicial to public policy'.

At trial, Sachs did not contend that the Minister was subject to a common law duty to hold a hearing at which Sachs might (either orally in writing) make representations prior to the issuing of the order. There was authority both in English and South African law to the effect that the common law imposed such an obligation upon government officals exercising powers which adversely

[28] Quoted in Hancock (1968), n. 23 above, p. 257.

[29] See pp. 176–177 above.

[30] The first instance and Appellate Division decisions are reported together at [1934] AD 11.

[31] A measure introduced by the Botha administration (see p. 142 above), and slightly amended at the instigation of the Hertzog government in 1930.

affected the rights of citizens (as section 1 undoubtedly did) if the statute granting the powers had not done so: in the words of Byles J. in *Cooper v Wandsworth Board of Works*, in such circumstances "the justice of the common law will supply the omission of the legislature".[32] However, rather than pursue an implicit common law right, Sachs premised his case on section 1(13), and contended that the Minister's duty to give reasons could not be satisfied unless the Minister revealed the information upon which his reasons were based.

Sachs' argument was rejected unanimously by a three-man court in the Transvaal provincial division.[33] His appeal was then unanimously dismissed in the Appellate Division, where judgment was given by Stratford A.C.J. After reviewing the facts, Stratford began his judgment by offering "a few general observations . . . upon the scope and nature of the enactment in question".[34] Stratford suggested that the Act was unusual:

> "There is no doubt that the Act gives the Minister a discretion of a wide and drastic kind, and one which, in its exercise, must necessarily make a serious inroad upon the ordinary liberty of the subject".[35]

Rather than seeing this as a reason for subjecting Ministerial action under the Act to strict scrutiny, Stratford suggested that the court was obliged to assume that parliament would have wished to minimise judicial interference with the implementation of the Minister's powers:

> "[The Act's] object is clear, it is to stop at the earliest possible stage the fomentation of feelings of hostility between the European and non-European sections of the community . . . [I]t will readily be seen that if the Minister's discretion is hampered by the obligation to submit his decision to the approval of a Court of law, the delay involved would defeat the whole object of the particular provision we are discussing".[36]

This expansive reading of parliament's intention led Stratford to conclude that the Minister was under no obligation to provide Sachs with the information on which the Minister has 'satisfied himself' that an exclusion order was appropriate. Nor, Stratford added, unnecessarily in the circumstances, did applicants in Sachs' position have a common law right to a hearing prior to the order being made. While such a right might be recognised as a general principle, it had been impliedly excluded by an Act such as this, which granted such wide powers concerning public safety to the Minister. This conclusion was reinforced by the presence of section 1(13). Stratford considered that a statutory requirement that the Minister explain his decision after it had been made necessarily implied that

[32] (1863) 14 CBNS 180. For further examples of English cases decide on this point by that time see *Board of Education v Rice* [1911] AC 179 and *Local Government Board v Arlidge* [1915] AC 120. In the South African context, see *de Verteuil v Kaggs* [1918] AC 557 and especially *Bignaar* (discussed at pp. 171–172 above) and the cases discussed therein.

[33] Tindall was one of the judges. He produced an opinion whose tone and substance was strongly reminiscent of his judgment in *Jooma*; see pp. 173–174 above.

[34] [1934] AD 11 at 36.

[35] *Ibid.* at 36.

[36] *Ibid.*

parliament had not intended any hearing to take place before the order was issued.[37]

The Status of the Union Act 1934

The *Sachs* judgment offered the coalition government a clear indication that its efforts to curb radical white political activity outside parliament could proceed largely unhindered by the prospect that the Appellate Division then saw itself as a staunch defender of individual liberties. In addition, the fused party offered, at least temporarily, the prospect of a parliament in which intra-white factionalism would be subordinated to the pursuit of the (white) national interest. This potential had been symbolically affirmed by the passage of the Status of the Union Act shortly before fusion took place.[38] The preamble to the Act announced that its purpose was to declare as a matter of South African law that South Africa was 'a sovereign independent state'.

Section 2 affirmed that "The Parliament of the Union shall be the sovereign legislative power in and over the Union". Section 4 confirmed that the King qua head of the Union's executive government was now legally rather than just conventionally bound to act upon the advice of his Ministers, while section 9 repealed the provision of the South Africa Act which required certain bills to be sent to the King for his assent in person rather than be approved on his behalf by the Governor-General.

The Act made no explicit reference to the entrenched clauses. However some members of the National party began to suggest that the passage of the Status Act did not simply confirm the unfettered sovereignty of South Africa as a nation, but also confirmed that its parliament now enjoyed unfettered sovereignty to pass any legislation (including issues covered by the entrenched clauses) by a simple bicameral majority vote. This was in essence the argument that Pollak had made concerning the Statute of Westminster, albeit one now rooted in South African rather than British constitutional soil. That the far right wing of the Nationalist party should desire such an outcome is understandable: the requirement of a two-thirds majority in a parliament which still contained a substantial number of SAP MPs committed to retaining the Cape's colour-blind franchise was an obvious impediment to such 'reform'. That it should conclude that the 1934 Act provided a legal tool with which to fashion that outcome is much less easy to comprehend.

The issue again turned on the meaning of 'parliament' in section 2. Was this parliament in the three part sense created by the constitution; or simply a replica of the Westminster legislature? The 1934 Act added nothing in legal terms to the debate surrounding the impact of the Statute of Westminster. If the 1931 Act had

[37] De Villiers, Beyers J.J.A. and Gardiner A.J.A. concurred.

[38] Moodie, n. 27 above, pp. 136–137.

indeed transformed South Africa's legislature into a copy of the United Kindom parliament, the legislature's mere declaration in 1934 of its bicameral, simple majority sovereignty just stated a fact which already existed. If, on the other hand, the Statute of Westminster had left South Africa with a three part parliament, the Status Act could not have altered this position. The 1934 Act was passed by the normal bicameral procedure. Thus, even if one accepted that sections 35, 137 and 152 could be impliedly repealed, that repeal could only be effected by parliament sitting in accordance with the section 152 provisions; i.e. by two-thirds unicameral majority.

In Hertzog's view, the 1934 Act had no impact on the validity of the entrenched clauses. He displayed no public sympathy for the argument that the Act offered a means to disenfranchise non-whites in the Cape by simple majority legislation. He condemned such whisperings among his own party in unequivocal terms: "the movement to reach solution of our native problem by such means deserves our disapproval in every respect. As for me, I must repudiate it absolutely".[39] Hertzog, it seemed, believed that *Ndobe* had been (at least in part)[40] a correct statement of the law prior to independence and continued to be so thereafter.

The Speaker of the house of assembly also expressed the view that the entrenched sections of the South Africa Act remained an effective part of South African constitutional law.[41] His opinion could have no significant legal effect, but would seem to be further cogent evidence that the majority of members of the 1934 parliament saw the Status Act as simply confirming that the impact of the Statute of Westminster was to have released South Africa's 1909 constitutional settlement from the control of the Westminster legislature: it was, *de facto* and *de jure*, a South African restatement of the Statute of Westminster.

While the passage of the Act had secured the fusion arrangements between Smuts and Hertzog, resulting in the formation of the 'United Party', Malan was unwilling to remain in a party which he considered to be betraying Afrikaaner interests. In December 1934 he and eighteen supporters considered the political situation sufficiently favourable to do what they had not done during the previous election: they left the National party and formed their own 'Purified National Party'.[42] Seven former SAP MPs (predominantly Natalians) had reacted to fusion by moving in the opposite direction and forming the Dominion Party: in their view Smuts had unacceptably compromised anglo interests.

[39] Quoted in Paton, n. 24 above, p. 158.

[40] It appears that Hertzog was still unwilling to acknowledge the distinction drawn in the constitution between existing and prospective voters.

[41] HAD 25 April 1934, c. 2736. See E. Kahn, 'Constitutional Law' (1951) *Annual Survey of South African Law* 1.

[42] Hancock (1968), n. 23 above, pp. 253–254: Davenport (1978), n. 22 above, pp. 224–230. The 'Purified Nationalist' label was coined by J.G. Strydom MP, who became a leading member of the new party both in the Transvaal and nationally; Moodie, n. 27 above, p. 138. The *Sunday Times*, highlighting resemblances between Malan's views and those of Hitler, rapidly gave the Purified Nationalists a less flattering name—the 'Malanazis'; Mervis, n. 25 above, p. 111.

This was perhaps an unnecessary step for them to have taken. Hertzog's subsequent denunciation of the Broederbond,[43] and of Malan's role within it, suggested that the Prime Minister was indeed sincere in his concern to reconcile anglo and Afrikaaner interests. Hertzog was particularly critical of the Broederbond's influence in schools, where he suggested children were being indoctrinated with propoganda aimed at undermining support for equal status between Afrikaaner and anglo-whites.[44] For Malan, the denunciation had a positive rather than negative effect, since it labelled him as the champion of 'Afrikaaner' interests and ideology. For the time being, both within parliament and in the country at large, Malan found himself the leader of the opposition.

The judicial role of the Privy Council

The Statute of Westminster had undoubtedly released the South African legislature from the control of its Westminster counterpart. What it had not done, however, was to release the South African courts from the control of the House of Lords qua the Privy Council. The South Africa Act 1909 had subjected the decisions of the Appellate Division to appeal to the Privy Council, and although this provision was not entrenched, the South African parliament had not thus far seen fit to deny litigants access to this extra-territorial judicial forum. The Privy Council very rarely heard appeals from South Africa; it had held in *Whitaker v Mayor of Durban*[45] in 1920 that the framers of the South Africa Act 1909 had intended that issues involving wholly domestic South African matters should be resolved by the South African courts. As a result, only five appeals had been held by the mid-1930s. The Status of the Union Act 1934 did not address the question, and the issue seemed not to be regarded as particularly significant in South African legal circles.[46]

It assumed much greater prominence shortly after the Status of the Union Act was passed. The Privy Council's decision in *Pearl Assurance Co v Government of the Union of South Africa*[47] managed both to antagonise moderate white opinion in South Africa and also provide a peg on which Malan's Purified Nationalists could hang a furious attack on British imperialism. The case involved a question of the calibration of damages in Roman-Dutch contract law. As such, it would have seemed (per *Whitaker*) to have been a matter that should have been resolved by the Appellate Division. That the Privy Council agreed to hear the appeal at all was thus seen in South African legal circles as an

43 See Moodie, n. 27 above, pp. 152–153; A. Hepple, *Verwoerd* (Harmonsdworth: Pelican, 1967), pp. 39–40. For a revealing account of the various networks that the Broederbond had created by this time see Hepple, *ibid*. ch. 7.

44 See Hepple, n. 43 above, pp. 68–69 for an account of this element of the Broederbond's activities.

45 [1920] 36 TLR 784.

46 D. Swinfen, *Imperial Appeal* (Manchester: Manchester University Press, 1987), ch. 4.

47 [1934] AC 570.

unwelcome break with tradition. That the Privy Council then went on to suggest that its members had a better understanding of principles of Roman-Dutch law than the majority of judges sitting on the Appellate Division was a cause of acute controversy. That the Privy Council expressed its view in typically diplomatic judicial language—"With all respect to the Chief Justice and the learned judge who formed the majority, their Lordships think that the conclusion cannot be supported"[48]—did nothing to assuage South African indignation.

Malan's party promptly introduced a resolution in the house urging an amendment to the constitution abolishing the right of appeal. Malan characterised the situation as one which revealed South Africa's "subservience to a higher foreign court".[49] Smuts, while evidently unhappy with the judgment and supportive in principle of ending the right of appeal, was unwilling to take that step in circumstances which would have offered Malan a political advantage. Hertzog was readily persuaded to adopt this viewpoint, as were the governing party's MPs. The resolution was defeated by eighty-two votes to fourteen.[50]

Pearl Assurance was also subjected to severe criticism in South African academic circles. Francois van den Heever, writing under the pseudonym of Aquilius, castigated the Privy Council both for erring in its understanding of Roman–Dutch law and for interfering in the issue in the first place.[51] Van den Heever had been appointed as Senior Law Adviser to the government in 1926, and had subsequently been a senior member of the South African delegation to the 1929 and 1931 Imperial Conferences where he played a major role in drafting the Statute of Westminster. His criticism of *Pearl Assurance* might readily have been seen as an indication that a newly independent South Africa might shortly wish to end the Privy Council's involvement with the shaping of its legal system.

The constitutional implications for South Africa of the Statute of Westminster were then further complicated by the judgment of the Privy Council in *Moore v Attorney-General for the Irish Free State*.[52] The *Moore* litigation focused on the constitutionality of the Irish legislature's decision in 1933 to end the Privy Council's appellate jurisdiction over the Irish courts. Moore contended that the relevant Irish Act, the Constitution (Amendment No. 22) Act 1933 was *ultra vires* the Irish constitution. The argument seemed poorly founded. Such an Act would undoubtedly have been unconstitutional as a matter of Irish law prior to the passage of the Statute of Westminster, since it would have been 'repugnant' to the British statute establishing the Privy Council's jurisdiction. As such, it would have contravened the Colonial Laws Validity Act 1865. However, the Privy Council concluded that this constraint on the Irish legislature no longer applied:

[48] [1934] AC 570 at 585.

[49] HAD, 25 February 1935, cc.2100–2101.

[50] Swinfen, n. 46 above, pp. 157–159.

[51] 'Immorality and Illegality in Contract' (1943) 60 *South African Law Journal* 468. See also R. Welsh, 'The Privy Council Appeals Act 1950' (1950), 67 *South African Law Journal* 67.

[52] [1935] AC 484.

> "The effect of the Statute of Westminster was to remove the fetter which lay upon the Irish Free State Legislature by reason of the Colonial Laws Validity Act. That Legislature can now pass Acts repugnant to an Imperial Act. In this case they have done so".[53]

The Irish government had chosen not to defend the action before the Privy Council, which suggested it would have ignored the decision even if judgment had been given in Moore's favour. But Lord Sankey's opinion added further fuel to the argument smouldering in South Africa as to the post-Statute of Westminster status of the South Africa Act's entrenched clauses. Strictly construed, *Moore* would seem to have little relevance to the South African question. It merely confirmed that, following the enactment of the Statute of Westminster and the granting of Irish independence, the Irish legislature could now make laws which were previously beyond its competence. No constitutional scholar would have denied that the South African legislature enjoyed similar powers. The crucial question, on which *Moore* shed no light, was whether the South African legislature was still obliged to respect the entrenchment procedures—not because they were the product of a British statute but because they were a fundamental provision of South Africa's now wholly domesticated constitutional structure ?

Within South Africa, a vocal strand of opinion—including the Malanites and some former Nationalist members of the United Party—portrayed *Moore* as a decision which confirmed that the entrenched clauses were no longer effective. From this perspective, the effect of the Statute of Westminster 1931 was not just to make South Africa a sovereign state, but also to give it a parliament that was sovereign in just the same sense as the British legislature—namely that it could make, amend and repeal *all* laws by a simple bicameral majority process. The entrenchment requirement was, to quote Lord Sankey, 'a fetter' which had been imposed by the Colonial Laws Validity Act and which had now been removed.

This viewpoint was arguably approved shortly after *Moore* by Sir Ivor Jennings, then perhaps the foremost authority among British constitutional lawyers. Jennings conceded that it was "at least arguable" that the 1931 Act "merely abolishe[d] the doctrine of repugnancy",[54] in which case South Africa's entrenchment provisions remained intact. Its parliament might be sovereign, but in respect of some laws that parliament had to act in ways other than by a simple bicameral majority.

However, he thought this argument was far weaker than that favoured by the Malanites. Jennings was led to this conclusion by the fact that the Statute of Westminster had explicitly preserved the various entrenched provisions of the Canadian, Australian and New Zealand constitutions, but was silent in respect of the entrenched provisions of the South African constitution. This omission,

[53] *Ibid*. at 498 per Viscount Sankey L.C.

[54] I. Jennings, 'The Statute of Westminster and Appeals to the Privy Council' (1936) 52 *LQR* 173 at 186.

he assumed, had to be construed in the light of *Moore* as a means by which the Westminster Parliament had repealed sections 35, 137 and 152 of the South Africa Act. The consequence of this was that the South African parliament was now competent to change any South African law by the simple majority bicameral procedure. Entrenchment was now no more than a "gentleman's agreement".[55]

Since *Moore* had made no reference to this issue, Jennings' argument was at best a process of speculation through extrapolation. His argument was also structured without reference to the intentions of the Westminster and South African legislatures. As noted above, the Malanite perspective did not seem to be embraced in 1931 by either parliament. It is, of course, 'at least arguable' that the Statute of Westminster had impliedly repealed the entrenched clauses of the South Africa Act. Yet it is also readily arguable that one would have expected so radical a change to South Africa's domestic constitutional arrangements to have been explicitly adverted to both in the Act itself and in the professed intentions of the politicians who determined its contents. There would have been no need to expressly preserve the entrenched provisions because none of the legislators involved with the drafting and passage of the 1931 Act ever assumed that their continued effectiveness was in question.

This analysis did not entail acceptance of the point that the Westminster parliament in some sense retained its former 'sovereignty' over the South African legislature. Rather it suggested that a legislative attempt by South Africa's parliament to overturn any of the entrenched clauses by a simple majority would have been illegal, not because such an Act would have been 'repugnant' to a British statute, but because it would have been 'repugnant' to a provision of the South African constitution. Insofar as the entrenchment procedures were a 'fetter' on the bare majority South African parliament, they were imposed not by the Colonial Laws Validity Act 1865, but were a fetter voluntarily adopted by the four colonies in 1909 and subsequently voluntarily readopted by the Union in 1931.

Arthur Berriedale Keith, then Professor of Constitutional Law at the University of Edinburgh, had served as a special adviser at the Imperial Conferences. His view on the post-independence status of the entrenched clauses was more equivocal than Jennings. He suggested that the Statute of Westminster *might* have turned the South African parliament into a carbon copy of the Westminster legislature, but this question remained to be decided.[56] In his view, *Moore* did not obviously support the proposition that Jennings advanced.

Quite where the Appellate Division's preferences—and, following *Pearl Assurance*, those of the Privy Council—would lie in answering this question

[55] I. Jennings, 'The Statute of Westminster and Appeals to the Privy Council' (1936) 52 *LQR* 173 at 187. Curiously enough, this was how Smuts had characterised the provisions in 1909; see p. 127 above.

[56] A.B. Keith, *The Governments of the British Empire* (London: Macmillan, 1935), ch. 2.

remained to be seen. One might also have speculated as to the force any such judicial pronouncement might have if it did not coincide with the wishes of the government of the day: the divergent responses of the legislatures of the Republic and the Free State to their respective judiciary's efforts to keep their powers within constitutionally designated limits remained a potent, if by now distant, illustration of the variable political status of the principle of the rule of law in southern African society.

For the moment, these rather rarified matters of constitutional law were of less significance to the development of white South Africans' political culture than the government's more exoteric initiatives in such fields as education policy. Hertzog's brief period as Education Minister in the Orange Free State had revealed that he—just like Milner—saw the content and delivery of the school curriculum as a crucial contributor to the maintenance of particular political ideologies. As Prime Minister in the 1930s, Hertzog presided over a marked 'Afrikanerisation' of both primary and secondary schooling.[57] The subject matter of school textbooks was increasingly tightly controlled by central government, and that control was excerised to produce a distinctly Afrikaner view of southern African history.[58] Thompson has suggested that the cumulative impact of this ideological initiative was to further consolidate the belief among all white South Africans that the role of non-whites in southern Africa had always been marginal and inferior to that of whites.[59] That marginality and inferiority was to be forcefully re-emphasised in 1936, in a controversy which eventually offered the Appellate Division the opportunity to give its opinion on the constitutional impact of the Statute of Westminster and the Status of the Union Act.

III. THE REPRESENTATION OF THE NATIVES ACT 1936

By the time he became Prime Minister in 1926, Hertzog had already been a major player on the South African political stage for over thirty years. He was well used, and apparently well-suited, to playing a long game. His failure to secure a two-thirds majority for his franchise reform bills in 1926 had not led him to abandon them, but rather to refer them for further study to a cross-party parliamentary select committee. The creation of the coalition government offered him another opportunity to bring his plans into effect, for it seemed more than likely that Smuts' long established track record of sacrificing even a

[57] Nominally, education remained a provincial responsibility (see p. 120 above), but central government's control of the fiscal purse strings rendered that particular decentralisation of political power somewhat illusory.

[58] Thompson (1995), n. 22 above, pp. 52–57.

[59] *Ibid*. Hertzog's aformentioned attack on the Broederbond was prompted in part by the resistance of those of its members who were teachers to Hertzog's preferred version of Afrikaner doctrine. His objection was evidently not to the use of schools for indoctrination *per se*, but to the indoctrination of ideas with which he did not wholeheartedly agree.

limited attachment to the principle of racial equality to the exigencies of retaining political power would lead the SAP to accept Hertzog's point of view.[60]

By 1935 Smuts and most other former members of the SAP were almost ready to accede to Hertzog's wishes. His proposed legislation would not entirely abolish Cape native blacks' right to vote. Rather it would permit them to elect one (white) member to the senate. Native blacks in Natal and the Transkei area of the Cape would gain the same entitlement. Blacks in the Transvaal and the Orange Free State would share a representative. The bill also proposed the creation of a Natives Representative Council, a nationwide body representing black interests and intended to communicate native sentiment to the government and—more importantly from Hertzog's perspective—to dilute and diffuse black antagonism to government policy. The franchise reform was to be tied to a separate land reform bill, which would purportedly have made substantial government funds available to purchase lands which would be designated exclusively for black occupation.[61] Under the proposed scheme, Cape blacks would most certainly be separate from white and coloured voters. What was similarly clear was that they would not be equal.

Hertzog's plans attracted a mixed reception in the English language press. The *Sunday Times* was more subtle in its language than it had been in opposing the entrenchment of the Cape francise in 1909:[62] it nonetheless took the view that native blacks were lucky to retain any rights to vote and could have no cause for complaint that they would in future do so on a separate roll. The *Rand Daily Mail* had latterly fallen under the relatively liberal influence of its new deputy editor, a young Englishman called Rayner Ellis, and a similarly minded political correspondent, George Heard. Ellis and Heard pushed the paper towards a line which reluctantly accepted the new measure as a *fait accompli* but considered that the long-term question of voting rights was far from settled.[63]

The bill provoked considerable opposition from black political groups.[64] D.D.T. Jabavu was the motivating force behind the calling of an 'All Africa Convention' which met in Blomfontein during December 1935. The AAC briefly held out the prospect of a unified black front in opposition to government

[60] The various machinations involved in constructing the compromise are clearly summarised in Davenport (1978), n. 22 above, pp. 218–222.

[61] The land bill could also plausibly be seen as a further extension of the long extant government policy of establishing native reserves as pools of cheap labour to supply factory and domestic workers for white South Africa's increasingly industrialised economy.

[62] See p. 123 above.

[63] Mervis, n. 25 above, pp. 186–192. Cf. the following extract from an Ellis editorial on the bill: "It might as well be understood at once that there is little right and less justice about this Bill, which is quite simply intended to take from the native as many political privileges as can be taken in view of the necessity for obtaining a two-thirds majority": *ibid.* at pp. 191–192.

[64] P. Rich, *State Power and Black Politics in South Africa 1921–1951* (London: Macmillan, 1996), ch. 6 details the response of black political groups to Hertzog's manouevrings. See also Davenport (1978), n. 22 above, pp. 220–224; J. Omer-Cooper, *History of Southern Africa* (London: Heinneman, 1987), pp. 179–181.

policy; representatives of over four hundred disparate groups attended the Convention. Hertzog proved however more than adept in intensifying existing tensions among the black political elite. Despite an initial rapprochement between Jabavu, the ANC and the ICU, black leaders rapidly found themselves divided—as were their forebears in 1913[65]—on the question of whether Hertzog's bills offered limited prospects of improving their supporters' economic and political prospects. Hertzog himself was of course the chief beneficiary of this fragmentation, although the hitherto white Communist party seized the opportunity to draw disaffected members of the ANC and the APO into its ranks.

Sir James Rose-Innes also returned to public prominence by orchestrating extra-parliamentary opposition among whites. He had been a founder member of the Non-Racial Franchise Association in 1929, and made a series of speeches denouncing both the bill and the *status quo*. His speech at the opening meeting of the Association was particularly trenchant:

> "We have not got democratic government now. We have the form of democracy, not the reality. In the Transvaal and Free State any white moron can vote, but no coloured or black man, however wealthy and civilised he may be. A white minority with manhood suffrage rule a black majority with no suffrage at all. That is the very negation of democracy".[66]

The official opposition in the house was hardly likely to resist such a bill, other than on the grounds that it was insufficiently draconian in its scope. Former SAP MPs in the United Party were however expressing some disquiet as a result of black and liberal white opposition to the bill, and Hertzog considered it prudent to offer a concession of sorts. The additional four Senators were to be retained, but in addition to this native black voters in the Cape, rather than being denied any vote for members of the house of assembly, would be placed on a separate electoral roll which would return three members to the house. The concession was sufficient for most of Smuts' supporters in parliament to follow his lead in supporting the bill. For some of them however, that was not the case, and the most eloquent opposition to the bill was to come from within the cabinet itself.

J.H. Hofmeyer was the nephew of the J.H. Hofmeyr who had been so important a figure in southern African politics at the turn of the century. He was also distantly related to Smuts. This Hofmeyr had been a child prodigy, conducting church services at the age of five, completing an undergraduate degree in his early teens, and writing a biography of his famous forebear when only seventeen. At nineteen, Hofmeyr took up a Rhodes scholarship at Balliol. On his

[65] See pp. 133–134 above.

[66] J. Rose Innes, *Autobiography* (Cape Town: OUP, 1949), p. 322. Smuts took the view that Rose-Innes' intervention served only to push the more moderately racist members of the white electorate away from the SAP and into Hertzog's camp: K. Hancock, *Smuts: Vol. 2 Fields of Force 1919–1950* (Cambridge: CUP, 1968), p. 260.

return to South Africa, he began to lecture at the newly-founded University of the Witwatersrand, and became its Principal at the tender age of twenty-four. Smuts then adopted Hofmeyr as his protege, much as Kruger had adopted Smuts, and appointed him administrator of the Transvaal just a few years later.

Hofmeyer's academic and administrative brilliance was accompanied by what might now be regarded as a stunted personality. He had an unusually intense relationship with his mother, who had even accompanied him to Balliol. At Oxford, Hofmeyr decided not to join the armed forces during the First World War, but rather made his contribution to the war effort by running the Balliol Boys Club—an organisation offering social and academic facilities to local working class youths. He never married, nor it appears had any sexual or serious emotional relationships with women, seemingly preferring the company of young boys in his leisure time.

Whatever his sexual or emotional preferences, Hofmeyr had established himself as a 'liberal' on race issues when he was elected to the house of assembly in a 1929 by-election. He then entered the coalition government as Minister of Education, the Interior and Public Health. His reputation had been much shaped by his involvement with several other young liberals, among them Oliver Schreiner, the barrister son of the former Cape Prime Minister W.P. Schreiner. The group had produced a collection of essays entitled *Coming of Age*, which seemed to reach back to the sentiments of the first Hofmeyr and John X. Merriman as a guide to handling South Africa's racial policies.

To be a 'liberal' on race matters at that time did not entail opposition to segregationist policies. Hofmeyr had little experience or knowledge of non-white races, and evidently little inclination to obtain any. He had, it might be noted, been the Administrator of the Transvaal when that province had introduced its stringent provisions against Asian traders.[67] His view of segregation when he was elected to the house was, however, that it should be a benevolent rather than exploitative form of racial separation. Hertzog's bill offered him the opportunity to clearly define his position.

The bill appeared to ignore the one remaining provision of the South Africa Constitution which had been substantively entrenched in 1909. As noted in Chapter 4, section 35(2) was drafted in terms which indicated that racial classification could not be deployed to remove any *existing voter* from the electoral register irrespective of the size of the parliamentary majority supporting the measure. Removal on racial grounds appeared to be permissible only in respect of *future voters*, and then only if (per section 35(1) of the South Africa Act) the measure attracted the support of two-thirds of the members of house and senate sitting in joint session.

Hertzog requested the Governor-General to convene a joint session of both houses to secure the bill's enactment. However, the government drew no distinction between existing voters and potential voters. All existing native blacks

[67] See pp. 170–172 above.

voters were to be placed on a separate roll, where they would in future be joined by any other blacks who subsequently met the Cape's then extant land and income criteria. Given De Villiers C.J.'s clear statement in *Ndobe* that there were no means by which Parliament could invoke racial classification as a justification for removing existing voters from the roll, the government's failure to acknowledge the distinction is quite startling, and becomes all the more so when one considers Hertzog's own expertise in and attachment to principles of entrenchment in constitutional law. The Prime Minister had evidently allowed questions of political advantage to override principles of constitutional law.

Hertzog framed his parliamentary defence of the bill in apocalyptic terms. It was intended, he claimed, to serve the highest of principles—that of national self-preservation. More precisely, he was concerned with white self-preservation in the face of what he portrayed as the threat of the black majority: a threat which could be realised either through miscegenation or the ballot box.

After some prevarication, Hofmeyr determined to speak against the bill at third reading. His position was a curious one. As Minister of the Interior, he would have had departmental responsibilty for steering the bill through the legislature. He would also have known that his speech could make no difference to the outcome of the vote. He had further taken the precaution—in the likely event that his views offended many of the United party's former Nationalist MPs—of establishing that he would not be asked to leave the cabinet as a result of his opposition. His argument then presented not an attack on discrimination *per se*, but rather a call for the defence of traditional understandings and a warning (reminiscent of those issued by his uncle) of the dangerous political consequences of black disenfranchisement:

> "I am not one of those who would necessarily stand or fall by the ideal of common citizenship as an absolute thing . . . If we were starting with a clean sheet it would certainly be possible to devise a system of separate representation in separate assemblies which would be fair and just . . . But we are not starting with a clean sheet. We are starting with the existence of a vested right which has been in existence . . . for more than eighty years. And once franchise rights have been given and exercised by a section of the community, then no nation save at a cost of honour and ultimate security should take away those rights without adequate justification".[68]

In Hofmeyr's opinion, Hertzog's appeal to white self-preservation did not amount to such a justification. Indeed, enacting the bill was likely to jeopardise rather than secure whites' political stability:

> "By this Bill we are sowing the seeds of a far greater potential conflict than is being done by anything in existence today . . . We have many educated and semi-educated Natives in South Africa . . . Now what is the political future for these people? The Bill says that even the most educated Native shall never have political equality with even the least educated and the least cultured White or Coloured man . . . [A]ll that this Bill

[68] HAD, 6 April 1936; quoted in Paton, n. 24 above, p. 176.

is doing is for those educated Natives is to make them leaders of their own people, in disaffection and revolt".[69]

The integrity of Hofmeyr's position might have seemed somewhat more convincing had he resigned from the government over the issue and made an active attempt to rally white opinion around what he evidently saw as 'fair and just' principles. Whether he would have found much support is debatable. The liberal *Rand Daily Mail* praised his speech, and he received a good deal of congratulatory correspondence from private individuals. From Smuts, from his fellow Ministers, and from most members of the United Party he received either silence or fierce criticism.[70]

Hofmeyr's opposition to the bill had been on the grounds that it was indefensible as a matter of morality. He did not contend that it was unconstitutional in the legal sense. The responsibility for raising this question would presumably fall—as it had in respect of the Land Act 1913 and the Native Administration Act 1927[71]—to a native black whose existing rights had been extinguished by the legislation. In 1936, that responsibility was accepted by a Mr Ndwlana.[72]

IV. *NDLWANA V HOFMEYR*

Hertzog's success in fashioning a two-thirds parliamentary majority for the Representation of the Natives Act 1936 did not bring the controversy over black African disenfranchisement to an end. Rather, the battle was joined in the courts. By a distasteful irony indicative of the rank hypocrisy of the nominal 'liberals' in the Smuts wing of the government, Hofmeyr—as Minister of the Interior—was the nominal defendant in the case. Mr Ndlwana's challenge was on the surface a curious one. The core of his argument was that the Act was *ultra vires* the constitution precisely because it had been passed by the two-thirds majority unicameral procedure. The Act should have been passed, he maintained, by the simple majority bicameral process. Mr Ndlwana contended that the section 35 procedure applied only to measures which (per section 35 itself) 'disqualified' individuals from the franchise on the grounds of their race.

[69] HAD, 6 April 1936; quoted in Paton, n. 24 above, p. 177–178.

[70] *Ibid.* pp. 182–185.

[71] In *Thomson v Kama* (pp. 148–149 above) and *R v Ndobe* (pp. 165–168 above) respectively.

[72] An earlier attempt—essentially raising the *Trethowan* argument—had been made by a Mr Masai, who had asked the Cape provincial division to issue an injunction preventing the Speaker sending the bill to the Governor-General after its third reading. The case was stillborn however, as it emerged that the bill had already been sent to the Governor-General when proceedings were issued. See *Masai v Jansen* [1936] CPD 361. The case was heard before two judges, Watermeyer and Centlivres JJ. Watermeyer's judgment, in which Centlivres concurred, intimated that Mr Ndlwana's suit was unlikely to succeed. Watermeyer suggested that even if the South Africa Act still required 'parliament' to function in particular ways to achieve certain objectives, no court had the power to require that the correct procedure be followed. Nor it seemed could a court hold any such procedurally flawed bill *ultra vires*. The efficacy of the constitutional guarantee would thus be wholly dependent on the voluntary acquiescence of members of 'parliament' to its terms.

In his view, the separate roll could not amount to a 'disqualification' because he retained the right to vote, albeit in a racially compartmentalised electorate. The Act should therefore have been passed by the simple majority, bicameral process.

Mr Ndlwana did not suggest that the entrenched sections of the constitution had been rendered ineffective by the Statute of Westminster. Echoing the views of Mr Speaker Jansen and Prime Minister Hertzog in 1934, his counsel suggested that any 'disqualification' on grounds of race would indeed have to be enacted through the enhanced majority mechanism: South Africa's parliament had not become a carbon copy of the British legislature just because South Africa had become an independent country. The Cape franchise and the equality of language provisions remained beyond the reach of bare legislative majorities.

Had Mr Ndlwana succeeded in his action, Hertzog's government would no doubt have been subject to the moderate inconvenience of finding the necessary parliamentary time for a new bill to be enacted. But there would manifestly be a majority for such a measure. Moreover, one might anticipate that the government (and most certainly the Malanites) would actually have welcomed a 'defeat' on this immediate question, since it would have confirmed that a bill placing Coloureds and Indians in the Cape on a separate electoral roll could also be passed by the simple majority formula. In the event, the first instance court and the Appellate Division delivered two quite extraordinary opinions which appeared to hand the government a victory in both the short and long term.

The first instance judgment

The suit at first instance was heard by a three-man court in the Cape Provincial Division. The Judge President of the court, Hendrik van Zyl,[73] authored an opinion in which his colleagues Centlivres (who had also sat in *Masai*) and Sutton JJ. joined without qualification. Van Zyl J.P. began with the historically incontrovertible assumption that while the legal root of the entrenchment provisions was an Act of the British Parliament, their political source was wholly southern African. He continued by noting—as had evidently been assumed by the British and South African governments in 1931—that the Statute of Westminster neither repealed nor altered the entrenched provisions. Thus far,

[73] Van Zyl was born in the Cape in 1876. He took a BA at the University of the Cape of Good Hope, and thereafter an LLB at Cambridge, where he achieved the improbable feat of being elected President of the Union while voicing strident opposition to British policy in the boer war. On returning to South Africa, Van Zyl began a career at the Cape bar, and was elected as an SAP member to the Cape house of assembly in 1905. Van Zyl supported Hertzog's departure from the Botha cabinet in 1912, and subsequently became a founding member of the Cape branch of the Nationalist Party. Smuts nonetheless offered him a seat on the Cape bench in 1920. He was appointed Judge President of the Cape Provincial Division in 1935.

Van Zyl J.P.'s judgment seemed to be proceeding towards a conclusion that the entrenched provisions remained effective.

He then promptly rejected Ndlwana's contention that the creation of a separate electoral roll for natives did not amount to a 'disqualification' within section 35(2). Van Zyl considered that the notion of 'disqualification' encompassed not just the right to vote *per se*, but also the manner in which that right was to be exercised. Section 35(2) clearly defined that right as one exercised in respect of a race-neutral electoral roll. Even if natives were to be granted voting rights of equivalent value to those they previously possessed, the very fact of their removal from the common roll disqualified them from exercising the right in the form that the South Africa Act had granted them.

But Van Zyl J.P. then cast doubt on the validity of De Villiers C.J.'s reasoning in *Ndobe* in respect of the permanent, substantive entrenchment of the franchise rights of voters already on the Cape's electoral register:

> "I must confess that I find great difficulty in accepting the view that before the passing of the Statute of Westminster the Union Parliament had no authority to remove names of voters from the roll by reason of race or colour only or to repeal or amend s.35(2)".[74]

He suggested (nothwithstanding the clear language of the South Africa Act) that *existing* voters could have been disenfranchised on grounds of their race through the same mechanism that parliament could use to deny *future* non-white voters access to the electoral roll—namely the two-thirds majority unicameral procedure. In effect, he concluded, there never was any substantive entrenchment of existing voting rights.

Van Zyl J.P.'s reasoning on this point has limited credibility, given the lack of ambiguity in the text of the South Africa Act. It may perhaps be explained simply by the sheer novelty, either to the English or Roman-Dutch (or Transvaal and Orange Free State) and even American constitutional traditions, of the proposition that there could be any political values which were *wholly beyond* the reach even of enhanced legislative majorities.[75] The Court seems to have assumed that the South Africa Act simply could not have been intended to bear the meaning that its text explicitly set out, and so searched—albeit unconvincingly—for an alternative explanation.

Van Zyl J.P. promptly spared himself the difficulty of having to defend his criticism of De Villiers C.J. by also observing that *Ndobe*—irrespective of the points of law it established—was irrelevant to the current case since any restrictions under which parliament might have had to labour prior to 1931 had been removed by the Statute of Westminster and the Status of the Union Act. Van Zyl J.P. did not make any reference to *Trethowan* in his judgment, a

[74] [1937] AD 229 at 233–234.

[75] The most deeply entrenched value in the American Constitution is that each state shall have at least two seats in the Senate. This provision cannot be changed unless the state concerned agrees to a reduction in its Senate representation: Art. 5.

case which might have been thought to contradict his argument. However one would presumably have expected the court to conclude that *Trethowan*—like *Ndobe*—was not relevant to the issue before it, since that case concerned a controversy which had arisen prior to the passsage of the Statute of Westminster.

Van Zyl J.P. found authority for his conclusion in the Privy Council's decision in *Moore*, from which he cited the above-noted quotation from Lord Sankey's judgment. He interpreted *Moore*, without any substantial explanation, as confirming that the Statute of Westminster had released the South African legislature from all 'fetters' imposed by the South Africa Act. These fetters evidently included the entrenchment provisions, for while these remained in the text of the constitution he categorised them as imposing only a 'moral obligation' and not a legal one on the South African parliament.[76]

In Van Zyl J.P.'s opinion, the constitutional position in which the South African parliament now found itself was that it could pass any law it wished in any way that it wished. In enacting a bill intended to abridge voting rights on the grounds of the voters' race, parliament could if it wished follow the two-thirds unicameral majority process, but might just as readily adopt the simple majority bicameral procedure if it preferred. In either case, the court had no authority to overturn the legislation.

Van Zyl's treatment of *Moore* was perhaps so brief because that case—notwithstanding Jennings' interpretation of it—provided no substantial authority for the proposition he was advancing. Lord Sankey's repugnancy quotation did however provide a superficially plausible justification for Van Zyl J.P.'s reasoning to observers whose constitutional illiteracy or mendacity could not conceive of a parliament in terms other than as a carbon copy of the Westminster legislature. Quite what constitutional purpose could have been served by the in effect 'optional' status which the Cape provincial division ascribed to the entrenched provisions was difficult to fathom. There was however little time for commentators or politicians to dwell on the adequacy of the court's reasoning, or the implications of its conclusions, for the case was immediately removed to the Appellate Division.

The Appellate Division judgment

The Appellate Division's judgment in cases such as *Rasool* and *Sachs* might plausibly be construed as indicating that the Court was not predisposed to obstruct governmental and parliamentary wishes. In *Ndlwana*, the appellate bench spent little time on dismissing the plaintiff's appeal. Stratford A.C.J.

[76] This was a precise echo of the conclusion reached by Sir Ivor Jennings, although Van Zyl did not allude explicitly either to Jennings' article or to the reasoning he used to sustain his conclusion.

delivered a judgment spanning less than two pages for a unanimous four-man court.[77] In Stratford's view, the question before him was a simple one:

> "[W]hether a Court of Law can declare that a Sovereign Parliament cannot validly pronounce its will unless it adopts a certain procedure—in this case a procedure impliedly indicated as usual in the South Africa Act".[78]

The answer to the question was evidently even more simple. In essence, it followed the lead given by Watermeyer and Centlivres JJ. in *Masai*:[79]

> "Parliament, composed of its three elements, can adopt any procedure it thinks fit; the procedure express or implied in the South Africa Act is so far as Courts of Law are concerned at the mercy of Parliament like everything else".[80]

Stratford A.C.J. followed Van Zyl J.P. in concluding that *Ndobe* was irrelevant to the question, as it had been decided before the Statute of Westminster was enacted. He did not explain why this was so, and made no reference either to the proceedings of the Imperial Conferences or to academic analyses of the impact of the 1931 Act. One must assume he attributed the previously binding effect of section 35(2) to the South African parliament's *de jure* subordination to the British Parliament. Once that subordination had been removed, the South African legislature mysteriously gained all the attributes of its British parent, notwithstanding any indications to the contrary in the constitution.

There is little legal merit in Van Zyl and Stratford's arguments. Neither seemed to recognise the obvious point that the South African constitution had always recognised that South Africa had *three* 'parliaments'. This viewpoint, as outlined above, suggests that the Statute of Westminster had two legal effects. The first was that the South African parliament was freed from the constraints imposed by the Colonial Laws Validity Act 1865—namely that it could not pass legislation repugnant to a British statute intended by the British Parliament to have effect within South African territory. In broader terms, the Statute of Westminster confirmed that South Africa as a *country* was now a sovereign state, free of British control.

Secondly, although the Act made no alterations at all to the substance of South Africa's internal constitutional arrangements, those arrangements were transformed from a matter both of British and South African law to a matter of South African law only. While the legal *source* of the constitution's entrenchment provisions had been altered, their *content* remained unchanged.

[77] The other judges were De Villiers J.A., De Wet and Watermeyer JJ.A. The intensely incestuous nature of the South African legal profession is neatly illustrated by the names of the firms of attorneys representing the government and the appellants; these being Van Zyl and Partners; Jan S. de Villiers & Son; and Marais and de Villiers.

[78] [1937] AD 229 at 238. Quite why Stratford A.C.J. claimed the procedure was only *impliedly usual* is a mystery. The text of s.35(2) *explicitly* presents an *invariable* rule.

The judgment did not consider the conclusion reached by the provincial division to the effect that the creation of a separate roll did indeed amount to a disqualification within s.35(2).

[79] See n. 72 above.

[80] *Ibid.* at 238.

In rejecting this argument, the Cape provincial division and the Appellate Division in *Ndlwana* were elevating the wishes of the existing and future simple parliamentary majorities over those of the Constitutional Convention of 1908 and of the Westminster and Union Parliaments in 1931. The courts were in effect denying the *constituent* status of the constitution. This is a particularly curious conclusion for the courts to have reached, given Van Zyl J.P.'s own recognition that the political source of South Africa's constitution lay in the Convention's deliberations.

The court's reasoning seemed to miss the distinction between a *sovereign nation* and a *sovereign legislature*. They were perhaps led down this path by the unfortunate argument of Mr Ndlwana's leading counsel[81] to the effect that the ultimate legal authority within the South African constitution continued to be the Westminster Parliament, since that Parliament retained—as a matter of British constitutional theory—the legal authority to repeal the Statute of Westminster and subject any or all of the Dominions to British control.

This was an absurd argument to make, for it denied the sovereignty both of the South African parliament and of the South African nation. In effect, it invited the courts to conclude that the only rationale which would justify upholding the entrenched clauses was one which characterised South Africa as—still—a British colony. A far more accurate characterisation, and one that would have been far less difficult for the courts to adopt, would have been to say that South Africa was, like the USA, a sovereign nation, but a nation whose central legislature was defined in different ways for different purposes by the nation's constitution. An even more appealing argument could have been found rather closer to home.

The insular nature both of Mr Ndlwana'a argument and the courts' respective conclusions might usefully be contrasted with the breadth of Kotze C.J.'s reasoning in *Brown v Leyds*,[82] a case which did not feature at all in the *Ndlwana* judgments. Kotze, it may be recalled, had drawn widely in *Brown* on constitutional principles from the USA and several continental European jurisidictions to illustrate the point that the allocation of national sovereignty to a bare legislative majority was an arrangement that few 'modern' constitutional settlements had made. Bare legislative majorities had generally been subject to constraints, to prevent them sweeping away what the framers of the constitutions concerned had regarded as 'fundamental' political principles. In the South African Republic, those principles had been firmly entrenched by demanding that *wetten* attract two-thirds majorities. It is curious that the case and the principle for which it stood was not deployed in *Ndlwana*. The obvious analogy would have been to argue that virtually all laws enacted by the South African parliament were *besluiten*, passed by a simple majority; the entrenched provisions were, in contrast, *wetten*, to be passed by an enhanced majority; and the

[81] Douglas Buchanan KC. By a strange irony, Mr Ndlwana's junior counsel was D. Molteno, a liberal barrister who subsequently occupied one of the native seats in the house created by the Act.

[82] See pp. 45–47 above.

South Africa Act itself had now been transformed into the newly sovereign nation's *Grondwet*.[83]

The reaction to *Ndlwana*

Such reasoning had made no stronger an impression upon the country's politicians than it had upon the members of the Cape provincial and Appellate Divisions of the Supreme Court. Political reaction to the *Ndwlana* judgment was generally muted. The principal reason for this would appear to be that while legislators and the government had been told that they had been labouring under a constitutional misapprehension, the judgment had no impact on the legislative outcome they had wished to produce. For, Hertzog, the case indicated that he need not—at least for legal reasons—have worked so long and so hard to secure the two-thirds majority he had assumed was necessary to enact his franchise reforms. From Smuts' perspective, the judgment perhaps confirmed the opinion he had voiced as long ago as 1909, that the entrenched clauses amounted in the long term to no more than a 'moral obligation' which legislators might repudiate as and when they thought fit.

The case attracted little detailed press coverage. The *Cape Times* accorded it a single column on page 13[84]—approximately half the space allocated to the evidently more pressing matter of 'Bad Teeth Among South Africans—Government to find out the causes'.[85] The top political story of the day was a continuing row between Malan and Hertzog over the national anthem. Two days later, the *Cape Times* ran a leader which expressed some concern about the implications of the judgment. The editorial suggested that Stratford A.C.J.'s opinion raised a:

> "serious question . . . [I]t would seem to imply that Parliament, without amending the South Africa Act, could, if it wished, suddenly adopt a method of referring any Bill to a joint sitting of both Houses of Parliament, even if the Bill had nothing whatever to do with questions in the case of which a joint sitting is specifically described in the South Africa Act".[86]

The concern seemed to be that a government with a majority in the house but in a minority in the senate could call a joint session and push through legislation by a simple majority, thereby sidestepping the section 63 requirements[87] and effectively removing the senate's role as a revising or delaying chamber. The *Ndlwana* judgment did indeed offer that possibility, but the *Cape Times'* leader,

[83] Albeit, curiously, a *grondwet* which was in most respects amendable by *besluiten*.

[84] Although it should be noted that at this time the first eight or so pages of the paper were given over to adverts.

[85] 6 April 1937.

[86] 8 April 1937.

[87] See pp. 110–111 above.

like the Appellate Division's opinion, did not get to grips with the question of what 'parliament' actually was.

Nor was the case subject to much adverse academic criticism.[88] The predominantly English language *South African Law Journal* did not offer any contemporaneous critique of the decision. Professor L. Coetzee published several articles in an Afrikaaner legal journal which argued that the Appellate Division's judgment was misconceived. He suggested that the court had failed to appreciate that the Statute of Westminster merely released South Africa qua country from the control of the Westminster Parliament. Once so released, South Africa was a sovereign state: and moreover a sovereign state with a sovereign legislature: but its sovereign legislature existed in two forms, the form being dependent upon the substance of the laws it wished to pass.[89]

The political significance and legal defensibility of *Ndwlana* were however rapidly obscured by political developments in Europe. The onset of the Second World War revealed the limits of consensus between Smuts and Hertzog and drew a clear and bitter dividing line between the Anglo and Afrikaaner factions of the white population and their respective representatives in parliament.

IV. THE SECOND WORLD WAR

By the early 1930s, Malan's vision of a pure Afrikaanerdom had come to be shared by a small group of young political activists. Many of these men had undertaken their graduate education in Germany, an experience which presumably did much to reinforce and legitimise any pre-existing sentiments they may have had concerning the superiority of the white race and the evils of British imperialism.[90] *Die Burger,* still the house journal of the Malanite fringe,[91] was forceful in its denuciation of claims that the Nazis were persecuting German Jews, as was a paper called *Die Transvaaler*, founded in 1936 and edited by Henrik Verwoerd.[92] Verwoerd was among the most prominent of these German-educated activists. He had returned from Germany to take up a psychology lectureship at the University of Stellenbosch. He had subsequently taken up a chair in social work, devoting his energies—in close association with

[88] Cf. H. Hahlo and E. Kahn (1960) *South Africa: The Development of Its Laws and Constitution* p. 153 (Cape Town: Juta & Co.) "By 1937 academic opinion was almost unanimous that entrenchment had ceased to be effective".

[89] 'Watte Registeem Beheers die Verhouding Tussen Owerheid en Onderdaan in die Unie, Roemins Hollands Reg of Englends Reg?' (1937) *Tydskrif vir Hedendagsee Romeins-Hollands Reg* 34; 'Die Wegtwende Orgaan van die Unie van Suid-Afrika' (1941) *Tydskrif vir Hedendagsee Romeins-Hollands Reg* 41. I have relied on G. Dold and C. Joubert, *The Union of South Africa* (London: Stevens and Sons, 1955), for a summary of Coertze's critique.

[90] L. Thompson, *The Political Mythology of Apartheid* (New Haven: Yale University Press, 1985), pp. 42–46. See also D. Posel, 'The Meaning of Apatheid Before 1948', in W. Beinart and S. Dubow (eds.), *Segregation and Apartheid* (London: Routledge, 1995).

[91] E. Potter, *The Press as Opposition* (London: Chatto and Windruss, 1975), pp. 145–146.

[92] Potter, n. 91 above, p. 46: Mervis, n. 25 above, pp. 225–227.

the Broederbond—to developing strategies to combat poverty among Afrikaaner whites. Verwoerd's preferred solution to that problem was straightforward, namely that the government should impose greater discrimination against non-whites in the labour market and the provision of welfare services.[93] His arrival in the public eye followed Hofmeyr's decision to admit five hundred German Jews to South Africa as political refugees. Verwoerd denounced the decision, speaking in terms of a 'Jewish menace' to the purity of the Afrikaaner race:[94] evidently it was no longer just blacks, coloureds and Asiatics who threatened white supremacy.

Malan had initially signalled clear disapproval of Verwoerd's anti-semitism. But by 1937 he had become convinced of the electoral appeal of rabid anti-Jewish propaganda. Malan became an advocate both of an end to any further Jewish immigration and of measures preventing Jews from engaging in certain professions and economic activities.[95]

With the 'Jewish threat' as an additional weapon in their propaganda armoury, the Malanites and their extra-parliamentary supporters garnered substantial popular support for their vision of a beleaugered Afrikaaner *volk* battling valiantly against the twin threats of a legacy of British imperialism and the prospect of swamping by non-white Africans when they managed—in close collaboration with the Broederbond—to assume *de facto* control over the centenary celebrations of the Great Trek.[96] Much as Kruger had adopted du Toit's mythologising of Slagtersnek to assert a boer identity against the British, so Malan and the Broederbond seized on the Great Trek as a myth to assert an undiluted boer identity against both the allegedly evermore anglicised version of Afrikanerdom represented by Smuts and many other members of the government[97] and the threat posed to Afrikaaners' economic interests by the increasing presence of native black workers in the country's rapidly urbanising economy.[98]

Malanite Afrikaanerdom was in effect assuming both the form and substance of what Moodie has referred to as a 'civil religion', in which fundamentalist Calvinist notions of the boers as 'a chosen people' spilled into the sphere of party politics, wherein the 'chosen people' were of course the Purified Nationalists and their supporters. The increasingly pervasive nature of the new 'civil religion' was further illustrated by the Broederbond's growing involve-

[93] See A. Hepple, *Verwoerd* (Pelican: Harmondsworth, 1967), pp. 29–31, 37–39.

[94] Paton, n. 24 above, pp. 193–194.

[95] Moodie, n. 27 above, pp. 166–167.

[96] The painstaking nature of the Broederbond's exploitation of the centenary—and the extraordinary emotional (and subsequently political) impact the events had on many white Afrikaners—are recounted in terrifying detail in Moodie, n. 27 above, ch. 9. See also Hepple (1967), n. 93 above, pp. 57–59.

[97] Thompson (1985), n. 90 above, pp. 39–40, 180.

[98] The threat was exacerbated by indications that black trade unionism was becoming an increasingly effective force. For illustrations of black workers' activities in the obvious area of heavy industry and the more unlikely field of domestic service see B. Hirsen, *Yours for the Union* (Johannesburg: Witwatersrand University Press, 1989), chs. 5, 7–8.

ment with Afrikaaner trade unionism. An umbrella organisation called the National Council of Trustees was established to provide financial and logistical support for the promulgation of Christian National doctrine among the Afrikaaner working class. The initiative built on the formation of an Afrikaaner Railworkers' union—*die Spoorbond*—in 1935, which combined militant defence of its members' economic interests with evangelistic promulgation of boer political ideology.[99]

These attacks from the political far right undermined Hertzog's position within the United Party, but offered no obvious and immediate threat to the government's continued electoral dominance. Nor did Hofmeyr's eventual resignation from the cabinet seem likely to jeopardise the party's electoral prospects. The resignation was triggered by Hertzog's decision once again to use—as he had for Pirow—the gift of one of the senate seats reserved for persons having a "thorough acquaintance with the reasonable wants and wishes of the Coloured races". The intended beneficiary on this occasion was A.P. Fourie, the former Minister of Commerce, who had lost his house seat in the 1938 election. Hofmeyr was of the opinion that Fourie had no such qualification. His resignation speech, in which he accused Hertzog of effecting "a prostitution of the Constitution . . . to assist the Government out of a temporary political difficulty"[100] was seen by many observers as a clarion call for liberal white opinion to rally against Smuts' evermore acquiescent stance towards Hertzog's racial policies. Hofmeyr himself remained unwilling to assume the leadership of such a movement however, and remained an unhappy and argumentative member of the United Party.

That status was eventually denied him in 1938, when he fought a virtually lone parliamentary campaign against the government's Asiatics (Transvaal Land and Trading) Bill.[101] The bill, introduced in response to a rising tide of white hysteria in the Transvaal over swamping by Indians, proposed that Indians as a group would not be permitted to increase either their commercial or residential landholdings in that province. In Hofmeyr's view, such measures were not only premised on weak factual grounds but were also more likely to exacerbate than ameliorate racial tensions. Such sentiments—and the parliamentary obstructionism which accompanied them—were too much for Hertzog to bear, and he arranged for Hofmeyr to be expelled from the party.

Smuts had argued in cabinet against Hofmeyr's expulsion, but was not prepared to make a public stand on the issue. Continuing and intensifying discrimination against South Africa's non-white races was evidently not a matter he regarded as sufficiently important to terminate his relationship with Hertzog. However, the Smuts/Hertzog alliance was not sufficiently strong to withstand the tensions created by the outbreak of the Second World War.

[99] Moodie, n. 27 above, pp. 170–171.
[100] Quoted in Paton, n. 24 above, p. 222.
[101] Hancock (1968), n. 23 above, pp. 298, 457; Paton, n. 24 above, pp. 239–244.

Hertzog's preference for South African neutrality in the event of a European war involving Britain had been an article of faith for him ever since 1914. He did not regard the spectre of Nazism as sufficent reason to change that view. Indeed, his protege Pirow had been embroiling the government in close economic links with Hitler's government, from which he had bought the planes to equip South Africa's emergent air force. Pirow had also developed close links with Salazar's fascist dictatorship in Portugal, a system of government of which he spoke with increasing approval. To classify either man as a Nazi at the outbreak of war might have been something of an exaggeration, but there was no doubt that both their personal inclinations and their view of South Africa's national interest would have led them to refuse to join Britain in waging war against Germany.

For Smuts, the converse beliefs were just as deeply engrained. There seemed little likelihood that he could remain in a government that would not enter the war on Britain's side.[102] Matters came to a head in early September 1939, when Hertzog presented a motion to the house. The motion maintained that South Africa's national interests were not as yet jeopardised by Germany's military adventurism, and that until such time as they were put in jeopardy, South Africa should not enter the war. Smuts immediately tabled an amended motion, advocating entry to the war precisely because it was in South Africa's national interest to do so.

Smuts carried the house by eighty votes to sixty-seven. The Governor-General, Sir Patrick Duncan,[103] accepted Hertzog's resignation as Prime Minister but refused his request to dissolve the house so that an election could be fought on the neutrality question. Duncan determined instead to invite Smuts to form a new government.[104] After a gap of fifteen years, Smuts was once again to be Prime Minister.

For Hertzog, the collapse of the United Party government signalled a personal political odyssey that moved him even further to the right. His initial response, having continued to defend Germany against charges of war-mongering even after the commencement of the Battle of Britain, was to seek realignment with the Malanites. This was achieved in January 1940: he was to serve as the leader of the Reunited Nationalists. Within a year, Hertzog's brand of racism had proved too tame for the Malanites. He resigned the leadership when his party refused to commit itself to the principle of equality between the white

[102] N. Mandela notes that at the time he regarded Smuts as "England's greatest advocate in South Africa", a contention Hertzog would presumably have accepted but which Smuts himself would have rejected: *Long Road to Freedom* (London: Abacus, 1995), p. 57.

[103] Duncan had been a member of the Unionist party in 1910. He entered Smuts' cabinet as Minister of Justice on the merger of the SAP and Unionists in 1920. Hertzog, presumably to his later regret, had appointed Duncan as Governor-General in 1937.

[104] See K. Heard, *General Elections in South Africa 1943–1970* (London: OUP, 1974), pp. 15–16. Duncan took the step of publishing a letter to Hertzog explaining his decision in the *Cape Times* of 5 September 1939; Hahlo and Kahn, n. 88 above, p. 174.

races.[105] His previously loyal lieutenant Havenga subsequently founded a 'moderate' Afrikaaner party.[106] But Hertzog, bizarrely, spent his final months of political life as a member of Pirow's newly founded and overtly Nazi New Order party.[107] The alliance was to be short-lived. Hertzog died in 1942. On the simple matter of longevity, as on so many other issues, Smuts had had the better of their rivalry.

War powers

Smuts' role in the Second World War, on both the domestic and international stages, was significantly less commanding than it had been in the First World War. While a close confidant of Churchill, he did not join the British war cabinet, and spent the greater part of the war in Africa. The war had nevertheless begun with an episode that indicated Smuts was willing and able to take close personal control of the South African war effort.

While Malan himself gave no indication that he would take positive steps actively to sabotage the war effort, Smuts took the view that members of the extreme fringes of the Afrikaaner nationalist movement did offer a real and immediate threat to South Africa's internal security. His preferred response to this threat was to intern the persons concerned. However, rather than seek statutory authority to imprison suspected Nazi sympathisers, Smuts claimed a power rooted in English common law—and transposed to South Africa—to carry out this policy. His position, in effect, was that in times of war the executive government (of which the Governor-General was *de jure*—and Smuts himself *de facto*—the head) was empowered to override peace-time constraints on its powers in order to secure the nation's safety. Smuts could no doubt have found a legislative majority, albeit perhaps a narrow one, for such a measure.[108] He would equally certainly have encountered fierce opposition from the Nationalists, for whom any such Act could readily be presented to the electorate as a British-motivated interference with Afrikaaners' civil liberties. For reasons of speed and expediency, the common law route was a more attractive proposition.[109]

[105] Verwoerd and Strijdom had been particularly enthusiastic in their efforts to force Hertzog and the more 'moderate' of his followers out of the re-united party, an enterprise in which they were assisted by the Malanite leader of the party in the Free State, C.R. Swart: Moodie, n. 27 above, pp. 193–194.

[106] For details of the creation of the party see the *Cape Times* and the *Cape Argus*, 28 May 1941.

[107] Manoeuvrings at this time among the various extremist Afrikaaner groups are outlined in Davenport (1978), n. 22 above, pp. 235–239. On Hertzog's embrace of Nazism see Moodie, n. 27 above, pp. 209–210.

[108] And did indeed do so later in the War Measures Act 1940. Malan and Hertzog fiercely opposed the bill, which was eventually subject to a drastic guillotine. It was carried by twenty votes in the house.

[109] Some seventy-six people had been detained by January 1940. The number subsequently rose (under the statutory scheme) to nearly 600 in 1943; see Hancock (1968), n. 23 above, pp. 338–340.

The legal basis of the power was, however, uncertain. The question came before the Transvaal Provincial Division in *Trumplemann and Du Toit v Minister for Justice and Minister for Defence.*[110] Greenberg—by now Judge President of the Transvaal court—delivered the court's opinion.[111] The court concluded that a declaration of war was sufficient to unlock executive powers which could not be drawn upon in times of peace:

> "There is an inherent right in every State, as in every individual, to use all means at its disposal to defend itself when its existence is at stake . . . Under such circumstances the State may be compelled by necessity to disregard for a time the ordinary safeguards of liberty in defence of liberty itself, and to substitute for the careful and deliberate procedure of the law a machinery more drastic and speedy to cope with an urgent danger".[112]

The internment of suspected subversives was a legitimate exercise of that power. Moreover, once satisfied that a state of war did prevail, the courts would take no steps to review the substantive or procedural regularity of exercises of such powers beyond asking the government to confirm that their use was intended to serve military purposes. In effect, the court was offering Smuts a virtually untrammelled discretion to snuff out all and any opposition to the war.[113]

The government nevertheless remained selective in the use it made of this judicially granted freedom. While potential spies and saboteurs were interned, the more 'moderate' body of Afrikaaner nationalist opinion found space both within parliament and in the press to denounce South Africa's continued involvement in the war. For some of Malan's supporters, this freedom was to prove a costly (if only in monetary terms) liberty.

South African nazis

The assistance lent by some boers to the German cause during the First World War was echoed on a smaller scale by some extreme right wing Afrikaaners in

[110] [1940] TPD 242. Pirow added to his already well-founded reputation as the champion of Afrikaaners' civil liberties by appearing as lead counsel for the internees.

[111] Schreiner J. concurred. On Schreiner, see p. 222 below.

[112] [1940] TPD 242 at 245.

[113] The judgment is described as "reprehensible" by D. Basson and H. Viljoen, *South African Constitutional Law* (Cape Town: Juta & Co, 1988), p. 249. Smuts had taken the precaution, lest the Appellate Division overturn the first instance judgment, of inserting an indemnity clause (as he had done in 1913 and 1922; see pp. 142 and 154 above) into the War Measures Bill 1940.

Observers of British constitutional law would no doubt see many similarities between the *Trumpelmann* judgment and the majority opinion of the House of Lords in *Liversidge v Anderson* [1942] AC 206. In *Liversidge*, the majority in the Lords ignored traditional understandings concerning the interpretation of legislation and afforded the Home Secretary effective powers to intern alleged subversives on the basis of no more than his own suspicions. See generally A. Simpson, *In the Highest Degree Odious* (Oxford: OUP, 1992). For an extended treatment of *Liversidge* and its impact in South Africa see D. Dyzenhaus (1991) *Hard Cases In Wicked Legal Systems* (Oxford: Clarendon Press).

the 1940s. The most notorious supporter of the German war effort was a man named Robey Leibbrandt, who went so far as to lead a small armed invasion against South African territory. Leibbrandt was subsequently charged and convicted of treason. He was initially sentenced to death, although the sentence, confirmed by the Appellate Division, was commuted to life imprisonment by the Smuts government.[114]

While Hertzog and even Malan might plausibly have rebutted claims that they were Nazis at the outbreak of war, just such an accusation was levelled against younger members of the Purified Nationalists. Perhaps ironically, given the fervour of Henrik Verwoerd's admiration for Hitler's government and the intensity of his hatred for Jews, Verwoerd seemed to take no pride in the label.[115] Indeed, when the *The Star* newspaper accused Verwoerd of being a stooge for the Nazi regime, Verwoerd was sufficiently outraged to sue the paper for libel.

The case of *Verwoerd v Paver* was heard in the Witwatersrand Local Division of the Supreme Court in 1943.[116] The case was in effect an action between the two newspapers.[117] *The Star's* article had specifically accused *Die Transvaaler* of persistently falsifying news stories in an effort to undermine South African support for the war effort. The falsifications were said to to have included the drawing of unsustainable suppositions from statements by government spokesmen, the deliberate misreporting of speeches made by leading Commonwealth politicians, including Smuts and Churchill, and misdescriptions of events involving the South African army. By a curious irony, given Verwoerd's aforementioned attitude towards Judaism, the case was tried by Millin J., a South African Jew who Smuts had appointed to the Witwatersrand bench in 1938.

The judgment in *Verwoerd* spans over sixty pages. Millin J. concluded that *The Star's* charges as to the falsification of news stories were in the main justified. He also considered that it was clear that *Die Transvaaler's* general policy was one which was calculated to assist the German war effort. This was perhaps not a difficult conclusion to reach. *Die Transvaaler* had made its position on the declaration and continuation of the war perfectly clear:

> "The National Party has always proclaimed that South Africa throughout its history, has had only one enemy of its freedom, namely, Great Britain, and that Germany has never yet attacked South Africa. That is why the declaration of war against Germany was so bitterly opposed and why the party has always, with all its might, both in

[114] *R v Leibbrand* [1944] AD 253. Smuts was no doubt conscious of the need to avoid providing the Malanites with a modern equivalent of Slaagtersnek; see p. 10 above.

[115] For an evaluation of the case for and against placing Verwoerd in the Nazi camp at this time see Hepple (1967), n. 93 above, pp. 208–219. Hepple—who was subsequently to emerge as a leading figure at the liberal end of the white political spectrum—appears to believe that the charge was justified.

[116] [1943] WLD 153. See Dugard, *Human Rights and the South African Legal Order* (Princeton: Princeton University Press, 1978), pp. 205–206; Mervis, n. 25 above, pp. 230–231; Hepple (1967), n. 43 above, pp. 213–216.

[117] On the tangled background to the case see Moodie, n. 27 above, pp. 220–224.

Parliament and outside, contested it. The party has declared that when it gains office it will immediately seek an honourable peace".[118]

The final pages of the judgment draw on a good many similar editorial comments in the newspaper between 1940 and 1943. Their overall effect, in Millin J.'s view, left the court with no choice but to conclude that *Die Transvaaler's* editorial comment was indistiguishable:

> "in tone or spirit from what the Germans were trying at this time to say to the people of the Union . . . [Verwoerd] did support Nazi propaganda, he did make his paper a tool of the Nazis in South Africa, and he knew it".[119]

The 1943 general election

The equation of Purified Nationalism with Nazism did not appear to inflict any significant damage on the Malanites' electoral fortunes. Smuts had called a general election for July 1943, calculating that the war situation was by now sufficiently favourable to the allied cause to secure the United Party a workable house majority. The outbreak of war had meant a speedy return to the cabinet for Hofmeyr, who served as Minister of Finance and Deputy Prime Minister when Smuts was abroad. His appointment to so senior a post provided an obvious target for the Reunited Nationalists. In conjuction with their continuous portrayal of Smuts as a man who cared more for the elitist trappings of British society than the economic cares of the Afrikaaner, the Malanites' characterisation of Hofmyer as Smuts' successor and the harbinger of a multi-racial democracy offered a potent force with which to build upon their electoral gains in 1938. That both claims were wholly ludicrous was of no significance to many voters. Malan also fought the 1943 election on the basis of a manifesto which advocated withdrawal not just from the war but also from the Commonwealth.

The United Party concluded an electoral pact with the Labour and Dominion parties in an attempt to prevent a splintering in the anti-Malanite and anti-Havenga vote. This proved, on the surface, a successful strategy. The United Party and its allies won 107 house seats to the Reunited Nationalists' forty-three. The bald figures indicated Smuts had secured a crushing victory. But in terms of the share of the vote won, the election result suggested that Malan was making huge advances.[120] Some thirty-six per cent of voters[121] supported the Malanite ticket. In the Cape, the Purified Nationalists secured forty per cent of the vote; and achieved over fifty per cent in the Free State. More ominous for the United Party was the fact that the Malanites were running a close second in a substantial number of small rural constituencies. Because of the traditional elec-

[118] 27 October 1941, quoted in [1943] WLD 153 at 207.
[119] *Ibid.* at 214–215.
[120] See generally Heard, n. 104 above, ch. 2.
[121] In contested seats.

toral loading in favour of rural constituencies, a modest increase in Purified Nationalist support in the countryside offered Malan a realistic prospect of victory at the subsequent election.[122]

Schools and sea and sand and soldiers—and segregation

The Appellate Division was given the opportunity to revisit the principles it had advanced in *Moller* in the 1940 case of *Seneque v Natal Provincial Administration.*[123] The plaintiff was the father of three children who had previously been accepted as 'European' by their local whites only school. A new headmaster had however required Mr Seneque to 'prove' their European identity by demonstrating that he, his wife, his parents, his wife's parents and his and his wife's grandparents were all of 'pure' European ancestry.[124] The provincial council had upheld this new policy, with the result that the children were excluded from the school.

The exclusion appeared to be in conformity with regulations passed by the Natal Provincial Council in 1929. These provided that children could be admitted to 'European' schools if:

> "the Head Teacher is satisfied by the guardians or parents that the child is of pure European ancestry for three generations on both sides . . . The onus of proof of European ancestry shall lie with the parents or guardians".

Seneque did not challenge the legality of the regulations *per se*. Nor did he ask the court to pass judgment on the question of whether his children were indeed 'European' within the meaning of the regulation. His primary contention was the much more modest one that the school and the provincial council were bound (or 'estopped') to respect the decision made by the original headmaster.

De Wet C.J.[125] accepted this argument. His conclusion was not based on clear precedent, nor on grandiose principles of racial equality. Rather, he held that it would be administratively impracticable to allow a child's racial status to be questioned every time a new headteacher took over the child's school. The

[122] Havenga's Afrikaner party did not win any seats in the 1943 election.

[123] [1940] AD 149.

[124] It will be recalled that the court in *Moller* did not define 'purity', although De Villiers C.J. had indicated that for the child to have one 'impure' grandparent would suffice to prevent her being 'European' for this purpose; see pp. 135–138 above. The Natal regulations seemed to be going much further than that.

[125] De Wet had been educated at Victoria College (subsequently Stellenbosch University) and Cambridge, where he took a first in Law. He began to practice as an advocate in Pretoria in the mid-1880s and then served on Botha's staff during the second boer war. He continued his association with Botha after the war, and was elected as a Het Volk member of the Transvaal legislature in 1907. He returned to practice rather than seek election to the house after Union, but returned to political life in 1913 as Minister of Justice in Botha's cabinet. He once again resumed a career at the bar after Hertzog's election victory in 1924. Hertzog's government appointed him to the Transvaal bench in 1932. The fusion government raised him to the Appellate Division five years later, and he became Chief Justice following Stratford's retirement in 1939.

Natal provincial council could surely not have intended such consequences to ensue. Once admitted, a child could only be removed if the headteacher satisfied the court that she/he was not European in the sense required by the regulation.

The majority—in an opinion authored by Watermeyer J.A.—rejected this argument, however. Such an estoppel could arise only if the child concerned was indeed 'European', which was a matter for the parent to prove. In the absence of such proof, successive headteachers retained the power to exclude pupils who were already attending the school. Perhaps surprisingly, Tindall J.A.—in one of his first Appellate Division opinions—concurred in this result, as did another recent appointee, Albert Centlivres.[126] Watermeyer J.A. began his judgment by professing:

> "a great deal of sympathy for the appellant . . . But however one's natural sympathies may incline one to regret that the question was ever raised in the case of the appellant's children, the matter must be decided according to ordinary legal principles".[127]

As De Wet C.J.'s dissent would indicate, those 'ordinary legal principles' were decidely uncertain. De Wet C.J. himself referred only to *Moller* in his opinion, and that case was of only limited relevance to the narrow question before the court in *Seneque*. Watermeyer J.A. did not refer to a single previous judgment in his opinion. This would suggest that the court had a blank legal sheet on which to author its conclusion. Neither statute nor precedent compelled the majority to reach the outcome it preferred.

Yet it would be far too simplistic, as it would be in respect of the 1900s, the 1920s and the 1930s, to regard *Seneque* as merely a typical example of the courts' unwillingness to deploy common law principle in such a way as invariably to require government authorities to diverge as little as possible from the notion of racial equality. Shortly after *Seneque*, the Cape Provincial Division was faced with a controversy in which there did seem to be compelling authority for upholding government-sponsored discrimination. But on this occasion, the common law proved to be a distinctly more substantial obstacle to segregationist policy and practice.

The judgment of the Cape provincial division in *R v Carelse*[128] addressed a rather more prosaic form of discrimination than was at issue in *Seneque*. The quaintly-named Seashore Act 1935 vested ownership of the seashore and the seabed (for a distance of three miles from land) in the Governor-General. The Act appeared to be primarily concerned with facilitating coastal public works projects. Section 10 of the Act empowered the Governor-General to issue regulations concerning, *inter alia*, 'the use of the sea shore and bathing in the sea'. Neither section 10 nor any other provision in the Act made any reference to racial matters.

[126] Who had concurred in the first instance judgment in *Ndlwana*.

[127] [1940] AD 149 at 158.

[128] [1943] CPD 242. For further comment see Dugard (1978), n. 116 above, p. 317.

In 1940, the Governor-General issued regulations demarcating different sections of the seashore for use by different parts of the community.[129] Persons using the 'wrong' section of the beach committed a criminal offence. Regulations made in respect of an area of the Cape coast known as The Strand, which stretched for some three and a half miles, designated some two miles for the use of 'Europeans' and the remainder for 'non-Europeans'. The European portions, which did not run in a continuous stretch, in the main had both sandy beaches and a sandy sea bottom, and all were served by access roads. The non-European sections had exclusively rocky beaches and sea bottoms, and in some areas the rocks were sharp and jagged following excavation and dumping works by building contractors. None of these areas were served by access roads.

Dan Carelse, a teenager, was one of several Cape Coloureds who challenged the regulations. He used the European section of the beach, and was arrested and subsequently convicted. His defence at trial had not been that he was a 'European', but that the regulations were *ultra vires* section 10 in that they were partial and unequal in their operation under the *Kruse v Johnson* formula.[130]

Davis J., with whom De Villiers J. concurred, considered that there could be no doubt, following *Moller* and *Rasool*, that parliament would have intended that the Governor-General could make regulations under section 10 which segregated areas of beach on the grounds of race. That racial classification *per se* was not unlawful, even though it had not been expressly authorised in the Act, was evident as a matter of implication from the social and cultural context in which the legislation was framed. After quoting from Lord DeVillier C.J.'s judgment in *Moller*,[131] Davis J. observed that:

> "After all, bathing is nowadays a social affair; people lie next to one another on the beach before and after bathing; childen play in and out amongst them. The same reasons which have led to a policy of keeping Europeans and non-Europeans apart in schools may well be thought, as it seems to me, to apply here".[132]

This presumption as to legislative intent did not however lead the court to uphold the regulations. Rather Davis J. concluded that the government's *implied* power to segregate on racial grounds was subject to substantive limits. *Rasool*, he reasoned, was authority for the proposition that race discrimination would be unlawful if: "coupled with an impartiality of treatment which is in all the circumstances manifestly unjust or oppressive".[133] In Davis J.'s view, the facts before the Court did indeed disclose such manifest injustice. Much against the wishes of the Cape Attorney-General, the judges had insisted on visiting the beaches. What they found there, according to the *Cape Argus*, led them to issue 'sharp words' to the Attorney-General when the hearing resumed: "It is

[129] See G. Lewis, *Between the Wire and the Wall* (Cape Town: David Phillip, 1987), pp. 171, 204.

[130] Carelse was represented by D.M. Buchanan and D.B. Molteno, who had acted for Mr Ndlwana in *Ndlwana v Hofmeyr*.

[131] The relevant passage is reproduced at p. 136 above.

[132] [1943] CPD 242 at 247.

[133] *Ibid*. at 253.

practically impossible to bathe with any degree of comfort anywhere on [the coloured] section if the tide be at all low. Reasonably safe surfing is out of the question".[134] The regulations were therefore *ultra vires*.[135]

While segregation on the Cape's beaches was, if only temporarily, relaxed, the country's armed forces continued to be rigidly divided along racial lines.[136] Smuts had initially not seen any merit in allowing non-white South African troops to bear arms in the conflict. By 1944 he had concluded that logistical pressures demanded that Coloureds at least be equipped with weapons. And if the threat of Japanese invasion of South Africa were to become imminent, Smuts also indicated that he would be willing to arm native blacks. This was presumably—given the judgment in *Trumpelmann and Du Toit*—a policy that he could have effected through common law emergency powers had it seemed (as was surely likely) that a legislative majority could not be found for such a measure. His cabinet, with Hofmeyr taking the lead, was unwilling to take this step.[137] Native black troops played no more active a role in the second world war than they had in the first.

Nor did the Smuts administration take steps even to halt, still less to reverse, the segregationist ethos that Hertzog's governments had intensified since the mid-1920s. The Factories, Machinery and Building Works Act 1941 empowered the government to force employers to provide racially segregated work and rest areas for employees.[138] The government also established a Commission of Inquiry into trans-racial marriage and sexual relations, with a view to extending the prohibitions introduced during the late 1920s.[139]

The war government's major initiative in respect of the Coloured population was the creation of a 'Coloured Advisory Council' in 1943. The Council was to consist of prominent Coloureds appointed by the government, who would advise on the most effective ways to address the housing, educational and social welfare needs of Coloured people. The APO offered its support for the Council, but in doing so triggered a clear split in the Coloured community. Many of its of its youngers members saw the Council both as a confirmation both of their existing political and economic inferiority to whites and an indication that that inferiority was likely to become more marked in future. From this viewpoint, the APO's long commitment to 'constitutional' methods was now proven to be a failure, and they began to embrace instead a far more assertive form of protest against segregationist politics.[140]

[134] *Cape Argus*, 15 May 1941, per Davis J.

[135] The initial hearing occurred in 1941. The parties returned to Court some two years later having arrived at a "gentleman's agreement" to re-allocate the beach in a way which satisfied all those concerned; *Cape Argus*, 30 March 1943.

[136] See Hirsen, n. 98 above, ch. 7.

[137] Hancock (1968), n. 23 above, pp. 370–372, 412–414.

[138] G. Lewis, n. 129 above, pp. 205–206.

[139] *Ibid.*

[140] See Lewis, n. 129 above, ch. 8 for an account of the intricacies of Coloured politicians' reactions.

The ANC's embrace of more forceful opposition to segregationist assertive had been stimulated by the Natives (Urban Areas) Consolidation Act 1945.[141] The economic imperatives imposed by the war had led the government tacitly to encourage native blacks to move to urban areas to work in industry. The 1945 Act signalled that that trend would not continue after the cessation of hostilities. Native blacks wishing to move to enter areas would be required to gain a certificate of approval from a labour bureau. This would be withheld if the person concerned had not been offered employment which the bureau considered appropriate. Appropriate employment did not however trigger a right to residence. That arose only (per section 10) if the native black concerned had worked in that urban area for the same employer for a ten-year period or had lived there lawfully for at least fifteen years.[142] Breach of the Act could be a criminal offence. The legislation also granted the police extensive enforcement powers; section 29, for example, permitted a police officer to arrest any person whom he believed to be 'idle' or 'undesirable'. If a court should consider that the person concerned possessed these characteristics, it could order his removal to a native reserve.[143]

VI. CONCLUSION

The legal efficacy of measures such as the Seashore Act, which couched their racial definition simply in terms of concepts like 'European' and 'non-European', turned in large part on the courts' readiness to accept that individuals such as Mr Carelse fell within one group rather than another. As suggested in previous chapters, the South African legal system was by 1945 awash with a variety of racial classifications, some statutory, some the product of the common law, and with a variety of yardsticks against which that classification might be measured. In *R v Radebe*,[144] the Appellate Division offered an authoritative opinion on how that second task was to be performed.

Radebe posed a question concerning the jurisdiction of Natal's 'Native High Court', a tribunal created in 1898 and retained after Union.[145] *Radebe* was one of several defendants who had been convicted of riot and affray in a hearing held within the native court system. He subsequently challenged his conviction on the basis that one of his co-accused, Dhoeki Singh, was not a 'native'. If this contention was correct, Radebe own's conviction would have been invalid as the trial itself would have been beyond the native court's jurisdiction.[146]

[141] See E. Landis, 'South African Apartheid Legislation I: Fundamental Structure' (1961) 71 *Yale LJ* 1 at 43–52; J. Dugard, *Human Rights and the South African Legal Order* (Princeton: Princeton University Press, 1978), pp. 74–75.

[142] The right was also extended to the wives and minor children of a qualified male.

[143] See Landis (1961), n. 141 above, p. 45 for cases dealing with the implementation of this Act in the mid-1950s.

[144] [1945] AD 591.

[145] See p. 89 above.

[146] As noted in Chapter 3, its jurisdiction reached only to criminal cases in which *all* the co-accused were natives.

The Natal Act had defined 'native' as: "all members of the aboriginal races or tribes of Africa south of the Equator". The parties to the action had accepted that Mr Singh was the illegitimate offspring of a 'native' mother and an Indian father. It was also accepted that he lived with natives, resembled a native in appearance, and had married a native woman according to native marriage laws. Radebe's counsel nevertheless maintained that Singh was *not* a native.

The Native High Court had concluded that Singh was a native by employing three tests: first, his 'blood or descent'; secondly, his 'appearance'; and thirdly, his 'habits or mode of life'. The court had concluded that since Singh's descent was not preponderantly non-native, and since his appearance and habits were those of a native, a native he must be. Radebe's conviction was therefore upheld. In a unanimous opinion, authored by Schreiner J.A., the Appellate Division reversed this conclusion and quashed the convictions of Radebe, Singh, and all the other co-accused.

Oliver Schreiner had been sitting on the Appeal Court for less than a year when the *Radebe* appeal was heard. He was the son of W.P. Schreiner, the former Cape Prime Minister who had championed the cause of South Africa's coloured citizens in Britain prior to the passage of the South Africa Act 1909.[147] After achieving a first in classics at the University of the Cape of Good Hope, Schreiner studied law at Cambridge (having, in deference to his father's break with Rhodes, pointedly declined to seek a Rhodes scholarship to study at Oxford). He was subsequently elected to a fellowship at Trinity College. Schreiner served as a captain in the First World War, was wounded on the Somme and awarded the Military Cross. He returned to South Africa to practice law and teach at the University of Witwatersrand. Despite his parentage, Schreiner took no formal role in party politics, although he had been active in liberal causes, having been one of the collaborators along with Hofmeyr in the *Coming of Age* project.[148] His elevation to the Transvaal bench in 1937 would seem to have owed more to his legal abilities than his political connections.[149] He had however already earned the opprobrium of the Malanites by his decision, as the first instance judge in the *Leibbrand* treason case, to impose the death sentence on the accused. His opinion in *Radebe* indicated that his view of the court's interpretive role shared appreciable common ground with the liberal political principles espoused by his father.

Schreiner J.A.'s survey of South Africa's racial classification laws revealed a heterogeneous, confusing and ill-defined set of principles. Some statutory definitions were indeed quite thorough, and permitted courts to draw straightforward conclusions as to a person's racial identity. Other definitions, however, used only such vague terms as 'European', 'Coloured', or 'Native'. This often resulted in wholly tautological legal concepts: "many statutory definitions by

[147] See p. 129 above.

[148] See p. 200 above.

[149] E. Kahn, 'Oliver Denys Schreiner—the Man and His Judicial World' (1980) *South African Law Journal* 566.

making use of the word 'native' in the definition succeed in defining the word 'native' in terms of the word 'native' and thereby introduce confusion".[150] He suggested that South African courts had exacerbated this confusion by failing clearly to establish which test should be applied to determine racial identity under such provisions. In Schreiner J.A.'s view, 'blood or descent' was the key criterion. 'Appearance' or 'habits of life' could at most be invoked as evidence of descent; they were not in themselves free-standing assessment criteria. Lord DeVilliers's statement in *R v Parrot* that racial status turned on whether or not the parents of a mixed-race child were married to each other was not regarded as helpful in resolving this question.

Mr Singh's descent was clear. The question which then arose was whether a person whose descent contained native and non-native blood in equal parts could be a 'native'. Schreiner concluded that the answer to this question had to be 'No':

> "I do not think that it is either logical or in accordance with the ordinary use of language to describe a person who is half-native, half Indian as a native by descent . . . though such a description might be apt when an appreciable, substantial or overwhelming preponderance of native blood existed".[151]

Schreiner J.A. was careful to limit his ruling to the definition of 'native' within the Natal native court legislation. Yet his judgment clearly had wider implications. In effect, he was suggesting that any legislation which used a racial classification based on the *exclusion* of particular races would be ineffective in respect of people whose parents' own descent was wholly of different racial groups. Thus, for example, an ordinance banning 'natives' from particular trams would not have been enforceable against Mr Singh. Such legislation would presumably have to be cast in positive, *inclusive* terms. An ordinance limiting particular trams to 'natives only' would presumably have excluded him.[152]

The *Radebe* decision posed a considerable threat to the legal validity of many of South Africa's ill-defined race classification laws. It also raised the possibility that many South Africans could for many purposes have no obvious racial identity at all. Were Mr Singh, for instance, to encounter a tram system which had carriages for 'Whites only', 'Natives only', 'Asiatics only' and 'Coloureds only' he would arguably have had to walk to his destination, since his 'descent' did not bring him within any of those four categories. More alarming still, from a racist white perspective, was the prospect that the Appellate Division might respond to such absurd situations by permitting mixed race individuals to invoke the most favourable of the various racial identities which mingled in their 'descent'. For the Purified Nationalists, pre-empting this possibility was to become a major plank of their policy programme.

[150] *Ibid.* at 604.

[151] *Ibid.* at 610–611.

[152] The *Radebe* ruling would not have been of any assistance to Mr Moller, Mr Seneque, or Mr Carelse for example, who were excluded from particular facilities not because they *were* 'natives' or 'coloureds', but because they *were not* 'European'.

The Appellate Division also took the opportunity in 1946 to nudge South Africa's laws concerning freedom of expression in a somewhat more liberal direction. *Die Spoorbond v South African Railways*[153] was a defamation action brought by the Railway Administration against the railway workers' union. The case was triggered by a *Spoorbond* claim that the Railway Administration regularly endangered the lives of passengers by permitting trains to be grossly overcrowded and to run at excessive speeds. The Appellate Division had concluded almost twenty years earlier in *Winter v South African Railways and Harbour*[154] that for the purposes of litigation the Railway Administration was to be equated with the Governor-General in Council—in effect the Prime Minister and cabinet. The issue before the trial court was a simple one: whether or not the government had the legal capacity to bring an action in libel to recover damages for attacks on its reputation.

Die Spoorbond, for whom Oswald Pirow appeared as senior counsel, maintained that there was no common law authority in any commonwealth jurisdiction supporting that proposition. It further argued that the reason for that absence of authority was clear; affording the government such a right would unduly suppress freedom of political speech, since critics of government policy would be deterred from voicing opinions or disseminating information by the prospect of losing a libel action.[155]

The trial court rejected this argument. Blackwell J. reasoned instead that the government was a corporate entity, similar in many respects to a private company. Since such companies undoubtedly had the capacity to sue in libel, he concluded by a process of analogy that the government must also have such a right. The Railway Administration received £1,000 damages.

The Appellate Division offered two judgments, by Watermeyer C.J. and Schreiner J.A. respectively,[156] both of which reversed Blackwell J.'s initial ruling. Watermeyer took some pains to confirm that his opinion was rooted more in Roman-Dutch legal principle than in English common law ideas. He observed that neither body of law contained any clear authority supporting the claim that government bodies could sue for libel in their corporate capacity. This seemed to him a strong reason for concluding that no such capacity existed. Nor did he accept that any compelling reason had been advanced to prompt the court to hold that South African common law should now recognise that changing political and social circumstances required such a capacity to be brought into being.

Schreiner J.A. reached the same conclusion as Watermeyer C.J., but he arrived at his destination via a rather more expansive route. In his view, there

[153] (1946) AD 999.

[154] [1929] SALR (AD) 100.

[155] Constitutional lawyers now characterise this argument as the 'chilling effect' on political speech, following the celebrated judgment of the US Supreme Court in *The New York Times v Sullivan* (1964) 376 US 255.

[156] Tindall J.A., Greenberg J.A. and Davis A.J.A. concurred in the Chief Justice's opinion.

were sound political reasons for the absence of legal authority supporting the Railway Administration's position:

> "I have no doubt that it would involve a serious interference with the free expression of opinion hitherto enjoyed in this country if the wealth of the State, derived from the State's subjects, could be used to launch against those subjects actions for defamation because they have, falsely and unfairly as it may be, criticised or condemned the management of the country".[157]

The appropriate way for the government to respond to such criticism was through political action, not through litigation.

Both judges agreed that individual ministers or government employees could institute libel proceedings in respect of stories which defamed them personally. They also suggested the government itself could bring an action in malicious falsehood to recover quantifiable economic loss caused by false and malicious press stories.[158] What it could not do, however, was sue in libel simply to vindicate its reputation.

The judgment was obviously of some significance to newspapers and political activists who wished to air critical views of any aspect of government policy, including its initiatives in respect of race relations. Its value was perhaps greater to the liberal white press than to more radical (and mainly non-white) groups, to whom the already extensive network of criminal restraints on political expression posed a more serious impediment to the dissemination of fact and opinion.

The decision also strengthened the Appellate Division's reputation as a law-making body which was *de facto* as well as *de jure* independent of the *government* of the day. As Schreiner J.A. had observed in his opinion, however, the South African constitution placed no impediment in the way of *parliament* if it decided that legislation should be enacted reversing the *Die Spoorbond* judgment.[159] The Smuts administration evinced no particular desire to invite parliament to act upon that suggestion, notwithstanding the fact that its policies, its competence and its integrity were subjected to constant attack by the Malanite press in the run up to the 1948 general election. That election was to prove a watershed in South Africa's constitutional development, provoking a series of political and legal controversies which were to trigger a crisis in the relationship between the cabinet and the Appellate Division over the apparently simple questions of what 'parliament' actually was and what legal powers that body possessed.

157 [1946] SALR (AD) 999 at 1013.

158 Malicious falsehood is a far less attractive proposition for defamed plaintiffs than libel. In the latter remedy, damage to reputation is presumed merely from the fact of publication and it is the responsibility of the defendant to prove either that the libel was true or that it was covered by the (limited) defences of fair comment or qualified privilege. In the former, damage is recoverable only for proven economic loss and it is for the plaintiff to prove both that the libel is false and that it was published with malicious motives.

159 [1946] SALR (AD) 999 at 1013–1014.

7

Harris v Donges (Minister of the Interior) No. 1: *The Immediate Context*

Smuts had begun the post-war era by advocating what seemed to be a remarkable break with dominant South African traditions. The Asiatic Land Tenure and Indian Representation Bill proposed that Indians in the Transvaal and Natal should be granted (white) representation in parliament. The Indians would be placed on a separate electoral roll, whose voters would return two senators and three members of the house. The bill was produced in response to continuing unrest in Natal, where whites were increasingly fearful that Indians were encroaching into white residential areas. The *quid pro quo* for the Indian vote was that Asians would be prevented from owning property in large areas of Natal.[1]

The bill was enacted by the bicameral, simple majority process rather than in accordance with the two-thirds unicameral majority procedure specified in section 35 of the South Africa Act. Smuts' choice of procedure excited little comment. This is unsurprising, given that the Appellate Division's decision in *Ndlwana* had indicated that the entrenched provisions were no longer effective. The lack of controversy over the procedure parliament used might alternatively or additionally be explained by a presumption that since Indians did not have the franchise *de facto* in Natal and were denied it *de jure* in the Transvaal, the Act enhanced rather than reduced their voting rights.

Smuts achieved a parliamentary majority for the bill, but at the cost of antagonising not just the Purified Nationalists, but also the Labour and Dominion Parties. Nor was South Africa's Indian population pleased by the Act. Many Indians embarked on a protracted civil disobedience campaign to oppose its provisions, an enterprise in which they enjoyed the increasingly vociferous support of the government of soon-to-be independent India.

The resurgence of Indian opposition to segregationist policies stimulated a marked intensification of the activities of the ANC. In December 1945, the ANC launched a 'Declaration of Rights' which urged the complete removal of all racial

[1] K. Hancock, *Smuts. Volume 2: Fields of Force 1919–1950* (Cambridge: CUP, 1968), pp. 464–468.

classifications in South African law.[2] The increasingly assertive nature of non-white political opposition was forcefully illustrated in the following year, when the native representatives on the Native Representatives Council[3] concluded that they played no meaningful role within the South African system of governance. Rather than continue to act as a buffer for native black hostility to the government, the Council voted to disband itself and backed the ANC's call for immediate abolition of racially discriminatory legislation.[4] More significantly still, substantial steps were taken by Indian, Coloured and native black political activists to launch joint campaigns against discriminatory government policies.[5]

The ANC leadership was however seen as unduly conservative by one faction of the party's younger members. A more radically inclined ANC Youth League was formed in 1944, committed if necessary to adopt far more confrontational tactics to redress racial discrimination. Nelson Mandela, Oliver Tambo and Walter Sisulu were among the League's earliest members.

Political unrest was matched by industrial upheaval. In 1946 some 70,000 black miners went on strike in the Rand. Legislation passed in 1942 had made any strike by black workers illegal. As in 1914 and 1922, Smuts eventually resorted to the deployment of armed police and soldiers to force the strikers back to work.[6]

The government's increasingly embattled state at home was mirrored by difficulties abroad. Smuts' taste for the world rather than domestic stage had been indulged after the war in his involvement with the foundation of the United Nations. He had played a prominent role in shaping the contents of the United Nations Charter, a document in which the notion of 'fundamental human rights' was an essential element. That South Africa's treatment of its non-white citizens was wholly irreconcilable with any sophisticated understanding of human rights had evidently escaped Smuts' attention. The paradox did not however prove so elusive to the mind of the Indian government, nor to other liberal democratic regimes. Smuts's early experiences at the United Nations were centred primarily on defending his government from constant attack.[7]

[2] N. Mandela, *Long Road to Freedom* (London: Abacus, 1995), pp. 109–111. Mandela records that the Indian campaign "became a model for the type of protest that we were calling for . . . [It] reminded us that the freedom struggle was not merely a question of making speeches, holding meetings, passing resolutions and sending deputations, but of meticulous organisation, militant mass action, and above all, the willingness to suffer and sacrifice": *ibid.* at p. 119.

[3] Established under the Representation of the Natives Act 1936; see pp. 197–202 above.

[4] Hancock (1968), n. 1 above, pp. 483–486.

[5] G. Lewis, *Between the Wire and the Wall* (Cape Town: David Phillip, 1987), pp. 230–231; Brookes and Macaulay, n. 45 below, pp. 147–148. For an account of an early (and partly successful) campaign see T. Lodge's account of the Alexandria bus boycotts in 1944 and 1945; *Black Politics in South Africa* (London: Longman, 1983), pp. 13–15. A slightly different perspective on the same event is provided in B. Hirsen, *Yours for the Union* (Johannesburg: Witwatersrand University Press, 1989), ch. 11.

[6] *Ibid.* at 117–118; T. Davenport, *South Africa: a Modern History*, 2nd edn. (Cambridge: CUP, 1978), pp. 241–243; Hancock (1968), n. 1 above, pp. 478–484: D. O'Meara, *Forty Lost Years* (Athens, Ohio: Ohio University Press, 1996), pp. 25–26; Lodge, n. 5 above, pp. 19–20.

[7] K. Heard, *General Elections in South Africa 1943–1970* (London: OUP, 1974), pp. 31–32.

Political instability at home, coupled with Nationalist indignation at criticism of South Africa abroad, presented Malan with a powerful cocktail to offer the electorate in 1948.[8] That Churchill had been so unceremoniously voted out of office by the British electorate in 1945—notwithstanding his contribution to securing victory in the war—was a poor omen for Smuts' own electoral chances, notwithstanding his success in negotiating a further electoral pact with the Labour party. The 1948 election was called for 26 May.

I. THE 1948 GENERAL ELECTION

Hofmeyr's relative liberalism again offered the National Party a further important line of attack during the 1948 general election campaign.[9] The propaganda deployed—that Hofmeyr would succeed Smuts and force whites to work for and marry native blacks—was as devoid of subtlety as it was of truth. Hofmeyr expressed a commitment to separate development and held out the long term prospect of the gradual incorporation of 'civilised' non-whites into the mainstream of political life. Yet anyone familiar with his record in office of accommodating his abstract principles to the reality of discriminatory legislation would have doubted that even these ideas would have found their way into bills promoted by a Hofmeyr government.

Malan had seemingly doubted that the National Party could win an outright majority in 1948. That it did so is testament in part to the electoral pact it made with Havenga's somewhat reinvigorated Afrikaner party, and in part to the effectiveness of its racial propaganda. Malan had made the point with little subtlety in his campaign speeches:

> "Will the European race in the future be able to, but also want to maintain its rule, its purity and its civilisation, or will it float along until it vanishes in the black sea of South Africa's non-European population?".[10]

But, ironically, Malan's success was substantially the result of Smuts' own political chicanery some forty years earlier. As noted in Chapter 4, the house of assembly's electoral system had allowed a thirty per cent variation in the size of the electorate in individual constituencies. That variation had always been implemented in a way that weighted rural votes more heavily than in urban areas. The system was the one Smuts had persuaded the West Ridgeway Commission to adopt for the Transvaal in 1906, in order to ensure that the *uitlanders* in the Johannesburg metropolitan area could not command an obvious majority of seats in the Transvaal's legislature. Smuts' manoeuvrings had had

[8] See O'Meara, n. 6 above, pp. 31–32.

[9] A. Paton, *Hofmeyr* (Cape Town: OUP, 1965), pp. 373–375. See also A. Pelzer, *Verwoerd Speaks* (APB Publishers: Johannesburg, 1966), pp. 14–16. On the campaign generally, and for detailed results of the voting patterns, see Heard, n. 7 above, ch. 3.

[10] Speech at Paarl on 20 April 1948; cited in Hancock (1968), n. 1 above, p. 500.

the desired effect in 1907 and again, applied to South Africa as a whole, in the 1910 general election. But by 1948, Smuts' natural support was disproportionately located in urban areas. Rural white South Africa now stood markedly to his political right. As a consequence, Malan was returned to power with a workable majority in the house of assembly having won barely forty per cent of the popular vote (see Table 7.1). The United and Labour parties had in contrast received fifty per cnt of the total votes cast. Their successes, however, had been by large majorities in urban constituencies. The Nationalist and Afrikaner MPs won their seats in predominantly rural constituencies with what were generally much smaller majorities. Smuts himself was defeated in his own constituency and—much like Botha in 1910—had to engineer a by-election in a safe seat to secure his return to the house.

Table 7.1 The 1948 General Election*

Party	*Votes*	*Seats*
National Party	41%	70
Afrikaner Party		9
United Party	51%	65
Labour Party		6

*Source: K. Heard, *General Elections in South Africa 1943–1970* (London: OUP, 1974), ch. 3, especially.

The Purified National government: the politicians

Malan's background, beliefs and early political career have already been outlined. At this juncture, it is perhaps helpful to focus briefly on several of his senior cabinet colleagues.

Theophilus Donges was to serve as Minister for the Interior in Malan's government. Born in 1898, Donges had taken an undergraduate degree at Victoria College,[11] and then read for both an LLB and LLD at London University. Rather than practice law full time on his return to South Africa in 1924, Donges became a journalist, serving as Malan's assistant editor on *Die Burger*. In addition to maintaining a part-time practice at the bar, Donges worked as a law teacher at Stellenbosch and was a leading member of the Afrikaner Broederbond. Donges' political activities closely followed Malan's. Initially a member of Hertzog's Nationalist party, he joined Malan in the Purified Nationalists following the

[11] Subsequently the University of Stellenbosch.

Smuts/Hertzog coalition. He entered the house of assembly in 1941, and moved straight into the cabinet as Minister of the Interior after the 1948 election.

Havenga resumed the role of Minister of Finance which he had played during the Hertzog administrations. By this point however, his previous fixation with maintaining the nominal value of the currency had abated. One of his first actions in the new Cabinet was to follow a devaluation of sterling in 1949, thereby triggering a further upswing in the country's economic well-being (or more accurately, the economic well-being of its white inhabitants).

Malan appointed C.R. Swart to serve as Minister of Justice. Swart had entered the house in 1931 as a member of the Malanite wing of the National Party. He refused to participate in the fusion project, and lost his seat, standing as a Purified Nationalist, in the 1938 general election. He became leader of the Purified Nationalist Party in the Free State in 1940, and returned to the house in a by-election the following year. Swart was firmly opposed to reunification with the Hertzogian Nationalists after the ourbreak of the Second World War, and was a prime-mover in securing Hertzog's departure from the leadership.

Johannes Strijdom entered the cabinet as Minister of Lands and Irrigation. Strijdom, born in 1893 in the Transvaal, had been in his early life successively an ostrich farmer, a civil servant and a lawyer. He had achieved the singular distinction (for a boer) of being disciplined for anti-British behaviour while at school, and was a prominent member of militant Afrikaaner political groups while an undergraduate at Stellenbosch. Strijdom formally entered political life as a National Party organiser in the Transvaal in 1920, and was elected to the house for the Transvaal seat of Watersburg in 1929. Strijdom followed Malan into the Purified Nationalist party after the Hertzog/Smuts fusion agreement, and subsequently became the party leader in the Transvaal. Strijdom was influential in securing the editorship of *Die Transvaaler* for Verwoerd in 1937. Thereafter the two men worked closely in tandem, with Strijdom focusing his energies on building an effective party machine and Verwoerd developing a coherent ideological programme for the party to adopt. Strijdom saw little merit in trying to find common ground with the United Party, and indeed was even opposed to the electoral accommodation Malan had made with Havenga in 1948. He had been a consistent advocate of South African republicanism and secession from the Commonwealth during his time in the house, although in his first year as a cabinet minister he devoted the bulk of his energies to his departmental responsibilities. Malan was already an old man in 1948, and Strijdom was widely regarded in the party as his heir apparent. Relations between the two men were however distinctly frosty. This was in part because of their divergent attitudes towards Havenga, but the tension also stemmed from Strijdom's evident impatience with Malan's purported respect for the parliamentary system of government and the procedural niceties that the system entailed. Strijdom's organisational success in the Transvaal had played a crucial part in the party's election victory: to be 'rewarded' with so minor a cabinet portfolio could readily be construed as an insult.

Henrik Verwoerd's labelling as a Nazi by the courts during the Second World War had not hindered his political career, even though the costs of the action had virtually bankrupted him. Verwoerd's parents were Dutch, and had emigrated to South Africa in 1903 when Verwoerd was two years old. His father's involvement with the Dutch Reformed Church meant that the family endured a peripatetic existence, living variously in the Transvaal, the Free State and Rhodesia. After taking bachelor's and doctoral degrees in psychology and philosophy, Verwoerd refused the offer of a scholarship to Oxford and pursued further studies in Germany. On returning to South Africa, he became a professor of psychology and subsequently head of the new department of social work at Stellenbosch. Verwoerd was an influential figure in the growth of the social work profession in South Africa, but by the mid-1930s he found the pull of political activity outweighing the attractions of academia. Rather than seek election to the house, he was persuaded to become editor of *Die Transvaaler*, where he developed an editorial line that was fiercely republican and segregationist in substance. Verwoerd stood unsuccessfully for a house seat in the 1948 election, but shortly afterwards entered the senate, where he initially made his mark with a lengthy speech outlining the rationale and implications of the government's race relations policies. To the vocal dismay of the most extreme wing of the party, Verwoerd was not immediately appointed to the cabinet. Malan soon bowed to the pressure from Strijdom and the Transvaal backbenchers however, and brought Verwoerd into the cabinet as Minister of Native Affairs in October 1950.

II. THE NATIONAL GOVERNMENT: THE INITIAL PROGRAMME

Malan's government held the view that it was charged with a divine mission to safeguard the survival of the Afrikaaner population.[12] Its main objective was to give legal expression to the ideological tenets of the christian nationalist philosophy to which Malan had begun to lend a coherent political shape as long ago as 1912. The doctrine was forcefully restated by the Dutch Reformed Church shortly after the 1948 election, in a pamphlet entitled *Fundamental Principles of Calvinist Political Science*.[13] Wilson and Thompson's suggestion that the Dutch Reformed Church could defensibly be portrayed as 'the National Party at prayer'[14] has appreciable force, but Malan's policy agenda went far beyond matters of theology.

To a considerable extent, the Nationalist agenda was centred on advancing the interests of the Afrikaaner *volk* within the white community. On the

[12] See generally D. O'Meara, *Forty Lost Years* (Athens, Ohio: University of Ohio Press, 1996), ch. 1; Moodie, *The Rise of Afrikanerdom* (London: University of California Press, 1975), p. 7 and ch. 12.

[13] See F. Troup, *South Africa: an Historical Introduction* (London: Methuen, 1972), pp. 287–290.

[14] 'Afrikaner Nationalism' in M. Wilson and L. Thompson (eds.), *The Oxford History of South Africa* (London: OUP, 1971), p. 372.

micro-symbolic level, this concern was evidenced by such gestures as freeing from gaol Robey Leibbrand, the Nazi saboteur convicted of treason during the Second World War.[15] But the government also addressed more practical, macro-level issues. By the end of the Second World War, South Africa (or more accurately white South Africa) was a wealthy country, but Afrikaaners possessed a disproportionately smaller share of that economic power than their anglo compatriots.[16] They were similarly 'disadvantaged' in terms of their share of positions of authority within the government service and the professions. The Afrikaaner Broederbond had been formed in 1918[17] in part as a long-term attempt to redress these imbalances. By 1948 it had made modest progress. The Nationalist Party's electoral victory promised far more rapid developments in the next few years. The new government anticipated that there would be a substantial expansion in public sector employment, all of which would be targeted at the hitherto impoverished and under-represented Afrikaaner. Recruitment to and promotion within the police force and the military would also in future be organised to further distinctly Afrikaaner—and at senior levels Broederbond—interests.[18]

The government's proposed economic policies had a 'socialist' tinge.[19] Much as Hertzog had appealed to white working class voters on the Rand in the 1920s, Malan had premised part of the party's electoral strategy in 1948 on a campaign against 'English-speaking' capitalist interests. The tactic had particular resonance in the Transvaal, where the promise of the nationalisation of key industries to be run in future for the benefit of the Afrikaaner *volk* rather than British shareholders struck a chord with many of the working class voters who had supported the United Party in 1943.

While countering the insidious influence of 'British' interests within the white population was an essential tenet of the Malanite programme, neutralising the threat of the non-white South Africans was its dominant theme. South African academics have conducted an intense debate in recent years over the extent to which the Malan government's racial policies represented a marked break with, rather than just an intensification of, previously segregationist practice.[20] The

[15] See the coverage—and criticism—of the release in The *Cape Times* on 10 September 1948.

[16] See O'Meara, n. 6 above, pp. 74–78.

[17] See p. 152 above.

[18] For an indication of the rapidity and ruthlessness with which these policies were followed in the early 1950s see O'Meara, n. 6 above, pp. 61–63.

[19] See especially A. Norval, *Deconstructing Apartheid Discourse* (London: Verso, 1996), ch. 3.

[20] Cf. Lewis, n. 5 above, at p. 261: "The [Purified] Nationalists did not invent segregation; in many cases they built on segregatory foundations laid well before 1948. What they did do, however, was greatly to extend and refine it". See also M. Wolpe (1995) 'Capitalism and Cheap Labour Power in South Africa', in W. Beinart and S. Dubow (eds.), *Segregation and Apartheid* (London: Routledge). Hancock (1968), n. 1 above, pp. 500–503. Mandela's view was that *apartheid* was "a new term, but not a new idea": he characterised the project as an intensification and systematisation of existing governmental policy and practice; *op. cit.*, at pp. 127–128. Malan himself suggested *apartheid* was little different from previous segregatory practices; it was "part and parcel of the South African tradition as practised since the first Dutch settlement at the Cape in 1652, and still supported by the large majority of white South Africans of the main political parties". Malan's comments were made in a letter he had written to an American clergyman, in which he accepted the

government itself had no qualms about coining a new label—*'apartheid'*—for the programme it wished to pursue. Malan had no doubts either as to the religious and moral legitimacy of the policy: "Apartheid is based on what the Afrikaner believes to be his divine calling and his privilege—to convert the heathen to Christianity without obliterating his national identity".[21] But just what *apartheid* was to mean in practical terms was a less clear cut matter.[22]

One strand of Nationalist discourse, and one faction of the Nationalist party, equated *apartheid* with complete separation—political, territorial and economic—of South Africa's various racial groups. This viewpoint was closely associated with an academic thinktank, SABRA, based at Stellenbosch University.[23] SABRA appeared to have overlooked the awkward economic fact that white South Africans owed much of their collective prosperity to their industries' ruthless exploitation of native black labourers. The removal of the black labour force would have had catastrophic short-term consequences for the South African economy.[24]

The alternative position was to impose segregation in the political and social senses, while continuing to draw on cheap black labour as a means to subsidise white South Africans' continually improving standard of living. This demanded the retention of the reserves as homes for a migrant black labour force. It also required—given the increasingly industrialised basis of the white economy—that substantial numbers of native black men and women be accommodated in urban areas close to their places of work. Additionally, it necessitated segregation within employment to ensure that only white workers could gain employment in skilled (and thence better paid) occupations.

Verwoerd's speech to the Senate in 1948 has been widely regarded as a blueprint for the *apartheid* programme.[25] Verwoerd identified the vision of wholly separate white and non-white societies as an 'ideal'. That ideal could never be realised, however, because white farmers and industrialists were dependent upon non-white labour. *Apartheid* would nevertheless involve taking more and more steps toward that ideal, even if the ideal itself could never be reached. The

latter's invitation to offer a defence of *apartheid*. The letter is reproduced in L. Kuper, *Passive Resistance* (London: Jonathan Cape, 1956), Appendix 1.

[21] *Ibid.* at p. 219.

[22] See especially D. Posel, 'The Meaning of Apartheid Before 1948: Conflicting Interests and Forces Within the Afrikaner Nationalist Alliance', in W. Beinart and S. Dubow (eds.), *Segregation and Apartheid in South Africa* (London: Routledge, 1995). Millner, writing from a more contemporaneous perspective, characterised it as both an ideal of white domination and a process in which: "Philosophical and theological arguments were now advanced to bolster the legal structure of race discrimination and the colour bar laws, hitherto incomplete, uneven and loosely co-ordinated, were now to be systematically revised and extended into a comprehensive caste system": 'Apartheid and the South African Courts' (1961) *Current Legal Problems* 280 at 281.

[23] The South Afrcan Bureau of Racial Affairs. See Posel, n. 22 above; Norval, n. 19 above, pp. 114–123.

[24] For a helpful overview of the changing dynamics of the economy in the twenty years preceding 1948 see S. van der Horst, 'The Changing Face of the Economy', in E. Hellmann and H. Lever (eds.), *Race Relations in South Africa 1929–1979* (London: Macmillan, 1979).

[25] The speech is reproduced in full in Pelzer, n. 9 above, pp. 1–19.

only alternative to *apartheid* was political equality. Steps in that direction, Verwoerd contended, would eventually lead to black domination of the white minority. Only *apartheid* could guarantee the pre-eminence of European civilisation in South Africa: "I want to state here unequivocally now the attitude of this side of the House, that South Africa is a white man's country and that he must remain the master here".[26]

Verwoerd outlined three short-term objectives within the *apartheid* programme. First, native blacks should be permitted to own land only in the native reserves. Secondly, non-whites who were required as labour for white farmers and industries outside the reserves should be required to reside in 'villages' designated solely for members of their race: "the Native in our urban areas must be regarded as a 'visitor', who will never have the right to claim any political rights or equal social rights with the Europeans in the European areas".[27] Thirdly, employment opportunities should also be segregated on racial lines, with some kinds of industrial work reserved solely for Europeans.

In Verwoerd's view, Smuts' government had already taken many dangerous steps towards equality:

> "What is the situation as it exists? Europeans and non-Europeans scattered and mingled about the whole of South Africa: Europeans and non-Europeans travelling mixed in the trams and the trains: Europeans and non-Europeans mixing are already in the hotels and places where meals are served; engaged more and more in taking possession of the theatres and the streets; . . . engaged in seeking learning which they do not use in the service of their own people, but . . . to try to cross the border line of European life, to become traitors to their own people".[28]

Verwoerd clarified the government's longer term objectives in a senate speech delivered shortly after he became Minister of Native Affairs.[29] The notion of 'separate development' underpinned the Malan administration's plans:

> "[T]he present government adopts the attitude that it concedes and wishes to give to others precisely what it demands for itself. It believes in the supremacy (*baaskap*) of the European in his sphere, but, then, it also believes equally in the supremacy (*baaskap*) of the Bantu in his sphere".[30]

The 'spheres' would be manifestly unequal in the short and mid-term. Verwoerd ignored[31] the presumably inconvenient fact that native reserves comprised less than fifteen per cent of the country's land mass, even though native blacks comprised some seventy plus per cent of the population. He nevertheless accepted that the black population could not be sustained in reserves built upon

[26] Pelzer, n. 9 above at p. 16.

[27] *Ibid.* at p. 9. A corollary of points 1 and 2 was that education, health and welfare services for particular racial groups would be available only in their own designated areas.

[28] *Ibid.* at pp. 14–15.

[29] The speech is reprinted in Pelzer, n. 9 above, pp. 20–30.

[30] *Ibid.* at p. 25.

[31] Beyond criticising Britain for failing to release the native protectorates to South Africa.

a subsistence agricultural economy. The government would take immediate steps to bolster agricultural productivity in native areas, and envisaged that the reserves would also develop their own industrial base in the fullness of time.[32] The reserves would also develop their own form of governance, along 'traditional' native rather than Western lines.[33] Many of these proposals, and in particular the promotion of 'native' forms of government, were soon given legal expression in the Bantu Authorities Act 1951.[34]

Verwoerd's blueprint would clearly take some considerable period to achieve. Verwoerd himself maintained that the length of time required would depend on 'the Bantu's own industry and preparedness to grasp this opportunity'. The legislative programme needed to implement *apartheid* would not long be delayed, but South Africa's non-white population was not the only 'problem' that the new administration was eager to address.

Consolidating Nationalist authority

Malan acted rapidly to enhance the Purified Nationalists' long-term prospects of retaining a parliamentary majority. Legislation enacted in 1949 granted parliamentary representation to the whites of South West Africa—notwithstanding the United Nations' continuing refusal to allow South Africa to incorporate the territory[35]—whose allegiance to the Nationalist programme was beyond doubt. Six members would be returned to the house and four to the senate. The Act was gerrymandering of the most flagrant kind. The average size of house constituencies was some 4,000 voters—less than half the average in the country as a whole. The over-representation of senators was on a similar scale. Gerrymandering was of course an integral feature of the Afrikaaner political tradition; Malan just took the idea rather further than Smuts or Hertzog had ever considered appropriate. Legislation was also enacted removing the limited franchise rights granted to Indians in 1946, rights which would have been likely to result in the election of United Party MPs.[36]

[32] The broad thrust of Verwoerd's plan subsequently received 'scientific' approval in the recommendations of a Commission of Inquiry chaired by an Afrikaner academic, Professor F.R. Tomlinson. The Commission produced a seventeen volume report in 1954. At the core of its recommendations, however, was a recognition that economic development in the reserves would demand substantial government investment in creating a 'native industrial economy'. Verwoerd seemingly never had any intention to provide such investment. See Ashforth, *The Politics of Official Discourse in Twentieth Century South Africa* (Oxford: Clarendon Press, 1990), ch. 5.

[33] Verwoerd took some pains to stress that the policy was in many respects an extension of, rather than departure from, Hertzogian principles.

[34] See generally A. Hepple, *Verwoerd* (Harmondsworth: Pelican, 1967), ch. 9.

[35] The manoeuvre represented a triumph of the *de facto* over the *de jure*. As Hahlo and Kahn observed some ten years later; "Today, while not a portion of the Union as such, the territory, whose exact juridical status is a mystery, is so closely connected with the Union as to be practically a fifth province": (1960) *South Africa: The Development of Its Laws and Constitution* p. 129 (Cape Town: Juta & Co.).

[36] The Malan administration also secured the abolition of the Native Representative Council, a body which had been virtually defunct since 1945.

The removal of non-European voters from the Cape's common roll would also have reinforced the Nationalist's electoral position, as the great majority of these voters supported the United Party. Malan made it perfectly clear that he wished to achieve this objective. The means by which he might do so were however less straightforward. In an exchange in the house with Hofmeyr, Malan accepted—notwithstanding the Appellate Division's judgment in *Ndlwana*—that legal opinion was divided over whether or not the entrenched clauses remained effective. He began by suggesting that his government would not disregard constitutional limitations: "If we decide to introduce a bill of this nature we shall certainly not do so without first having obtained the very best legal advice in this connection".[37] In the event that such advice made it clear that the entrenched provisions no longer applied, the government would proceed by seeking a simple bicameral majority for the measure.

Three weeks later however, Malan indicated that if the advice was that the entrenchment provisions remained effective, his government would adopt a wholly unconstitutional means to evade them:

> "If the finding was that [entrenchment] was still legally valid . . . we shall have to go to the people with a referendum, to ask the people for leave to set aside this legal provision and to solve this question if necessary with a majority of less than two-thirds".[38]

The referendum device no doubt fitted closely with the Nationalist's perception of themselves as enjoying a mandate from the 'people', and since it seemed quite likely that the government could find some support among United Party voters on the single issue of non-European disenfranchisement, majority support would presumably be forthcoming. Yet the referendum mechanism had no constitutional basis whatsoever. If the entrenched clauses were still in force, they could not be removed by a plebescite. Perhaps unsurprisingly, the advice offered by the government's Law Advisers, the chief of whom at the time was a man named L.C. Steyn, concluded that *Ndlwana* was correctly decided, and the entrenched clauses had been rendered inoperative by the Statute of Westminster.[39]

Malan was not the only member of the house who sought 'the very best legal advice' on this issues. Abraham Bloomberg was a United Party MP, sitting for the Castle constituency in Cape Town, who headed a firm of attornies in the city. He had formerly been Mayor of Cape Town, and had strong links with the city's coloured community. Bloomberg engaged three of the Cape bar's most prominent liberal lawyers, Graeme Duncan KC, Donald Molteno and Harry Snitcher,[40] to produce an opinion. Their conclusion was that *Ndwlana* was wrongly decided. The Statute of Westminster had freed South Africa qua

[37] HAD, 1 September 1948, c.1369.

[38] HAD, 21 September 1948, c.2947.

[39] The advice is contained in an undated and unsigned memorandum, a copy of which can be found in the Molteno papers at BC 579 G2.3.17.

[40] Molteno had argued for the plaintiff in *Ndlwana*. Snitcher was a member of the Communist party, who had stood unsuccessfully against Bloomberg in the 1948 election.

nation from British control, but had had no impact on its internal constitutional structure. Parliament thus remained 'bound' by the entrenched provisions,[41] and the Appellate Division would in turn be bound to invalidate any purported Act which removed non-Europeans from the common roll unless that Act had been passed by a two-thirds unicameral majority at third reading.[42] In the event that South African courts upheld such an Act pased by a bare bicameral majority, the opinion had no doubt that the Privy Council would reverse the domestic judgment. The principal authority on which the opinion relied was *Brown v Leyds*. Given the fate which subsequently befell that judgment at the hands of a bare Volksraad majority, *Brown* was a curious precedent for Duncan *et al.* to invoke. It was chosen evidently to stress the point that entrenchment of basic moral values was an indigenous element of Afrikaaner political culture.[43]

The government did not take any immediate steps to follow its Law Advisers' opinion. It did however take one precautionary measure. A simple two clause statute passed by parliament in 1950, The Abolition of Appeals to the Privy Council Act, ensured that British judges would no longer serve as South Africa's highest Court of Appeal. The Act might be seen in part as a belated response to the indignation triggered in South African legal circles by the *Pearl Assurance* decision.[44] It seems however likely that the Act also had a more forward-looking purpose, in that it removed the possibility, alluded to by Duncan, Molteno and Snitcher in their opinion for Bloomberg, that the Privy Council might at some future date hold that *Ndlwana* had been wrongly decided.

The Suppression of Communism Act 1950, a product of Swart's tenure at the Ministry of Justice, was a rather misleadingly named measure. The Act's definition of 'communism' was sweeping in its terms. In addition to identifying Marxian socialism imposed by a dictatorship of the proletariat as a 'communist' concept, section 1 stated that 'communism':

> "includes, in particular, any doctrine or scheme which aims at bringing about any political, industrial social or economic change within the Union by the promotion of disturbance or disorder, by unlawful acts or omissions or by the threat of such acts or omissions; or . . . which aims at the encouragement of feelings of hostility between the

[41] The inference being that the South Africa Act created a bicameral simple majority parliament which was subjected to some limits on its powers, rather than having created several different parliaments.

[42] The opinion—dated 30 July 1948 and titled *Ex parte Bloomberg*—is filed in the Molteno papers at BC 579 G2.3.2.

[43] Harry Snitcher, interview with Ian Loveland, August 1998. Smuts was apparently reluctant to litigate on the point, fearing that if the government were defeated on the issue it would follow Kruger's example and seek ways to reduce the courts to an irrelevance in constitutional terms. Smuts recalled that after *Brown v Leyds* he had suggested to Kruger that the judgment might expediently be side-stepped simply by packing the Volksraad with government supporters: Dennis Cowen, recalling a discussion he had with Smuts in 1949, in an interview with Ian Loveland in August 1998. On Cowen, see pp. 264–7 below.

[44] See R. Welsh, 'The Privy Council Appeals Act 1950' (1957) *South African Law Journal* 67.

European and non-European races of the Union, the consequences of which are calculated to further the achievement of any object referred to [above]".

The Act declared the Communist party to be an unlawful organisation, and provided for the seizing of its assets. Any person who continued to be a member of the party or to advocate its policies after the Act came into force committed a crime punishable by a gaol term of up to ten years. The legislation gave the Governor-General the power to issue proclamations declaring any other organisation unlawful if he considered it was propagating 'communist' principles. The group's assets could then be seized, and membership or support for such an organisation after the proclamation was issued would also be a criminal offence. In a reversal of traditional Anglo-American legal principle, a person accused under the Act was to be regarded as guilty until such time as a court had found her innocent.

Section 5 empowered the Governor-General to dismiss any member of a provincial assembly, the house or the senate, or to prevent any person becoming a member of those bodies, if she was a 'communist' under the terms of the Act. Sitting members who had previously espoused 'communist' sentiments could not be dismissed as long as they did not profess such beliefs after May 1950.

The Act gave the government sweeping powers of search and seizure. Under section 7, the Minister could authorise officials to:

> "without previous notice at any time enter upon any premises whatsoever and make such investigation and enquiry as he deems necessary . . . [and] require from any person the production then and there . . . of any document or of any copy of any periodical or other publication which is on the premises".

The Minister was also permitted (under section 6) to ban the printing or dissemination of any periodical which he considered was propagating 'communist' doctrine. The Act also borrowed provisions previously found in section 1 of the Botha government's Riotous Assemblies Act 1914: section 9 allowed the Minister to prohibit *any* assembly or gathering which he believed might further the interests of 'communism', or ban specific individuals from attending any such gathering; while section 10 empowered him to restrict the movements of any individual who he was satisfied was furthering 'communist' objectives.[45] Unlike the 1914 Act, however, sections 9 and 10 of the 1950 legislation did not require the Minister to offer any *ex post facto* reasons for his decision. The government no doubt assumed, following the reasoning of the Appellate Division in *Sachs v Minister of Justice*,[46] that no question arose that such a duty (nor a

[45] The ss.9 and 10 powers rapidly became known as 'banning orders'. Mandela, one of the first victims of the powers, described his bans as "a kind of walking imprisonment . . . My bans extended to meetings of all kinds, not only political ones. I could not, for example, attend my son's birthday party"; n. 2 above, pp. 155, 166. See also E. Brookes and J. McAulay, *Civil Liberties in South Africa* (Cape Town: OUP, 1958), pp. 61–63.

[46] Discussed at pp. 189–191 above.

duty to give the affected individual a hearing prior to the issuance of the order) could be implied into the Act as a matter of common law.

Donges and Malan had made it clear that they regarded the advocacy of racial equality as 'encouraging hostility among the races'. It was also clear that the government expected that strikes by black workers (though not by whites) would amount to 'disturbance', 'disorder' or an 'unlawful act' under section 1.[47] The Act also had the effect of attaching draconian penalties to such minor offences as, for example, committing a breach of the peace, obstructing a highway, or entering a railway carriage or beach designated for the use of another race. If done in the furtherance of 'communist' objectives, such activities could now be punished by substantial custodial sentences.

The Act was clearly intended to suppress *any* political activity which advocated the recasting of South Africa's race relations on a non-discriminatory basis, an ambition which was not the exclusive concern of 'communists' as that term would then have been understood in most western democracies.[48] Strauss, who was shortly to replace Smuts as leader of the United Party,[49] offered a confused opposition to the bill. The United Party declared itself in favour of the suppression of communism as a substantive ambition, but objected to the draconian powers the Act gave the government to achieve that end.

It had initially seemed that the Communist Party had sidestepped the Act by the simple expedient of dissolving itself before the legislation came into force. This ploy seemed to have enabled it both to save its assets from seizure, and to permit its one MP, Sam Kahn—elected as a Native member under the terms of the 1936 Act—to retain his seat in parliament. Swart's response was to introduce an amendment to the Act the following year which gave it retrospective effect; anyone who had ever been a 'communist' was now caught by its terms.[50] The significance of the Act becomes all the more apparent when one considers the explicitly racial policies which the government requested parliament to enact, since the terms of the Act suggested that any opposition to government racial policies should be construed as 'communism'.

The legal boundaries of discrimination

The South African courts had experienced considerable difficulties even in the early years of the Union in deciding just what the legislature meant when it used

[47] Kuper (1956), n. 20 above, pp. 61–62. The Act exempted strikes conducted pursuant to the terms of the Industrial Conciliation Act 1937. This measure, promoted by the Hertzog/Smuts government during the fusion era, was limited only to white workers; see Hancock (1968), n. 1 above, p. 478.

[48] Dugard, *Human Rights and the South African Legal Order* (Princeton: Princeton University Press, 1978), pp. 155–156; 'Racial Legislation and Civil Rights', in E. Hellmann and H. Lever (eds.), *Race Relations in South Africa* 1929–1979 (London: Macmillan, 1979). Norval offers an illuminating insight into the way in which the Malan government invoked the label of 'communism' to describe any view that diverged from its own orthodoxies, n. 19 above, pp. 136–140.

[49] Smuts died in September 1950 following a period of severe physical incapacity.

[50] Davenport (1978), n. 6 above, pp. 263–265.

such terms as 'European', 'Native' or 'Coloured' in discriminatory statutes.[51] Those difficulties were compounded by parliament's occasional use of the notion of 'descent' or 'parentage' as a calibrator of racial identity, by its increasingly frequent use of tribal sub-classifications of native blacks, of geographical sub-classifications for Asians and of notions of 'general reputation' as an alternative means of constructing racial identity. This legislative melange was in turn complicated yet further by the increasingly complex genetic and cultural heritages of many of South Africa's inhabitants. In 1948, the South African 'law' of racial classification was in a wholly chaotic state, in which particular individuals could find themselves simultaneously possessing several different racial identities: one might be a Bantu for employment purposes, a Native in respect of housing, a Coloured when cross-racial sexual relations were in issue, or simply a 'non-European' if one wanted to get on a tram.[52] One might have thought that the Appellate Division's decision in *Radebe* had given the Nationalists an incentive for promptly rationalising the classification system along lines which facilitated rather than obstructed segregationist policies. If *apartheid* was to be both an effective system of racial separation and oppression, but also one which could plausibly be claimed to be ordered in its principles and application, a more uniform system of classification would presumably have to be introduced.

The Population Registration Act 1950

Theophilus Donges was the Minister responsible for piloting the the Population Registration Act 1950 through parliament. The Act's preamble announced that it was intended "To make provision for the compilation of the Population of the Union; for the issue of Identity Cards to persons whose names are included in the Register; and for matters incidental thereto". Section 13 provided that the identity cards would record a person's name and sex, her racial classification, her nationality, an identity number and a recent photograph. Under section 18, failure to produce a valid identity card to the police within seven days of being requested to do was made a criminal offence, punishable by up to six months' imprisonment.

The bulk of the Act was concerned with the procedures through which racial classification would be determined. These procedures appeared quite complex. The original designation was to be made by a government official, the Director of Census. Section 2 required the Director to compile a national register. This was (per section 8) to be a public document, available for inspection at local magistrates' offices. Section 11 provided that persons aggrieved by their own classification, *or that of another person*, could contest the decision before a classification board. The board was to consist of a judge or magistrate and two other white appointees. Applicants were required to pay a £10 fee, which was

[51] See particularly pp. 221–223 above.

[52] See A. Suzman, 'Race Classification and Definition in the Legislation and Union of South Africa' *(1960) Acta Juridica* 339.

forfeit if their appeal was unsuccessful. The board held oral hearings, at which applicants were entitled to speak and be represented by counsel. A further appeal then lay to the relevant provincial division of the Supreme Court, and thereafter to the Appellate Division.

The complexity of the Act's procedures was not however matched by the sophistication of its substantive definition of racial identity. Section 5(1) stated simply that: "Every person who is included in the register shall be classified by the Director as a white person, a coloured person or a native, as the case may be". Section 19 further provided that: "A person who in appearance is obviously a white person shall for the purposes of this Act be presumed to be a white person until the contrary is proved". The legislation made no further attempt to define 'white', 'coloured' or 'native', although section 5(2) gave the Governor-General power by proclamation to sub-divide the 'coloured' and 'native' categories into ethnic sub-divisions.

Donges evidently anticipated that the Appellate Division's emphasis on 'descent' in *Radebe* should not be the test of racial identity for this legislation: "The Act stipulates that a person's appearance or social associations will be the deciding factor in the classification . . . [A]ncestry will not even be referred to".[53] The Minister's assumption that his view of the Act's meaning was authoritative indicated that the government saw little scope for judicial interpretation. Whether the courts would share that view remained to be seen.

Mandela's recollection of his experiences as an attorney representing clients who believed they had been wrongly classified under the Act suggests that its initial implementation owed little to rigorous, scientific evaluation. In one case, he found himself arguing that a 'Coloured' client had been erroneously classifed as a 'native':

> "I had formidable documentary evidence to establish my client's case . . . But the magistrate seemed uninterested . . . He stared at my client and gruffly asked him to turn round . . . After scrutinising my client's shoulders, which sloped down sharply, he nodded to the other officials and upheld the appeal. In the view of the white authorities in those days, sloping shoulders were one stereotype of the Coloured physique".[54]

It might plausibly be suggested that the procedural rigour which the Act ostensibly imposed on classification decisions was intended as a smokescreen to disguise the substantive anarchy that the tripartite test would produce. Ambiguity and uncertainty over racial designation served a useful governmental purpose. At a simple level, the dividing line between 'white' and 'coloured' led substantial numbers of 'coloured' South Africans to attempt to 'pass' for white.[55] Many of those who were successful were necessarily removed from the

[53] HAD, 8 March 1950, c.2521.

[54] See n. 2 above, at p. 175.

[55] As Lewis points out, this issue was a constant thorn in the side of the APO's attempts to construct a vigorous 'Coloured' identity (1987), n. 5 above. See also Kuper (1956), n. 20 above, pp. 66–67, who suggests that such 'passers' were among the most rigorous of *apartheid's* supporters.

campaign against segregationist legislation since they had gained an obvious material stake in its retention. A similar effect could be perceived on the Coloured/native borderline.[56] Furthermore, the process itself absorbed substantial amounts of the time and effort of anti-*apartheid* campaigners in activities which were effectively legitimising in a micro context the very system to which they were so opposed at a macro level.[57]

The Group Areas Act

The Population Registration Act was directed at segregating races through the aggregation of decisions about particular individuals.[58] The Group Areas Act, in contrast, swept *apartheid* onto the South African landscape with a rather broader brush. The Act was essentially an extension of Smuts' Asiatic Land Tenure Act 1946.[59] Its was targeted at all races, and empowered the Governor-General, acting on the advice of the Minister of the Interior and a body called the Group Areas Board,[60] to proclaim specific areas for the sole occupation[61] of ownership of particular racial groups. The legislation followed the Population Registration Act 1950 in identifying three racial groups: whites, coloureds and natives.[62] However section 2(2) empowered the Governor-General to sub-divide the coloured and native groups into 'ethnic, linguistic or cultural' sub-groups if he so wished. The designation of a given area would not become effective until at least one year after the Governor-General issued a proclamation reserving it for a particular group. When that time had expired, members of a racial group other than the one identified by the Governor-General committed a criminal offence by retaining occupancy or ownership of any property in the area. Section 34 provided that such offences could be punished by a fine and up to two years' imprisonment.

[56] Cf. Norval's comment that a multifaceted classification system enabled the government to engineer "internal racisms and divisions between the members of oppressed communities", n. 19 above, p. 108.

[57] Some five years after the Act came into effect, the government acknowledged that several thousand people had received different clasifications under different Acts. It also accepted that some 90,000 people were still awaiting classification; E. Landis, 'South African Apartheid Legislation I: Fundamental Structure' (1961) 71 *Yale LJ* 1 at pp. 14–15.

[58] For accounts of the Act, at varying levels of legal detail see E. Landis, 'South African Apartheid Legislation I: Fundamental Structure' (1961) 71 *Yale LJ* 1 at 20–29; Dugard (1978), n. 48 above, pp. 60–61. Brookes and Mcaulay, n. 45 above, pp. 18–22 also provide a useful insight into the way in which the legislation was initially used.

[59] Davenport (1978), n. 6 above, pp. 258–259.

[60] The body was initially called the 'Land Tenure Advisory Board'. It consisted of seven members, all appointed by the Minister.

[61] Section 4 made a general exception for *bona fide* employees, domestic servants and guests, be they in private homes or commercial establishments. The Minister was also empowered by s.14 to issue permits authorising particular individuals to reside in an an area zoned for a different racial group.

[62] Wives and female cohabitees, irrespective of their own race, were classified in the same group as their husband/partner.

The Act also extended to companies, which would be assigned to the particular racial group into which the persons holding a controlling interest in the company concerned belong.[63] Nor could the legislation be circumvented through the device of having the land concerned held in trust for a member of the 'wrong' group. Individuals or companies which attempted to do so also committed a criminal offence. Once the designation became effective, occupants/owners of the wrong racial group would have some three months to sell their property. If they had not done so by that time, the Governor-General was empowered to sell their properties at auction on whatever terms he thought fit.

The Act's ostensible purpose was to facilitate separate development of the races within urban areas by segregating residential neighbourhoods. In practice it was used almost immediately as a device forcibly to remove native blacks and coloureds from the more valuable areas of land and enable whites to move in. Curiously, given the Appellate Division's opinion in *Thompson v Kama*,[64] no serious contention was made either by the United Party or non-white political groups that the Act could impinge indirectly on the Coloureds' voting rights in the Cape, and so should have been enacted through the two-thirds unicameral majority procedure. The *Ndlwana* rationale had it seemed sunk deeply into politicians' understandings of constitutional requirements.

Discrimination in the labour market[65]

The Native Building Workers Act 1951 was to serve as the government's initial vehicle for introducing *apartheid* within the blue collar labour market. The Act could be seen as an extension of the principle introduced by the Botha government in the 1911 Mines and Works Regulations and subsequently given statutory form by the first Hertzog government.[66] This legislation, however, reached not just to mines but to many forms of employment in urban areas. Section 15 prohibited the employment of native blacks in towns and cities in certain occupations in areas other native locations on any task involving 'skilled work'. The Act offered a long, detailed definition of skilled work. This included *inter alia* bricklaying, carpentry, painting and plumbing. The Act also provided, lest parliament had omitted any relevant trade, that the Governor-General could declare any other activity to be 'skilled work' within section 15. If native blacks wished to engage in such types of work, they would have to return to the reserves to do so. The Act ensured that in white areas, blacks could undertake only the most menial and the most poorly paid of employment.

[63] The provision was clearly intended to plug the loophole identified by the Appellate Division in *Dadoo Ltd v Krugersdorp Municipal Council*; see pp. 156–157 above.

[64] See pp. 148–149 above.

[65] See Brookes and Macaulay, n. 45 above, ch. 7.

[66] See pp. 140–141 and 160–161 above.

On sex, marriage and parliamentary hospitality across the racial divide

The Prohibition of Mixed Marriages Act 1949 and the Immorality Act 1950 were rather shorter measures.[67] The 1949 Act prohibited (with prospective effect) marriages between 'European' and 'Non-Europeans'. Any such marriage would be void. A person who knew he/she and his/her intended spouse were not both Europeans or Non-Europeans was guilty of perjury. A mixed marriage would be permissible only if both parties believed themselves to be either Europeans or non-Europeans, and that both parties were: "in appearance obviously what [they] profess to be" *and* that they habitually consorted with Europeans or non-Europeans respectively. Fewer than 100 mixed marriages had taken place per year during the 1940s. The Malan government nevertheless justified the Act on the basis that non-whites were attempting to 'infiltrate' the white race and corrupt its blood line.[68] Verwoerd's celebrated *apartheid* speech in 1948 had stressed that the government was: "emphatically opposed to any mixture of blood between the European and the non-European races".[69]

Donges had offered the house several reasons for supporting the bill. He suggested it was beyond argument that members of all racial groups regarded inter-marriage as an 'evil': the legislation was thus: "designed to give concrete expression to public opinion".[70] The Act would assist the morally 'weaker' members of the white community from succumbing to the temptation of racial inter-mixing, and would spare the innocent children of such unions the social opprobrium that their mixed race heritage would carry with it.

Smuts' opposition to the bill rested on grounds of practicality rather than principle. He accepted that: "if there is one thing on which all South Africans are agreed it is this, that racial blood mixture is an evil".[71] Smuts also accepted that it would be a straightforward matter to prevent such mixtures in respect of Indians and native blacks. 'Coloureds', however, were not susceptible to identification in so clear a manner. So many people existed on the borderline between 'white' and 'coloured' that the inevitable consequence of the Act would be the working of harsh and often arbitrary injustice against a great many individuals.

Donges reiterated his 1949 arguments in respect of the 1950 Act, which amended the legislation promoted by Hertzog's government in 1927 criminalising pre- and extra-marital sexual relations between 'Europeans' and 'Natives'.[72] Malan's government wished to replace the term 'Native' with 'Non-European'. The penalties remained unchanged; up to five years' imprisonment for the male concerned, and up to four years for the female. The Act employed a different classification test from the 1949 Act. Section 3 retained the 'obvious appearance'

[67] See Dugard (1978), n. 48 above, pp. 68–69.

[68] Dugard (1978), n. 48 above, pp. 68–69.

[69] Quoted in Pelzer, n. 9 above, p. 4.

[70] HAD, May 1949, c.6168. On the importance of the legislation as a rallying point for the *apartheid* project within the Afrikaaner community see Norval, n. 19 above, pp. 125–128.

[71] *Ibid*. at c.6175.

[72] See p. 161 above.

criterion, but the 'habitual consorting' criterion was replaced by that of 'general acceptance and repute'.

Neither the 'European' nor 'Non-European' designation featured in the Population Registration Act. The government's failure to co-ordinate its racial classification criteria across different Acts might be thought a consequence of incompetence or oversight. Yet it might also be suggested that the use of different substantive tests in respect of different aspects of social and economic life assisted government efforts to diffuse, deflect or deter unified non-white opposition to the *apartheid* programme.

Pursuit of the *apartheid* project did not always require the government's parliamentary majority to pass bills, however. In February 1951, Senator W. Ballinger, a native representative, had entertained a senior Indian diplomat to lunch in the house's restaurant. The house's catering committee—on which the Nationalists had a majority—subsequently resolved that non-Europeans could be entertained in the house only if sponsored and accompanied by a cabinet minister.[73]

White press reaction

Like much of South Africa's commerce and industry at this time, the white press was disproportionately owned and staffed by 'British' interests. To a limited extent, ownership was indeed vested in what were nominally British companies, for whom the South African media offered an attractive overseas investment. But from a Nationalist perspective, the problem posed by the 'British' press was produced by non-Afrikaaner white South Africans. The Argus group and the *Rand Daily Mail* group continued to exercise an effective duopoly over the English language press, and neither conglomerate was well-disposed towards the Malan government and the principles for which it stood.

In the final months of the Smuts' government, a United Party MP and the Nationalist opposition had urged that an inquiry be set up to explore ways of controlling 'unpatriotic' press coverage of race relations issues.[74] Smuts had seen no need for such measures, a stance which one might attribute either to a sincere belief in press freedom or the expedient consideration that the newspapers concerned were primarily anti-Nationalist in orientation.[75] Once in government, the Nationalists returned to the issue.

The *apartheid* programme had attracted much critical coverage in the English language media. The *Rand Daily Mail* was by then edited by Raynor Ellis, whose tentative liberalism of 1936[76] had hardened some twelve years later into

[73] *Rand Daily Mail*, 2 March 1951.

[74] E. Potter, *The Press as Opposition* (London: Chatto and Windruss, 1975), p. 54.

[75] W. Hachten and A. Giffard, *The Press and Apartheid* (Madison, Wisc: University of Wisconsin Press, 1984), pp. 49–50. The following paragraphs draw heavily on ch. 3 of Hachten and Giffard's book.

[76] See p. 198 n. 63 above.

contempt for the Nationalists and disdain for the United Party. His views were closely reflected in the paper's coverage of political issues,[77] with the result that the *Mail* became the chief focus of the Nationalists' attacks.

The government's view was that such press criticism was ill-founded and intolerable. In November 1949, F.C. Erasmus, then Minister of Defence, argued that the government had been subjected to a 'slanderous press campaign' which was intended to promote suspicion, anatagonism and hostility between Anglo and Afrikaaner whites.[78] Erasmus' complaints were rapidly followed by a major set-piece debate early in 1950, in which ministers and Nationalist backbenchers took turns to accuse the press of being British-dominated, of wilfully misrepresenting government policy, and of attempting to incite hostility between whites and non-whites.[79]

The debate took place at a point when relations between the government and the press had reached a new low. The British government had refused once again to hand over the Native Protectorates to South Africa after the 1948 election. The *Sunday Express* (one of the *Rand Daily Mail* group) had indicated its evident approval and understanding of this refusal by running a cartoon showing Malan inviting black representatives of the three protectorates into a house in which, unseen by those outside, a white man was viciously beating a black man with a stick while another black man lay dead in the corner. Rather than regard this cartoon as part and parcel of the political process, Strijdom had denounced the cartoon as "sabotage of South Africa", and the government initiated a prosecution for incitement of hostility between blacks and whites against the *Sunday Express* under section 29(1) of Hertzog's 1927 Native Administration Act.[80] The paper's editor and the cartoonist were convicted at trial in the magistrate's court and each fined £50.

The paper then appealed against the conviction to the Transvaal provincial division. In *R v Sutherland and Others*,[81] Murray and Ramsbottom JJ. quashed the conviction in forceful terms. The court held that the magistrate had erred in accepting the government's contention that a person 'intended' to promote racial hostility between whites and non-Europeans simply because the engendering of such hostility was a natural and probable consequence of his/her words or actions. Sutherland contended that the cartoon was intended to draw attention to the *Sunday Express*' belief that "European oppression of natives by

[77] But evidently not as fully as it might have been. Mervis relates that during the passage of the Immorality Act 1950, Sam Kahn, a native representative, had revealed that a prominent Nationalist MP had fathered a child by a coloured woman and had been ordered by a court to pay maintenance. With the agreement of the United Party leadership, Kahn's comments were expunged from Hansard. Pressure was also placed on the English language press not to report the story. Ellis, like all his editor colleagues at other papers, complied with the request not to publish the story, *The Fourth Estate* (Johannesburg: Jonathan Ball, 1989), pp. 284–286

[78] See *The Times*, 29 November 1949. For a critique of the Nationalist view of the press at this time see Scrutator (1952), 'The English Press as Villain' *Forum* 52 (June).

[79] HAD, 31 January 1950, c.414.

[80] See Potter, n. 74 above, p. 121; Mervis, n. 77 above, pp. 269–272.

[81] [1950] 4 SALR (TPD) 66.

or with the approval of the Government was rife".[82] Murray J. concluded that if such an intention was a reasonable inference on the facts, no offence under section 29(1) had been committed. He then illustrated this principle with an analogy which in effect—and perhaps by design—would have been most unpalatable to the government:

> "Presumably a Samuel Wilberforce inveighing against the evils of slavery in his endeavours to secure its abolition could scarcely have been said to have deliberately purposed to create hostility between slave and slave owner, whatever feelings might have been aroused in the minds of his listeners by his condemnation of the evils of slavery".[83]

The court considered that the cartoon was no more than "an attack on the present government and its policy"—an action which was not at present an offence under South African law.[84]

The *Sunday Express'* leader in response to the judgment was serious rather than triumphalist in tone. It suggested that had the court found in favour of the government "There would arise a curious and dangerous position in which it would be virtually impossible to criticise the Government's Native policy without being accused of intending to create hostility between the races".[85]

It was not just *apartheid* which caused difficulties in press/ government relations, however. Malan took great offence at the *Mail's* decision to report that he had entered hospital to undergo prostate surgery early in 1950. The Prime Minister considered that such matters were not a subject in which the public had any legitimate interest. On this occasion, despite again being pressurised by United Party MPs not to run the story, the *Mail*—alone among the English language press—did so.[86]

A Press Commission, chaired by the son of former Judge President Van Zyl of the Cape provincial division, and himself Judge President of the Cape, was established in 1950, charged in particular with examining how best to prevent the press publishing 'reckless statements, distortion of facts or fabrication'.[87] As the Johannesburg *Star* saw it, the Commission was a barely veiled threat to press freedom.[88] The Commission's investigations focused almost exclusively on the English language press.[89] It seemed wholly to overlook the intimate

[82] *Ibid.* at 72.

[83] *Ibid.* at 71.

[84] See also *R v Nkalto* [1950] 1 SALR 26 (CPD), in which the Cape provincial division held that an ANC activist who called for non-constitutional methods of resistance to *apartheid* laws could not be convicted under s.29(1) if his words might reasonably be construed as an attack on the principle of white supremacy. To attack white supremacy was not *per se* to promote feelings of racial hostility between blacks and whites.

[85] 13 August 1950.

[86] Mervis, n. 77 above, pp. 286–288.

[87] *Ibid.* at 54; Mervis, n. 77 above, pp. 278–281.

[88] Verwoerd in particular would have had strong reasons for wishing to see *The Star's* editorial freedom curtailed; see pp. 214–216 above.

[89] C. Merret, *A Culture of Censorship* (Pietermarizburg: University of Natal Press, 1994), pp. 36–40.

linkages between the government and the Afrikaaner press. Malan cut his formal ties with *Die Burger* when he became Prime Minister, but his influence on its editorial policy was barely diminshed.[90] Strijdom was intimately involved in the management of a Transvaal paper called *Dagbreek*, while Strijdom, Verwoerd, Donges and Swart also sat on the board of the company which controlled *Die Transvaaler*.[91] As Elaine Potter has suggested, the selective nature of the Commission's attentions reflected the cabinet's perception of the problem the press posed:

> "[The] Government came to see the apartheid ideology not merely as the policy of a political party which chanced to be in office, but as a fundamental 'truth' against which only the blasphemous spoke. The importance of this for the press was the growing tendency to identify all opposition to apartheid with subversion and all criticism of its defenders with treason".[92]

Malan's objective appears to have been to frighten the press into self-censorship rather than to introduce restrictive legislation. Malan was prepared to adopt informal methods of signalling his displeaure, however. He withdrew briefing privileges for the *Rand Daily Mail* in 1950, a step which marked the beginning of a gradual and eventually total exclusion of the English language press from any informal channels of communication with government ministers, backbench Nationalist MPs and senior civil servants.[93]

The cabinet saw some appreciable public relations benefit, both internally and internationally, in being able to claim that South Africa's media was 'free' of overt governmental control.[94] The strategy did not initially bear any fruit.[95] The English language press continued to offer largely hostile coverage of *apartheid* laws, and so made itself a constant source of irritation to the government. There was no doubt that the government could muster a parliamentary majority for legislation imposing strict controls on press freedom: the only question—in the light of many newspapers' evident refusal to toe the government's line—was whether it would take steps to do so.

III. JUDICIAL 'RESPONSES' TO *APARTHEID*

Malan's administration may have been infuriated by press coverage of its policies, but it showed not the least sign of allowing such criticism to sway it from its course. Yet the passage of legislation did not guarantee that the government's wishes would invariably have legal effect. The statute concerned had still to be

90 Potter, n. 74 above, p. 202.
91 *Ibid*. pp. 70–73.
92 *Ibid*. p. 102.
93 *Ibid*. pp. 138–139.
94 *Ibid*. pp. 128, 208.
95 Although see Potter, n. 74 above, pp. 102–108 for an indication that the Commission's activities deterred some papers from running stories critical of government policy.

interpreted by the courts. The possibility remained that a court might conclude that Act's text did not actually bear the meaning that the government had intended. Similarly, it was conceivable that the language parliament had used might be regarded by a judge as insufficiently explicit in its terms to rebut traditional common law understandings in respect of racial equality. The Nationalists' electoral victory had brought with it the power to control the composition of the Supreme Court at both provincial and Appellate level. There did not appear to be any serious support within the government's ranks in the first years of the Malan administration for any attempt to remove reputedly 'unsympathetic' judges from the bench; but little time was to pass before at least some of the less constitutionally conservative of the government's supporters began to find an 'independent' judiciary a source of considerable irritation and inconvenience.

Tindall J.A., among the most forceful of judicial advocates of race neutral common law principles, retired from the Appellate Division in April 1949. He was replaced by Oscar Hoexter. Hoexter was the son of a German Jewish doctor father and a Dutch schoolteacher mother. Like Schreiner, he obtained a first in Classics at the University of the Cape of Good Hope, and thereafter went to Cambridge, where, under Keynes' tutelage, he gained a double first in economics and was elected President of the Union. He took his LLB on returning to the Cape. From 1918 to 1938 Hoexter combined a career both at the bar and in academia, before being appointed to the bench in South West Africa in 1938.

Radebe v Hough

Hoexter had indicated that he shared Tindall's attachment to a colour-blind understanding of the common law through his judgment (when he was serving as an acting appellate judge) in *Radebe v Hough*.[96] Radebe, a native black, had been shot in the penis during a melee with several other black South Africans. In a subsequent civil action, he had been awarded some £16 damages for pain and suffering against his assailant. The trial judge had accepted that the injury suffered was quite severe. Mr Radebe had been rendered impotent for some months. He was no longer impotent by the time of the trial, but suffered severe discomfort when he had an erection. He also experienced acute burning pains during urination. The trial judge explained the low sum awarded, notwithstanding the gravity of the injury, in the following terms:

> "[O]ne must take into consideration the standing of the person injured. For instance, in the case of a native . . . I should most certainly not award the same amount for pain and suffering as I would for the same pain and suffering of a person who had more culture and, for instance, I would award a larger sum for damages in the case of an injury to a European woman than I would for a native male, and so too in the present

[96] [1949] 1 SA 380 AD.

> case, if it had been a European of some standing I would have awarded greater damages".[97]

The trial judge could have pointed to some legal authority for the principle he had followed.[98] However, the Appellate Division unanimously concluded that the principle could not be reconciled with the requirements of the South African common law.

Hoexter issued the sole judgment. He saw no logical basis for assuming that a plaintiff's experience of physical injury was affected by his financial, social or cultural status: "Most decidely it cannot be determined by reference to his race".[99] Evidence that a given individual was atypically sensitive or insensitive to pain might have a bearing on the quantum awarded under this head of damages, but classification by class for these purposes was wholly inappropriate. Mr Radebe had suffered a serious injury, for which the sum of £200 was a suitable recompense.

Sachs v Donges

Radebe v Hough did not impinge directly upon government policy, even if lent the common law an ideological bent with which the Malan government would have found little empathy. The Appellate Division's decision in *Sachs v Donges*[100] struck in contrast at the core of the government's policy agenda. Sachs, it may be recalled, had been a leading white anti-discrimination activist since the 1930s.[101] In the late 1940s, a good deal of his time and energy had been devoted to criticising segregation policies at foreign fora, especially international meetings of trade union bodies. Donges decided that this potential source of embarassment to the government could be removed by the simple expedient of revoking Sachs' passport, which would effectively prevent him from leaving the country. Sachs refused to surrender his passport when asked to do so, and sought a court ruling that Donges had no power to take the passport away.

The issuance of passports in Britain had always been conducted under the government's prerogative (i.e. common law) powers rather than under statutory authority.[102] South Africa had adopted this system in 1909, and its parliament had not since placed the matter on a statutory basis. Donges claimed that the way in which the government exercised these prerogative powers was not sub-

[97] [1949] 1 SA 380 AD at 384–385.

[98] See *Jojo v William Bain & Co Ltd* [1941] SR 72; *Mkize v The South British Insurance Co. Ltd* [1948] 4 SALR 33.

[99] [1949] 1 SA 380 (AD) at 385.

[100] [1950] 2 SA 265.

[101] See pp. 189–191 above.

[102] On the prerogative in general see I. Loveland, *Constitutional Law* (London: Butterworths, 1996), ch. 4.

ject to review in the courts, and that the issuance of passports was a privilege granted by the government which could be withdrawn at any time for any reason. The Minister was able to point to considerable English and South African authority to sustain the first point, and to decisions of the Cape and Transvaal provincial divisions[103] explicitly upholding his second contention. Sachs accepted that he had no right to be issued with a passport, but argued that the granting of a passport afforded him certain rights, which the government could revoke only if he breached the terms on which the passport was issued.

The Minister's claim was upheld in the Witwatersrand local division. But in the Appellate Division, it was rejected by a three to two majority. The majority, Watemeyer C.J.[104] and Greenberg and Schreiner JJ.A., approved Sachs' argument. A passport conferred valuable rights on its holder: without it, foreign travel was virtually impossible. It was issued for a fee, and with the sole condition that it would be cancelled if it was altered or mutilated in any way. The majority thus concluded that a passport was *de jure* a contract between its holder and the government: it could only be revoked if its holder breached the terms on which it was issued. Since Sachs had not done so, Donges had no power to revoke it.

It would have been quite consistent with previous authority, both English and South African, for the majority to have supported the Minister's claim. Its decision to an extent broke new constitutional ground, insofar as it placed new restraints on previously unhindered government actions. The majority was clearly not prepared to assume that the common law required judges to be deferential to governmental policy preferences on such matters. The dissenting judges, Centlivres and Van den Heever JJ.A., did in contrast adopt just such a deferential stance. Centlivres considered that English authority pointed firmly towards the conclusion that the courts had no legitimate role to play in supervising the issue and revocation of passports. Van den Heever reached the same conclusion on the basis of Roman-Dutch legal principle.[105]

R v Abdurahman

The decisions in both *Radebe v Hough* and *Sachs v Donges* were made as a matter solely of common law. In this context, the judges' discretion was not

[103] *Sasseen v Minister of the Interior* [1942] CPD 546 and *Dadoo v Minister of the Interior* (unreported, Transvaal Provincial Division, 15 October 1948).

[104] Ernest Frederick Watemeyer had been born in the Transvaal in 1880. He initially studied at Stellenbosch, and then took degrees in mathematics and law at Cambridge. He joined the Cape bar in 1905, and was appointed to the Cape provincial division by the Smuts government in 1922. The Fusion government promoted him to the Appellate Division in 1937, and he became Chief Justice in 1943. He had no obvious party political affiliations, and had built a reputation as an able exponent both of English and Roman–Dutch law by the time he reached the appellate bench.

[105] Cf. Hahlo and Kahn, n. 35 above, p. 170: "The extent to which the prerogative . . . rests on principles of English or Roman Dutch law is a matter of dispute".

constrained in any degree either by the text of legislation or presuppositions as to legislative intent. The Appellate Division was afforded the opportunity to reveal how, if at all, the outcome of the 1948 election and the Malan government's subsequent policy programme had affected judicial understandings of common law principles in respect of statutory interpretation in *R v Abdurahman*,[106] a case which came before it in 1950.

In August 1948, the Railway Administration[107] made its first contribution to the government's intensified segregation programme by designating a number of first class carriages on Cape routes for 'Europeans Only'. Other first class carriages were open to members of any race. The Administration presumed that its power to adopt this policy had been granted by legislation initially passed during the First World War and then amended by parliament during the first Hertzog administration. The Railways and Harbours Regulation, Control and Management Act 1916, section 3 (as amended in 1926) permitted the Administration to make regulations allowing it to allocate any railway facility: "for the exclusive use of males or females, persons of particular races, or different classes of persons or natives". Section 36(b) then provided that it was a criminal offence for any person to use any facility which had been designated for the exclusive use of members of another race.

Regulation 20 of 1946 (issued during the final Smuts administration) was purportedly an exercise of the section 3 power. It provided, *inter alia*, that:

> "The Administration may, whenever it deems expedient, reserve any train or portion of a train for the exclusive use of males or females, or persons of particular races, or different classes of persons or natives".

The August 1948 designation was in turn presumed by the Administration to be a lawful exercise of the powers claimed under regulation 20.

The new rules were to come into force on 16 August. Under a front page headline which announced 'Segregation era begins', the *Cape Times* reported that railway staff had been placing covered signs reading 'Europeans Only: Slegs Blankes' on first class carriages for the past few days: at midnight on 15 August, the signs were uncovered. The *Cape Times* reported that the Railway Administration had suggested there would be a one month 'period of grace' before the new rules were enforced. Its coverage of events at Cape Town's main rail terminus the next day seemed to confirm this: "There were some glaring breaches of the new regulations, but ticket collectors appeared to turn a Nelson's eye on offenders".

The new rules had been vigorously criticised by a newly emergent pressure group, the Springbok Legion, composed of ex-serviceman, white and coloured, who had been politically radicalised by their wartime experiences. The Legion condemned the segregation as the "first measure of a policy designed to remove

[106] (1950) 3 SA 136 (AD).

[107] As noted in the earlier discussion of *Die Spoorbond* at pp. 224–225 above, the Railway Administration's legal persona in litigation was that of the Governor-General in Council.

all rights from non-Europeans. It will culminate in their disenfranchisement . . . It is contrary to all morality, in direct conflict with the fundamentals of civil liberty".[108]

Non-white opposition to the rules coalesced on 19 August, when the communist party and several coloured and Asian groups formed the 'Train Apartheid Resistance Committee'[109] (TARC). On 6 September, some 400 members of TARC marched on the Cape Town Railway station. The front page headline in the *Cape Times* recorded: "Plan to Oppose Apartheid: Volunteer Force of Resisters: Lively Scenes in Station".

The 'lively scenes' had involved a series of speeches by leading members of the TARC, including A.E. Abdurahman, then the General Secretary of the APO and the nephew of the Abdurahman who led the APO in the early part of the century. The *Cape Times* reported that Abdurahman had told the crowd: "Our struggle must go on until no non-white is left alive or we share with the whites the ruling of our country . . . Go home in an orderly manner, but you can get into any coach, 1st, 2nd or 3rd class". A substantial number of protesters boarded the 'whites only' carriages of a train to Fishhoek. A substantial contingent of police thereafter physically prevented other protestors from boarding any trains. Abdurahman and nine of his colleagues were subsequently prosecuted for incitement to commit a breach of the peace and to breach section 36(b).[110] The trial ended on 12 October. Nine of the ten accused were acquitted. Abdurahman was convicted, and the conviction was upheld in the Cape Provincial Division.

The Appellate Division joined unanimously in an opinion authored by Centlivres J.A.[111] Albert Centlivres (1887–1966) had been appointed to the Appeal Court bench in 1939. His legal career had begun in 1906, when he was awarded a Rhodes scholarship to New College, Oxford, where he took both a BA and the BCL degree. His early career at the Bar in the Cape was interrupted by the First World War. Rather than take a commission, Centlivres served under Smuts and Botha as a private in the South West Africa campaigns. He thereafter returned to South Africa to resume his career as an advocate. In 1920, he abandoned private practice to begin a career as a parliamentary draughtsman. He was appointed to the Cape bench in 1935, where, notably, he had concurred in Van Zyl J.P.'s decision in *Ndlwana*. That judgment, together with his concurrence in *Seneque* and his dissenting opinion in *Sachs v Donges*, might have suggested that his understanding of constitutional and common law would lead

108 The Legion predictions were lent added force on 4 September, when the *Cape Argus* reported a speech by Eric Louw, the Minister of Economic Affairs at a party meeting in Beaufort West, in which he confirmed that train *apartheid* was only the begining of a systematic, all-embracing segregation programme.

109 See Lewis, n. 5 above, pp. 259–260, 266; Lodge, n. 5 above, pp. 39–40.

110 Had these events occurred after 1950, Abdurahman could presumably also have been charged with offences under the Suppression of Communism Act; see pp. 237–238 above.

111 [1950] 3 SA (AD) 136.

him to be sympathetic towards the government's interpretation of its legal powers. Any such assumption was soon shown to be misplaced.

Centlivres J.A.'s judgment in *Abdurahman* addressed two questions. Abdurahman would be innocent of any offence if either regulation 20 itself was *ultra vires* section 3 or if the particular designation made by the Railway Administration exceeded the authority that regulation 20 bestowed. Centlivres J.A.'s argument began by returning unequivocally to the *Kruse v Johnson* principle of 'partial and unequal' operation between classes. Regulation 20 and/or the designation would have that effect if they produced a substantial inequality of treatment between European and non-European passengers.

In what appears initially a strained use of language, Centlivres accepted that parliament did indeed intend in 1916 to permit 'discrimination' between the races in respect of railway facilities. However, he refused to accept that 'discrimination' entailed partial or unequal treatment. Rather the concept encompassed only racial separation on a basis of substantially equal treatment. Regulation 20 was therefore not *ultra vires per se*, because one could envisage certain types of discrimination which would be *intra vires* section 3:

> "If the Administration reserves one or more first class coaches for Europeans only and one or more first class coaches for non-Europeans only (according to their respective reasonable requirements) and restricts the use thereof to European and non-Europeans respectively, there could be no ground of complaint in law. Similarly . . . no objection could be raised in law to reservation of some first class coaches for Europeans and non-Europeans on alternate trains respectively".[113]

The judgment indicated that the requirement laid out in *R v Carelse*[114] that 'partial and unequal' treatment required substantial inequality between the races was perhaps too high a test; anything more than a *de minimis* inequality might suffice to make an executive action unlawful. However Centlivres did not overrule the *Carelse* test, for he considered that the inequality produced by this particular designation was indeed substantial:

> "in that Europeans have the right to use any portion of every train running on the routes in question while non-Europeans are allowed to use only the unreserved portion, and non-Europeans only are liable to criminal sanction".[115]

Centlivres' line of argument did however lead him to overrule *George v Pretoria Municipality*.[116] He suggested (with some delicacy) that the reasoning deployed in the majority judgments in *George* was "difficult to follow",[115] and then proceeded to quote at length and with approval from Bristowe J.'s dissenting opinion in that case.

[112] (1943) CPD 242.

[113] [1950] 3 SA (AD) 136 at 149.

[114] [1950] 3 SA (AD) 136 at 148.

[115] See pp. 146–147 above.

[116] (1950) 3 SA (AD) 136 at 146. He observed, *contra* the empirical assumptions made by the majority in *George*, that there would have been no white demand for whites-only trams if there had not been substantial non-white demand to use trams.

Dugard has suggested that *Abdurahman* should be construed as a forceful judicial reassertion of a common law principle of racial equality, and thus a signal of—if not judicial defiance—then of common law obstructionism to the government's apartheid programme:

> "The decision contrasts sharply with that of *Rasool*, in approach if not in principle, in that the judicial process of choice was consistently exercised against the administration".[117]

The comment touches forcefully on the complex, often internally contradictory nature of the South African common law's treatment of racial classification. Centlivres' references to *Rasool* made it clear that he considered the case to have been correctly decided, on the basis that the segregation imposed in Post Offices had not produced substantial inequality between the races.[118] It does seem clear that in *Abdurahman* the Court—for it was a unanimous judgment—was favouring one well-established strand of common law doctrine over another.[119] The Court could with equal felicity have found authority for concluding either that the legislation did authorise partial treatment or that the inequality created by the designation was not substantial. Alternatively, the Court could have fastened on the less securely established common law principle that the mere classification of people by racial groups amount to 'partiality' in the *Kruse v Johnson* sense, even if the treatment meted out to each group was identical.[120]

Dugard's proposition seems eminently defensible, but the force of the point it makes should not be over-estimated. Centlivres' judgment indicated quite clearly that the government could expect that existing statutory powers authorising racial classification in the provision of public services would be construed by the courts not just to permit separation on the basis of strict equality, but also separation on the basis of minor inequality. Should the government wish to go further, and introduce substantial inequality of provision between the races, or to exclude one or more races entirely from particular facilities, it would have to introduce a carefully worded bill to that effect into the legislature and ensure that the bill attracted majority support in the house and senate. The

[117] Dugard (1978), n. 48 above, pp. 316–317.

[118] The important (and unanswerable) question which then arises is whether Centlivres would have concluded, had *Rasool* been re-argued, that the inequality was indeed substantial. As noted above, Rasool had conceded there was an equality of service for the purposes of his appeal.

[119] See also H. Corder, *Judges at Work* (Cape Town: Juta & Co, 1984), pp. 149–150. It is ostensibly difficult to reconcile Centlivres' judgment here with his opinion in *Seneque* (pp. 217–218 above). Corder suggests that the latter case illustrates Centlivres' pre-occupation with legal technicality to the exclusion of more amorphous 'political' considerations. That analysis would seem equally applicable to the *Abdurahman* opinion; *ibid.* at p. 161. Milner, writing in 1961, applauded the sentiment underlying the judgment, but seemed to doubt its legal integrity, commenting that Centlivres' suggestion that parliament did not intend to impose unequal services contained "a heavy element of fiction"; n. 22 above, p. 289.

[120] See the opinions of Bristow J. and De Villiers J.P. in *Williams and Adendorff v Johannesburg Municipality* (1915) TPD 106; discussed at pp. 144–146 above.

Abdurahman principle was thus an impediment to the extension of *apartheid* principles, but only a temporary and readily surmountable impediment.

An independent judiciary?

Nor did the government appear to regard *Abdurahman* as a manifestation of a form of judicial resistance to *apartheid* which had to be addressed by direct and immediate measures. Centlivres was appointed as Chief Justice—nominally by Swart but *de facto* by the cabinet—later in 1950 when Watermeyer C.J. retired. Previous governments had accepted as a matter of tradition that Chief Justiceship should pass to the longest serving Appellate Division judge on the death or retirement of the previous incumbent. However, the government was not under any constitutional or statutory duty to follow this practice. That it was prepared to do so offered it an opportunity to suggest both to an internal audience and to the outside world that *apartheid* and respect for the rule of law—or at least for the institutional independence of the judiciary from the executive—were not necessarily mutually exclusive concepts.

The Malan government's first appointments to the Appellate Division lent further force to this supposition. Francois Van den Heever was born in 1894. He took a BA degree at Transvaal University College in 1916, before beginning a career as a language teacher. He shortly afterwards joined the civil service and took the LLB degree of the University of South Africa through private study. As noted in Chapter 6, Van den Heever was appointed as Senior Legal Adviser to the government in 1926. He had played a prominent part in the drafting of the Statute of Westminster. He was subsequently appointed to the bench of the Orange Free State provincial division in 1938, and became its Judge President in 1948. His promotion to the Appellate Division followed in October that year. Van den Heever had built a substantial reputation as an academic lawyer by this time, having published two major textbooks and a substantial number of articles in legal journals. He also enjoyed a reputation, writing in Afrikaans, as a poet of some distinction. While Van den Heever was undoubtedly an 'Afrikaner', there was no obvious reason to assume he had been promoted because Swart expected him to act as a mere cipher for the government's wishes. Van den Heever's dissent in *Sachs v Donges* might have given Swart reason to believe that he had appointed an 'ally' to the appellate bench, but that judgment offered a flimsy base for any uncategorical predictions as to van den Heever's understandings of South African common and constitutional law.

Henry Fagan, who replaced Watermeyer, was also manifestly an Afrikaner in his political and cultural outlook. Born in 1899, Fagan had been educated at Victoria College and London University. He was called to the Cape bar in 1914, but spent the next few years as an assistant editor at *Die Burger*, where he forged strong links with Malan. After taking a law lectureship at Stellenbosch, Fagan pursued a career combining academia, journalism, literature and legal practice with considerable distinction. His election as a Nationalist member of the House of Assembly followed in 1933. Fagan was not however a Malanite. He remained loyal to Hertzog after fusion, and—after acting as leading counsel for the government in *Masai* and *Ndlwana*—served as Minister of Native Affairs in the fusion government. Although Fagan followed Hertzog into opposition on the outbreak of the Second World War, he subsequently drifted back towards the centre ground of white politics. Smuts had appointed him to the Cape bench in 1943. Fagan was regarded if not as a liberal then certainly as a 'moderate' on race issues. He had chaired a Commission of Inquiry set up by the Smuts government to make recommendations concerning the future direction of native policy. Verwoerd had condemned the report, which recommended a very incrementalist approach to economic and political integration, in his 1948 senate speech.[121] There was thus no reason to suppose that Fagan would be predisposed to bend or break legal principles to assist the government's cause.

Cynical observers of the Malan's government's attitude towards the independence of the judiciary might nevertheless have been concerned by the provisions of the Criminal Procedure Amendment Act 1948. The Act was one of the first measures that parliament passed after the 1948 election. Its concern was in the main with technical matters of court jurisdiction. However, section 1 empowered the Governor-General to raise the number of judges sitting in the Appellate Division to whatever figure he found expedient. The provision could readily be explained as a way of easing the Court's workload, but it was certainly possible that section 1 might in future be invoked to boost the size of the court for less principled reasons without requiring the government to endure the potential embarassment of having to promote new primary legislation.

In one of the most influential of studies of the South African judiciary, Professor Hugh Corder has suggested that the weight of judicial decision in the pre- and immediately post-war eras:

> "does not seem to lend support to the arguments of the majority of commentators who sing the praises of a judiciary seeking to protect the interests of all those who appeared before it, regardless of racial origin. On the contrary, the [Appellate Division] seems to have identified itself with contemporary social conventions, as embodied in legislation, as far as matters of race were concerned".[122]

That conclusion seems rather overstated, for two reasons. The first is that this position perhaps underestimates the extent to which courts operating in what was essentially a neo-British administrative law tradition *must* be constrained by a presumption of deference to legislative texts. If parliament has made clear its desire to enact a racist 'social convention' in the literal words of an Act, there is no legitimate scope for a court to obstruct the implementation of the

[121] See Davenport (1978), n. 6 above, pp. 244–245; Hancock (1968), n. 1 above, pp. 488–490. On Verwoerd's view of the Fagan report see Pelzer, n. 9 above, pp. 12–13. For a less jaundiced view, see Ashforth, n. 32 above, ch. 4; Norval, n. 19 above, pp. 110–116.

[122] (1984), n. 118 above, p. 168.

legislation concerned. To do so, the court concerned would in effect have to engage in revolution.

Evaluation of the common law's adherence to a colour-blind rule of statutory interpretation could thus only be made in respect of legislation which was textually ambiguous. In such circumstances, there is manifestly scope for a court to construe a statutory provision in ways which either accommodate or frustrate the government's understanding of the powers which the legislation was intended to grant. In these cases, as this and previous chapters have suggested, the courts' longer term record was distinctly inconsistent. Dugard is perhaps nearer the mark than Corder in his suggestion that both the reasoning and the outcome of cases such as *Abdurahman* were "a far cry from the decision of the Court in *Moller*".[123]

It may also be suggested that a more appropriate gauge for measuring judicial attitudes to racial inequality is offered by cases raising matters purely of common law. In such litigation, judicial autonomy was not in the least constrained by a need to legitimise the outcome of a case in terms either of the text used by legislators or the intention that legislators purportedly had in mind when fashioning a particular statute. Measured against this yardstick, the judiciary's performance as a guardian of a race-neutral perception of legalism is rather more impressive. Rose Innes' judgment in *Tsewu* stands out as a particularly forceful illustration of this viewpoint, as does, some forty years later, the Appellate Division's judgment in *Radebe v Hough*. The common law traffic was manifestly not flowing in only one direction. The judgment in *Louw v Kielblok* offered a powerful illustration of the court bending common law principle to accommodate white racist sentiment, but it is hard to extract from decisions of this type a more general presumption that judicial attitudes did indeed identify themselves in any systemic fashion with 'contemporary socal conventions' concerning race at any point in the first half of the twentieth century.

The second alternative gauge would of course be provided by litigation in which the *competence* of 'parliament', rather than its *intention*, was being called into question. On this issue, of course, South African constitutional law rested on foundations wholly dissimilar to those existing in Britain, since the South Africa Act had created several functionally distinct legislatures. This far in this book, we have encountered only four cases in which that argument was raised: *Thomson v Kama*, *R v Ndobe*, *Masai v Jansen* and *Ndlwana v Hofmeyr*. In both *Thomson* and *Ndobe*, the Appellate Division had clearly accepted that its judicial duty lay in upholding the the race neutral terms and spirit of the franchise provisions of the 1909 constitutional settlement, even in circumstances where narrow parliamentary majorities would have favoured an alternative course.

Masai and *Ndlwana*—in which Centlivres had issued a concurring judgment at first instance—had pointed the Appellate Division in a different direction.

[123] Dugard (1978), n. 48 above, p. 318. For *Moller*, see pp. 134–138 above. The case also offers a pointed contrast with the Transvaal trams cases discussed in Chapter 5.

But, as was suggested in Chapter 6, *Ndlwana* could readily be regarded as a poorly reasoned decision. As such, it might be construed as a simple example of judicial acquiescence to political pressure. That construction would however be somewhat unfair, given that so many commentators—among them 'liberal' South Africans and British academics—had subsequently accepted that the Statute of Westminster did indeed free the South African parliament from the 'fetters' of the constitution's entrenched provisions.

It also has to be noted that *Ndlwana* did not actually present the courts with a governmental and legislative attempt to defy the entrenched provisions of section 35(1) of the constitution. The Representation of the Natives Act had after all been passed by a two-thirds majority: both the *Thomson* and *Ndobe* courts would presumably have regarded it—at least in respect of future voters—as a wholly constitutional initiative. One must assume, given the judgments issued in *Ndlwana*, that had Hertzog deliberately sought to have the 1936 bill enacted through the bicameral simple majority procedure, the courts would have allowed him to do so; not because they were simply kowtowing to political pressure, but because they sincerely (if mistakenly) presumed that such a course was now demanded by the constitution.

By 1951, the prospect that the courts might be faced with the twin constitutional difficulties of a powerful argument that *Ndlwana* should be overruled *and* a government determined to establish that the judgment was correct was no longer remote. For Malan, the time had come to purge South Africa's political landscape of one of the most important symbols of the Cape's colour-blind legal tradition. And for defenders of the Cape franchise, a thesis had at last been advanced which forcefully concluded that *Ndobe* rather than *Ndlwana* offered a correct analysis of South African constitutional law.

8

Harris v Donges (Minister of the Interior) No. 1: *The Litigation*

Within the flood of legislation which had gushed out of South Africa's parliament in the first two years of the Malan administration, the contents of the Separate Representation of Voters bill 1951 appeared to add an acute, symbolic force to the *apartheid* tide. Malan had signalled his intentions to address Coloured voting rights in a house speech in 1949.[1] He suggested that Coloured voters en masse were a corrupt and immature electorate, whose votes could be won either through bribes or trickery. This presented a severe problem in constituencies where there were sufficient coloured voters to swing the outcome in a close fought contest between the Nationalists and the United Party. Some two years were however to pass before the government's proposed solution to this "problem" was unveiled.

I. THE SEPARATE REPRESENTATION OF VOTERS BILL

On explaining the bill to the house,[2] Donges asserted that the government possessed an electoral mandate for the policy it contained. The bill expressed:

> "the determination of the white electorate of South Africa to perpetuate the white race in South Africa, in the interest not only of South Africa and the world, but also in the interests of the non-Europeans in our own country".[3]

South Africa, he noted, contained some 2,700,000 whites, 1,000,000 Coloureds, 300,000 Indians and 9,000,000 native blacks. This demographic reality had meant that "the fear of political domination by the non-Europeans has hung like a dark cloud over this country".[4] The cloud was evidently growing darker because native blacks and Coloureds had been inter-marrying, thereby triggering a potentially enormous long term increase in the size of the Coloured population.

This prospect became the more alarming, Donges continued, when one considered that the Coloured voters had apparently habitually 'sold' their votes to

[1] See G. Lewis, *Between the Wire and the Wall* (Cape Town: David Phillip, 1987), pp. 265–266.

[2] The following passage draws on Donges' speech at second reading: HAD, 25 April 1951, c.5381 *et seq*.

[3] *Ibid*. at 5381.

[4] *Ibid*. at 5382.

the highest bidder at election time. This predisposition to corruptibility caused antagonism in the white community, particularly in those constituencies where the Coloured vote was large enough to determine the outcome of the contest. Moreover, the vote was 'a sham and a fraud' for the Coloured people themselves. Having been offered electoral bribes at election time, the Coloured voters promptly found themselves forgotten by the victorious candidate until the next election came round. Worse still, white fears of Coloured political influence were expressed in an unwillingness on the whites' part to assist the economic and social development of the Coloured population.

Donges explained that the solution to these problems lay in separate electoral arrangements for Coloureds: "One of the underlying principles of Apartheid is to remove the points of contact [between the races] as far as possible, because it is the points of contact which are the points of friction".[5] Coloureds would no longer be voting fodder for manipulative white politicians; whites would no longer fear non-white domination; and the economic and social progress of the Coloured people would be enhanced. There were, the Minister observed, sound precedents for this policy. Not only did it resemble the constitutional position in respect of Maoris in New Zealand, but it was also in perfect accord with the proposals of the 1905 South African Native Affairs Commission.[6]

The bill again departed from the race classification criteria laid down in the Population Registration Act 1950. While it recognised 'natives' and 'whites', it used the term 'non-European' rather than 'Coloured'. The definitions employed were similarly confused. One was a 'non-European' if one was not a white or a native. The definition of 'native' followed that used in the Representation of Natives Act 1936.[7] 'White' "means a person who in appearance obviously is, or who is generally accepted as, a white person, but does not include a person, who, although in appearance obviously a white person, is generally accepted as a non-European". Quite what the courts would make of such concepts in the light of the *R v Radebe* decision[8] remained a matter for speculation.

The *consequences* which the Act sought to impose upon 'non-Europeans' were far clearer. Section 2 of the Act required the Minster of the Interior to compile an electoral roll on which all existing Cape Coloured voters were to be placed. The property qualifications for Cape Coloured voters remained intact, and Coloured voters who met those qualifications in the future could also be placed on the new electoral roll. The list was then to be divided into four constituencies, each of which would return one member to the house.[9] Section 4

[5] *Ibid.* at c.5387–5388.

[6] See pp. 66–67 above.

[7] See pp. 197–200 above.

[8] See pp. 221–223 above.

[9] The Act did not amend s.26 of the South Africa Act, which meant that the person elected had to be a 'European'. The house constituencies did not have to be of equal size; the usual 15% deviation above or below a strict numerical mean was permitted (s.6). The new electoral roll was also to be divided into two parts for the purposes of returning two members to the Cape provincial assembly.

also required the Minister to draw up an electoral roll containing only white voters. The implication of sections 2 and 4 would seem to be that the common roll in the Cape was therefore abolished, and two new rolls were created in its place. Section 7 of the Act then required the Governor-General to appoint an additional senator who would have 'a thorough acquaintance with the reaonable wants and wishes' of the non-European population in the Cape. The new registers were not to come into force until another general election had been held.

No change was made to the voting rights of the few non-whites who were registered on the electoral rolls in Natal. However, section 13(3) provided simply that no further non-whites could be registered in that province. Sections 14–19 of the Act established a 'Board for Coloured Affairs', consisting of eleven non-European members and representatives of several government departments.[10] The Board's role would be to advise the government on matters affecting the non-European population and to act as 'an intermediary' between non-Europeans and the government.

Malan's proposal in respect of Coloured voting rights differed little in form from Hertzog's 1936 legislation on native electoral qualifications. Where Malan diverged from Hertzog, however, was in his view of how the bill might be enacted. Having availed themselves of 'the very best legal advice',[11] Malan, Donges and Strijdom had indicated repeatedly[12] that they considered it quite lawful for parliament to repeal section 35 by the simple majority procedure. The government maintained (ignoring Van Zyl J.P.'s conclusion in *Ndlwana*) that the bill did not introduce a 'disqualification' within the meaning of section 35; if anything it enhanced Coloured voters' electoral power.[13] But even if was a disqualification, the effect of the Statute of Westminster and the Status of the Union Act was (and here the government followed its Law Advisers' opinion)[14] to have transformed the South African legislature into an exact replica of the British Parliament.

This conclusion seemed entirely consistent with the Appellate Division's judgment in *Ndlwana* and with Smuts' approach to the 1946 legislation. That *Ndlwana* was simply bad law was not a proposition that Malan's government was likely to embrace. It was most certainly not going to accept Van Zyl J.P.'s suggestion in *Ndlwana* at first instance that parliament could choose to use the two-thirds unicameral procedure if it so wished, for no such majority for the bill would have been forthcoming.

[10] Eight members were to be elected by voters on the Cape's new non-European electoral roll. The other three (one for each northern province) were to be chosen by the Governor-General (s.14).

[11] See p. 236 above.

[12] Strijdom had first made the government's view on this point clear in a speech at Lydenburg in the Transvaal on 9 October 1948, in which he suggested that the government was prepared to defy the constitution if need be; *Cape Times*, 12 October 1948.

[13] HAD, 25 April 1951, c.5934.

[14] See p. 236 above.

Strijdom had also suggested, however, that the government would proceed by the simple majority route even if the constitution did indeed require the 'two-thirds majority in joint sitting' formula to be followed: "The continued existence of white South Africa demands it and therefore we must".[15] Unlike the position sketched out by Malan in 1948, Strijdom's preferred course of action did not involve a referendum to seek the approval of white voters. Strijdom enjoyed Swart's support on this matter. The Minister of Justice had evidently also forgotten the 'moral commitment' to entrenchment that he had offered the house in 1931.[16] 'British' perceptions of the rule of law and the express sentiments of the framers of the South African constitution could not be permitted to stand in the way of Strijdom's *baaskap* view of *apartheid*.[17] Whether Malan would willingly pursue a course that entailed outright defiance of the courts, should the Appellate Division conclude that *Ndlwana* was incorrectly decided, remained to be seen.[18]

Havenga had in contrast intimated that he considered the government was both legally and morally obliged to seek a two-thirds majority for the bill. South Africa's parliamentary rumour mill was rife at this time with suggestions that Havenga was appalled by the neo-Nazism displayed by Strijdom and Verwoerd, and was seriously contemplating crossing the floor to create a new coalition with the United Party.[19] He did not however do so. Nor did he insist that his continued membership of the cabinet be contingent on the government accepting that the section 35 procedure be followed. Havenga's intellectual position appeared increasingly untenable by this point. In July 1950, he had publicly vowed not to support legislation, even if submitted for approval by a two-thirds unicameral majority, which involved a diminution of the coloured voters' political rights.[20] Given that Van Zyl J.P.'s opinion in *Ndlwana* had clearly identifed a separate roll as a diminution, Havenga had seemingly ruled out support for a separate roll for coloureds. His initial attempt to square this political circle was to argue that the issue of diminution had not yet been settled. The obvious

[15] Quoted in A. Paton, *Hofmeyr* (Cape Town: OUP, 1971). The Dutch Reformed Church lent an explicitly theological base to the government's programme. The Rev. P. Viljoen, the Moderator of the DRC, opened its annual synod in Pretoria in April 1951 with a speech informing listeners that: "The struggle in Africa was not between black and white, but between Christendom and Heathendom, between God and Satan . . . God has implanted the urge towards race purity in our hearts and we would be unfaithful to God and to our past to deviate from that"; reported in the *Cape Argus*, 5 April 1951.

[16] See p. 183 above.

[17] Strijdom saw no need to dress *apartheid* up in the language of separate development. For him the concept simply denoted white superiority and non-white subordination in all spheres of social, economic and political life.

[18] Some suggestions were aired that Malan was ready to pursue this course for fear that Strijdom would resign from the Cabinet and challenge his leadership if he did not do so; *Natal Mercury*, 20 April 1951.

[19] Paton, n. 15 above, at p. 405. See also K. Hancock, *Smuts. Volume 2: Fields of Force 1919–1950* (Cambridge: CUP, 1968), pp. 515–516.

[20] *Cape Times*, 26 July 1950.

inference was that he was more concerned to stay in the cabinet than to defend the voting rights of coloured electors.[21]

The weight of academic opinion supported the government's viewpoint. *Ndlwana* was seen as determinative of the issue in the narrow sense, and more broadly, approval was given to the rationale deployed in *Ndlwana* that the Statute of Westminster had imbued the South African legislature with all the qualities of its British creator.[22] That so many academic lawyers—and not simply South African supporters of the government—held this view is most surprising. The rationale underpinning this perspective was the casual equation of a sovereign state with a parliament competent to make any laws by a bare majority. Since few sovereign states had adopted this form of constitutional settlement, the casualness of the equation in respect of South Africa seems wholly unjustified. From a British perspective, the argument made little concession either to political or legal logic. Britain's former colonies had in the main entered independent status—and many of its remaining colonies were approaching it—with constitutional foundations which placed justiciable restraints on bare parliamentary majorities. None had explicitly been constituted with a legislature which was a perfect replica of its British creator. That Afrikaaners should embrace the principle is also at best ironic and at worst simply mendacious, given that the Orange Free State's constitution had specifically rejected it, and that the Republic's constitution had been racked with ambiguity on the question. But by the spring of 1951, the Malan government had been given reasons to think that the entrenchment provisions might continue to be effective.

The Cowen thesis

Despite the evidently awkward precedent offered by Smuts' approach to the 1946 Asiatic land tenure legislation, the leadership of the United Party itself maintained—premising its views on the Bloomberg opinion—that sections 35, 137 and 152 retained their legal force. There was little obvious academic or judicial support for this proposition, notwithstanding the fact that its contention was undoubtedly correct. But by the time the Separate Representation of Voters bill was issued, a forceful legal argument had at last been made in South African circles to the effect that *Ndlwana* had been misconceived. The thesis was

[21] Ben Tindall was appalled by this stance. In a letter to Schreiner he asked: "One hesitates to impute dishonesty, but how can any intelligent man say that the change involves no diminution of the political rights of coloured men qualified to vote ? . . . What a country! What politicians!": Tindall to Schreiner, 15 October 1950: Schreiner papers.

[22] Pollak's views have already been canvassed. In addition see K. Wheare, *The Statute of Westminster and Dominions Status*, 4th edn. (Oxford: Clarendon Press, 1949), H. May, pp. 240–245; *The South African Constitution*, 2nd edn. (Cape Town: Juta and Co, 1949); W. Kennedy and H. Schlosberg, *The Law and Custom of the South African Constitution* (London: Stevens and Sons, 1935), pp. 99–100.

advanced by D.V. Cowen, Professor of Comparative Law at the University of Cape Town, in a short monograph, *Parliamentary Sovereignty and the Entrenched Provisions of the South Africa Act*.[23]

Cowen identified a number of flaws in the 'orthodox' position, a position perhaps best represented by *Ndlwana* itself and Walter Pollak's 1931 article.[24] The first flaw was the presumption that the efficacy of the entrenched clauses had ever been dependent on the continued existence of the 'repugnancy provisions' of the Colonial Laws Validity Act 1865. That legislation, Cowen maintained, had been concerned only with preventing South Africa qua nation, or any of its internal law-making organs, from making laws incompatible with another British statute. The meaning of 'parliament', in contrast, was solely a matter of internal South African constitutional law, which law was found in the South Africa Act itself. Such internal constitutional matters could not have been affected by the Statute of Westminster, since that legislation, which repealed the Colonial Laws Validity Act in respect of Dominion laws, had been enacted only to alter the legal relationship between the Dominions qua nations and the United Kingdom Parliament.[25]

Cowen argued that the South Africa Act *defined* 'parliament' in several different ways. That definition varied according to the *function* 'parliament' was seeking to perform. One version of 'parliament' was able to enact legislation by the bicameral simple majority process. Another version of parliament could overcome senate opposition to a bill approved in the house through the section 63 unicameral process. And a third version of parliament could amend the entrenched provisions of the South Afria Act through the two-thirds majority unicameral procedure. All three bodies were 'parliament', but only if the measures they enacted corresponded with the functional limitations imposed on their respective powers by the South Africa Act itself.

From this perspective, Cowen argued, the Privy Council's decision in *Moore* was an irrelevance to questions concerning the status of the entrenched clauses. In contrast, the Privy Council's approval of the Australian High Court's judgment in *Trethowan* was virtually on all fours with the situation pertaining in South Africa, both prior and subsequent to the country's independence. The South African parliament was not *bound* by the entrenched clauses—rather it was *defined* by them. For the purposes of amending the entrenched provisions, 'parliament' existed only in the 'manner and form' specified by the South Africa

[23] (Cape Town: Juta & Co, 1951). Cowen was also the son-in-law of Patrick Duncan, the Governor-General appointed by Hertzog who had refused to grant Hertzog a dissolution of parliament after the United Party split over the question of entry into the Second World War; see pp. 211–212 above.

[24] See pp. 185–187 above.

[25] Cowen here borrowed Coke C.J.'s formulation of the mischief rule of statutory interpretation in *Heydon's Case* (see p. 182 above) to determine the meaning of the Statute of Westminster. The 'mischief' in question in 1930–1931 had been the subordinacy of the Dominions as countries to the United Kingdom. That the Dominions' own constitutions might place restraints on the legislative power of bare parliamentary majorities was not a 'mischief' within the contemplation of the 1931 Act.

Act, namely in the two-thirds unicameral majority process. If a matter within the scope of sections 35, 137 or 152 was in issue, there was no bicameral simple majority parliament.

Cowen maintained that the 'manner and form' technique of entrenchment was concerned in essence not with *how* legislation was passed, but with *who or what* was competent to pass it. The distinction is an important one. From the first perspective—which was essentially the position arrived at by Duncan *et al.* in the Bloomberg opinion—entrenched measures become a deviation from the legislative norm, and might thus be felt to lack legitimacy. From the second viewpoint, they represent an alternative or additional or even perhaps superior normalcy within the constitutional structure, and might thus be thought more secure in political terms.

Cowen took pains to stress at the outset of his monograph that his argument did not mean that South Africa qua country was in any sense subordinate to the United Kingdom:

> "I would emphasise that I accept fully and unreservedly that South Africa is today a sovereign State and that the Union Parliament possesses sovereign legislative power in and over the Union. But . . . the bald statement that the Union Parliament is the sovereign lawmaking body in the Union does not end the matter; for the vital question remains: 'What is the Union Parliament?' ".[26]

Cowen politely suggested that advocates of the orthodox theory had been 'overawed and misled' by the emotive force attached to the notion of sovereignty, and had quite failed to recognise the distinctions between a sovereign nation, a sovereign nation possessing a legislature exercising sovereign power by a simple majority process, and a sovereign nation in which lawmaking power over different issues had been granted to different legislative bodies; (even if, as in South Africa, those different legislative bodies comprised the same individuals). Straford A.C.J. and his then colleagues in the Appellate Division had themselves fallen into this trap in *Ndlwana*: "The major—though inarticulate—premise in the judgment of Stratford ACJ is that the Union *Parliament* is of exactly the same nature as the United Kingdom *Parliament*".[27] The Court's conclusion was therefore "palpably wrong", and should not be followed in future.

The unavoidable conclusion which flowed from Cowen's thesis was that if the Separate Representation of Voters bill were to be 'enacted' by a simple bicameral majority, the Appellate Division[28] would be obliged to hold that it was not an 'Act' at all, since it had not been passed by the appropriate version of 'parliament'. Cowen's analysis was in large part legalistic in tone and content, but he concluded with an explicitly moral or political argument:

[26] Cowan, n. 23 above, at p. 3.

[27] *Ibid.* at p. 45; original emphasis. Cowen presumably meant 'unarticulated' rather than 'inarticulate'.

[28] A provincial division bench could not do so, since it would be bound by the Appellate Division's own decision in *Ndlwana*.

"The same conclusion could however be reached on the basis that the South Africa Act is a fundamental declaration of the will of the South African people. That Act was forged after much travail at a National Convention. At the request of the four self-governing colonies, it embodied the essential terms of a contract entered into between them to unite for the purposes of government. Accordingly it would not be a contention without force that the South Africa Act is a British Act in form only, but in substance a constitution created by the will of the South African people".[29]

That Professor Cowen was not advancing a radical critique is readily demonstrated by his assumption that the 'South African people' were properly represented by the Convention delegates. With the very limited exception of the more affluent of non-white men in the Cape, the electorates which had chosen those delegates were wholly white and wholly male. Cowen's thesis—and its enthusiastic endorsement by, in particular, the *Rand Daily Mail*[30]—was however an unwelcome irritant to the Malan government; in the longer term because it raised the possibility of defeat in the courts; but more immediately because it gave the government's parliamentary opponents a plausible legal stick with which to attack the bill.[31]

The parliamentary opposition

Hofmeyr's death in December 1948 robbed the United Party of its most influential critic of National Party policy. The brunt of the opposition's challenge was borne by Strauss. Strauss had greeted the introduction of the bill into the house by asking the Speaker to rule if such a measure could be passed by the bicameral procedure. In a long speech,[32] in which he quoted extensively from Cowen's arguments and skirted delicately around the Appellate Division's judgment in *Ndlwana*, Strauss maintained that the Statute of Westminster had turned South Africa into a sovereign state, but had had no impact whatsoever on its internal constitutional arrangements. This view was supported, Strauss argued, by the expressed intentions of the 1929–1930 Imperial Conferences, by the 1931 joint resolution, by Mr Speaker Jansen's 1934 ruling, and by Hertzog's decision to use the unicameral two-thirds majority process to enact the Representation of the Natives Act 1936.[33]

[29] Cowan, n. 23 above, at p. 49.

[30] Mervis, *The Fourth Estate* (Johannesburg: Jonathan Ball, 1989), pp. 303–304.

[31] Cudgels were immediately taken up by the Natal provincial council, which debated and approved a motion in March 1951 which condemned the bill as a breach of the constitution; see the *Cape Times*, 21 March 1951.

[32] HAD, 8 March 1951, c.2586 *et seq*. Evidently too long for some members; the *Cape Times* of 9 March reported that: "It is doubtful whether more than a few legal minds in the galleries and in the chamber understood the close reasoning of the lawyers on the floor. Members on both sides of the House, including two Ministers, quite openly dozed off in the early part of the debate".

[33] Strauss' argument subsequently derived some further support from the view of the Parliamentary Draftsman, A.J. Pienaar, who had told the senate that parliament could only pass legislation on this issue if it complied with the procedural requirements laid out in ss. 35 and 152. See

The Speaker, J.C. Conradie, delivered his ruling on Strauss' motion a month later.[34] Conradie stressed that he was not performing a judicial function, but merely determining procedure within the house. He found—unavoidably—that the weight of academic opinion[35] was against Strauss' argument. He also considered that *Moore* and *Ndlwana* lent great support to the government's position. The 1931 joint resolution was of no assistance; it was merely a resolution, that either chamber could revoke at any time. Mr Speaker Jansen's 1934 opinion shared the same ephemeral status: and indeed he felt that Jansen had changed his view on this question following *Ndlwana*. In combination, these factors led Conradie to assume that the bill could proceed through the bicameral, simple majority process:

> "When this is the conclusion not only of so many constitutional authorities, but also the considered and unanimous judgment of the highest court in the land as expressed by ACJ Stratford, far be it from me to differ".[36]

Malan greeted the ruling with a scarcely veiled threat to the courts in general and to the Appellate Division in particular:

> "If the court should decide to declare this Act of Parliament invalid . . . it would be a serious matter for Parliament and for the country. It would mean the undermining of Parliament's sovereignty; it would mean that the judicial authority had assumed powers belonging to the legislature".[37]

After alluding to the *Brown v Leyds* controversy and advising the courts not to follow Kotze's example, Malan concluded by saying "I hope no crisis of that nature will arise in the Union of South Africa. I do not expect for a moment that it will happen".[38] Malan was evidently anticipating that the Appellate Division might invalidate the Act. But that prospect remained some months away. In the short term, the bill had first to be piloted through the house and the senate.

Strauss' attack on the bill subsequently moved to its merits as well as the process through which it was being enacted. Much of Strauss' energy was directed towards driving a wedge between Havenga and Malan. Playing on the intimacy of Hertzog and Havenga's relationship, Strauss made many references to Hertzog's repeated commitments to keep Coloureds on the common roll. This bill, he argued was a betrayal of those commitments. He also broadened

E. Kahn, 'Constitutional Law' (1951) *Annual Survey of South African Law* 1 at pp. 3–4. Hahlo and Kahn note that the government chose to ignore Pienaar's advice entirely; *South Africa: the Development of Its Laws and Constitution* p. 155 (Cape Town: Juta & Co, 1960).

[34] HAD, 10 April 1951, c.4201 *et seq.*

[35] He drew on arguments by Pollack (p. 185 above), Wheare (p. 185 above), Jennings (p. 195 above) and Kennedy (p. 179 above).

[36] HAD, 10 April 1951, at c.4219. See E. Kahn, 'Constitutional Law' (1951) *Annual Survey of South African Law* 1.

[37] HAD, 17 April 1951, c.4584. Havenga had hoped to resolve his own difficulties over the 'diminution' question by following the Speaker's ruling on that point. Conradie did not however reach it. Elevating expediency over principle, Havenga announced he had decided himself that no diminution was involved; *Rand Daily Mail*, 18 April 1951.

[38] *Ibid.*

his attack by invoking wider moral principles: "a breach of these pledges [i.e. the common roll] amounts to the breaking of the word of honour of the white man to a section of the non-European people".[39] There were also, he suggested, more pragmatic reasons for opposing the bill, for in a very real sense it undermined rather than strengthened the white community's long-term political security: "We are seeing that the non-Europeans today are doing what has never been done before in the history of South Africa. They are forming a united anti-European bloc".[40] The United Party's arguments did not sway the government from its chosen course. Nor did they detach any Nationalist MPs from the government side. The bill was passed by both house and senate sitting separately. The Governor-General gave his assent on 15 June.

The extra-parliamentary opposition

As Strauss had observed, the Separate Representation of Voters bill lent further momentum to the emergent trend for black, Coloured and Indian political activists to make common cause against government policy.[41] A group of Coloured political activists had initially mobilised themselves under the auspices of a body known as the National Convention Co-ordinating Committee (NCCC), chaired by George Golding. The NCCC had announced that it would limit itself to 'constitutional' methods of opposing the bill, foremost among which was the sending of a petition to all members of the house and senate, urging them not to support the proposed legislation.[42] A campaign was also begun to raise funds for a legal challenge to the bill should it be enacted. The NCCC had also sent a delegation to meet with Donges at the end of February. He had been wholly unresponsive to their concerns, and then indicated in a speech at a party meeting in Robertson on 2 March that he did not really take their case seriously: "The Coloured man was never much interested in his vote, whereas now he is assured of his food, housing and his own representation".[43]

The NCCC was not the only pressure group to emerge. The APO, ANC and a collection of other trade union and community groups established a Franchise Action Council (FAC) early in 1951.[44] The Council promptly began a campaign of protest, industrial action and civil disobedience. The organisation staged a massive rally in Cape Town in March 1951,[45] and engineered a

[39] HAD, 25 April 1951, c.5407.

[40] *Ibid.* at c.5409.

[41] T. Davenport, *South Africa: a Modern History*, 2nd edn. (Cambridge: CUP, 1978), pp. 262–265; Lewis, n. 1 above, pp. 262–264.

[42] *Cape Argus*, 1 March 1951.

[43] *Cape Argus*, 3 March 1951.

[44] See the report in *The (Cape) Guardian*, 15 February 1951. *The (Cape) Guardian* was effectively the house journal of the South African Communist Party, although it had of course, following the passage of the Suppression of Communism Act 1950, ended any *de jure* linkage with the party.

[45] The *Cape Times* reported that some 8,000 people marched peacefully through Cape Town on the day of the bill's first reading; 9 March 1951.

widely supported general strike among Coloured workers and shopkeepers in April.[46]

The FAC was from the outset a multi-racial enterprise. J.S. Moroka, then President of the ANC, called a press conference in Cape Town in which he called for trans-racial co-operation: "In South Africa, it is necessary that all Coloureds, Indians and Africans should come together and fight any issue that is aimed at the oppression of any one section".[47] Yousef Dadoo, a leading figure in the Indian political community, was equally forthright in offering his people's support. He dismissed the bill as "a fraudulent piece of legislation to rob the coloured people of the only political right which protects them from the utterly desperate plight of the African".[48] The disbanded communists were also prominent participants in the FAC. Sam Kahn had announced at the FAC's inaugural meeting that it should pursue a long-term agenda: "It is our task to turn South Africa from a backward country to a first class democracy. It is a question of freedom and liberty or baaskap and slavery for the non-European people".[49] The NCCC, having been so peremptorily dismissed by Donges, proved receptive to these overtures. Its leaders began negotiations with the FAC early in March to merge the two groups.[50]

The emergence of a solely white, non-communist pressure group was more unexpected. The 'Torch Commando' was an organisation of the Second World War veterans led by a Battle of Britain fighter pilot called (ironically) Malan.[51] The Commando attracted the support of former Chief Justice De Wet,[52] one of the four Appellate Division judges in *Ndlwana*. His support presumably implied that he had come to doubt that *Ndlwana* was correctly decided. The Commando was brought into being as a direct response to the government's efforts to disenfranchise the Cape Coloureds, but rapidly embraced a more wide-ranging programme of race-neutral principles. In addition to organising petitions, processions and demonstrations, the Torch Commando engineered a 'United Democratic Front' with the Labour and United Parties, and promised briefly to reinvigorate the traditions of Cape liberalism among the white community. The promise did not however last for long. A riot following a demonstration in Cape Town in May 1951 enabled the government to brand the Torch Commando as a subversive force, while its

[46] N. Mandela, *Long Road to Freedom* (London: Abacus, 1995), pp. 141–142; Lewis, n. 1 above, pp. 267–268; T. Lodge, *Black Politics in South Africa* (London: Longman, 1983), pp. 40–41.

[47] *The (Cape) Guardian*, 15 February 1951.

[48] *Ibid.*

[49] *Ibid.*

[50] *Cape Argus*, 3 March 1951.

[51] Malan was the third highest ranking 'Ace' in the Royal Air Force; D. O'Meara, *Forty Lost Years* (Athens, Ohio: Ohio University Press, 1996), pp. 20–21. On Malan and the foundation of the Torch Commando see J. Mervis, 'The Torch Commando' (1952) *The Forum* 4 (May).

[52] Many of the judges then sitting in the Supreme Court were apparently 'startled' by De Wet's move; L. Blackwell, *Blackwell Remembers* (Cape Town: Howard Timmins, 1971), p. 158.

refusal to allow Coloureds to join its ranks undermined its credibility in the eyes of its more liberal adherents.[53]

The demonic status which Malan's ministers had bestowed on the English language press was reinforced by its coverage of the legislation. In April 1951, Ben Schoeman, the Minister of Labour, denounced the English language newspapers en masse: "in article after article they present the British standpoint. There is only one way to describe them. They are British provincial newspapers. Their spiritual home is in England".[54]

The *Cape Times* saw no merit in the bill, and spoke approvingly of the way in which non-white voters had opposed its provisions. Commenting on the marches and protests in Cape Town, the *Times* argued that:

> "[T]he non-Europeans demonstrated their self discipline and thereby re-emphasised the fact, so often conveniently forgotten or glossed over, that they are fundamentally a law-abiding and responsible community, which in itself is a powerful argument in favour of entrusting them with the responsibility of the franchise".[55]

For the *Cape Argus*, the bill had ramifications above and beyond its impact on the Coloured franchise: "What is at stake is not only the rights of 48,000 Coloured voters. The Bill wounds, in our opinion, national morality and the sanctity of a compact for nationhood".[56]

Donges' second reading speech attracted vitriolic criticism:

> "Never has the bareness, the hollowness of Nationalist contentions been more painfully if unconsciously revealed. The shallow theories, the unsupported assertions, the misleading presumptions, the dogmatic self-importance and the underlying spiritual and moral tribalism of the New Nationalism, were all cruelly exposed".[57]

Notwithstanding such attacks on its integrity, the government continued to resist the temptation to introduce legislation expressly controlling the activities of mainstream newspapers. It was however prepared to use the powers granted by section 6 of the Suppression of Communism Act[58] to ban one of its most

[53] See K. Heard, *General Elections in South Africa 1943–1970* (London: OUP, 1974), pp. 51–53; Davenport (1978), n. 41 above, pp. 20–261. *Die Burger* took particular satisfaction from the Torch Commando's own embrace of *apartheid*: "People who loudly demand that their political opponents must comply with principles and a policy which they themselves avoid like the plague deserve the deepest contempt"; translation taken from *The (Cape) Guardian*, 18 October 1951.

[54] Reported in the *Cape Times*, 9 April 1951.

[55] 9 March 1951.

[56] 10 April 1951. The *Argus* echoed a view that had perhaps best been expressed by the *Natal Witness* when the bill was first published: "[I]mportant as the rights of coloured voters are, what is at stake is something very much more important: it is the whole future of our constitution and the security of all rights established under it"; 26 February 1951. The *Witness* returned to the theme on 3 April: "Like the iceberg, which conceals by far the greater and more dangerous part of its mass beneath the water, the greater and worse part of what is in store for the coloured voters is concealed in the murky but not impenetrable depths of the official Nationalist mind".

[57] 26 April 1951.

[58] See p. 238 above.

virulent critics, the left-wing weekly newspaper *The Guardian*.[59] Sam Kahn, the 'former' communist who served as a Native representative in the house was also—following an amendment to the original 1950 Suppression of Communism Act—removed from the house.[60] His seat was promptly won by Brian Bunting, a former communist standing as an independent. Bunting sat in the the house for a year, until he too was removed because of his communist sympathies.[61]

Malan's administration showed no signs of bowing to either white or black political pressure, whether applied in parliament, in the press or on the streets. The fate of the 'Act' would be determined in the courts. On 22 June, two members of the Appellate Division offered the government additional grounds for thinking that its bill might not survive judicial scrutiny.

Swart and Nicol v De Kock

Shortly after the 1951 bill was introduced to the house, the Appellate Divison had begun to hear argument in *Swart and Nicol v De Kock*.[62] In 1949 the Transvaal Provincial Council, then dominated by the Strijdomite faction of the Nationalist Party, had introduced its own intra-white variation on Verwoerd's theme of *apartheid*. A 1949 Ordinance moved away from the Hertzogite notion of educational bi-lingualism, and insisted instead that all children (whether in state or private schools) should be educated in whichever of the two official languages they were most proficient.[63]

The ordinance was challenged by the Bishop of Pretoria on behalf of privately-run catholic schools in the Transvaal, and by the father of a child at a state school who wished his daughter, even though her home language was Afrikaans, to be educated in English. Both plaintiffs contended that the ordinance breached section 137 of the South Africa Act 1909, which had guaranteed equal status to the English and Dutch/Afrikaans languages. That equal status had also been protected by one of the procedurally entrenched clauses in the Act. The Bishop initially contended that even if the ordinance was valid in respect of state schools, it could not have that effect in relation to private institutions. The Transvaal Provincial Division had invoked section 137 to invali-

[59] See *The (Cape) Guardian*, 18 October 1951. *The Guardian* then engaged in a game of cat and mouse with the government, reappearing (and being banned once more) successively as *Advance* and *New Age*; E. Potter, *The Press as Opposition* (London: Chatto and Windruss, 1975), pp. 114–115. See also C. Merret, *A Culture of Censorship* (Pietermarizburg: University of Natal Press, 1994), ch. 3.

[60] Merret, n. 59 above, p. 23.

[61] Brian Bunting, interview with Ian Loveland, August 1998.

[62] [1951] 3 SA 589.

[63] On the background to the case see T. Moodie, *The Rise of Afrikanerdom* (London: University of California Press, 1975), pp. 242–245, 282–283; A. Norval, *Deconstructing Apartheid Discourse* (London: Verso, 1996), pp. 132–133.

date the ordinance in respect of private schools, but upheld its application to schools in the state sector.

On appeal, a five-man bench[64] in the Appellate Division unanimously accepted that it was part of the court's constitutional role to safeguard individual rights against unlawful governmental interference. All five judges also agreed that the provincial council could not apply the ordinance to private schools since that would abridge section 137 rights. However the court held only by a three to two majority that the ordinance was valid in respect of state schools. Schreiner and Hoexter considered that the ordinance was also invalid in relation to state schools.

The judges' reasoning on the substantive question before the court need not detain us here. Nor is the relevance of the judgment to the status of section 35 *vis-à-vis* a simple bicameral parliamentary majority readily apparent. The National Party had not at any point contended that provincial councils were not subject to substantive limits on their powers. However, in the course of their opinions, both Centlivres and Schreiner had indicated that they considered, notwithstanding *Ndlwana*, that the entrenched clauses were still effective. Centlivres made the point rather obliquely:

> "In construing s.137 of the South Africa Act I shall, therefore, start from the standpoint that the section gives the individual the right to call on the judicial power to help him to resist any legislative or executive act which offends against that section".[65]

The reference to '*any*' legislative act raised the inference that parliament acting bicamerally by simple majority, as well as provincial councils, was subject to judicial supervision.

Schreiner was more explicit. He observed that:

> "the duty of the courts is to ensure that the protection of [s.137] is made effective unless and until it is modified by legislation in such a form as under our constitution can validly effect such modification".[66]

The reference to the '*form*' in which legislation might be enacted was obviously directed towards the entrenched clauses, for Schreiner continued by stating that he might be prepared to recognise a distinction between 'ordinary' (i.e. simple bicameral majority) and 'extraordinary' (i.e. two-thirds unicameral majority) Acts of parliament:

> "we are not concerned in this case with the question whether s.137 could be modified by ordinary Parliamentary legislation or whether extraordinary legislation under s.152 of the South Africa Act would still be required".[67]

It was soon to become apparent, however, that the question of 'parliament's power' to modify the entrenched clauses would shortly be a question of considerable concern to the judges of the Appellate Division.

[64] Centlivres C.J., Schreiner, Hoexter, Van den Heever and Fagan JJ.A.
[65] [1951] 3 SA (AD) 589 at 601–602.
[66] *Ibid.* at 611.
[67] *Ibid.*

II. THE JUDGMENT

Shortly after the bill received the Governor-General's assent, four Cape Coloured voters began court proceedings to challenge the legality of the 1951 Act. Their suit was financed by the United Party.[68] The four were Ganief Harris, Edgar Franklin, William Collins and Edgar Deane. Ganief Harris was a bricklayer, employed by the Cape Town City Council and a prominent member of the Muslim Malay sub-group within the coloured community. William Collins was a general merchant and a member of the Cape Town city council. He had also served as the Treasurer of the National Convention Co-ordinating Committee. Edgar Deane, who had long been active in Cape political and trade union circles, was the General Secretary of the Cape Furniture Workers Union and had also been the Secretary of the National Convention Co-ordinating Committee. Edgar Franklin was a baker's van driver and active trade unionist. He had given a speech at a rally against the bill at Cape Town City Hall in April 1951, in which he had accused the goverment of igniting "a spark of hatred" against the coloured people among whites, and claimed that: "The government is doing this to us because it fears the progress of the coloured people".[69]

The plaintiffs were represented by Duncan, Molteno and Snitcher, instructed by Bloomberg & Co. Their arguments were straightforward. They claimed first that the Act disqualified them from the electoral register on the grounds of their race. Secondly, they contended that the South African constitution permitted parliament to pass such an Act only by the unicameral two-thirds majority procedure specified in the South Africa Act 1909. Their suit maintained unambiguously that *Ndlwana* was wrongly decided. They argued that the effect of the Statute of Westminster 1931 was simply to free the South African parliament from the shackles imposed by the British Colonial Laws Validity Act; it had no impact on South Africa's internal constitutional arrangements. The plaintiffs invited the courts to reverse *Ndlwana*; to hold that South Africa's legislature was not a carbon copy of the United Kingdom Parliament; and to conclude that, if only in a very small area of policy, the support of a simple majority of members in each house would not be sufficient to give a bill the force of law.[70]

Their suit was dismissed in the Cape Provincial division in a judgment issued on 26 October 1951.[71] The three-man court, which included De Villiers

[68] It is not entirely clear how the four came to be the plaintiffs. Harry Snitcher's recollection is that the four men all had strong political links with Bloomberg, and that he had arranged for them to act as nominal plaintiffs on the United Party's behalf; intereview with Ian Loveland, August 1998.

[69] *Cape Times*, 28 April 1951.

[70] The argument was different from the 1948 Bloomberg opinion in two ways. First, no reference was made to *Brown v Leyds*. Secondly, counsel adopted Cowen's terminology to the effect that the entrenched clauses identified a particular parliament rather than restrained the bicameral parliament.

[71] A brief note of the case appears in the appendix of [1951] 4 SALR 707. It was not fully reported. The account and quotations which follow are taken from the report in the *Cape Times* of 27 October 1951. For observers who—like the Minister of Labour Ben Schoeman—regarded the *Cape*

J.P.[72] and Steyn J., unanimously followed *Ndlwana*, in holding that the South African parliament was now sovereign within South Africa just as the United Kingdom Parliament was sovereign within the United Kingdom. The Cape provincial division had little alternative in this respect; it was clearly bound by the previous decision of the Appellate Division. If *Ndlwana* was decided in error, it was an error only the Appellate Division could correct.

The court nonetheless offered the plaintiffs some grounds for believing that their appeal might succeed. De Villiers J.P. observed that he did not consider that the entrenchment point had been fully argued in *Ndlwana*. He also intimated that he harboured doubts about Stratford A.C.J.'s characterisation of sections 35, 137 and 152 of the South Africa Act as merely procedural devices, given that the Appellate Division had so clearly identified them as rules of substantive law in *Ndobe*. Steyn J. also expressed reservations about the implications of the government's argument that the Statute of Westminster had swept away the entrenchment provisions; if the entrenchment provisions no longer applied, then on what basis could one suggest that any other limits could be applied to parliament's law-making competence, even, for example, to the extent of requiring that a bill receive bare majority support in both houses?

The case was scheduled for argument before the Appellate Division in March 1952. In the interim, the government extended the reach of *apartheid* through less legally controversial means. In October, the cabinet decided that it would no longer provide public funds to support the South African Association of Fine Arts (SAAFA) if SAAFA did not introduce *apartheid* in its galleries. The threat was extended to the University of Cape Town Ballet and the International Society for Contemporary Music. Only the third of these bodies immediately announced that it would rather lose the government's financial support than segregate its performers and audiences.[73] But while South Africa's arts establishment did little to obstruct the segregation programme, the Appellate Division, with the *Harris* appeal pending, gave the government additional cause to consider that *apartheid* was being subjected to consistent judicial assault.

Times as a 'British provincial newspaper (see p. 271 above)—the fact that the coverage of the judgment was pushed off the front page (and the second and the third) by a detailed analysis of the British general election results would perhaps not have come as a surprise.

[72] This being another Jean Etienne De Villiers. This De Villiers, born in 1894, had taken a BA and BCL at Oxford, before beginning a career combining practice at the Cape bar with lecturing at the University of Cape Town. He was appointed to the Cape bench by the Fusion government in 1939 and was promoted to be Judge President of the division by Swart in 1949. As De Villiers' sentiments in *Harris* made clear, he could not be regarded as a cypher for Nationalist sentiment. The third member of the court was Newton Thompson J. The Steyn on the court was G. Steyn, and should not be confused with L.C. Steyn, the government's senior legal adviser.

[73] See the *Cape Times*, 29 October, 30 October and 1 December 1951; *The (Cape) Guardian*, 8 November 1951.

On transport, sex and marriage across the racial divide—again

Notwithstanding the political climate created by the passage of the Separate Representation of Voters Act, Centlivres' Court evidently felt sufficiently secure in its independence to continue to interpret legislation in ways which manifestly contradicted the Malan government's preferences. The issue before the Appellate Division in September 1951 in *Tayob v Ermelo Local Road Transportation Board*[74] concerned a local authority's refusal to issue a taxi-driver's licence under the terms of the Motor Carrier Transportation Act 1930 to an Asian applicant to carry white passengers. The applicant was permitted instead to carry only non-white passengers. The authority argued that it had taken account of 'public opinion' in deciding to withhold the licence: white passengers would simply not be comfortable about being driven by an Asian driver.[75] The authority also added that the area required only three taxis for white passengers and, as chance would have it, three white drivers had applied for licences at the same time as Mr Tayob. All were granted licences. Centlivres issued the Appellate Division's unanimous judgment. He held that 'public opinion' was not a legitimate factor for local authorities to take into account when making decisions of this sort insofar as it is expressed racist sentiments. Following *Abdurahman*, Centlivres observed that such racism was permissible only if clearly authorised by the statute concerned. No such authorisation could be found in the Act. In consequence, the authority's refusal was unlawful. A licence might legitimately be refused on the basis of an applicant's failings as a taxi-driver, but the applicant's racial identity had no bearing on that question.[76]

Matters of racial identity were in contrast crucial to the issue before the Appellate Division in *R v Ormonde*.[77] The defendants were allegedly a European male and a non-European female. They had been prosecuted and convicted under the Immorality Act 1950. Each was sentenced to three months' hard labour, suspended for three years. The prosecuting authorities contended that the male defendant was a European (a designation which the defendants did not contest). They did however contest the prosecution's claim that the female defendant was a non-European. As noted above,[78] that Act had specified that "non-European means a person who in appearance obviously is, or who by general acceptance and repute is a non-European".

[74] (1951) 4 SA 440 (AD). For further discussion see Dugard, *Human Rights and the South African Legal Order* (Princeton: Princeton University Press, 1978), pp. 317–318.

[75] A less candid objective would presumably have been to increase employment for whites by excluding Asians from this line of work.

[76] In *Williams and Adendorff*, Bristow J. had indicated that a multi-racial public opinion might approve segregation, a premise which Centlivres manifestly rejected in *Tayob*; (see p. 146 above). More starkly still, Centlivres' judgment expressly disapproved Wesells J.'s conclusion in *George* that a council could legitimately pander to the racism of its white voters; (see p. 147 above).

[77] [1952] (1) SA (AD) 272. Judgment issued on 5 December 1951.

[78] See p. 244 above.

The Magistrate had heard evidence in respect both of the female defendant's appearance and her 'reputation'. In respect of her appearance, he had concluded that she:

> "suffered the hereditary disability of retaining a decided trace of colour combined with slightly prominent cheekbones, nostrils and hair which collectively imparted a coloured appearance; this gave rise to the question whether she was obviously coloured".[79]

The magistrate also heard evidence from the male defendant to the effect that both defendants regularly consorted with other 'Europeans' and patronised 'European' social facilities,[80] and, conversely, from the female defendant's mother that she was generally accepted as 'Coloured'. The magistrates's conclusion had been that the combination of the female defendant's appearance and her mother's evidence meant that she was a non-European in terms of the 1950 Act.

A unanimous Appellate Division bench quashed the conviction. Fagan J.A. delivered the judgment, with Van den Heever, Greenberg, Schreiner and Hoexter concurring. Fagan began by drawing attention to the multiplicity of racial classifications then extant under South African law, and stressed that his conclusion was limited to the 1950 Act. However, he then followed the rationale that presented itself after *R v Radebe* in concluding that the female defendant had no racial identity under the terms of that legislation.[81] He held that the magistrate had erred in concluding that it was sufficient for the prosecution to prove the *negative fact* that the female defendant *was not a 'European'*. Deciding what she was not did not amount to deciding what she was. Rather the prosecution had to prove the *positive fact* that she *was a 'non-European'*. If there was doubt concerning *either* the defendant's appearance or her 'reputation', the prosecutions's case was not made out. On these facts, the magistrate's own view had been that the female defendant's appearance 'raised' the question of whether she was 'obviously non-European', but evidently did not answer that question in the affirmative. Similarly, the male defendant's evidence as to the female defendant's reputation raised doubt under that criterion. The existence of doubt on either therefore precluded proof of the positive racial identity which the Act required.

Fagan's judgment would no doubt have infuriated the government. He then compounded that annoyance by explaining that he had arrived at his conclusion not by a strict, literalist interpretation of the text of the Act, but by making presumptions as to parliament's intentions. Parliament, he suggested, appreciated that it would have amounted to a 'grave injustice' for this Act to be applied to

[79] *Ibid.* at 277. The male defendant had testified that the female defendant "has the appearance of a European *even after she has washed her face*"; *ibid.* at 276 (emphasis added).

[80] Including a 'Europeans only' section of beach at The Strand; see *R v Carelse* at pp. 219–220 above.

[81] See pp. 221–223 above.

individuals about whose racial status there was any uncertainty. Many thousands of people might fall into that category. None of them could be convicted.[82]

To Malan's government, which appeared to equate the wishes of its majorities of members in the house and senate with 'parliament', such judicial sentiments would have appeared outrageous. Any expectation Swart might have had that Fagan qua judge would prove a friend to the government's programme was firmly rebutted by the *Ormonde* decision. The governing party would certainly not have been predisposed to accept that 'parliament' had intended the results that Fagan held the Act had created. The case would no doubt have intensified rather than diminished the Nationalists' concern about the Appellate Division's approach to the forthcoming *Harris* appeal.

Harris No. 1: the Appellate Division

Andries Beyers QC was leading counsel for the government. Beyers had read law at Stellenbosch. On graduating he became private secretary to F.W. Beyers,[83] before he began an academic career as a law lecturer at Stellenbosch University in 1928. He went to the Cape bar in 1936 and immediately served as Henry Fagan's junior counsel on the government side in *Ndlwana*. Beyers took silk ten years later, by which time he had built a formidable reputation as a criminal lawyer. Beyers was joined by J.T van Wyk QC, D.P. De Villiers, and a member of the senate, G. Wynne.[84]

As in the provincial division, Graeme Duncan led the case for the appellants, joined once again by D.B. Molteno and Harry Snitcher, the three times unsuccessful parliamentary candidate for the Communist party.[85] Duncan had by this time consolidated his reputation as the leading courtroom advocate of liberal political principles. In the English language press, both the substance of his argument before the Appellate Division—essentially a reprise of his first instance brief—and the way in which it was delivered attracted warm and enthusiastic support. The *Cape Argus* perhaps led the field with coverage that managed to be adulatory of Duncan, supportive of his argument, and entirely patronising to his clients:

[82] For further comment see E. Landis, 'South African Apartheid Legislation I: Fundamental Structure' (1961) 71 *Yale LJ* 1 at 11–12; H. Hahlo, 'European or Non-European?' (1952) *South African Law Journal* 116. Hahlo suggested Fagan was splitting linguistic hairs to reach the result, but stopped short of accusing the court of obstructing the government's wishes.

[83] See p. 158 above.

[84] Wynne, a graduate of Rhodes University and a Rhodes Scholar at Oxford, was by 1950 a prominent advocate and a leading figure in the Cape National party. He had previously stood unsuccessfully for election both to the Cape provincial council and the house, and was appointed to the senate in March 1951.

[85] "At one stage in my life I though that I was the most effete candidate ever . . . [In 1948] I realised that politics was standing in the way of my practice and my life. I then took a decision that it was either politics or the law. I chose the latter": Harry Snitcher, interview with David Borgstrom, July 1998.

"Gradually you could see the argument taking shape. It grew as a well laid brick wall grows under the hands of the master; smoothly interknit, seemingly unbreakable . . . It was a complicated, cautious argument, avidly followed by the judges and the legal fraternity, though often over the heads of the public packing the gallery.

And from the gallery, dark faces and red and black fezzes looked down into the court, doubtless missing many of the finer legal points the barrister was making, but knowing that he was fighting to retain for them an old liberty".[86]

The Court

The 'finer legal points' of Duncan's argument were presumably not going to elude the intellectual grasp of the judges. Centlivres still held the post of Chief Justice when *Harris* was decided. Oliver Schreiner also remained on the Appellate Division bench. The four other members of the court at that time were Leopold Greenberg, Oscar Hoexter, Francois van den Heever and Henry Fagan.

Leopold Greenberg (1885–1964) had followed a less star-studded route to the bar than Centlivres, Hoexter and Schreiner. He had read law as a part-time student in the Cape, before being called to the Cape bar in 1908. His career flourished, and in 1924 he achieved the dual distinction of becoming a King's Counsel and being appointed to the Transvaal bench. His promotion to the Appeal Court was rather less rapid, eventually coming in 1943. As noted in previous chapters, Greenberg had marked himself out, as had Ben Tindall, as a trenchant judicial advocate of South African common law as an anti-discriminatory legal tool.[87]

With the exception of Centlivres, whose role in *Ndwlana* and comments in *Swart and Nicol* suggested he had once felt that sections 35, 137 and 152 of the constitution were no longer effective but had now changed his mind, only one of the judges on the Appellate Bench had been directly involved in the three previous cases concerning the reach of the constitution's entrenched clauses. Fagan had acted as leading counsel for the government in *Masai* and *Ndlwana*. Centlivres did not select him to sit as one of the quorum of five in *Harris No. 1*, although there is no obvious indication that Centlivres felt that Fagan's role in *Masai* and *Ndlwana* would compromise his ability to decide *Harris* in a dispassionate way. Schreiner and Greenberg could plausibly have been classified as 'liberals' on race matters; their judicial careers indicated that they assumed that common law rules and principles of statutory interpretation required courts to seek 'colour-blind' outcomes to litigation in the absence of explicit parliamentary instructions to the contrary. Hoexter and Van den Heever did not fall quite so clearly into this category, but Hoexter's opinions in *Radebe v Hough* and *Ormonde*, and Van den Heever's in the latter case, indicated that neither judge

[86] 1 October 1951.

[87] For brief biographies of the other judges, see p. 253 Centlivres, p. 222 (Schreiner), p. 256 (Van den Heever), p. 249 (Hoexter).

was predisposed to sacrifice his convictions as to legal principle in order to accommodate governmental preferences. Yet it was by no means clear that the judges' views on matters of common law and statutory interpretation would have any bearing on the *Harris* litigation. If the case raised a question unlike any other they (aside from Centlivres) had ever tried, there was no obvious reason to assume that past decisions could serve as a reliable guide to the judgments they would issue.

E.C.S. Wade's opinion

Malan's government did not regard the *Ndlwana* decision and the existing academic works supporting the Appellate Divisions's reasoning in the case as a sufficient bolster for the legitimacy of its point of view. It took the added precaution of seeking an opinion from one of the most eminent of British constitutional lawyers at the time, Professor E.C.S. Wade of Cambridge University.[88] In the late 1930s, Wade had written an introduction to the ninth edition of the leading English constitutional law textbook of the time, A.V. Dicey's *Introduction to the Study of the Law of the Constitution*.[89] Wade had written approvingly of the Appellate Division's judgment in *Ndlwana*, in terms both of its reasoning and outcome. Having become even more esteemed in the years since the introduction was published, Wade was an obvious ally for Malan's government to recruit.

Malan had tried to make sure that the resultant opinion would be favourable to his cause by couching the task Wade accepted in heavily loaded terms:

> "To what extent is there English authority for the rule that the will of Parliament as expressed in an Act of Parliament cannot be questioned in a court of law . . .
>
> Why has the repeal of the Colonial Laws Validity Act 1865 had the effect of rendering the entrenched sections (Ss. 35, 137, 152) of the South Africa Act ineffectual?".

That any academic at a British university could accept a brief that manifestly had no other purpose than to facilitate the imposition of racist oppression by a neo-fascist regime is quite extraordinary. Wade was not even being asked in the second question for his opinion on the merits of the *Harris* litigation, but to confirm that the government's viewpoint was correct. Nor was there any reason to assume that the first question had any bearing on the *Harris* issue, given that it was not the constitutionality of an Act of the British Parliament that was being called into question. But rather than question the premise of the brief, Wade produced an opinion that was as unctuously fulsome in its support for the Malanite position as it was feeble in its grasp of constitutional law and theory.[90]

[88] The opinion is reproduced as an appendix in G. Marshall, *Parliamentary Sovereignty and the Commonwealth* (Oxford: Clarendon Press, 1957). References in the text which follows are to that source.

[89] (London: Macmillan, 1939). On Dicey and his influence on British constitutional law scholarship see I. Loveland, *Constitutional Law* (London: Butterworths, 1996), chs. 2 and 3.

[90] Marshall offers a rather less abrasive critique of the opinion; (1957), n. 88 above, pp. 187–190.

The opinion addressed a range of issues, and found that all of them could be resolved unambiguously in the government's favour. Wade even doubted the proposition that the entrenched sections were implicated in the passage of the 1951 Act at all. In his view, the removal of Coloured voters onto a separate electoral register was not a 'disqualification' within the meaning of section 35: "it merely allocates [Coloured voters] as hitherto, to a certain division of a single register of voters, as it does the European voters".[91] His opinion made no allusion to the point that Van Zyl J.P. had clearly held to the contrary in *Ndlwana*.[92]

Wade began his analysis on the broader issue of the validity of the entrenched provisions with the bizarre assertion that only federal constitutions could contain super-majoritarian values which could be protected by a country's courts. There is no reason as a matter of constitutional theory why this should be so. Wade offered the USA as his proof of this proposition, citing it as the country which first recognised the concept of judicial review of legislative power against a supra-legislative yardstick. It is admittedly easier to identify majority and minority interests within a federal nation, as such interests are often disproportionately concentrated within particular state or provincial boundaries. It is admittedly also true that the Framers of the American constitution were concerned to safeguard the allocation of authority they had granted to the national and state governments respectively. What Wade neglected to mention however, was that a good deal of the 'fundamental law' of the USA was initially designed not to protect state powers against the national government, but to protect the rights of *individual citizens* against a national legislature that might temporarily be controlled by a party representing the tyrannically inclined wishes of a narrow electoral majority. That particular moral concern is as readily applicable to a unitary as to a federal state. This was indeed an essential tenet of the Afrikaaner constitutional tradition. Wade also omitted to mention that the pre-Union constitution of the Orange Free State (which was most certainly not a federal country) rested on precisely the same moral basis that the *Harris* plaintiffs contended underpinned the South African constitution.[93]

Wade also conveniently overlooked the fact that the first American case to articulate the judicial review doctrine, *Marbury v Madison*[94] in 1803, had nothing whatsoever to do with national/state governmental relations. Its concern rather was with whether Congress had the power—and here the reasons for Wade's selective amnesia becomes apparent—to alter the jurisdiction of the federal courts in a manner that contradicted the provisions of the Constitution.[95]

[91] *Ibid.* at p. 258.

[92] See p. 204 above.

[93] Wade would also have found, had he bothered to look, unitary states with supra-majoritarian fundamental rights protected by the courts in Portugal, Norway, Greece, Italy and Ceylon; see D. Cowen, 'Legislature and Judiciary—Part Two' (1953) 16 *Modern Law Review* 273 at 286.

[94] (1803) 5 US (1 Cr) 137.

[95] Wade also stated matter of factly that the US Supreme Court had 'assumed' the power, a choice of words which implies that the Court in *Marbury* took it upon itself to take a power which the Constitution had not granted it. This rather overlooks the facts that the Constitution does offer a

Having laid these weak and unstable foundations for his analysis of the impact of independence on South Africa's internal constitutional arrangements, Wade then proceeded to build a tottering structure of jurisprudential sophistry and ineptitude in which to accommodate the government's preferences. The opinion promptly dealt with the apparently awkward political fact that the house and senate had resolved in 1931 that they did not wish independence to 'derogate' from the continued vitality of the entrenched provisions. For Wade, the use of the word 'derogate', rather than 'amend' or 'repeal' was of great significance:

> "This may be regarded as confirming the view that the Statute of Westminster did not change the South Africa Act but that it made the change possible on the initiative of the Union Parliament acting as a sovereign legislature".[96]

One might doubt that such subtleties had impressed themselves upon legislators' minds in 1931.[97] But the significance of the absurd meaning Wade attached to 'derogate' was trivial compared to the consequences flowing from the meaning he attached to 'parliament'.

Wade's argument did not distinguish between the sovereignty of a country and the sovereignty of its 'parliament'. Such a distinction would of course be inapplicable to the United Kingdom, where national sovereignty and parliamentary sovereignty are congruent phenomena. This evidently led Wade to assume that the implication one should draw from the Statute of Westminster was not simply that the Act turned the Dominions into sovereign states, but that it turned their legislatures into sovereign parliaments in the British sense. In Wade's view, this implication could only be rebutted by express terms to the contrary, such as were provided by the 'saving clauses' in respect of the Canadian, Australian and New Zealand constitutions.

Wade was of course correct in claiming that the union parliament was a sovereign legislature. But the obvious flaw in his analysis—which repeated the error made by Pollak, by the courts in *Ndlwana*, by Wheare and by Jennings—was that of assuming that 'parliament' in an independent South Africa could mean only a carbon copy of the Westminster legislature, rather than, as Cowen contended, a legislature which existed in three quite distinct forms. Thus Wade stated, again quite correctly, that the absence of any explicit saving clause in the Statute of Westminster in respect of sections 35, 137 and 152 meant that the

textual basis for the *Marbury* decision and that many of the Framers of the Constitution at the Philadelphia Convention considered that the Court would have to exercise such a power; see especially Alexander Hamilton's 'Federalist No.78', reproduced in C. Rossiter (ed.), *The Federalist Papers* (New York: Mentor, 1961).

[96] See Marshall, n. 88 above, at pp. 237–238.

[97] Or indeed in 1950. See the obvious meaning attached to the term 'derogate' in s.5(5) of the Suppression of Communism Act 1950. Section 5 empowered the Minister to dismiss any office holder who he considered was propagating communist ideology. Section 5(5) provided that this general power should not 'derogate' from ss. 68 and 101 of the South Africa Act 1909, which respectively provided that Provincial Administrators and Supreme Court judges could only be dismissed by the house and senate. Clearly the 1950 Act did not give the minister power to dismiss judges.

"Union Parliament can legislate without restriction on its powers".[98] But this contention once again ignores the main issue—namely what was 'parliament' in South Africa?

Wade did not at any point explicitly explain why South Africa's parliament should be assumed to be a precise copy of its British counterpart; but this assumption underpins his entire argument. The omission is perhaps the result of the structure of the task he was asked to perform. Wade spent the first half of his opinion answering the first question that Malan's government posed, namely confirming the incontestable point that the Westminster parliament's sovereignty was exercisable through the bicameral, simple majority process. Having thereby normalised the notion that a sovereign parliament acted in this way, he then engaged in a jurisprudential sleight of hand to shift attention to the powers of the South African parliament without stopping to ask if the concept of 'parliament' might bear different meanings in different constitutional contexts. In essence, his critique rested on the assumption that the label one attached to a legislative body was a conclusive determinant of its power *and* that the label could bear only one (British) meaning.

This can justifiably be regarded as rather poor legal scholarship. It would also seem to depend upon a distinctly 'imperialist' set of cultural assumptions; namely that the British system of parliamentary sovereignty is a norm from which no former colony would diverge. This presents something of a paradox: a government which in ideological terms had built its electoral identity on anti-British sentiment was hijacking a British principle to override the much more identifiably Afrikaaner assumption that bare legislative majorities should not be endowed with sovereign legal authority.

Malan did not publish Wade's opinion prior to the litigation.[99] This may be because he was aware of the paradox that it presented, or because he had appreciated the flimsiness of the opinion's conclusions. As is clear from the arguments offered by Beyers and van Wijk at trial, however, Wade's views were selectively employed to sustain the contention that *Ndlwana* had been correctly decided.

Argument

Graeme Duncan closely followed Cowen's analysis.[100] Cowen himself was sitting just behind Duncan and Molteno, playing what one paper referred to as a 'consultancy' role. Duncan received few interventions from the bench. He restated the thesis that the South Africa Act had created several distinct

[98] See Marshall, n. 88 above, at p. 257.

[99] *Ibid.* at p. 187.

[100] Harry Snitcher recalls that "Cowen sat in on many of our consultations, and we listened carefully and appreciated his opinion. But we certainly didn't just accept his viewpoints and adopt them as our own just because he came to the conclusion we wanted. As counsel you always consider these things for yourself and build from there"; interview with David Borgstrom, July 1998.

'parliaments', and that the Statute of Westminster, while turning South Africa into an independent state, had done nothing to redefine its various parliaments into a single body along the lines of the United Kingdom's legislature. In consequence, if an 'Act' was passed by the 'wrong' parliament, it was not an Act at all, and the courts would be obliged to declare it invalid.

Beyers, in contrast, endured an extensive and searching interrogation from all five judges. He had begun by accusing Duncan of following an 'American' argument, which could have no application to South Africa. He subsequently took the opportunity to disparage Cowen: "I am not being personal, but Professor Cowen is not nor has he ever been a professor of constitutional law. He is a professor of comparative law".[101] His own academic support, Beyers suggested, was more weighty: "I have a long list of people who ought to know what all this is about. They all say the same thing—that the Union Parliament is no longer bound by the provisions of the South Africa Act".[102]

Beyers' style was evidently rather repetitive: as the day wore on, Centlivres became increasingly irritated by his embellishment of his written brief: "You have not made much progress. I think you had better follow your own argument, or you will never finish".[103] The day's proceedings ended with an acrimonious exchange:

Beyers:	"Parliament today can get rid of the whole South Africa Act by . . .".
Centlivres:	"You have already said that several times".
Beyers:	"I don't think so".
Centlivres:	"My memory is pretty good".

Beyers' difficulties continued the next day, when all five judges subjected him to abrasive questioning. Hoexter quizzed him vigorously on the distinction between a sovereign state and a sovereign parliament, while Schreiner offered him an elementary lecture on the nature of the separation of powers. Centlivres again displayed impatience with the government's line of argument. This was shown most clearly when Beyers sought to invoke *Ndlwana* as an authority. Beyers began by quoting from the judgment:

Beyers:	"Inasmuch as parliament is now the supreme and sovereign lawmaking body in the Union . . .".
Centlivres:	"Here was a categorical statement of the effect of the Statute of Westminster at the beginning of the judgment without any statement of the reason for arriving at the conclusion".
Beyers:	"But it is a decision, not an assumption".
Centlivres:	"It is remarkable that a statement like that should be made as soon as counsel appeared in court. There does not seem to have been any argument on that statement".
Beyers:	"Both counsel argued on that preliminary point".

[101] *Johannesburg Star*, 22 February 1952.
[102] *Ibid.*
[103] *Ibid.*

Centlivres:	"I called for the registrar's record. Mr Buchanan argued from the time the court met up to 11 am and Mr Fagan for fifteen minutes. Then the court adjourned. Judgment was given at noon".[104]

While the Chief Justice's style of intervention suggested he saw little merit in Beyers' argument, it was van den Heever who led the government's counsel to accept that his argument that no court could look behind an Act of Parliament would lead to lunatic consequences:

Van den Heever:	"What would the legal effect be if the two Houses sat with the Convocation of the University of Cape Town and passed a bill?"
Beyers:	"If it were signed by the Governor General, it could not be questioned in a court of law".[105]

At the end of the five days of oral argument, it seemed that the plaintiffs had made a more favourable impression on the Court than had the government. Little time would elapse before such a presumption was put to the test.

Judgment

The Appellate Division issued only one opinion.[106] The judgment was authored by the Chief Justice, and was joined without qualification by the four other members of the court. Centlivres C.J. identified two central questions for the court to answer. The first was whether the entrenched clauses were still effective, notwithstanding the Appellate Division's previous conclusion in *Ndlwana*. The second was whether, in the event that the court now believed *Ndwlana* to have been wrongly decided, it was possible and desirable for the Appellate Division to overrule the *Ndlwana* judgment.

Centlivres' C.J. judgment offers a fascinating survey of both (explicit) legal principle and (implicit) political theory. It is perhaps as interesting for what it leaves unsaid as for the arguments that were expressly employed. The conclusions that the court reached were straightforward: the entrenched provisions were still effective; *Ndlwana* had been wrongly decided; and the Appellate Division was not only empowered but also obliged to reverse its previous judgment. The route which Centlivres C.J. followed to reach these conclusions was, however, a rather more circuitous affair.

On stare decisis

Centlivres C.J.'s judgment in *Harris* made no allusion at any point to his own concurring opinion at first instance in *Ndlwana*. Nor did he refer on any occasion to *Brown v Leyds*. This might be thought a curious omission given that

104 *Johannesburg Star*, 25 February 1952.
105 *Ibid*.
106 [1952] 1 The Times Law Reports 1245.

Brown posed exactly the same questions, and offered just the same answers, as the *Harris* litigation: namely were entrenched constitutional provisions still effective notwithstanding judicial authority maintaining that they were not; and if they were so effective, could that previous judicial authority be overturned?

As a matter of strict law, *Brown v Leyds* was of no particular significance to the *Harris* question, given that it was decided in a country that no longer existed. Centlivres C.J. did however refer to the pre-Union constitutional tradition of the similarly extinct Orange Free State to buttress his opinion at one point. This selective resort to boer constitutional history may be explained by the court's perception of contemporary *realpolitik* in South Africa. It might have been thought politically imprudent for the court to invoke *Brown* as even a persuasive authority, both since the eventual outcome of that controversy was the obvious subordination of the Republic's judiciary to the Volksraad and because the judgment was perceived within Afrikaaner mythology as an instance of a 'British' attempt to control boer political autonomy. Graeme Duncan's original resort to the case had, it may be recalled, been abandoned when *Harris* reached the courts. The legal status of the Free State's constitution had never been subjected to such pressures, and would thus appear a more defensible analogy for the court to adopt.

Yet Centlivres C.J. did draw heavily and explicitly on the ideas of Kotze C.J. to sustain his own argument on the question of whether the Appellate Division was entitled to overrule its own decisions.[107] Had the Appellate Division considered itself in a position analogous to that then occupied by the House of Lords within the British constitutional system, it would have enjoyed little scope to reverse *Ndlwana*. The House of Lords' preference for a wholly rigid concept of *stare decisis* was confirmed in the 1898 case of *London Tramways v London County Council*.[108] For a unanimous House of Lords, Lord Halsbury claimed that the judgments of that court bound not only all inferior courts, but also the House of Lords itself. He acknowledged that such rigidity would sometimes produce unjust solutions to given problems because the common law could not be adapted to meet changing social conditions or to acknowledge errors in previous decisions:

> "but what is that . . . as compared with the inconvenience—the disastrous inconvenience—of having each question subject to being reargued and the dealings of mankind rendered doubtful by reason of different decisions, so that in truth and in fact there would be no final court of appeal".[109]

Centlivres C.J. did not accept that the Appellate Division was bound to embrace this theory. The Chief Justice found a more palatable *stare decisis*

[107] Denis Cowen suggested to me that Kotze had by this time widely been accorded the status of a sage on legal matters, and was not associated—notwithstanding *Brown*—with anti-boer sentiment; interview with Ian Loveland, August 1998.

[108] [1898] AC 375.

[109] *Ibid.* at 380.

prescription for the South African courts to follow in an academic article written by Kotze in the *South African Law Journal*.[110] South African common law was a blend of both English and Roman–Dutch principle, and "the practice of Roman-Dutch law is far removed from the doctrine recently affirmed by the House of Lords—viz that it is absolutely bound by a previous decision on a question of law".[111]

Centlivres C.J. accepted that the interests of legal certainty should make the Appellate Division "very reluctant to depart from one of its own decisions".[112] It should nonetheless be prepared to hear arguments to the effect that a previous decision was wrongly decided. Should those arguments seem compelling, the court would not just be entitled to reverse itself, it would be bound to do so.

This methodology could justifiably be seen as a subtle exercise in diffusing or wrongfooting potential governmental (and Afrikaaner) hostility to the conclusions that the court eventually reached. His argument characterises British principle as clumsy and essentially unjust, and portrays Roman–Dutch law as a more sensitive jurisprudential tool. This tool is then used to facilitate departure from a previous decision that favoured contemporaneous Afrikaaner sentiment.

Whether Centlivres C.J. was indeed so 'politicised' in his approach is of course a matter for speculation. It is much more likely that he would have characterised his reasoning on the *stare decisis* issue as wholly non-political in nature; namely that the court had been presented with a choice between two irreconcilable legal positions and had ultimately (as it was bound to do) favoured the position which seemed most securely rooted within the South African constitutional tradition. The *stare decisis* point was however a preliminary matter in the *Harris* litigation; the more pressing question, once it had been established that *Ndlwana could* be overruled, was whether it *should* be?

Was the separate roll a 'disqualification' on grounds of race?

The court spent little time in rejecting the claim that placing Coloured voters on a separate roll did not amount to a 'disqualification' on grounds of race. Centlivres C.J. was unimpressed by van Wyk's (and Wade's) argument that the Act simply redefined the Coloured voters' qualifications, and gave them a more than equivalent electoral influence than they had enjoyed on the common roll. He held that section 35 created a guarantee of specific rights, not of their equivalents.[113] Indeed, he concluded that the Act would work a disqualification not just on Coloured voters, but also on European voters, since its effect was in essence to abolish the common roll altogether and create two new ones, for Europeans and Coloureds respectively. On this point, Centlivres' argument

[110] 'Judicial Precedent' (1917) 34 *South African Law Journal* 281.
[111] [1952] 1 The Times Law Reports 1245.
[112] *Ibid*. at 1250.
[113] "[van Wyk's] argument suggests that a spoliator may deprive me of my property with impunity if he is prepared to give something of equal or greater value in return"; *ibid*. at 1251.

followed Van Zyl J.P.'s reasoning in *Ndlwana*. He also found common ground with *Ndlwana* in concluding that De Villiers C.J. had been incorrect in *Ndobe* to suggest that the rights of existing voters could not be abridged on racial grounds by any law-making process whatsoever. His reasoning on this point was no more convincing that that deployed by Van Zyl J.P. in *Ndlwana*, a failing which is perhaps surprising in the light of the clarity which he subsequently brought to his analysis of the central question before the court.

The status of the entrenched clauses

Centlivres C.J.'s survey of the text of the Statute of Westminster and the intentions of the various governments and legislators involved in turning the recommendations of the Imperial Conferences into legal form led him to conclude that the Act's objective and result was to confirm that the Dominions *as countries* were in future to enjoy comparable legal powers to those possessed by the United Kingdom. Rather than adopt the 'literal rule' of statutory interpretation, he followed the mischief rule. Having identified the parameters of that rule by drawing on *Heydon's Case*,[114] Centlivres then concluded that the 'mischief' before legislators in 1931 was that the conventional equality which the Dominions and the United Kingdom enjoyed as countries following the Balfour Declaration in 1926 was not reflected in their legal relationship. The purpose of the Statute of Westminster was therefore to ensure that the United Kingdom and Dominions would in future be "autonomous *communities* within the Empire, equal in status, in no way subordinate to one another".[115] Centlivres had no doubt that the Statute of Westminster had achieved this result. South Africa as a country was no longer in any way subordinate to the United Kingdom, but "the fact that these mischiefs were removed does not result, as I shall show, in any modification of sections 35 and 152 of the South Africa Act".[116]

Centlivres C.J. regarded as a fallacy the presumption that the parliament of a Dominion "must necessarily be a replica of the British Parliament".[117] There was certainly no historical underpinning for this assertion in respect of South Africa's legislature. Its creators in 1909—and this label included both the four colonial assemblies as well as the United Kingdom legislature—had clearly provided that it would function in three different forms. Centlivres C.J. saw the 1931 house/senate resolution as an affirmation of this principle. And while the Statute of Westminster had granted the South African 'parliament' increased powers,[118] it had made no explicit alterations to the way in which that 'parliament' had to function to exercise those powers.

[114] See p. 182 above.
[115] [1952] 1 The Times Law Reports 1245 at 1255; emphasis added.
[116] *Ibid.*
[117] *Ibid.* at 1258.
[118] i.e. to legislate extra-territorially and to pass Acts repugnant to British statutes.

The judgment argued that if the Statute of Westminster had been intended to have that effect, its text would have said so explicitly. The change contended for by the government was far too radical to be achieved as a matter of implication. Indeed, Centlivres doubted that even the text of the Statute of Westminster construed without reference to the events leading up to its enactment could sustain such an implication:

> "in my opinion one is doing no violence to language when one regards the word 'Parliament' as meaning Parliament sitting either bicamerally or unicamerally, in accordance with the requirements of the South Africa Act".[119]

Nor was he prepared to accept that this implication could be supported by the absence of 'saving clauses' for sections 35, 137 and 152 from the text of the 1931 Act. In Centlivres C.J.'s opinion, South Africa had no need for any such saving clause, because the continued vitality of the entrenched clauses had never been in doubt in the minds of the governments and legislators whose deliberations had led to the enactment of the Statute of Westminster.[120]

The court found no support for the government's contentions in *Moore*, on which Andries Beyer placed considerable reliance. Centlivres C.J. read *Moore* as confirming simply that the Statute of Westminster empowered a Dominion parliament to pass legislation repugnant to a British statute. The case had no bearing at all on the question of how a Dominion's own constitution defined its 'parliament' for the purposes of passing legislation on a given subject.

Centlivres C.J. considered that Beyers' arguments were at root premised on the same constitutionally illiterate ground as Douglas Buchanan KC had advanced in *Ndlwana*; namely that if the court concluded that the entrenched clauses were still effective, it would in essence be saying that South Africa as a country remained subordinate to the Westminster Parliament. Centlivres C.J. dismissed this argument as nonsensical, lacking a basis either in theory or historical practice:

> "To say that the Union is not a Sovereign state, simply because its Parliament functioning bicamerally has not the power to amend certain sections of the South Africa Act, is to state a manifest absurdity. Those sections can be amended by Parliament sitting unicamerally. The Union, is therefore, through its legislature, able to pass any laws it pleases, and it would be as false to say that the Union is not a sovereign State as it would have been to claim that the Orange Free State was not a sovereign State on the ground that it was provided in section 26 of its Constitution that no amendment could be made to it save by a three fourths majority of the *Volksraad* in two successive annual sessions".[121]

119 *Ibid.* at 1258. Centlivres noted, as Pollak and Wade had not, that the implication of the government's argument would be that s.63 could be circumvented without the need for further legislation.

120 Centlivres presumably had the benefit on this point of being able to hear directly from the horse's (i.e. Van den Heever's) mouth just what the Hertzog's government and the South African legislature hoped to achieve through enactment of the Statute; on Van den Heever's role in 1931 see p. 256 above.

121 *Ibid.* at 1262.

Nor, Centlivres C.J. continued, were examples of this principle confined to the southern African experience:

> "To go further afield it would be surprising to a constitutional lawyer to be told that that great and powerful country, the United States of America, is not a sovereign independent country simply because its Congress cannot pass any legislation which it pleases".[122]

The judgment concluded by noting that 'parliament' did indeed have the power to repeal section 35. But if the government wished the policy outlined in the 1951 bill to become law, it would have to convene a joint session of parliament and persuade two-thirds of the members of the house and senate to vote in favour of its ideas. The measure purporting to be an 'Act' for the separate representation of voters did not possess that legal status: the constitution left the Appellate Division with no option but to declare it invalid. At the end of his judgment, Centlivres appeared to try to dilute the impact of what might readily be regarded as a fierce criticism of the legal abilities of the *Ndlwana* court. He suggested that counsel in that case had failed to draw the court's attention to the full significance and complexity of the argument surrounding the status of the entrenched clauses:

> "It seems to me with great respect that [the *Ndwlana*] Court *per incuriam* pronounced a decision on a question of vital constitutional importance without hearing argument for and against the main conclusion at which it arrived. Even if it did hear any argument on this vitial question, that argument lasted a very short time . . . (This short argument contrast strangely with the argument in this case which lasted six days . . .) [I]t is clear that there was not placed before the Court on that occasion the mass of materials which counsel on both sides placed before this Court in the present case".[123]

III. THE REACTION

The suggestion that the *Harris* court was impliedly impugning the competence of its predecessor did not feature prominently in the government's immediate reaction to the judgment. Malan's response bore a distinct resemblance to the way in which Kruger had reacted to *Brown v Leyds*.[124] On the day that judgment was issued, Malan made a statement to the house.[125] He informed the house that the Appellate Division had:

> "created a constitutional position which cannot be accepted. Neither Parliament nor the people of South Africa will be prepared to acquiesce in a position where the leg-

[122] On Van den Heever's role in 1931 see p. 256 above.

[123] [1952] 1 *The Times Law Reports* 1245 at 1265.

[124] See pp. 46–47 above. The *Cape Argus* of 21 March spoke of 'ominous echoes' of the former episode. The *Natal Daily News* was more explicit: "It is back to Krugerism, back to the Transvaal Republic where that battle over the sanctity of the courts resulted in a pyrrhic victory for Kruger"; 21 March 1952.

[125] HAD, 20 March 1952, cc. 3124–3126.

islative sovereignty of the lawfully and democratically elected representatives of the people is denied, and where an appointed judicial authority assumes the testing right".[126]

He continued by suggesting that it was neither 'fair nor right' to impose such an onerous burden on a court, for no matter how carefully its members strained to be impartial they would never be able to avoid the appearance of prejudice. The government would be "grossly neglecting its duty towards the people if it allowed such a situation to continue".[127]

The following day, Malan issued a statement which proposed prompt remedial action:

> "As soon as possible the Government will introduce legislation to ensure:
>
> A—That the sovereignty of parliament as representing the will of the electorate will be placed beyond all doubt.
>
> B—That in view of the conflicting judgments of the Appeal Court there should be clarity and finality by establishing that the courts do not have the testing right.
>
> C—That consequently the courts of the country should be protected against the danger of being involved in constitutional issues of a political nature".[128]

Malan also announced that the solution would have retrospective effect, dating back to 1931. Quite how the Prime Minister envisaged that he would achieve this objective was unclear. An Act merely announcing that *Harris* was wrongly decided and reinstating the 1951 legislation would presumably not have been recognised by the Appellate Division unless passed by a two-thirds unicameral majority—a majority which the government manifestly did not command, notwithstanding its attempt to pack the house and senate with South West African Nationalist MPs. Professor Cowen also cast some doubt on Malan's understanding of the notion of a 'sovereign electorate'; that the Nationalists commanded a majority in both the house and senate did not mean that they commanded majority support even among the small minority of South African adults who were eligible voters.[129] Nor indeed was it a self-evident truth that

[126] *Ibid.*

[127] *Ibid.* Louw, Minister for Economic Affairs, displayed a weak grasp of constitutional theory in his denunciation of the decision, in maintaining that only federal states recognised the principle of judical review of legislation. He then revealed a similarly weak grasp of English history; "A few hundred years ago the English House of Commons finally triumphed in its legal struggle with the courts. It is strange in this enlightened age of free parliamentary government that our own Parliament should now be engaged in a similar strugggle": *Cape Times*, 22 March 1952. As any competent historian could have told the Minister, it was the king rather than the courts against which the House of Commons was ranged in the English revolution, and the revolution established the supremacy of Parliament—of which the King and the House of Lords were essential parts—not simply of the Commons; see Loveland (1996), n. 89 above, ch. 2. The *Natal Daily News* was distinctly unimpressed; "Mr Louw posing as a constitutional lawyer is the only comic relief in this grave situation": 22 March 1952.

[128] Quoted in E. Kahn, 'Constitutional Law' (1952) *Annual Survey of South African Law* 1 at 9.

[129] Cf. the comment by E. McWhinney: "One of the more ironic features of the current crisis in South Africa is that the principle of parliamentary sovereignty . . . which has its philosophic justification at the present day in the concept of Parliament as the embodiment of the popular will, should now be invoked by a legislature which is itself not fully representative, and in an endeavour to

'sovereignty' and narrow electoral majoritarianism should be construed as coterminous concepts.

Malan had invoked *Ndlwana* in support of his view that courts did not have 'the testing power', evidently blind to the irony of employing one judicial precedent to justify the rejection of another.[130] It does not appear however that he seriously entertained the idea of deploying the Nationalists' parliamentary majority to dismiss any or all of the Appellate judges. Such a response would arguably have been legal,[131] but Malan evidently assumed that it could not be defended as a legitimate exercise of political power. Nor did Malan seem immediately attracted to the obvious expedient, now available to him under the terms of the Criminal Procedure Act Amendment Act 1948,[132] of appointing lawyers sympathetic to the government's standpoint as additional Appellate Division judges to create a new judicial majority supporting the *Ndlwana* analysis of the entrenched clauses.

Centlivres C.J. and his colleagues might also have been less than impressed that this new legislation—whatever it might be—was intended to 'protect' judges against accusations of political bias. Malan was evidently unable to appreciate or unwilling to acknowledge that the rationale underpinning *Harris* was that the constitution had removed certain issues from the mainstream arena of bare majoritarian politics: in upholding this principle, the Appellate Division was necessarily standing *above* the ordinary political process.

For Coloured voters in the Cape, the decision meant that they remained able, for the time being, to continue to participate in the ordinary political process. The FAC welcomed the judgment, but doubted that it would settle the issue: "It is however obvious that the National Party is determined to carry out its fascist programmes . . . Like the Nazis before them, they are determined to implement to the full their barren, undemocratic policy of racial oppression".[133] The plain-

abridge representation still further": 'The Union Parliament, the Supreme Court, and the "Entrenched Clauses" of the South Africa Act' (1952) *Canadian Bar Review* 692 at 721.

[130] Strijdom took the opportunity to attack what he regarded as the United Party's hypocrisy over the entrenchment issue. At a public meeting (attended primarily it seems by the government's opponents) at Sea Point in Cape Town on 25 March, he observed that barely five years earlier the Smuts government had promoted the Asiatic Land Tenure and Representation bill through the bicameral procedure. Since that Act removed Indians from the common roll in Natal, it manifestly breached s.35. Yet the then government had seen no need to follow s.35's specified procedures; *Pretoria News*, 26 March. See pp. 226–227 above.

[131] Section 101 of the South Africa Act had provided that judges could be removed by the Governor-General in Council on the grounds of 'misbehaviour or incapacity' following an address from both houses of parliament. This provision presented Malan with an obstacle that had not impeded Kruger in 1897. It was at best debatable that Centlivres had 'misbehaved' simply by reversing *Ndlwana*, and most unlikely that any of the existing Supreme Court judges would uphold such a dismissal were it to be challenged in court. The government could however have promoted a bill dismissing the judges concerned, and might have expected such a measure would gain majority support in both house and senate.

[132] See p. 257 above.

[133] *The (Cape) Guardian*, 27 March 1952. Writing in the same issue, Sam Kahn suggested (certainly optimistically and probably naively) that Malan had overplayed his hand by issuing veiled threats to the Court: "Dr Malan has committed a colossal political blunder in deciding to kick the

tiffs certainly regarded the case as simply a battle in what might prove a protracted war. Edgar Franklin greeted the judgment as "a great victory, but the fight is not over. We still have to see what the government will do next. If the government should now take unconstitutional steps, we can no longer say what the Coloured people will do".[134]

For native blacks, and for Indians and Coloureds elsewhere, the option of participation in the 'normal' political process was manifestly not available. Other alternatives were however vigorously pursued. The ANC had waged a widespread and intensive campaign of protest and civil disobedience against both the 1951 Act and the increasing panoply of discriminatory legislation with which parliament was surrounding it. Early in 1952, the ANC launched a co-ordinated 'Defiance Campaign', in which thousands of activists volunteered to break segregatory laws in the full expectation that they would be arrested, prosecuted and jailed for doing so.[135] The ANC's recruits included Coloureds and Indians as well as native blacks. The campaign was intended to be non-violent; protestors even went so far as to inform the police of when and where their law-breaking activities would occur. Malan had remained quite unmoved by the threatened protests;[136] his response had simply been to warn the ANC that the government would not hesitate to use any means at its disposal to prevent disturbances to public order.[137]

The Torch Commando's internal feuding had meant that its high profile on the extra-parliamentary political stage enjoyed only a short run, but its activities did seem to contribute to a stiffening of resolve within the United Party leadership. Strauss appeared increasingly willing to see the franchise issue as one which was rooted less in technical concerns of constitutional law, and more in substantive considerations of constitutional morality. Whether he would be able to carry his party in this direction, and whether the party could carry a majority of the white electorate, remained to be seen. For the moment, the political ball lay squarely in the government's court.

Courts in the teeth . . . The savage and malicious attacks that are now being made by leading Nationalists not only on the Courts themselves but upon the judges are a threat to all democratic institutions that exist in South Africa".

[134] *Cape Times*, 21 March 1953.

[135] Mandela, n. 46 above, pp. 145–160; Dugard (1978), n. 74 above, pp. 212–213; E. Brookes and J. Macaulay, *Civil Liberties in South Africa* (Cape Town: OUP, 1958), pp. 77–80; Lodge, n. 46 above, ch. 2. For a detailed account of the immediate background and conduct of the campaign, and an analysis of its links with Gandhi's earlier activities in South Africa (pp 86–87 and 139–140 above) see L. Kuper, *Passive Resistance* (London: Jonathan Cape, 1956), chs. 4, 5 and 1 respectively. For details of the campaign itself, with extensive reference to contemporaneous news coverage, see C. Heyns, *A Jurisprudential Analysis of Civil Disobedience in South Africa* (Pretoria: University of Pretoria Ph.D, 1991), pp. 163–200.

[136] Kuper raises the possibility that this stance may have been facilitated by the rather cursory coverage that the white English language press accorded to the Defiance Campaign's activities; (1956), n. 135 above, p. 131. The criticism is a rather curious one, insofar as Kuper's own account of the campaign is premised largely on white newspapers' coverage of events.

[137] Mandela records that the ANC leadership regarded this response as tantamount to a declaration of war, n. 46 above, pp. 145–146.

Much of the English language press was, at might have been expected, fulsome in its support of the Court's decision.[138] The *Cape Argus* of 21 March denounced the cabinet as "acolytes in the temple of apartheid" and castigated Malan for suggesting that the judgment raised political rather than legal issues. The *Natal Daily News* greeted the judgment as "a shattering blow to the government".[139] For the *Cape Times* "the forcing through Parliament of the Coloured Vote Bill was the disreputable strategem of a group of disreputable politicians".[140] A *Times* leader on 24 March regarded Malan's threat to reverse the decision as even more contemptible: "By what right does a minority party with fascist tendencies set about tearing the foundations of our country to shreds?". The *Pretoria News* was particularly critical of Malan's reaction to the judgment: "There can have been few statements as ill-advised and unstatesmanlike".[141] The *Rand Daily Mail* was similarly scathing on 21 March:

> "The government has received a sharp, and we hope salutary rebuff. But even if the Appeal Court had decided the other way, a legal victory for the government would not alter the fact that its methods constituted a grave breach of faith".

The *Mail* lost no time in intensifying its criticisms of the cabinet's *bona fides*. Strijdom was the target of its most forceful attack.[142] During a house speech in April 1952, Strijdom claimed that violent scenes at a recent United Party meeting had been staged by the United Party itself with a view to falsely pinning blame for the action on the Nationalists. The *Mail's* investigation of the incident led Raynor Ellis to conclude that the Nationalists had indeed caused the disruption, that Strijdom had known this, and that he had lied to the house when casting blame on the United Party. Ellis subsequently published a leader—titled simply 'Mr Strijdom Lied'—in which he invited the Minister to sue for libel. Strijdom did not accept the challenge.

The Afrikaans press, predictably, was overtly critical of the Court's decision. *Die Vaderland* suggested that: "It seems as if the Appeal Court has exceeded its jurisdiction", and objected to parliament being "hobbled by theories that it make it subject to the testing right".[143] *Die Burger* announced that "It is of supreme importance, both for the country and for the Appeal Court, that the Government take steps to place the legislative sovereignty of Parliament beyond all doubt. In this matter the Government can count on strong support".[144] *Die Burger's* leader either misunderstood or wilfully misrepresented the judgment,

[138] Although in some of them the judgment shared top billing with outrage over another government initiative—the removal of the H.M. designation from the ribbons worn by sailors on their caps. The Monarch's 'disappearance' was variously seen as a gross discourtesy and an indicator of the government's republican ambitions; see *The (Johannesburg) Star*, 21 March and the *Natal Daily News*, 22 March.

[139] 21 March.

[140] 21 March 1952.

[141] 21 March.

[142] See Mervis, n. 51 above, pp. 294–297 for a detailed account of this episode.

[143] Translation taken from *The (Johannesburg) Star*, 21 March 1952.

[144] 21 March 21 1952.

which had repeatedly stressed that the South African parliament was indeed a sovereign law-maker.[145]

Die Burger's ignorance or mendacity was however shared by *Die Transvaaler*. Its 21 May edition portrayed the government's defeat as just another stage in the Afrikaaner *volk's* long struggle for freedom from the British: "The Cape Coloured vote is the last vestige of the Cape-British liberalism in our political system. In 1948 the nation gave a mandate for its removal and the mandate will be carried out". The paper enthusiastically predicted that: "There can be no doubt that the necessary steps will be taken to place the sovereignty of Parliament above doubt".[146]

Harris was front page news in many British newspapers. Malan would perhaps have found some solace in the *Daily Telegraph's* leader on 20 March:

> "For reasons which are perfectly understandable, if not always justifiable, Dr Malan and his followers have sought to segregate the African and Coloured population of the Union. But those who condemn them out of hand only sharpen the conflict they affect to deplore".

Such out of hand condemnation was however promptly forthcoming from the *Sunday Express* on 23 March, which was particularly forceful in criticising the Malan government: "Courts overruled, judges discredited, the electorate manipulated. Where have we heard all this before. In the pre-war Germany of Hitler and the Italy of Mussolini".[147] The view was echoed by the *News Chronicle*, which described the Court's decision as "a blow struck for justice".[148] The *Manchester Guardian* was similarly critical: "If the Nationalists seek to override or amend the Court's decision they will have set out on a desperate course".[149]

The *Guardian's* view was echoed by Germany's *Welt am Sonntag*, which suggested that Malan would be 'abandoning democracy' if his government attempted to prevent the courts from questioning parliament's decisions.[150] In the USA, the *New York Times* of 22 March applauded:

> "the firm and wise judgment that has been rendered in South Africa. Any other ruling would have overthrown the whole concept of the safeguarding of individual rights. Thus matters that belong in the constitutional field would have been prominently placed in the political field".

Academic reaction was broadly supportive of the *Harris* result. Professor Cowen greeted the decision as a substantial vindication of the position he had

[145] This point was made extremely carefully on the front page of the *Pretoria News* of 21 March. A lengthy analysis of the judgment by its (unnamed) political correspondent stressed that the judgment affirmed parliament's sovereignty, but held that parliament existed in two forms: "To argue that the Appeal Court is trying to take over the sovereign power of Parliament is absurd".

[146] Translation taken from *The (Johannesburg) Star*, 21 March 1952.

[147] 23 March 1952.

[148] 21 March 1952.

[149] 20 March 1952.

[150] 23 March 1952.

advocated earlier that year.[151] The great flaw in the government's position, he observed, was that it had subscribed to the 'naive confusion' so prevalent in South African political circles that a sovereign nation had to possess a (bicameral simple majority) sovereign legislature. The great stress that its counsel had laid on British constitutional principle was at best an irrelevance, since there was no obvious reason to assume that South Africa's parliament was a replica of the British legislature in all respects. 'Sovereignty' was a 'slippery and delusive' concept, the subtleties of which the government had been unable to grasp or unwilling to acknowledge.[152]

The government also faced the embarassment of seeing some of the authorities on whose arguments Andries Beyers had relied announce that they had on reflection decided that *Harris*, rather than *Ndlwana*, was the correct statement of the constitutional position. Perhaps the most significant change of mind came from former Chief Justice de Wet, who had sat as a judge of appeal in *Ndlwana*. In an interview with the *Cape Argus* on 22 March, De Wet observed that he doubted that *Ndlwana* supported the position that the government maintained; but if it did do so, it was wrongly decided:

> "I am pleased that the Court now . . . could come to the conclusion that the entrenchment clauses are more than a matter of procedure and could give legal validity to the strong moral obligations which were undertaken on all sides at the time of the passing of the Statute of Westminster. I quite agree with the Chief Justice that this decision in no way detracts from the sovereignty of Parliament".[153]

Two days later, the *Argus* reported that Henry May, the author of *The South African Constitution*, had also recanted his former view that the Statute of Westminster had repealed the entrenched clauses. In the next edition of his book, May was to praise Cowen's thesis as "one of the most brilliant and important pamphlets in modern constitutional law".[154]

The judgment was also warmly received by various foreign academic commentators. In Britain, Professor G. Keeton of University College London

[151] 'Legislature and Judiciary—Part One' (1952) 15 *Modern Law Review* 282; (1953), n. 93 above.

[152] Cf. a note in the (1952) *Law Quarterly Review* 285, which acknowledged that the fact that legal root of the South African Constitution lay in a British statute "seems to imply a certain degree of foreign domination" (at 287). The note went on to suggest that such claims were merely 'an emotional attitude' given that South Africa was a sovereign state after 1931. Moreover, as the article pointed out, if the entrenched clauses of the consitution were invalid because of their 'foreign' origin, so was every other provision of the South Africa Act; "If one clause can be disregarded by the government in power because it is restrictive in nature then all other clauses can be disregarded whenever it becomes politically convenient to do so": *ibid.*

[153] 22 March 1952. De Wet's views were also run as front page leads in the *Natal Daily News* and the *Pretoria News*.

[154] H. May, *The South African Constitution*, 3rd edn. (Cape Town: Juta & Co., 1955). May also recounts an extraordinary episode involving Mr Ndlwana. Shortly after *Harris* was decided, an (unidentified) newspaper ran an 'interview' with Mr Ndlwana, in which he castigated the 1937 Court for having decided his case wrongly and demanded damages. The interview was a complete fabrication. Ndlwana sued the paper for defamation and received a substantial settlement out of court; *ibid.* p. 47.

dismissed the Malan government's arguments on national sovereignty as "electioneering devices and not sober arguments".[155] He was equally dismissive of the Nationalists' general political agenda, seeing it as little more than a reassertion of the boer extremism that had been a contributory cause of the second boer war. On the merits of Centlivres C.J.'s judgment, he was rather more circumspect. Keeton limited himself to a survey of competing views,[156] and did not offer his own opinion of which was the better legal argument.[157]

Erwin Griswold, Dean of the Harvard Law School,[158] was considerably more forthright. He congratulated Centlivres C.J. on producing "a great judgment, deserving to rank with the best work of the judges who have contributed to the field of constitutional law".[159] Professor Zelman Cowen, an Australian academic, embraced the decision as one which was "clearly correct",[160] and which moreover imparted useful lessons to both British and Australian constitutional reformers concerned with safeguarding fundamental political values from bare legislative majorities.

H.R.W. Wade, then a fellow of Trinity College, Cambridge, and subsequently to be regarded in some quarters as the most eminent of Britain's constitutional lawyers, offered a curious critique of the judgment in the *Cambridge Law Journal*.[161] In an article primarily concerned with the continuing authority in British constitutional law of the doctrine that Parliament could legislate on any topic through the bicameral simple majority plus royal assent procedure, Wade suggested that *Harris* had no defensible legal base. Rather, he argued "the court had reached the ultimate boundary of the legal system, and had in substance to take a political decision".[162] What Centlivres had done, he concluded, was to 'invent' a justification for his judgment because the Court was faced with a constitutional 'vacuum'.[163] Wade was evidently not convinced that both the text of the South Africa Act and the intentions of its framers provided a sound foundation for the judgment. Nor did he address De Villiers C.J.'s judgment in *Ndobe*, beyond citing it in a footnote. Wade conceded that the Appellate Division had found itself in a 'revolutionary' situation, though he gave the

155 'The Constitutional Crisis in South Africa' (1953) *Current Legal Problems* 22 at 34.

156 Primarily those of E.C.S. Wade and Professor Cowen.

157 E.C.S. Wade's initial comment reported in the South African press was that the judgment was simply wrong; *Bantu World* 29 March 1952. In the foreword to the 10th edition of Dicey, published in 1959, Wade appeared to have come round to the view that Cowen's thesis, and thus the *Harris No. 1* judgment, were if not correct, then certainly defensible in terms of South African constitutional law; (London: Macmillan, 1959), pp. lx–lxiii.

158 E. Griswold, 'The "Coloured Vote Case" in South Africa' (1952) 65 *Harvard LR* 1361.

159 *Ibid.* at 1374. The force of Griswold's legal argument was rather undermined by the silly suggestion that British courts might impose substantive constraints on the powers of Britain's parliament (*ibid.* at 1369 and n. 22).

160 Z. Cowen, 'Parliamentary Sovereignty and the Limits of Legal Change' (1952) 26 *Australian Law Journal* 237 at 239.

161 'The Basis of Legal Sovereignty' (1955) *Cambridge Law Journal* 177.

162 *Ibid.* at 192.

163 *Ibid.* at 192.

impression that it was the members of the Court, rather than the Malan government and the bare parliamentary majority, that were the revolutionaries.[164] The article also managed to maintain a magisterial detachment from issues with a more prosaically political hue. Its reader, if she were unfamiliar with the facts of *Harris*, would not have discovered that the case concerned voting rights or racial discrimination. She would be faced, one assumes, with an intellectual vacuum of Wade's own making.

Centlivres C.J.'s reasoning, if not the result to which it led him, was subjected to a more coherent attack in the *Canadian Bar Review*. Edward McWhinney, an Australian barrister and academic then at Yale Law School, criticised the judgment for its 'legalistic' rather than 'constitutional' basis. McWhinney noted (quite accurately) that Centlivres had referred throughout his opinion to 'the South Africa Act' rather than to 'the South African constitution'. This labelling was a legal fiction which concealed a political truth; namely that the continued vitality of the entrenched provisions should be rooted in the endorsement by South African legislators in 1931 of the compromise on the Cape franchise made at the 1908 Constitutional Convention which was the *sine qua non* of South Africa coming into being.[165]

McWhinney suggested that the judgment would have had greater legitimacy if it had explicitly identified an indigenously (and wholly) South African *grondwet* in which to root its defence of the entrenched provisions. There is some force to this argument, but it rather overlooks the fact that such an argument emerges as a necessary implication from the tenor and the text of Centlivres C.J.'s opinion. Rather than, as McWhinney suggests, ignoring the political dimension of the dispute before it, the Appellate Division could be seen as playing a quite sophisticated political hand by refusing to engage with such overtly 'political' conceptions. For the Court to have proclaimed what was in effect a new source of fundamental law which only it could identify might have lent greater weight to Malan's contention that the judges were usurping constitutional power.[166] Legalistic analysis is admittedly a limited tool, but in the context of the constitutional challenge presented to the court by the 1951 Act, it was both a familiar and a reliable one. Whether it could continue to be an adequate tool was likely to depend primarily on the nature of the legislation that Malan would propose to 'remedy' the malaise he assumed that *Harris No. 1* had introduced into the constitutional system.

[164] Cf. his comment at *ibid*. 192; "In disregarding the manifest will of the 'sovereign legislature', they made it clear that it was for them, the court, to say what a valid Act of that legislature was".

[165] E. McWhinney, 'The Union Parliament, the Supreme Court and the Entrenched Clauses of the South Africa Act' (1952) 30 *Canadian Bar Review* 692.

[166] Which was in essence the argument made by H.R.W. Wade in response to the judgment.

IV. CONCLUSION

The Malan government did not regard the *Harris* judgment as any reason to reflect upon the merits of its intended programme. Unfettered by the enhanced majority requirments of sections 35 and 152, parliament promptly enacted the Bantu (Abolition of Passes and Co-ordination of Documents Act) 1952.[167] Despite its title, the Act did not abolish passes in any meaningful sense. Rather it replaced them with an identity card containing the holder's fingerprints and employment details.[168] Failure to produce the documents whenever requested to do so was made a criminal offence, punishable by up to one year in jail. All native blacks over the age of sixteen, male and female, had to carry such documents.

While the government had not made any immediate attempt to pack the Appellate bench with its own supporters, there were indications that it regarded this as a viable long term tactic. In 1950, Swart had appointed L.C. Steyn to the Transvaal bench.[169] Steyn, born in 1903, had taken a BA, LLB and LLD at Stellenbosch. He initially began a career as an academic lawyer at Stellenbosch, during which he articulated a strong preference for removing English common law influences from South African jurisprudence, and returning to a 'pure' form of Roman–Dutch law,[170] before entering the Cape bar in 1928. Rather than go into private practice, Steyn immediately took a post in the government legal sevice. He was appointed Attorney-General of South West Africa in 1931, and subsequently became an adviser to the Department of Justice. He was appointed as the government's Senior Legal Adviser in 1944, and represented the government at the United Nations and before the International Court of Justice.[171] In 1946, Steyn published a major work on statutory interpretation, *Die Uitlig van Wette*, which was notable for its virtually complete refusal to acknowledge that principles derived from English law had any legitimate role to play within the South African legal system.[172] The book also indicated that Steyn's personal preference was for judges to interpret ambiguous legislation in favour of the government's view of what a given Act was intended to achieve, rather than in

[167] See Dugard (1978), n. 74 above, pp. 75–77: Brookes and Macaulay, n. 135 above, pp. 55–71.

[168] This card held more extensive information than the card required under the terms of the Population Registration Act 1950; see p. 240 above. Verwoerd described his Act as one which would "provide every Native with a handy little holder for his identification card in the form of a little pocket book in which the most important data concerning him will appear, as for example his employment contract and tax receipts"; quoted in A. Pelzer, *Verwoerd speaks* (Johannesburg: APB Publishers, 1966), p. 51.

[169] L.C. Steyn should not be confused with G. Steyn, who by that time been sitting for some years on the Cape provincial bench, and who had heard *Harris* at first instance; see p. 275 above.

[170] Dugard (1978), n. 74 above, pp. 9, 287.

[171] *Ibid*. pp. 286–287.

[172] I have relied in the following paragraph primarily on E. Cameron, 'Legal Chauvinism, Executive-Mindedness and Justice—L.C. Steyn's Impact on South African Law' (1982) 99 *South African LJ* 38.

vigorous defence of individual liberties. This was perhaps best illustrated by Steyn's forceful critique of Rose Innes C.J.'s Appellate Division judgment in *Dadoo v Krugersdorp Municipal Council*.[173] Steyn criticised the Court in *Dadoo* for 'clinging to the precise terms of the law', thereby evading its substantive purpose and producing a result which 'offends one's sense of justice'.[174] Whether Steyn's concept of 'justice' was premised on the need to enforce racial segregation, or on the assumption that judges should adopt a deferential stance towards the wishes of the executive, is unclear. But either or both explanations would presumably have made him an attractive candidate for high judicial office from Malan's perspective.

Steyn's elevation to the bench provoked outrage among the Transvaal bar, many of whose members doubted that he was either willing or able to discharge his judicial duties with the requisite degree of independence from the government's wishes.[175] This potential incursion into the perceived independence of the judiciary paled however into insignificance when the government eventually announced the steps it proposed to take to reverse the *Harris No. 1* judgment.

[173] See pp. 156–157 above.

[174] The translation is taken from Cameron, n. 172 above, at 63.

[175] Dugard (1978), n. 74 above, pp. 9–11. Some advocates simply refused to appear before courts over which he presided.

9

Harris v Minister of the Interior No. 2

I. THE HIGH COURT OF PARLIAMENT BILL

Despite its minority share of the popular vote in the 1948 election, Malan's government had consistently maintained that its *apartheid* programme represented the 'will of the people' and that it possessed a mandate which obliged it to ensure that these policies were implemented. The Appellate Division had, in the government's view, illegitimately frustrated the will of the people in *Harris No. 1*. The obstacle it presented therefore had to be removed.

Malan's 'remedy' for *Harris No. 1*—The High Court of Parliament bill—was unveiled to an incredulous parliamentary and extra-parliamentary opposition in April 1952. The government had decided to ask parliament (by bicameral simple majority) to create a new 'court of law' possessing jurisdiction to hear appeals from any decision of the Appellate Division which had concluded that an 'Act of Parliament' was invalid.[1] Clause 3 of the bill provided that the new court was to be composed of every member of the house and senate, and could operate with a quorum of fifty members. It would have a 'President' appointed by the Governor-General. Clause 5 announced that any Minister of State could refer an Appellate Division judgment invalidating an Act to the 'court' within six months of the judgment having been given. Clause 6 made provision for this 'appeal' to be heard by the 'Judicial Committee' of the 'court', a body comprised of ten members, appointed by the President, of whom four would have to be present for the committee to have a quorum. The committee could make (by simple majority) such recommendations as it thought appropriate to the 'court'. Under clause 8, the 'court' (acting by simple majority of members present) could then make any order it thought fit in respect of the impugned Appellate Division judgment. Such an order would be "final and binding, and shall be executed in every respect as if it were a decision of the Provincial or Local Division of the Supreme Court".

The full text of the bill had not been published when Donges sought leave to introduce it to the house on 22 April. This was in itself something of a departure from previous practice. One would generally not assume that the house could reach an informed decision as to whether a bill should proceed if its members had not been apprised of its proposed terms. Instead of the text of the bill, Donges offered the house his own exposition of its aims and contents.

[1] Enacted as s.2 of the High Court of Parliament Act 1952.

The first 'basic principle' underlying the bill was:

> "to vest in the democratically elected representatives of the electors, as representing the will of the people, the power to adjudicate finally on the validity of laws passed by Parliament . . . [B]y constituting the High Court of Parliament in this way, the principle of responsibility, the principle of accountability to the sovereign will of the electorate is placed beyond all doubt".[2]

A court composed of members of parliament, in addition to representing the will of the people, would have the further advantage, Donges suggested, of safeguarding the Appellate Division from accusations of political bias when it dealt with constitutional questions. On this point, Donges referred approvingly to the British system, noting that under the British constitution a judgment such as that given in the *Harris* case could never be produced.

Donges maintained that the need for a reform of this nature had arisen for two reasons. The first, unsurprisingly, was that the Appellate Division's overruling of *Ndlwana* in *Harris No. 1* had created confusion and uncertainty in the law. The second, bizarrely, was that the abolition of appeals to the Privy Council enacted by Parliament in 1951 had created an unfortunate legal void above the Appellate Division—a void which this new 'court' would fill: "All that we do in this Bill is to substitute *mutatis mutandis* the High Court of Parliament for the old Privy Council".[3]

The minister argued that the bill should not be seen as an attack either on the existing courts or on the principle of the rule of law: "Where after all is the 'smashing of the courts'? Where is the rule of law destroyed when you are instituting a new court of law?".[4] Nor was it correct to say that the bill necessarily made legislators judges in their own cause, for by the time that a case came before the High Court of Parliament the composition of the house and senate could be quite different from their composition at the time that the Act in question was passed. Nor (and here Donges seemed to enter the realm of fantasy) should it be assumed that a High Court of Parliament drawn from the current house and senate would necessarily overrule *Harris* and re-instate *Ndlwana*. It might on the contrary confirm that *Harris* was correctly decided.

Strauss denounced the proposal in strident terms:

> "This is not a court that has been created. This is not a judicial body at all, a body that will give judicial pronouncements . . . No, Sir, this is a political court; this is a bogus court; . . . a bogus court set up in order to express the will of the Caucus of the Nationalist party".[5]

[2] HAD, 22 April 1952, cc. 4108–4109.

[3] *Ibid.* at c.4120.

[4] *Ibid.* at c. 4122.

[5] *Ibid.* at c.4125. The point was pursued in a more prosaic vein by the leader of the Labour Party: "At least when the Cabinet appoints an Appeal Court, the members are appointed from men who are barristers . . . [the judges] go there for the honour and to serve the country and divest themselves, as far as I suppose any man can, from any political opinion they may have had . . . But here we have a court which is going to be set up by the Cabinet . . . They must and they will put on that court men

Donges' references to the British situation were an irrelevance, designed only to mislead a credulous public. Strauss noted that it was also rank hypocrisy for the government to invoke the constitutional principles of a country for which it had never expressed any sympathy in an attempt to legitimise its subversion of the South African constitution:

> "[F]or the last 20 years and more we have heard from the opposite side . . . that we must do away with that system of what was called British Jewish democracy, and on the other hand we heard a lot about the model Republics of the Free State and the Transvaal. But this afternoon we heard from the Minister that we should go back to the Mother Parliament. Now he does not ask us to look back to the constitution of the model Republic of the Orange Free State. We know why not. The constitution of the model Republic of the Orange Free State contained entrenched clauses".[6]

At second reading on 5 May 1952, Donges continued to invoke the sovereignty of the people and British perceptions of the sovereignty of Parliament to justify the bill. He also regurgitated arguments deployed in E.C.S Wade's opinion for the *Harris* case to buttress the government's position. Donges further contended that the mere fact that members of the High Court of Parliament might not be legally qualified to sit as judges did not mean that the body could not be a court. Magistrates, assessors on Water Courts, and members of juries were not judges either, but no-one disputed that the bodies in which they sat were courts. The minister also drew upon the principle that many legislative assemblies retained the power to act in a judicial capacity in respect of the impeachment of their own members. The USA, Norway, France and the former Orange Free State were all identified as countries whose constitutions recognised 'courts' of this sort.

In reply, Strauss contended that the Minister's speech suggested that the government had accepted that the High Court of Parliament could not accurately be described as a 'court' in the traditional sense of the word. Strauss emphasised that the United Party remained committed to 'constitutional' methods of opposing the bill. On this question, he argued, the United Party had adopted a more morally defensible position than the ANC, for whose 'Defiance Campaign'[7] Strauss expressed no sympathy at all; "as far as the United Party are concerned, we condemn in the strongest possible terms the proposed defiance of so called unjust laws by the ANC".[8] The government's subversion of the constitution was however no less reprehensible, and Strauss warned Malan of the potentially violent consequences which might ensue if the Appellate Division was to declare the High Court of Parliament invalid and the government refused to accept its decision. The spectre then arose, Strauss argued, of a *coup d'etat*.[9]

who will vote the way the government wishes it, they will be party hacks. . . and they will act in a way to insult the law as we know it in this country": J. Christie, HAD, 22 April 1952, cc. 4137–4138.

[6] *Ibid.* at c.4126.

[7] See p. 293 above.

[8] HAD, 5 May 1952, c. 4940.

[9] The second reading took place in the midst of a massive deployment of police and soldiers in

There was, as had been the case in respect of the Separate Representation of Voters bill the previous year, no likelihood that anything said in the house would move the government either to withdraw or substantially amend its proposed legislation. Nor was the government swayed by critical comments in the mass and academic media, both in South Africa and from abroad.

Reaction to the bill

The publication of the bill had triggered an outbreak of violent affrays within the white political community. A United Party meeting at Stellenbosch on 23 April was abandoned following a sustained attempt by government supporters to shout down and intimidate the speakers and audience. Similar scenes had occurred at a United Party meeting at Alberton the previous day. United Party members complained that the police had been noticeably reluctant to restrain or eject the Nationalist party's supporters.[10]

Much of the English language South African press resorted to virulent denunciation of the bill and of the motives that lay behind it. The *Rand Daily Mail's* coverage was typified by a cartoon published on 17 April which simply showed a Nationalist politician standing in front of a mirror—the reflection he faced was that of Hitler. The Nazi theme was echoed in the *Cape Times*, which had accurately predicted the bill's contents a week before it was published. Its leader on 16 April, referring to proceedings in an opposition debate on the constitutional crisis announced that:

> "The course of the establishment of despotism was clearly seen yesterday. There was the pseudo-legal cloak, the jeers and adolescent interjections from a disciplined mass of Government speakers, and the attempt to describe resentment and criticism of the Government's actions as an 'incitement'. Hitler was cruder. He did not describe the opponents of the onward march of Nazi tyranny as inciters: he called them communists. The principle is the same".[11]

The paper subsequently described the bill itself as "a veiled attempt to bypass the entrenched clauses . . . an insult to the intelligence of the judiciary".[12]

The British press criticised the bill both in prose and—perhaps more effectively—in cartoons. The *Daily Herald* ran a sketch by Low showing Malan

and around the legislature. Malan maintained that the police presence was the initiative of the police themselves, who had uncovered information that violent attacks might be made on Nationalist MPs by opponents of the bill. Strauss suggested that the police presence was a clumsy, government-engineered smear to discredit the Torch Commando, the Labour Party and the United Party by presenting them as harbingers of violence and unrest.

[10] *Cape Times*, 24 April 1952.

[11] The *Cape Times* also gave prominence to the decision of J.G. Benade, a three-time Mayor of Blomfontein and formerly a leading figure in Havenga's Afrikaner party, to join the United Party. Benade denounced the Malan government for its 'refusal to abide by our constitution and the rule of law'; 15 April 1952.

[12] 22 April 1952.

forcing Centlivres into a jail cell full of blacks, while Vicky in the *London News Chronicle* showed a cartoon of the High Court of Parliament in which every member was Malan.[13]

The government's resolution was not shaken by the barrage of press criticism at home and abroad. In a speech at a party meeting in Rondebosch in the Cape on 29 April, T.H. Viljoen, Minister of Education, told his audience that a government which accepted *Harris No. 1* would not be 'worth its salt'; "How can we abide by that decision and say that Parliament, the voice of the people, was subordinate to the veto right of five judges, not elected by the people, but appointed and paid by the Government".[14] Nor was the government deterred by the bill's evident lack of academic support. In Britain, Professor Keeton suggested that the passage of the 'Act' had moved the issue "beyond the point where compromise is possible".[15] Erwin Griswold of Harvard Law School had greeted the bill as "an obvious subterfuge",[16] and speculated that it would not survive judicial scrutiny.

Harris, Collins, Deane and Franklin evidently shared Griswold's opinion, for shortly after the 'Act' came into effect on 3 June 1952, they initiated proceedings in the Cape provincial division with a view to having the measure declared invalid. At the same time, the Malan government referred the Appellate Division's judgment in *Harris No. 1* to the Judicial Committee of the High Court of Parliament. The intensity of the conflict in which both 'courts' found themselves embroiled was further highlighted at the end of June, when some 45,000 whites marched in protest against the Act in Durban.[17]

II. THE 'JUDGMENTS' OF THE CAPE PROVINCIAL DIVISION AND THE HIGH COURT OF PARLIAMENT

The provincial division heard argument in *Harris and Others v Minister of the Interior and Another* (hereafter referred to as *Harris No. 2*) on 11–13 August, and delivered its judgment on 29 August. The High Court of Parliament produced its opinion on *Harris No. 1* on 28 August. The two decisions were delivered in a time of increased political tension, in both the white and non-white communities.

By 1952, a young black lawyer named Walter Sisulu had become a leading figure in the ANC and was one of the most prominent of anti-*apartheid* activists.

[13] Vicky evidently liked the theme. On 24 April the *News Chronicle* ran another of his cartoons, this one showing a British Cabinet composed entirely of Churchills, intended to convey the Prime Minister's supposed dominance within a lack-lustre government.

[14] *Cape Times*, 24 April 1952.

[15] 'The Constitutional Crisis in South Africa' (1953) *Current Legal Problems* 22 at 35.

[16] 'The "Coloured Vote Case" in South Africa' (1952) 65 *Harvard LR* 1361 at 1374.

[17] H. May, *The South African Constitution*, 3rd edn. (Cape Town: Juta & Co., 1955), p. 61. May described the demonstration as "the greatest meeting ever held in South Africa": *ibid*.

He was well used to appearing in the lower courts as an attorney,[18] along with his partner in the law firm of Sisulu and Mandela. In 1952 however, Sisulu and Mandela appeared in court as the defendants in a criminal trial. They were prosecuted under the terms of the Suppression of Communism Act 1950 for, *inter alia*, inciting people to challenge the pass and identity card laws and the provisions segregating access to public facilities.[19] The initial hearing before a magistrate in Johanesburg was scheduled for late August.

On 26 August, several hundred students, many of them Europeans, had been arrested after having marched on the Johannesburg Magistrates Court in protest at Sisulu and Mandela's arrest. Fighting had broken out among white supporters and opponents of the government, and over 400 protestors were arrested.[20] The leadership of the United Party had condemned the protest for its unconstitutional methods,[21] a stance which to many observers might readily have been construed as a call for acquiescence to the Malan administration's own departure from 'constitutional' modes of governance.

The United Party had, however, refused to participate in the hearings held by the Judicial Committe of the High Court of Parliament in the 'appeal' against *Harris No. 1*. The committee's membership was thus limited to six Nationalist MPs. Malan, in a surreal nod to the concept of 'judicial independence', had disqualified himself from the proceedings on the grounds that he had an interest in the outcome.[22] These six MPs heard argument on the Minister's behalf, but the plaintiffs were not represented. To no-one's great surprise, the Judicial Committee concluded that *Harris No. 1* was wrongly decided. The Committee 'held' that the Appellate Division had erred by assuming that the South Africa Act should be regarded as 'fundamental law' within the South African constitutional order. The correct approach, as argued by Pollak, Jennings and Wheare and confirmed in *Ndlwana*, was that the passage of the Statute of Westminster had left the newly independent South African nation with a parliament which exercised sovereign authority along British lines. There was thus no 'fundamental law' within the South African constitution. *Harris No. 1* should therefore be reversed.

Centlivres C.J. had not explicity used a 'fundamental law' argument in *Harris No. 1*. His method had ostensibly been premised rather on an orthodox if unusual technique of statutory interpretation. The Judicial Committee may well

[18] The equivalent of the English solicitor, who then had far more limited rights of audience than a barrister. There were few black attorneys in South Africa at that time, and hardly any black advocates; Dugard, *Human Rights and the South African Legal Order* (Princeton: Princeton University Press, 1978), pp. 12–13.

[19] Ironically, Sisulu and Mandela's main 'offence' was urging native blacks to assume that the Bantu (Abolition of Passses and Co-ordination of Documents) Act 1952 (see p. 299 above) did indeed abolish passes, and so passes need no longer be carried. For an account of the trial see N. Mandela, *Long Road to Freedom* (London: Abacus, 1995), pp. 155–159.

[20] *Rand Daily Mail*, 27 August 1952.

[21] Cf. D.B. Michell, the UP's leader in Natal: "If this disobedience campaign is successful, the white people of this country will rally behind the government": *ibid.*

[22] *Cape Times*, 28 August 1952.

have been correct in assuming that the 'fundamental law' thesis was a hidden determinant of the Appellate Division's reasoning, but its failure to address the *Harris No. 1* judgment in its own (legalistic) terms did little to rebut suggestions that the committee was not really 'a court' at all.

In London, those suggestions were typified by a leader in *The Times*: "The High Court of Parliament has given the judgment it was created to pronounce . . . It was automatic, and having been forseen, it does not change the political situation".[23] The *Cape Times* was less restrained in its opinions. Its leader on 28 August was titled 'Humiliation'. The leader referred disparagingly to the High Court of Parliament as:

> "Mr Swart's committee, [comprising] two professional politicians, two county attorneys and two junior advocates. Their draft was referred to a motley collection of farmers, teachers, dentists and professional politicians presided over by an undistinguished lawyer . . . The best will in the world will not disguise that South Africa yesterday witnessed the humiliation of an episode unprecedented in the civilised world, an episode which will forever be a dark page in our history".

Government officials nonetheless placed great faith in the legality of the 'court's' authority. Some weeks prior to the 'judgment' being issued, Donges had instructed the electoral officer of Cape Town to remove non-European voters from the common roll and to draw up a separate, coloureds-only roll. The *Harris* plaintiffs sought an immediate injunction from the Cape provincial division against these actions. The court forbade the removal of coloured voters from the common roll, but allowed the compilation of the separate roll to proceed.[24]

If Malan had hoped however that the High Court of Parliament's 'judgment' would persuade the judiciary to acquiesce to the wishes of the Nationalists' parliamentary majority, he was swiftly to be disappointed. On the following day, the Cape provincial division announced that the High Court of Parliament Act was in itself a measure having no legal effect.

As in *Harris No. 1*, the first instance judgment in *Harris No. 2* was not fully reported in the South African Law Reports.[25] The same three judges heard the case: De Villiers J.P., Newton Thompson J. and Styen J.[26] They were, once again, unanimous in their opinion. But on this occasion, their unanimous judgment was delivered in the plaintiffs' favour. De Villiers J.P. delivered a narrowly reasoned judgment, which closely followed the argument submitted for the plaintiffs by Graeme Duncan. The 'Act' tried to empower the 'High Court of Parliament' to determine the validity of legislation affecting the entrenched rights. It could only do so if it had itself been passed by the section 152 procedure. Since it had not been passed in this way, it was invalid.

[23] 28 August 1952.

[24] *Pretoria News*, 15 August 1952.

[25] There is merely a brief note on the decision in the appeals pending section; 1952 (4) SALR 153. For contemporaneous comment see E. McWhinney, 'The New High Court of Parliament' (1952) *Canadian Bar Review* 734.

[26] Again, this was not L.C. Steyn, but G. Steyn.

Newton-Thompson J. issued a separate concurrence in which he indicated that Centlivres C.J. had indeed pursued a 'fundamental law' analysis in *Harris No. 1*, and that he had been right to do so. In Newton-Thompson J.'s view: "the founders of our constitution thought fit to follow the American example by entrenching clauses 35, 137 and 152 of the South Africa Act".[27] He also concluded, following the American model, that the protection of entrenched rights was a constitutional responsibility entrusted to "the *established* courts of justice".[28] The inference of his judgment appeared to be that the High Court of Parliament could not be regarded as a 'court' in this constitutional sense.

The *Rand Daily Mail* greeted the judgment enthusiatically, suggesting that the government should call a general election, resign and offer voters the chance to pass their own judgment on its 'extraordinary antics' since March 1951.[29] Malan initially made no comment on the provincial division judgment. Erasmus was less restrained. In a party meeting at Vryheid in the Free State he condemned the decision, asking his audience: "Has the British way still a right in South Africa? Is the dead hand of the conqueror not buried yet?".[30]

Notwithstanding Erasmus' apparent fury, the government implicitly acknowledged the legitimacy of the provincial division's conclusion by filing an appeal to the Appellate Division.[31] Malan and Donges did not regard simple defiance of the court's judgment as a viable or desirable option at this juncture. But the situation that thereby arose was quite bizarre. Should the government's appeal to the Appellate Division be unsuccessful, would it then refer that judgment to the High Court of Parliament, notwithstanding the Appellate Division's conclusion that the High Court of Parliament had no authority to hear such an appeal? In the house, Malan repeatedly refused to give Strauss an assurance that the government would respect the Appellate Division's judgment. If it were to refuse to do so, Strauss' predictions about a *coup d'etat* and the prospect of violent unrest might be proven well-founded. The government's hopes evidently rested on a belief that the Appellate Division would uphold the Act—and thereby sacrifice the principle it had enunciated in *Harris No. 1*—rather than strike it down and thereby run the risk of triggering a profound political crisis. Such hopes did not appear to be well-founded.

[27] Quoted in McWhinney (1952), n. 25 above, 739. Quite who these 'founders' were is a point to which we shall return.

[28] *Ibid.* (emphasis added).

[29] 30 August 1952.

[30] *Cape Times*, 30 August 1952. That the court was rejecting the 'British way', and rather upholding the constitutional ideals of the former Orange Free State, was an irony that appeared to have escaped the minister's attention.

[31] May described this as a 'blunder', suggesting that in filing the appeal the government also implicitly conceded that the Appellate Division did indeed possess a 'testing right'; (1955), n. 17 above, 61.

III. BEFORE THE APPELLATE DIVISION

Andries Beyers again acted as leading counsel on the government's behalf, and was again assisted by van Wyk and de Villiers. The government did not afford the Appellate Division the courtesy of accepting that *Harris No. 1* was correctly decided, but its counsel evidently saw little point in asking the court to reverse its previous decision.[32] Beyers proceeded instead on the assumption that the entrenchment provisions embraced only issues of '*substantive*' law; i.e. voting rights and language equality. They did not, he contended, reach to matters of '*adjectival*' or '*procedural*' law which determined how those substantive rights were to be protected. Beyers maintained that the creation of the 'High Court of Parliament' was a matter wholly of adjectival law. It was thus a body that parliament was competent to create through the bicameral, simple majority legislative procedure. Since the courts had no power to question the substantive wisdom of legislation enacted through the appropriate legislative procedure, the 1952 Act was beyond judicial scrutiny. For Harris and his colleagues, Graeme Duncan simply reiterated the argument he had successfully made at first instance.

The judgments

The personnel occupying the seats in the Appellate Division had not altered in the brief period between the conclusion of *Harris No. 1* and the beginning of *Harris No. 2*. Centlivres remained as Chief Justice; Greenberg, Schreiner, Hoexter and Van den Heever also heard the appeal. But in contrast to the judgment delivered in *Harris No. 1*, the decision produced by the Appellate Division in *Harris No. 2* offered five separate opinions.[33] The judges were unanimous in the result that they reached: the High Court of Parliament Act had no legal force. There were also marked similarities in the reasoning that each member of the Court adopted to sustain his respective conclusion. There were nevertheless important differences in the detail of the arguments offered, differences which to an informed observer might have pointed the Malan government in the direction of a legislative strategy which would successfully achieve the objective frustrated in *Harris Nos. 1 and 2*.

Centlivres C.J. delivered the first opinion. There was, from the outset of his judgment, a significant symbolic shift in the language that he used. In *Harris No.*

32 Harry Snitcher recalled that the plaintiffs' legal team felt that Beyers' discourtesy to the Court on this point immediately undermined the force of his argument; interview with David Borgstrom, July 1998.

33 The opinions closely followed ideas which the various judges had circulated amongst themselves in *Harris No. 1*. Copies of Van den Heever's, Greenberg's, Schreiner's and Centlivres' thoughts in *Harris No. 1* are to be found in the Schreiner papers.

1, the Chief Justice had referred to the South Africa Act 1909 as 'the Act', a nomenclature which might be thought to have unfortunately imperialist overtones. In *Harris No. 2*, he referred unwaveringly to 'the Constitution'.[34] The different label was presumably more than just an exercise in semantics. By rooting his analysis in the 'South African Constitution' rather than 'Imperial legislation', Centlivres was implicitly disarming attacks on the legitimacy of the court's decisions which portrayed the judgments as confirmation of South Africa's continuing subordination to Britain.

One might see a similar rationale underlying the absence of any reference to the British parliament as the creator of the South African Constitution. Centlivres C.J. used instead the much more ambiguous concept of the 'authors' of the Constitution. He at no point identified just who he meant by this; was it to be the Imperial Parliament; or the parliaments of the four colonies; or the Constitutional Convention; or an admixture of the above.

What was clear was that Centlivres now expressly acknowledged, as he had not done in *Harris No. 1*, that the constitution recognised the notion of 'fundamental' law. To that extent, the High Court of Parliament had accurately analysed the basis of his reasoning in the first *Harris* case. Where the judicial committee had erred—as Newton Thompson J. implied at first instance in *Harris No. 2*—was in assuming that 'fundamental' law had no part to play in the South African constitutional order.

Centlivres C.J. accepted that the entrenched clauses were such 'fundamental laws'. The question which then arose was how were such laws were to be protected? In his view, providing that protection was a duty imposed on the courts. This conclusion seemed more assumed than argued. Centlivres did not (and could not) identify an explicit textual basis for the assertion. Nor did he invoke the traditions of the Orange Free State as a basis for this conclusion.[35] His opinion alluded to the Appellate Division's recently issued judgment in *Swart NO and Nicol v De Kok*[36] as a South African authority for the proposition that the courts were obliged to protect entrenched rights against executive or legislative infringement.[37] The government would presumably have been distinctly unimpressed by an 'authority' that was barely a year old, and was in any case Centlivres' court's own invention. The Chief Justice also referred very briefly to two Privy Council decisions confirming a judicial power to review the constitutionality of Acts passed by colonial legislatures.[38] These latter cases would seem to be rather inapposite precedents, both in legal and presentational terms, since both convey notions of South African subordination to British authority.

[34] With a capital 'C'.

[35] He might readily have referred, for example, to the position advanced by Melius De Villiers, the Chief Justice of the Free State, in 1897; see pp. 48–52 above.

[36] See pp. 272–273 above.

[37] Centlivres' argument here raises the inference that he had foreseen the type of question that he would be presented with in *Harris No. 2* when writing his opinion in *Swart*, and had deliberately planted a conclusion to which he might refer back at a future date.

[38] *James v Commonwealth of Australia* [1936] AC 578 and *The Queen v Burah* [1878] 3 AC 889.

Having established (if only to his own satisfaction) that the 'testing power' rested in the courts, Centlivres C.J. dismissed as 'a startling proposition' Andries Beyers' contention that section 152 did not govern procedural or adjectival legislation. The proposition was startling because it would mean that parliament acting by a simple, bicameral majority could 'render nugatory' the substantive rights themselves:

> "in other words, the individual concerned whose right was guaranteeed by the Constitution would be left in the position of possessing a right which would be of no value whatsoever . . . There can to my mind be no doubt that the authors of the Constitution intended that these rights should be enforceable by the Courts of Law".[39]

This 'intention' (on the part of unidentified 'authors') was once more assumed. The only authorities offered for the point were two archaic English cases. Quite why these were thought valid comparators was not explained, although one of the cases concerned did deal with a governmental attempt to abridge existing voting rights.[40]

The Chief Justice nonetheless felt able to conclude that the Constitution demanded that entrenched rights be defensible before a court of law. Centlivres C.J. considered that a proper construction of the 1952 Act gave "good reason for thinking that the manifest intention of the Act was to provide for a reconsideration by the High Court of Parliament of the issue raised in [*Harris No. 1*]".[41] The question which then arose was whether the High Court of Parliament was indeed a court of law. In Centlivres' opinion, the answer was unequivocably 'No'.

That the Act described the body as a 'Court of Law' was an irrelevance: the Appellate Division's duty was to look "at the substance of the matter".[42] On substantive grounds, the body created by the Act possessed features which were irreconcilable with traditional understandings of the concept of a 'court'. Prominent among these was the fact that the 'judges' would sit in judgment on legislation which they as legislators had enacted. Centlivres also pointed to the fact that only Ministers, and no other parties to litigation, could appeal to the new body. Moreover, the body's judgment could have the effect of repealing section 152 of the Constitution, a task which had been reserved by the constitution to a unicameral two-thirds majority of parliament. In effect, the 'court' was simply parliament acting by a bare majority. The decision of the provincial division should therefore be upheld.

[39] [1952] 4 SA 769 at 780–781. Van den Heever J.A. expressed similar sentiments. He observed that Andries Beyers argued that substantive constitutional rights would still stand "although by the amendment of adjective law their enforcement may have become impossible. How rights so prostrate can be said to remain 'standing' I cannot grasp"; at 791. The argument, in both text and substance, is closely comparable with the analysis of the constitutional order of the Orange Free State offered by Melius De Villiers some fifty years earlier; see pp. 48–52 above.

[40] This being *Ashby v White* (1703) 92 ER 126; for comment see I. Loveland, *Constitutional Law* (London: Butterworths, 1996), pp. 243, 294–296. The other case was *Dixon v Harrison* (1740) 124 ER 958.

[41] [1952] 4 SA 769 at 779.

[42] *Ibid*. at 784.

Hoexter J.A. closely followed Centlivres C.J.'s reasoning. In his view, entrenched rights had to be subject to judicial protection. Like Centlivres, he rather skirted the issue of the source of that protection. But he had no doubt that the High Court of Parliament "is nothing but a joint sitting of the two Houses of Parliament".[43] He cited additional reasons for that conclusion to those offered by Centlivres. The members of the court were not impartial in the sense traditionally required of judges. Nor were they invariably possessed of any, still less substantial, legal qualifications and experience.

Greenberg rooted the source of the testing power in the intentions of the 'authors' (again undefined) of the South Africa Act:

> "it must be borne in mind that when the authors of the South Africa Act provided the safeguard, implicit in sec. 152, of recourse to Courts of Law, they must have had in mind the elements of the judicial system in existence at the time of the Union".[44]

These elements were not present in the High Court of Parliament. Its members did not have to be either impartial or legally qualified. Greenberg J.A. did however explicitly observe that he assumed that parliament would be able by a simple bicameral majority to create a court which exercised appellate jurisdiction over the Appellate Division. As long as the substantive features of that body complied with traditional understandings of the judicial role, the legislation concerned would not be subject to judicial reversal.

Van den Heever J.A. pushed that argument rather further:

> "As ordinarily constituted Parliament has unlimited power to reorganise the judiciary. It can create a Court or Courts superior to the Appellate Division and confer upon them such jurisdiction as it thinks fit".[45]

Nor was parliament bound to create courts in the image of those that had existed in southern Africa at the time of the Union. 'Courts' might take many forms, and it was no part of the Appellate Division's constitutional function "to criticise the wisdom or equity of a measure passed in the exercise of that power by a comparison of the Court established with courts answering to some preconceived standard".[46]

There were however limits to parliament's discretion. In a rather tautological vein, Van den Heever J.A. held that a 'court' had to be 'a court'. Deciding whether a body was a 'court' might be a difficult task. It was more straightforward to establish that a body did not merit such a designation. And a body could not be a 'court' if it was in substance—as was the body created by the 1952 Act—parliament acting by a simple majority.

Van den Heever's substantial role in drafting the Statute of Westminster perhaps left him better placed than anyone else involved in the case to appreciate

[43] [1952] 4 SA 769 at 795.
[44] *Ibid.* at 786.
[45] *Ibid.* at 791–792.
[46] *Ibid.* at 792.

the impact that independence was to have on the South African constitution. He went rather further than other members of the Appellate Division in seeking a South African root for the judicial power to protect entrenched rights. He echoed Centlivres C.J.'s labelling in referring to the South Africa Act as the South African constitution, a constitution moreover which created parliament, defined its substantive powers, and defined the procedures through which those substantive powers could be exercised. Entrenched rights could therefore be removed only by section 152 procedures. For parliament to do so by the bicameral simple majority procedure would not be a lawful act, but 'a revolution'. He dismissed as 'British bias' "the thought that since such a power resides in the legislature in Britain our Parliament as ordinarily constituted must necessarily have it too".[47]

Oliver Schreiner's concurrence approved his colleague's conclusions, and also accepted that the High Court of parliament was not a 'court'. However he then suggested that it was beyond parliament's powers, when acting through a bicameral simple majority, to create a 'court' (even a 'proper' court in the traditional sense) competent to reverse the judgments of the Appellate Division if the motive behind the Act was to evade the section 152 provisions:

> "it might very well be (I need put it no higher) that the Act in question would be held to be invalid because it would involve a radical departure from the judicial hierarchy set up in the Constitution and a grave impairment of the protective system implicit in s.152".[48]

IV. THE REACTION

Schreiner's judgment in *Harris No. 2* indicated that he doubted that the episode had yet reached a conclusion. The plaintiffs' initial reaction to the judgment revealed similar concerns. Speaking on his co-litigants behalf, Edgar Deane reported that they were all 'relieved' by the Court's decision. They also expressed the hope—if not the expectation—that the government would now leave the Cape franchise alone: "For nearly three years the question of the Coloured Franchise has kept us in anxiety and we pray that it will never confront us again".[49] The Torch Commando was markedly more sceptical, warning the government's opponents not to allow the judgment to lull them "into a false sense of security and think that the constitution has been saved".[50]

Malan did not offer any immediate comment on the judgment, although both Havenga and Sauer were quick to pledge that the government would not

[47] *Ibid.* at 791. Van den Heever, the most obviously 'Afrikaner' member of the bench, must have been aware that this was a particularly sharp accusation to level against Malan's avowedly anti-British government.

[48] *Ibid.* at 788.

[49] *Cape Times* 14 November 1952.

[50] *Ibid.*

contemplate any unconstitutional action to overcome the Court's decision. Malan appeared at a public meeting the next day to announce that the government would accept the judgment, but did not intend to let the matter rest: "We are going to appeal to a higher authority—an authority above courts and above Parliament, namely the electorate".[51] Malan also accused the United Nations and the Indian government of fomenting unrest among South Africa's non-white population, and hinted that the Soviet Union was also attempting to destabilise the country.[52]

The *Cape Times* ran an internally contradictory series of articles on the judgment. On 13 November, its leader suggested that *Harris No. 2* would "bring to a close a series of the most important constitutional hearings in the Union's history". The next day, its leader condemned the Separate Representation of Voters Act as "an egregious error and a blatant breach of faith", decried the High Court of Parliament Act as 'squalid trickery', and praised the Court's judgment in *Harris No. 2* as "the only tolerable outcome of a shameful episode in South African history". In contrast, a page one story headlined 'MOMENTOUS DECISIONS FACING SOUTH AFRICA' assumed that the 'shameful episode' had not yet run its course. The story suggested that the Cape franchise would be the central issue at the next election, and speculated that the tool which Malan would use to break the constitutional impasse would be an Act placing an additional forty or so Nationalists in the senate.

International press coverage of the judgment suggested Malan's government would find few supporters overseas. In Germany, the *Frankfurter Rundschau* applauded the Court's decision: "The five South African Supreme Court judges have shown to the world what a really independent judiciary means to all of us . . . Western democracy stands or falls with an independent judiciary".[53]

The judgment was a page one story in the *New York Times*, where it was covered under the headline 'TOP TRIBUNAL VOIDS PARLIAMENTARY COURT CREATED BY MALAN'. The paper reported that the Appellate Division's decision had triggered a split within the cabinet over how the government should proceed:

> "The verdict confronts Prime Minister Malan with a grave choice—whether to abide by the Constitution or defy the law and create what the opposition leader J.G. Strauss said would be anarchy".[54]

[51] *Cape Times*, 14 November 1952.

[52] *New York Times*, 11 November 1952.

[53] Translation taken from the *Cape Times*, 14 November 1952.

[54] 14 November 1952. The paper also ran a lengthy interview with Gerhardus Jooste, South Africa's Ambassador to the United Nations, where South Africa had been under constant attack, especially from India, for its *apartheid* programme. Jooste's defence of his country, and of his government, was as vigorous as it was incredible: "Racial discrimination is more repugnant to the people of South Africa than to almost any other population in the world . . . The tension alleged to exist in South Africa has been exaggerated beyond belief . . . The more intelligent of the non-whites here have repeatedly expressed their thanks to our government for what they see as a genuine attempt to protect their rights as well as our own, and to diminish the risk of conflict".

The judgment attracted substantially less coverage in Britain. *The Times* simply reported it without comment.[55] The *Manchester Guardian* also confined itself to reporting the decision. Its long leader on South Africa on 14 November made no mention of the case at all, but dwelt instead on the country's continuing difficulties in the United Nations. The *Daily Telegraph* combined the two issues. Malan's government 'deserved criticism' for promoting the High Court of Parliament Act, but the paper felt (apparently forgetting the limited reach of the franchise in South Africa) that the South African electorate was "incomparably better qualified than the UN Assembly to decide the Coloured vote issue".[56]

Within the academic community, Erwin Griswold reiterated his praise of the Appellate Division in an article in the *Harvard Law Review*.[57] He applauded the "steadfast way" in which the Appellate Division had upheld constitutional principles in the face of considerable governmental and legislative pressure.[58] In Oxford, Professor Wheare had also revised his earlier opinion[59] of the impact of South African independence on the entrenched clauses. *Harris No. 1*, he now suggested:

> "asserts the logical priority of a constitution over the institutions it has created and whose nature and powers it describes and determines . . . The procedure referred to in the entrenched sections was part of the definition of the Union Parliament and not a limitation on the powers of an exclusively bi-cameral Parliament".[60]

Writing in the *Canadian Bar Review*, McWhinney greeted the judgment as 'courageous and swift', although he was unconvinced by the rigour of the judges' respective arguments as to the constitutional source of the reservation of the power of review to ordinary courts.[61] He also seemed to accept, in contrast to his critique of *Harris No. 1*, that the Appellate Division was now engaged in an avowedly political as well as legal conflict; the Court "has administered a sharp rebuff to Prime Minister Malan in the carrying out of his Apartheid policy".[62] He nonetheless concluded that the opinions of all of the judges except Schreiner offered the government a way forward: "Could the South African Parliament by further enactment, validly empower some new body, possibly an existing court of law, to review decisions of the Appellate Division that might prove unfavourable to its policies".[63]

55 14 November 1952.

56 14 November 1952.

57 'The Demise of the High Court of Parliament in South Africa' (1953) 66 *Harvard LR* 864.

58 *Ibid.* at 871 and 872.

59 See p. 185 above.

60 K. Wheare, *The Statute of Westminster* (Oxford: Clarendon Press, 1953), p. 346. Wheare's change of heart was the lead story in the *Cape Times* of 24 March 1953, reported gleefully under the headline " **'Nats' Court Authority Recants**".

61 E. McWhinney, 'The Court Versus the Legislature in the Union of South Africa' (1953) 31 *Canadian Bar Review* 52 at 64.

62 *Ibid.* at 62.

63 *Ibid.* at 55. By 'parliament', McWhinney presumably meant parliament in its bicameral, simple majority form.

The decisions in *Harris No. 1* and *No. 2* were also afforded a warm reception by a leading textbook on South African constitutional law, published in 1955.[64] Gilbert Dold, a barrister, and C.P. Joubert of the law faculty at the University of Pretoria, firmly endorsed Cowen's analysis of the Statute of Westminster, severely criticised the Provincial and Appellate Division judgments in *Ndlwana*, and—in a somewhat hyperbolic vein—applauded the Centlivres court for its 'impartiality and honesty' in the *Harris* cases: "Boldly and loyally have the South African courts adhered to the fundamental principle of administering justice, *fiat iusticia ruat coelum*, in discharging their duty to declare and apply the law".[65]

V. RACE DISCRIMINATION AT COMMON LAW

While comment on the *Harris* litigation dominated the political, mass media and academic stages, the escalating tension between the Appellate Division and the Malan government was further intensified by the Court's evident determination to restate and extend the common law principles it had laid down in *R v Abdurahman*. In two judgments issued in March and April 1953, the Appellate Division indicated that the government could not expect the common law to smooth South Africa's path towards realisation of the *apartheid* ideal.

Separate but equal revisited: *R v Lusu*

The increasingly rigid legislative policing of native black civil disobedience campaigns—and particularly the threat of a conviction under the Suppression of Communism Act 1950—did not entirely quell efforts by the ANC and other groups to challenge *apartheid* laws. The defendant in *R v Lusu* was an ANC activist who had entered and thereafter refused to leave a 'Europeans only' waiting-room at Cape Town railway station.[66] In 1949, the Malan government had promoted an amendment to the 1916 railway legislation. As amended, section 7 of the Act empowered the railway authority to:

> "reserve any railway premises (including conveniences) or any portion thereof, or any train or any portion of a train for the exclusive use of males or females or persons of particular races, or different classes of persons or Natives".

Section 36 of the Act (as amended in 1949) made it a crime for any person not to leave premises designated for the use of a different gender or ethnic group when asked to do so by a railway employee.

[64] G. Dold and C. Joubert, *The Union of South Africa* (London: Stevens & Sons, 1955).

[65] *Ibid.* at p. 100.

[66] Dugard (1978), n. 18 above, pp. 212, 318; L. Kuper, *Passive Resistance* (London: Jonathan Cape, 1956), pp. 59–60.

Section 7's explicit reference to 'races' and 'class' would seem to preclude judicial review of any designation of specific facilities to particular races on *Kruse v Johnson* grounds. Mr Lusu's defence at his trial had however drawn squarely on the *Abdurahman* principle. He maintained that the facilities for whites and native blacks were substantially unequal, in which case the "Europeans only" designation was unlawful. At trial, in August 1952, the presiding magistrate accepted this argument, and acquitted Mr Lusu.

It was not immediately clear how the government would proceed. A senior railway official described the situation—with some understatement—as "extremely delicate at the moment".[67] Nor was it obvious that the acquittal was welcomed even by the supposedly liberal English language press. The *Rand Daily Mail's* leader on the case had been distinctly equivocal:

> "Separation and discrimination are not yet synonomous terms. True, there are people who see in separation itself all the components of discrimination, but that may often be an extreme view. Clearly, there are circumstances where a case can be made for separation, provided it is tempered with justice".[68]

The government subsequently appealed on a point of law to the Cape provincial division. Its argument (Andries Beyers and D.P. de Villiers again acted as its counsel) was that *Abdurahman* was not a controlling authority. That case, it was contended, had concerned a statutory power for the Railway Administration to 'make regulations' under section 4 outlining schemes of segregation. In this case, the section 7 power was simply to designate facilities on an *ad hoc* basis, without the need for regulations. Beyers argued that this type of power afforded government bodies a virtually unfettered discretion, and certainly a discretion which was sufficiently elastic to encompass the provision of substantially unequal facilities. This argument had been rejected by a majority in the provincial division, which considered *Abdurahman* to be a binding authority. One judge however, Hall J.,[69] had held that *Abdurahman* did not apply to these facts. In his view, the Railway Administration did indeed possess an 'untrammelled' discretion under section 7.

On 23 March, Centlivres C.J. delivered an opinion for a four to one majority[70] in the Appellate Divison upholding the provincial division's conclusion. He accepted that Beyers' contention 'merits serious consideration'. But having

[67] *Rand Daily Mail*, 27 August 1952.

[68] *Ibid.*

[69] Hall was born in England, and emigrated to the Cape when a teenager. He did not attend university, but began a career in the civil service. He subsequently qualified as an attorney, before taking an LLB at Stellenbosch and joining the Cape bar in 1921. His professional and academic specialisation was in water law, an area in which he published extensively and gained an LLD degree from Stellenbosch. Between 1943 and 1949 he was also the editor of the *South African Law Journal*. Swart had appointed him to the Cape bench in 1949. Acute observers of Hansard might wonder if Donges' references to 'water courts' at second reading of the High Court of Parliament bill foreshadowed a greater role for Hall should the *Harris* controversy not have been settled to the government's liking at that stage.

[70] Schreiner, Hoexter and Greenberg concurred.

granted the argument such consideration, the Chief Justice concluded that it was ill-founded. While there was undoubtedly a distinction in *form* between the section 4 and section 7 powers in the Act, their *substance* was essentially the same:

> "In each case, the question at issue is the same: Did Parliament intend that the right of reservation, whether conferred by a regulation made under the authority of s.4 or conferred by the Act itself in s.7 could be exercised in such a manner as to result in partial or unequal treatment between males and females, persons of particular races or different classes of persons?".[71]

Centlivres C.J. concluded that this could not have been parliament's intention. If the government's contention were correct, the Railway Administration could—and here Centlivres drew on a hypothetical example—use section 7 to deny any facilities at all to particular racial or gender groups. Such an absurd result could not have been intended. Segregation was therefore *ultra vires* section 7 if the segregated facilities provided were not of broadly equal quality. If the government wished the Railway Administration to provide unequal facilities, it would have to convince parliament to pass legislation explicitly authorising that result.[72]

The *Lusu* judgment was—post-*Abdurahman*—wholly consistent with existing common law principle. Yet it would seem beyond dispute that the then majority of members of parliament would have intended that the legislation should authorise unequal treatment; from their perspective *Lusu* and *Abdurahman* would have appeared as blatant examples of illegitimate judicial activism. Such was certainly the view taken by *Die Burger*, for which the case was the lead story on three consecutive days, reported (respectively) under the headlines:

> 'APPEAL COURT—NO APARTHEID ON CAPE STATION';
> 'VIOLENT REACTION TO APPEAL COURT JUDGMENT';
> 'WHAT ARE THINGS COMING TO IN SOUTH AFRICA?'.[73]

The cabinet made little attempt to disguise its fury at the judgment. Sauer, the Minister of Transport, made a speech on the day in which judgment was delivered in which he declared that the decision was "a shock to the whole country": the next day, Malan announced that he considered the situation "intolerable".[74]

[71] [1953] (2) SA 484 at 490.

[72] Centlivres also issued a specific rebuke to Hall J. for failing to follow *Abdurahman*. Van den Heever J.A. was however willing to distinguish the former case from the one now before him. He did not accept Andries Beyers' legal argument, but suggested that there was a *factual* distinction between the two cases. *Abdurahman* had been concerned with *trains*: this case was concerned with *premises*. In his view, it was plausible to argue that parliament did not intend to permit the provision of substantially unequal facilities on trains, because the Railway Administration could easily reorganise its rolling stock to provide equal facilities. Constructing new premises, however, was a much more difficult and expensive affair. It might well be thought that parliament did not intend the equal treatment principle to impose so onerous a burden on the Administration.

[73] The translations are taken from the *Cape Times*, 28 March 1953.

[74] The comments were reported in *Die Burger*. The translation is taken from discussion of *Die Burger's* coverage of the case in HAD, 20 August 1953, c.2026. See also the *Cape Times*, 24 March 1953 for further reports of Sauer's reaction.

Once again, Malan found himself promising that his government would take steps to reverse an Appellate Division judgment. And once again, he found the justification for so doing in the wishes of 'the people':

> "South Africa does not intend to depart from this traditional form of apartheid, which, in fact, has always been accepted by the non-Europeans except for an extremist minority. If the National Party wins the next election, we shall rectify the matter without delay, and in a way that will leave no doubt about the wish and intention of Parliament and the people".[75]

While Malan suggested that the problem the government faced lay in the Court's *decision*, several of his cabinet colleagues indicated that the problem lay rather with the *Court itself*. Louw, the Minister for Economic Affairs, characterised the four-man majority in *Lusu* as unthinking liberals, who might be 'honest' but were nonetheless blind to 'certain facts and circumstances' of South African life.[76] Schoeman and Naude[77] made speeches indicating that the government was ready to engage in court-packing. Naude was quite explicit on this point at a party meeting in Johannesburg on 28 March. If the court did not change its ways:

> "The Government would be compelled to resort to the practice in future of appointing only judges who were favourably disposed to its legislation, which I for one would much regret, as I prefer appointments by the government of the day to be on their merits".[78]

The judicial room for manoeuvre of which the Appellate Division took advantage in *Lusu* was contingent upon parliament's failure to employ explicit language in its discriminatory statutes. But, other than in respect of the very limited exceptions provided by the Constitution's entrenched clauses, such judicial decisions could readily be reversed by a bare parliamentary majority. Shortly after the *Lusu* judgment was issued, that parliamentary majority was reconstituted on a basis that was substantially more favourable to the Malanite cause.

The 1953 general election

Malan called the 1953 general election for April.[79] The Nationalist campaign was essentially an attack upon the Appellate Division's decisions in *Harris Nos. 1 and 2* and *Lusu*. Its manifesto, entitled *Democracy in Danger*, proclaimed that 'the people' were the supreme authority, and that the nationalist house and senate majorities were the democratic representatives of the people. The court was

[75] *Cape Times*, 25 March 1953.
[76] *Ibid*.
[77] The Minister of Labour and the Minister of Health respectively.
[78] *Cape Times*, 29 March 1953.
[79] See generally K. Heard, *General Elections in South Africa 1943–1970* (London: OUP, 1974), ch. 4.

thus acting against the wishes of parliament, the will of the people, and the spirit of the constitution. The manifesto ended with a ringing call to arms:[80]

"Save the Will of the People
Save Democracy
The National Government Represents the People".

The United Party had formed an uneasy alliance with the Torch Commando and the Labour Party in a so-called United Front for the 1953 election. Its campaign focused on a portrayal of the Malan government as a despotic force, to which the Appellate Division had offered brave and wholly constitutional resistance.

The *Lusu* case had been the subject of considerable Nationalist propaganda during the election campaign. The decision was portrayed quite mendaciously as requiring an end to segregation in all public facilities, be they railway stations, schools or hospitals. Sauer, the Minister of Transport had attacked the Appellate Division as 'the six old men', custodians of obselete values which had no legitimacy in the *apartheid* era. The term was redolent of the attack made by (ironically) liberal commentators on the US Supreme Court in the 1930s, when it repeatedly quashed New Deal legislation promoted by President Roosevelt. Roosevelt's initial cure for the problem posed by 'the nine old men' who sat on the US Supreme Court was to pack the bench with his own supporters. Whether Sauer's phrase betrayed a similar plan on the Malan's government part remained unclear. No such plans figured in the government's election manifesto. But during a rally at Port Elizabeth in the Cape, Donges echoed Naude's pre-election suggestion that the government was considering adopting the 'American expedient' of simply appointing judges who shared the governing party's views on the legal question. The tactic would be, he suggested "distasteful, but the people were tired of legal subtleties".[81] Swart had voiced similar distaste for the Appellate Division's frustration of government policy, asking: "Is it right that I, who appoint the judges, should have to go to them to ask whether they approve of a law which I want to pass in Parliament?".[82]

The opposition's strategy did not however prove successful. On the *Lusu* issue, Strauss had offered the rather vague promise that a United Party government would introduce 'fair segregation' on the railways. He had been rather more forthcoming on the government's repeated attacks on the Appellate Division's judgments: "The truth is that these persistent attacks on our courts are direct evidence of the Nationalists' desire to stage a diversion in order to

[80] Quoted in Heard, n. 79 above, p. 55.

[81] Quoted in HAD, 25 April 1955 at c.4434. The government subsequently introduced a bill in July 1953 which—presumably acting on the hints offered by Van den Heever and Greenberg in *Harris No. 2*—proposed that the Appellate Division be 're-organised' into criminal, civil and constitutional divisions. Additional judges would be appointed to the new court. Malan evidently considered that accusations that the new judges would simply be government placements made it inadvisable to pursue the initiative.

[82] *Ibid.* at c. 4440.

obtain power and thereafter to put an end to the impartiality and independence of our judiciary".[83]

In terms of votes cast, the United Front secured a narrow majority over the Nationalists. Malan's share of the vote had nevertheless increased substantially since 1943. Its distribution, disproportionately located in small, rural constituencies, again ensured that the Nationalist Party (which had by now reabsorbed Havenga's Afrikaner Party) won a majority of seats in the house.[84] This time, its tally rose to ninety-four (of 159). The United Party's strength in the house fell from sixty-five to fifty-seven. The Labour party secured five seats. The three communal seats allocated under the Representation of the Natives Act 1936, were won by two independents and a former communist. Malan's claim that his government enjoyed a mandate to implement the will of the people was voiced evermore strongly.

Lusu was one of the new government's first targets. Malan's second administration promptly responded to its electoral success by promoting the Reservation of Separate Amenities bill, a measure which parliament rapidly enacted. The Act provided in the most explicit of terms for the provision of unequal public facilities for different races.[85] Section 2 authorised any person who was in charge of a public vehicle or public facility to set aside any part of it "for the exclusive use of persons belonging to a particular race". Section 3 then provided that no such separation would be invalid 'merely' on the grounds that:

> "(a) no such [facility] has similarly been set apart . . . for the exclusive use of persons belonging to any other race or class; or
>
> (b) any such [facility] is not substantially similar to or of the same character, standard, extent or quality as the [facility] set apart . . . as aforesaid".

Swart had begun the second reading debate on the bill with an extraordinary gesture. Earlier that year, the daughter of Sir Stafford Cripps, the Chancellor of the Exchequer in Atlee's Cabinet, had married a native black African. Swart began the debate by brandishing a photo of the couple before the house. The marriage was, he said, 'disgusting'. Were such a thing ever to happen in South Africa, it would signify the end of white civilisation.[86]

The Minister of Justice then embarked upon a sustained criticism of the Appellate Division. *Lusu* itself was dismissed as 'a curious decision'. Swart obliquely attacked the Court by suggesting that the decision was 'probably' *bona fides*. He confirmed however that the government and the Court held fundamentally different views as to the meaning of the statute concerned:

[83] *Cape Times*, 30 March 1953.

[84] Havenga was the only member of his former party who had been nominated by the Nationalists to contest an obviously winnable seat.

[85] T. Davenport, 'Civil Rights in South Africa 1910–1960' (1960) *Acta Juridica* 11; Dugard (1978), n. 18 above, pp. 64–68.

[86] The United Party did not attack the substance of Swart's comment. Nor did the *Cape Times*, which suggested merely that as a tactic it was ill-considered; 7 August 1953. Swart's sentiments were echoed by other Nationalist MPs; cf. Herman Martins, who denounced "the disgusting marriage of Peggy Cripps to a Nigerian blanket kaffer": *ibid*.

"Although the Court held that its judgment was in accordance with the will of the legislature there was probably not a single member present when the Act was passed who would agree with this view".[87]

Strauss chose not to lead the opposition case, leaving the task instead to Lawrence, the United Party's spokesman on justice issues. The United Party's 'opposition' to the measure was muted. Lawrence did not condemn segregation *per se*:

"[W]e recognise that in carrying out that policy there may be a need for partiality; there may be a need for partiality in fact and partiality in administration . . . [I]t is not practicable or wise or necessary to give exactly the same facilities to every section".[88]

The United Party's attack on the government was limited to accusing it of negligence in failing to close the legal loopholes which *Lusu* had exposed, and accusing it also of acting improperly in its subsequent criticism of the courts.[89]

Following the passing of the 1953 Act, there could now be no doubt that the *Lusu* principle would no longer control the provision of public services. Yet it seemed that as soon as the Malan government had persuaded parliament to stitch one judicially created tear in the statutory fabric of segregation, the Appellate Division unpicked another of what the government had presumably regarded as *apartheid*'s common law seams. On the day that the *Lusu* judgment had been issued, the Appellate Division began to hear argument in *Pretoria North Town Council v A1 Electric Ice Cream*. Judgment was delivered shortly after the 1953 election.

Asiatic traders in the Transvaal revisited: *Pretoria North Town Council v A1 Electric Ice Cream*

Dugard has suggested that *Lusu* represented the culmination of "an enlightened judicial movement towards substantial equality of treatment".[90] There is some force in this contention, although the larger step on that particular journey was taken in *Abdurahman*. *Lusu* was at most a modest extension of that earlier decision. The Appellate Division's virtually contemporaneous opinion in *A1 Electric Ice Cream* offers clearer and more forceful evidence of 'enlightened' judicial law-making. For not only was the *substance* of that decision markedly unpalatable to Nationalist politicians, but the *method* by which it was reached was far more unconventional than the technique employed in *Lusu*.

[87] *Cape Times* 7 August 1953.

[88] HAD, 20 August 1953, c.2034.

[89] Cf. E. Potter, *The Press as Opposition* (London: Chatto and Windruss, 1975), p. 22: "On the major issue of post-1948 politics, namely race policy, the two parties were in fundamental agreement; both were deeply committed to a policy of white supremacy and they differed only in the practical details of implementation".

[90] (1978), n. 18 above, p. 68.

Chapter 5 focused briefly on a series of judgments by the Transvaal courts in the late 1920s and early 1930s arising from the Transvaal provincial council's efforts to prevent Indian residents operating as traders within the province.[91] The initial provincial legislation concerning the licencing of Asian traders had required councils to provide reasons for their refusal to grant licences and had specified the grounds on which refusal could be based. In three cases, the courts had overturned licensing refusals which offered no reason for the refusal, which disclosed racial prejudice in the decision-making process, or which were premised on reasons so extraordinary that they could not be construed other than as an attempt to conceal racial bias.[92] The provincial council had then replaced the relevant ordinance with new legislation which did not require any reasons for refusal to be given. In *Jooma v Lydenberg Rural Licensing Board*[93] the court subsequently held that neither the South African constitution nor South African common law contained any implied presumption that government agencies had to offer reasons for the decisions they reached. The absence of reasons could thus not be construed as indicating that the refusal of a licence was motivated by racial bias. In effect, while the court confirmed that racial bias was an unlawful motive, it set the aggrieved applicant a virtually impossible task to establish that the council's decision had been determined by that consideration.[94]

The courts' incapacity to interfere with licensing decisions was however challenged in 1953 by the A1 Electric Ice Cream Factory in Pretoria. A1 Electric had a virtually monopoly of the ice cream-making industry in the Pretoria area. Ice cream sales were made primarily by individual hawkers, each of whom required a licence under the 1932 Transvaal ordinance. Until the late 1940s, hawkers in the Pretoria North municipality had been almost wholly European, and experienced no difficulty in getting the requisite licence. From 1949 onwards however, A1 Electric found that Europeans were increasingly unwilling to take on the job, and decided to allow native blacks to hawk its wares. Of the dozen or so native blacks who applied for licences in 1950, 1951, and 1952, none were successful. One licence was given to the sole European applicant. The council refused to offer reasons for the refusals, beyond saying that they were not motivated by racial prejudice. Nor would it reveal to an attorney engaged by A1 Electric on the rejected applicants' behalves if its refusals were premised on information which the applicants might have been able to rebut.

Tindall J.'s judgment in *Jooma* would seem to sustain the council's position. However, when the case came before the Transvaal Provincial Division, Dowling J. quashed the refusal, on the basis that, notwithstanding the 1932

[91] See pp. 170–174 above.

[92] *Bignaar v Municipal Council of Rustenberg*, *Nanabhay v Municipal Council of Johannesburg* and *Patel v Witbank Town Council* respectively; see pp. 171–174 above.

[93] (1926) TPD 477.

[94] South African law was perfectly in tune with its contemporaneous English counterpart: the English courts had not at that time offered any indication that the common law imposed a general duty to give reasons on government decision-makers.

amendment to the ordinance, the council's failure to give reasons for so striking a pattern of refusals created an inference that they had acted in bad faith; in pursuit either of a racially discriminatory policy or a policy to ban ice cream sales altogether in the Pretoria North area, neither of which motives was explicitly permitted under the terms of the ordinance. The appeal was heard by a three-man bench,[95] Schreiner, Fagan and Greenberg JJ.A. Although Greenberg himself had issued several judgments in the Transvaal in the 1930s quashing refusals of licences, he did not author the Court's opinion in this case, but concurred in a judgment issued by Schreiner.

Schreiner concluded that *Jooma* was wrongly decided. He accepted that Tindall J. had been right in assuming that the council was not obliged to give reasons for its decisions. The council was nonetheless under an obligation to make its decisions according to rules of 'reason and justice' rather than according simply to its members' personal whims. In Schreiner's view, the pattern of unexplained refusals before the court in this case had entitled Dowling J. to infer that the council was acting in pursuit of improper motives. If it wished the refusals to be upheld, it would have to offer the court legitimate explanations for the decisions reached.

The judgment clearly runs wholly counter to the legislative trend followed by parliament since the 1948 election. There could be not the least doubt that both central government and the Transvaal provincial council would have wished *Jooma* to be upheld. Nor is there much room for doubt that the Appellate Division could have sustained *Jooma* without departing from orthodox legal principles. The case could therefore readily be seen as judicial obstructionism of *apartheid* policy.

That argument gains additional weight when one considers the authorities on which Schreiner relied. He suggested that Tindall's error in *Jooma* was explained largely by his failure to consider two *English* decisions, from 1891 and 1892 respectively,[96] dealing with local authorities' licensing powers arising under legislation couched in similar terms to the 1932 Transvaal ordinance. In Schreiner's view, these cases confirmed that even the most loosely cast executive discretion had to be exercised within bounds set:

> "according to law, and not humor. It is to be, not arbitrary, vague and fanciful, but legal and regular. And it must be exercised within the limit, to which an honest man competent to discharge his office ought to confine himself".[97]

It would rarely be appropriate for a court to infer that those limits had been transgressed if it had only a single instance of refusal before it, but in this case the court was presented with a systemic pattern of refusals. In combination, these were sufficient to sustain the presumption that the council was concealing an illegal motive.

[95] *Pretoria North Town Council v A1 Electric Ice Cream Factory (Pty) Ltd* [1953] 3 SALR 1.

[96] *R v London County Council, ex parte Akkersdyk; ex parte Fermenia* (1891) 1 QB 191; *Sharp v Wakefield and Others* [1891] AC 173.

[97] Per Lord Halsbury in *Sharp v Wakefield and Others* [1891] AC 173 at 179.

The Appellate Division was not of course bound even to consider, still less to follow, the principles outlined in these English decisions. And given the steps which the Malan administration had persuaded parliament to take to sever its links with British law-making institutions, the court's invocation of those judgments might easily be seen as a blatant sign of judicial distaste for the *apartheid* programme.

The case meant that either parliament (or the provincial council) would have to produce legislation (or an ordinance) explicitly approving racial bias as a reason for refusing the grant of licences. There was presumably little scope for believing that either body would be too embarassed to do so. The task would nevertheless embroil either or both of them in time and effort which they could readily have been spared if the Appellate Division had upheld Tindall's reasoning in *Jooma*.

VI. CONCLUSION

Lusu and *A1 Electric Ice Cream* were in one sense judgments that could readily be separated from *Harris Nos. 1 and 2*. Both were cases involving points of administrative rather than constitutional law: the target of judicial scrutiny was the executive branch of government rather than the legislature. Yet in both cases, the Appellate Division could readily have produced decisions which accommodated *apartheid* sentiments without violating accepted understandings of South African common law principles. The judgments were rooted in a line of common law reasoning which the government would undoubtedly consider illegitimate. As such they were—if only to a limited extent—a judicial defiance of executive preferences. But observers who regarded these two cases as a signal that the Appellate Division was steeling itself to manipulate or develop administrative law principles in order to engage in a constant war of attrition with the Malan government in defence of liberal values[98] would have been rapidly disabused of the notion by the Court's decision in *R v Sisulu*[99] at the end of May 1953.

Mandela and Sisulu had been convicted of breaching the Suppression of Communism Act towards the end of 1952.[100] Their contention that their involvement in the Defiance Campaign did not amount to communism, and was thus outside the terms of the Act, was rejected by the trial court. Sisulu and Mandela were sentenced to three months' imprisonment, suspended for two years. The judge, Rumpf J., whom Mandela described as "fair minded and reasonable",[101] made a point of stressing that the defendants had been found guilty of 'statutory communism', rather than of communism as the term was

98 Cf. Griswold (1952), n. 16 above.
99 [1953] 3 SA 276 (AD). For further comment see Dugard (1978), n. 18 above, pp. 156–157.
100 See pp. 305–306 above.
101 See n. 19 above, p. 159.

ordinarily understood. Rumpf justified the suspension of the sentence on the grounds that the defendants had consistently urged their followers to limit themselves to peaceful, non-violent forms of protest. He also granted the defendants leave to appeal.

Greenberg, serving temporarily as Acting Chief Justice, delivered the Appellate Division's opinion.[102] Sisulu's defence rested on an elaborate argument as to the textual meaning of section 1 of the Act. In essence he contended that parliament's references in section 1 to doctrines aiming at bringing about 'political industrial or socio-economic change' or 'encouraging feelings of hostility between the European and non-European races'[103] had to be read as particular manifestations of the earlier reference in section 1 to 'communism' as a Marxist-Leninist ideology. Since the defendants were not marxists in the orthodox sense, their advocacy of social reform could not be communist.

Greenberg rejected this argument. He began by asserting that the court was not competent to form its own opinion as to what was meant by 'communism'. It must rather find that definition in the statute. He then offered an interpretation of the Act which was very indulgant of the government's wishes. Greenberg held that the complex nature of the Act's definition of communism indicated that the government had foreseen it might be difficult to convince a court that defendants were Marxist-Leninists in the traditional sense. The broader definitions should thus be seen as a governmental invitation to parliament to enact formulae which would be sufficiently wide-ranging to facilitate conviction. Greenberg recognised that this approach could lead to what might be thought bizarre results. A campaign by the (white) National Council of Women in support of divorce law reform which involved unlawful marches or fly-posting would be 'communism' as defined in the Act. The court should nevertheless not succumb to the temptation of giving section 1 a narrower meaning:

> "it may well be that the law-giver did not realise that the language used in these provisions would cover the acts involved in the hypothetical instances cited . . . But I know of no principle which justifies a court in such circumstances in allowing the factor of unforeseen results to outweigh the conclusion at which it has arrived".[104]

Greenberg's method here is of course quite irreconcilable with Centlivres C.J.'s use of hypothetical examples in *Lusu*.[105] In that case, an absurd and unforeseen hypothetical result was considered a good reason for not following the literal wording of an Act. Nonetheless, both judgments suggested that Malan's government would have to resort to the expedient (if verbose) strategy of promoting bills couched in the most expansive terms if it wished to ensure that its policy preferences were not to be impeded by the courts' invocation of

[102] Schreiner, Hoexter, Van den Heever and Fagan concurred.

[103] See p. 237 above.

[104] [1953] 3 SA 276 (AD) at 290–291.

[105] See also Centlivres' and Fagan's use of just the same method in *Swart and Nicol v De Kock*; pp. 272–273 above.

traditional administrative law principles. One might thus doubt that *Sisulu* could be taken as an indication that the Appellate Division had decided to be more accommodating to the government's wishes.

At the end of 1953, with Centlivres once again heading the bench, the Appellate Division invoked just such a traditional administrative law principle to interpret the Suppression of Communism Act in a way which, for the government, would have been as infuriating as it was unexpected. The defendant in *R v Ngwevela*[106] was the President of the ANC's regional organisation in the Western Cape: he had also been a prominent member of the FAC, and had participated very visibly in the Defiance Campaign.[107] As a result of his activities, he had been served by Swart with a banning order under section 9 of the 1950 Act. He had subsequently defied the order and had been tried and convicted for so doing. Section 9, it may be recalled, was largely a verbatim repetition of section 1(12) of the Riotous Assemblies Act 1914.[108] Unlike the earlier Act however, it did not require the Minister to give *ex post facto* reasons for his decisions. There was a strong Appellate Division authority—in *Sachs v Minister of Justice*[109]—for the proposition that legislation of this sort did not carry with it an implied *common law* duty on the Minister either to grant affected individuals a hearing prior to making the order, or to offer reasons for the decision made.

Mr Ngwevela's primary contention before the Court was that his conviction was invalid because the banning order Swart had served on him was *ultra vires* the 1950 Act, insofar as he should have been granted a hearing before the order was made. *Sachs* might have been thought to present a severe obstacle to this argument, but Centlivres, for a unanimous court, embraced it with alacrity. In *Harris No. 1*, Centlivres had taken the bold step of formally overruling Stratford A.C.J.'s opinion in *Ndlwana*. His judgment in *Ngwevela* did not go so far as *de jure* to overrule Stratford's judgment in *Sachs*, but it left little doubt that he considered the earlier decision to be misconceived both in its method and its result.

Centlivres distinguished the issue before the Court in *Ngwevela* from that which had faced his predecessor in *Sachs* on several grounds. As noted in Chapter 6, Stratford had in part premised his conclusion that the 1914 Act did not demand that individuals be granted a hearing before an exclusion order was made on the ground that section 1(13)'s *ex post facto* reason-giving obligation necessarily implied that parliament had not intended a pre-decision hearing to be held. The government had undoubtedly omitted a version of section 1(13) from the 1950 bill to reduce still further the legal obstacles that the implementation of its policy would face. Yet Centlivres attributed an entirely different meaning to the absence of such a clause in the 1950 legislation. In his view, the omission of the *ex post facto* reason-giving provision strongly implied that the

106 [1954] 1 SA 123.

107 See *The (Cape) Guardian*, 15May 1952, for biographical information about Mr Ngwevela.

108 See p. 238 above.

109 See pp. 189–190 above.

generally applicable common law duty on a government official to hold a hearing prior to making a decision adversely affecting an individual's rights had *not* been impliedly excluded in respect of section 9.

He found further support for this conclusion by drawing a second distinction between the *Ngwevela* and *Sachs* scenarios. Stratford had considered in *Sachs* that the delay occasioned by a pre-decision hearing would fatally undermine the purposes of the 1914 Act. This indicated that parliament had not intended a hearing to be held. Centlivres applied this test to section 9 and—notwithstanding the fact that section 9 was directed at precisely the same activities as section 1(12) of the 1914 Act—concluded that such a delay would not have the effect of severely obstructing achievement of the Act's purposes. Unless an emergency had arisen, which was not the case on the present facts, a hearing was quite compatible with the overall scheme of the Act. The banning order had thus been *ultra vires*, and Mr Ngwevela's conviction had to be quashed.

While Centlivres took care to couch his opinion in terms of an agreement with Stratford's approach in *Sachs*, the differences between the two judgments are both manifest and profound.[110] Stratford's court in *Sachs* appeared to draw little distinction between parliament (acting lawfully through the bicameral simple majority process) and the government, and approached its interpretive and common law functions in a vein which seemed designed to accept rather than question the government's perception of its legal powers. In *Ngwevela*, Centlivres evidently adopted a quite different starting point; namely that parliament and the government were wholly distinct entities, and that parliament—irrespective of the government's wishes—could never be assumed to have compromised common law entitlements unless it said so in the most explicit of terms.[111]

Promoting the most unambiguous and precisely-worded of statutes might enable the government to overcome the obstacles presented to it by judgments such as *Lusu* and *Ngwevela*, but that solution would not assist it in reversing or by-passing *Harris Nos. 1 and 2*. Those cases would apparently continue to stand as a symbolic irritation to National Party sentiment. But the Cape's common electoral roll was—in practical terms—a tiny element of the *apartheid* programme. Malan certainly did not regard the judicial obstructionism (if such it was) evidenced in *Lusu* and *A1 Electric Ice Cream* as sufficient reason to stop inviting parliament to enact still more legislation aimed at taking the country nearer to Verwoerd's *apartheid* ideal.

[110] I owe a debt to David Dyzenhaus' book, *Hard Cases in Wicked Legal Systems* (Oxford: Clarendon Press, 1991), for bringing these two cases to my attention.

[111] It could be suggested that *Ndlwana* and *Harris No.1* display a similar 'separation of powers' dichotomy, in that *Ndlwana* drew no distinction between the different 'parliaments' created by the constitution while *Harris No. 1* placed that difference at the heart of its reasoning.

The Criminal Law Amendment Act 1953

The government moved rapidly to quell the ANC's growing civil disobedience campaign. Swart had adverted to increased severity in the government's handling of protests in mid-November 1952, when he announced that he had instructed police to open fire first on protestors if they found themselves in a riot situation.[112] Early in the new year, the cabinet took more formal steps by pushing the Criminal Law Amendment Act 1953 through parliament.[113] The statute made it an offence for any person to violate or advocate violation by anyone else of any existing law for the purposes of attempting to persuade parliament or the courts to repeal or modify an existing law. The Act provided penalties of whipping and up to five years' imprisonment. There might at first sight seem little point in passing such an Act, since the breaking of an existing law would in itself attract a legal sanction. However, much unlawful protest of this sort has traditionally involved breaches of only trivial laws; obstructing the highway would be a typical example. Such trivial offences carried only trivial punishments, and could not be expected to deter committed proponents of reform. In the South African context, the obvious law for protestors to break was the Bantu (Abolition of Passes and Co-ordination of Documents) Act 1952, which imposed a maximum penalty of one month's imprisonment. Some 8,000 ANC activists had been gaoled for breaching this Act and other segregationist legislation in the course of the ANC's 'Defiance Campaign'.[114] The 1953 Act followed the method introduced by the Suppression of Communism Act 1950 and effectively transformed a politically motivated breach of the 1952 Act or any other minor measure into a major crime. The Act also posed severe problems for the English language press. Journalists and editors were now faced with the prospect that articles which criticised government policy—or even those which reported other people's opposition to such policy—could be construed as 'advocacy' of law-breaking and so render their authors and publishers liable to serious criminal penalties.[115]

The government's continued efforts to disenfranchise coloured voters had spurred the formation of a new coloured pressure group, the South African Coloured People's Organisation (SACPO) in Cape Town in 1953. SAPCO grew out of the FAC;[116] and its leaders expressed willingness to find common ground with the ANC, and indicated that SACPO might prove a more militant organisation than the APO. Edgar Deane was to serve as its Chairman.

[112] *Cape Times*, 15 November 1952.

[113] Dugard (1978), n. 18 above, pp. 174–175, 212: E. Brookes and J. Macaulay, *Civil Liberties in South Africa* (Cape Town: OUP, 1958), pp. 80–81; Kuper, n. 66 above, pp. 62–63.

[114] Dugard (1979), n. 18 above; Mandela, n. 19 above, pp. 145–160: Brookes and Macaulay, n. 113 above, pp. 80–81; C. Heyns, *A Jurisprudential Analysis of Civil Disobedience in South Africa* (Pretoria: University of Pretoria Ph.D, 1991), pp. 187–195.

[115] Potter, n. 89 above, p. 117.

[116] T. Lodge, *Black Politics in South Africa* (London: Longman, 1983), p. 69.

SACPO's emergence had been preceded by the creation of the Congress of Democrats (COD), a small left-wing white party committed to multi-racial opposition to *apartheid*, which offered a political home both for former communists and the most liberal faction of United Party supporters.[117] Neither SACPO nor COD offered any obvious and immediate threat to the government, but both had the capacity to serve as a continuing irritant to the cabinet and as a focus for potentially more serious long-term opposition.

'Bantu education'

By 1953, the government's pursuit of Verwoerd's idealised vision of *apartheid* had moved on to consider the question of native blacks' education. Verwoerd regarded schooling as an essential ingredient of the separate development recipe:

> "Good racial relations are spoilt when the correct education is not given. Above all, good racial relations cannot exist when the education is given under the control of people who create wrong expectations on the part of the Native himself . . . It is therefore necessary that Native eduction should be controlled in such a way that it should be in accord with the policy of the State".[118]

As noted in previous chapters, most non-white children had received their formal education at 'mission schools' rather than in publicly-funded institutions. Missions schools were a pale imitation of their white, publicly-funded counterparts. They were nevertheless an imitation; and this, to Verwoerd, was wholly unacceptable. It may be recalled that Verwoerd's first major speech on *apartheid* had condemned those non-whites who saw education as a means to equip themselves with 'European' values. In the Bantu Education Act 1953, Verwoerd promoted a policy which would 'save' native blacks from this temptation.

The Act removed such limited public subsidies as the mission schools received, and required all schools to obtain a licence from the Minister of Native Affairs before they could lawfully operate. That licence would be refused if the school's syllabus or ethos was considered to be 'unsuitable' for native children. Verwoerd contended that a 'European syllabus' created unreasonable expectations on the part of native students, since it equipped them to perform roles which were denied them in later life because of the segregated nature of South Africa's economy and political system.[119] Verwoerd maintained that this

[117] T. Lodge, *Black Politics in South Africa* (London: Longman, 1983), pp. 62, 69.

[118] Quoted in L. Thompson, *The Political Mythology of Apartheid* (New Haven: Yale University Press, 1985), p. 52. See also Brookes and Macaulay, n. 113 above, ch. 8. On the 'Christian-National' underpinnings of the Act see *ibid.* at pp. 112–113 and Moodie, *The Rise of Afrikanerdom* (London: University of California Press, 1975), pp. 271–272.

[119] Lodge, n. 116 above, pp. 114–117; A. Norval, *Deconstructing Apartheid Discourse* (London: Verso, 1996), pp. 133–134.

created two distinct problems: first, it deprived the native community of the kind of educational provision which would enable it more efficiently to perform the role that *apartheid* had assigned it; and secondly, it created a group of malcontent 'educated natives' who devoted their intellectual energies to questioning the legitimacy of a segregated society and sowing seeds of discord among their less educated peers.

The appropriate syllabus would be one which limited itself to teaching students to: "read, write and do arithmetic through the mother tongue, and give them the beginnings of Afrikaans and English, along with religious education . . . handicraft, singing and rhythm".[120] This syllabus was intended not just to deflate the expectations of students, but also of teachers. In the long term, only native black teachers would be permitted to teach native black pupils. Verwoerd considered it essential that the government assume direct control of teacher training institutions for native black teachers. Their own education should not expose them to 'European' values, but should simply enable them to become proficient in teaching the limited curriculum suitable for native black children. The native teacher, who had hitherto been among the most discontented of native blacks, would have to:

> "learn not to feel above his community so that he wants to become integrated into the life of the European community, and becomes frustrated and rebellious when this does not happen and tries to make his community dissatisfied because of such misdirected and alien ambitions".[121]

Whether Verwoerd sincerely believed that such 'reforms' would produce a more 'satisfied' and thence quiescent native black population in the long term is open to question. It was however quite clear that the Act's short term impact was to provoke further and more intense non-European opposition to government policy.[122] The ANC was by this time conducting a serious internal debate on the desirability and practicality of maintaining its commitment to a non-violent form of protest and challenge. The Bantu Education Act, which announced the government's long-term commitment to an even more intense subordination of the native black population, lent further force to the arguments of those members of the ANC for whom 'constitutional' methods of protest now seemed a worthless enterprise.

On civil liberties

The government had nonetheless taken further steps to respond promptly to any such protests by promoting a 'Public Safety' bill early in 1953. The bill proposed

[120] A. Pelzer, *Verwoerd Speaks* (Johannesburg: APB Publishers, 1966), pp. 76–77.
[121] *Ibid.* at p. 74.
[122] For an account of black parents' and children's efforts to resist the new school regime see Lodge, n. 116 above, ch. 5.

that the Governor-General be given the extraordinarily wide-ranging power—whenever he felt that the ordinary law of the land was inadequate to ensure public safety and preserve public order—to: "make such regulations as appear to him to be necessary for providing for the safety of the public and the maintenance of public order". Such regulations, which included powers of imprisonment without trial, could have retrospective effect. In 'urgent' situations, the powers could be exercised by the Minister of Justice. The Act essentially granted the government quasi-legislative authority to deal in any way it thought fit with any individual, group or event that it considered to be offering effective or embarassing opposition to any facet of government policy.[123]

The government also persevered with its oblique efforts to cajole the English language press into adopting a less oppositional stance towards government policy. In 1954 Malan established a 'Commission of Inquiry In Regard to Undesirable Publications'. The Commission was initially presented as being concerned only with obscenity and pornogaphy, but its remit was rapidly broadened to include political news coverage.[124] The Commission recommended that a Publications Board be established, endowed with the power to prohibit publications which were 'undesirable'. For the sake of certainty and ease of administration, the Commission recommended that the definition of 'undesirable' be a matter solely for the Board: the courts should have no role in this area. The government evidently had no immediate intention of acting upon the recommendations; rather it left them hanging in the political ether as an indication of how the law governing the press might be reformed if criticism of *apartheid* continued unabated.

Political realignment in white society

Malan's patience with criticism within parliament had, however, worn thin. Amendments to the Suppression of Communism Act introduced in 1954 enabled the government to exclude former communists from the house of assembly. Sam Kahn, a native representative, had already been removed from the house under a similar power, as had his successor, Brian Bunting. A third former 'communist' elected as a native representative, Ray Alexander, was prohibited even from taking up her seat.[125]

Despite the evident lack of attachment to the spirit of the constitution that was revealed by such manoeuvrings, Malan considered himself bound after the government's defeats in *Harris Nos. 1 and 2* by the letter and the spirit of

[123] Cf. Millner's critique of the Act as one which "enables the Government . . . to rule by decree with virtually unlimited power . . . In this measure . . . the growth of executive power which has characterised the apartheid policy culminates in the reduction of the judiciary to complete impotence": 'Apartheid and the South Africa Courts' (1961) *Current Legal Problems* 280 at 295.

[124] Potter, n. 89 above, pp. 108–110; C. Merrett, *A Culture of Censorship* (Pietermarizburg: University of Natal Press, 1994), ch. 3.

[125] Merrett, n. 124 above, pp. 24–25.

section 35. His government re-introduced the Separate Representation of Voters bill in 1953 and 1954. On each occasion, Malan accepted that the measure could be enacted only by the 'two-thirds majority in joint session' procedure. On each occasion, despite Malan's attempt to detach a sufficient number of MPs from the United party opposition, that majority was not forthcoming.

Malan's tactics did however have the useful side effect of splitting the United Party. Six of its members were expelled after they held discussions with Malan concerning the terms on which they would support the separate representation bill. Preliminary agreement was reached on an amendment to the 1951 bill which would leave existing coloured voters on the common roll, while introducing a separate roll for new voters.

Rather than join the Nationalists, the expelled MPs formed themselves into the Conservative Party.[126] The United Party also lost some rank and file members to the left. The Liberal Party was founded in the summer of 1953. It was an avowedly multi-racial party, committed to a gradual move towards a universal adult franchise. Its only parliamentary members, however, were native representatives in the house and senate. There seemed little prospect of it winning a seat in a white constituency. The Labour Party also moved in a markedly liberal direction after the 1953 general election, building a political platform which was both socialist and colour-blind in nature.[127]

Malan also succeeded in driving a wedge between the coloured community's various political groups. He began this strategy in the summer of 1953, when representatives of small coloured interest groups were invited to meet with Malan, Havenga and Donges to discuss their concerns. The *Rand Daily Mail* of 18 August reported what seemed to be a significant coup for the government:

> "That they as a group did not derive any benefit from the existing franchise system was the opinion of a group of Malays led by Mr Ganief Harris . . . Mr Harris said that he had previously held other views . . . but that he was now convinced of the desirability and the need for a separate voters' roll".

Subsequent press coverage suggested Malan had exaggerated Harris' 'conversion', which was allegedly extracted as a *quid pro quo* for a government assurance that mosques in District Six of Cape Town—a coloured area which was to be designated as 'white' under the Group Areas Act—would not be demolished if Harris withdrew his opposition to the separate roll.[128] Harris' own standing within the coloured political community was nonetheless irreparably harmed by the episode.

[126] For a "horse's mouth" account of the split see the speech of P.B. Bekker at HAD, 11 May 1955, c.5410 *et seq*.

[127] On these party manoeuvrings see Heard, n. 79 above, pp. 73–77.

[128] Cf. the editorial in the *Natal Witness* of 19 August which quoted an unidentified spokesman for the Cape Malay community: "Our religion is everything to us. We have nothing to barter but the vote. The Government wants the vote. We are prepared to give it up if only we can be assured that our mosques will be spared".

Nothwithstanding these fragmentations of the former United Front and the coloured community, the balance of political forces within the house indicated that the entrenchment of the Cape Coloured vote would continue to be effective. In a further attempt to attract United Party support, Malan established a Coloured Vote Commission. This was *de facto* a joint parliamentary select committee, chaired by Donges and containing eleven Nationalist and seven opposition members.[129] The Commission's immediate effect was to foster further tension between coloured groups on the question of whether or not they should submit evidence to it. In the medium term, the government was able to use such submissions, as it had done with Mr Harris, to misrepresent the extent to which some coloured groups accepted the legislation.[130] It was particularly successful in suggesting that George Golding, the first Chairman of the NCCC and now leader of a group called the Coloured People's National Union, shared Harris' (alleged) views. Golding eventually denied the claim, but not before the white press had presented its readers with substantial 'evidence' that many coloured voters supported the government's plans.[131]

The Commission proved ineffective in garnering cross-party support for the government. Its final report, approved by the eleven Nationalist MPs and rejected by the seven opposition members, simply recommended re-enactment of the 1951 bill. A joint sitting was convened, but the government had no prospect of securing the necessary two-thirds majority.

In November 1954 Malan, by now eighty years old, resigned as Prime Minister. Donges' prospects of succeeding him as party leader had been irrevocably damaged by his failures in *Harris*. Malan had favoured Havenga as his successor, and tried to manage his retirement in a way that minimised Strijdom's chances of becoming party leader.[132] The Transvaal faction of the party (which now had some forty-three of the party's house seats compared to the Cape's thirty) was not however prepared to see its leader shouldered aside. Malan's preference was rejected, and the party turned instead to Strijdom,[133] a man for whom the niceties of constitutional law and principle were something to be exploited rather than respected. Strijdom's view of *apartheid* was also less sophisticated than the approach favoured by Verwoerd: for him *baaskap* was a concept less concerned with the separate development of the races than with the continued subordination of blacks, coloureds and Indians to the wishes of the whites.[134] The Appellate Division, however, was Strijdom's immediate concern.

[129] *Rand Daily Mail*, 3 October 1953.

[130] See especially the report in the *Natal Daily News*, 14 April 1954.

[131] Edgar Deane, now Chairman of SACPO, managed to avoid misrepresentation of his views. He maintained at the outset of the Commission's inquiries that: "The suggestion that [we would accept] a separate roll on the lines envisaged by the government would be ridiculous if it were not so dangerous in its implications": *Cape Times*, 28 May 1954; *Natal Mercury*, 28 May 1954.

[132] See P. O'Meara, *Forty Lost Years* (Athens, Ohio: Ohio University Press, 1996), pp. 89–90 for details of the manoeuvrings.

[133] Heard, n. 79 above, pp. 70–71.

[134] On the growing tensions between Verwoerd and Strijdom see Heard, n. 79 above, pp. 71–73.

Among his first actions as Prime Minister were the promotion of two bills which were intended to achieve, through what were ostensibly in technical legal terms entirely constitutional means, the ends that had eluded Malan and Donges in *Harris Nos. 1 and 2*.

10

Collins v Minister of the Interior

Strijdom persisted in refusing to accept that the *Harris* cases confirmed that 'parliament' was the sovereign law-maker in South Africa. Shortly after the 1953 election, he had suggested in a speech at a party conference that the government's intention was 'to break the courts'.[1] In December 1953, the leaders of the Nationalists' four provincial parties (Strijdom in the Transvaal, Malan in the Cape, Swart in the Free State, and Havenga in Natal) had issued a joint statement which proclaimed that the Nationalist party and the South African people were engaged in a 'struggle for freedom'. The *Harris* decisions were portrayed as placing the South African nation in a situation of 'constitutional slavery', with the master evidently being the 1909 British parliament. The government's efforts to free the nation from this plight would be, the ministers pledged, 'forceful and unrelenting'.[2]

In May 1955, in a more temperate vein, Strijdom told the house that if *Harris* was not overruled:

> "this parliament is not sovereign and it is not all powerful because then there is a body above it, namely the Appeal Court, which can say you may not do this and you many not do that . . . And therefore we are determined to continue the struggle until finality has been reached".[3]

Strijdom has generally been regarded as less intellectually able than his four predecessors as Prime Minister of South Africa.[4] It nonetheless seems difficult to accept that he believed the statement he made to the house to be true. And if he did so believe, he evidently did not appreciate (notwithstanding Van den Heever J.A.'s allusion to the point in *Harris No. 2*) that his equation of 'parliament' only and invariably with a simple bicameral majority betrayed an oddly British bias. Strijdom did not, however, allow his intellectual shortcomings or poorly developed sense of irony to deflect him from his pursuit of *apartheid* ideals.

The government's dissatisfaction with—and intolerance towards—the courts had grown still more intense as a result of an episode involving the Transvaal courts in July, August and September 1954. Early in 1954, Professor Z.K. Matthews, a leading ANC intellectual, mooted the idea of calling a multi-racial

[1] Cited in HAD, 25 April 1955 cc.4440–4441.
[2] Quoted in HAD, 23 May 1955 c.6050.
[3] HAD, 23 May 1955 cc. 6039–40; quoted in G. Marshall, *Parliamentary Sovereignty and the Commonwealth* (Oxford: Clarendon Press, 1957), p. 231.
[4] See D. O'Meara, *Forty Lost Years* (Athens, Ohio: Ohio University Press, 1996), pp. 89–91 for a markedly unflattering portrayal (by Strijdom's peers) of the fifth Prime Minister's abilities.

'People's Congress' to design a new constitutional settlement for South Africa. The Congress of Democrats expressed support for this idea, and scheduled a multi-racial conference in late July 1954 in Johannesburg to consider proposals on which such a settlement might be based.

The conference was a private meeting rather than a public rally; entrance was by invitation only. A substantial contingent of Johannesburg police nevertheless forced its way into the meeting, and the officers refused to leave when asked to do so. The organisers immediately sought an injunction from the Transvaal provincial division, prohibiting the police from attending the proceedings unless they could show lawful cause for their presence. Blackwell J. granted an interim injunction, pending a full hearing on the matter. The subsequent litigation, *Wolpe v O.C., S.A. Police, Johannesburg,* was heard before Rumpf J. in August 1954.[5]

The police could not adduce any statutory authorisation for their entry into the meeting. They relied instead on a claimed common law power to enter any premises whenever they suspected that a criminal offence was likely to be committed. In respect of the COD conference, the anticipated 'criminal offences' were that 'banned persons' would participate in the meeting, that a conspiracy would be hatched to overthrow the existing system of government, and that seditious speeches would be made. The principal authority for the police's contention was a 1935 English decision, *Thomas v Sawkins*,[6] in which the court held that police officers enjoyed a common law power to enter a *public* meeting whenever they had reasonable grounds for suspecting that a breach of the peace might occur or seditious speeches might be made. *Sawkins* had been vigorously criticised in contemporaneous British legal journals as making an unwarranted intrusion into individuals' freedom of speech and assembly, and was seen as creating a rationale for permitting the police to enter *private* meetings under similar circumstances.[7]

Rumpf J. accepted this rationale in *Wolpe*. In his view, a well-founded fear of sedition was sufficient to empower the police to enter private meetings:

> "A seditious speech is a serious offence and is directed against the public order. If the police had reasonable grounds for suspecting that such speeches would be made at such a meeting . . . and that their presence would prevent them being made, then to my mind it was a reasonable exercise of their duty to attend the meeting notwithstanding protest and notwithstanding the fact that it was not a public meeting and that there would be no immediate disturbance of the peace.

[5] [1955] (2) SA 87. Rumpf had been the presiding judge in Mandela and Sisulu's 'communism' trial; pp. 325–326 above). The *Wolpe* litigation attracted considerable comment in the South African academic legal press; see E. Brookes and J. Macaulay, *Civil Liberties in South Africa* (Cape Town: OUP, 1958), ch. 3; E. Kahn, 'Right of Police to Attend Private Meeting' (1954) *Annual Survey of South African Law* 14; 'Police Attendance at a Private Meeting' (1955) *South African LJ* 134; B. Beinart, 'Police Powers' (1955) *Butterworths South African LR* 157.

[6] [1935] 2 KB 249.

[7] A. Goodhart, '*Thomas v Sawkins*: a Constitutional Innovation' (1936) *Cambridge LJ* 22; E. Wade, 'Police Powers and Public Meetings' (1937) *Cambridge LJ* 175.

In my opinion, the freedom of the individual must in such circumstances give way to the interests of the state".[8]

The police declined to produce any evidence to substantiate their claim that they had reasonable grounds for such a belief. Thus, on this occasion, the interim injunction was upheld. Rumpf J.'s opinion nonetheless amounted to a considerable extension of police authority. His judgment did not however go far enough for the cabinet, which rapidly promoted legislation extending the police's newly identified common law powers of entry and search of private premises.[9]

Perhaps the most revealing aspect of the episode, however, was Swart's attack on Blackwell J.'s initial decision. Blackwell J. would appear an ideal candidate for antagonising the Nationalist government. Born in Australia, Blackwell had come to South Africa as a child and completed his education in Cape Town. After serving with distinction in the army during the First World War, Blackwell pursued a career at the bar and as a SAP and subsequently United Party MP. After retiring from the bench, he became a Professor of Law at Fort Hare College.[10] In 1928, he had promoted a private member's bill to enfranchise women: unlike the measure subsequently introduced by Hertzog's government, Blackwell's bill did not contain a colour bar. He had been expelled from the United Party by Hertzog in 1938 along with Hofmeyr for assisting Hofmeyr in opposing the government's Asiatics (Transvaal Land and Trading) bill.[11] He was appointed by Smuts to the Transvaal bench in 1943, amid some Nationalist rumblings that he was a 'political' nominee.[12]

Swart claimed in the house that Blackwell had 'failed to do his duty' in the case. The Minister maintained that Blackwell had been given several days' advance warning of the application, and had deliberately declined to notify the police of the impending action. Swart also claimed that when the police did finally appear before Blackwell, the judge had admonished them with the comment that "I want you to know that we are not a police state yet". Blackwell, who had by this time retired and gone to live in Rhodesia, denied the claims. He invited Swart to repeat the allegations outside the house, intimating that the Minister would be sued for defamation if he did so. Swart declined the invitation,[13] but evidently saw nothing improper in a cabinet Minister accusing a

[8] Rumpf's judgment was delivered in Afrikaans. This translation is taken from Beinart (1955) *op. cit.* at p, 162.

[9] See Brookes and Macaulay, n. 5 above, pp. 31–35.

[10] Fort Hare was a college solely for black students. Its emphasis on equipping students with a clasical 'liberal' legal education would of course have been anathema to a government which had promoted the Bantu Education Act.

[11] See p. 211 above.

[12] Blackwell had been the first instance judge in *Die Spoorbond*; (see pp. 224–225 above). His decision that the government could sue the union for libel presumably did little to endear him to Purified Nationalist politicians.

[13] *Rand Daily Mail*, 31 March 1955; *Cape Times*, 31 March 1955.

Supreme Court judge of being motivated by political bias in discharging his judicial functions.[14]

Further concern as to the government's elastic understanding of the 'independence' of the judiciary was raised following Greenberg's retirement at the end of 1954. Swart appointed L.C. Steyn as his replacement. Steyn had done little in his few years on the Transvaal bench to indicate that he possessed outstanding juristic talents. The suspicion that his promotion owed more to Swart's assessment of his willingness to tailor legal principle to political expediency would hardly seem unwarranted.

Strijdom also proved himself less phlegmatic than his predecessor when faced with criticism in the English language press. In August 1954, Strijdom told a Nationalist rally that some English language newspapers were engaged in a conspiracy to incite non-whites to break the law by offering support for such initiatives as the Defiance Campaign and criticising the government's various efforts to disenfranchise coloured voters.[15] Like Malan, however, Strijdom was not ready to let a hostile press deflect him from his chosen course. Shortly after this speech, his government offered its critics in parliament and the white media a still more draconian target to attack.

I. THE LEGISLATION

It was not initially clear if Strijdom felt that his 'opponent' in the 'struggle' to which he alluded in the house in May 1955 was the British, the Appellate Division or rather the Consititution itself.[16] Directly to attack either the court or the Constitution remained a politically problematic exercise even in the aftermath of the 1953 election. This largely explains why the government had by now decided to try to achieve the 'finality' that Strijdom sought through rather more oblique means than those favoured by Malan. As noted above, Malan had flirted briefly in July 1953 with a bill which would have altered the composition of the Appellate Division, but the initiative was not proceeded with after the 1953 general election. Strijdom resuscitated this measure in a rather different form in 1955, and made plans to couple it with legislation which offered the government a means to ensure it could gain a two-thirds majority for the Separate Representation of Voters bill.

[14] Blackwell gives his side of the story in L. Blackwell, *Blackwell Remembers* (Cape Town: Howard Timmins, 1971), pp. 161–162. In his version of events, the police officer concerned admitted he had no lawful authority for his action, but was carrying out an order from Swart.

[15] W. Hachten and A. Giffard, *The Press and Apartheid* (Madison, Wisc: Univeristy of Wisconsin Press, 1984), pp. 55–56.

[16] Swart seemed to think the United Party was the enemy. At a rally on 13 May, he told supporters that the opposition was the source of South Africa's constitutional difficulties: "The United Party has looked for trouble and has provoked us. Now we must hit hard. The people's patience has been exhausted": *Johannesburg Star*, 14 May 1955.

The Appellate Division Quorum Act 1955

The Appellate Division Quorum bill was introduced into the house on 29 March 1955. It was a simple two clause bill. It proposed that section 110 of the consitution should be amended. As noted in Chapter 4, section 110 had provided that a quorum of three Appellate judges was required to hear appeals from cases decided by a single judge, while a quorum of five (reduced to four in 1927) was necessary in cases heard by two or more judges at first instance. The new bill envisaged that the quorum would be increased to five in all but one type of case. An eleven judge court would be required whenever "any Act of Parliament (which includes any instrument which purports to be and has been assented to by the Governor General as such an Act) is in question". The additional judges would, of course, be appointed by the government.

The Cabinet had attempted to minimise the quantity of press attention the initiative would attract by announcing the new appointments to the court—in advance of publication of the bill—at the same time as Havenga's successor as Minister of Finance, Louw, introduced the 1955 budget. The English language papers did not attack the competence or integrity of the new appointees, but saw little room for doubt that the expanded court was the next stage in the *Harris* controversy. For the *Cape Times*, the increase in the size of the court was 'bewildering' and had an unmistakably political hue.[17] The *Cape Argus* expressed concern that the policy:

> "hints at a renewal of the constitutional crisis . . . The Minister may have some good reason for acting in this abrupt way [but] . . . the method of the fait accompli is surely the last that should be followed in dealing with one of the highest institutions in the land".[18]

The *Pretoria News* was less reticent in linking the bill to the *Harris* litigation. Under a leader headlined 'Confusion of Courts and Politics', the paper—perhaps somewhat naively—was unsure if the new Court would help or hinder the government's efforts to disenfranchise Coloured voters: "But if the Government did not hope there would be some effect it is extraordinarily difficult to understand why they have taken the step they have just announced".[19] *The*

[17] 26 March 1955. On 16 January, the paper had predicted that any enlargement of the Court to overturn or bypass *Harris* would be futile, since there were no judges on the High Court bench "who will so casually disgrace themselves and their honourable profession". Oswald Pirow, perhaps better versed in the niceties of far right politics, had been less naive. Within the Strijdom faction, he had suggested, was a large contingent of *bantjisoekers* (opportunists) who "had already dealt out among themselves all the best jobs, from Party organisers to judges of the Supreme Court"; recalled in a *Cape Times* leader of 6 June 1955.

[18] 26 March 1955.

[19] 28 March 1956. *The (Johannesburg) Star* was equally circumspect about the predelictions of the new judges, noting it would be "idle as well as improper to try to anticipate how the new Appeal Court would in fact decide when the constitutional issue is once more brought to the test". It was not at all circumspect in condemning the increased size of the Court *per se*, accusing the government of setting off down a "dangerous path for South Africa . . . The status and reputation of its whole judicial system, the basis of all ordered freedom, might receive a shattering blow"; 26 March 1956.

(Johannesburg) Star also identified a more prosaic concern; the present court chamber in Blomfontein did not seem to be big enough to seat eleven judges on a single elevated bench.[20]

What was unknown to the public and the press at that time however, was that the bill had prompted a vitriolic exchange of letters between Centlivres and Swart.[21] Swart had made no attempt to seek Centlivres' opinion on the bill prior to its publication. Rather he sent the Chief Justice a letter on 23 March which informed Centlivres that the government had already decided on the reforms to be introduced. The letter invited Centlivres' comments on the bill, though quite what impact such comments could have on the contents of what seemed to be an unshakeable government plan is unclear.

Centlivres and four of his colleagues[22] were outraged both by the terms of the bill and the government's failure to seek their opinion of the proposed changes. Centlivres described the government's behaviour on the latter point as 'reprehensible and censurable'. The Chief Justice did not pass any comment on the proposal for a quroum of eleven in cases involving the validity of legislation,[23] but observed that he and his four colleagues did not believe that a quorum of five in all other cases would increase the court's efficiency. Steyn had refused to associate himself with the viewpoints expressed in the letter. He suggested there was some merit in the government's proposals and saw no point in opposing what was evidently a *fait accompli*.[24]

Swart's response, in a letter headed 'STRICTLY CONFIDENTIAL AND PERSONAL' was bucolic:

[20] 26 and 28 March 1956.

[21] The exchange is reproduced in C. Forsyth, *In Danger for Their Talents* (Cape Town: Juta & Co., 1985), Appendix A.

[22] Schreiner, Hoexter, Van den Heever and Fagan.

[23] Forsyth has convincingly suggested Centlivres adopted this course in order to stand aloof from 'political' issues; n. 21 above, pp. 15–16. It would seem most unlikely that Centlivres had not considered Roosevelt's efforts to pack the US Supreme Court in the 1930s by increasing its membership from nine to fifteen. The then Chief Justice of the USA, Charles Hughes, had effectively torpedoed Roosevelt's plans by publicly rebutting the President's suggestion that the increase in personnel was a necessary efficiency measure. The plan was thereby exposed as a crude attempt to interfere with the independence of the judiciary, a scheme so unpalatable that even a substantial number of Roosevelt's supporters in the House and Senate refused to support it; see L. Fisher, *Constitutional Dialogues* pp. 209–215 (Princeton: Princeton University Press, 1988), pp. 209–215; *Constitutional Rights* 2nd edn. (New York: McGraw-Hill, 1995), ch. 19; M. Nelson, 'The President and the Court' (1988) *Political Science Quarterly* 267. Unlike Hughes, Centlivres did not publish his views to a wider audience, thereby sparing the government some considerable embarassment.

The suggestion that Centlivres saw no role for judges to indulge in 'politics' is reinforced by Professor Cowen. Just after *Harris No. 2*, Erwin Griswold sent Centlivres—as a Christmas gift—a copy of a book of essays by American academics and judges called *Jurisprudence in Action*. The book is largely concerned with exploring the political underpinnings of law. Centlivres passed the book on to Cowen, along with a comment that he could not see its relevance to his judicial responsibilities. He subsequently sold the book at a garage sale. It was bought by Cowen; Cowen, interview with Ian Loveland, August 1998.

[24] Schreiner was infuriated by this stance. In a private memorandum, he likened the bill to the measures adopted in Nazi Germany, and suggested that Hitler's rise to and continuation in power had owed much to the inertia of the public in the face of apparent *faits accompli*; memo dated 27 March 1955, reproduced in Forsyth, n. 21 above, at p. 251.

> "You and your colleagues who associate themselves with this remark [the 'reprehensible and censurable' point], apparently do not yet realise that it is the task and prerogative of the Government and Parliament to prescribe and define policy and legislation and not that of the Court; and where you, out of politeness or as a result of other good reasons, are asked to make comments or give advice, [it is] nevertheless most certainly expected that you will consider the relative positions of Government and Judiciary and that your comments will not exceed the approved limits, as occurred in this case".[25]

The new court

While Malan had foresworn any crude attempts to pack the Appellate Division bench in the early years of his administration, Strijdom's comments during the 1953 general election campaign[26] had indicated that he had no such qualms. Announcing the additional members of the expanded Court prior to the bill beginning its parliamentary passage had proven a not particularly subtle but nonetheless effective way to blunt opposition to the bill, since it thereby became difficult for some of the bill's opponents to attack the integrity of the enlarged court qua institution without at the same time being seen to impugn the integrity of the court's prospective members.[27]

Quite how much 'integrity' those appointees possessed is very much open to question.[28] That any lawyer who embraced a meaningful commitment to an independent judiciary could in good conscience accept a seat on a Court that had no purpose other than to override that independence is a contention that beggars belief. Swart's protestations in the house that the packed court might uphold the principles laid down in *Harris No. 1 and No. 2*[29] rang as hollow as Donges' suggestion during the passage of the High Court of Parliament bill that that 'court' might approve the Appellate Division's *Harris No. 1* judgment. Disinterested observers would readily have found grounds for assuming that the new appointees would be inclined to interpret their obligations as judges in a manner which would facilitate rather than obstruct government policy. E.M. de Beer was sixty-three years old in 1955. He was born in the Orange Free State, where he became simultaneously involved in Nationalist politics and legal practice after taking his law degree at London University. In addition to building a wide-ranging practice at the bar, de Beer served on Blomfontein Town Council in the 1920s and 1930s, and sat as a Nationalist member of the Free State provin-

[25] Swart to Centlivres, 1 April 1955; reproduced in Forsyth, n. 21 above, at p. 250.

[26] See p. 336 above.

[27] See for example Strauss' press statement on 25 March, reported in the *Pretoria News*, 26 March 1956.

[28] May was somewhat equivocal on this point. At one point in his textbook he observed that the impartiality of the new judges "cannot be, and is not, in doubt". However he had concluded the preceding paragraph by asking "why the judges had been appointed in advance and why many eminent senior judges had been passed over": *The South African Constitution*, 3rd edn. (Cape Town: Juta & Co., 1955), p. xiii.

[29] HAD, 25 April 1955, c.4431.

cial council from 1936 to 1939. He was appointed to the Free State provincial division in 1939, becoming its Judge President in 1948. He was by 1955 a very experienced and senior, if not particularly distinguished, member of the judiciary. He had sat as an acting Judge of Appeal in 1953 and 1954, during which time he had concurred (one assumes to the government's displeasure) in Centlivres' *Ngwevela* opinion. De Beer's attractiveness to the government seemed to owe much to his views on *Harris No. 1*. De Beer had had discussions with Swart prior to his appointment concerning the government's intended strategy to overcome the *Harris* decisions. De Beer had by this time already made his disagreement with *Harris No. 1* quite clear. He was evidently concerned that if he was subsequently invited to reverse *Harris No. 1*, his reputation for 'independence' would be severely compromised. Swart had promised him that the government would not attack *Harris No. 1* directly, an undertaking which the Minister of Justice later characterised to the house as 'helping De Beer with a personal problem'.[30]

Frederick Reynolds had been called to the Cape bar in 1911 at the age of twenty-three. Born and schooled in the Cape, Reynolds took his law degree at Rhodes University, and subsequently developed a diverse practice at the bar. By the mid-1950s, he was a leading member of the Cape bar, where he was regarded as a man of rigidly conservative political values. He had previously declined an appointment to the bench, but had accepted Swart's invitation to sit in the Eastern Districts local division in October 1948. Reynolds' subsequent promotion to the Appellate Division, at the age almost of seventy and after barely six years' experience on the provincial bench, smacked rather loudly of a Faustian bargain in which the judge brought his legal career to an end having reached the peak of his profession in return for assisting the government to bring the *Harris* episode to a satisfactory conclusion.

H.H.W. De Villiers was also an elderly man, being some sixty-four years old in 1955. De Villiers had undergone a wide-ranging education. His career had also been eclectic. He had worked as a farmer, teacher and journalist before being called to the Pretoria bar in 1922. The Smuts government had promoted him to the Transvaal provincial division in 1945. He was not obviously a National party stooge, but nor was his elevation obviously due to his juridic talents. That he was the brother-in-law of a government Minister might be thought a germane factor in his appointment.

Clarence Brink had built his legal reputation as much as an academic lawyer as an advocate. Born in 1897, Brink had been raised and educated in the Orange Free State. He began to practise at the bar in 1922, but in 1929 he was appointed as Head of the Faculty of Law at the University College of the Free State, a

[30] The episode is recounted in G. Mulligan, 'The Senate Act Case' (1957) 54 *South African LJ* 7. The accommodation reached between Swart and De Beer did not come to light prior to De Beer's appointment. For comment see the *Rand Daily Mail*, 26 January 1957. Swart's defence of the negotiations was offered to the house on 25 January 1957. The opposition's supposition was that the government had clandestinely made similar agreements with all of the new appointees.

position which he retained until 1948, when he had been appointed by Swart to the Free State bench. Brink had apparently also had conversations with Swart on the question of whether he would be asked to overrule *Harris No. 1*, and had seemingly received assurances that this eventuality would not arise.[31]

D.O.K. Beyers had been a judge for barely four years when he was appointed to the Appellate Division. Swart had chosen him to sit in the Griqualand West Local Division in 1951. Beyers was perhaps the most obviously partisan of the government's new appointments, but he was run close in this regard by the final proposed member of the court.

The sixth appointee was Cyril Hall, the water law expert,[32] whose pro-segregation judgment at first instance in *Lusu* had been so explicitly criticised by Centlivres and then warmly praised by Swart. He too might readily be thought to have a less than resolute attachment to those questions of constitutional propriety which impeded government policy.[33]

In a vein reminiscent of some of its members' refusal to appear before Steyn on his appointment to the Transvaal provincial division in 1950, the Johannesburg Bar Council criticised the appointments in outspoken terms. The Bar Council's press release was the lead story in the *Rand Daily Mail* on 23 April, which ran it under a triple headline:[34]

"RAND BAR CONDEMNS MOVE TO ENLARGE APPEAL COURT —
Not a Genuine Attempt to Strengthen Court —
JUDGES OF GREATEST EMINENCE EXCLUDED FOR POLITICAL REASONS".

The Bar Council did not attack the appointees individually, but in effect accused them of being governmental lackeys by condemning the enlargement of the Court as a crude political device. It was:

> "dangerous and unpatriotic to imperil for the sake of mere political expediency the great esteem in which the highest court is held . . . We are forced to conclude that the Government is moved solely by the hope that it will obtain the decision it desires on the constitutional question from the new eleven judge court".[35]

Strijdom's response in the house was equally forthright. After characterising the Johannesburg Bar Council as unrepresentative of the legal profession both in the Transvaal and the country as a whole, the Prime Minister condemned its 'unsavoury' and 'scandalous' remarks and ended with a promise of retribution: "I only hope that none of those people will ever get the idea that they have proved that . . . they are fit to be appointed as judges".[36]

[31] See Forsyth, n. 21 above, pp. 23–25.
[32] For a brief synopis of Hall's career see p. 317 n. 69 above.
[33] Harry Snitcher recalled that many members of the Cape bar regarded Hall as the most partisan of all the appointees; interview with Ian Loveland, August 1998.
[34] Original emphases.
[35] The Bar Council also renewed its criticism of Steyn, reiterating its view that he was unduly deferential to government wishes and querying his "unusually rapid elevation to the Appeal Court".
[36] HAD, 24 April 1955, cc. 4444–4445.

The passage of the legislation

Swart had begun the second reading debate on 25 April by suggesting that the bill was primarily concerned with procedural difficulties. It was 'not fair' that, because of section 110's provisions concerning quora in the Appellate Division, some of that court's most important decisions were rendered by a bench containing only three judges, while those dealing with lesser issues might have to be heard by a five-man panel. It would be much 'fairer', he suggested, if a quorum of five was required for all cases.

This rationale was quickly forgotten however, when Swart acknowledged that the bill was "connected, of course, with the so-called constitutional crisis which we had in South Africa".[37] The 'crisis', he maintained was the fault not of the government, nor of 'parliament', but of the Appellate Division. Its reversal of *Ndlwana* in *Harris No. 1* was intolerable on several constitutional grounds. *Harris No. 1* was the source of great political and legal uncertainty for the government. Having proceeded for fifteen years on the basis that *Ndlwana* correctly defined parliament's powers, members of the government and the legislature now found that their assumptions were ill-founded, and had to face the possibility that *Harris No. 1* itself might be reversed in future. Such arbitrary shifts in basic constitutional understandings were as unwelcome to 'the man in the street' as they were to government ministers, for if the Appellate Division could so readily change its mind on such large questions might it not also be feared that it would do so on a host of minor matters. Furthermore, Centlivres' suggestion in *Harris No. 1* that the Appellate Division's judgment in *Ndlwana* was reached *per incuriam* was an insult to the four judges sitting in that case.

Strijdom echoed his colleague's arguments. He reserved his most intemperate comments for the Chief Justice. He suggested that Centlivres' *per incuriam* argument was an "undeserved libel and insult", which in effect was saying that "those four eminent judges in 1937 were such bad judges that from pure negligence and neglect of duty they gave a wrong decision".[38] The Prime Minister was either ignoring or overlooking De Wet C.J.'s comments after *Harris No. 1* to the effect that he now considered his concurrence in *Ndlwana* to be misconceived.[39] One of the other three judges who sat in the Appellate Division in *Ndlwana*, Jean Etienne de Villiers had died in 1947. Former Chief Justice Stratford had died in January 1952, before *Harris* was decided. One could thus only speculate as to whether or not they would have concurred in De Wet's change of mind. Watermeyer was still alive at this point, having retired to live in Hermanus, but did not seem to offer any public statement about the judgment.

37 HAD, 25 April 1955, c.4427.

38 HAD, 25 April 1955, cc. 4451–4452.

39 See p. 296 above. Subsequent Nationalist contributors to the debate did refer to De Wet's post-*Harris* comments, but maintained that his involvement with the Torch Commando necessarily made him a unacceptably partisan figure.

From the opposition front bench, Strauss argued that Swart's procedural justification for the bill was quite spurious. The bill's purpose was simply to subvert the constitution by packing the existing court. It was likely to be followed, Strauss suggested, by a similar measure designed to pack the senate with government supporters. The whole "sordid and debased"[40] episode, which had begun with the 1951 Separate Representation of Voters bill, was entirely of the government's making.

Strauss did not attack the court's new members in personal terms. Other opposition MPs were not so reticent. The most forceful attack on the bill came from Leo Lovell, the Labour Party member for Benoni. Lovell suggested that the bill should be analysed according to the precepts of the 'mischief rule' of statutory interpretation:

> "Now what is the mischief? The mischief was a quorum of five . . . and this magic number of eleven is going to remedy that mischief . . . Mr Speaker, this trick of the Government is obvious to a child; this strategem of the Government. Six outvote five, and six and five is eleven. There you have the magic behind the number eleven".[41]

In vituperative terms, Lovell endorsed the protest made about the new court by the Johannesburg bar, and urged that the bill be rejected because the enlarged quorum would "prove an irresistable temptation to the government with its record of contempt for the independence of the judiciary to pack the courts with servile judges or paid officials".[42] In effect, Lovell contended, the government had responded to its failure in 1952 to turn parliament into an appeal court by promoting legislation which was intended to turn the Appellate Division into a parliament: "The Prime Minister and his party have tried to introduce a two party system in the court, just as they have it in this House, with six members on one side and five on the other".[43]

Swart had remained quite unmoved by the torrent of opposition criticism which the bill had provoked. The measure was, he contended, a perfectly legitimate response both to the United Party's previous concerns about the constitutional propriety of the High Court of Parliament *per se* and to the Appellate Division's judgment in *Harris No. 2*: "When we passed the High Court of Parliament Bill, their argument was that we should have a proper court. They said that that court was not a proper court. Here we are now forming a proper court".[43a]

Centlivres and his colleagues evidently did not share the view that the enlarged Appellate Division constituted 'a proper court'. Forsyth records that, with the exception of Steyn, the existing appellate judges had contemplated a mass resignation in protest at the measure, but were persuaded against this course by Greenberg.[44] They did, however, institute a blatant 'boycott' of the

[40] HAD, 25 April 1955, c. 4438.
[41] *Ibid.* at c.4446.
[42] *Ibid.* at c.4467.
[43] *Ibid.* at c.4471.
[43a] *Ibid.* at c. 4485
[44] See n. 21 above, p. 17. Forsyth's source for this claim is not identified.

new appointees. This was in some respects a quite trivial affair, involving such measures as a refusal to socialise with the new judges. In a more significant vein, Centlivres determined to ensure that the 'second team', which included the previously appointed Steyn, was marginalised when he chose five-man quorums for appeal cases. (The Chief Justice's room for manoeuvre on this issue was soon reduced by Van den Heever's death). But such strategies would not of course be available to him in cases questioning the validity of legislation.

Centlivres had for example not selected Styen to sit in *R v Kahn*, a case in which judgment was delivered on 9 May. Sam Kahn was the former communist MP, who had been removed from the house under the amended 1950 Suppression of Communism Act. Kahn was also subjected to a banning order. In July 1954 he had attended a party given by Brian Bunting at Bunting's house in Cape Town. As a banned person under the Act, Kahn was prohibited per section 5 from attending any 'gathering'. The government regarded the party he attended as a 'gathering'.[45] Kahn was prosecuted and convicted under section 5, the magistrate taking the view that any assembly of people for any purpose was a gathering under section 5. The conviction was upheld in the Cape provincial division.[46] Giving judgment for a unanimous court, Centlivres quashed the conviction.[47] In a brief opinion, the Chief Justice held that the meaning of the term 'gathering' was structured by the purposes of the Act. People who assembled together for purposes unrelated to the furtherance of 'communism'—such as, in this instance, a social event—were not attending a gathering within the meaning of section 5.[48]

The concern that the government anticipated that the Appellate Quorum legislation would produce a quiescent Appellate Division—which, with the exception of Steyn, the previously six-man Court manifestly was not—was exacerbated by the passage of yet more legislation curtailing what had traditionally been regarded (at least by white South Africans) as basic civil liberties. An 'independent' Appellate Division might subject such statutes to rigorous interpretive scrutiny: a 'packed' court could not be expected to share such sensibilities. The Departure from the Union Regulation Act 1955 made it a criminal offence, punishable by a gaol term of up to two years, for any citizen to leave South Africa without being in possession of a passport. The Act was a belated response to the Appellate Division's decision in *Sachs v Donges*.[49] The Act provided, in stark terms, that passports were to be issued—and withdrawn—at the

[45] Cf. Mandela's comment at p. 238 n. 45 above.

[46] [1955] (1) SA 692.

[47] [1955] (3) SA 177. The case, which had been argued in March, was one of the last in which Van den Heever participated.

[48] Brian Bunting recalled that the 'party' had been arranged so that Kahn could debrief other communists and sympathisers on his recent experiences abroad. It was manifestly a political gathering; "But we were half-expecting a police raid. So when we heard the knock at the door we all started dashing to the kitchen and bringing in cups of tea"; interview with Ian Loveland, August 1998.

[49] See p. 250 above.

apparently unfettered discretion of the government. The Act was ostensibly introduced to supplement the Suppression of Communism legislation; the government claimed that black ANC activists and some radical coloureds and whites had been travelling to the Soviet Union or China to gain political and military skills with which to destabilise South Africa's political structures. The Act was more likely to be of use however as a means of pressurising white liberals (such as Sachs and Kahn) to refrain from criticising government policy:[50] an ANC activist seeking Soviet military training was unlikely to bother with a passport and even less likely to be deterred by the threat of two years' imprisonment.[51] Whether the government could by such measures eventually succeed in creating a tame opposition within white political society remained to be seen. It had, it seemed already taken steps to create a tame judiciary. Its next step on the route towards the reversal of *Harris* was to create a tame senate.

The Senate Act 1955

The senate bill, introduced to the house on 11 May 1955, was a rather more textually substantial measure than its Appellate Division predecesor. The bill outlined two main objectives. The second of these was to replace section 63 of the South Africa Act. Section 63 had made provision for the convening of a joint session of the house and senate to vote on the passage of bills that had been passed on two occasions by the house but thereafter blocked by the senate.[52] The amended section 63 would remove the joint sitting process, and simply provide that any bill which had twice been passed by the house (in different calendar years) and twice blocked by the senate could be sent directly to the Governor-General for his assent. The proposal was broadly analogous to the situation introduced in Britain by the Parliament Act 1911, which permitted the Commons to override a Lords veto in most circumstances, and—in comparison with the bill's first objective—occasioned little political controversy.

That first objective was to increase the size of the senate and to alter the way in which its members were elected. As noted in Chapter 4,[53] the senate had originally contained some forty members: eight from each province, elected by single transferable vote by the members of provincial councils; and eight appointed by the Governor-General, four of whom were to 'thoroughly acquainted with the reasonable wishes' of the coloured races. By 1955, the senate had increased in size to forty-eight members; four representing native blacks through the method introduced by the Native Representation Act 1936, and four representing South West Africa. The structure of the senate was a modest concession to

[50] See Brookes and Macaulay, n. 5 above, pp. 69–71.

[51] Cf. Mandela's account of one of Sisulu's trips to eastern Europe and China at this time; *Long Road to Freedom* (London: Abacus, 1995), pp. 184–185.

[52] See p. 110 above.

[53] See pp. 110–111 above.

federalist sentiment in a unitary state, in that it afforded each province, irrespective of its population, equal political representation. The removal of the section 63 process undermined that concession to a small extent, but the rest of the bill envisaged a much more radical departure from 'federal' principles.

The new bill proposed markedly to dilute the senate's provincial equality provisions. Native and South West African representation in the senate would remain unchanged, but the process through which other senators would gain office was to be significantly amended. The bill proposed that the Governor-General should in future be able to appoint sixteen rather than eight senators; eight of whom should be 'thoroughly acquainted with the reasonable wishes of the coloured races'.[54] The number of provincial representatives would in future crudely reflect each province's population. The bill proposed that the number of each province's house and provincial assembly seats[55] be added together and then divided by five to arrive at the provinces permitted total of senators. Under this scheme, the Cape would have twenty-two senators; the Transvaal twenty-seven; and the Free State and Natal would each have eight.[56] This would produce a senate of eighty-nine members in all (see Table 10.1). The provincial senators would then be elected by an 'electoral college' comprising the members of each province's provincial council and its house representatives. Election would be by the simple majority system rather than the single transferable vote process; a party with a majority (no matter how small) in the respective electoral college could thus ensure that only its members sat in the senate. When the bill was introduced, the Nationalists would have had clear majorities in the Cape, Transvaal and Free State electoral colleges.

Table 10.1 The composition of the reformed senate

Province	*House seats*	*Provincial council seats*	*Senate seats*
Cape	54	54	22
Transvaal	68	68	27
Natal	16	25	8
Orange Free State	16	25	8
South West Africa	6	—	4
Native senators	—	—	4
Appointed senators	—	—	16
Total			89

[54] As noted in previous chapters, the 'thorough acquaintance' proviso did not prevent Prime Ministers appointing whoever they wished to these seats; see pp. 165 and 211 above.

[55] Section 70 of the South Africa Act had provided that the number of provincial councillors should match the number of that province's representatives in the house, subject to no province having fewer than twenty-five councillors.

[56] No province would have fewer than eight senators.

Strauss had tried to derail the bill at first reading by moving an immediate amendment to the effect that the new senate would have no power to participate in legislation affecting the entrenched clauses.[57] He suggested that the bill was just one further part in an elaborate legal scheme to overturn *Harris No. 1*; a scheme that had begun with the Appellate Quorum bill and would continue with additional, as yet unannounced, legislation. The details of the bill were not yet available, but Strauss saw no room to doubt the bill's purpose. It would be 'steamrollered through' parliament: "in order not to establish the sovereignty of Parliament, which is beyond all doubt, but in order to establish the sovereignty of the Nationalist party".[58]

Strauss made some attempt to divorce his critique of the bill from the coloured voters issue. Reform of the senate would be in any circumstances an event of major constitutional significance. Echoing Smuts' critique of the much milder measure promoted by Hertzog's government in 1926, Strauss suggested that reform should be a matter in which the government accepted an obligation to proceed only if it had secured broad cross-party support for its proposals.[59] The attempt to sever the senate bill *per se* from the *Harris* controversy was however unsustainable. Strauss' critique rapidly returned to the point he had made in the Appellate Division bill debates—that the government was engaged in the laborious process of constructing a complex legislative scheme, enacted piecemeal in successive statutes, to overturn *Harris No. 1*. This scheme, the final instalments of which remained as yet unannounced, amounted to a vile debasement of South Africa's constitutional traditions:

> "Until now it was a great honour to be a judge of the land in this country. A different impression is now being created by . . . this Government. Up to now it was a great honour to be a member of this House and of the Other Place under our constitution. What will happen when . . . Senators by the dozen are brought into existence in order to create a two thirds majority for this government".[60]

The Labour, Conservative and Liberal parties also expressed clear opposition to the bill. Members of each party portrayed it as an immoral attempt to flout constitutional safeguards. The bill was nevertheless approved at first reading by some 82 votes to 53.

At second reading on 23 May, Donges again adopted the now familiar strategy of invoking British precedent to justify the government's reforms. There had, he observed, been several episodes in British constitutional history when a government with a Commons majority had altered or threatened to alter the composition of the House of Lords in order to ensure its policies were enacted.[61]

[57] HAD, 11 May 1955, c. 5404 *et seq*.
[58] HAD, 11 May 1955, c. 5407.
[59] See pp. 161–162 above.
[60] HAD, 11 May 1955, cc. 5407–5408.
[61] The episodes being the ratification of the Treaty of Utrecht in the early 1700s; the passage of the Great Reform bill in 1832; and the dispute over the 'People's Budget' in 1909–1911. See further I. Loveland, *Constitutional Law* (London: Butterworths, 1996), chs. 6–7.

Donges also suggested that the structure of the house and senate were out of line with most other commonwealth legislatures. In South Africa, the ratio of lower to upper house members was over three to one, whereas in Canada, Australia and Britain that ratio was under two to one. To increase the size of the senate would therefore merely be to bring South Africa's legislative arrangements into approximate conformity with those of its Commonwealth counterparts, and moreover, with those of such countries as Ireland, Denmark, France and Belgium.

Nor did Donges see any great difficulty about rejecting the principle of provincial equality in the senate. This was he suggested an unwelcome 'federal' concept, which had unhappily 'crept in' to the 1908 Convention's debates. The initial ten-year entrenchment of the senate's composition contained in section 25 of the South Africa Act indicated that the Convention's members did not regard its structure or composition as inviolate. This conclusion applied as much to the senate's size as the way in which its members were chosen. In a unitary state such as South Africa, population was the only defensible basis for determining electoral representation.

Donges was not inclined, however, to try to conceal the government's intentions. Enlarging the senate was the only way for the government to fulfil the mandate it had been given by 'the people' in two successive general elections to implement the Separate Representation of Voters bill:

> "I want to ask on my part what other alternative is there still open which we on this side have not yet tried? What other alternative is there still by which the mandate of the electorate can be carried out? . . . [T]he position we are in today demands drastic measures. The country wants to put an end to all this quarrel and strife of the past five years . . . I am therefore sure it welcomes the effort by the Government to cut through the constitutional knot".[62]

Strijdom's speech was a particularly blunt affair. He maintained that the entrenched clauses had been imposed by the British government on the unwilling colonies. After reiterating the Pollak thesis to explain why *Harris No. 1* was wrongly decided, he then accused the Appellate Division of involving itself with 'politics', and thereby triggering the constitutional crisis. In an extraordinary illustration of the 'Christian-National' underpinnings of his government's programme, the Prime Minister claimed that the National Party enjoyed a mandate for the disenfranchisement of coloured voters not just from the electorate, but also from God:

> "God Almighty controls the Destiny of our people. He is sovereign. We recognise Him and any Government which is in power is in power by his will . . . [W]e sit here because it was at that time the will of the Almighty that the Government should rule. Everything happens according to his will".[63]

[62] HAD, 11 May 1955, at cc. 6015 and 6019.

[63] HAD, 25 May 1955, cc. 6219–6220, quoted in Marshall, n. 3 above, at p. 235. See also the speech at a party meeting in Johannesburg of the Minister of Labour, Senator T. de Klerk, reported

Donges had it seemed initially hoped that the mere threat of the bill would induce the United Party to support a re-introduced Separate Representation of Voters bill.[64] Strauss rapidly made it clear that his party would not do so. Strauss' attack on the bill again traversed familiar ground, although his language was by now becoming increasingly intemperate. He imputed the charge of Nazism against the government by accusing it of 'jackbooting'[65] the bill though parliament. The bill would not enhance the power of parliament, but would rather, by creating so many 'fake senators':

> "make [parliament] a mere tool in the hands of the political bosses in this country . . . [W]hat they are setting out to do here is to make the political bosses in the National Party the real sovereigns of this country. It is to establish the sovereignty of the Nationalist Party".[66]

United and Labour party MPs had apparently not yet accepted that parliamentary opposition to the bill was a futile exercise. Strauss in particular voiced the hope that determined and principled resistance to the government's subversion of the constitution would bring the party increased support at the next general election. This was, as Strijdom and Donges both suggested, both an unrealistic and hypocritical stance for the opposition to adopt. The long-term electoral trends pointed towards increased support for the Nationalists among the white population, more and more of whom were seeing and enjoying the economic benefits accruing from *apartheid*. Similarly, it was absurd for the United Party to present itself as the champion of 'democracy' without at the same time offering an immediate commitment to enfranchise all of South Africa's adult citizens, irrespective of their race. As Strauss knew as well as Strijdom, such a commitment would have ensured the party's almost complete annihilation at the next election. If the United Party was to succeed in its opposition to the bill, it would do so as a result of the deliberations of the Appellate Division rather than its own efforts in the house and senate. The bill passed its third reading: "by 79 votes to 46 amid roars of applause from the Nationalists and shouts of 'scandal' and 'Heil Strijdom' from the Opposition".[67]

'Parliament's' competence to change the composition of the Senate

The United Party had some cause for believing that some members of the Appellate Division might regard the Senate Act as unconstitutional. There was no doubt that parliament was competent to alter the composition of the senate.

in the *Cape Argus* of 16 May 1955: "We are taking this step because we are Calvinists who believe that God is sovereign and hands over that sovereignty to the legal rulers of the land. We therefore have the right to determine what must be done, and nobody—even if it is the highest court—has received that power from the Creator of heaven and earth".

[64] *Rand Daily Mail*, 11 May 1955.

[65] HAD, 25 May 1955, at c. 6030.

[66] *Ibid*. at c. 6025.

[67] *Cape Times*, 15 June 1955.

As noted in Chapter 4, section 25 of the South Africa Act had substantively entrenched the original rules concerning its membership for ten years. Thereafter, its structure and membership was a matter for parliament to determine. So much was uncontentious. The pertinent question which again arose, however, was what did section 25 mean by 'parliament' when it stated that "Parliament may provide for the manner in which the Senate shall be constituted".

In the government's view, the section 25 'parliament' was the simple majority, bicameral legislature. This was indeed the body that had created four additional senators for South West Africa in 1949. The bill's opponents conceded that this definition would be correct in respect of any change to the senate's composition which was unconnected with governmental attempts to alter the constitution's entrenched clauses. It was claimed by some United Party MPs, however,[68] that if the intention underpinning the bill was to circumvent sections 35, or 137 or 152, then the only 'parliament' which could restructure the senate was the unicameral, two-thirds majority legislature. The argument was built largely on the Appellate Division's judgments in *Harris No. 2*. To allow the bicameral, simple majority parliament to pack one (or both) of its chambers in order to engineer a two-thirds unicameral majority for the purposes of removing entrenched rights would render such rights 'nugatory'.[69] Whether such an argument would convince the 'first team' judges, still less any of their new colleagues on the now enlarged Appellate Division bench, remained to be seen. But by the end of the summer, the bill had received the Governor-General's consent.

Extra-parliamentary reaction to the bill

Strijdom's pursuit of 'finality' had prompted a small group of Afrikaaner academics to found a new political party, the South African Bond (SAB). While the SAB declared itself broadly sympathetic to the Nationalist programme, it deplored the government's efforts to subvert the constitution through the Senate and Appellate Division Acts. The SAB enjoyed a brief burst of publicity, but looked unlikely to make any substantial inroads into the government's electoral support.[70]

A more long-lasting, if only symbolic, manifestation of opposition within the white community, was offered by the Women's Defence of the Constitution

[68] The argument was also implicit in Strauss' intervention during the first reading debate.

[69] In a precursor of this thesis, United Party MPs had argued during the abortive joint sessions Malan called after *Harris No. 2* that the South West African senators were not competent to vote on the bills, as they were themselves appointees whose presence in 'parliament' had been intended to pack the Nationalist benches. The Speaker was unimpressed by the argument; see Marshall, n. 3 above, pp. 234–235, esp at n. 3.

[70] K. Heard, *General Elections in South Africa 1943–1970* (London: OUP, 1974), p. 79, n. 3 above, Marshall, n. 3 above, p. 235.

League, which was founded in May 1955.[71] The League was more commonly known as the 'Black Sash'. The name derived from the organisation's preferred form of civil disobedience, which was for its white, middle class women members silently to picket government buildings and parliament, clad in white dresses and black sashes, in symbolic mourning for the anticipated 'murder' of the original constitution.[72]

The Archbishop of Cape Town, Dr Geoffrey Clayton, also entered the public debate. He too likened the government to Nazis. He accused the cabinet's members of not being 'real' christians, and castigated Strijdom for his claims that the government's agenda was divinely inspired.[73]

The English language press had in the main been fiercely critical of the bill. The most vigorous condemnation was made shortly after the bill was enacted by the *Johannesburg Star*. In an article headlined 'The Senate Disgrace', the *Star* launched a scathing attack both on the government and the putative new members of the enlarged senate:

> "There has been no more undignified spectacle in the history of South African politics than the scramble among Nationalists for seats in the Senate under the new dispensation. If anything more were needed to expose the shabbiness of the Senate Act device it was the stampede of would-be politicians for the pickings in the new make believe chamber that will pass for a constituent part of the central institution of democracy . . .
>
> They are volunteering—for a handsome fee[74]—to do the dirty work of the Nationalist government".[75]

The paper was subsequently sued for defamation by two would-be senators, each of whom claimed some £10,000 in damages. The then editor of *The Star*, Horace Flather, regarded the suit as a test case brought on behalf of the forty-one new Nationalist senators, all of whom would subsequently launch similar proceedings.[76] Flather did not see himself, or his paper, as an inveterate opponent of the government; he described Donges as a long-standing friend, with whom he had broken only after the Minister had pushed the senate bill through parliament. He nonetheless saw the bill as "a dangerous connivance",[77] and one

[71] See generally C. Michelson, *The Black Sash of South Africa* (Cape Town: Juta & Co.). T. Davenport, *South Africa: a Modern History*, 2nd edn. (Cambridge: CUP, 1978), p. 274; J. Omer-Cooper, *History of Southern Africa* (London: Heinneman, 1987), pp. 204–205.

[72] The movement had begun with more orthodox measures, such as mass meetings and petitions to government ministers. The so-called 'haunting' strategy was subsequently adopted because of its eminently non-aggressive but hugely embarassing impact on government ministers. Spink records for example that ministers flying back into the country took to leaving the airport terminal through a non-white entrance to avoid the women's picket: K. Spink, *Black Sash* (London: Metheun, 1991), ch. 2.

[73] *Cape Times*, 11 June 1955.

[74] Senators received the then very substantial sum of £1,400 per year (author's footnote).

[75] Quoted in *Pienaar and van Schoor v Argus Printing and Publishing Co. Ltd* [1956] (3–4) SALR 508 at 508–509.

[76] Flather recounts the episode in his autobiography; *The Way of an Editor* (London: Purnell, 1977), pp. 158–162.

[77] *Ibid.* at 158.

which should be exposed to furious criticism in the press. He was determined to defend the action, irrespective of the potentially enormous costs a defeat might entail.

Pienaar and van Schoor v Argus Printing and Publishing Co. Ltd was eventually heard before Ludorf J. in the Witwatersrand local division in April 1956. *The Star* ran a variety of defences: that the story was true; that it was fair comment; and—building on the *Die Spoorbond* principle[78]—that the South African common law should not permit politicians to sue for libel in respect of political criticism. Ludorf J. resolved the case in the plaintiffs' favour, but granted them a manifestly pyrrhic victory. The judge awarded the plaintiffs £100 damages. He explicitly noted that the award to these plainitffs was sufficient to vindicate the reputations of all the new senators, and warned that: "subsequent plaintiffs in the Supreme Court would run a grave risk in regard to the award of costs which the Court would make".[79] The judgment offered a clear indication that the government could not expect the courts to allow its supporters to use the existing libel laws to chill press criticism of government policy.

As might be expected, the English and Afrikaans press had afforded the senate bill markedly different reactions. For *Die Transvaaler*, a packed senate was: "so small a price to pay for the ending of the constitutional struggle that it is really regrettable that this method was not used before".[80] *Die Burger* was similarly enthusiastic, describing the bill as: "the best and least dislocating measure remaining to end this situation after the repeated and patient efforts of the government".[81] For the *Cape Argus*, in contrast, the senate bill was a device which would *de facto* abolish 'Parliament' and effectively grant the government unaccountable and uncontrollable legislative powers.[82] In the *Rand Daily Mail's* opinion, the bill was "a coup d'etat dressed up in quasi-legal form . . . Once this bill becomes law there is no reason why the Government should ever hold an election again".[83]

Julius Lewin, a senior lecturer in law at the University of the Witwatersrand,[84] suggested that the newly enlarged senate would shortly be summoned to provide Strijdom with a two-thirds majority for a new Separate Representation of Voters bill. He doubted that this was however the main purpose behind the 1955 legislation. The government was more concerned to establish its superiority (acting through its parliamentary majority) over the courts. By so doing, it would confirm that the 'rule of law' as it existed in South Africa meant no more than obedience to the government's wishes. It would no longer function as a set of substantive, apolitical principles regulating both the substance and conduct

78 See pp. 224–225 above.

79 [1966] (3–4) SALR 508 at 509–510.

80 15 May 1955; translation taken from the *Cape Argus* of 16 May 1955.

81 15 May 1955; translation taken from the *Cape Argus* of 16 May 1955.

82 11 May 1955. Two days later, the *Argus'* leader column once again invoked the comparator of Nazism to criticise the government's behaviour.

83 13 May 1955.

84 J. Lewin, 'The Struggle for Law in South Africa' (1956) *Political Quarterly* 176.

of the government which judges would enforce and, perhaps more importantly, legislators would respect. Lewin argued that Strijdom's government regarded the South African judiciary's attachment to the rule of law—as evidenced by decisions such as *Lusu*, *Tayob* and Blackwell J.'s preliminary holding in *Wolpe*—as "an unfortunate legacy of British colonial government in the nineteenth century".[85] In this respect, the government was simply upholding a long established boer tradition, evidenced by Slagtersnek and Kruger's response to *Brown v Leyds*, of dispensing with principles of substantive legality whenever they proved politically inexpedient.

Lewin's critique was a polemic. It made no reference to the pre-Union constitutional traditions of the Free State, for example, nor to Hertzog's consistent respect (in procedural terms) for the entrenched provisions. It nevertheless conveyed the point that the Malan and Strijdom administrations marked a clear departure from the Hertzogian brand of Afrikaner Nationalism. The packing of the Appellate Division, and the subsequent packing of the senate, indicated that:

> "the rule of law will continue to prevail only in the most technical sense. The deeper meaning that the term has historically borne in politics and in jurisprudence will become a thing of the past. South Africa may retain the outward forms of constitutional government, but its substance will have gone the way of its spirit, which has already departed from the scene".[86]

While the Appellate Division and senate bills were particularly acute causes of dismay to white commentators such as Lewin, they were, in comparison with many other ingredients of *apartheid*'s legislative programme, issues of minor significance to the ANC. The collapse of the Defiance Campaign in 1953 had temporarily derailed attempts for non-whites and white liberals to form a common, extra-parliamentary opposition to government policy. The setback was shortlived. Notwithstanding the outcome of the *Wolpe* litigation, the People's Congress initiative launched by the ANC early in 1954 attracted considerable cross-racial support. The plan received backing from SACPO, the Congress of Democrats and the South African Indian Congress. After an extensive consultation campaign, the 'Congress of the People' was convened at Kliptown in the Transvaal in late June 1955.[87] The Congress' main objective was to adopt the 'Freedom Charter', an idealised constitutional settlement for a democratic, multi-racial South Africa. The Charter was an exhortatory document rather than a detailed blueprint for reform. This perhaps explains why it so effectively caught the imagination not only of non-whites in South Africa but also of substantial swathes of public opinion in other western democracies. It would also seem to have breached the provisions of the Suppression of Communism Act, a

[85] *Ibid.* at pp. 176–177.

[86] *Ibid.* at p. 181.

[87] For an 'insider's' account of the process leading up to the Congress and the Congress itself see Mandela, n. 51 above, pp. 199–207. Mandela was under a banning order at the time, and observed proceedings (in disguise) from a safe distance.

fact which its supporters could not have expected to escape the government's attention.

In the short term, however, Strijdom's cabinet had fixed its gaze on more readily soluble questions. Just as *Lusu* had been reversed by the Reservation of Separate Amenities Act 1953, so the Appellate Division's equally (to Nationalists) unpalatable decision in *Tayob* was overruled: the Motor Carrier Transportation Amendment Act 1955 made explicit provision for local authorities to allocate trading licences on a racially discriminatory basis.[88]

At the same time, Verwoerd intensified an extraordinary, almost surreal, propaganda campaign intended to convince native blacks and the outside world that non-whites also supported *apartheid*. The Department for Native Affairs published a journal, *Bantu*, which was devoted largely to publishing praise from black tribal leaders for government policy. The June 1955 issue ran a poetic eulogy to Verwoerd, evidently scripted by a black admirer, which began with the following verse:

Dr Verwoerd
Minister of Native Affairs
I

Dr Verwoerd, thou art the Shepherd of the black races,
Thou art the defender of the Bantu, our rock, our mountain,
Thou art our refuge and our shield.
The mountain that saves us, our refuge,
The Saviour who rescued us at time of need.

The poem continued in like vein for four further verses. It had not, the Department maintained, been an officially sponsored initiative.[89]

Centlivres on the rule of law and the South African constitution

While the appellate quorum and senate bills had excited furious opposition in white political circles, the four remaining members of the *Harris* court (plus Fagan) maintained a diplomatic silence on the constitutional propriety or otherwise of the government's actions. Oliver Schreiner recorded his views in an unpublished memorandum, filed among his personal papers. His fear was that democracy, in even the limited sense of that term employed in South Africa, was under immediate threat: "The principle of changing governments will disappear and the judiciary will lose all semblance of independence from the executive. The strain upon the Union must grow".[90]

It would not then have been regarded as appropriate for judges in South Africa (nor indeed in Britain) to make direct, extra-judicial comments on the

[88] See the *Rand Daily Mail*, 17 May 1955.

[89] The whole text is reproduced in A. Hepple, *Verwoerd* (Pelican: Harmondsworth, 1967), p. 108.

[90] Memo dated 11 May 1955; reproduced in Forsyth, n. 21 above, at p. 253.

merits of the government's legislative programme,[91] but Centlivres in particular was offered a platform from which he could, if only obliquely, give an indication of his views on the current state of the South African constitution. In September 1955, Ervin Griswold hosted a conference at the Harvard Law School in celebration of the two hundredth anniversary of the birth of John Marshall, one of the first and most influential Chief Justices on the American Supreme Court. Centlivres was invited to deliver a speech at the conference, and chose as his subject 'The South African Constitution and the Rule of Law'.[92]

Centlivres began his address with a declamation that one might have thought was aimed squarely at the Strijdom government. Much of the world, he observed, did not enjoy the benefits of democratic government, but was ruled by:

> "autocracies which set the State above the individual and which deny their citizens the fundamental rights of an independent judiciary, freedom of movement within and outside the limits of their own country, freedom of speech, freedom of the press, freedom of assembly, freedom of association and freedom to elect representatives of their own choice".[93]

In what might be regarded as a barely coded attack on the Appellate Division Quorum Act, Centlivres noted that it would be quite legal for a bare parliamentary majority to pass legislation allowing the government to dismiss judges whenever it wished to do so. Such legislation would however be 'unconstitutional' in the moral sense. The same failing would attach he suggested—in an evident reference to the Senate Act—to any bicameral legislation which made "a radical alteration" to the constitution without having been explicitly adverted to in a government's election manifesto.[94] This strident start to his speech might have led some observers to conclude that the Chief Justice was indicating that he would regard a legislative attempt to circumvent *Harris* as an immoral, if not illegal, venture. Yet one might readily assume that Strijdom's cabinet would consider this an encouragement rather than a deterrent. It had already shown it was unmoved by political disapproval; the prospect that South Africa's Chief Justice would find such legislation distasteful was of minor significance as long as he did not declare it illegal. Centlivres offered the government further encouragement by stressing that South Africa's understanding of the rule of law required that: "the Court is not concerned in any way with the policy of the Act,

[91] Donges' attack on the Appellate Division's judgment in *Lusu* (p. 321 above) and Swart's denunciation of Blackwell J.'s role in *Wolpe* (p. 338 above) suggested it was becoming acceptable in South Africa for government Ministers to make direct—and critical comments—on judicial decisions.

[92] The speech is published in (1956) *Butterworths South African LR* 3.

[93] *Ibid.* at p. 3.

[94] Swart, it may be recalled, had invoked Asquith's 1911 threat to pack the House of Lords with Liberal peers as a precedent justifying the senate bill. Centlivres observed that Asquith had made reform of the Lords the key element of his party's manifesto in the second 1910 election. Centlivres stopped short of pointing out that the senate act had not featured in the Nationalists' 1953 election programme. The obvious inference was that the Strijdom government had no 'mandate' for the senate legislation.

the validity of which is attacked": he also reiterated the point he had made in the *Harris* cases that "Parliament is omnipotent".[95] Perhaps most significantly, he concluded by noting that the continued vitality of 'democratic'[96] principles in South Africa depended not on the courts, but on "an enlightened electorate".[97]

For the cabinet, such matters as reversing *Tayob* or reading betweeen the lines of the Chief Justice's abstract musings on constitutional principle were little more than fleeting distractions from the main business in hand—changing the personnel of the senate. And from the government's perspective at least, the 'electorate' charged with performing that particular task was to prove most 'enlightened'.

The new senate

Section 1 of the Senate Act had empowered the Governor-General to dissolve the senate at any time before the end of 1955. The power was promptly used after the bill was enacted, and 'elections' for the new senate were scheduled for November 1955. As might have been expected, the result of that election was that the new senate contained an overwhelming majority of Nationalist members. The United Party had decided not to boycott the senate, in contrast to its boycott of the High Court of Parliament. It took all eight of the Natal seats. Strauss had justified the policy on the grounds that in the (hugely unlikely) event that a handful of Nationalist MPs did not approve of abolition of the common roll, the presence of eight United Party Senators might be sufficient to deprive the government of the requisite two-thirds majority.[98]

Prior to the election, the Nationalists held twenty-nine of the senate's forty-eight seats—a majority of ten. After the election, it held seventy-seven of the new senate's eighty-nine seats—a majority of sixty-five. The total membership of the two houses prior to the election was 201, of whom 117 were Nationalists.

[95] *Ibid*. at 5 and 7.

[96] The Chief Justice manifestly adopted a narrow view of 'democracy'. That the bulk of South Africa's population was not afforded the right to vote was evidently not something he saw any need to discuss.

[97] *Ibid*. at 15. Some indication of how 'enlightened' the electorate might be was offered in August and September. Strauss had provoked a furore among opposition ranks by a statment in June that the United Party could not commit itself to reversing whatever measures the government took to disenfranchise coloured voters. Strauss was evidently making a technical point: if the Nationalists managed to destroy the entrenched clauses, the South Africa Act offered no way to restore them. Both Collins and Deane appreciated this point, and approved Strauss' statement; *Natal Daily News*, 14 June 1955. However, due primarily to his equivocal response to initial criticism of what he had said, his comment was widely taken to mean that a United Party government would not restore the common roll. One United Party backbencher, Dr Bernard Friedman, accused Strauss of weakness and prevarication and resigned his (safe) seat to fight a by-elction as an independent against a United Party candidate on the sole issue of restoring the common roll. Friedman lost the election, and in so doing handed a valuable propaganda tool to the Nationalists: *Cape Argus*, 16 June 1955; *Cape Times*, 17 June 1955; *Rand Daily Mail*, 18 August 1955.

[98] *Cape Times*, 11 June 1955.

The newly enlarged parliament contained 241 members in all, of whom 166 were Nationalists. It now seemed that Strijdom could command a two-thirds majority in a unicameral sitting of 'parliament'. The government wasted little time in putting this supposition to the test.

II. THE SOUTH AFRICA ACT AMENDMENT ACT 1956

The Governor-General convened a joint session of the house and senate for February 1956. The matter before the joint session was the government's South Africa Act Amendment bill. The preamble observed that the measure would be passed in accordance with section 152 of the South Africa Act. The bill had just five clauses, and would occupy barely a page of the parliamentary roll. It was both clear in its terms and straightforward in its intended effects.

Clause 1 proposed that *Harris No. 1* should be overruled with retrospective effect:

> "The Separate Representation of Voters Act 1951 . . . shall have the force of law with effect from the date of commencement of this Act, which date shall for all purposes be deemed to be the date of commencement of the first aforementioned Act".[99]

Clause 2 addressed the 'testing right' of the Supreme Court, and appeared to affirm that the court had such powers in respect of the constitution's two remaining[100] entrenched provisions:

> "No court of law shall be competent to enquire into or pronounce upon the validity of any law passed by Parliament other than a law which alters or purports to alter or repeal the provisions of section *one hundred and thirty-seven* or *one hundred and fifty-two* of the South Africa Act 1909".

The bill was greeted by a headline in the *Cape Argus* which announced that the retention of two of the entrenched clauses, coupled with an explicit recognition of the courts' testing power in relation to those sections of the constitution, represented a "Big Compromise by Nationalists on the Sovereignty Issue".[101] The *Argus* also commissioned a series of articles by Profesor Cowen, in which, drawing heavily on American examples, he laid out the case for the principle of a judicial power to review legislation against constitutional yardsticks. The *Cape Times* couched its opposition to the bill in terms which hinted at a shift towards a more radical understanding of democracy than it had previously adopted. Its leader on 14 February argued that:

[99] The retrospective nature of the Act would mean that, if it were upheld by the courts, the separate roll would come into immediate existence, since the anticipated general election (referred to in the 1951 Act and held in 1953) had already occurred.

[100] The expectation being that s.35 of the constitution would have been removed by s.1 of this Act.

[101] 3 February 1956.

"A system like that in the Union where there is democracy for whites and varying degrees of authoritarian government for non-whites is unstable in practice and morally indefensible in a country which proclaims itself Christian".[102]

The government's evident indifference to English language press coverage of the bill was, however, forcefully illustrated by the staging of yet another house debate lambasting the biased and subversive nature of its coverage of political issues.[103] Strauss could therefore be assured of substantial media support when he asserted that: "The attitude of the United Party remains one of determined opposition and we shall fight the measure with all the vigour and skill at our command".[104]

The joint sitting

That the United Party commanded insufficient vigour and skill to sway the cabinet from its chosen course was not in doubt. Strijdom, opening the debate, quickly took the opportunity to reiterate the 'divine basis' of the government's mission:

"Our attitude is that, subject only to the supreme sovereignty of God, Parliament, as the instrument of the people through which they give expression to their will and desires in the political sphere, is the highest authority, so far as State institutions are concerned, to which all, and consequently also the courts, are and must be subordinate".[105]

The session had barely begun when disorder erupted in the public gallery. Members of Black Sash had started a silent picket of the parliament buildings

[102] Three days later, its leader offered the curious suggestion that the government had embraced racism, at least against Coloureds, as a matter of practical rather than 'principled' politics; "If by any chance it had happened that the large majority of the coloured voters voted Nationalist, we should not have had the High Court of Parliament swindle, this Senate, the present Appeal Court or this dreary joint sitting".

[103] Strauss had denounced the government's attacks on the press as hypocritical. Recalling Verwoerd's role as editor of *Die Transvaaler* during the Second World War, when he was found to have falsified news stories (see pp. 214–216 above), Strauss remarked that Verwoerd's subsequent elevation to the senate indicated that the government did not consider a regard for the truth as a necessary element of the journalist's ethical code. He subsequently provoked a furore on the government benches by observing that becoming a senator was "in those days [1948; i.e. before the passing of the Senate Act] an honourable position"; *Cape Times*, 3 February 1956.

[104] *Cape Argus*, 3 February 1956.

[105] *Joint Sitting of Both Houses of Parliament* (hereafter *JS*) 15 February 1956, c. 40. The 'will and desires' of the Afrikaaner people on matters of race relations were chillingly illustrated by a story run in the *Cape Times* and *Cape Argus* on 2 February . Two white farmers had been convicted of beating two black workers to death. The trial judge in the Griqualand West local division, Diemont J., told the acused that "You have not the slightest right to assault your labourers in this fashion. We are not living in an age of slavery". The conviction, however, was for culpable homicide, not murder. The sentences imposed were four and six month gaol terms, suspended for three years, and fines of £100 and £150. That the prosecuting authorities had not sought a murder conviction, and the laughable sentence imposed by the judge, indicated that 'the age of slavery' may have passed *de jure*, but *de facto* it retained considerable influence on the legal system at local levels.

several days before legislative proceedings began. On the first day of debate, a small contingent of Black Sash activists had quietly pinned sashes to their dresses as Strijdom rose to speak, and were forcibly ejected from the gallery. The women were eventually permitted to return—but were not allowed to wear their sashes.[106]

The *Natal Mercury*, an English language daily paper,[107] had run a highly critical editorial on 14 February 1956 in response to the joint sitting, which argued that "This is not a Parliament as we have been brought up to know it".[108] This was met by a threat from the Speaker that its press privileges within the house and senate would be withdrawn. The threat was sufficient for the newspaper to apologise shortly afterwards.[109]

The joint sitting lasted for two weeks. The speeches made by government ministers, Nationalist backbenchers and members of the opposition traversed familiar ground, as did the English language press' coverage of the bill's passage. The outcome was of course never in doubt. The South Africa Act Amendment Act was passed at third reading by the necessary two-thirds majority. Once again, the controversy was removed to the courts.

III. THE *COLLINS* LITIGATION

Strauss had announced on 14 February that the United Party would support a court action challenging the legality of the Senate Act and/or the 1956 legislation. By mid-1956, when proceedings were initiated, only one of the four original *Harris* plainitffs was continuing the litigation. Mr Collins had decided not to challenge the constitutionality of the Appellate Quorum Act. There was little scope to argue that the expanded Appellate Division was not a 'court' in the sense identified by four of the judges in *Harris No. 2*. Schreiner's suggestion in that case that even a 'proper' court might be regarded as unconstitutional if it had been created to undermine entrenched rights was considered too flimsy a base on which to build a challenge to the Act.[110]

[106] Spink, n. 72 above, pp. 40–41.

[107] The *Mercury* was an independent paper, not part either of the Argus or Rand Daily Mail groups.

[108] Quoted in Marshall, n. 3 above, p. 236.

[109] Brookes and Macaulay, n. 5 above, p. 87: E. Potter, *The Press as Opposition* (London: Chatto and Windruss, 1975), p. 158: *Cape Argus* 21 February 1956.

[110] Had Collins pursued this option, several intriguing jurisdictional questions would have arisen. One might have asked firstly *which* 'Appellate Division' was competent to hear an eventual appeal. If it was the eleven-man court, would the new appointees have had to disqualify themselves from hearing the case on the grounds that they had a personal interest in its outcome? If the answer to those two questions was 'Yes', could the 'new' Appellate Division have raised a quorum of eleven to hear the appeal? If it could not, presumably the Act's fate would have been settled by whatever decision was offered at first instance. Alternatively, it might be suggested that any such challenge to the Act would have had to have been heard by the 'old' five-man Appellate Division. See May (1955) *op. cit.* pp. xiii-xiv.

Something of Schreiner's method nonetheless informed the strategy that Collins eventually decided to adopt. Collins was once again represented by Graeme Duncan, D.B. Molteno and Harry Snitcher. His challenge presented the Senate Act and the South Africa Act Amendment Act as interlinked legislation. While they might, as free-standing measures, be immune from constitutional challenge, they should properly be seen as simply parts of an overall scheme to 'render nugatory' the voting rights entrenched in section 35. In essence, Collins' argument was that the passage of the 1956 Act revealed that the 1955 Act had no purpose other than to furnish the government with a two-thirds unicameral majority. As such, it could itself only have been passed by the two-thirds majority procedure.[111]

The implications of this argument were far-reaching. Narrowly construed, it would mean that the new senate was not a 'senate' for the purposes of sitting in joint session to amend or repeal sections 35, 137 or 152 of the constitution. In consequence, the 1956 Act was void as it had not been enacted in accordance with the entrenched clauses. Broadly construed, the argument suggested that South Africa was currently without a 'senate' at all, in which case no new legislation on any topic could be enacted.[112]

Andries Beyers was no longer acting as lead counsel for the government. His loyal if unsuccessful service during *Harris Nos. 1 and 2* had been rewarded with an appointment to the Cape bench in 1955. Swart had bestowed the same gift on J.T. Van Wyk, who had assisted Beyers in the earlier cases. D.P. de Villiers, the junior member of the government's legal team in *Harris Nos. 1 and 2*, served as lead counsel for the Minister.

The first instance judgment

The Cape provincial division delivered its judgment on 18 May 1956. The case was heard by a three-man court; Jean Etienne De Villiers J.P. and Newton Thompson and Van Winsen JJ. The court unanimously dismissed Mr Collins' argument.[113] It held that the Senate Act was a measure that was clearly within the competence of 'parliament' acting bicamerally. That the motive underlying the Act, and its subsequent indirect effect, was to create a two-thirds majority for the government in a unicameral sitting was immaterial. It was no part of the court's constitutional role to invoke considerations of motive to invalidate

[111] Cf. May (1955), n. 28 above, p. xii: "The intention of the Framers of the South Africa Act was that Parliament, both in the Assembly and in the Senate, should reflect in a substantially fair degree the political opinion of the country; not to create an artificial two-thirds majority when nothing like a two-thirds majority exists in the electorate".

[112] This latter construction does not seem to have been seriously embraced by any participants in or commentators on the litigation or the Acts which preceded it.

[113] Once again, the judgment was not fully reported in the law reports. A summary is provided at [1956] 3 SALR 511. For comment on the judgment see Mulligan, n. 30 above. For a verbatim record of the judgment see the *Cape Argus*, 18 May 1956; *Cape Times*, 19 May 1956.

legislation whose 'pith and substance' fell squarely within the powers of a bicameral legislature.

The presentation of the opinion in itself represented a break with tradition, insofar as the court issued a single opinion signed by all three judges. Hitherto, unanimous judgments were arrived at by the device of judges concurring in the opinion of the judge who authored their decision. Strijdom was unconcerned by such technical niceties. For his government, it was the substance of the judgment that counted. In a press release issued shortly after the decision was given, he announced that the government was "pleased with the judgment and hoped that it would bring about finality and stability in the constitutional issue that has arisen as a result of the 1952 decision of the Appeal Court".[114] Strijdom's hope for finality was misplaced: the case was promptly removed for further consideration by the Appellate Division.

The Appellate Division

Centlivres remained as Chief Justice when *Collins* was argued before the Appellate Division on 15–19 October 1956: judgment was issued on 9 November.[115] Of the other judges who had sat in *Harris No. 2*, Schreiner and Hoexter also sat in *Collins*. They were joined by Fagan, Steyn and the six 'second team' appointees. The Chief Justice himself was to deliver the majority judgment, which eight of his ten colleagues supported.

The hearing

The hearing began on 15 October. De Beer J. immediately caused some consternation during de Villiers' opening argument by revealing his discussions with Swart prior to his appointment. De Villiers QC intimated that the government was prepared to argue that *Harris No. 1* was wrongly decided. De Beer thereupon interjected, asking counsel: "Are you aware that certain members of this Court accepted appointment on the clear understanding that the propriety of that judgment would not be attacked".[116]

De Beer did not indicate whether these 'certain members' included all six of the new Appellate judges, but his comments were sufficient to confirm that Swart's protestations during the passage of the Appellate Division Quorum bill that the new judges were wholly independent of the government—and so might uphold *Harris No. 1* should it be the subject of future challenge—were simply a lie.

Following De Beer's comment, de Villiers sought instruction from the government. He subsequently informed the court that he had been explicitly

[114] *Rand Daily Mail*, 19 May 1956.
[115] [1957] (1) SA 552.
[116] *Cape Argus*, 15 October 1956.

instructed not to question the correctness of *Harris No. 1* unless asked to do so by the court, and apologised that he had alluded to the issue at all, thereby bringing the first day of the hearing to what the *Rand Daily Mail's* court reporter characterised as "an extraordinary and dramatic conclusion".[117]

Duncan began his argument by referring to a 'packed' senate. He was promptly pulled up on this nomenclature by Schreiner:

Schreiner: "When you use the word 'packed' it may have an emotional content. I understand it to mean an ad hoc Senate".
Duncan: "That is so my Lord".
Schreiner: "Better to use a colourless expresion".[118]

Schreiner and Duncan thereafter engaged in what Duncan referred to as a 'philsophical' debate about the reach of parliament's power, including the question of whether it had the power to abolish itself. Steyn and de Villiers JJ.A. chose a more prosaic line of questioning. In their view, the crucial issue seemed to be whether the court had any power to look beyond the text of the Senate Act in order to discern its purpose. Duncan maintained that the Court was entitled to "strip the Act of words to get at its true essence",[119] an approach to the interpretive function which Steyn himself had traditionally shown some inclination to embrace, albeit only when such a technique produced an outcome in the government's favour.[120]

De Beer made clear during the course of Duncan's argument that he had little sympathy with Collins' suggestion that the courts should not permit the government to circumvent section 35's provisions. He suggested that the fact that voting rights had not been substantively entrenched indicated that the Framers of the constitution had not regarded their preservation as a 'solemn undertaking':[121]

> "What solemnity is there in the guarantee when the Act envisages and lays down the procedure for removing the Cape Coloured voters from the roll? That being so, would there be a solemn guarantee? Was it not simply political subterfuge? What I am saying is that their consciences must have been elastic".[122]

Such imputations of subterfuge and elasticity would seem quite accurate in respect of at least some of the delegates at the Convention. More pertinently in

117 *Rand Daily Mail*, 16 October 1956.

118 *Cape Argus*, 15 October 1956.

119 *Ibid*.

120 See p. 299 above.

121 De Beer was of course in error in not recognising that the rights of existing voters were so protected by s.35. This point, which is expressed with perfect clarity in the text of the South Africa Act, had been made by the Appellate Division in *Ndobe*. De Beer was however in good company in perpetuating this misunderstanding. As noted above, the first instance courts and the Appellate benches in both *Ndlwana* and *Harris No. 1* had failed to accept the principle of substantive entrenchment for the franchise rights of existing voters.

122 Cited in Mulligan, n. 30 above, p. 10. As Mulligan observed, De Beer's approach suggested that observers of the Convention's proceedings were left with the unpalatable choice of concluding that the constitution's framers were either 'incredibly stupid' or 'incredibly dishonest'; *ibid*.

the present circumstances, they indicated that even if De Beer was prepared to accept that the court should follow the intention of the framers of the constitution, his own interpretation of that intention was unlikely to lead him to find the Senate Act unlawful. His colleagues in the second team made few contributions to the discussion.

Judicial questioning of de Villiers' argument came almost wholly from 'the first team'. Hoexter pressed him on whether the government's argument in this case necessarily implied that the equal language rights still 'entrenched' in the consitution could also be removed by a dual sitting involving the expanded senate. De Villiers conceded that this assumption was correct.[123]

Fagan's concern was to establish if the government accepted there was any objective criteria against which to assess if a 'senate' was a 'true senate' within the meaning of the constitution. De Villiers agreed that there must be such criteria, but he could not assist Fagan in suggesting what they might be. He was equally reticent when asked by Centlivres: "If Parliament were to pass an Act abolishing the present Senate and setting up a new one consisting of 100 members put there by the majority party, would that be a Senate"? In reply, De Villiers could say only: "It may not. I cannot now give an exact answer".[124] Graeme Duncan interjected at this point, offering a negative definition of a senate (and seemingly forgetting Schreiner's earlier advice regarding nomenclature): "The essential character of a Senate is that it is not a packed Senate".[125] De Villiers QC was rather more forthcoming to Centlivres' hypothetical question as to whether a legislative attempt to add 100 government nominees to the house would mean that the house was no longer a 'house of assembly'. de Villiers was willing to accept the absence of an electoral basis for membership might lead to this conclusion.[126] The apparent scepticism which Centlivres, Schreiner, Hoexter and Fagan displayed towards de Villiers' argument may have indicated to some observers when argument ended on 19 October that the Court was likely to split seven to four in favour of the government when judgment was handed down, thereby re-igniting the controversy over whether or not the Appellate Division Quorum Act had created a 'packed' court. Such indications were, however, to prove quite misleading.

The majority opinion

The Court's judgment was issued on 9 November, at a time when the attention of both the English and Afrikaaner language press, and indeed of the government and opposition, was focused primarily on foreign events: the Soviet Union had just invaded Hungary, while the French and British governments had embarked upon their ill-fated military intervention in the Suez crisis.

[123] *Cape Argus*, 17 October 1956.
[124] *Rand Daily Mail*, 17 October 1956.
[125] *Ibid.*
[126] *Ibid.*

Centlivres began his judgment by briefly reviewing the history of the *Harris* controversy. He then observed that neither the Senate Act nor the South Africa Act Amendment Act, if construed as separate statutes, could be regarded as invalid. The Senate Act did not *per se* alter section 35 or section 152 of the South Africa Act, and while the 1956 Act did have this effect, it had been passed in evident conformity with the entrenched provisions. There could not however be any doubt that:

> "the sole reason why the membership of the Senate was increased was because it was desired to provide the Government with a two thirds majority at a joint sitting of the two houses".[127]

While this conclusion was beyond doubt, Centlivres also observed that it was of little relevance to the present litigation. If parliament sitting bicamerally had plenary power to restructure the senate in any way it wished, its motives for so doing were not an issue on which the court was competent to pass judgment.

It was clear that the bicameral parliament's powers under section 25 were subject to the section 152 provisions. A bicameral parliament could not, for example, pass legislation which limited membership of the senate only to Afrikaans or English speakers. Such a measure would contravene section 137, and would therefore have to enacted by the unicameral procedure. The Senate Act 1955 did not however have any such effect.

The Chief Justice then turned to Graeme Duncan's suggestion that the 1956 Act was invalid because the two-thirds majority it had received in the joint sitting included the votes of a senate which had been 'artificially created' solely to furnish such a majority. Centlivres promptly rejected the argument, noting that "I know of no authority for justifying such a construction".[128]

This might seem a curious rationale for Centlivres to adopt. There would manifestly not be any South African authority for that contention, since the circumstances had never before arisen. One might equally suggest that there was no authority for the conclusion that the majority of the Appellate Division had reached in *Harris No. 2*, but that had not precluded Centlivres from reaching it.

Centlivres' evident wish to see a lack of authority as an obstacle to Collins' case rather than an opportunity for it to be made was indicative of what seemed to be a markedly more conservative jurisprudential approach than the one he had favoured in *Harris No. 2*.[129] His judgment in *Harris No. 2* had effectively rested on two principles that he found to be implied in section 152. The first

[127] [1957] (1) AD 552 at 565.

[128] *Ibid*. at 556.

[129] There was also a noticeable shift in the terminology that the Chief Jusice used in *Collins*. As noted in Chapter 9, Centlivres in *Harris No. 1* had referred constantly to 'the South Africa Act' rather than 'the constitution'. In *Harris No. 2*, he had spoken unfaiingly of the 'constitution'. In *Collins*, he reverted to 'the South Africa Act'. The word 'constitution' does not appear in his judgment at all. There is no obvious explanation for the change. One might speculate that it was an oblique attempt to imply that the government's manoeuvrings had deprived South Africa of a constitution in any meaningful sense, and merely reduced its fundamental laws to the status of ordinary legislation.

implication was that the entrenched rights had to be protected by a court. The second was that 'a court' possessed certain objective criteria which the High Court of Parliament lacked. However he was not willing to accept that section 152 contained any such implied restraints on the composition and role of the senate. While a 'court' had to be independent of the executive and legislature, and be composed of members learned in the law, a 'senate' need not be an elected body at all, still less a body that was broadly representative of electoral opinion in the country at large. 'Senate' was evidently a label that was devoid of objective, constitutional meaning:

> "[I]t cannot in my opinion be said that the reconstituted Senate is not a Senate in the ordinary sense of the word. Even if the Senate Act had reconstituted the Senate by enacting that the Senate should consist entirely of Government supporters whose names were set forth in the Act it would still have been a Senate within the meaning of . . . s. 152".[130]

The plaintiff was in error, the Chief Justice continued, in assuming that his judgment in *Harris No. 2* was of any assistance in this case. The Senate Act had not rendered Mr Collins' entrenched rights 'nugatory' in the same way that the High Court of Parliament Act had done. That Act had launched a direct assault on section 35. The Senate Act, in contrast, threatened section 35 in an indirect way: "A further legislative step had to be taken in order to destroy appellant's rights and that step was in conformity with the proviso to section 152".[131]

That the 'further step' was part of a legislative scheme was of no constitutional significance:

> "The conclusion at which I arrive on the whole case is that the legislative scheme which was adopted is not open to attack in law. Each step taken in the scheme was taken in accordance with the provisions of the South Africa Act and the scheme as a whole was designed in such a way that [the Separate Representation of Voters Act] would be validated in accordance with . . . ss. 35 and 152 of the South Africa Act".[132]

Steyn's concurrence

Steyn agreed with the result that the majority reached, but chose to offer a brief opinion of his own. He began by observing—correctly but unnecessarily—that procedural entrenchment did not create immutable rights, but rather left those rights at the mercy of a two-thirds parliamentary majority. He could not however find any indication in the text of the Constitution[133] that parliament for those purposes was anything other than the house and senate as they happened to be defined by bicameral legislation at the time of the joint sitting. If the app-

[130] [1957] (1) AD 552 at 567.
[131] *Ibid.* at 569.
[132] *Ibid.* at 570.
[133] In marked contrast to Centlivres, Steyn referred throughout his judgment to the 'Constitution', and never to the 'South Africa Act'.

pellant's argument was correct, enormous difficulties would be placed in the path of any (bicameral) parliamentary attempt to modify the composition of either the house or the senate, be it through the redrawing of constituency boundaries, a change in the voting system or a (non-racial) change in the franchise qualification. This suggested that entrenchment was underpinned more by political than legal mechanisms. Steyn suggested that Collins' argument meant if the indirect effect of any such measure was to weaken the protection afforded to section 35 rights, the court would be obliged to hold that it could be passed only by a two-thirds unicameral majority. Steyn's argument was premised on a substantial misrepresentation of the contentions that Graeme Duncan had made, but was indicative of Steyn's evident predisposition to see the continued vitality of the entrenched provisions as a matter for the political rather than legal sphere of the constitution. This he suggested, was a perfectly plausible reading of the intentions of the framers of the constitution:

> "[T]he constituent Legislature . . . may well have considered that the sanctions of the electorate would provide an adequate and more appropriate curb for the purposes which the limitation in question would serve".[134]

Schreiner's dissent

Schreiner had indicated in *Harris No. 2* that his perception of the constitutional rationale underpinning the entrenched clauses required the Appellate Division fiercely to question the merits of any bicameral legislation which appeared to threaten their effectiveness. In *Harris No. 2*, Schreiner implied that even a 'court' that was created bicamerally for the purposes of overriding sections 35, 137 and 152 would not be competent to pass judgment on the constitutionality of bicameral legislation which removed or abridged entrenched rights. In *Collins*, he argued that this methodology was as applicable to a 'senate' as it was to a 'court':

> "the crucial issue is whether 'Houses of Parliament' in the second proviso to s.152 includes a House created by Parliament *ad hoc*, that is in order to produce by nomination or similar device a two-thirds majority at a joint sitting".[135]

Schreiner did not accept that the new senate was in all senses a 'senate' simply because the 1955 Act identified it as such. He saw no obstacle to parliament (acting bicamerally) endowing any institution with the status of a senate for the purposes of enacting future legislation through the bicameral process:

> "But in respect of matters falling within [s.152] any legislative action which detrimentally affects the position of those who are entitled to the protection of ss. 35 and 137

[134] *Ibid.* at 585. One might wonder if Steyn had read Centlivres' Harvard speech, in which the Chief Justice had referred to 'an enlightened electorate' as the ultimate guarantor of constitutional values; see p. 359 above.

[135] *Ibid.* at 571.

> must conform to the requirements of [s.152], as a matter of substance and not merely as a matter of form".[136]

The inquiry as to substance could not be answered simply by examining the texts of the constitution and the 1955 and 1956 Acts. Rather, it demanded that the court examine the circumstances which had led to the passage of the Acts in question. Those circumstances clearly revealed a persistent effort by the government to reverse, *de facto* if not *de jure*, the Appellate Division's decision in *Harris No. 1* and thereby 'render nugatory' the section 35 voting rights.

In contrast to the position adopted by Centlivres, Schreiner insisted that section 152 impliedly required that a senate for section 35 and section 152 purposes had to possess certain "objective qualities".[137] He did not specify what these 'objective qualities' were. He was neverthless sure that an *ad hoc* senate could not possess them, and suggested that he drew this conclusion from the intentions of the framers of the constitution:

> "[S.152] was intended to furnish a real and not merely a theoretical protection against Parliamentary majorities acting bicamerally. *Prima facie*, the framers of the Constitution did not intend that Parliament, that is, in effect, the Government acting through its majority, should have the power by bicameral legislation to convert an insufficient majority into a sufficient one, merely by invoking the procedure of nomination or its equivalent".[138]

Like Centlivres, Schreiner accepted that there was no authority governing the issue of whether or not parliament acting bicamerally could achieve through a legislative scheme of several nominally discrete 'Acts' an objective it could not achieve through a single measure. But while the Chief Justice assumed that the lack of authority meant that parliament could do so, Schreiner drew the opposite conclusion. A 'piecemeal approach' did not shield the component parts of such a legislative scheme from the taint of invalidity. Such a strategy on 'parliament's' part was no more than "a scheme to defraud": to allow it to succeed would "surrender substance to form": "the Court", he suggested, "should not easily be persuaded that the Constitution contains so obvious a weakness".[139] In substance, the Senate Act 1955 and the South Africa Act Amendment Act 1956 were one piece of legislation.

Schreiner indicated that Steyn was incorrect in assuming that acceptance of this argument precluded any bicameral reform of the composition of either the house or the senate. Such a reform which did not disclose, either on its face or in the circumstances of its enactment, that it was part of a scheme to circumvent the entrenched clauses would not subsequently be rendered invalid just because

[136] [1957] (1) AD 552 at 572.

[137] *Ibid.* at 573.

[138] *Ibid.* at 574. In contrast to the position adverted to by De Beer during oral argument (see n. 122 above), Schreiner's view requires observers to assume that the framers of the constitution were neither stupid nor dishonest.

[139] *Ibid.* at 574, 575 and 576 respectively.

it had enabled a government to muster a previously non-existent two-thirds majority. The question of invalidity only arose where there was a direct and immediate linkage between the various Acts concerned. Had a bicameral parliament passed the Senate Act in 1955, and had some substantial time elapsed before a unicameral parliament passed the South Africa Act Amendment Act, neither Act would necessarily be regarded as invalid.

Yet on the facts disclosed by the *Collins* case, there was no doubt that the 1955 and 1956 were interlinked parts of an overall legislative plan to evade section 152. As such, the 1956 Act was an unconstitutional piece of legislation because it had not been passed by a unicameral sitting of the two houses of parliament in the sense required by section 152.

Reaction to the judgments

Strijdom greeted the judgment with restrained approval. In a speech to party members at Nylstrom, he announced that the government was "thankful that an end has come to a long and difficult struggle and that our difficult task has eventually been successfully fulfilled".[140] With a view perhaps to placing his own manouevres in the pantheon of boer history, Strijdom indicated that the 'struggle' had begun not with *Harris No. 1*, but with Kotze C.J.'s judgment in *Brown v Leyds* some sixty years earlier. Whether through mendacity or incomprehension, Strijdom persisted in casting 'the struggle' in terms of establishing the legal supremacy of 'parliament' over the courts. He refused to accept the 'two parliaments' thesis. He also noted that it was 'very interesting' and 'very important' that three of the four remaining *Harris No. 1* judges had decided *Collins* in the government's favour.

Strauss was careful not to criticise the Appellate Division for upholding the Senate Act. Rather he condemned the Act itself as a measure which had done "a grave injustice to the coloured people".[141] He also intimated that the United Party might be preparing to adopt a more liberal stance on electoral matters: "It is our duty to create an upper house which will be truly democratic and representative of the people of South Africa, not of one section, no matter what their colour or creed".[142]

The *Cape Argus* greeted the judgment with a leader titled "Triumph is failure".[143] It suggested that even within the limited sphere of the white political community, South Africa could no longer be regarded as a democratic society:

> "Why limit this form of representation to the Senate? Why not double the number of members of Parliament and include in the Cabinet all members of the *Broederbond*? Why not give the Nationalist Party all the seats in a province if it wins a majority of

[140] *The Friend*, 27 November 1956.
[141] *Cape Argus*, 12 November 1956.
[142] *Ibid.*
[143] 10 November 1956.

> them? A Government so little concerned about providing a one party state cannot be too scrupulous about other steps they may have to take in future to keep in power".

The *Rand Daily Mail* relegated its report of the judgment to the bottom right-hand corner of its front page: its lead stories focused on the escalating crises in Hungary and Suez. The paper made no criticism of the judgment itself, regarding the majority's opinion as a necessary acquiescence to the letter of the law. It nonetheless spoke warmly of Schreiner's dissent: "It may not express the law, but it does show knowledge of the facts of life".[144]

Members of Black Sash attacked the government in more tangible ways. A note was pinned to Strydom's office door in the parliament building, which announced, in terms reminiscent of Zola's famous letter during the Dreyfus Affair that:

> "We accuse you the Prime Minister and your cabinet of destroying the constitution of the Union and destroying all faith in the honour of white South Africa. We women of South Africa accuse you of these crimes against our country. Your lust for power has betrayed South Africa".[145]

In contrast to their copious reporting of Black Sash activities, neither the *Cape Times*, the *Rand Daily Mail* nor the *Cape Argus* offered any extensive coverage of the Coloured community's reaction to the judgment. This seems to be because by this point most non-white political activists, along with radical white opinion, regarded the case as an irrelevance. By late 1956, *The Guardian* (having been shut down by Swart under the Suppression of Communism Act) was appearing as the *New Age*. Its October and November issues carried no coverage at all either of the hearing or the judgment.[146] The ANC's energies at this time were directed towards organising a major trans-racial conference in Blomfontein to protest against the government's apparent wish, following the publication of the Tomlinson Report, to accelerate and intensify segregation in land occupation and employment.[147] The conference attracted delegates from several hundred organisations, and called for an inter-racial United Front to oppose government policy. It was dismissed as an irrelevance by *Die Transvaaler*, which reported that it was attended merely by "a number of Natives and a couple of Europeans".[148]

144 10 November 1956.

145 *Cape Argus*, 10 November 1956.

146 A long article under the headline 'A Day at Court' in the 1 November issue dealt not with *Collins* but with a typical day's proceedings in the Cape Town Magistrates Court.

147 On Tomlinson see p. 235 above, n. 32.

148 8 October 1956. The ANC's deliberations were, in contrast, approvingly received in the *Cape Times*. The conference was praised for being "commendably objective in its study of the [Tomlinson] report: its reasons for rejection were calmly stated and closely argued". The paper was also warmly approving of the ANC's evident disiclination to seek to replace white domination with black domination: "It is remarkable that, in the present political climate, these leaders should still be capable of exercising this restraint on their people . . . But this restraint cannot for ever be proof against repressive legislation and the contemptuous deafness of white authority": 11 October 1956.

In Britain, the judgment received extended coverage and comment in *The Times*. As well as reviewing the judgments in some detail, *The Times* devoted its leader to the case, under the title 'Disentrenchment'. The leader described the Senate Act device as "a way of defeating the intention of the lawmakers . . . the National Convention of 1908 . . . without transgressing the form of the law". The judgment, which the paper thought the Court had little choice but to produce, represented the culmination "of a course of tortuous sharp practice pursued from one unscrupulous device to another over a period of five years".[149] The *Daily Telegraph* ran a short feature article on the case, in which it criticised the judgment as an "unhappy decision" and, warning that it was "dangerous to build a state without a safety valve", predicted that Coloureds would now be more readily inclined to find common cause with native blacks in increasingly militant opposition to the government. The *Manchester Guardian*, preoccupied with its coverage of Suez and Hungary, made no comment on the case, and devoted only a few lines to reporting the judgment.

In academic circles, both in South Africa and abroad, the government's strategy and the Appellate Division's response attracted an equivocal reception. G.H. Le May, Professor of Local Government and Public Administration at the University of the Witwatersrand, greeted *Collins* as an indicator of "a transformation in the constitutional structure of the Union".[150] It was a transformation, he suggested, that lacked legitimacy from either an abstract or practical perspective. Le May was concerned primarily to address Strijdom's claim that the government enjoyed a 'mandate' for its legislation. That the government did not enjoy the support of an electoral majority dealt a severe blow to this claim,[151] but the doctrine itself rested on deeply flawed foundations:

> "In the first place it assumes a static society, in which political problems and their answers are clearly discernible . . . and can be answered by a simple negative or affirmative. It assumes an all-knowing electorate, which has considered all questions fully and disinterestedly. It assumes that a single cross upon a ballot paper is an indication that a voter has endorsed each item upon a political programme. All these assumptions are without foundation".[152]

In Le May's view, recent events in South Africa had confirmed that the reality of the mandate doctrine was that it provided an oligarchic cabal within the governing party with an ostensibly convincing legitimator for the enactment of its own political preferences. 'The will of the people' had no objective, ascertainable existence. Rather it functioned as a mantra which a party commanding a bare parliamentary majority might invoke to attack the propriety of

[149] 10 November 1956.

[150] 'Parliament, the Constitution and the Doctrine of the Mandate' (1957) *South African LJ* 33 at 34.

[151] Rather like Centlivres' speech at Harvard, Le May's critique glossed over the fact that the South African electorate comprised barely 10% of the population.

[152] See n. 150 above, at 40.

any opposition, be it from within the legislature, in the courts, in the press or on the streets to any aspect of government policy.

H.R.W. Wade, writing in the *South African Law Journal*, was broadly supportive both of the government's strategy and the court's response.[153] As Donges had done in the house, Wade pointed to the government's threat to pack the House of Lords in 1832 and 1911 as offering a legitimate pedigree for the Senate Act. The majority on the court, he suggested had no choice but to deliver judgment upholding the 1956 Act. Schreiner's dissent, while deserving respect, was tainted with 'considerable artificiality'. For the majority to have adopted it would have compromised the court's reputation as 'a dispassionate arbiter' in the eyes of the public.

In contrast to Wade, Geoffrey Marshall, then a Fellow of Nuffield College, Oxford, and subsequently to become one of the foremost authorities on commonwealth constitutional law and practice, saw little merit in the majority's reasoning *in toto*, and none at all in Centlivres' efforts to distinguish the issue before the court in *Collins* from the one it faced in *Harris No. 2*.[154] Marshall was particularly perplexed by Centlivres' suggestion that the efficacy of the entrenched clauses was dependant upon political rather than legal forms of protection, given that the Court's judgment in *Harris No. 2* was premised largely on the assumption that the constitution demanded that the entrenched rights be afforded judicially enforceable safeguards. Marshall also suggested there was a marked inconsistency between Centlivres' willingess to look to the purpose and intention of the High Court of Parliament Act in *Harris No. 2* and his refusal to apply the same technique to the Senate Act in *Collins*.

Marshall appeared to see rather more merit in Schreiner's dissent, which he described as taking "a line which stands in sharp contrast to the majority view and has a closer affinity on the question of construction to the unanimous decision of the court in [*Harris No. 1*]".[155] This view was echoed by Mulligan, writing in the 1957 *South African Law Journal*, who characterised Schreiner's opinion as "well expressed and persuasive".[156]

Marshall concluded his analysis of the episode by characterising the *Collins* judgment as "a judicial withdrawal from the position established by the unanimous decisions of the Supreme Court bench of 1952".[157] So much is entirely clear. A rather more interesting question is why the three members of the first

[153] 'The Senate Act Case and the Entrenched Sections of the South Africa Act' (1957) *South African Law Journal* 160.

[154] See n. 3 above, esp. at pp. 242–248.

[155] *Ibid.* at p. 242.

[156] See n. 30 above, at p. 10. For a less flattering critique of the dissent, written with the benefit of many years of hindsight, see M. Wiechers, 'The Fundamental Laws Behind Our Constitution', in E. Kahn (ed.), *Fiat Iusticia: Essays in Memory of Oliver Deneys Schreiner* (Cape Town: Juta & Co, 1983). In Britain, Schreiner's dissent was dismissed as 'curiously obtuse' by Louis Blom-Cooper, then Legal Correspondent of the *Manchester Guardian*, in an appraisal of Schreiner's career published on his retirement in 1960: 30 December 1960.

[157] Marshall, n. 3 above, at p. 248. By 'Supreme Court', Marshall presumably meant the Appellate Division.

team did not align themselves with Schreiner, thereby producing the split in the government's favour which the United Party had predicted would arise during the passage of the Appellate division quorum legislation.[158] Writing some five years later, M.A. Millner of University College London found no answer to the question: "The explanation of the collapse of judicial resistance at this point is puzzling".[159] Millner, like Marshall, found the formal explanation of Centlivres' evident change of constitutional heart unconvincing.

Yet it is plausible to argue that Centlivres' 'withdrawal' was rooted solely in legalistic considerations. Marshall's point concerning the Chief Justice's refusal to look beyond the form of the legislation in *Collins* while having done so in *Harris No. 2* is soundly based in itself. However, it rather overlooks the fact that Centlivres used this technique in *Harris No. 2* only as a preliminary step. Having concluded that the purpose behind the High Court of Parliament Act was to reverse *Harris No. 1*, Centlivres then suggested that the final question to be answered was whether the 'High Court' was in fact a 'Court' at all. He could have applied precisely the same approach to the Senate Act and still have decided in the government's favour by concluding that the 'ad hoc' senate was nonetheless a senate.

But, as Marshall and Millner suggested, it is equally obviously the case that Centlivres could have answered that final question in *Collins* differently, and concluded a packed senate was not a senate for the purposes of amending or repealing the entrenched sections of the South Africa Act. As has been stressed repeatedly in the past four chapters, the tension between the Nationalist governments and the Appellate Division stemmed in part from the Court's refusal to allow ambiguities in statutory or constitutional texts and principles always, as seemed to be Steyn's instinctive preference, to be resolved in accordance with the government's wishes. As Schreiner's dissent in *Collins* made clear, that ambiguity had not wholly disappeared when that case reached the Court.

It is perhaps misleading to suggest that Centlivres underwent a change of heart between *Harris No. 2* and *Collins*. It would be more accurate to assume that the government had fashioned a constitutional device which was compatible with the Chief Justice's own understandings of legal principle. Centlivres' own papers, deposited at the University of Cape Town, do not contain any material relating to the *Harris* saga which might cast further light on his reasoning. Nor do such personal papers as have been left by other members of 'the first team' reveal a hitherto hidden explanation. A letter in Oliver Schreiner's archive from his sister Dot, dated 12 November 1956, conveyed disappointment but not surprise at the outcome of *Collins*:

> "I have just seen the report of the failure of the Senate Act appeal and your own dissenting judgment. I know how proud Dad would have been . . . I don't understand how you came to stand alone. I thought it would be five real judges against six bogus

[158] See p. 346 above.

[159] 'Apartheid and the South African Courts' (1961) *Current Legal Problems* 280 at 297.

ones. But I suppose Albert [Centlivres] saw things differently. He has always seemed to me absolutely honest and sincere".

Harry Snitcher, the only one of the counsel involved in the case still alive in 1998, had no doubt that all three cases were decided on strictly legal grounds,[160] a contention which gains considerable force when one considers that Snitcher was an active member of the Communist Party in the 1940s. There is nothing to support the contention that 'politics' in any crude party sense altered the way in which Centlivres, Hoexter and Fagan approached their task.[161]

IV. THE AFTERMATH

Centlivres remained on the court for only a short time after the *Collins* judgment. He retired from the bench in 1957. He did not retire wholly into obscurity, but retained a role in public life as Chancellor of the University of Cape Town. As Chancellor, he added his voice to the (rather lacklustre and wholly unsuccessful) campaign to dissuade the government from introducing *apartheid* into the university sector, a policy initiated by the absurdly named Extension of University Education Act 1959.[162] The demonic status he had acquired in the government's eyes was forcefully illustrated in 1964. Following allegations that political detainees were being tortured in prison, the United Party had urged the government to establish a Commission of Inquiry, chaired by Centlivres, to investigate the allegations. The proposal was scornfully rejected by the then Minister of Justice, John Vorster, who had openly been a Nazi supporter during the Second World War and had been imprisoned for treasonable activities by the Smuts government. Vorster maintained that Centlivres could not be trusted with such a responsibility: "Mr Centlivres associates with all the Leftist-Liberal groups. There is no doubt that Centlivres is a Leftist. He moves in ultra-liberal circles. The Liberal Party is his spiritual home".[163]

For Oliver Schreiner, the forceful dissent he offered in *Collins* carried a personal cost. On Centlivres' retirement, Schreiner was the senior appellate judge. On all previous occasions, the Chief Justiceship had passed to the longest serving member of the Court. There was no legal requirement that this be done, but successive governments appeared to have accepted the principle as an unshakeable convention of constitutional practice. It was not, however, unshakeable to the Strijdom government. Schreiner was passed over for the position. His papers

[160] Interview with David Borgstrom, July 1998.

[161] Both Harry Snitcher and Dennis Cowen nonetheless observed that, with the exception of Schreiner, the members of the 'first team' had by 1956 been considerably worn down by the government's continued antagonism towards them. Cowen recalls that Centlivres in particular aged visibly even in the short space of time between *Harris No. 1* and *No. 2*; interviews with Ian Loveland, August 1998.

[162] C. Merret, *A Culture of Censorship* (Pietermarizburg: University of Natal Press, 1994), pp. 32–33; A. Norval, *Deconstructing Apartheid Discourse* (London: Verso, 1996), pp. 134–135.

[163] *Rand Daily Mail*, 12 March 1964.

contain extensive correspondence from members of the legal profession and the public expressing outrage and sympathy at this turn of events. Ben Tindall described the decision as 'a grave injustice', while noting: "It is a consolation, to me at any rate, to know that you will be on the court for four more years to help save it from further deterioration". He also received commiserations from further afield:

Royal Courts of Justice
The Strand
London

My dear Oliver,

I have been meaning to write to you for a long time . . . I have seen with dismay that you have not been appointed to succeed Centlivres as Chief Justice. I say no more because I am not sure whether our letters to South Africa are opened—it is a pretty pass that I should have this feeling—so I will not write of the great issues in which you have participated.[164]

Yours,

Tom Denning

Hoexter, the next most senior judge, was also passed over, evidently because his judgments in *Harris Nos. 1 and 2* had made him extremely unpopular with the government.[165] His own view was apparently that the Appellate Division was beyond saving. In a letter to Schreiner, he wrote that there was considerable truth in a friend's suggestion that:

"the difference between you and me is that you want to help the Appellate Division to recover, whatever the circumstances may be, while I would prefer to let it go to pot in certain circumstances. I agree with you that the appointments in the Provincial Divisions over a period of six or seven years have been such that it will be very difficult to find suitable candidates for the Appellate Division".[166]

The post was eventually offered to Henry Fagan, the third most senior judge on the court. Fagan's initial reaction was to reject the offer, which he described in a letter to his wife as "a large shock . . . so unthinkable that [it] came like a bolt from the blue".[167] In a letter to Swart, he wrote:

"Your [offer] presents me with a very difficult choice. Judge Schreiner is not only the senior judge after the present Chief Justice, but he has also been a member of the Appellate Division for many years longer than me . . . Furthermore, there is the consideration that if I am appointed over his head just after the Senate case in which he

164 Denning to Schreiner, 2 January 1957.

165 See Forsyth, n. 21 above, pp. 25–28; E. Kahn, 'Oliver Deneys Schreiner—the Man and His Judicial World' (1980) *South African LJ* 566. Hoexter retired into relative obscurity, devoting much of his remaining energies to assisting blind South Africans to get enhanced access to library materials. Hoexter eventually died in 1970.

166 Hoexter to Schreiner, 1 April 1958: Schreiner papers.

167 Fagan Papers, letter dated 16 November 1956 (David Borgstrom's translation).

gave the only dissenting opinion, the impression will be created for the public that I have been rewarded and he is being punished for judicial attitudes which we expressed and which we both arrived at in honest belief".[168]

After discussions with Schreiner, Fagan decided to accept the post, largely it seems to prevent the mantle passing to Steyn, a scenario which Hoexter described some months later as "an unpleasant thought".[169] Centlivres had urged Fagan to reject the offer on the basis that to accept would in effect allow the government to use him to do "an ugly thing":

"He even came up with the plan that we all, the whole bunch of us judges, must decide that we would refuse the offer, to whomever it was made, as an effort to force the government's hand and to compel them to appoint Oliver".[170]

Fagan evidently thought the plan ridiculous. He nonetheless consulted with his colleagues. None of the new appointees would agree to the strategy. L.C. Steyn's opposition was particularly trenchant: "Lukas [Steyn] said . . . that Albert just wants to make a protest against the government . . . and it is not our job to prescribe to the government in matters that lie with them".[171] Fagan thus accepted the post with misgivings, which were reinforced by adverse press coverage in the *Sunday Express*: "I myself still feel as if my head is spinning—sick about Oliver, scared about the work and the responsibility, and unhappy while people (I rather want to hide from everyone) congratulate me with broad smiles and every post delivery brings a pack of congratulatory letters".[172] Fagan retired as Chief Justice in April 1959. He did not, however, leave public life, but decided to re-enter politics as the leader of the newly-founded National Union Party. The NUP was intended to provide a political home for Nationalist supporters who had been troubled by Strijdom's disregard for constitutional proprieties. It fought the 1961 election in an uneasy alliance with the United Party, but made no significant impact and rapidly disintegrated.[173] Fagan himself spent his final years sitting as a United Party senator, a postion he used to promulgate a moderate policy of racial conciliation which had strong echoes of the proposals he had made in the 1940s.[174]

Steyn received his 'reward' for his loyal service to the *apartheid* cause in 1959, when he was appointed Chief Justice following Fagan's retirement.[175] Schreiner was once again passed over for the appointment, as was Hoexter, who had by

[168] Fagan to Swart, 16 November 1956: Fagan papers.

[169] Hoexter to Schreiner, 30 April 1958: Schreiner papers.

[170] Letter from Fagan to his wife, 22 November 1956: Fagan papers (David Borgstrom's translation).

[171] *Ibid.*

[172] Letter from Fagan to his wife, 2 December 1956: Fagan papers (David Borgstrom's translation).

[173] Potter, n. 109 above, pp. 171–172.

[174] See his lengthy articles in the *Johannesburg Star*, 28 and 29 August 1962.

[175] Andries Beyers' fortunes proved similarly favourable. Having sat on the Cape provincial bench since 1955, he was subsequently elevated to the Appellate Division in 1959.

then also accumulated over ten years' service on the bench. Under Steyn's stewardship, the Appellate Division embarked upon a jurisprudential journey into craven deference to governmental preferences. In a long series of judgments dealing with race discrimination and civil liberties issues, Steyn's court jettisoned existing common law principles and designed new ones to minimise the possibility that a governmental action would be found to be beyond the powers granted by a particular statute.[176] In *Cassem v Oos-Kapse Komittee van die Groepsgebiederaad*,[177] Steyn held that members of an Indian community to be displaced following the designation of its neighbourhood as a whites-only locale under the Group Areas Act had no right to be heard by the decision-maker prior to the designation. Steyn's concern to facilitate the implementation of the Group Areas Act extended to matters of substance as well as procedure. In *Minister of the Interior v Lockhat*,[178] Steyn concurred in a judgment which held that parliament envisaged that applying the Act would impose substantial inequalities on particular groups of displaced residents, notwithstanding the fact that no such intention was expressed in the text of the legislation. Steyn also concurred in a series of majority judgments in the early 1960s which offered extremely expansive interpretations of the government's powers of detention under various pieces of emergency legislation aimed at liberal political activists. In *Roussow v Sachs*,[179] Steyn's court held that a detainee had no right to books or writing materials while in gaol. The Act concerned was silent on the point. The Court held that prisoners were impliedly denied such facilities; to grant them would relieve the tedium of detention and so reduce the intensity of the offender's punishment. Similarly, in *Schermbrucker v Klindt NO*, a majority held that it had no power to order gaolers to produce a prisoner on whose behalf it was alleged that he was being subjected to continuing torture: "interference with that detention which may negative the inducement to speak is likely to defeat the purpose of the legislature".[180]

In the context of a continuing curtailment of civil liberties even within the limited confines of the white community, the United Party itself became an evermore declining force in South African politics:

> "The acquiescence of the Opposition in the system on which the government's legitimacy was founded, in addition to the fundamental agreement about principles, left the Opposition without purpose or policy, and it became a minority party with diminishing relevance. Even within the framework of White politics, it ceased to be a political Opposition; it offered no credible alternative to the government".[181]

[176] The brief selection of cases that follows is drawn primarily from the extended critique offered in E. Cameron, 'Legal Chauvinism, Executive-Mindedness and Justice—L.C. Steyn's Impact on South African Law' (1982) 99 *South African LJ* 38.

[177] [1959] 3 SA 651 (A).

[178] [1961] 2 SA 587 (A).

[179] [1964] 2 SA 551 (A). The prisoner was Albie Sachs, the son of Solly Sachs.

[180] [1965] 4 SA 606 at 619; quoted in Cameron, n. 176 above, at p. 58.

[181] Potter, n. 109 above, p. 26.

Strauss was forced to resign as leader by senior figures in the party late in 1956. His replacement was Sir de Villiers Graf. Graf's appointment suggested that the United Party would seek to challenge the Nationalists by moving markedly to the political right. He had marked himself out as a decidely non-liberal member of the party in 1950, when he had proposed an amendment to the Suppression of Communism bill which would have imposed the death penalty on convicted 'communists'. As the *New Age* sarcastically observed: "Even the Minister of Justice, Swart, thought this was a bit extreme".[182]

The United Party's rightward drift brought it little benefit at the polls. In the 1958 general election, the National Party won some ninety-seven house seats to the fifty-three won by the United Party and its allies. Perhaps most significantly, the government substantially extended its support within urban communities.[183] Had that trend continued in the longer term, the government might well have found that its elusive two-thirds majority could have been obtained without the need to alter the composition of the senate.

The election results added further momentum to the United Party's decline. The mantle of opposition within the white population passed instead to the newly-founded Progressive party and thence—given the Progressives' evident inability to win a significant number of house seats[184]—to the press. The mantle was seized particularly firmly by the *Rand Daily Mail*; the liberal direction which it had taken under the editorship of Raynor Ellis was pursued at a faster rate by his successor, Laurence Gandar.[185]

The *Mail's* sister paper, the *Sunday Express*, joined the attack from time to time. In 1956 and 1957 it ran a protracted campaign against the evident propensity of many members of the cabinet to retain directorships in companies which did business with the government. Strijdom in particular was subjected to criticism for having an interest in a printing company which was awarded substantial government contracts.[186] The paper's headline on 24 November 1957 read:

"STRIJODM USES POSITION AS PREMIER TO BOOST PRIVATE BUSINESS: AND IT PAYS OFF . . . PROFITS SOARING".

Such stories evidently had no adverse impact on the government's electoral appeal. But Strijdom did not live to enjoy the fruits of his constitutional victory and evident immunity to press criticism of his ethical failings for very long. He had been in declining health for some years, and died in August 1958. The battle for the succession threatened briefly to rupture the party on geographical lines: Verwoerd (Transvaal), Donges (Cape) and Swart (the Free State) all considered themselves worthy successors.[187] That Verwoerd emerged victorious

[182] 29 November 1956.

[183] Heard, n. 70 above, pp. 232–233.

[184] It won just one seat in the 1961 election.

[185] This was certainly the view of the government. For its attacks on the white press in the 1961 election campaign see Potter, n. 109 above, pp. 168–170.

[186] Mervis, *The Fourth Estate* (Johannsburg: Jonathan Ball, 1989), pp. 328–332.

[187] See Hepple (1967), n. 89 above, pp. 139–144 for an account of the campaign.

owed much to his ability to avoid making personal enemies in the party, but was also attributable in part to his status as the foremost target of attack from the English language press: to be the government's 'chief villain' in the eyes of the *Rand Daily Mail* gave an appreciable boost to Verwoerd's Prime Ministerial ambitions.[188]

Once installed as Prime Minister, Verwoerd acted quckly to take the country further along the path to the 'ideal' of a fully segregated state. The Promotion of Bantu Self-Government Act 1959[189] substantially extended the native self-government programme initiated under the Bantu Authorities Act 1951. In an attempt to undermine united black opposition to the government, the 1959 Act created eight 'autonomous' 'Bantustan' homelands, occupying small and scattered patches of poor quality land in the country's rural areas.[190] Each Bantustan was nominally governed by its indigenous tribal population, although in effect these tribal authorities enjoyed little effective political power and were almost wholly dependent financially on the (very limited) largesse of the white government.[191] The Act also abolished the native black representation in the house and senate which had been introduced by Hertzog's 1936 legislation, on the grounds that there was no need for such representation now that blacks had been granted their own homeland governments.

Verwoerd also moved promptly to sever South Africa's few remaining formal ties with Britain. The creation of a South African republic had long been among the foremost of his political ambitions. It was achieved in 1960, when a narrow majority of the white electorate voted to replace the Queen as Head of State with a State President.[192] Swart was subsequently installed as the first occupant of the new office. In the following year, stung by criticism of *apartheid* from the leaders of most other Commonwealth nations, Verwoerd led South Africa out of the Commonwealth into a situation of almost total international isolation.

Like Strijdom before him, Verwoerd did not live as long as he might have expected. His assassination by a deranged white parliamentary employee in 1966 triggered Donges' final—and again unsuccessful—bid for the leadership of the National Party. In the extraordinary circumstances of the time, Donges could perhaps have been regarded as the 'moderate' candidate. Purified Nationalists had of course never had much regard for moderation, and as Verwoerd's successor in 1966 the party chose not the ageing Donges, but John Vorster, the then Minister of Justice and former Nazi collaborator.

188 Potter, n. 109 above, pp. 152–153.

189 See Hepple (1967), n. 89 above, ch. 13.

190 Cf. the premable to the Act: "Whereas the Bantu peoples do not constitute a homogenous people, but form separate national units on the basis of language and culture". For a discussion of the government's approach see Ashforth, *The Politics of Official Discourse in Twentieth Century South Africa* (Oxford: Clarendon Press, 1990), pp. 176–180. See also D. Cowen, *The Foundations of Freedom* (Cape Town: OUP, 1961), ch. 2.

191 See, for an opposition perspective, Mandela, n. 51 above, pp. 222–225.

192 Of an electorate of 1.87 million, some 850,000 voted in favour of a republic, and 775,000 voted against. See Hepple (1967), n. 89 above, pp. 173–179 and Heard, n. 70 above, ch. 6 for an account of the process.

By this time, Mandela and most other senior members of the ANC were detained in jail, having been convicted of offences under the Suppression of Communism Act and the Departure from the Union Regulation Act 1955. Mandela and over 150 of his colleagues had previously been arrested and charged with high treason in December 1956. The government's case was premised largely on the terms of the Freedom Charter, a document which it maintained evinced the ANC's involvement in a conspiracy violently to overthrow the existing system of government. The preparatory examination of the case before a Johannesburg magistrate, conducted in the glare of national and international press scrutiny, lasted almost a year. The full trial began in July 1958 in Pretoria before a three-judge panel headed by Rumpf J. Pirow was to serve as lead counsel for the prosecution.[193] The verdict was delivered in March 1961. To the government's dismay, and the ANC's delight, Rumpf concluded that South African law did not regard the advocacy of fundamental political reform as treason. The accused were consequently acquitted.[194]

Shortly thereafter, the ANC decided to initiate a campaign of violent resistance to *apartheid*. After co-ordinating a minor series of sabotage attacks on government property, Mandela and Sisulu were again arrested in 1962. On this occasion, they were convicted, and sentenced to gaol terms which would eventually stretch for almost thirty years into the future.

Black opposition to government had indeed fragmented by the early 1960s, although not along the bantustan lines Verwoerd had envisaged. At the 1958 ANC conference, a group of radicals led by Robert Sobukwe denounced the Freedom Charter as a betrayal of black African nationalism. Sobukwe and his colleagues subsequently founded a new black political grouping, the Pan Africanist Congress (PAC), which was resolutely opposed to trans-racial collaboration and much more indiscriminate in its choice of targets for its campaigns of violence.[195]

The PAC was nonetheless far more selective in its choice of victims than the Verwoerd government. The government began the new decade by declaring a state of emergency under the terms of the Public Safety Act 1953. The declaration was made following the slaughter of sixty-nine black men, women and children at Sharpeville in March 1960.[196] The carnage was inflicted by a small, panicky contingent of police, who allegedly became fearful for their safety during a mass demonstration organised by the PAC.

[193] Pirow died midway through the proceedings. Mandela observes, extraordinarily, that the defendants had developed an affection for Pirow during the trial: n. 51 above, p. 274.

[194] Mandela, n. 51 above, chs. 27–39. The trial undermined still further, if that were possible, the Verwoerd government's international reputation. Merret notes that *The Times* condemned the trial as " 'the violent outburst of an authoritarian regime in panic', and even the *Daily Telegraph* questioned the way in which the arrests had been effected", n. 162 above, pp. 28–29.

[195] Mandela, n. 51 above, pp. 266–268.

[196] Merret, n. 162 above, pp. 41–44; Mandela, n. 51 above, pp. 278–283; L. Thompson, *A History of South Africa* (New Haven: Yale University Press, 1995), pp. 210–211.

In the face of widespread condemnation of his government in international press and political circles, Verwoerd maintained simply that the demonstration was the result of a communist conspiracy. It was the 'communists', and not the police—and most certainly not the government—who bore responsibility for the deaths. The white electorate seemed unperturbed by the escalating internal tension and greater international opprobrium that the massacre triggered. The Nationalists actually increased their representation in the house in the 1961 election, gaining two additional seats. By then however, the significance of the *Harris* cases had already begin to fade into an increasingly distant historical background.

V. CONCLUSION

In comparison with the enormity and intensity of the struggles which were to shape South Africa's destiny in the decades following Sharpeville, the drama played out in the courts, in the press and within 'parliament' as the *Harris* saga ran its course seems to offer almost mundane, even trivial political fare. This is not to belittle the substantive importance of the Cape franchise itself, nor to suggest that litigation in defence of supposedly 'fundamental' individual rights is an essentially worthless task in societies whose constitutions afford sovereign legal authority—albeit by indirect means—to narrow legislative majorities. The point rather is to underline the ultimately political as opposed to legal nature of the forces which led to the creation of the *apartheid* state in South Africa in the 1950s and 1960s and subsequently to its fall and dismantlement in the 1990s.

This is, nonetheless, a book concerned primarily with law, written by an academic lawyer for a predominantly legally-minded audience. The *Harris* litigation may have occupied only a small part of South Africa's constitutional landscape. Yet as the following chapter suggests, this is not to say that within the admittedly sometimes narrow field of constitutional law, this particular historical episode cannot offer us valuable lessons, providing principles for structuring the content and role of both constitutional and common law within democratic societies which cut not just across space but also across time.

11

Constitutionalism, Parliamentary Sovereignty and the Common Law

There is an obvious temptation in a book of this sort to devote the final chapter to an attempt to provide a new critique of what seems ostensibly to have been the project's main foci of attention: namely the role of the South African courts within the segregationist and subsequently apartheid eras; and, in a more theoretical vein, the extent to which common law (and constitutional law) in South Africa operated as a source of authority independent of, even antagonistic to, executive (and legislative) power. That task has however already been admirably performed by several South African commentators,[1] all possessing personal and professional experience of their subject which markedly outstrips my own.

The way I have chosen to tell this particular story may lead some South African commentators to re-evaluate aspects of their country's legal history, but my primary audience in writing this book was always intended to be British rather than South African. This was only in (small) part because I felt British law students remain unfortunately ignorant of the legal and political legacies their predecessors bequeathed to generations of South Africans. The dominant motivation was to use the *Harris* saga as a yardstick against which to measure Britain's constitutional future rather than its past. The comparison cannot in many important senses be a precise one. For all the flaws which one might attribute to the modern constitutional order in the United Kingdom,[2] a charge of moral degeneracy on the scale offered by the societies governed successively by the Botha, Smuts, Herzog, Smuts (again), Malan, Strijdom and Verwoerd administrations simply cannot plausibly be laid. Nonetheless, it seems plausible to suggest that the *Harris* litigation, and the politico-juridical history which preceded and surrounded it, speak with extraordinary clarity to both legal and moral concerns which pervade contemporary critiques of the British constitutional settlement. In matters both of substance and of process, a contextual study of *Harris* offers modern Britain an invaluable illustration of the ideals to which our constitution might aspire and of the evils it should labour to avoid.

[1] A. Sachs, *Justice in South Africa* (London: Sussex University Press, 1973); J. Dugard, *Human Rights and the South African Legal Order* (Princeton, NJ: Princeton University Press, 1978); H. Corder, *Judges at Work* (Cape Town, Juta & Co., 1984); C. Forsyth, *In Danger For Their Talents* (Cape Town: Juta & Co., 1985); and D. Dyzenhaus, *Hard Cases in Wicked Legal Systems* (Oxford: Clarendon Press, 1991) being the leading (English language) examples.

[2] I have outlined my views on these flaws in I. Loveland, *Constitutional Law* ch. 15 (London: Butterworths, 1996); some are discussed further below.

1. ELECTORAL APPORTIONMENT

It would be a substantial oversimplification to attribute the Purified Nationalist's successes in implementing *apartheid* to the structure of South Africa's electoral system. The Malanites' route to power and their subsequent retention of office were conditioned by a myriad of factors: by the ideological legacy left within white political culture by a century of governance in which racism had been accepted both internally and by Britain as a legitimate moral value; by the immense economic utility—to whites—of racially segregated markets in land and labour; by the ambiguity and hypocrisy inherent in the United Party's attitude towards racial matters;[3] and by the obstacles hindering the emergence of a cross-party, non-white political opposition. Nonetheless, the Nationalists' initial seizure of governmental power in 1948 was greatly facilitated by the inherently inegalitarian basis—even within the wholly white electorate—of South Africa's electoral apportionment rules. As noted in Chapter 7, the party's house majority was won with the support of barely forty per cent of votes cast, and with the positive endorsement of only thirty-three per cent of eligible voters. The *Harris* cases themselves revolved around the legality and legitimacy of constitutional principles which could be amended only by supermajoritarian legislative procedures. This pivotal issue tended to obscure political comment on two other questions: namely whether a constitution should afford such protection against bare legislative majorities to so few 'fundamental' rights; and whether one could in any event defensibly describe Malan's administrations as representing a majority of the South African electorate.[4] The first of those two issues, which is concerned with ensuring that some 'extraordinary' government powers are reserved to super majorities, will be discussed further below. For the moment, the second, which is concerned with ensuring that 'ordinary' governmental powers are reserved to simple majorities, merits closer consideration.

It would be absurd to suggest that the range of political choices likely to be embraced by a majority or large minority of the British electorate is in substantive terms closely comparable to that entertained by the South African electorate in the 1940s, 1950s and 1960s. Yet it is equally facile to ignore the fact that the outcomes of the 1948, 1953 and 1958 South African elections pose a constitutional question with a universal resonance. The question is a simple one. To what extent should national electoral systems be designed in order to reduce, rather than to enhance, the probability that governmental power can be won by

[3] It is entirely possible that had the United Party clung to power in the 1948 election, it would have attempted to defuse the electoral threat offered by the Nationalists by adopting Malanite policies. Smuts, Strauss and de Graaf rather than Malan, Strijdom and Verwoerd may thus have become the architects of apartheid.

[4] That the South African electorate was itself wholly unrepresentative of the South African people is a point that need hardly be reiterated.

a political party (or coalition of parties) which does not enjoy the support of a majority of eligible voters?

As noted in Chapter 4, the delegates at the 1908 southern African constitutional convention had given serious consideration to adopting an electoral system based on a form of proportional representation. The same matter received similarly serious consideration in Britain shortly thereafter, but no legislation was forthcoming.[5] We thus retain today the same model of voting system that we bequeathed to South Africa nearly one hundred years ago; namely that seats in the House of Commons are allocated to some 650+ geographically distinct constituencies, each of which returns the candidate who receives the largest number of votes.

The contemporary critiques of this model are too obvious, and have been made too frequently, to demand more than cursory attention here. The House of Commons (Redistribution of Seats) Act 1949 Schedule 2 (as amended) grants the power to define constituencies to a Boundary Commission which operates *de jure* and *de facto* independently of the government of the day.[6] But the Act does not require mathematical equivalence in constituency sizes. It identifies an 'electoral quota' for each constituency; i.e. the national total of eligible voters divided by the number of constituencies. The quota is presently some 65,000 voters. However there is—unlike under the terms of the Act of Union which limited variations in constituency sizes to some fifteen per cent above or below the relevant provincial quota—no obvious legal limit to the disparities in the sizes of individual constituencies. Substantial deviations from the quota are permissible if: "the size, shape and accessibility of a constituency, appear to render a departure desirable". No legal challenge is permissible to a government's decision to accept a Boundary Commission's recommendations,[7] and the courts have shown themselves unwilling to entertain any challenge to the recommendations themselves.[8]

In practice, the Act produces vast discrepancies in constituency size. In 1987, more than 100 seats deviated from the quota by over twenty per cent. At the various extremes were the Orkney and Shetland constituency with barely 31,000 voters, and the Isle of Wight with over 98,000.[9] Such variations provoke criticisms of anti-democratic practice, on the grounds that the system ignores the principle of 'one vote one value'.[10] In simple terms, the votes of, for example, Orkney residents in the 1987 general election were 'worth' more than three

[5] See D. Butler, *The Electoral System in Britain 1918–1951* ch. 1 (Oxford: Clarendon Press, 1953).

[6] See Loveland (1996) *op. cit.*, n. 2 above, pp. 262–267; J. Craig, 'Parliament and the Boundary Commissions' (1959) *Public Law* 23.

[7] Section 4(7) contains an explicit ouster clause to this effect; see S. De Smith, 'Boundaries between Parliament and the Courts' (1955) 18 *MLR* 281.

[8] See *R v Boundary Commission, ex parte Foot* [1983] QB 600.

[9] P. Norton, *The British Polity* (London: Longman, 2nd edn. 1991) p. 94.

[10] See especially H.R.W. Wade, *Constitutional Fundamentals* ch. 2 (London: Stevens and Sons, 1980).

times as much as those of Isle of Wight residents, since both constituencies returned only one MP. In general terms—as Smuts found to his benefit in 1907 and 1911 and to his detriment in 1948—this model bestows great benefits on a party whose supporters are disproportionately concentrated in small constituencies.

There is—perhaps surprisingly—little indication that any South African government attempted to gerrymander constituency boundaries through creative use of electoral cartography above and beyond retaining the distortions built into the system in 1909.[11] This contrasted quite markedly with the experience of the United States, where—at the time the *Harris* cases were being decided—many States engaged in the most extraordinarily blatant boundary manipulation in order to safeguard white, rural and small town control of their legislatures. It was not until the mid-1960s that such defects were cured; the cure being effected not by the States themselves, nor by the federal government, but by the Supreme Court's creative interpretation of the federal constitution.[12] Chief Justice Earl Warren had encapsulated the principle underpinning the Court's intervention in apportionment issues in the pithy phrase: "Legislators [should] represent people, not trees or acres".[13] That principle led the court to insist that single member constituencies for both national and state legislatures should contain approximately equal numbers of voters.

The United Kingdom's current apportionment criteria, even if not subject to direct party political manipulation in the way that afflicted constituency design in many American states in the 1960s, undoubtedly contain appreciable scope for indirect political bias. This arises most obviously and systemically in favour of rural rather than urban areas: 'trees and acres' are, if only to a limited extent, enfranchised under our present system.[14] And if there is a marked difference in the economic and party political demography of urban and rural communities, that indirect bias is necessarily embedded in the party political make-up of the Commons. That South Africa's rural white voters were consistently more reactionary and bigoted than their urban counterparts is perhaps a general rather than universal truth, and not one which has any obvious bearing on contemporary British society.[15] But unless one is convinced by the reactionary cultural values which led Merriman in the early 1900s to advocate a (colour blind) high threshhold franchise tied to land-ownership in the Cape, or by the cultural paranoia and racism which at the same time led Kruger to disenfranchise

[11] Malan of course used the more direct route of creating additional seats, with tiny electorates, in South West Africa; see p. 00 above.

[12] See *Baker v Carr* 369 US 186 (1962); *Gray v Sanders* 372 US 368 (1963); *Wesberry v Saunders* 376 US 1 (1964); *Reynolds v Sims* 377 US 533 (1964).

[13] *Reynolds v Sims* 377 US 533 (1964).

[14] Although one can readily identify very small urban constituencies in Britain's contemporary political landscape.

[15] Although it will perhaps come as little surprise to urban observers of the so-called Countryside Alliance which appeared on the British political stage in 1998, in defence of such values as the hunting of stags and the retention of vast EC subsidies for farmers to produce chemically polluted food.

urban-dwelling *uitlanders* and all non-whites in the Republic, there seems to be little to weigh in the scales in favour of the proposition that where one lives in modern Britain should markedly affect the value of one's vote in parliamentary elections.

It seems barely credible that there is still any need to allude to episodes of foreign constitutional history to highlight the intrinsically unsatisfactory—and instrumentally dangerous—character of our apportionment laws. Yet quite clearly the principle of one 'one vote one value' has no dominant force within the contemporary British constitution. For a brief period prior to and immediately after World War II, Britain's apportionment rules recognised the ideal—even if it did not lead to the reality—of ensuring that constituencies were of approximately equal size. If we are to retain our existing electoral system, it would not seem a radical proposition to suggest that Parliament should promptly enact legislation which returns to that principle.

The argument in favour of such reform becomes the more compelling, since, as was the case in South Africa, the potential shortcomings of the apportionment process are much exacerbated by the way in which votes are counted. Contrary to popular belief, the House of Commons in modern Britain has never been controlled by a single party enjoying only bare majoritarian support. But this is not because post-war governments have possessed large electoral majorities. Rather it is because all of them have been elected on the basis of having only the largest minority share of the popular vote. Like Malan and Strijdom administrations, no recent British government has ever succeeded in garnering more than fifty per cent of the votes case in a general election. And when one takes into account the fact that only some eighty per cent of eligible voters actually participate in those elections, one is left with the ostensibly bizarre proposition (for a democratic country) that the huge Commons majorities enjoyed by the 1983 and 1987 Conservative and 1997 Labour governments enjoyed the positive electoral support of barely thirty-three per cent of people entitled to vote. Just as, one might repeat, did the governments led by Malan and Strijdom.

The massive votes/seats discrepancy is a direct consequence of our constitution's continued acceptance of the 'first past the post' counting system in single member constituencies. Within an individual constituency, there will always be a mismatch between votes cast and seats won in contested elections unless every voter supports one candidate, since there is only one seat to win. But the wasted vote problem is much exacerbated when one aggregates the results of all 650+ constituency elections. In post-war British elections, candidates have frequently won constituencies with substantially less than fifty per cent of the votes cast, because the majority of electors have split their vote among several other parties. In the 1997 election some thirty-two candidates were returned with less than forty per cent of the vote; a further 250 gained only between forty and fifty per cent; a similar number managed to achieve a bare majority; while the number of candidates attracting overwhelming support in their constituencies (i.e.

over sixty-six per cent) was barely 100.[16] The so-called 'landslide' victory won by the Labour party in 1997 was achieved with a share of barely forty per cent of the popular vote. Since turnout was only seventy-one per cent, the government's majority of 179 in the House of Commons actually received the positive approval of only thirty per cent of the electorate.

This is unfortunately not an anomaly but a normalcy within our modern electoral system. A substantial minority of votes are always 'wasted'. And this problem would not, of course, be eliminated simply by ensuring that constituencies were of equal size. In a single MP constituency system, there are no direct rewards for coming second. Thus voters whose preferred political party enjoys substantial support on a nationwide basis are effectively disenfranchised both as individuals and as a collectivity, except in those few constituencies where their party's concentration of support is atypically high. The handicap thus suffered by the Liberal party in modern Britain has obvious parallels in the inability of South Africa's Liberal and Labour parties to win appreciable numbers of seats in the house of assembly. Small parties whose support is geographically concentrated may fare less badly. Scots, Welsh and Northern Irish nationalists, for example, do not contest seats outside their respective countries, and so are less acutely affected by the wasted vote problem. For this reason, both the Dominion and Conservative parties, based in Natal, were able to achieve parliamentary representation which bore some resemblance to their share of the popular vote.

Curtice and Steed's fascinating analysis of the 1997 United Kingdom election results suggests that the distortive effect of the electoral system is in fact increasing.[17] Labour support is becoming both increasingly concentrated in geographical terms and—crucially—that concentration is occurring in small constituencies. The average size of the electorate in seats won by Labour in 1997 was some 6,500 lower than in seats won by the Conservatives. There is perhaps a certain notion of rough justice in these results; namely that Labour voters are now enjoying the benefits that accrued to Conservative supporters between 1979 and 1992. But the argument that an electoral system is acceptable because it periodically allows both major parties to acquire wholly unrepresentative Commons majorities would seem to lack a legitimate constitutional foundation.

As was the case with South Africa's Nationalist administrations in the 1940 and 1950s, the minority electoral support won by the Thatcher and Blair governments hands them in effect unimpeded control of the legislative process. The contemporary House of Lords is no more an obstacle to a government with a huge Commons majority than was the (pre-1955) senate to Malan and his successors; and the Queen's assent to bills is no less readily forthcoming than was that of South Africa's Governor-General.

As noted above, most of the *apartheid programme* had no 'constitutional' dimension, in the sense that the relevant laws could legally be enacted by a bare

[16] Figures extracted from D. Butler and D. Kavanagh *The British General Election of 1997* (London: Macmillan, 1998) Appendix 1.

[17] Appendix 2 of Butler and Kavanagh *op. cit.*

parliamentary majority. With the exception of the Cape franchise laws, they were part and parcel of the 'ordinary' legislative process. In Britain, of course, every political or moral value is subject to amendment or repeal by a bare parliamentary majority.[18]

Manifestly, no modern British government has been predisposed to pursue the tyrannical, egregiously racist policies favoured by all South African administrations prior to the revolution of the 1990s. Nor is there any indication that such propensities are likely to emerge in the foreseeable future. That our governments—and effectively our Parliament—represent only a minority of the population is therefore not constitutionally problematic if the height of one's constitutional ambition is the avoidance of tyranny and egregious racism.

Yet it might readily be thought that a country which prides itself on being a modern democratic society should pitch its constitutional standards at a markedly higher level. As I have suggested elsewhere at some length,[19] and will reiterate briefly below, I see little merit in our constitution's continued acceptance of the principle that 'Parliament', through the mechanism of a bare bicameral majority and the royal assent, may enact laws on any subject matter it wishes. But if one is to retain such a legislature, it would not seem outlandish to expect that the government which controls that legislative majority also enjoys majority electoral support. That expectation obviously points towards the adoption of a new electoral system premised on a variation of proportional representation which closely ties the number of Commons' seats a party wins to the number of votes it attracts. Until the election of the Blair administration in 1997, no post-war government had given any indication that it would give serious consideration to enacting such a reform. The current government's promise that a referendum will be held on the question of electoral reform within the next few years offers the possibility that Commons majorities will in future represent electoral majorities. The Jenkins Commission proposals offer only a modest step towards proportionality. Their true importance, however, lies merely in their adoption by the government. If the change to the electoral system is enacted, its most significant consequence will be that the Labour party will win many fewer seats at the next general election than it would have done under the old system. This may in turn require a future Labour government to limit its legislative ambitions to objectives which can garner at least some support from opposition parties. It is an unusually 'democratic' government indeed that is prepared to promote legislation which will undermine rather than reinforce its hold on political power.

There is obviously no unassailable basis for believing that the adoption of a strictly proportional electoral system in the Act of Union would have precluded enactment of segregationist and subsequently *apartheid* legislation in South Africa. All the white political parties supported—to varying degrees—racist

[18] It seems now to be generally accepted that United Kingdom courts will not apply domestic legislation which breaches directly effective EC law. This is discussed further below.

[19] (1996) *op. cit.*, n. 2 above, ch. 15.

legislation. And it is not implausible to suggest that the Purified Nationalists might have been able to gain through coalition by the mid-1950s the bare parliamentary majority they gained under the electoral system South Africa then employed. Nor is it beyond doubt that a different electoral system would have effectively safeguarded the entrenched clauses. Hertzog was after all able to attract virtually unanimous parliamentary support for the Representation of the Natives Act 1936. Moreover, the seepage of right-wing members of the United Party towards the Malanite camp on the disenfranchisement issue, coupled with the Nationalists' steadily growing electoral support throughout the 1950s, suggest that the necessary super-majority of voters would, sooner rather than later, have embraced the cause of constitutional amendment.

What seems rather less open to question is the suggestion that the present British government's evident willingness to increase the probability that a Commons majority represents a majority of voters is a very modest constitutional aspiration indeed. Just as, one might readily think, is its desire to eliminate a perpetual party political bias in that legislature's second chamber.

II. A SECOND LEGISLATIVE CHAMBER

Centlivres' had observed during the *Collins* hearing that a wholly appointed senate, within which all the appointees were government supporters, would nevertheless be a 'senate' within the meaning given to that term by the Act of Union. The Chief Justice presumably offered this hypothetical scenario as an indication of legislation which might exceed the 'moral' boundaries of constitutionalism even if it remained within the legal competence of a bare parliamentary majority. While the South African polity may indeed by this time have been thoroughly 'wicked'[20] in most important respects, its controllers still paid lip-service to notions of 'democratic' governance: even Strijdom's administration did not think it defensible to limit membership of the senate to legislators who were nominated directly by the government.

It thus seems rather odd that, in 1998, Britain's Labour government was suggesting that the House of Lords should be reformed—if only for an interim period—along just those lines. The bulk of the criticism levelled at the House of Lords in recent times has focused on its composition rather than its powers. On that latter point, there appears to be widespread agreement that a second chamber should be markedly inferior in terms of its power to the Commons, and that the powers the Lords currently possesses are adequate. Its power of legislative veto is limited essentially to bills intended to postpone or abolish general elections. In respect of other bills, it can merely delay enactment, generally for a year but for only a month in respect of money bills. The purpose of the delaying power is clear; namely to force a government and the Commons majority to

[20] See Dyzenhaus *op. cit.*, n. 1 above.

reflect on the merits of a proposed Act and to give breathing space for press and public opinion on the measure to be made known. The Lords is also widely presumed to have a valuable legislative role to play in scrutinising the details of government bills which may have received insufficient examination in the Commons, in providing a forum for debate on issues of general concern, and, through its select committees in producing expert reports on a variety of subjects. These presumptions all rest on the expectation that because members of the Lords are not subject to the pressures of seeking re-election, all these functions will be performed in a spirit which is markedly less hidebound by concerns of party discipline than is the behaviour of members of the Commons. The Lords, in short, is idealised qua collectivity as a forum which might provide an expert and impartial complement to the House of Commons.[21]

That the ideal is subverted by the hereditary basis (and so pro-Conservative bias) of most of its members, and the manifest intellectual shortcomings of many members of the aristocracy, are the issues to which the Blair government is currently addressing itself. The rationale guiding reform of the composition of the upper house would appear simple; having identified the purposes one wishes the Lords to serve, one must then devise a process for choosing its membership that would seem to maximise the likelihood that those purposes would be achieved. That process would need to produce two outcomes: firstly that the membership as a collectivity was not controlled by any single political party (and especially not the party that controlled the Commons); and secondly that the membership as individuals occupied their seats on a meritocratic basis—whether those merits be evidenced by success in an electoral contest or as recognition of past achievement in other walks of life.

Many western societies—including perhaps ironically South Africa in 1909—have sought to achieve these outcomes by electing members of a second chamber on a regional basis, thereby seeking to make an anti-majoritarian virtue rather than a pro-minoritarian vice out of geographical inconsistencies in their societies' internal political demography. In the absence of any attempt to restructure the United Kingdom's constitution on a (quasi)-federal basis, that particular route to establishing the 'independence' of the Lords from the Commons is not available.[22] Three options thus present themselves: that all members of the Lords be appointed: that they be elected by a system which differs from that used by the Commons and which is most unlikely to produce a single party majority; or that they be appointed by a mixture of the first two methods.

Given the present government's commitment to entertain the possibility of reforming the Commons electoral system, introduction of an elected second

[21] See generally Loveland (19996) *op. cit.*, n. 2 above, ch. 6.

[22] The creation of a Scots 'parliament' and Welsh and Northern Irish Assemblies is of little assistance in this regard, since the overwhelming majority of the United Kingdom's population lives in England. A 'federal' solution would demand the sub-division of England into several discrete regions.

chamber would seem precipitate.[23] Options two and three are thus ruled out in the short term. That the Blair administration seems attracted to option one would not seem unreasonable, were it not for fact that the government also initially seemed to be attracted to the idea that the Prime Minister should make all the appointments. That no British Prime Minister might in practice use such monopolistic powers to create a packed upper house is no reason for designing an appointment system which would permit that result in theory. The most obvious legal innoculation which our constitution might take to ward off that particular political disease would be allocate appointment powers not just to the Prime Minister, but also—in shares broadly proportionate to their share of the Commons vote over the previous twenty years—to the leaders of all other political parties represented in the lower house. Should it be thought desirable to reserve a tranche of Lords seats or avowedly non-party political peers, such appointees might take their seats following nomination by the Prime Minister and approval by the Leader of the Opposition.

A device of this sort clearly does not preclude the possibility that members of an upper house would simply act along party lines. It would however seem to preclude the possibility of single party majorities, a reality which if maintained in the long term might lead the chamber's members to embrace the principle that they owe their legislative loyalty to their country rather than their party:[24] and might even persuade the leaders of political parties to offer up nominees whose chief virtues were something other than party loyalty. The Blair government's more recent proposal to establish an all-party parliamentary select committee to assess the merits of the Prime Minister's nominees may prove a similarly efficacious solution to this particular problem, especially if the government resists the temptation to grant itself a committee majority. Whether the committee can achieve the desired level of 'a(party)political' orientation obviously remains to be seen, but the initiative promises to mark a significant step towards a more pluralist constitutional structure.

III. THE 'INDEPENDENCE' OF THE JUDICIARY

The frequency with which the 'first team' judges on the Appellate Division, and their like-minded colleagues on the various provincial benches, were subject to public and private attack by government ministers, backbench MPs, and pro-government (i.e. Afrikaaner language) newspapers was a prominent feature of

[23] Even if this were not the case, the arguments against an elected Lords or 'Senate' are powerful. An elected second chamber brings with it an obvious danger. If its members are chosen by a method which makes them more representative of voters at large than MPs who sit in the Commons, it might quickly come to be seen as a more legitimate source of governing authority than the lower house. The constitutional stage would thus be set for the upper house to challenge rather than complement its nominally more powerful partner.

[24] An objective which might be facilitated by ensuring that appointments were for terms substantially in excess of the Commons electoral cycle.

constitutional discourse in South Africa during the 1950s. Those attacks varied in their intensity and in terms of the nature of the substantive judicial 'ill' they wished to cure, but they shared a common theme; namely that the judges were overstepping the boundaries of their proper constitutional role because they persistently offered interpretations of the law (be it constitutional law, legislation, or common law) which differed from those favoured by the government. The more intemperate of these attacks questioned the bona fides and integrity of the judges concerned. The less hyperbolic critiques suggested that the judiciary was unable or unwilling to adapt traditional legal orthodoxies in a way that properly responded to changed political circumstances. But both strands of complaint rested on the assumption that the government's status as the elected government—and specifically as the promoter of legislation or the executor of prerogative powers—per se entitled it to expect that its understandings of its legal powers would be accepted by the courts. In essence, this discourse attempted to redefine the separation of powers; parliament would do as the government wished it to do; statutes meant what the government wished them to men; and insofar as the courts had an independent constitutional role to play, that role was limited to developing the common law in ways which facilitated achievement of the government's objectives.

Much the same kind of discourse was offered by members of the Major government and backbench Conservative MPs during the early and mid-1990s in respect of judicial decisions which happened to hold ministerial actions unlawful.[25] *M v The Home Office*,[26] the *Pergau Dam* case,[27] *R v Criminal Injuries Compensation Board, ex parte Fire Brigades Union*,[28] and *R v Secretary of State for Social Security, ex parte Joint Council for the Welfare of Immigrants*[29] resulted in outcomes which would hardly have surprised any commentator possessing even a rudimentary understanding of English administrative law. The attack on these decisions revealed an extraordinary degree of constitutional illiteracy (or—less extraordinarily—mendacity) on the part of backbench Conservative MPs.[30] The rationale for this criticism of the courts appeared to rest—in a precise echo of Nationalist MPs' attacks on the Appellate Division in South Africa in the 1950s—on the assumption that the preferences

[25] See J. Griffith, *The Politics of the Judiciary* (London: Fontana, 5th edn., 1997) pp. xiii–xvii, 320–325; I. Loveland, 'The War Against the Judges' (1997) *Political Quarterly* 162.

[26] [1993] 3 WLR 433. The judgment established that the Home Secretary, in both her personal capacity and in her official capacity as part of the Crown, could be the subject of interim injunctions and, more dramatically, could be held in contempt of court for failing to honour assurances made to a judge by counsel on her behalf.

[27] [1995] 1 All ER 611. In which the High Court held that a proposed grant of some £300 million of overseas aid to Malaysia was unlawful as it did not represent an economically 'sound' use of public funds.

[28] [1995] 2 AC 513.

[29] [1996] 4 All ER 385.

[30] Including *The Times*; see Loveland (1997) *op. cit.*, n. 25 above. See especially the Commons debate immediately following the *Joint Council for the Welfare of Immigrants* case at *HCD*, June 24 1996 cc. 37–48.

of the majority party in the Commons enjoy the same constitutional status as the most precisely drafted of statutory provisions. It seemed not to occur to these Conservative MPs—any more than it did to Nationalist MPs in South Africa fifty years ago—that a judge who rejects that analysis is not attacking the *de jure* sovereignty of (P)parliament, but is rather questioning the *de facto* usurpation of that sovereignty by the executive.

One basic constitutional virtue that seems to be cast in sharp relief by the *Harris/Collins* decisions—and the various administrative law judgments which surrounded them—is that our concept of the independence of the judiciary must possess both negative and positive dimensions. The negative facet is more readily achievable and generally uncontroversial; it requires merely that a judge is not a government or opposition lackey. The positive half of the couplet is both more elusive and more contentious, and demands in effect that judicial duties are discharged in accordance with moral precepts which transcend considerations of party politics.

The appointment of judges

One notable element of the *Harris* controversy was the relative ease with which the Malan and Strijdom governments were able to bypass the entrenched terms of the constitution, and to reverse the common law presumptions surrounding the interpretation of legislation, by packing the courts with sympathetic judges. Notwithstanding the delicacy with which much of the South African press approached the question of the political allegiances of the six 'second team' judges appointed to the Appellate Division in 1955,[31] there is little doubt that Strijdom expected—and with evidently good reason—that his nominees would regard their constitutional duty as to dismiss rather than uphold any legal challenge to the Senate Act and the South Africa Act Amendment Act 1956.

The furore which surrounded the passage of Strijdom's Appellate Division Quorum Act highlights the immense importance of ensuring in all professedly democratic nations that the process of selecting senior members of the judiciary minimises the likelihood that individual judges, and the bench as a collectivity, be biased in favour of one major political party at the expense of another. As John Griffith and Roy Jenkins among others have noted, the practicalities of judicial appointments in modern Britain have left far behind the old and evidently not then dishonourable tradition that a seat on the bench be allocated as a reward for loyal party political service.[32] Nor has there been in recent times any suggestion that governments have systematically appointed judges on the

[31] See pp. 342–344 above.

[32] R. Jenkins, *Asquith* (London: Collins, 3rd edn., 1986) pp. 38–40; Griffith (1997) *op. cit.*, n. 25 above, pp. 8–12. Cf. the new orthodoxy, as recently expressed by Sir John Laws; "Even outside court, a judge should no doubt appear to favour no political party, lest his extra-curial opinions be perceived to infect his decisions in court"; 'Law and Democracy' (1995) *Public Law* 72 at p. 74.

basis of presumptions about the political predispositions which the appointees might bring to bear on their interpretation of statutes and development of the common law.[33] Nonetheless, in legal terms, the British government's control over the appointment and dismissal of High Court and appellate judges is no less extensive than that exercised by Malan and his successors in respect of the South African Supreme Court.

As is the case with appointments to the House of Lords qua legislative chamber, however, there seems little merit in retaining a judicial selection system which is manifestly open to abuse on party political grounds simply because that abuse has not occurred in recent times. Proposals for reforming the process of selecting judges have generally borrowed heavily from the American model, in which federal judges are nominated by the President but appointed by the Senate, whose Judiciary Committee is charged with the responsibility of establishing the nominee's fitness for office. That the Senate's inquiries are frequently akin to an ordeal by fire for the nominee,[34] and that they receive much attention in newspapers and on television—leaves one with the impression that access to high judicial office in the USA is more properly seen as a trust granted by the people rather than—as in Britain—a gift bestowed by the government. The process also ensures that even the interested layperson in the USA has a fair idea of the career history and jurisprudential suppositions that Supreme Court judges take with them to the bench, a situation which contrasts markedly—and very favourably—with the state of public knowledge in Britain about the judges who sit in the House of Lords, still less of those in the Court of Appeal and High Court. The administration of justice in Britain may be open in the sense that the press and the public court are almost always physically accessible to a public audience and have their proceedings reported in the press. But our courts are generally mysterious, opaque fora when one moves to consider the identities and backgrounds of the judges who preside over them.

While the American model ensures a substantial degree of transparency in the judicial appointment process, it does not necessarily preclude the indulgence of party political bias. That it has done so in the past dozen or so years is a result of the Presidency and the Senate being controlled by different political parties. In those circumstances, appointment depends either on the President nominating a candidate who is obviously acceptable on a bipartisan basis or on the candidate herself convincing a sceptical and perhaps hostile Senate audience either that she will leave her personal political baggage behind when she reaches the court, or that her juristic brilliance is sufficient to outweigh any concerns that

[33] Such suggestions are sometimes aired about specific appointments; cf. Griffith's comment on Lord Donaldson's appointment as Master of the Rolls in 1982; (1987) *op. cit.*, n. 25 above, p. 17.

[34] The hearings conducted into the candidacies of Robert Bork and Clarence Thomas being obvious examples. For an unsurprisingly critical view of the Bork hearing see R. Bork, *The Tempting of America* (New York: Free Press, 1990) chs. 14–15. For less partisan coverage see D. Savage, *turning Right* (New York: Wiley, 1992), ch. 4; R. Dworkin, *Freedom's Laws* (Cambridge, Mass.: Harvard UP, 1996) ch. 12. On Thomas see Dworkin *op. cit.*, ch. 15. For an extended treatment of the nomination see J. Mayer and J. Abramson, *Strange Justice* (New York: Houghton Mifflin, 1994).

Senators might hold about her political predilections. In an era where the President's party also controls the Senate, the system may do little more than ensure that the nominee's face and resume are brought to the public's attention.

Thus in the British context, where the government virtually always has a sizeable majority in the Commons, the American model has little to commend it as a vehicle for eliminating the possibility that a government might succumb to the temptation of indulging its power to allow party political bias to influence the appointment of members of the judiciary. It seems unlikely that any government would concede the point that a Commons/Lords equivalent to the USA's Senate Judiciary Committee should contain an anti-government majority. This raises the obvious possibility that most committee members would be predisposed to approve the government's nominee. This in turn, unless the committee extended extensive interrogatory powers to opposition members or contained several independently-minded nominees from the government party—is likely to ensure that candidates for judicial office are spared rigorous questioning. The independence and authority of all select committees are widely regarded as inadequate by legal and political commentators,[35] and there is no reason to suppose that a Commons judiciary committee would buck this particular constitutional trend.

To query the adequacy of modern Britain's judicial appointment process is not to cast doubt on the party apolitical integrity of High Court judges; nor even to suggest that they might have been found lacking in some necessary judicial quality had their nomination for office process been examined by backbench MPs with the rigour often favoured by the Judiciary Committee of the US Senate. The question which arises is rather whether our constitutional arrangements should afford any scope even for the *possibility* that a government could use its appointment powers for partisan ends.

A simple mechanism to eliminate this possibility would be to require that appointments to the High Court bench, to the Court of Appeal and to the House of Lords, be made in pairs. One would be nominated by the Prime Minister, the other by the Leader of the Opposition, each of whom would have to consent to the other's choice before an appointment could be made. There seems no good reason why that consent should not be withheld until such time as the nominee has faced examination by a parliamentary select committee.

The common law as a guarantor of conservative political morality

There is no doubt some value in increasing general public awareness of the identities and career backgrounds of High Court judges. It is something of an oversimplification to suggest that there is less need for transparency in the process used to appoint senior judges in Britain than in the USA, since our courts exercise substantially less constitutional power than their (federal) American

[35] See the sources cited in Loveland (1996) *op. cit.*, n. 2 above, ch. 5.

counterparts. It is rather easy, by focusing on the fact that we regard our Parliament as a sovereign law maker, to underestimate the enormous legal authority that the common law[36] bestows upon the judiciary to shape the development of our constitutional law.

The various administrative law cases that came before the Appellate Division immediately prior to and during the *Harris* litigation bring this point home very forcefully. It is quite clear that Malan and his successors controlled South Africa's (simple majority) 'parliament' in a political sense. The size of the Nationalist majority in each house, coupled with the tightness of the party's internal discipline, guaranteed that the government was able (with the exception of matters covered by the entrenched provisions) to enact whatever policy preferences it wished. In the legal sense, however, that 'control' proved much more elusive. For it is equally clear that the mere process of enactment did not in itself convert government policy into 'law'. The latter status was acquired only after the relevant legislative text had passed through the interpretive filter of the South African common law. And it need hardly be repeated that the end product which emerged from the courts in the 1950s was frequently not to the government's liking.

The trans-national and trans-historical significance of this point is to redirect our attention towards a concern which ought to have equal resonance within the British constitutional structure, but which has rather been under-emphasised because of the easy assumption that the constitution of modern Britain—unlike *apartheid* South Africa—exists in the context of a broadly democratic polity. The concern is, of course, what we mean by the notion of the separation of powers and—relatedly—by the principles of the rule of law and the sovereignty of parliament.

It need hardly be stated that the British constitution has never in practice adhered to a purist understanding of the separation of powers. Our dilute model nonetheless rests on the theoretical assumption that 'parliament' can be distinguished *de facto* or *de jure* from the government, with the latter—as is dictated by the doctrine of parliamentary sovereignty—occupying a distinctly inferior position to the former. A purist understanding of the theory would then suggest that statutes are enacted because their sponsor (the government) has convinced an open-minded legislative audience that the policies contained in the Acts best serve the national interest. The role assigned to the courts is then to ensure that Parliament—and indirectly the electorate—is protected from governmental encroachment into areas of activity that have not been authorised either by statute or the common law.

[36] In which I include principles of statutory interpretation. Obvious recent examples of the courts introducing marked changes to our understanding of public law principles would include *Council for the Civil Service Unions v Minister for the Civil Service* [1985] AC 374; *R v R*—(rape: marital exemption) [1991] 4 All ER 481: *Pepper v Hart* [1993] 1 All ER 42: *R v Secretary of State for Transport, ex parte Factortame* [1991] 1 AC 603: *M v Home Office* [1993] 3 WLR 433.

The model is of course extraordinarily difficult to apply in situations where—as in modern Britain—there is no meaningful *de facto* separation between parliament and the executive. In that context, the legitimating force underpinning legislation is not that it necessarily serves a consensual national interest, but that it expresses the preferences of whichever electoral 'majority' currently controls the House of Commons. That rationale closely accords with the arguments advanced by the Nationalist governments of South Africa in the 1950s.

What we seem to have witnessed in 1950s South Africa is an Appellate Division refusal to accept this empirical corruption of the pure theoretical model by a government determined to use its parliamentary majority to impose radical, minoritarian values on society. What we might surmise from the South African experience in the 1940s and 1950s is that when two pillars of a tripartite constitutional orthodoxy are revealed to have increasingly unstable foundations, the custodians of the third might readily be expected to shore up society's political superstructure by digging their own pillar more deeply into its moral base.

To express the matter rather differently, the administrative law judgments of the Centlivres Court reveal a process in which the common law moved to occupy the political space created by the government and legislatures' abandonment of their 'proper' constitutional functions.[37] For Nationalist politicians, this judicial colonisation of a newly vacated constitutional terra nullius[38] was simply a matter of judges indulging a personal, (party) political bias. The judges were 'liberals' or 'anglophiles' who—whether deliberately or because they could not help themselves—deployed their political beliefs in a systematic attempt to sabotage government policy.

Even ardent opponents of *apartheid* would have to concede that the Centlivres Court on occasion presented the government with a significant obstacle. However, the obstacle was not the personal politics of the judges; it was rather their understanding of political ethos of the common law. In the jurisprudential sense, judgments such as *Abduhrahman*, *Lusu*, *Ormonde*, *Tayob* and *A1 Electric Ice Cream* were deeply conservative, insofar as they were arrived at through the orthodox application of long-established interpretive principles—albeit that they were principles which were not uncontested within the South African jurisprudential tradition. But these decisions were also intensely conservative in the political sense, in that they bluntly impeded—if only temporarily—the government's pursuit of a radical policy agenda by subjecting its legislation to an interpretive filter still tinted by the less egregiously racist political culture which had informed the first forty years of South Africa's history. In

[37] Lord Woolf of Barnes expressed the point less melodramatically in respect of more recent English experience; "It is one of the strengths of the common law that it enables the courts to vary the extent of their intervention to reflect current needs, and by this means it helps to maintain the delicate balance of a democratic society"; (1995) '*Droit Public*—English Style' *Public Law* 56 at 58.

[38] See pp. 5–8 above. To pursue the analogy further, one might suggest that the terrain was not empty, but rather peopled by 'uncivilised' inhabitants.

essence, it appears that the Appellate Division decided in these cases not to view 'parliament' as a statutory text, nor as an institution promoting government policy, but as an idealisation of a particular type of political development; namely one in which the legislature was presumptively deferential to long established moral values, and in which that presumption could be rebutted only by the most overtly radical statutory language.

This point is perhaps one that merits further consideration in the British context. For—and here we reach a point often overlooked by critics of judicial activism whose world view is limited to Britain with occasional glances at the USA, Canada and Australia—is that the judicial conservatism of the Centlivres Court was ranged against the political right rather than the political left. It has long been an article of faith among the more politically radical members of Britain's legal community that the common law and the judges who control it are suffused with a deeply rooted sense of conservatism on social, economic and civil liberties issues. The point is perhaps best and most famously put by John Griffith: "Judges today mostly reflect moderate Conservative opinion of the middle 'consensus' years of this century".[39] This conservatism,[40] when manifested in the form of judicial decisions which obstruct government policy-making, is regarded as an intrinsically unsatisfactory state of affairs, evidently for two inter-linked reasons. The first is that since governments are elected on the basis of a universal franchise their policy preferences enjoy a greater degree of legitimacy than the judiciary's understanding of the common law; consequently the courts should always be willing to modify common law principles[41] to accommodate shifts in electoral sentiment. The second objection—which rather confuses conservative jurisprudence with the quite different phenomenon of reactionary morality—is that courts thereby stand in the way of achievement of a more 'democratic' polity.

One lesson that detailed exposure to the *Harris* saga might bring home to advocates and opponents of constitutional reform in modern Britain is that the alternative to political and legal conservatism is not a socialist utopia, to which we will as a society be led by elected legislators whose constant embrace of truth and justice will be secured by ensuring that they are constantly accountable to our apparently wise, benevolent and essentially egalitarianly inclined electorate. That our elected politicians possess such virtues, still less the suggestion that they can be found in conspicuous quantities among successful electoral minorities within the general public are—to put the matter kindly—assertions which seem to lack an obviously defensible political base. What we might instead consider is that the most likely alternative to a centrist, conservative version of social democratic governance in our contemporary society is a significant lurch to the political right; a lurch engineered by a large minority whose distinguish-

[39] (1997) *op. cit.*, n. 25 above, p. 328.

[40] Griffith drops the large 'C' in conservatism in the paragraph immediately following the one from which the above quotation is drawn.

[41] Again, I include within this concept rules of statutory interpretation.

ing political characteristics are above average wealth, an ingrained sense of racism, a manifest intolerance of alternative political ideologies and appreciable enthusiasm for the erosion of civil liberties.

This might suggest that the first task of reformers who wish to move a society's political culture to the left is to secure its centre against successful attack from the right. That is a process to which a conservative understanding of the common law would prove an important ally. Yet the chief criticism that can be levelled at the Griffith thesis—and at the younger analysts who continue to support it[42]—is that it facilitates rather than impedes the advance of reactionary political values. It has this effect because it deploys a really rather naive view of the inter-relationship of 'law' and 'politics' in elevating the moral bona fides of the latter above those of the former. In essence, *The Politics of the Judiciary* critique (albeit unintentionally) legitimised Thatcherism and the policy agenda pursued by the Major governments by creating the impression that electoral approval in a mature democracy such as modern Britain necessarily lends governmental initiatives a morally irreproachable foundation.

In so doing, this analytical perspective runs the risk of lapsing into just the kind of supine legal positivism that characterised L.C. Steyn's approach to public law and statutory interpretation.[43] In the post-*Collins* era, that approach eventually transformed the Appellate Division into little more than an agent of the government. It is not much of an answer to this criticism to suggest that judicial deference is appropriate only when elected bodies are pursuing 'enlightened' policies, since that particular quality is not one which possesses—certainly in matters of detail—either an objective or an ahistorical base.

Yet whether applied in 1950s South Africa or modern Britain, judicial conservatism in this sense can do no more than temporarily obstruct and delay the effective implementation of the wishes of a bare parliamentary majority, be it of the left or the right. Judges whose conservative understanding of the common law led them to impede government policy would presumably offer justifications for so doing ostensibly rooted in orthodox common law principles. To some informed observers, that strategy would contain 'a heavy element of fiction'.[44] From 'fictional' it is but a short step to 'dishonest', and from there it is really no distance at all to 'undemocratic', since the judicial lawmaking process in issue can easily be characterised as neither transparent nor publicly accountable.

But the contention that such judicial obstructionism is therefore 'undemocratic' is oversimplistic. It is—to borrow from Centlivres' exchange with Andries

[42] See for example K. Ewing, 'A Bill of Rights: Lessons from the Privy Council', in W. Finnie, C. Himsworth and N. Walker (eds.), *Edinburgh Essays in Public Law* (Edinburgh: Edinburgh University Press, 1991): K. Ewing and C. Gearty *Civil Liberties Under Thatcher* (London: OUP, 1990); A. Tomkins, *After the Scott Report* (Oxford: Clarendon Press, 1997).

[43] See particularly the critiques by Sachs *op. cit.*, n. 1 above, and Dugard (1978) *op. cit.*, n. 1 above.

[44] This being Millner's description of Centlivres' reasoning in *Adburahman*; see p. 255 n. 118 above.

Beyers in *Harris No. 1* over the status of *Ndlwana*[45]—an assertion and not a conclusion. One might plausibly argue that such judicial behaviour reinforces the values of transparency and accountability within the democratic process. By forcing the government to promote further legislation to achieve its preferred radical objectives, the courts require legislative majorities to reflect further upon the acceptability of the course they pursue. They also afford electors the opportunity through the scrutiny of such legislation to reach more informed conclusions about the merits of government policy.[46] In that limited sense, the common law engineers a state of (weak) procedural entrenchment for conservative political values.

Nonetheless, even if a court should adopt this strategy, the point would soon be reached in modern Britain—as it was in Malan's South Africa—at which the judiciary is faced with the stark choice of deference or defiance in respect of the government's legislative intent. Its capacity to defend conservative values has only limited potential. It is dependent on the presumption that there is a legal gap between a given statutory text and the government's political objectives in promoting it. In other words, the court's conclusion has to be not that the legislative majority *cannot* do x, y or z, but that—thus far—it *has not* done so. In circumstances where the legislative majority and its electoral supporters are not deflected from their chosen course by a court's judgment and are willing to re-enter the legislative arena to pursue it, the courts must either concede that a conservative value has now been dispensed with or steel themselves to provide the moral basis for revolution. An effective constitutional safeguard against political extremism necessary requires that the judiciary is provided with an supra-legislative and super-majoritarian source of legal authority, in terms of which it can both legitimise its own conclusions and simultaneously undermine the legislature's constitutional bona fides. In an abstract sense, this is the battle that the Centlivres Court fought and won over the Cape franchise by invoking the two-thirds majority requirement as a legitimating moral yardstick for its judgments in *Harris Nos. 1 and* 2. That the battle was eventually lost in the practical sense is not a demonstration that super-majoritarian constitutional settlements are a worthless enterprise, but rather an illustration of the point that their creators need to be possessed of rather more foresight (or integrity) than the delegates to South Africa's constitutional convention.

[45] See p. 284 above.

[46] Even if we were to accept the accuracy of the first assertion however, it does not necessarily follow that the behaviour it condemns is constitutionally undesirable. Rather it may mean that we have to reconcile ourselves to the uncomfortable fact that while such judgments would be a constitutional evil in an abstract sense, they amount to a lesser constitutional evil than decisions which—in eschewing any element of 'fiction'—allowed governments to implement extremist policies.

V. CONSTITUTIONS AS 'FUNDAMENTAL' LAW

The notion of legally entrenched moral values lies at the core of the *Harris* litigation. It is of course a notion that has enjoyed minimal currency within the British constitutional tradition, wherein it has always been accepted:[47] firstly that a bare majority of the Commons and Lords, having received the Monarch's assent to their wishes, might enact legislation on any subject matter whatsoever; and secondly that no British court possesses the power to 'test' the constitutionality of any such legislation against supra-parliamentary criteria. The British courts' reaction to the United Kingdom's accession to the European Communities has latterly led to some minor modification of those orthodoxies—discussed further below—but there has been little serious suggestion, be it by politicians, judges or academic lawyers to the effect that the moral values articulated in the law of the EC are entrenched in UK law in the sense that Parliament cannot repeal them all by removing this country from the EC altogether.[48]

Both the political left and right have consistently and vociferously dismissed the constitutional desirability of having such entrenched rights in the United Kingdom. Their argument has an obvious appeal. It starts from the ostensibly incontrovertible premise that the constitution's most important task is to ensure that the country is governed according to 'democratic' principles. It then makes the following assertions. Entrenched rights necessarily empower senior judges to overturn unconstitutional legislation. Legislators are elected by 'the people', are thus 'democratic' lawmakers and so necessarily produce 'democratic' laws.[49] Judges are not elected by the people, and are thus not 'democratic' lawmakers and so necessarily produce 'undemocratic' laws. Entrenched rights are therefore 'undemocratic' in principle.[50] A secondary argument, again premised on supposedly democratic principles—is that entrenchment necessarily makes modern society the prisoner of the political values espoused by its predecessors.[51]

[47] Other than, on occasion, by a few heretically minded academics; see particularly T. Smith, 'The Treaty of Union as Fundamental Law' (1957) *Public Law* 99: T.R.S. Allan, 'Legislative Supremacy and the Rule of Law' (1985) *Cambridge LJ* 111; *Law, Liberty and Justice* (Oxford: Clarendon Press, 1993).

[48] I have—somewhat frivolously and speculatively—made that suggestion elsewhere: see 'Parliamentary Sovereignty and the EC: the Unfinished Revolution?' (1996) *Parliamentary Affairs* 571.

[49] The argument is usually accompanied by the supposition that the composition of the Lords must be reformed to purge Parliament of its 'undemocratic' elements, and by the assumption that the Queen presents no substantive threat to 'democratic' governance because she always acts on the advice of her elected Ministers. That the Commons is a grossly unrepresentative institution is generally glossed over. For an exception see Tomkins *op. cit.*, n. 42 above, pp. 266–275.

[50] The United States supposedly offers the most fertile ground for this thesis, with the series of Supreme Court decisions which invalidated Roosevelt's initial New Deal legislation being held up as a prime example of this perniciously anti-democratic trend.

[51] See for example Sir Stephen Sedley, 'Human Rights: a Twenty-First Century Agenda' (1995) *Public Law* 386.

These are of course precisely the arguments invoked by Malan, by Strijdom and by Verwoerd in response to *Harris Nos. 1 and 2*, a factor which might suggest opponents of entrenched rights in the United Kingdom should pause to give their position further thought. It is no answer for them to assert simply that the South African analogy is inappropriate because the United Kingdom has a universal franchise and is therefore presumptively a 'democratic' country, while South Africa prior to the 1990s never possessed that status.

Such a response rests on three presumptions. The first is that the notion of 'democracy' is at root but minimally concerned with matters determining the citizenry's substantive legal entitlements, and is instead overwhelmingly concerned with matters of political process. Thus as long as all citizens have a right to vote, and as long as that vote is counted in a fashion which is not grossly distortive of collective public sentiment and which does not institutionalise a marked bias in favour of one particular political ideology,[52] the laws made by the elected legislature will necessarily be democratic. The second is that there is no need to entrench even the laws guaranteeing the integrity of the electoral process, for society's moral commitment to its preservation is so intense that no electoral or legislative majority would ever wish to undermine it. The third presumption is that electoral and legislative majorities in the United Kingdom will always be sufficiently 'enlightened' not to pursue policies which would infringe those other fundamental substantive legal entitlements of the citizenry which in most 'democratic' nations, not blessed it seems with such enlightened voters and legislators, can only be safeguarded by entrenched, judicially enforceable protections.

All three premises seem to adopt an extraordinarily optimistic (or, more perjoratively, naive) view of our political culture and a similarly stunted view of the substance of democracy. It is readily apparent, for example, that a universal franchise is of very limited value in electoral systems which apportion seats in a grossly biased fashion, or in a society which places partisan restrictions on freedom of political expression, or under a constitution which permits disenfranchisement consequent upon conviction for a 'crime' while placing no limits on the type of behaviour (for example political dissent) which a bare legislative majority can criminalise. In such circumstances, the process right, deprived of substantive reinforcement, can be quite illusory. The second premise is intrinsically quite bizarre, amounting in effect to a claim that there is no need to entrench those values legally because they are already entrenched morally. The third seems simply to be blind to history, assuming that politicians would never pander for electoral advantage to bigoted or intolerant public sentiment.

The suggestion that entrenchment necessarily binds society to the values of past generations is also quite fallacious. That argument would have great force if entrenchment meant only that particular values were substantively fixed for

[52] These of course being the minimum substantive rights needed to lend meaning to the process rights.

all time and that no constitutional mechanism to amend them existed. It has minimal force if the purpose of entrenchment is simply to afford limited procedural protection to the values concerned. To borrow the analysis Denis Cowen invoked in *Harris No. 1*, procedurally entrenched rights do not *restrain* modern societies but rather *define* them, by clearly delineating the boundaries of their political morality. The only sense in which such entrenched rights[53] amount to a restraint is that a society cannot carelessly toss aside the moral principles that its previous generations held so dear. If it wishes to reject them it can do so, but it should leave them behind only after having constructed a broad consensus in favour of change.

Legitimising the principle

Quite how modern British society might go about the process or redefining itself in this way is of course a large question. It is, to be more precise, three large and inter-related questions. Namely which values should be accorded 'fundamental' constitutional importance; by what legal mechanism should that status subsequently be protected; and through what political method could we effect the 'revolution' needed to bring such change about?

The what . . .

One of the inevitable difficulties attending any attempt to engineer constitutional reform in a mature and stable democracy is that initiatives invariably proceed in a piecemeal fashion. The linkage between different facets of the constitutional structure may simply not be appreciated by legislators—or, if recognised, may be ignored. The ongoing British debates about reforming the Commons' electoral system and the altering composition of the House of Lords are obvious examples of this problem. Much of the discontent over the present electoral system stems from the fact that it affords unfettered legislative authority to bare parliamentary majorities which represent only electoral minorities. Objections to this consequence would be much less forceful if that bare parliamentary majority exercised only limited legislative authority. And the more limited that authority, the less objectionable the principle of bare parliamentary majoritarianism becomes. To approach the issue from the other direction, one might suggest that the more scope that an electoral system gives for a national legislature to be controlled by minoritarian interests, the more compelling is the argument for limiting that legislature's capacity to make laws by a bare majority. And as the size of the controlling minority diminishes, so the range of issues subject to bare majority legislation should also be reduced.

[53] I use the term here to encompass super-majorities of 66% to 75%. Once the majority necessary for change exceeds 75%, one is really entering the realm of *de facto* if not *de jure* substantive entrenchment.

This is not the place to offer yet another exhaustive shopping list of the 'fundamental' rights which—from a particular moment of space, time and political ideology—it would seem beneficial for the United Kingdom to adopt in a new constitutional settlement. The *Harris* episode in South Africa perhaps enables us to identify a few such values with little difficulty and to expect that their preservation would attract multi-party support in our present polity. A universal franchise producing some approximate correlation between votes cast and seats won, extensive protection for political expression, and a prohibition on racial and gender discrimination would be the obvious example. The addition of the other principles articulated in the European Convention on Human Rights might now also appear to be relatively uncontroversial, given that they have been incorporated into domestic law as additional grounds of review in respect of government action. Similar protection would also have to be extended to the process (newly refashioned on a bipartisan basis) of appointing judges and altering the composition of the legislature. A more contentious (and perhaps more important) value would be the creation of a federal rather than unitary state, which allocated substantial power to sub-central elected bodies and required such bodies' consent to its reduction. The regionally derived differences in political opinion among the British population are rather less starkly drawn than those held by whites in the four southern African colonies. They are nonetheless significant, and there seems no obvious reason why in a country of some sixty million people that psephological diversity should not be permitted simultaneous access to meaningful governmental power.[54]

. . . and the how . . .

It was suggested above that understandings of democracy which focus upon issues of lawmaking procedure to the virtual exclusion of substantive limits on ordinary lawmaking powers are severely flawed. But to adopt the converse view in defence of 'fundamental rights' is equally problematic. One lesson the *Harris* litigation does *not* impart is that entrenchment through enhanced parliamentary majorities is futile because entrenched substantive rights could always be overturned through such indirect procedural techniques as packing the courts with judges—or the legislature with MPs—whose loyalty lies to a governing bare majority rather than to the constitution. It does however tell us that affording a given substantive right that status is in itself a wholly inadequate means of protecting the right concerned. The enhanced parliamentary majority technique of entrenchment does not automatically cure the problem of bare majoritarian or minoritarian legislation; it may simply relocate the problem to a political arena one, two or more steps removed from the substantive value in issue. The warning that the *Harris* litigation imparts to advocates of a programme of con-

[54] I have addressed this issue in some depth in I. Loveland, 'Local Authorities', in R. Blackburn and R. Plant (eds.), *Constitutional Reform Now* (Harlow: Longmans, 1988).

stitutional reform in the United Kingdom which creates supra-parliamentary, fundamental rights is that entrenchment mechanisms must ensure that bare majoritarianism and minoritarianism are substantively disabled rather than just symbolically displaced. A sophisticated understanding of the many interlinked strands of the lawmaking process is an essential pre-condition of effective entrenchment.

To offer a simple example, Strijdom's success in bypassing the entrenched nature of the Cape franchise by packing the Appellate Division and the senate would not have been available to him if the framers of the Act of Union had had the foresight (or inclination) to entrench with similar rigour provisions which guaranteed that the members of both institutions could be chosen only on a bipartisan basis. Thus a requirement that any legislation changing the composition of the senate or the house required a two thirds unicameral majority might well[55] have prevented enactment not just of the 1955 Senate Act, but also Hertzog's 1927 legislation and Malan's 1948 bill to create four senators for South West Africa.

A device to prevent packing of the courts would be slightly more complicated, but does not call for a particularly exotic flight of the constitutional imagination. An obvious cure for the 'packing' problem would have been for the constitution to have adopted the device suggested above—namely that appointments to the provincial division and promotions to the appellate division be made in pairs. One judge would be appointed by the Prime Minister, the other by the Leader of the Opposition, each of whom would have to approve the other's nominee. This requirement would itself have had to have been entrenched by the enhanced majority procedure. But one might then question whether it would ever be desirable to place the power to alter entrenched rights in the hands of the same lawmakers (albeit more of them) who are entrusted with enacting ordinary legislation. That solution to the entrenchment question has obvious dangers. Such legal and political currency as the Nationalists could muster for their views in *Harris Nos. 1* and *2* lay in no small part in the confusion that could be engendered in the public (i.e. white electorate's) mind by the 'three parliaments' structure adopted by the South African constitution. In exoteric terms, no obvious distinction could be drawn between these functionally discrete bodies. They comprised exactly the same people, meeting in exactly the same place, at exactly the same time. For observers not versed in the subtleties of constitutional law and theory, the assertion that the bodies would have to act in different ways is not immediately compelling. This type of mono-institutional entrenchment is also open to a further objection—namely that the (from the public's perspective) potentially blurred edges of each 'parliament's' jurisdiction diverts attention from the political significance of legislative proposals intended to alter 'fundamental' law.

[55] As I suggested above, it is possible that the requisite majority may have been forthcoming; see p. 391 above.

The inference thereby raised is that entrenchment mechanisms and the ordinary legislative process need to be institutionally as well as functionally discrete phenomena. If structured in this way, their activities they cannot possibly be confused with the 'ordinary' legislative process. Nor, relatedly, could the constitution's various 'fundamental' laws be confused with those enjoying only non-fundamental status. Perhaps equally importantly, an extra-parliamentary device precludes the possibility that fundamental laws could be changed instantaneously, for it would ensure that the issue in question was widely discussed and reflected upon.[56]

These imperatives are easily met in a federal constitutional structure, where—as in the USA—the task of constitutional amendment (and thus the exercise of sovereign legal power) is entrusted to a 'people' comprised of super-majorities of both the States and the national Congress. The constitution of a unitary state would perhaps best meet this objective by granting powers of constitutional amendment to a super-majority of the electorate in an issue-specific referendum. Parliament's role in the process could then sensibly be reduced simply to one of initiating proposals for change. If the requisite referendum majority were set at a level which manifestly precluded the possibility that it could be achieved by the supporters of a single political party, there is no obvious objection to allowing Parliament to initiate referenda by the simple majority legislative process. The enhanced majority referendum device also has the benefit of denying a political party the opportunity—so readily seized by Malan and Strijdom—of equating its legislative majority with the 'people'.

The more difficult issue that faces advocates of entrenchment—even assuming that they manage to surmount the hurdle of deciding which substantive values are to be protected—is that of deciding how deeply rooted that protection should be; and, relatedly, of deciding if a new constitutional settlement should recognise a hierarchy of entrenched rights, some of which would be more deeply protected than others.

. . . and the means to the end

Much of what has been said in the preceding section is applicable only to the realm of abstract theorisation. Its practical significance is limited largely to those few occasions when a nation professing a wish to establish a democratic polity finds itself writing upon a blank constitutional sheet. Such a scenario is manifestly not going to arise in the United Kingdom, where the legitimacy of any shift towards the recognition of judicially enforceable fundamental rights must be sensitive to the accumulated traditions—both legal and political—arising from the country's long history of generally peaceful and consensual governance.

[56] Although this concern could of course be met by the type of intra-legislative entrenchment procedures deployed in the Orange Free State; pp. 48–50 above.

Much the most controversial—and from an academic lawyer's perspective much the most interesting—question is whether the courts possess the moral and legal authority to invoke the common law as a device to protect 'fundamental rights'; not simply from the actions of government[57] but also from incursion by Parliament. The controversy and the interest has been stimulated by the UK's membership of the EC, and particularly by the judgment of the House of Lords in the *Factortame* litigation,[58] in which the court held that it would 'disapply' domestic legislation that was implicitly inconsistent with directly effective EC law. The opinion offered by Lord Bridge attempted to reconcile this nominally radically conclusion by explaining that the European Communities Act 1972 had impliedly inserted into every subsequent statute concerned with EC matters an invisible clause to the effect that the courts should not apply any part of the Act that conflicted with EC law. Parliament, in Lord Bridge's view, had 'voluntarily limited its sovereignty' in 1972.

As H.R.W. Wade has pointed out, this reasoning makes very little sense, whether as an excursion in legal theory or as a recipe for practical politics. The obvious problem with Lord Bridge's reasoning is that if Parliament has managed in 1972 to entrench the European Communities Act, on what basis can one sensibly maintain that it could not now or in the future entrench other legislation as well: "the new doctrine makes sovereignty a freely adjustable commodity whenever Parliament chooses to accept some limitation".[59]

This is perhaps not as alarming a spectre as it may appear. *Factortame* entrenchment is—it seems—of an extremely weak procedural kind. It does not take the form of requiring super-majorities within Parliament, nor that there be resort to any extra-parliamentary device, but merely requires that a bare parliamentary majority expresses itself in unusually blunt language. A new Merchant Shipping Act which said in section 1 that it was intended to repudiate the UK's obligations under the Common Fisheries Policy would presumably have been applied by Lord Bridge and his colleagues.[60] It certainly could not have been disapplied through the judicial techniques used in *Factortame No. 2*.

Factortame need not therefore be read as suggesting that Parliament has granted itself within the UK a power equivalent to that granted to colonial

[57] There seems little doubt that the courts have episodically claimed such a power at various stages in the past 100 years through the device of subjecting government actions which interfere with such rights to a more exacting standard of scrutiny to establish if it has a defensible common law or statutory root. See for example the cases surveyed in S. de Smith, Lord Woolf and J. Jowell, *Judicial Review of Administrative Action*, (London: Sweet and Maxwell, 1995) pp. 325–330. What amounts to such a right is, of course, a judicially determined matter.

[58] *R v Secretary of State for Transport, ex parte Factortame (No. 2)* [1991] 1 AC 603.

[59] 'Sovereignty—Revolution or Evolution' (1996) 112 LQR 568 at 573.

[60] That type of entrenchment obviously does not satisfy the requirements of Community membership, which demand that the supremacy of EC law be permanently (i.e. throughout the period that the member state remains within the community) entrenched within member states' legal systems. If the courts were to disapply that hypothetical Act, we would have arrived at a deeper form of entrenchment for EC law, and one that met EC requirements; i.e. that Parliament could not breach EC law while the UK remained a member of the community.

legislatures in section 5 of the Colonial Laws Validity Act 1865 to entrench particular values by altering the legislative manner and form required to change them. As I have suggested elsewhere,[61] an entrenchment device of this sort is a monstrous creation, as it would enable a bare legislative majority enjoying only minority electoral support to set such high thresholds for the repeal of its preferred laws that they could never be altered.[62] But one might of course note that if Parliament was able to create even a very weak form of entrenchment in 1972, might it not be able to create much stronger entrenchment devices in future?

Wade's conclusion that *Factortame* therefore amounts to a 'judicial revolution' is initially enticing, but on closer inspection has several weaknesses. The first is that he seeks to buttress his analysis by invoking *Harris No. 1* as an authority:

> "Just as in the *Harris* case the South African judges elected to carry over the old entrenched clauses into the new constitution . . . so in *Factortame* the House of Lords elected to allow the Parliament of 1972 to fetter the Parliament of 1988 in order that Community law might be given the primacy which practical politics obviously required".[63]

The comparison is really not a valid one. However one explains *Factortame*, it is undoubtedly an innovative judgment. *Harris No. 1*, in contrast, was an intensely conservative decision which was firmly rooted in South(ern) African constitutional law and tradition and buttressed by copious legal authority from other Commonwealth jurisdictions. In simple terms, the Appellate Division did not hold that there was a 'new' constitution at all; rather it concluded that, contrary to the beliefs of the Malan government and its own per incuriam decision in *Ndlwana*, the 'old' constitution was still very much in existence.[64]

More problematic however, is the assumption—which Wade initially made his 1955 discussion of *Harris*—that explanations for judicial behaviour can be reduced to question of 'ultimate political facts'. In advancing new understandings of their powers *vis-à-vis* the legislature, it is suggested, the courts are simply adapting to new political realities. To put the matter crudely, law follows politics; and our membership of the EC has presented the courts with a new 'ultimate political fact'.

The claim is not particularly enlightening. Indeed it might be thought quite misleading. The *Harris* saga does rather strongly suggest that—in situations other than those of violent revolution—the legitimacy of that new 'ultimate' political fact is substantially dependent upon the legal defensibility of the process through which a society moves from one understanding of its constitutional structure to another. T.R.S. Allan's analysis of *Factortame* is more satisfactory

[61] (1996) *op. cit.*, n. 2 above, ch. 15.

[62] *Ibid.* pp. 612–613.

[63] (1996) *op. cit.*, n. 59 above, at 574.

[64] The Appellate Division obviously accepted that—post 1931 — South Africa was a new country, but it did not make the elementary error of confusing changes in South Africa's status *vis-à-vis* other states with changes in its internal constitutional dynamics.

on this issue.[65] Allan has long offered a rather isolated voice in our constitutional discourse to the effect that orthodox understandings of parliamentary sovereignty are, and always have been, ill-conceived.[66] Allan's suggestion that our current constitutional settlement permits the courts to disapply legislation which is irreconcilable with the concept of the rule of law offers a fascinating point of departure for abstract discussion.[67] The power of his argument is obviously contingent on what we might mean by 'the rule of law'. We might easily accept—taking *Harris No. 2* as our guide—that legislation purporting to grant a select committee of the House of Commons appellate jurisdiction over judgments of the House of Lords would fall into this category. So, presumably, would an Act which established a new Supreme Court whose judges were all barristers who had in the immediate past been MPs representing the governing party.

Identifying the limits beyond which the courts should not permit Parliament to go is of course a difficult exercise. Barendt's suggestion that a judge might legitimately invalidate 'evil' legislation would perhaps command wide assent—until such time as we asked ourselves what we meant by 'evil'.[68] Murray Hunt's recently published and influential work, *Using Human Rights Law in English Courts*,[69] places such analyses on rather more justiciable moral grounds by suggesting that international human rights treaties provide an appropriate yardstick against which to measure the legitimacy of any such judicial innovation.

Rather unfortunately—but understandably—recent musings by our senior judges in the academic press on matters of constitutional theory have tended to resort to outlandish examples of parliamentary extremism to illustrate scenarios

[65] 'Parliamentary Sovereignty: Law, Politics and Revolution' (1997) 113 *LQR* 443. Although Allan's suggestion that Wade's view of *Factortame* is readily undermined by reference to *Anisminic v The Foreign Compensation Commission* [1969] 2 AC 147 seems poorly founded. In *Anisminic*, the House of Lords ignored an unambiguous ouster clause in the Foreign Compensation Act 1950 by the transparently mendacious technique of concluding that the statutory text in issue did not mean what it obviously meant. This is a rather different strategy, albeit a no less dishonest one, than was deployed in *Factortame*, insofar as its supposed constitutional root lies in an abstract principle of the rule of law (i.e. that courts should determine the meaning of statutes) rather than in (as with the European Communities Act) an earlier statute.

[66] See particularly (1983), 'Parliamentary Sovereignty: Lord Denning's Dextrous Revolution' *OJLS* 22; (1985) *op. cit.*, n. 47 above; (1993) *op. cit.*, n. 47 above.

[67] Even so his vision of the issues at stake in the controversy is uncomfortably limited. Allan's critique, like Wade's, and indeed like most of the debate around *Factortame*, is marked by just the same insularity that Melius de Villiers identified a century ago in respect of *Brown v Leyds*; (see pp. 50–51 above). For many politicians the issue has been the relationship between Parliament and 'Brussels'. For academic lawyers it has been about the relationship between Parliament and the UK courts. (H.R.W. Wade's discussion of the litigation—like his critique of *Harris* in 1955—makes no mention of the individual citizen's interest in the case; (1996) *op. cit.*). What has rather been forgotten is that this particular constitutional episode was triggered by the deliberate decision of a xenophobic minoritarian government to use its Commons and Lords majorities to enact a crudely segregationist economic policy which—in addition to clearly breaching the Treaty of Rome—was intended to bankrupt several business enterprises and throw many people into unemployment and poverty. It would be a very strange view of 'democracy' which nonetheless accorded legitimacy to such behaviour.

[68] E. Barendt, *An Introduction to Constitutional Law* (Oxford: Clarendon Press, 1998) p. 105.

[69] (Oxford: Hart Publishing, 1997).

in which a court might legitimately disapply legislation. Sir John Laws, now a member of the Court of Appeal, has made the most extensive and wide-ranging journies into this field,[70] but has not thus far specified the type of Acts he had in mind. Nor are the concrete examples given by some other judges very enlightening. Disenfranchisement of a substantial section of the population or the complete abolition of the courts' power to review the legality of government action are favoured examples of the type of Act a court might refuse to apply.[71] Outside the confines of the classroom, this scenario does not take us very far. This is in part because a direct parliamentary assault on the extent of the franchise or a complete abolition of judicial review is so unlikely in political terms that it is hard to conceive of a government and legislature that would embark on such a course.[72] Moreover, if a government did ever promote such legislation, one would expect it already to have used its own powers to pack the courts with sympathetic judges before the constitutionality of the Act was called into question. Such extra-judicial commentaries would be rather more illuminating if the hypothetical statutes their authors advanced embraced somewhat less outlandish political scenarios. A parliamentary attempt by a minoritarian government to withdraw the UK from the EC without the unanimous consent of the other member states would perhaps be a more helpful example. The withdrawal would breach EC law and would also deprive many millions of citizens of a valuable panoply of economic, social and political rights. Eliciting the views of our more radically inclined judges on the 'constitutionality' of such a statute—or perhaps on one repealing the Race Relations Act 1976 or granting the government a power to detain alleged 'terrorists' for several days without charge solely on the basis of a police officer's untested suspicions—might provide a more empirically pertinent grounding for theorisation.

It would seem clear that even the most extreme of legislative measures which the courts will face in the foreseeable future will do no more than bite at the boundaries of political consensus rather than leap far beyond them. In those circumstances, it is difficult to envisage any further (r)evolution in the courts' understanding of the sovereignty of Parliament. The apparently entrenched

[70] 'Is the High Court the Guardian of Fundamental Constitutional Rights?' (1993) *Public Law* 59; 'Judicial Remedies and the Constitution' (1994) 57 *MLR* 213; 'Law and Democracy' *Public Law* 72; 'Meiklejohn, the First Amendment and Freedom of Speech in English Law', in I. Loveland (ed.), *Importing the First Amendment* (Oxford: Hart Publishing, 1998).

[71] See Lord Woolf, 'Droit Public—English Style' (1995) *Public Law* 57 at pp. 67–69. Lord Woolf expressly limits his discussion to 'politically unthinkable' legislation, an approach which rather makes one wonder why the issue is worth thinking about.

[72] English judges engaged in such philosophising seem to be fixed with rather limited political vision; see for example Lord Browne-Wilkinson, 'The Infiltration of a Bill of Rights' (1992) *Public Law* 397. One wonders for example if Oliver Schreiner, placed in a contemporary British context, would have seen an indirect but nonetheless impermissible assault on the franchise in the community charge legislation, which, by linking the electoral register with liability to pay local taxes undoubtedly had an indirect impact on voting rights for the most impoverished members of the community. Nor is it difficult to maintain an argument that the abolition of the GLC and metropolitan county councils by the Local Government Act 1985 impacted upon voting rights, albeit not for the Commons.

position of EC law may well be the sole exception to the orthodox rule, having achieved that status largely because it offers our courts several convenient anchorage points above and beyond the common law[73] on which to secure the *Factortame* rationale.

No other source of 'fundamental law' can presently lay claim to such persuasive sources of external validation. Without this reinforcement, it is difficult to conceive of any plausible legislative innovation that might prompt a court to claim a hitherto non-existent common law power. For it to do so would trigger—if not a constitutional crisis—at least a period of acute political controversy. This would indicate that we should not be looking to the judiciary as a source of fundamental legal principle.

As suggested above, any attempt to impose super-majoritarian entrenchment of any 'fundamental laws' through the device of bare majoritarian legislation enacted by Parliament as it is currently composed could make not any serious claim to constitutional legitimacy. A parliamentary effort to do so through bipartisan legislation would presumably a more securely 'democratic' base; and its claim to legitimacy would become stronger as the size of the parliamentary majority supporting it increased. Yet even if such a constitutional '(r)evolution' attracted virtually unanimous legislative approval, it would still suffer the handicap of not possessing any clear institutional cleavage between ordinary and extraordinary laws and lawmaking procedures.

This would suggest that any new constitutional settlement would have to be fashioned by an extra-parliamentary Assembly or Convention. The proposals offered by the Liberal Democrat proposal at the 1992 general election went some way to meeting this meeting this goal,[74] although the party's decision to limit membership of its Constitutional Assembly solely to members of the Commons is surely a weakness.

That MPs might form a substantial contingent of any such Assembly seems an uncontroversial proposition, especially if the process were to begin following upon a more modest reform of the Commons' electoral system which produces a closer correlation than at present between a party's representation in the lower house and its level of electoral support. The addition of members of the newly created assemblies in Scotland, Northern Ireland and Wales would lend such an enterprise a more consensual political base. As would, no doubt, the inclusion of those of our lawmakers whom we currently assume to stand outside the party political process—the judges.

Nor should we be deterred from such a project even if we accept the traditionalist argument that Parliament's sovereignty is irremovable. Rather we might re-direct our attention from disabling aspects of Parliament's power to disabling Parliament itself. A plausible solution to this difficulty—albeit inelegant in theoretical terms—is for our present Parliament to disable itself by

[73] Namely the ECA 1972 and the institutions of the community, particularly the European Court of Justice itself.

[74] Described in Loveland (1996) *op. cit.*, n. 2 above, pp. 624–630.

apportioning all its powers to the desired sub-Parliamentary bodies. This would include the allocation of the power of constitutional amendment to a manifestly super-majoritarian, extraordinary lawmaking body—'the people'—defined in a way which makes it unlikely that it will legislate on a frequent basis. As matter of legal theory, Parliament would still 'exist'. But there would be no way for it to act, and no way for it to be brought back into being by any of the subordinate bodies it created other than the people themselves. And when it comes to exercising this power, we might seek to define 'the people' in a fashion that imposes an extremely high degree of entrenchment indeed. This would leave us with the rather bizarre constitutional structure as a matter of theory: 'the people'—being the creation of Parliament—are technically its subordinate, yet they are also the only lawmaker that can call their creator back into being.

VI. CONCLUSION

The constitutional prescription offered here is essentially a pessimistic one. It views the process of constitution building as largely an exercise in negativity: not as a task which celebrates the best in human nature but one which fears the worst, in which the participants' main responsibility is not to encourage their electors to do good but to minimise the likely political impact of their propensity to do evil. The British people take a continuing political risk in maintaining a constitutional structure within which untrammelled legal authority can be wielded by the representatives of so few of their number. The risk is hardly comparable to that taken by those societies which adopt similar constitutional settlements but which lack the historical tradition of a broadly consensual political process which modern Britain has enjoyed. Overnight tyranny is not a prospect of which we need have any fear. A more pertinent worry is that a series of intolerant legislative majorities may push our country incrementally, in a ratchet-like process, in a direction which exposes our children to a governmental system which we would regard as less and less enlightened, and towards which—by dint of accumulated experience—their critical faculties have become increasingly enfeebled. From that perspective, our continued embrace of our constitutional orthodoxies makes us guilty of a thoroughgoing abdication of our moral responsibilities. We seem almost to celebrate our unwillingness to identify the values we hold most dear and attempt to protect them accordingly. It appears as yet that only a minority—albeit a growing minority—of our population consider the experience of British political history a sufficient reason for desiring a super-majoritarian constitutional settlement. If this book is to have any worth beyond that of relating an interesting story to curious readers, it may be in convincing more of our citizens that the political evils our constitutional orthodoxies bequeathed to several past generations of South Africans are sufficient reason to recast those orthodoxies into a more substantively defensible legal form better to protect future generations of Britons.

Bibliography

Abel, R., *Politics By Other Means* (London: Routledge, 1995).
Akehurst, M., *A Modern Introduction to International Law* (London: George Allen and Unwin, 1982, 4th edn.).
Allan, T.R.S., 'Parliamentary Sovereignty: Lord Denning's Dextrous Revolution' (1983) *OJLS* 22.
—— 'Legislative Supremacy and the Rule of Law' (1985) *Cambridge LJ* 111.
—— *Law, Liberty and Justice* (Oxford: Clarendon Press, 1993).
—— 'Parliamentary Sovereignty: Law, Politics and Revolution' (1997) 113 *LQR* 443.
Ashforth, A., *The Politics of Official Discourse in Twentieth Century South Africa* (Oxford: Clarendon Press, 1990).
Bailes, H., 'Military Aspects of the War' (1980) in Warwick (ed.), *infra.*
Bailyn, B., *The Ideological Origins of the American Revolution* (Cambridge, Mass: Harvard UP, 1969).
Basson, D. and Viljown, H., *South African Constitutional Law* (Cape Town: Juta & Co., 1988).
Beinart, B., 'Parliament and the Courts' (1954) *Butterworths South African LR* 134.
—— 'Police Powers' (1955) *Butterworths South African LR* 157.
—- 'The Rule of Law' (1962) *Acta Juridica* 99.
Beinart, W., *Twentieth Century South Africa* (Oxford: OUP, 1994).
—— and Dubow, S. (eds.), *Segregation and Apartheid* (London: Routledge, 1995).
—— —— 'The Historiography of Segregation and Apartheid', in Beinart and Dubow *supra.*
Beloff, M., *Britain's Liberal Empire 1897–1921* (London: Methuen, 1969).
Bennet, T., 'African Land—a History of Dispossession', in R. Zimmerman and D. Visser (eds.), *Southern Cross: Civil Law and Common Law in South Africa* (Oxford: Clarendon Press, 1996).
Blackwell, L., *Blackwell Remembers* (Cape Town: Howard Timmins, 1971).
Blanch, M., 'British Society and the War' (1980), in Warwick (ed.), *infra.*
Blom-Cooper, L., 'The South African Treason Trial' (1959) 8 *ICLQ* 59.
Bork, R., *The Tempting of America* (New York: Free Press, 1990).
Brookes, E. and Macauly, J., *Civil Liberty in South Africa* (Cape Town: OUP, 1958).
Browne-Wilkinson, Lord, 'The Infiltration of a Bill of Rights' (1992) *Public Law* 397.
Bryce, J., *Studies in History and Jurisprudence* (Oxford: Clarendon Press, 1901).
Butler, D., *The Electoral System in Britain 1918–1951* (Oxford: Clarendon Press, 1953).
—— and Kavanagh, D., *The British General Election of 1997* (London: Macmillan, 1998).
Cameron, E., 'Legal Chauvinism, Executive-mindedness and Justice—LC Steyn's Impact on South African Law' (1982) *South African LJ* 99.
Cell, J., *The Highest Stage of White Supremacy* (London: Cambridge UP, 1982).
Centlivres, A., 'The South African Constitution and the Rule of Law" (1956) *Butterworths South African LR* 3.

Chafee, Z., 'Freedom of Speech in Time of War' (1919) *Harvard LR* 932.

Coetze, L., 'Watte Registeem Beheers die Verhouding Tussen Owerheid en Onderdaan in die Unie, Romeins Holland Reg of England Reg?' (1937) *Tydskrif vir Hedendagsee Romeins-Hollands Reg 34.*

—— 'Die Wegtwende Orgaan van die Unie van Suid-Afrika' (1941) *Tydskrif vir Hedendagsee Romeins Hollands Reg 41.*

Corder, H., *Judges at Work* (Cape Town: Juta & Co., 1984).

—— 'The Judicial Branch of Government: an Overview', in D. Visser (ed.), *Essays on the History of Law* (Cape Town: Juta & Co., 1989).

Corwin, E., 'The *Dred Scott* decision in the light of contemporary doctrines' (1911) *American Historical Review* 52.

Cowen, D., *Parliamentary Sovereignty and the Entrenched Provisions of the South Africa Act* (Cape Town: Juta & Co., 1951).

—— 'Legislature and Judiciary—Part One' (1952) 15 *Modern Law Review* 282.

—— 'Legislature and Judiciary—Part Two' (1953) 16 *Modern Law Review* 273.

—— 'The Entrenched Sections of the South Africa Act: Two Great Legal Battles' (1953) *South African LJ* 238.

—— *The Foundations of Freedom* (Cape Town: OUP, 1961).

Cowen, Z., 'Parliamentary Sovereignty and the Limits of Legal Change' (1952) 26 *Australian LJ* 237.

Craig, J., 'Parliament and the Boundary Commissions' (1959) *Public Law* 23.

Crawford, J., *The Creation of States in International Law* (Oxford: Clarendon Press, 1979).

Davenport, T., 'Civil Rights in South Africa 1910–1960' (1960) *Acta Juridica* 11.

—— *South Africa* (London: Macmillan, 1978, 2nd edn.).

De Smith, S., 'Boundaries Between Parliament and the Courts' (1955) 18 *MLR* 281.

De Villiers, M., 'The Relationship of the Judicial to the Legislative Authority' (1897) *Cape LJ* 38.

De Villiers, R., 'Afrikaner Nationalism', in Wilson and Thompson (eds.), (1971) *infra.*

Dean, W., 'Reason and Prejudice: the Courts and Licencing Bodies in the Transvaal', in E. Kahn (ed.), *Fiat Iustitia: Essays in Memory of Oliver Denys Schreiner* (Cape Town: Juta & Co., 1983).

—— 'Our Administrative Law: a Dismal Science' (1986) 2 *South African Journal of Human Rights* 164.

Dicey, A., *An Introduction to the Study of the Law of the Constitution*, 9th edn., by E.C.S. Wade (London: Macmillan, 1939).

Dold, G. and Joubert, C., *The Union of South Africa* (London: Stevens and Sons, 1955).

Dubow, S., *Racial Segregation and the Origins of Apartheid* (London: Macmillan, 1989).

Dugard, J., *Human Rights and the South African Legal Order* (Princeton: Princeton University Press, 1978).

—— 'Racial Legislation and Civil Rights', in E. Hellman and H. Lever (eds.), *Race Relations in South Africa 1929–1979* (London: Macmillan, 1979).

Dworkin, R., *Freedom's Laws* ch. 12 (Cambridge, Mass: Harvard UP, 1996).

Dyzenhaus, D., *Hard Cases in Wicked Legal Systems* (Oxford: Clarendon Press, 1991).

Ewing, K., 'A Bill of Rights: Lessons from the Privy Council', in W. Finnie, C. Himsworth, and N. Walker (eds.), *Edinburgh Essays in Public Law* (Edinburgh: Edinburgh University Press, 1991).

Ewing, K. and Gearty, C., *Civil Liberties Under Thatcher* (London: OUP, 1990).

Fagan, H., *Collected Letters and Papers*, University of Stellenbosch.
Fenberg, H., 'The 1913 Native Land Act in South Africa: Politics, Race and Segregation in the Early Twentieth Century' (1993) *International Journal of African Historical Studies*.
Fisher, L., *Constitutional Dialogues* (Princeton: Princeton University Press, 1988).
—— *Constitutional Rights* (New York: McGraw Hill, 1995, 2nd edn.).
Fitzpatrick, P., 'The Constitution of the Excluded', in I. Loveland (ed.), *A Special Relationship* (Oxford: Clarendon Press, 1995).
Forsyth, C., *In Danger For Their Talents* (Cape Town: Juta & Co., 1985).
Flather, H., *The Way of an Editor* (London: Purnell, 1977).
Frehling, W., 'The Founding Fathers and Slavery' (1972) *American Historical Review* 81.
Gilbert, M. (ed.), *Lloyd George* (New Jersey: Prentice Hall, 1968).
Godfrey Phillips, G., 'The Dominions and the United Kingdom' (1929) 3 *Cambridge LJ* 164.
Goodhart, A., '*Thomas v Sawkins*: a Constitutional Innovation' (1936) *Cambridge LJ* 22.
Gordon, J., 'The Judicial Crisis in the Transvaal' (1898) 14 *LQR* 443.
Grant, J., 'Judicial Control of Legislation' (1954) 3 *American Journal of Comparative Law* 186.
Gray, H., 'The Sovereignty of Parliament Today' (1953) 10 *University of Toronto* LJ 54.
Grigg, J., *Lloyd George: the People's Champion* (London: Eyre Methuen, 1978).
Griswold, E., 'The "Coloured Vote Case" in South Africa' (1952) 65 *Harvard LR* 1361.
—— 'The Demise of the High Court of Parliament in South Africa' (1953) 66 *Harvard LR* 864.
Grundlingh, A. 'Collaborators in Boer Society', (1980) in Warwick (ed.), *infra*.
Hachten, W. and Giffard, C., *The Press and Apartheid* (Madison, Wisc: University of Wisconsin Press, 1983).
Hahlo, H., 'European or Non-European?' (1952) *South African LJ* 116.
Hahlo, H. and Kahn, E., *South Africa: the Development of Its Laws and Constitution* (Cape Town: Juta & Co., 1960).
Hancock, K., *Smuts Volume 1: the Sanguine Years* (Cambridge: CUP, 1960).
—— *Smuts Volume 2: the Field of Force* (Cambridge: CUP, 1968).
Heard, K., *General Elections in South Africa 1943–1970* (London: OUP, 1974).
Hepple, A., *Verwoerd* (Harmondsworth: Pelican, 1967).
Hexham, I., 'Afrikaner Nationalism 1902–1914', (1980) in Warwick (ed.), *infra*.
Heyns, C., *A Jurisprudential Analysis of Civil Disobedience in South Africa* (Ph.D thesis: Faculty of Law, University of Pretoria, 1991).
Hirsen, B., *Yours for the Union* (Johannesburg: Witwatersrand University Press, 1989).
Hobsbawm, E., *Industry and Empire* (Harmondsworth: Penguin, 1972).
Hunt, M., *Using Human Rights Law in English Courts* (Oxford: Hart Publishing, 1997).
Hyam, R., *Elgin and Churchill at the Colonial Office 1905–1908* (London: Macmillan, 1968).
—— 'British Imperial Policy and South Africa 1906–1910', (1980) in Warwick (ed.), *infra*.
Innes, J. Rose, *Autobiography* (Cape Town: OUP, 1949).
Irvine, Lord, 'Judges and Decision-Makers: the Theory and Practice of *Wednesbury* Review' (1996) *Public Law* 59.
Jenkins, R., *Sir Charles Dilke* (London: Collins, 1958).

Jenkins, R., *Mr Balfour's Poodle* (London: Heinemann, 1968).
—— *Asquith* (London: Collins, 3rd edn., 1986).
—— *Gladstone* (London: Macmillan, 1995).
Jenks, E., 'The Imperial Conference and the Constitution' (1929) 3 *Cambridge LJ* 13.
Jennings, I., 'The Statute of Westminster and Appeals to the Privy Council' (1936) 52 *LQR* 173.
Jennings, R., *The Acquisition of Territory in International Law* (Manchester: Manchester University Press, 1963).
Joshi, P., *The Tyranny of Colour* (London: Kennikat Press, 1973).
Judd, D., *Balfour and the British Empire* (London: Macmillan, 1968).
Judd, D. and Slinn, P., *The Evolution of the Modern Commonwealth 1902–1980* (London: Macmillan, 1982).
Kahn, E., 'Constitutional Law' (1951) *Annual Survey of South African Law* 1.
—— 'Constitutional Law' (1952) *Annual Survey of South African Law* 1.
—— 'Right of Police to Attend Private Meeting' (1955) *Annual Survey of South African Law* 14.
—— 'Police Attendance at a Private Meeting' (1955) *South African LJ* 134.
—— 'Oliver Denys Schreiner—the Man and His Judicial World' (1980) *South African LJ* 566.
Katzenellenbogen, S., 'Reconstruction in the Transvaal', (1980) in Warwick (ed.), *infra*.
Keeton, G., 'The Constitutional Crisis in South Africa' (1953) *Current Legal Problems* 22.
Keith, A., *Responsible Government in the Dominions* (Oxford: Clarendon Press, 1912).
—— *The Constitutional Law of the British Dominions* (London: Macmillan, 1933).
—— *The Governments of the British Empire* (London: Macmillan, 1935).
Kennedy, A., *Salisbury 1830–1903* (New York: Kraus Reprint Co., 1971).
Kennedy, W., 'The Imperial Conferences, 1926–1930. The Statute of Westminster' (1938) 48 *LQR* 191.
Kennedy, W. and Schlosberg, H., *The Law and Custom of the South African Constitution* (London: Stevens and Sons, 1935).
Koss, S. (ed.), *The Pro-Boers* (Chicago: University of Chicago Press, 1973).
Kotze, J., 'Judicial Precedent' (1917) 34 *South African LJ* 281.
Kruger, D., 'The British Imperial Factor in South Africa from 1870–1910' in L. Gann and P. Dignan (eds.), *Colonialism in South Africa* (Cambridge: CUP, 1969).
Kuper, L., *Passive Resistance* (London: Jonathan Cape, 1956).
Landis, E., 'South African Apartheid Legislation I: Fundamental Structure' (1961) 71 *Yale LJ* 1.
—— 'South African Apartheid Legislation II: Extension, Enforcement and Perpetuation' (1962) 71 *Yale LJ* 371.
Lawrence, H., *Collected Papers and Letters*, University of Cape Town.
Laws, J., 'Is the High Court the Guardian of Fundamental Constitutional Rights?' (1993) *Public Law* 59.
—— 'Judicial Remedies and the Constitution' (1994) 57 *MLR* 213.
—— 'Law and Democracy' (1995) *Public Law* 72.
—— 'Meiklejohn, the First Amendment and Freedom of Speech in English Law', in I. Loveland (ed.), *Importing the First Amendment?* (Oxford: Hart Publishing, 1998).
Le May, G., 'Parliament, the Constitution and the Doctrine of the Mandate' (1957) *South African LJ* 33.

Legassick, M., 'British Hegemony and the Origins of Segregation in South Africa 1901–1914', (1995) in Beinart and Dubow (eds.), *supra*.
Levy, L., (ed.), *Essays on the Making of the Constitution* (New York: OUP, 1987).
Lewin, J., 'The Struggle for Law in South Africa' (1956) 27 *Political Quarterly* 176.
Lewis, A., *Gideon's Trumpet* (New York: Vintage, 1964).
—— *Make No Law* (New York: Vintage, 1991).
Lewis, G., *Between the Wire and the Wall* (Cape Town: David Phillip, 1987).
Lloyd, T., *The British Empire 1558–1995* (Oxford: OUP (1996), 2nd edn.).
Lodge, T., *Black Politics in South Africa Since 1945* (London: Longmans, 1983).
Lofgren, N., *The Plessey Case* (New York: OUP, 1992).
Loveland, I., 'Introduction: Should We Take Lessons From America', in I. Loveland (ed.), *A Special Relationship* (Oxford: Clarendon Press, 1995).
—— *Constitutional law* (London: Butterworths, 1996).
—— 'Parliamentary Sovereignty and the EC: the Unfinished Revolution' (1997) *Parliamentary Affairs* 567.
—— 'A Free Trade in Ideas—and Outcomes?', in I. Loveland (ed.), *Importing the First Amendment* (Oxford: Hart Publishing, 1998).
—— 'Local Authorities', in R. Blackburn and R. Plant (eds.), *Constitutional Reform Now* (Harlow: Longmans, 1998a).
Lumb, R., 'Native Title to Land in Australia: Recent High Court Decisions' (1993) 42 *ICLQ* 84.
McCloskey, R., *The American Supreme Court* (Chicago: University of Chicago Press, 2nd edn., 1994) ch. 2.
McWhinney, E., 'The Union Parliament, the Supreme Court and the Entrenched Clauses of the South Africa Act' (1952) 30 *Canadian Bar Review* 692.
—— 'The New High Court of Parliament' (1952a) 30 *Canadian Bar Review* 734.
—— 'The Court Versus the Legislature in the Union of South Africa' (1953) 31 *Canadian Bar Review* 52.
Mallet, C., *Herbert Gladstone* (London: Hutchinson & Co., 1932).
Malz, E., 'Slavery, Federalism and the Structure of the Constitution' (1992) *American Journal of Legal History* 466.
Mandela, N., *Long Walk to Freedom* (London: Abacus, 1995).
Marks, S. and Trapido, S., 'Lord Milner and the South African State' (1979) 8 *History Workshop* 50.
Marriot, J., *The Evolution of the British Empire and Commonwealth* (London: Nicholson and Watson, 1939).
Marshall, G., *Parliamentary Sovereignty and the Commonwealth* (Oxford: Clarendon Press, 1957).
Marquard, L., *The Story of South Africa* (London: Faber and Faber, 1955).
Matthews, E., 'Legislation Relating to Marriage or Sexual Intercourse between Europeans and Natives or Coloured Persons' (1921) *South African LJ* 313.
May, H., *The South African Constitution* (Cape Town: Juta & Co., 2nd edn., 1949).
—— *The South African Constitution* (Cape Town: Juta & Co., 3rd edn., 1955).
Mayer, J. and Abramson, J., *Strange Justice* (New York: Houghton Mifflin, 1994).
Meintjes, J., *President Paul Kruger* (Cassell: London, 1974).
Merret, C., *A Culture of Censorship* (University of Natal Press: Pietermarizburg, 1994).
Mervis, J., 'The Torch Commando' (11952) *The Forum* (May) 4.
—— *The Fourth Estate* (Johannesburg: Jonathan Ball, 1989).

Michelson, C., *The Black Sash of South Africa* (Cape Town: Juta & Co., 1975).
Millner, C., 'Apartheid and the South African Courts' (1961) *Current Legal Problems* 280.
Molteno, D., *Collected Letters and Papers*, University of Cape Town.
Moodie, T., *The Rise of Afrikanerdom* (London: University of California Press, 1975).
Morgan, K., *Keir Hardie* (London: Macmillan, 1975).
Mulligan, G., 'The Senate Act Case' (1957) *South African LJ* 7.
Nelson, M., 'The President and the Court' (1988) *Political Science Quarterly* 267.
Note, 'Editorial' (1952) 68 *Law Quarterly Review* 285.
Norval, A., *Deconstructing Apartheid Discourse* (London: Verso, 1996).
O'Kere, B., 'The Western Sahara Case' (1979) 28 *ICLQ* 296.
O'Meara, D., *Forty Lost Years* (Athens, Ohio: Ohio University Press, 1996).
Omer-Cooper, J., *History of Southern Africa* (London: Heinemann, 1987).
—— 'The Mfecane Survives Its Critics' in C. Hamilton (ed.), *The Mfecane Aftermath* (Johannesburg: University of Witwatersrand Press, 1995).
Pakenham, T., *The Scramble for Africa* (London: Abacus, 1992).
Paton, A., *Hofmeyr* (Cape Town: OUP, 1965).
Pelzer, A., *Verwoerd Speaks* (APB Publishers: Johannesburg, 1966).
Pheko, S., *South Africa—Betrayal of a Colonised People* (London: ISAL Publications, 1990).
Pirow, O., *James Barry Munnik Herzog* (Cape Town: Howard Timmins, 1946).
Pollak, W., 'The Legislative Competence of the Union Parliament' (1931) 48 *South African LJ* 269.
Porter, A., 'British Imperial Policy and South Africa 1895–9', (1980) in Warwick (ed.), *infra*.
—— *The Origins of the South African War* (Manchester: MUP, 1980a).
Porter, B., 'The Pro-Boers in Britain', (1980) in P. Warwick (ed.), *infra*.
Posel, D., 'The Meaning of Apartheid Before 1948', in Beinart and Dubow (eds.), (1995) *supra*.
Potter, E., *The Press As Opposition* (London: Chatto and Windrus, 1975).
Rich, P., 'Ministering to the White Man's Needs: the Development of Urban Segregation in South Africa 1913–1923' (1978) *African Studies* 177.
—— *State Power and Black Politics in South Africa 1921–1951* (London: Macmillan, 1996).
Richardson, P., 'The Recruiting of Chinese Indentured Labour for the Transvaal Gold Mines 1903–1908' (1977) 18 *Journal of African History* 87.
—— and Van-Helten, J., 'The Gold Mining Industry in the Transvaal 1886–1899', (1980) in Warwick (ed.), *infra*.
Roberts, A. (ed.), *The Cambridge History of Africa Volume 7 from 1905 to 1940* (Cambridge: Cambridge University Press, 1986).
Roskam, K., *Apartheid and Discrimination* (Leyden: AW Sythoff, 1960).
Ross, R., *Adam Kok's Griquas* (Cambridge: CUP, 1976).
Rossiter, C. (ed.), *The Federalist Papers* (New York: Mentor, 1961).
Sachs, A., *Justice in South Africa* (London: Sussex University Press, 1973).
Savage, D., *Turning Right* (New York: Wiley, 1992).
Sedley, S., 'Human Rights: a Twenty-First Century Agenda' (1995) *Public Law* 386.
Shaw, G., *Some Beginnings* (London: OUP, 1975).

Schreiner, O., *English Law and the Rule of Law in South Africa* (London: Stevens and Sons, 1967).

—— *Collected Letters and Papers*, University of the Witwatersrand.

Schreuder, D., *Gladstone and Kruger* (London: RKP, 1969).

Schwarz, B., *A History of the United States Supreme Court* (Oxford: OUP, 1995).

Simons, H. and Simons, R., *Class and Colour in South Africa 1850–1950* (Harmondsworth: Penguin, 1969).

Spink, K., *Black Sash* (London: Methuen, 1991).

Stewart, W., *J. Keir Hardie* (London: ILP, 1921).

Suzman, A., 'Race Classification and Definition in the Legislation of the Union of South Africa 1910–1960' (1960) *Acta Juridica* 339.

Swanson, M., 'The Sanitation Syndrome: Bubonic Plague and Urban Native Policy in the Cape Colony 1900–1909', (1995) in Beinart and Dubow (eds.), *supra.*

Swinfen, D., *Imperial Appeal* (Manchester: Manchester University Press, 1987).

Thompson, L., 'Constitutionalism in the Boer Republics' (1954) *Butterworths South African LR* 49.

—— *The Unification of South Africa 1902–1909* (Oxford: Clarendon Press, 1960).

—— 'Great Britain and the Afrikaner Republics', (1971) in Wilson and Thompson (eds.), *infra.*

—— 'The Compromise of Union', (1971a) in Wilson and Thompson *infra.*

—— *The Political Mythology of Apartheid* (New Haven: Yale University Press, 1985).

——*A History of South Africa* (New Haven: Yale University Press, 1995).

Tomkins, A., *After the Scott Report* (Oxford: Clarendon Press, 1997).

Trapido, S., 'The Origins of the Cape Franchise Qualifications of 1853' (1964) *5 Journal of African Studies* 37.

—— 'The Origins and Development of the African Political Organisation' (1969) *Institute of Commonwealth Studies* 1.

Troup, F., *South Africa: an Historical Introduction* (London: Metheun, 1972).

Van Alstyne, W., 'A Critical Guide to *Marbury v Madison* (1969) *Duke LJ* 1.

Van den Heever, P., 'Immorality and Illegality in Contract' (1943) 60 *South African LJ* 468.

Van der Horst, S., 'The Changing Face of the Economy', in E. Hellman and H. Lever (eds.), *Race Relations in South Africa 1929–1979* (London: Macmillan, 1979).

Wade, E.C.S., 'Police Powers and Public Meetings' (1937) *Cambridge LJ* 175.

Wade, H.R.W., 'The Basis of Legal Sovereignty' (1955) *Cambridge LJ* 177.

—— 'The Senate Case and the Entrenched Sections of the South Africa Act' (1957) 74 *South African LJ* 166.

—— (1980) *Constitutional Fundamentals* (London: Stevens and Sons).

Walker, A., *Lord De Villiers and His Times* (Constable & Co. Ltd.: London, 1925).

Walshe, A. and Roberts, A., 'Southern Africa', (1986) in Roberts (ed.), *supra.*

Warwick, P. (ed.), *The South African War* (London: Longman, 1980).

—— 'Black People and the War', (1980) in Warwick (ed.), *supra.*

Welsh, R., 'The Privy Council Appeals Act 1950' (1950) 67 *South African LJ* 67.

Wheare, K., *The Statute of Westminster* (Oxford: Clarendon Press, 1931).

—— *The Dominions as Sovereign States* (Oxford: Clarendon Press, 1938).

—— *The Statute of Westminster* (Oxford: Clarendon Press, 5th edn., 1953).

Wiechers, M., 'The Fundamental Laws Behind Our Constitution', in E. Kahn (ed.), *Fiat Iustitia: Essays in Memory of Oliver Denys Schreiner* (Cape Town: Juta & Co., 1953).

Wilson, J., *A Life of Sir Henry Campbell-Bannerman* (London: Constable, 1973).
Wilson, M. and Thompson, L. (eds.), *The Oxford History of South Africa* (Oxford: Clarendon Press, 1971).
Wolpe, H., 'Capitalism and Cheap Labour Power in South Africa', (1995) in Beinart and Dubow, *supra*.
Woodward, C., *The Strange Career of Jim Crow* (New York: OUP, 1966).
Woolf, Lord, 'Droit Public—English Style' (1995) *Public Law* 57.
Zander, M., *The Lawmaking Process* (London: Butterworths, 4th edn., 1995).

Index